ASCENT®

CENTER FOR TECHNICAL KNOWLEDGE

3DEXPERIENCE CATIA 2022x Introduction for Managers and Reviewers

Learning Guide

1st Edition

ASCENT - Center for Technical Knowledge®
3DEXPERIENCE CATIA 2022x
Introduction for Managers and Reviewers

1st Edition

Prepared and produced by:

ASCENT Center for Technical Knowledge
630 Peter Jefferson Parkway, Suite 175
Charlottesville, VA 22911

866-527-2368
www.ASCENTed.com

Lead Contributor: Mark Potrzebowski

ASCENT - Center for Technical Knowledge (a division of Rand Worldwide Inc.) is a leading developer of professional learning materials and knowledge products for engineering software applications. ASCENT specializes in designing targeted content that facilitates application-based learning with hands-on software experience. For over 25 years, ASCENT has helped users become more productive through tailored custom learning solutions.

We welcome any comments you may have regarding this guide, or any of our products. To contact us please email: feedback@ASCENTed.com.

AS-3DE22-IMR1-SG // RS-3DE22-IMR1-SG

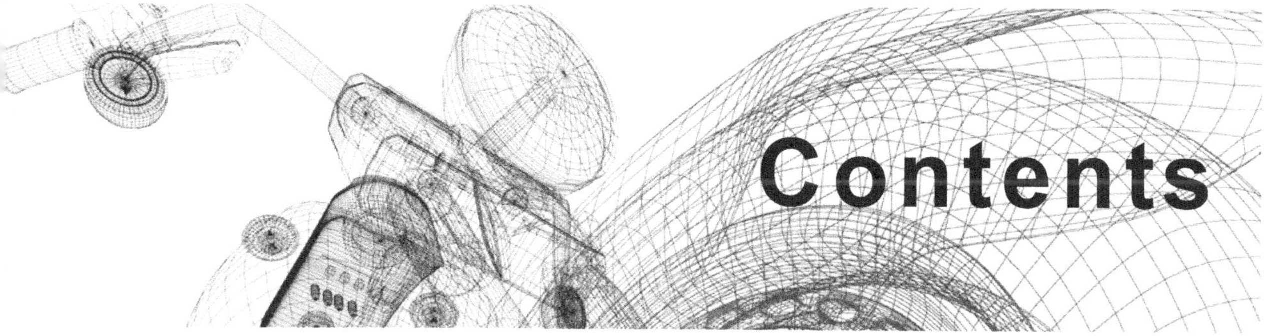

Contents

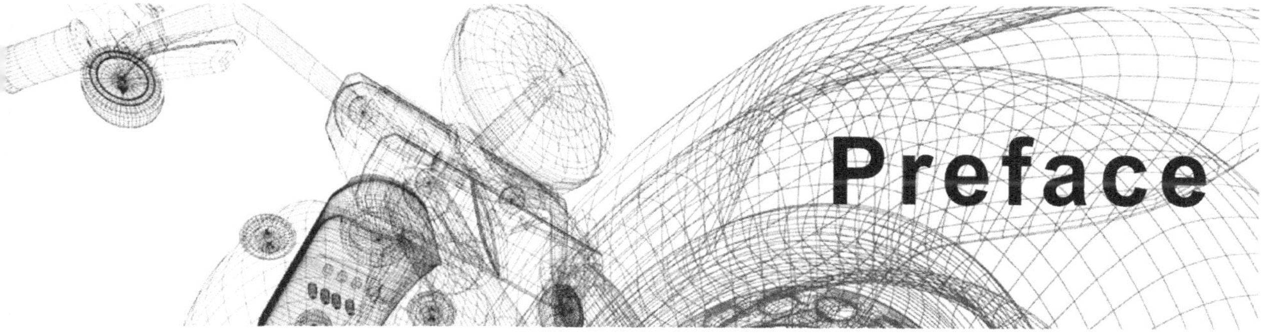

Preface

The 3DEXPERIENCE CATIA 2022x: *Introduction for Managers and Reviewers* guide introduces you to the interface and analysis capabilities of CATIA within the 3DEXPERIENCE platform. This guide, with numerous practice exercises, focuses on the concepts of measurement, analysis, image capture, and drawing creation.

Topics Covered

- Overview of Parametric Design Process
- Customization of CATIA within the 3DEXPERIENCE Environment
- Feature Management Using the Hide/Show, Activate/Deactivate Functions
- Obtaining Part Information
- Assembly Design App and assembly creation techniques
- Performing measurements and clash analyses
- Creating and viewing cross sections
- Creating and managing annotations
- Image raptures
- Creating Slides
- Drawing view creation
- Creating and Constraining Sketch Geometry
- Adding Material with Pad and Shaft Features
- Removing Material with Pocket and Groove Features

Prerequisites

- Access to the 3DEXPERIENCE CATIA 2022x platform, including access to the CATIA Part Design, CATIA Assembly Design, CATIA Drafting, ENOVIA Collaborative Lifecycle, ENOVIA Product Finder, and ENOVIA Design IP Classification apps.
- Permission to import 3DXML files.

Note on Software Setup

This guide assumes a standard installation of the 3DEXPERIENCE platform using the default preferences during installation. Lectures and practices use the standard software templates and default options for the Content Libraries.

Lead Contributor: Mark Potrzebowski

Mark Potrzebowski has been a trainer and curriculum developer in the PLM industry for over 14 years, with experience on multiple CAD systems, including Pro/ENGINEER, Creo Parametric, Inventor, and CATIA. Trained in Instructional Design, Mark uses his skills to develop instructor-led and web-based training products. Prior to joining ASCENT, Mark worked as a Technical Trainer with a focus on CATIA, Creo, and PLM systems. Mark holds a Bachelors degree in Computer Graphics Technology from Purdue University, West Lafayette, Indiana.

Mark has been the Lead Contributor for *3DEXPERIENCE CATIA 2022x: Introduction for Managers and Reviewers* since 2021.

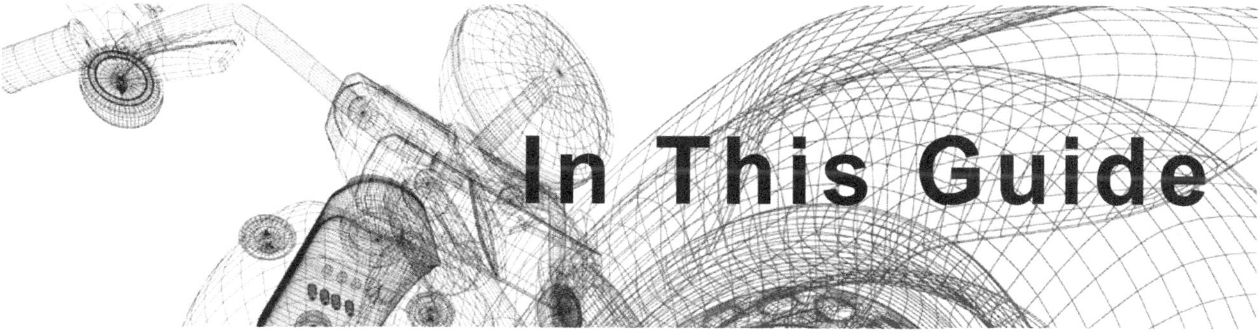

In This Guide

The following highlights the key features of this guide.

Feature	Description
Practice Files	The Practice Files page includes a link to the practice files and instructions on how to download and install them. The practice files are required to complete the practices in this guide.
Chapters	A chapter consists of the following - Learning Objectives, Instructional Content, Practices, Chapter Review Questions, and Command Summary. • **Learning Objectives** define the skills you can acquire by learning the content provided in the chapter. • **Instructional Content**, which begins right after Learning Objectives, refers to the descriptive and procedural information related to various topics. Each main topic introduces a product feature, discusses various aspects of that feature, and provides step-by-step procedures on how to use that feature. Where relevant, examples, figures, helpful hints, and notes are provided. • **Practice** for a topic follows the instructional content. Practices enable you to use the software to perform a hands-on review of a topic. It is required that you download the practice files (using the link found on the Practice Files page) prior to starting the first practice. • **Chapter Review Questions**, located close to the end of a chapter, enable you to test your knowledge of the key concepts discussed in the chapter.

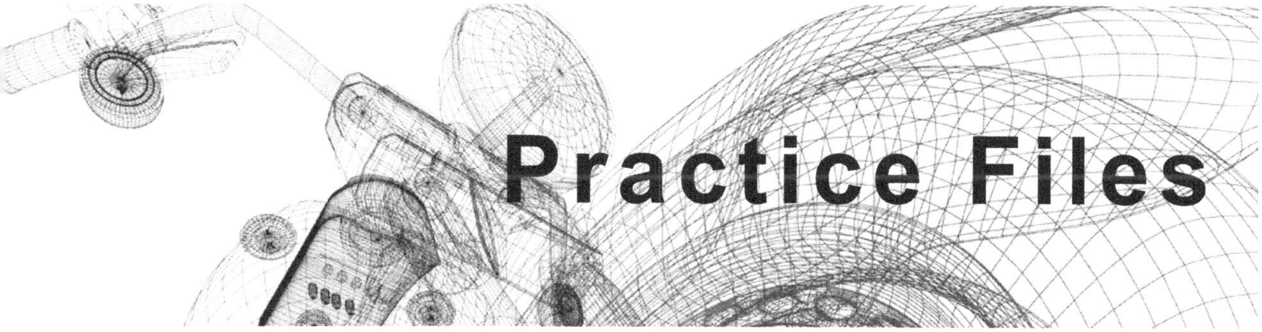

Practice Files

To download the practice files for this guide, use the following steps:

1. Type the URL ***exactly as shown below*** into the address bar of your Internet browser to access the Course File Download page.

   Note: If you are using the ebook, you do not have to type the URL. Instead, you can access the page simply by clicking the URL below.

   https://www.ascented.com/getfile/id/dimorphorchisPF

2. On the Course File Download page, click the **DOWNLOAD NOW** button, as shown below, to download the .ZIP file that contains the practice files.

3. Once the download is complete, unzip the file and extract its contents.

   The recommended practice files folder location is:
   C:\Managers and Reviewers Practice Files

   Note: It is recommended that you do not change the location of the practice files folder. Doing so may cause errors when completing the practices.

Stay Informed!

To receive information about upcoming events, promotional offers, and complimentary webcasts, visit:

www.ASCENTed.com/updates

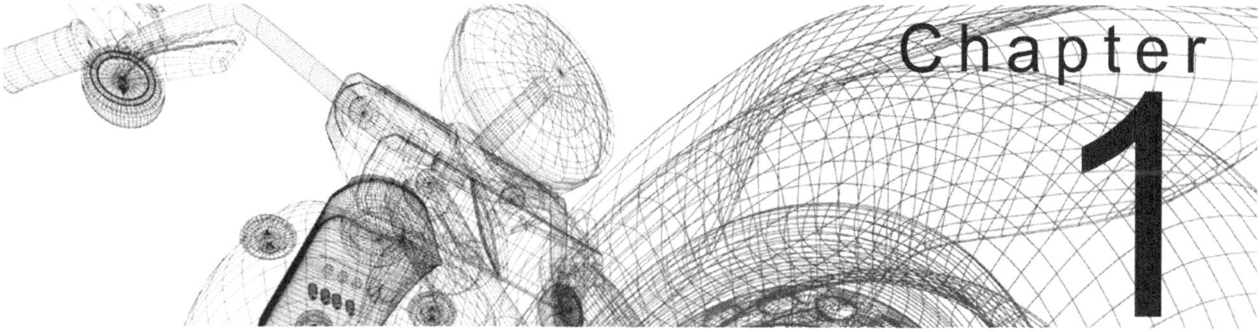

Chapter 1

Solid Modeling Overview

This chapter provides an overview of solid modeling, where you use features and parameters to build a model. The relationships created with these features and parameters can be used to establish the design intent on the model. You learn how CATIA maintains associativity between the model, assemblies, and drawings. You gain familiarity with the CATIA user interface and learn how to customize it, making it more efficient to work with.

Learning Objectives in This Chapter

- Understand the basics of solid modeling.
- Understand feature-based modeling.
- Understand the parametric and associative nature of CATIA.
- Understand how and why you capture a model's design intent during modeling.
- Become familiar with the CATIA user interface.
- Learn how to work with a model by opening it, customizing the display settings, and selecting entities.
- Learn how to access the online help system.

1.1 Fundamentals

Solid Modeling

CATIA is used to create three-dimensional (3D) solid models. The software *understands* that the model is *filled* with material. With a solid model, you can perform the following:

- Obtain the mass properties of a part.
- Determine if components in an assembly interfere with one another.
- Create cross-sections of an assembly or display part cross-sections in a drawing. Instead of manually *drawing* the views on the drawing, you can reference the part model to generate views and show the dimensions from the 3D geometry, as shown in Figure 1–1.

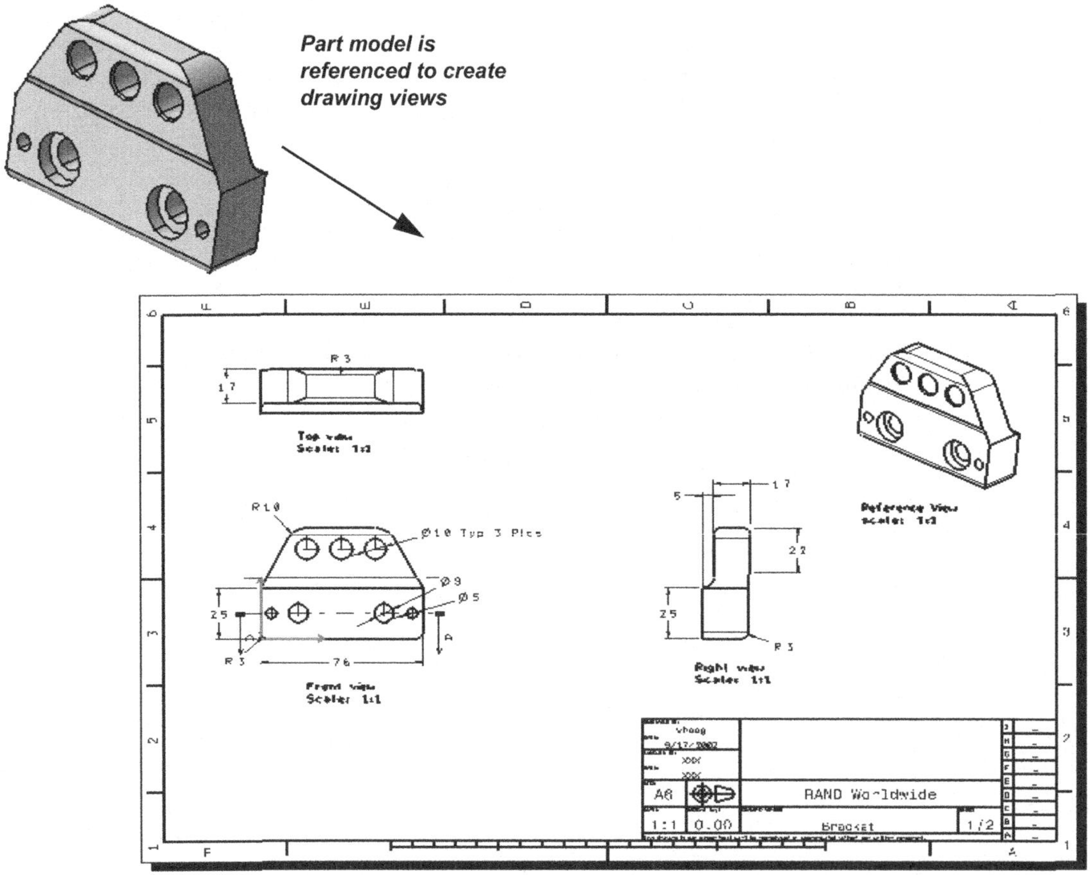

Figure 1–1

This process also applies to assemblies, as shown in Figure 1–2. You can locate existing part and assembly models relative to one another.

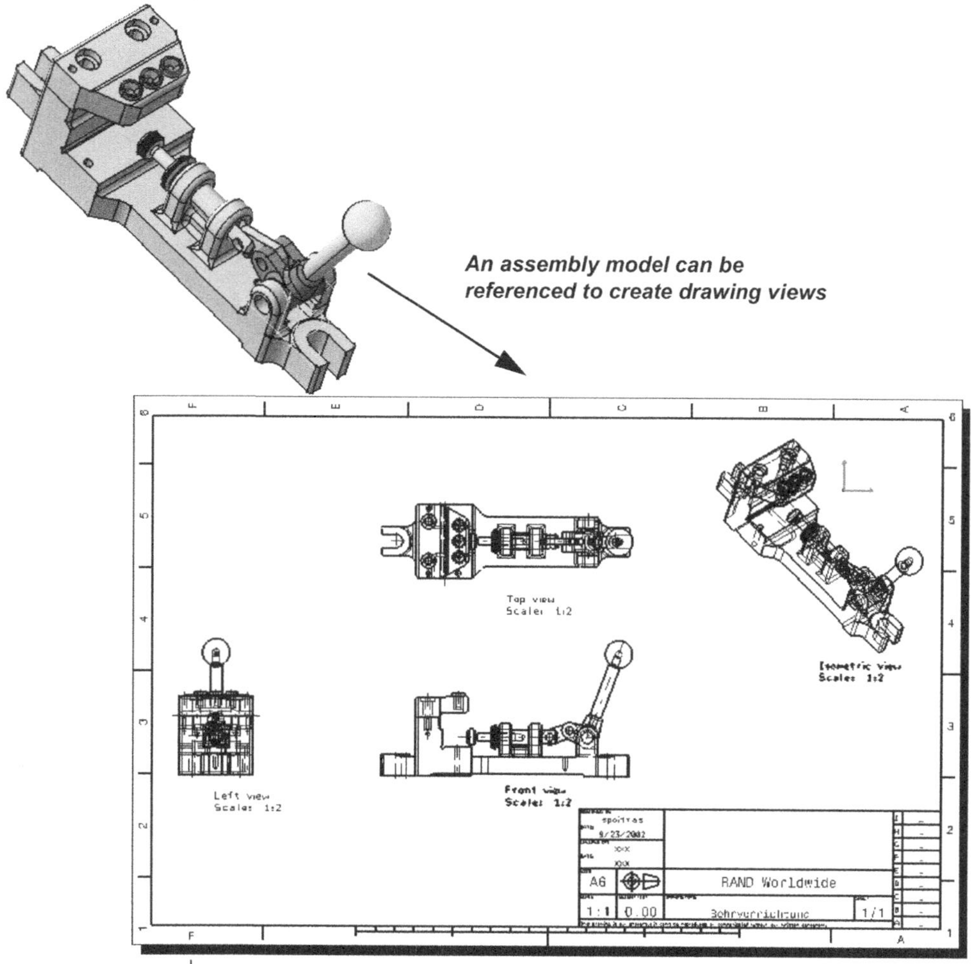

Figure 1–2

Feature-Based

The solid model evolves as features are created, one by one, until the geometry is complete. The part model (shown in Figure 1–3) is constructed by consecutively creating the following features:

1. Create a sketch.
2. Create a Pad feature.
3. Draft several walls of the part using a Draft feature.
4. Remove sharp edges of the geometry by creating a Fillet feature.
5. Create a Shell feature to hollow out the part.

6. Create another Pad feature to act as a cylindrical boss.
7. Center a Hole feature on the cylindrical Pad.
8. Duplicate the boss and hole to create the second boss, as shown in Figure 1–3.

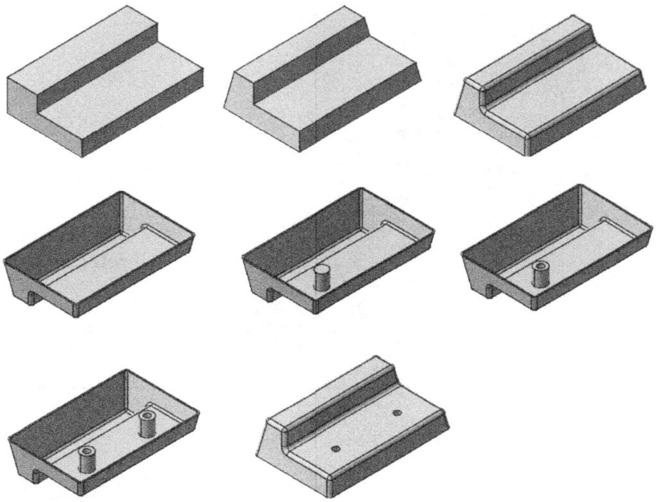

Figure 1–3

You can organize features based on the design intent by initially defining the overall size, major geometric shapes, and then later the finishing details.

Parametric

Features created in CATIA are parametric. All of the dimensional constraints used to define a feature's shape are considered *parameters* and are accessible at any time. Double-click on a feature to display its dimensional constraints and change any of those values to alter the geometry. The dimensional value that positions the Pocket feature (shown in Figure 1–4) has changed. The position of the feature updates to reflect the design change.

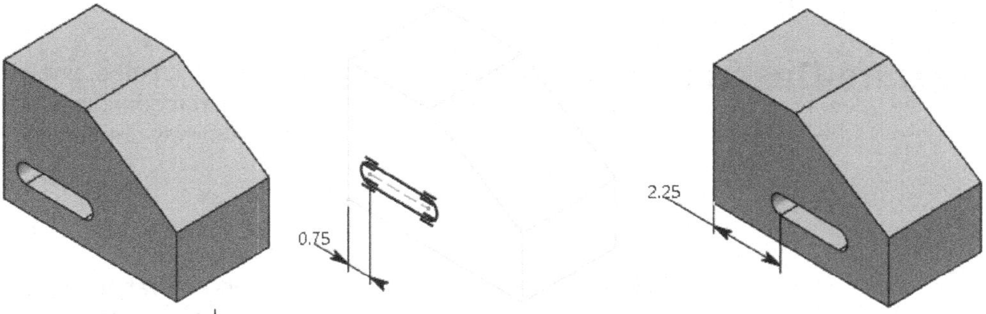

Figure 1–4

Associative

Drawings are created by referencing a model. When the model is changed, any drawings of that model are automatically updated the next time they are opened. Similarly, changing a part model is automatically reflected in the assembly. Also, changes made in the assembly update in all other modes in CATIA, as shown in Figure 1–5.

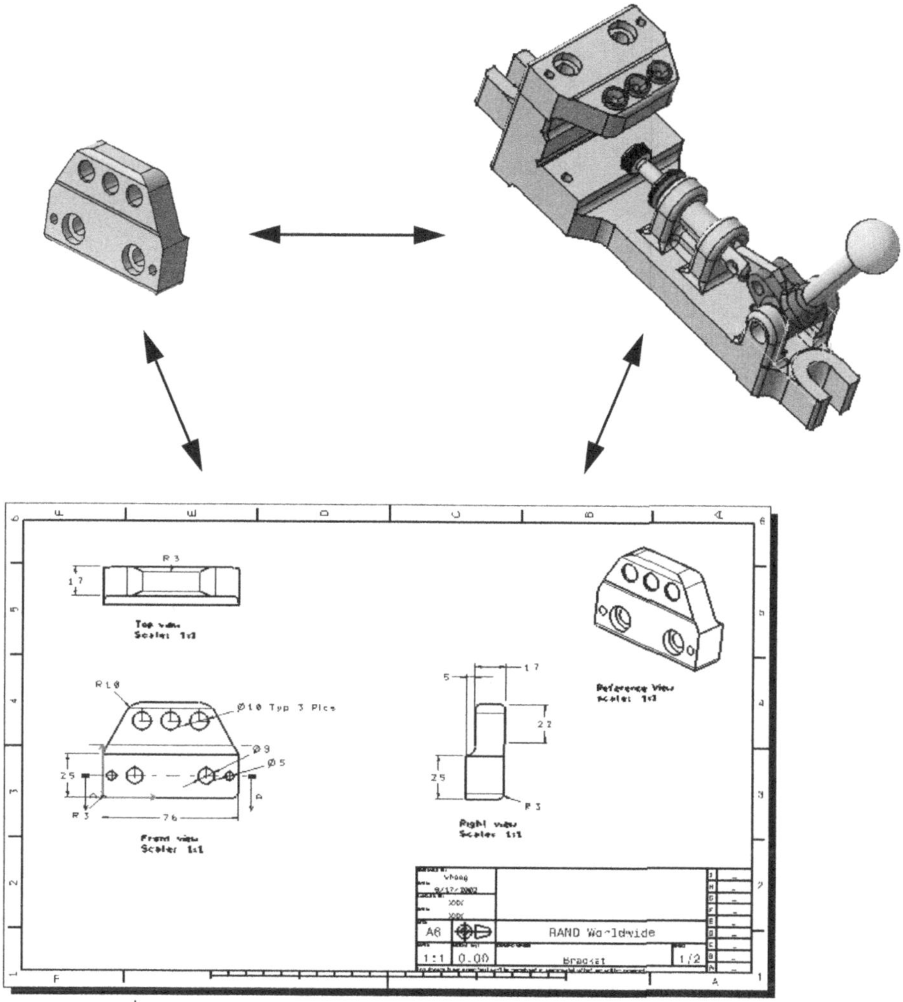

Figure 1–5

Associativity creates a dependency between models. The part models referenced by an assembly and/or drawing must be retrievable to work with the assembly and/or drawing.

1.2 Design Intent

The key to building parametric, feature-based, solid models is to ensure that they have a flexible and predictable behavior. This process is known as capturing *design intent*.

Method 1

One method of capturing design intent is to determine the feature's dimensioning scheme. Figure 1–6 shows an example of a part with a hole. When the Pad feature increases in length, the design intent of the hole determines how it behaves. If the hole is dimensioned to the end of the Pad, the hole moves to remain a distance of 3.00 from that end. If the hole is dimensioned to the face, it remains a distance of 6.00 from that face.

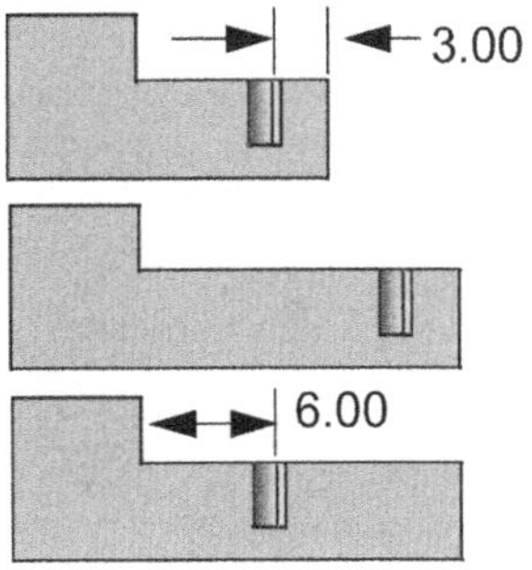

Figure 1–6

Method 2

A second method of capturing design intent is to select an option to limit your feature. A part with a hole is shown in Figure 1–7.

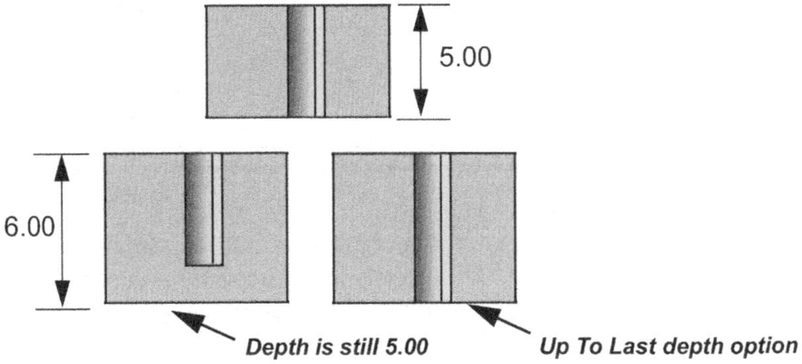

Figure 1–7

The design intent is for the hole to pass through the entire model. When the Pad changes from 5.00 to 6.00, the resulting geometry displays differently depending on how the hole is limited. If the hole was created with a depth of 5.00, it no longer passes though the entire part. It must be changed to maintain the design intent. A better solution is to set the limit of the hole using **Up To Last** option and ensure that it always passes through the part, regardless of the height of the Pad feature.

Method 3

A third method of capturing design intent is to create symmetrical geometry. The design intent for the part (shown in Figure 1–8) is to have the Pocket remain at the center of the part.

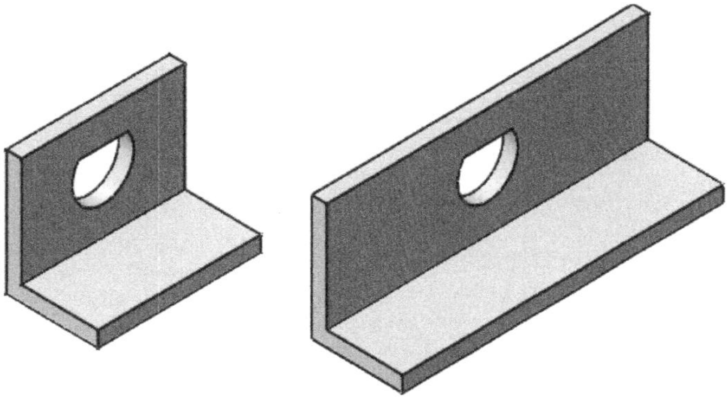

Figure 1–8

Constraining the Pocket from either end of the Pad feature does not capture the design intent. Constructing the Pad and Pocket relative to a center datum reference is preferable.

1.3 User Interface

Screen Layout, Quick Start

When you launch 3DEXPERIENCE, you are presented with a welcome screen, as shown in Figure 1–9.

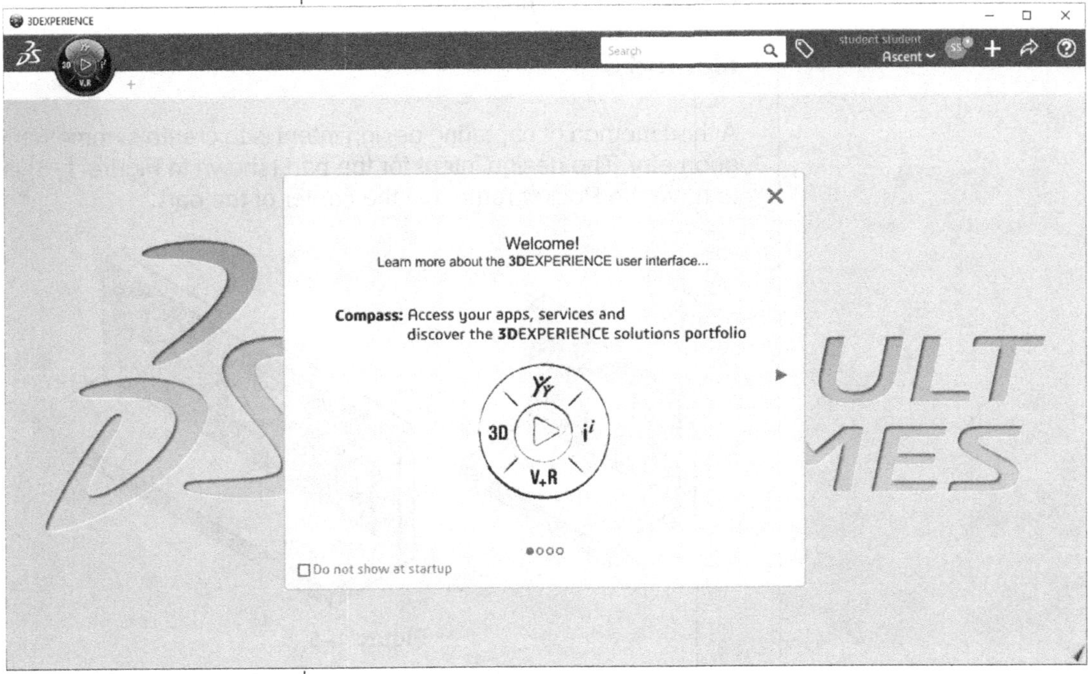

Figure 1–9

This welcome screen has multiple pages, accessed by the arrows on the side or the circular buttons at the bottom, as shown in Figure 1–10. The circular buttons allow you to move to a specific page.

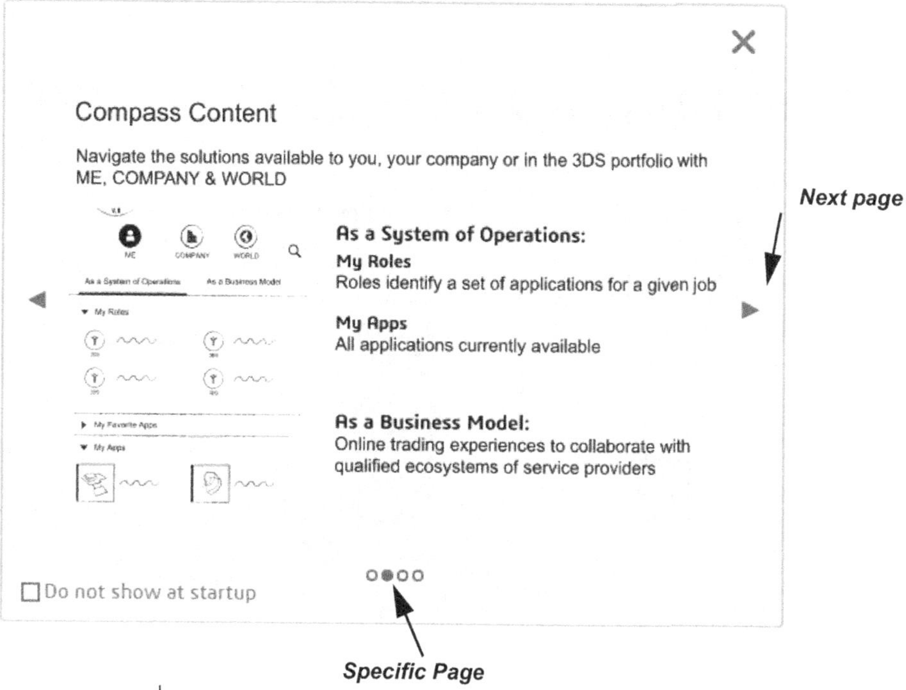

Figure 1–10

You can click through this welcome screen to discover the basics of the 3DEXPERIENCE user interface. If you do not want to see this screen when 3DEXPERIENCE launches, select **Do not show at startup**.

Screen Layout

When you open a model in 3DEXPERIENCE CATIA Part Design, the screen displays as shown in Figure 1–11. The major areas of the interface that are labeled are discussed in the following topics.

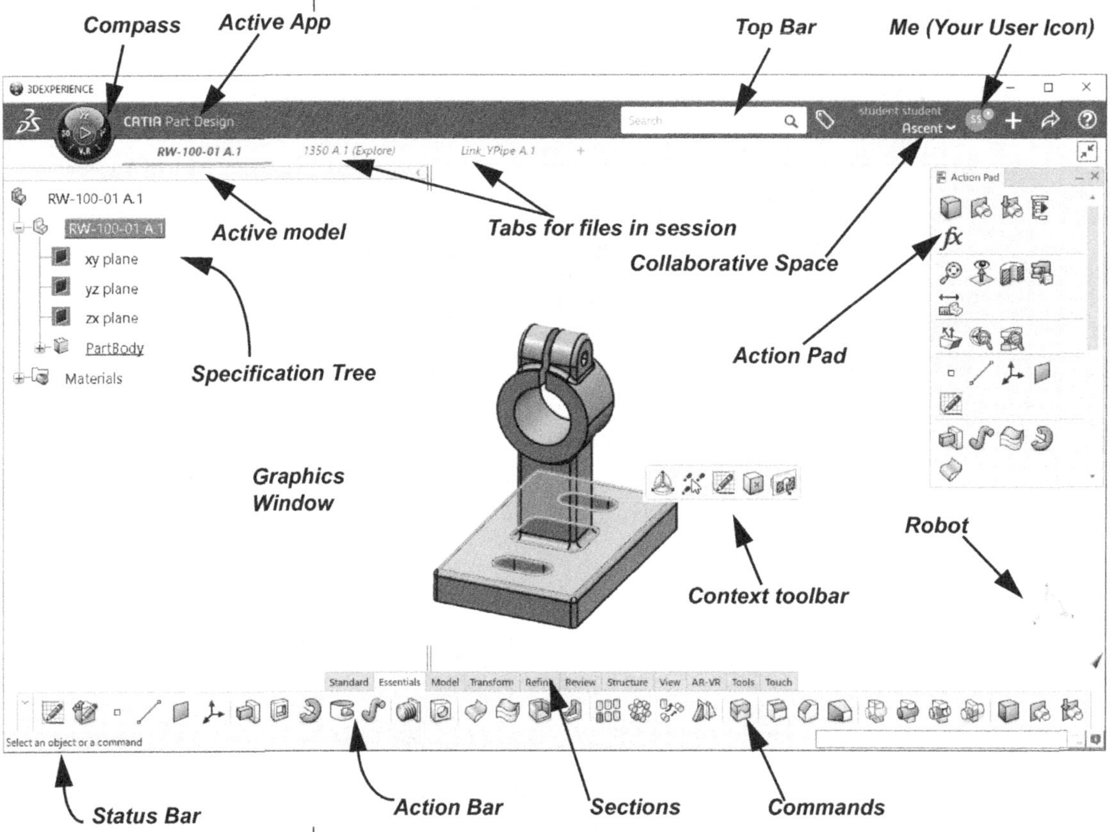

Figure 1–11

Commands

The primary way of interacting with the software is to select icons in the Action Bar, Action Pad or Context toolbar. You can customize the interface by arranging the location of the toolbars and selecting the icons to display.

Compass

The Compass enables you to access various apps. The Compass is broken into two functional areas. The inner circle named the (Play) button and the outer ring named (Roles, Apps and Solution Profile).The outer ring allows you to switch between Rolls and Apps freely, while the play button allows you to interact only with the applicable apps. Some of the major categories in the 3DEXPERIENCE platform system are shown in Figure 1–12.

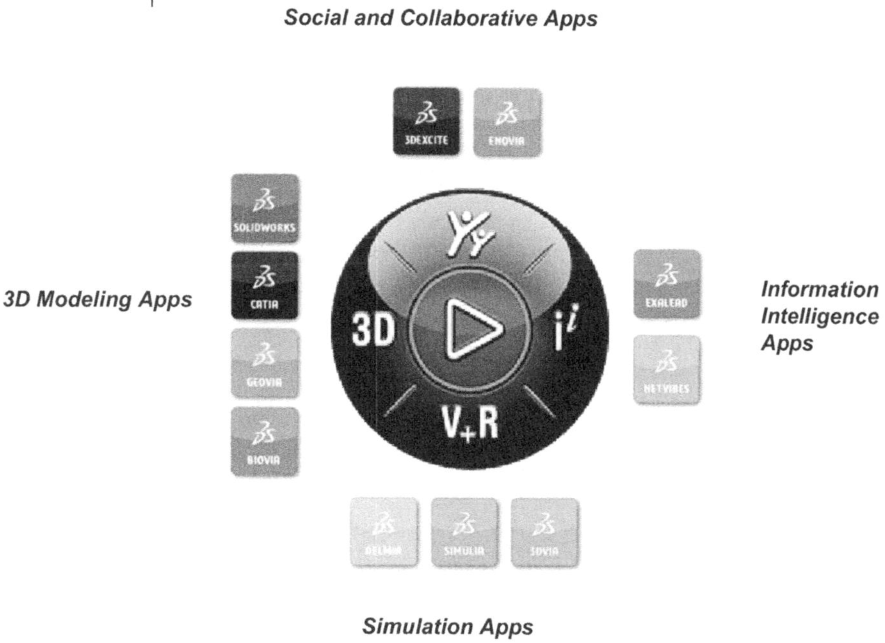

Figure 1–12

Search Bar

The Search Bar enables you to look up CATIA files within the engineering database. Searches can include wildcard (*) use (as shown in Figure 1–13) and can be refined in various ways. The wildcard (*) is not needed at the beginning or the end of the text because it is implied.

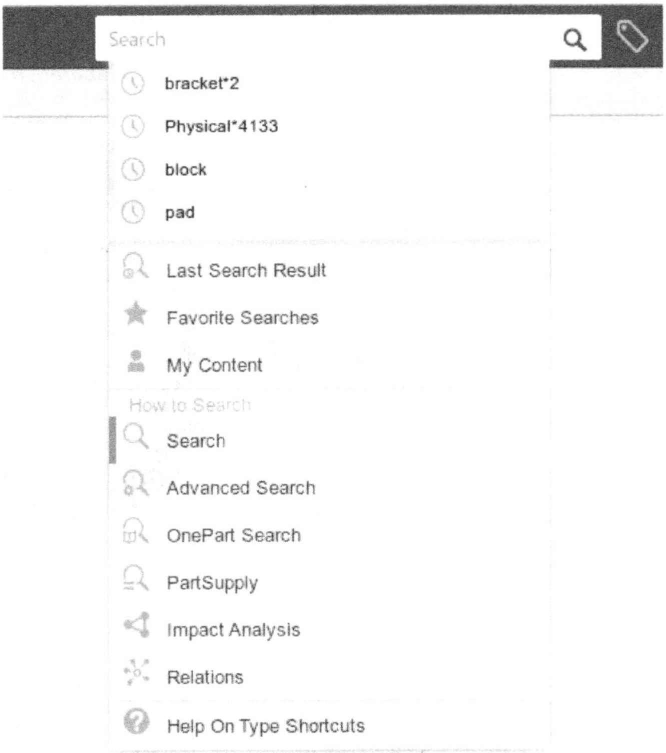

Figure 1–13

Specification Tree

The specification tree is available when working with parts, assemblies, and drawings. It displays a variety of information about the model and displays the features of the part in the order in which they were created, as shown in Figure 1–14. This provides quick access to parameters, functions, materials, and commonly used measurements.

The specification tree can be quickly toggled on and off by pressing <F3>.

Figure 1–14

Robot

The Robot is available for part and assembly models. It displays in the upper right corner of the model window and can perform various functions, as shown in Figure 1–15. The Robot is used to:

- Freely rotate the model in all three directions.
- Rotate the model in a plane.
- Pan along one direction.
- Pan in a plane.
- View down an axis direction by selecting the X, Y, or Z letter. Selecting again flips the view in the opposite direction.

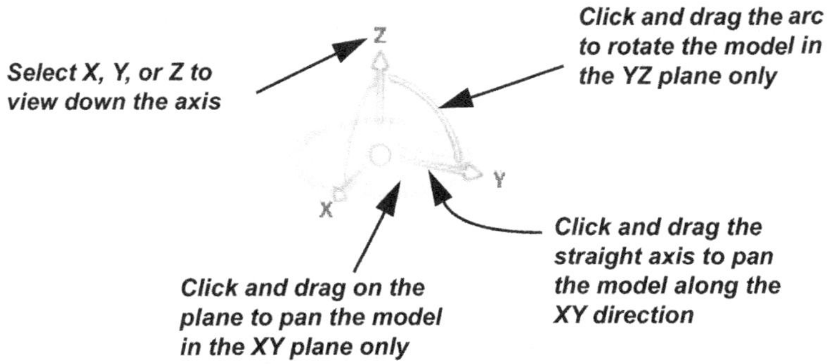

Figure 1–15

Tabs

Multiple objects can be open at the same time. Each object is presented in its own tab, and you can switch back and forth between objects simply by selecting the tab name.

Tabs can also be subdivided into smaller windows called widgets, as shown in Figure 1–16.

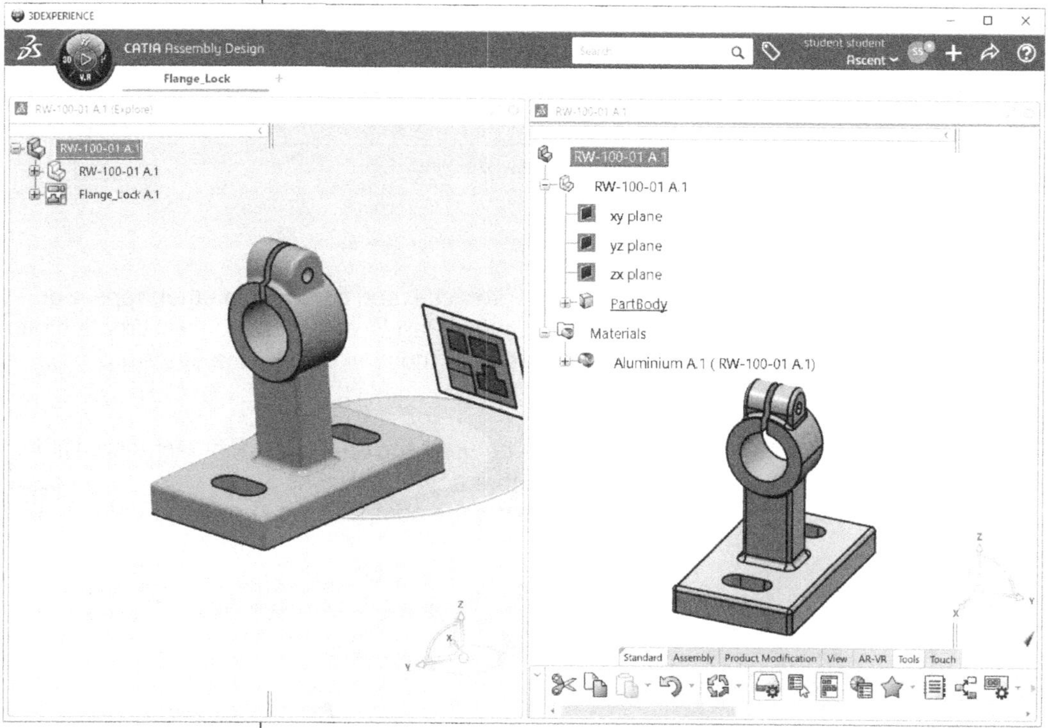

Figure 1–16

You can access options for controlling the display of widgets by right-clicking on the tab where they are stored, as shown in Figure 1–17.

Figure 1–17

Apps

An app is a set of tools used to complete certain tasks. The apps used in this course are described as follows:

Icon	Application Name
	Part Design
	Drafting
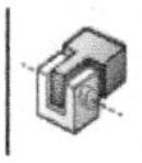	Assembly Design

Additional apps are accessed from within other apps. For example, when in the Part Design app, you will create sketches for features. To create those sketches, the system places you into the Sketch app.

Other apps can be used for Analysis, Manufacturing, Digital Mock Up, and other advanced tasks. The name of the active app is displayed next to the compass, as shown in Figure 1–18.

Part Design app is active

Figure 1–18

1.4 Working with Models

ViewModes

Although you are working with a solid model, you can change how the geometry displays. These options can be accessed using  (View Modes) found in the *View* section of the Action Bar, as shown in Figure 1–19.

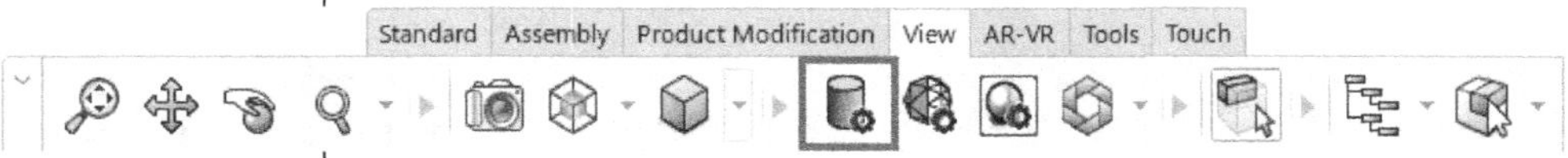

Figure 1–19

Selecting  (View Modes) will display the View Modes window, where the user can change the look of the model with standard predefined rendering styles. By selecting one of the many named cylinder shaped icons at the top of the window, the models look will quickly change as shown in Figure 1–20. By expanding the arrow next to **Shading** simple customizations can be made.

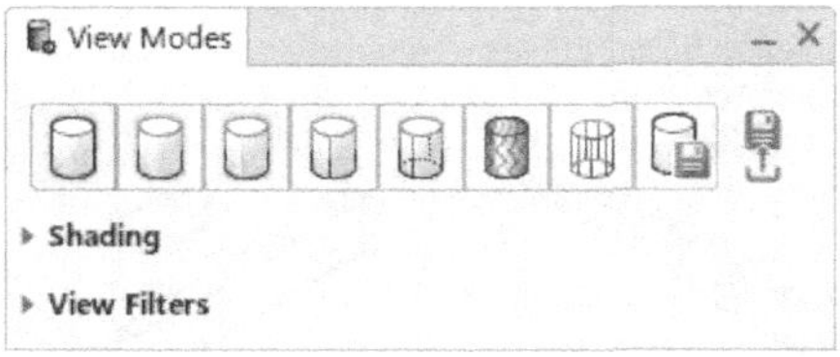

Figure 1–20

Figure 1–21 shows an example of each icon listed in the View Mode window. The **Customized View Mode** option enables you to configure the display with all options to suit your preferences, such as with hidden edges shown, with the material shown, or with faceted faces.

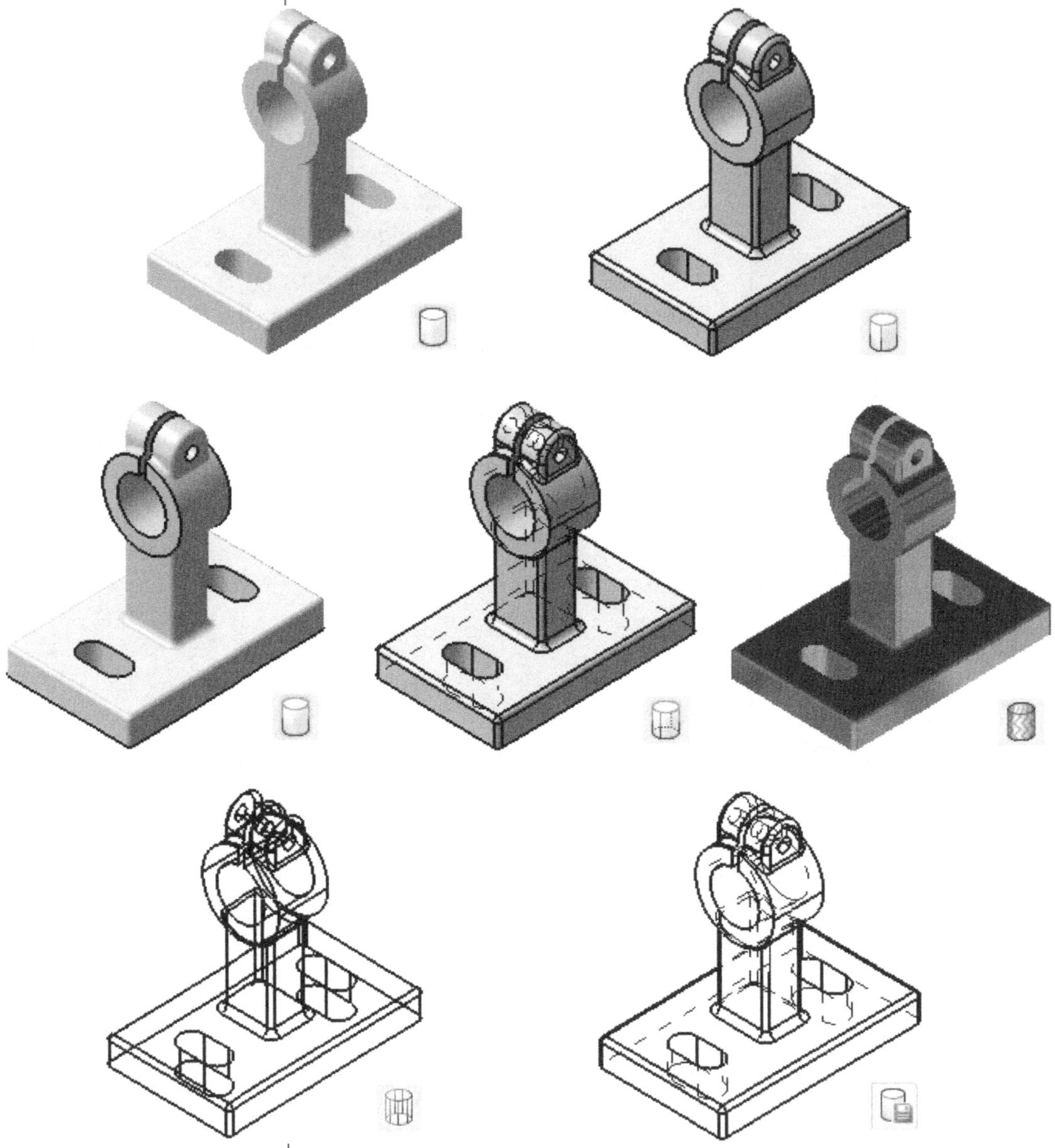

Figure 1–21

Model Navigation

To thoroughly inspect your models, you must learn how to reorient the model, zoom in and out, and pan. There are several methods to navigate a model.

- The Quick Views options in the *View* section of the Action Bar contain predefined model orientations enabling you to view the model from commonly used orientations. Figure 1–22 shows the available Quick Views.

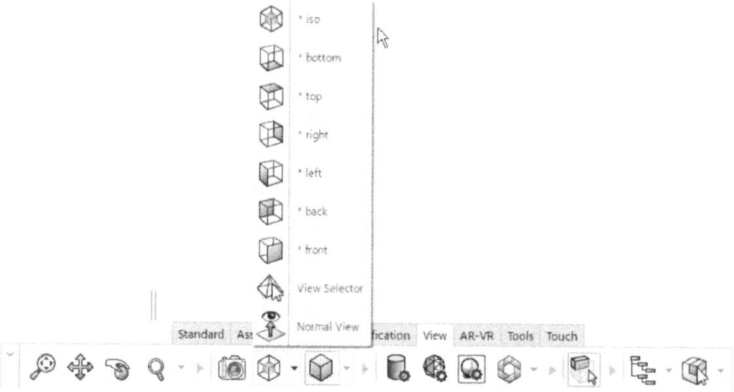

Figure 1–22

To dynamically navigate the model, you can use specific toolbar icons, menu commands, or mouse shortcuts. The navigation functions are listed as follows:

Icon	Function	Mouse
	**Pan**	Hold Middle
	**Rotate**	Hold Middle + Hold Right or Hold Middle + Hold Left
	**Zoom In/Out**	Hold Middle + Click Right or Hold Middle + Click Left
	**Zoom Area**	N/A
	**Fit All In**	N/A
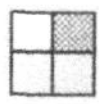	**Create Multi-view**	N/A
	**Re-center on Geometry**	Click Middle on required geometry

Use the **Re-center on Geometry** function to rotate the model around a specific location on the model or geometry. Click the middle mouse button on the required geometry or model location to re-center the model. Then, use the **Rotate** function to spin the model around the centered geometry.

Preselect Navigator

The **Preselect Navigator** tool enables you to select geometric entities that are hidden or difficult to select on a model. The software lists all entities that exist beneath the current cursor position and enables you to scroll through this list to select the required entity.

How To: Use the Preselect Navigator

1. Position the cursor over the geometry that you want to select.
2. Press the <Up Arrow> or <Down Arrow>. The software lists all entities that are beneath the current cursor position, as shown in Figure 1–23. A display window opens, indicating the currently highlighted entity.

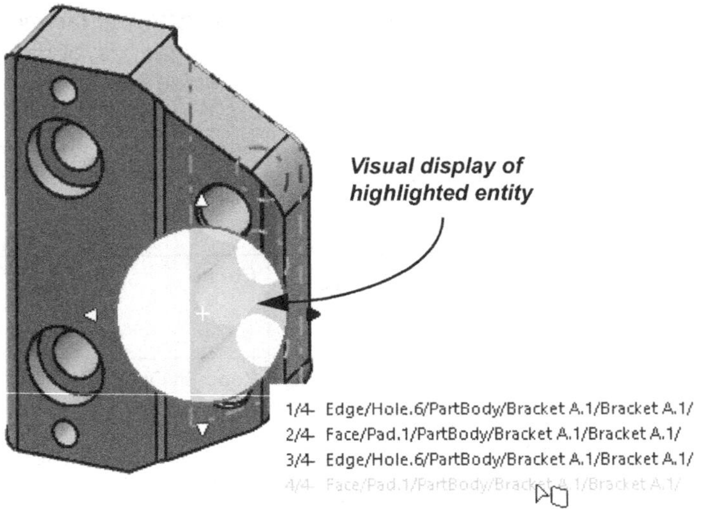

Figure 1–23

3. To scroll through the list, continue pressing the <Up Arrow> or <Down Arrow>. Press the <Left Arrow> and <Right Arrow> to navigate the possible selections for the active component only. You can also navigate the list using the cursor.
4. To select an entity for further operation, select it from the list using the cursor or press <Enter>.

An alternative method is as follows:

1. Position the cursor over the geometry that you want to select.
2. Press and hold <Alt> and then select the model. The software lists all of the entities that are beneath the selection point.
3. Move the cursor to make the appropriate selection. This option is controlled through the **Preselect in Geometry View** option, located in **Me>Preferences>Common Preferences>2D 3D View Display>Selection>Selection**, where Me is your user icon in the Top Bar of the 3DEXPERIENCE window.

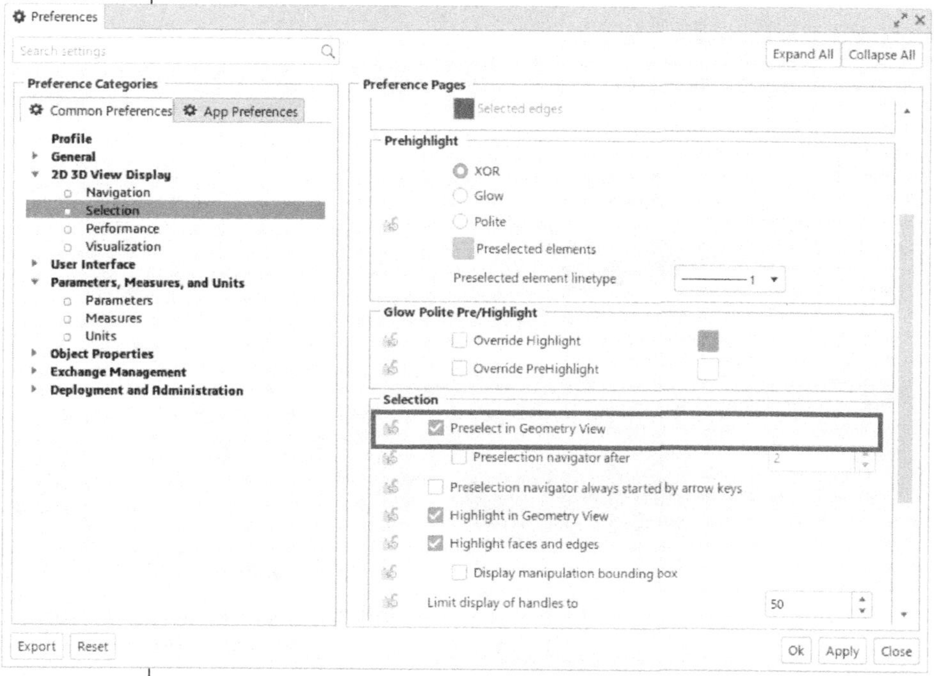

Figure 1–24

1.5 Online Documentation

Online documentation is very useful and easily accessible. To learn about any function, press <F1> when working with that function. This will open the User Assistance window that provides some basic information about that function. For additional information, click on **More help on this topic** at the bottom of the window, and the entire help topic displays on an Internet browser, as shown in Figure 1–25.

Figure 1–25

Online documentation usually includes structured practices that you can follow to gain hands-on experience with a particular function. At the top of the practice, the name of the component used in the practice displays as a blue hyperlink.

Practice 1a

Viewing a Part

Practice Objectives

- Open a part model and view it from different orientations.
- Change the display settings for the model.
- Investigate associativity between parts, drawings and assemblies.

In this practice, you will open an existing model and work with various visualization tools. You will also change the geometry of a model by editing parameters and deleting features, and note how these changes update in drawings and assemblies.

Task 1 - Import a CATIA part.

1. In the Top Bar, click (Add)>**Import**.
2. In the Import dialog box, click **(Open).**
3. Browse to and select **Flange_Lock_Drawing.3dxml** and click **Open**.
4. Ensure the settings in the Import dialog box match those shown in Figure 1–26.

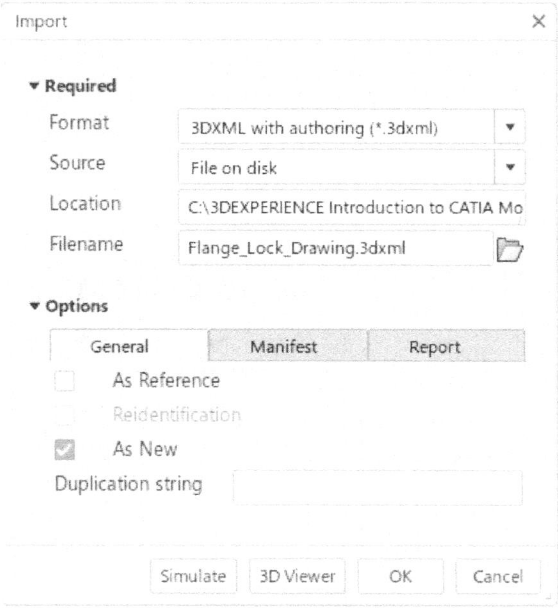

Figure 1–26

5. Click **OK**.
6. The Import Progression dialog box opens momentarily, as shown in Figure 1–27.

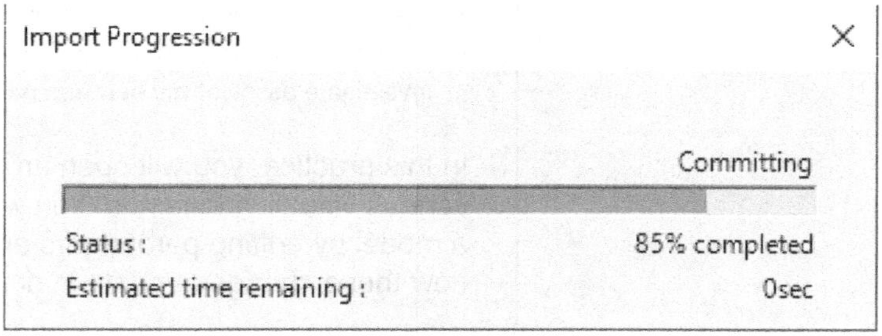

Figure 1–27

7. Then the Operation Report window displays showing the import was successful as shown in Figure 1–28.

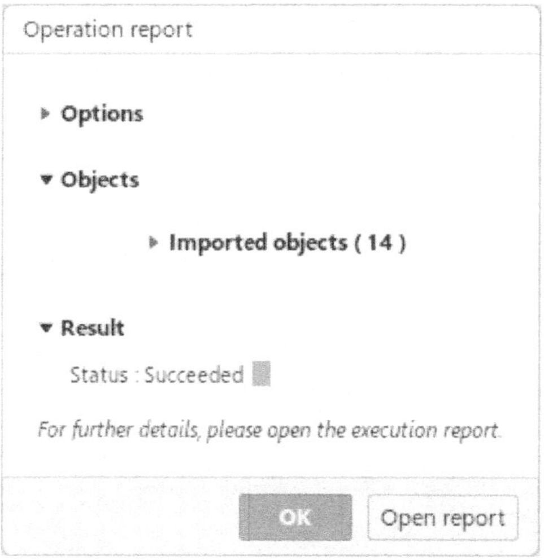

Figure 1–28

8. Click **OK** in the OperationReport dialog box.
9. In the specification tree, right-click **RW-100-01** and select **Open**.

10. The part displays as shown in Figure 1–29.

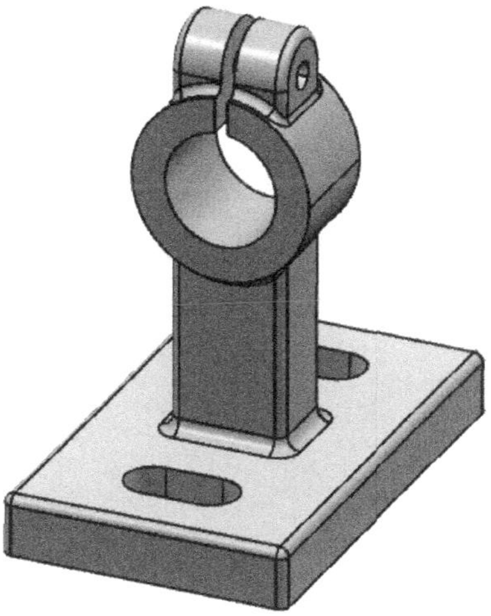

Figure 1–29

Task 2 - Change the display of the model.

1. In the *View* section of the Action Bar, select (View Modes). This will open a View Modes window, as shown in Figure 1–30, and select (Shading).

Figure 1–30

2. Repeat Step 1 to set the display to  (Shading With Sharp and Smooth Edges),  (Shading With Material), and  (Shading With Edges and Hidden Edges).

3. Set the display to  (Customize View Mode).

4. Set the options, as shown in Figure 1–31. The model displays as shown in Figure 1–32.

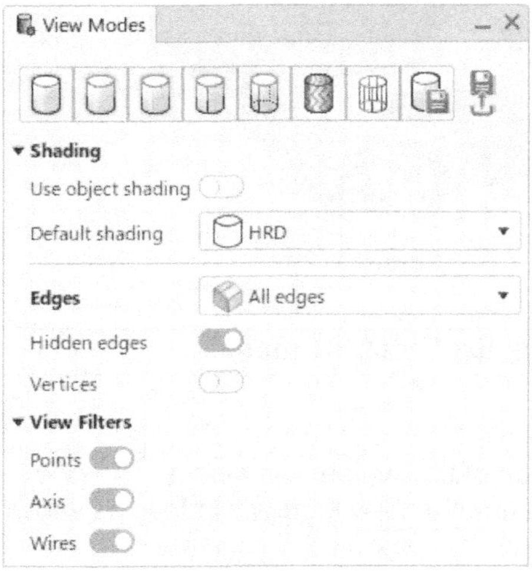

Figure 1–31

Figure 1–32

Task 3 - Use the Quick Views toolbar to change the model orientation.

1. Click  (Shading With Sharp and Smooth Edges) to set the display to **Shading With Sharp and Smooth Edges**.

2. Close the View Modes window by selecting  (close) in the right corner.

3. Change the display to **Front** by clicking (* front) in the flyout menu, as shown in Figure 1–33.

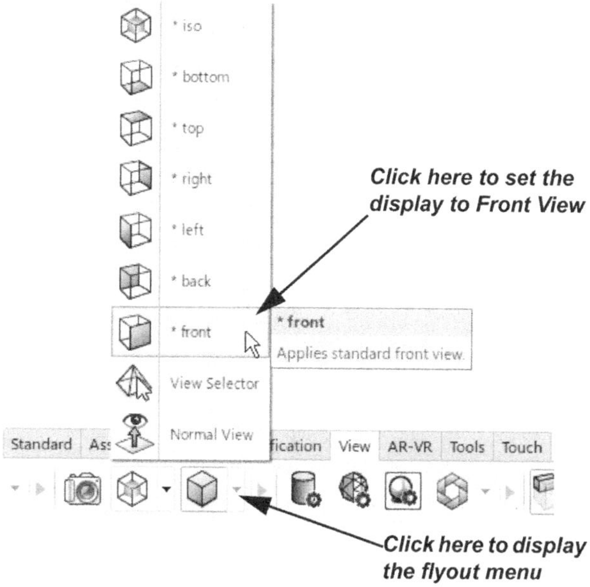

Figure 1–33

4. Repeat Step 2 for the (* back), (* right), (*left), (* top), and (* bottom) quick views.

5. Return to the (* iso) view.

Task 4 - Use the toolbar icons and menus to zoom, pan, and spin the model.

1. Click (Zoom In Out), select on the screen (keep the mouse button in) and drag upward to zoom into the model.

2. Click (Fit All In) to fit the model in the window.

3. Click (Zoom In Out), select on the screen (keep the mouse button in) and drag downward to zoom away from the model to zoom out.

4. Click the small arrow next to (Zoom In Out) and select (Zoom Area).

5. Use the left mouse button to draw a box around the area you want to zoom in to, as shown in Figure 1–34.

In some cases, the zoom area box does not display on the screen, although the functionality works correctly.

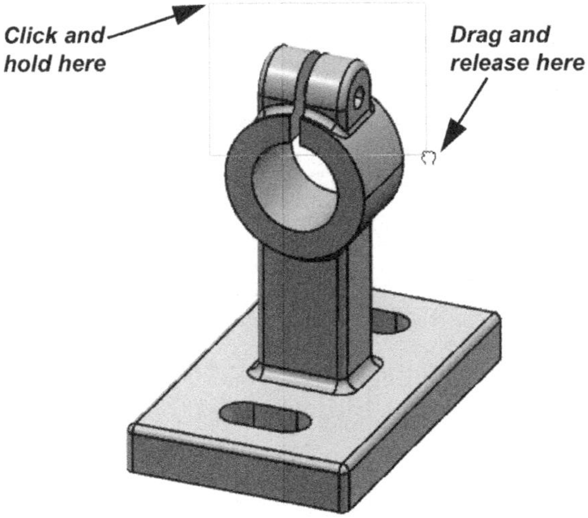

Figure 1–34

6. Click (Pan) to pan the model.

7. Click and drag the cursor around the screen, and the model follows your movements. Note that you must click the icon each time you want to pan.

You learn additional ways of panning and zooming later in the practice.

8. Click (Fit All In) to fit the model in the window.

9. Click (Rotate) to rotate the model. Hold the left mouse button and move the cursor to rotate the model. The **Rotate** tool behaves in the same manner as the **Pan** tool in that you must click the icon each time you want to rotate the model.

Task 5 - Use the robot to dynamically rotate and pan the model.

1. Click (* iso) to return to the Isometric view.

2. Click and drag the curved edge of the XY plane to rotate the model about the Z-axis only, as shown in Figure 1–35.

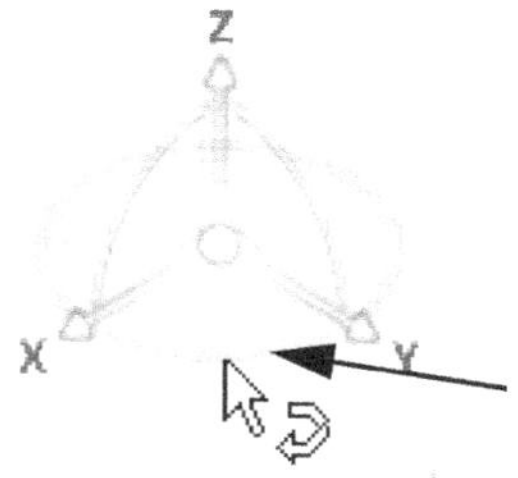

Figure 1–35

3. Repeat Step 4 for the other two curved edges.
4. Return to the Isometric quick view.
5. Click and drag the X-, Y-, and Z-axes of the compass to translate the model along that direction, as shown in Figure 1–36.

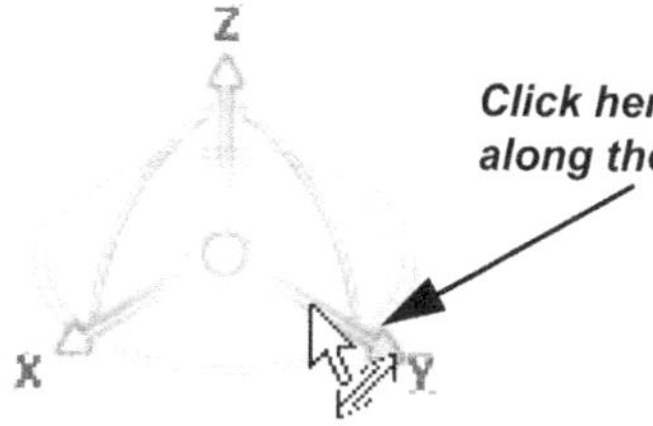

Figure 1–36

Task 6 - Use the mouse to dynamically rotate, pan, and zoom the model.

Click (Fit All In) to center your model in the graphics window.

Try repeating these mouse shortcuts when possible.

1. Return to the Isometric quick view and fit the entire model in the window.
2. Hold the middle mouse button and move the cursor to pan the model.
3. Hold the middle mouse button and then left-click (or right-click) once. Move the cursor up and down to zoom in and out.
4. Press and hold the middle mouse button and then press and hold the left mouse button (or right mouse button) simultaneously, and move the cursor to rotate the model.

Task 7 - Use the specification tree to review the model geometry.

1. In the specification tree, select **Multipad.1** (you might need to expand PartBody by clicking the **+** symbol). The feature highlights in green in the tree and blue on the model, as shown in Figure 1–37.

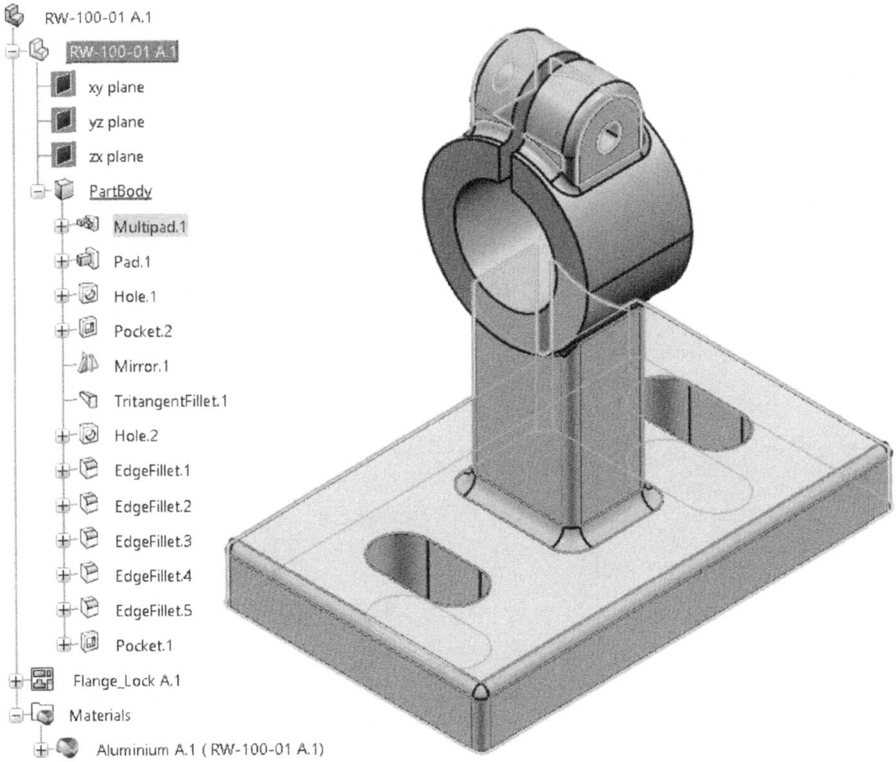

Figure 1–37

2. Repeat Step 1 for each feature under the PartBody branch (i.e., Pad.1, Hole.1, Pocket.2, Mirror.1, etc.). The selected feature is highlighted on the model and in the specification tree.

If you accidentally change the focus to the specification tree, you must understand how to activate the model.

3. Press <F3> several times to hide and show the specification tree.

4. Another method to hide and show (referred to as Pinning and Unpinning) the specification tree, is to select the arrow shown in Figure 1–38.

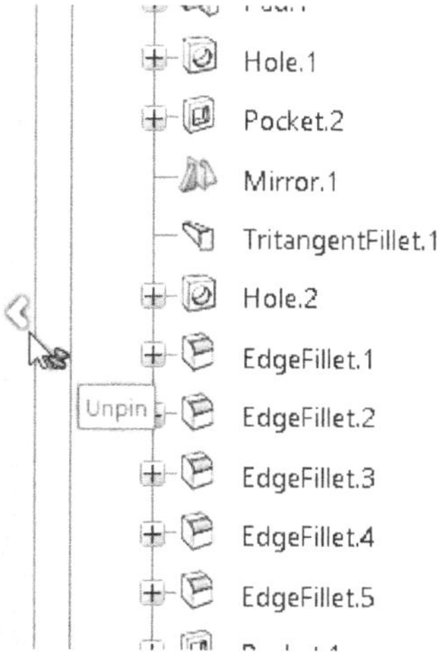

Figure 1–38

Task 8 - Change the size of several features.

1. Place the cursor over the large fillet at the base of the neck to highlight it, as shown in Figure 1–39. Double-click on it to display the radius dimension.

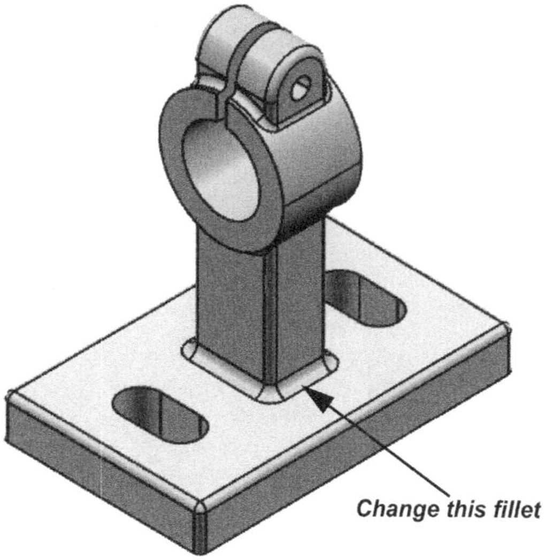

Figure 1–39

2. In the Edge Fillet Definition dialog box, change *Radius* to **6.00 mm (0.236 in)**, as shown in Figure 1–40. Click **OK**.

Figure 1–40

3. In the specification tree, double-click on **Hole.1**.

4. In the Hole Definition dialog box, change the *Diameter* to **13.00 mm (0.512 in)**, and click **OK**. The updated model is shown in Figure 1–41.

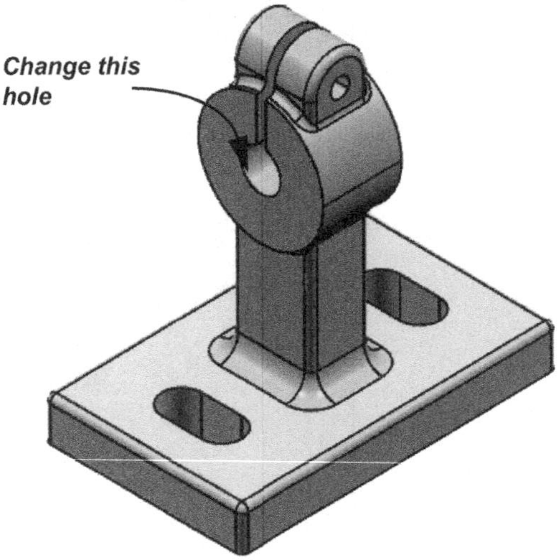

Figure 1–41

Task 9 - Delete features.

1. Select the edge fillet shown in Figure 1–42.

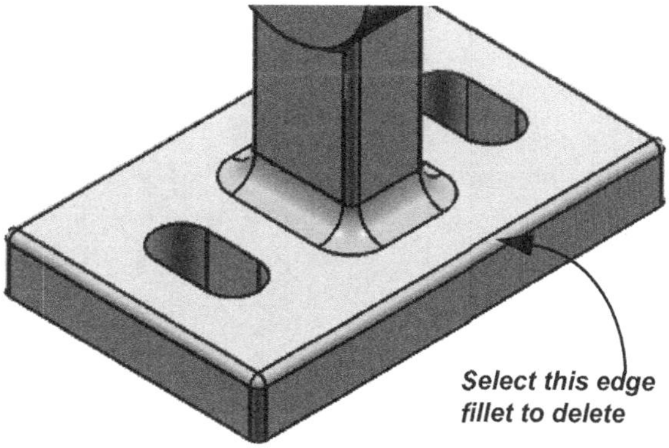

Figure 1–42

2. Right-click and select **Delete**.

3. Delete **Sketch.6** from the specification tree, as shown in Figure 1–43.

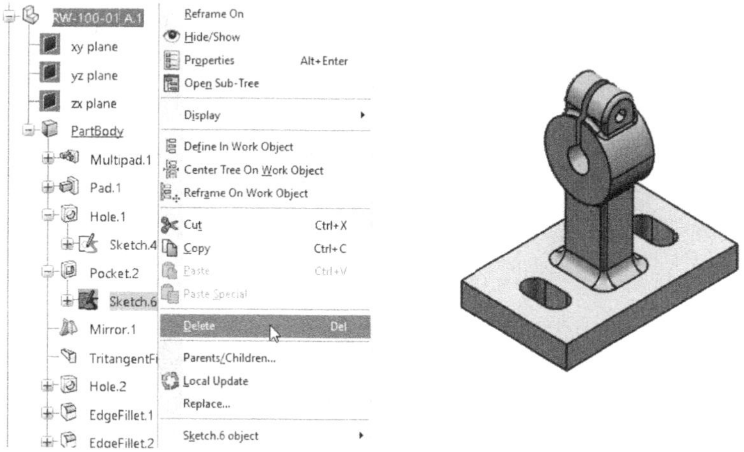

Figure 1–43

4. The Delete dialog box opens, as shown in Figure 1–44. It prompts you that the sketch is a parent feature and when deleted, its children are also deleted.

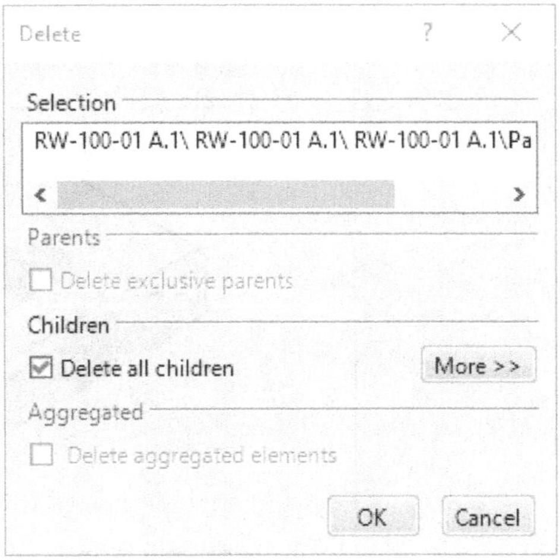

Figure 1–44

5. Click **OK**. The model displays as shown in Figure 1–45.

6. Click (Undo) to undo the deleting operations. The model displays as shown in Figure 1–46.

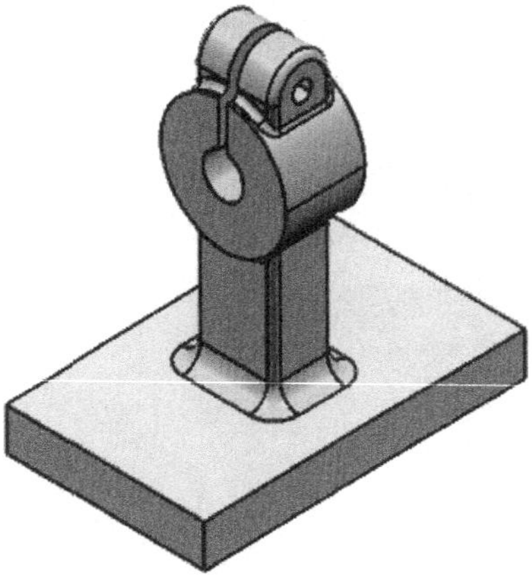

Figure 1–45

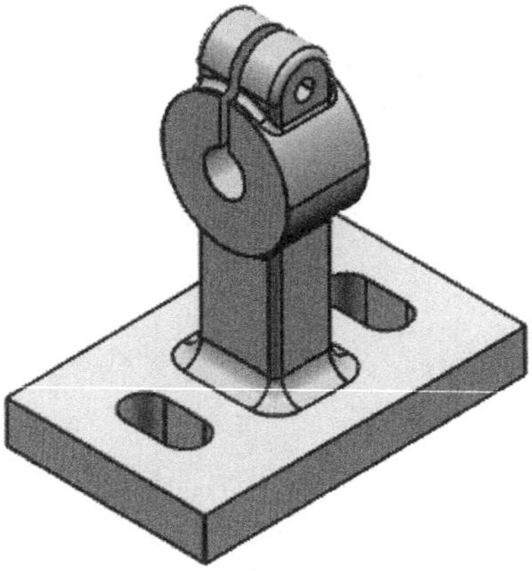

Figure 1–46

Task 10 - Cause a feature to fail.

1. In the specification tree, double-click on **EdgeFillet.2**.
2. Modify the radius of the fillet to **30.00 mm (1.181 in)** and click **OK**.

   The radius of the fillet is too large and causes the **EdgeFillet.2** feature to fail. An Update Diagnosis dialog box opens, as shown in Figure 1–47.

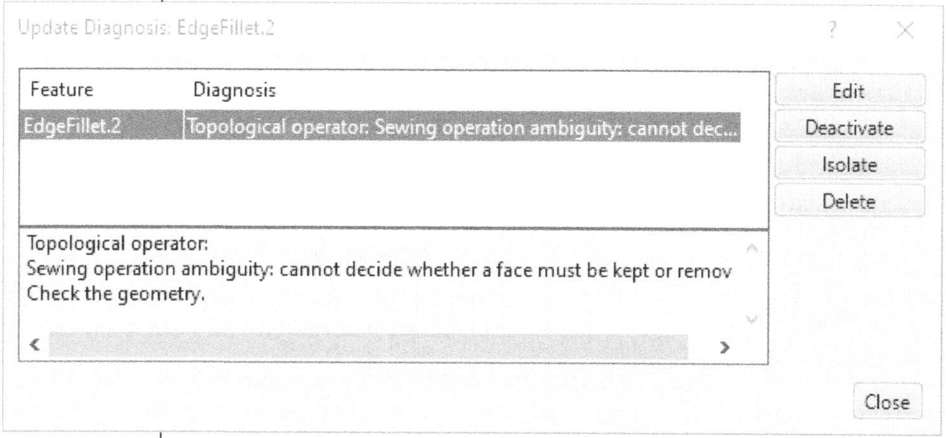

Figure 1–47

3. Select **Close**, and undo the changes made to the Fillet feature and resolve the failure by clicking (Undo).
4. Click (Share)>**Save** to save the model.
5. Close the part tab.

Chapter Review Questions

1. "Solid modeling evolves as features are created one by one until geometry is complete," best describes which attribute?
   a. Parametric
   b. Associative
   c. Feature Based
   d. None of the above
2. Parametric can best be described as:
   a. Changes made in one mode of CATIA update throughout the other modes of CATIA.
   b. Solid models evolve by creating features, one by one, until the geometry is complete.
   c. Three-dimensional solid models.
   d. Dimensional constraints define a feature's shape, are considered *parameters*, and are accessible at any time.
3. After editing the dimensions of a part model, you must open all drawings referencing that part and make the same dimensional changes.
   a. True
   b. False
4. The specification tree is useful because:
   a. It provides quick access to parameters, functions, materials, and commonly used measurements.
   b. It is available when working with parts, assemblies, and drawings.
   c. It displays the features of the part in the order in which they were created.
   d. All of the above.
5. CATIA part files have a ______ filename extension.
   a. .PRT
   b. .Part
   c. .CATPart
   d. .CATProduct

6.  enables you to view the Isometric view of the model.
   a. True
   b. False

7. To pan the model using the mouse, you press and hold which mouse button?
   a. Left
   b. Right
   c. Middle

8. To zoom the model using the mouse, press and hold the middle mouse button and click either the left or right mouse button.
   a. True
   b. False

9. Which tool can be used to zoom in or out on the shown geometry so that it fills all the available space?
   a. 
   b. 
   c. 
   d. 

10. You can open multiple windows in a CATIA session.
   a. True
   b. False

Answers: 1c, 2d, 3b, 4d, 5c, 6b, 7c, 8a, 9a, 10a

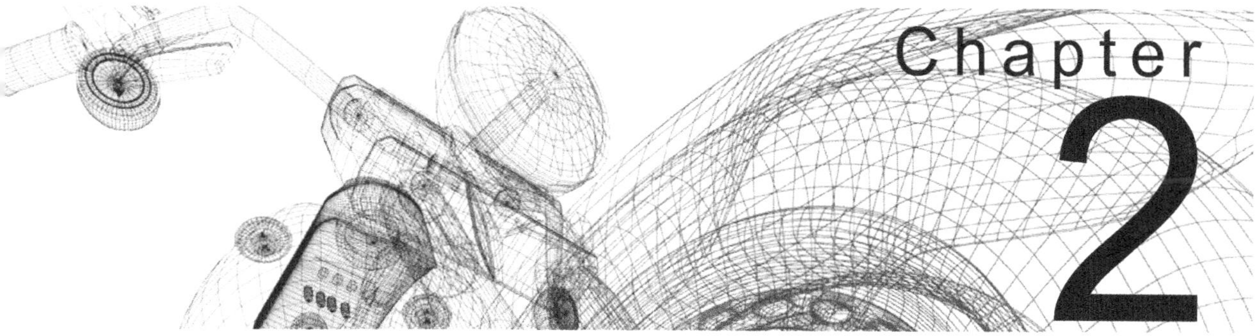

Chapter 2

Feature Management

CATIA provides several tools to simplify the display of your model. Three of these tools are Search, Hide/Show, and Activate/Deactivate. Using these tools will increase your overall efficiency. You can also use Selection Sets to quickly select groups of features at the same time.

Learning Objectives in This Chapter

- Use Search in complex models to find specific objects.
- Show and hide features to simplify the display and make working with complex models more efficient.
- Understand how hidden features display in the specification tree.
- Learn how to Activate and Deactivate objects.
- Learn how to group features using selection sets.

2.1 Search for Features

In complex models with a large number of features, locating specific features in the model might become difficult. The **Search** tool enables you to locate and select the feature in the specification tree using a variety of search parameters.

- Press *<Ctrl>*+*<F>* to perform a search. The Search dialog box opens and it displays the results of a sample search for a feature with a name containing the string **Rib,** as shown in Figure 2–1.

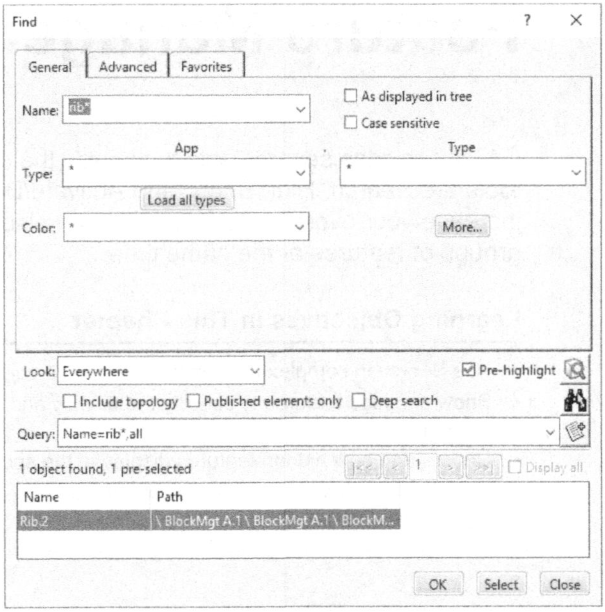

Figure 2–1

When you select the found objects, the features are highlighted in the main window and specification tree. The feature can be selected for use in the current operation by clicking **Select**.

- The *Advanced* tab provides options to define more search parameters.
- The *Favorites* tab provides access to search results that have been stored using  (Add to favorites).

2.2 Hide and Show

CATIA contains two default display spaces - invisible and visible. You have been working in visible space. As you create additional features and your models become more complex, the display area of the screen becomes cluttered. To simplify the display, the **Hide** and **Show** commands can be used to move features between the two spaces.

A model with all elements visible is shown in Figure 2–2.

Sketches are normally hidden after they are referenced by a feature. They are shown here for illustration purposes.

The display shows many elements that no longer need to be shown.

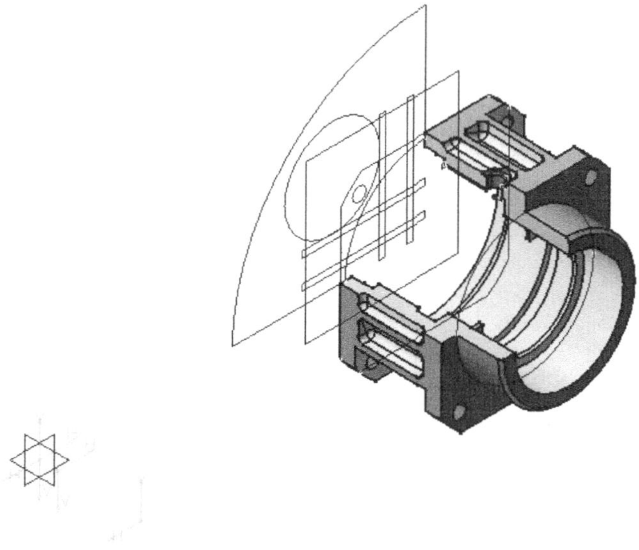

Figure 2–2

The model shown includes all of the sketches, lines, and reference planes. Individual features can be moved from the visible space to the invisible space by using one of the following methods:

- Select the feature in the display area or in the specification tree, right-click, and select **Hide/Show**. When a feature is switched to the invisible space, it no longer displays. However, the features still exist.

To select all elements of a particular type, select the top-level model, right-click and select **ModelTitle object>Show** or **Hide** then select the required element type, as shown in Figure 2–3.

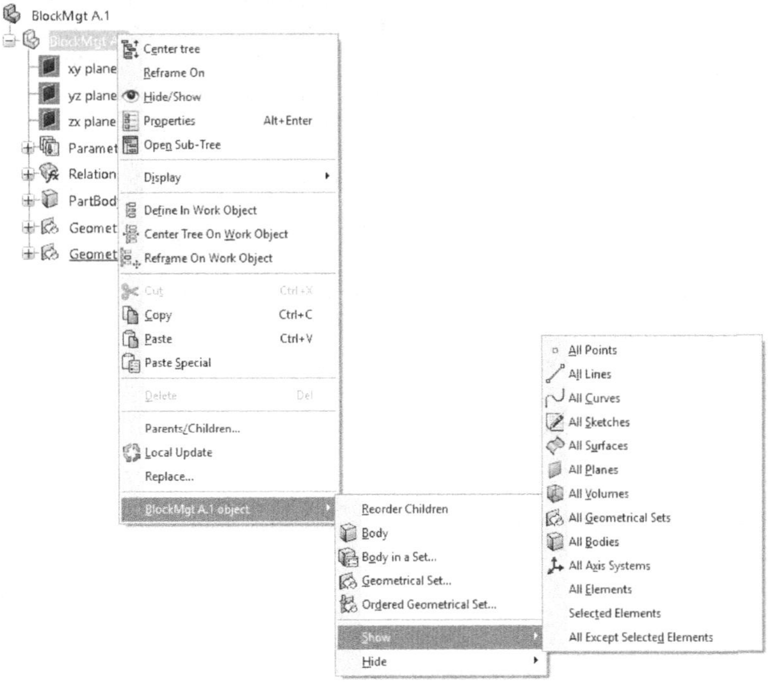

Figure 2–3

As a result, the display area is much less cluttered. Figure 2–4 shows the same model as the one shown in Figure 2–2, except that all sketches, planes, points, and axis systems are hidden from visible space.

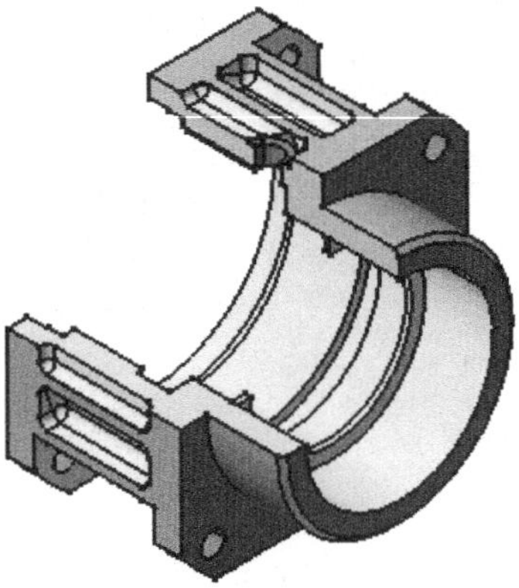

Figure 2–4

Indication of Hidden Features

The specification tree displays hidden features as faded or grayed icons, as shown in Figure 2–5.

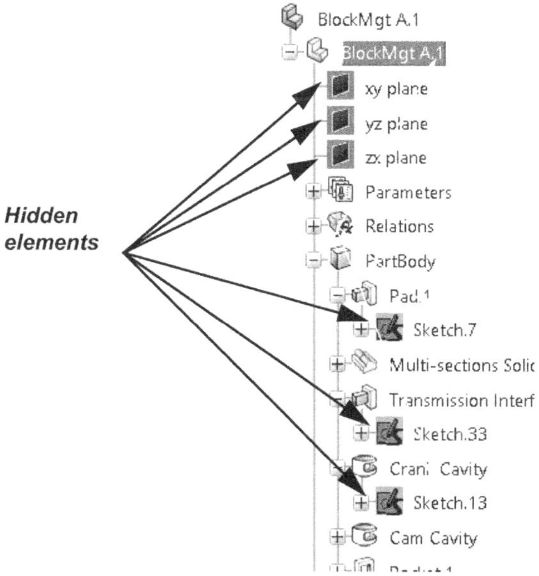

Figure 2–5

- To swap between the visible working space and invisible working space, click  (Swap Visible Space) in the lower-right corner of the graphics area. Hidden features are shown in a separate working space (i.e., invisible). Click the icon again to return to the visible working space.

- To make individual features visible after they have been hidden, select them in the specification tree, right-click and select **Hide/Show**.

Tips and Techniques

Use the **Hide/Show** command carefully. Although no real harm can be done to your model, the **Hide/Show** command can produce unexpected results if you select inactive features, or select the wrong types of features.

- A feature in the specification tree that affects the mass properties of the model cannot be hidden without hiding all solid features. To control the display of solid features independently, the feature must be deactivated.

2.3 Activate and Deactivate

If features are deactivated, the update sequence time decreases.

When features are added to the model, the software updates them with any changes made. When a change occurs that forces subsequent features to change drastically, the update can fail. To deactivate a feature and help solve an update failure, select the feature, right-click and select the feature object name (e.g., **Pocket.3 object**), and then select **Deactivate**, as shown in Figure 2–6.

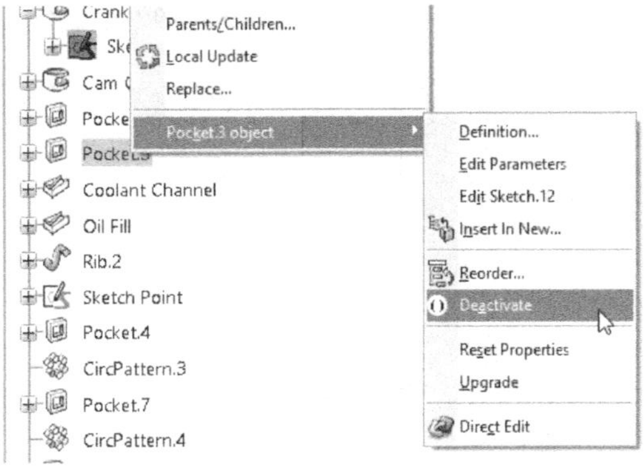

Figure 2–6

The **Deactivate** option temporarily removes the feature from the update sequence. This enables you to keep the feature as currently defined, without deleting it. The feature icon displays with a deactivation symbol in the specification tree, as shown for the **Hole.1** object in Figure 2–7.

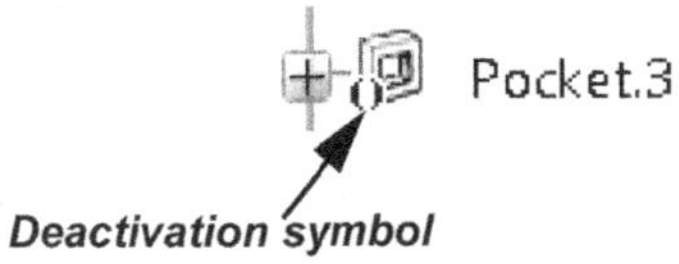

Figure 2–7

You can modify any previous features to help solve an update failure. Once solved, the feature can be returned to the update sequence by selecting it in the specification tree, right-clicking the feature object name, and selecting **Activate**.

Features should only be deactivated temporarily. If they are not required, they should be deleted from the model.

You can use the **Deactivate** option to:

- Reduce the chance of unwanted parent/child relationships.
- Make models run faster.
- De-feature the model for Finite Element Analysis purposes.
- Try alternative designs for a feature.

To avoid accidentally referencing a Fillet feature when creating additional features, deactivate the Fillet feature on your model, as shown in Figure 2–8. Deactivating fillets is one way to help CATIA run faster for modeling design and Finite Element Analysis.

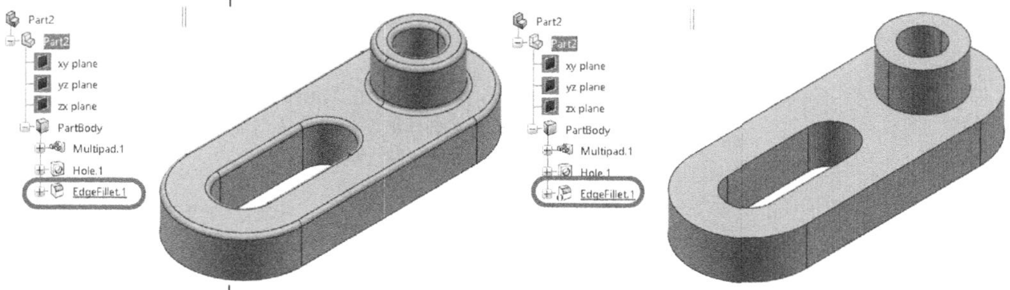

Figure 2–8

Once the design is finalized, it is recommended that you delete all unused features, rather than keep them deactivated in the model. If not deleted, these features can unnecessarily increase file size and cause confusion to someone else using this file at a later time.

Parent/Child Considerations

If a parent feature is selected for deactivation, its children must also be deactivated. Child features that are impacted by deactivating the parent are highlighted in the specification tree and the model. Figure 2–9 shows the **Hole.1** feature selected for deactivation and the Deactivate dialog box. The EdgeFillet feature on the edge of the hole is a child feature and would also have to be deactivated.

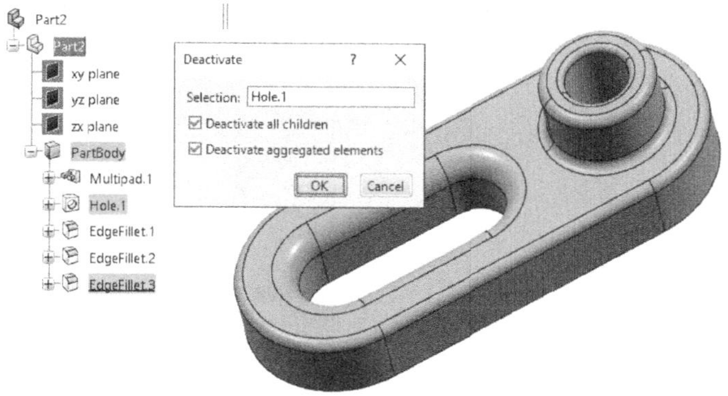

Figure 2–9

2.4 Creating Selection Sets

Selection sets enable you to define groups of features that can be quickly selected at the same time. This function is ideal for groups of features that are selected often. For example, you can quickly deactivate and activate fillet, chamfer, and other dress-up features by adding them to a selection set.

The Selection Sets options, found in the *Tools* section of the Action Bar, are shown in Figure 2–10. It can be hidden if you don't click the expand arrow.

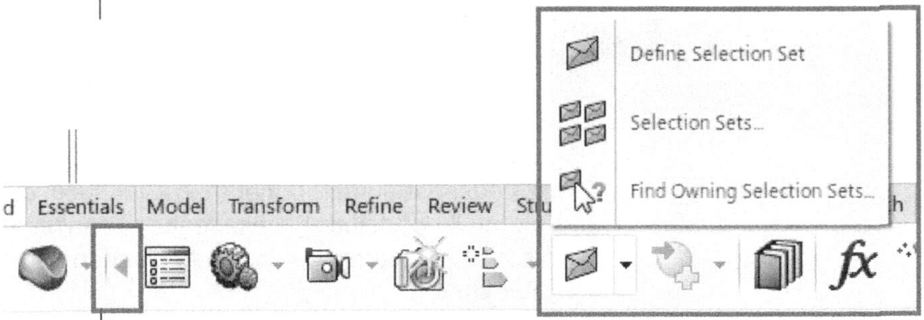

Figure 2–10

How To: Create a Selection Set

1. Click (Define Selection Set) to create a selection box. The Selection Sets Edition dialog box opens, as shown in Figure 2–11.

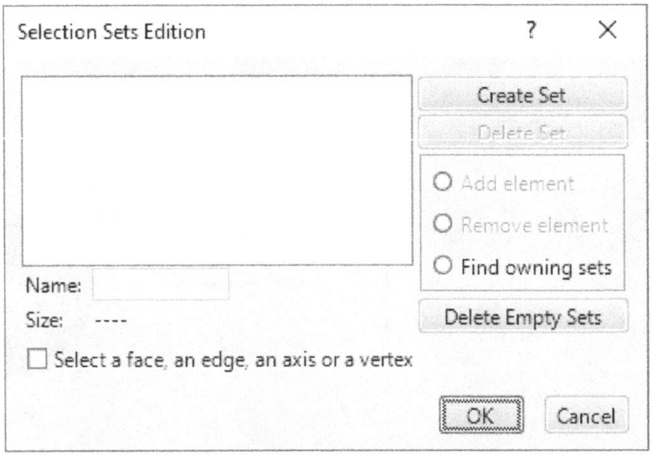

Figure 2–11

2. Click **Create Set** and enter a name for the set in the *Name* field.
3. With the new set highlighted, select the **Add element** option. Select features in the specification tree to add to the set. The **Select a face, an edge, an axis or a vertex** option, enables you to select geometry from the model.
4. Click **OK** to complete the creation of the set.
5. Click  (Selection Sets) to select a feature. The Selection Sets Selection dialog box opens, as shown in Figure 2–12.

Figure 2–12

6. Select the set from the list and click **Select**. Close the dialog box to complete the selection.

Practice 2a Feature Management

Practice Objectives

- Simplify the model display using the **Hide/Show** commands.
- Activate and deactivate features.
- Create and use selection sets.

In this practice, you will use feature management techniques to modify a part. You will use the **Hide/Show**, **Activate/Deactivate** and **Selection Set** commands. In addition, you will learn the properties of these commands and how they affect the model display.

Features are selected for visual clarity.

Task 1 - Hide reference geometry and sketch features.

1. Import **BlockMgt.3dxml**.
2. In the *BlockMgt (Explore)* tab, right-click **BlockMgt** in the specification tree and select **Open**. Note that the reference elements and feature sketches are also displayed.
3. View the invisible space by clicking (Swap Visible Space) in the lower right corner of the graphics area. The background changes to the invisible space color. Some measurements are hidden in the model. Therefore, they display in the invisible space as shown in Figure 2–13.

Note the Invisible Space color in this example is gray. Your system may differ.

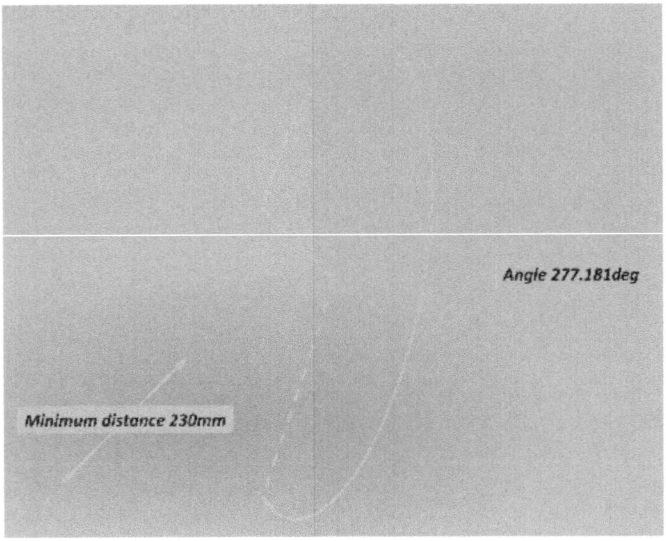

Figure 2–13

4. Return to the visible space by clicking (Swap Visible Space).

5. In the specification tree, using <Ctrl>, select the three default reference plane features.

6. Right-click over any of the selected planes and select **Hide/Show**. The planes are removed from visible space and added to invisible space.

7. The icons for the three planes display in the specification tree with grayed backgrounds, as shown in Figure 2–14.

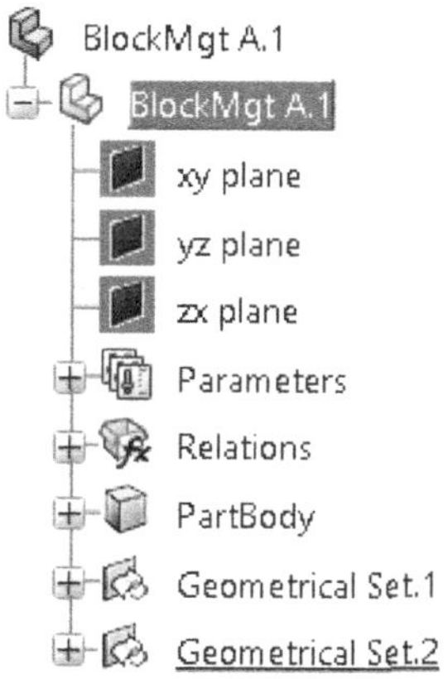

Figure 2–14

8. Click (Swap Visible Space) to switch to invisible space, and note that the planes are shown.

9. Click (Swap Visible Space) again to switch back to visible space.

Note that all hidden feature icons are grayed in the specification tree.

10. By default, sketches that are used to create other features, such as pads, grooves, pockets, etc., are automatically hidden from display. Currently, they are all set to display. In the specification tree, **right-click BlockMtg A.1** and select **BlockMtg A.1 object>Hide>All Sketches** to remove all sketches from visible space. The model updates, as shown in Figure 2–15. If the part turns red without updating, you will need to select (Update) to update it.

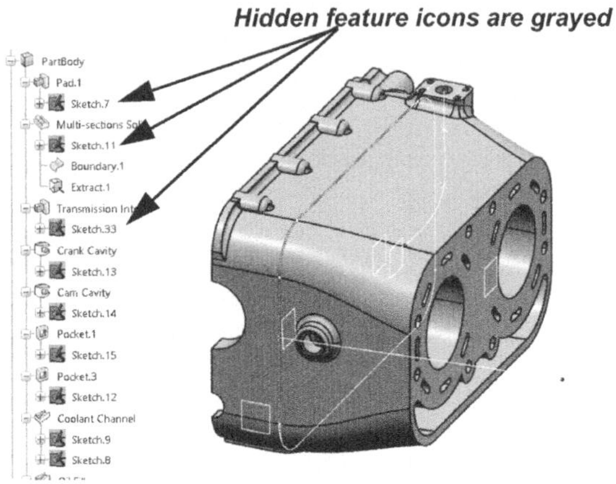

Figure 2–15

11. Reference geometry features are still set to display in visible space. Right-click on **Geometrical Set.1** and select **Geometrical Set.1 object>Hide Components**.

12. Click (Swap Visible Space) to switch to invisible space. The hidden space displays as shown in Figure 2–16.

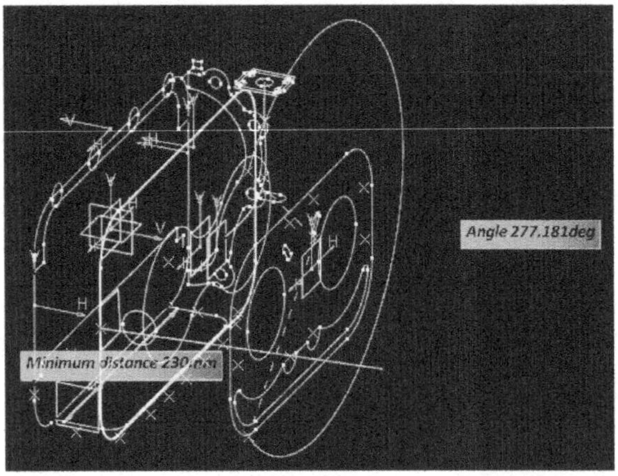

Figure 2–16

13. Switch back to visible space.

Task 2 - Attempt to hide a Hole feature.

1. Select the **Hole.5** feature in the specification tree, right-click and select **Hide/Show**. If you are unable to locate the feature in the specification tree, you can select any other solid feature to hide.

   Note that the contents of the PartBody switch to invisible space. Solid features cannot be hidden or shown independently from the rest of the PartBody solid features.

2. Select the **Hole.5** feature in the specification tree again, right-click and select **Hide/Show** to return PartBody to visible space.

Task 3 - Deactivate the Hole feature.

Design Considerations

As shown in Task 2, individual solid geometry features cannot be hidden independently. However, you can deactivate the individual solid features independently.

1. Right-click on the **Pad.8** feature in the specification tree and select **Pad.8 object>Deactivate**.

2. Note that since this feature has children, the **Deactivate all children** option is automatically enabled, as shown in Figure 2–17.

*Select the **Deactivate aggregated elements** option to deactivate all geometry grouped below the main element node being deactivated.*

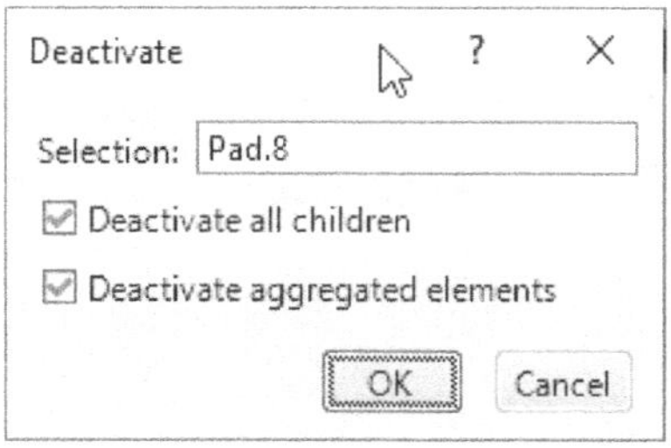

Figure 2–17

3. Click **OK** in the Deactivate dialog box.

The Pad.8 feature and its children are deactivated and removed from visible space, as shown in Figure 2–18.

Deactivation symbol displays on feature icon

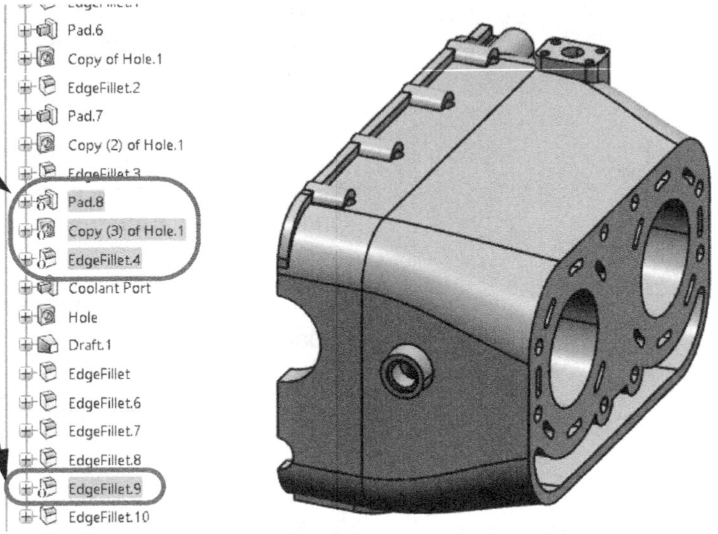

Figure 2–18

The feature is not switched to invisible space because it is deactivated and therefore no longer updates with the rest of the model. In the specification tree, select the deactivated **Pad.8** feature. Right-click, and select **Pad.8 object>Activate**.

4. The **Activate all children** and **Activate aggregated elements** options are enabled by default, as shown in Figure 2–19.

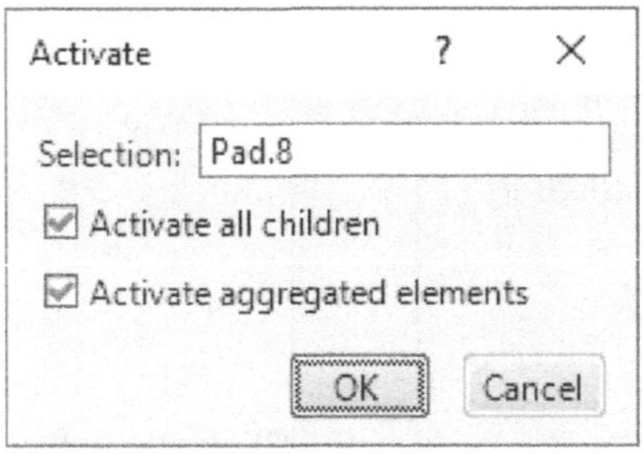

Figure 2–19

5. Click **OK** then click in the background to clear the selection. The model returns to the active state.

Task 4 - Deactivate the Fillet features.

1. Select the *Tools* section of the Action Bar.
2. Near the middle of the Action Bar, click .
3. The Action Bar expands as shown in Figure 2–20.

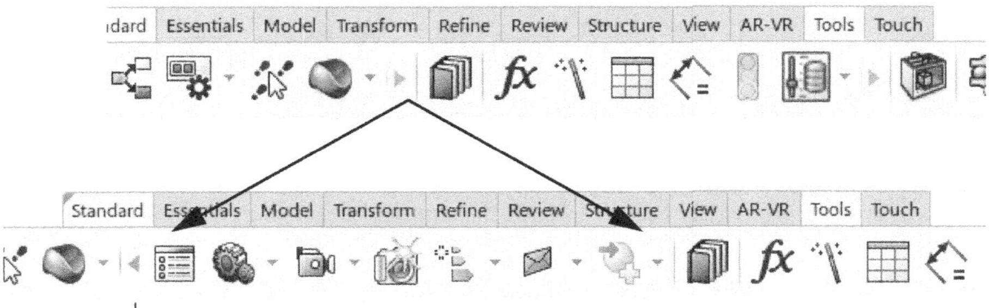

Figure 2–20

4. Click (Define Selection Set). The Selection Sets Edition dialog box opens.
5. Click **Create Set**.
6. Enter **FilletSet** in the *Name* field. Select the **Add element** option as shown in Figure 2–21.

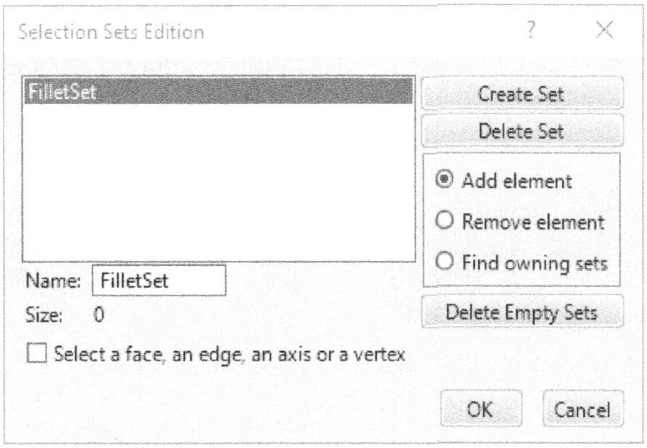

Figure 2–21

Design Considerations

You must perform a search operation to locate the Fillet features to add to the selection set. Searching is the most efficient way to locate and select all of the Fillet features in the model.

7. **Press <Ctrl> + <F>**. The Search dialog box opens.

8. In the *App* drop-down list, select **Part Design** and in the *Type* drop-down list, select **Fillet**. The Search dialog box opens as shown in Figure 2–22.

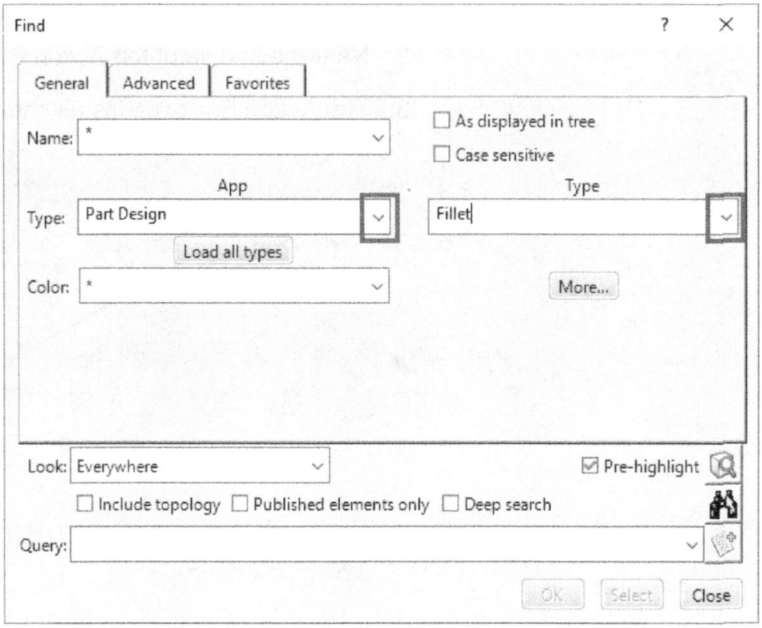

Figure 2–22

9. Click (Find and Select) to start the search. The results of the search is shown in Figure 2–23.

10. In the Selection Sets Edition dialog box, *Size* updates to **10**, as shown in Figure 2–23.

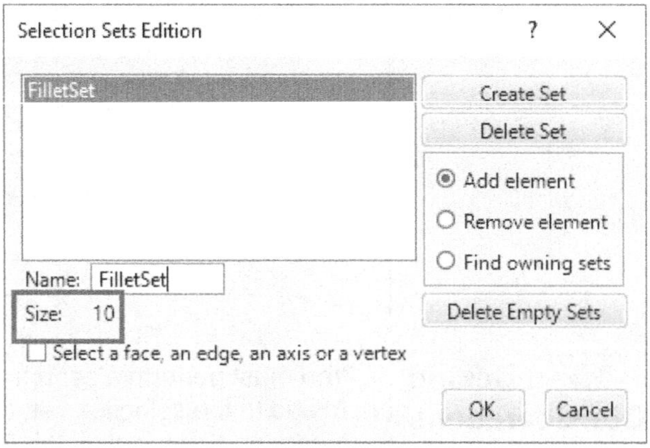

Figure 2–23

11. Click **OK** to close the Selection Sets Edition dialog box. The Fillet features should still be selected.

12. Right-click on any of the selected features in the specification tree and select **Selected objects>Deactivate**. The Fillet features are deactivated from the model, as shown in Figure 2–24.

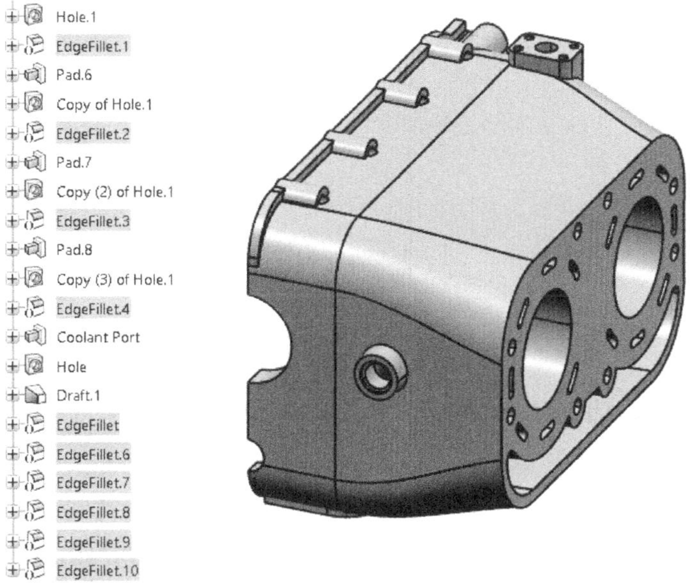

Figure 2–24

13. Clear the Fillet features by clicking in the background.

You can also click (Selection sets) to open the Selection Sets Selection dialog box.

14. Click (Find Owning Selection Sets). The Selection Sets Edition dialog box opens as shown in Figure 2–25.

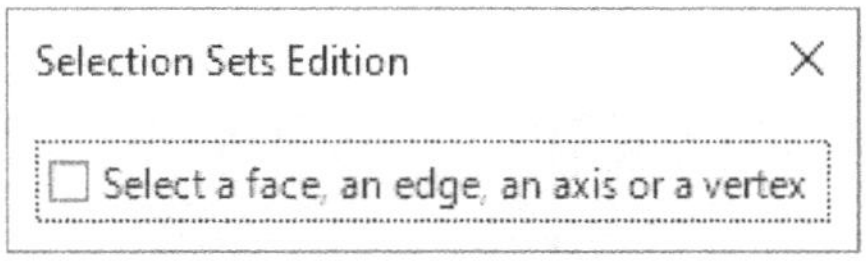

Figure 2–25

15. In the specification tree, select any of the Fillet features. The Selection Sets Selection dialog box opens as shown in Figure 2–26.

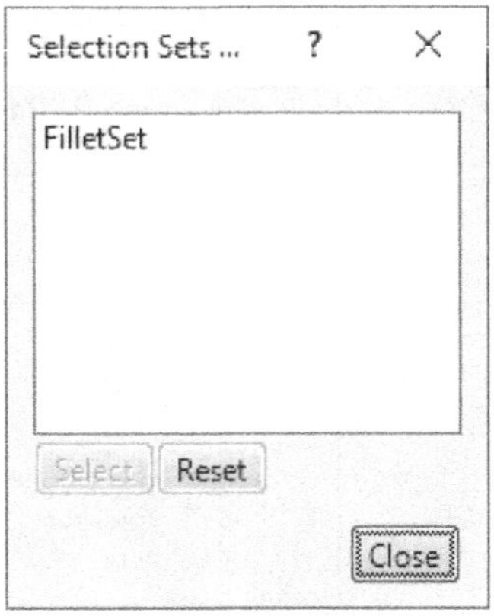

Figure 2–26

Design Considerations

When many unnamed or ambiguous selection sets (e.g., groups of fillets) exist and are difficult to distinguish, use **Find Owning Selection Sets** to locate the required set. Selection sets are accessed through the **Selection Sets** icon. Therefore, remember to name your selection sets meaningfully.

16. In the list, select **FilletSet** and click **Select**. Close the Selection Sets Selection dialog box to complete the selection. The Fillet features are highlighted in the specification tree.

17. Right-click on a Fillet feature in the specification tree and select **Selected objects>Activate**.

18. Save the file and close the tab.

Chapter Review Questions

1. Which of the following feature types are not visible on screen when hidden using the **Hide/Show** command? (Select all that apply.)
   a. Points
   b. Planes
   c. Sketches
   d. Pads
2. Deactivating a feature does not modify children of that feature.
   a. True
   b. False
3. When you deactivate a feature, it continues to be part of the update sequence.
   a. True
   b. False
4. Visible space contains any features that are shown. Invisible space shows features that have been hidden.
   a. True
   b. False
5. A selection set can be used to select individual edges.
   a. True
   b. False
6. By default, sketches that are used to create other features, such as Pads, are automatically hidden from display.
   a. True
   b. False

Answers: 1abc, 2b, 3b, 4a, 5a, 6a

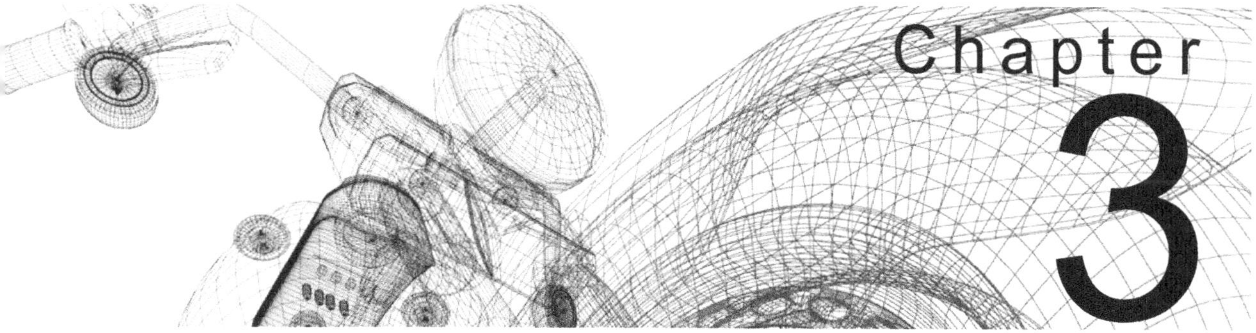

Chapter 3

Part Information

CATIA provides you with several tools that can be used to obtain information about a part's measurements and inertia. You can also use the feature investigation tools to determine how the model was constructed.

Learning Objectives in This Chapter

- Use measure entities.
- Update measurements that result from a model modification.
- Learn how to measure between items.
- Understand Standard, Chain, and Fan modes.
- Apply material to a model.
- Measure 2D and 3D inertia.
- Position a section plane to visualize a 3D section of the model.

3.1 Measuring Items

Click  (Measure Item) in the *Tools* section of the Action Bar, to open the Measure In Part dialog box, as shown in Figure 3–1.

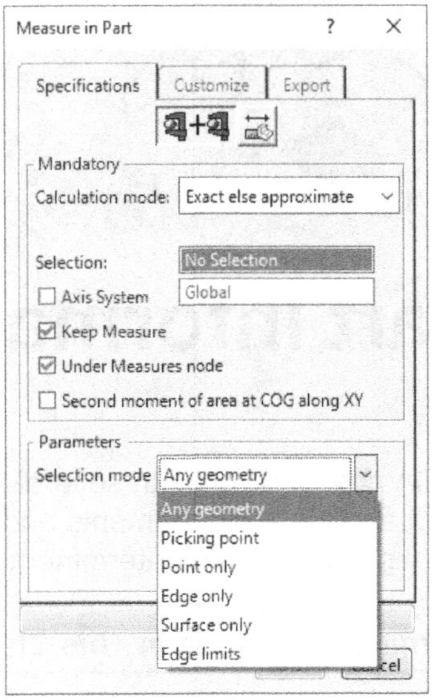

Figure 3–1

The **Measure In Part** tool is a one-click measurement tool that enables you to select one of the following items in the specification tree or on screen to measure:

- **Any geometry**: (Default) Enables measurement between any geometric entities.
- **Picking point:** Measures distance between points selected on defined geometric entities.
- **Point only:** Measures distance between points. Dynamic highlighting is limited to points.
- **Edge only:** Measures distance and angles between edges. Dynamic highlighting is limited to edges. All edge types are supported.
- **Surface only:** Measures distance and angles between surfaces. Dynamic highlighting is limited to surfaces.
- **Edge limits:** Measure the distance to edge extremity points.
- **Thickness:** Measure body thickness at any location.

The calculated results depend on what you select and what result settings are in place. The results for a curved surface are shown in Figure 3–2.

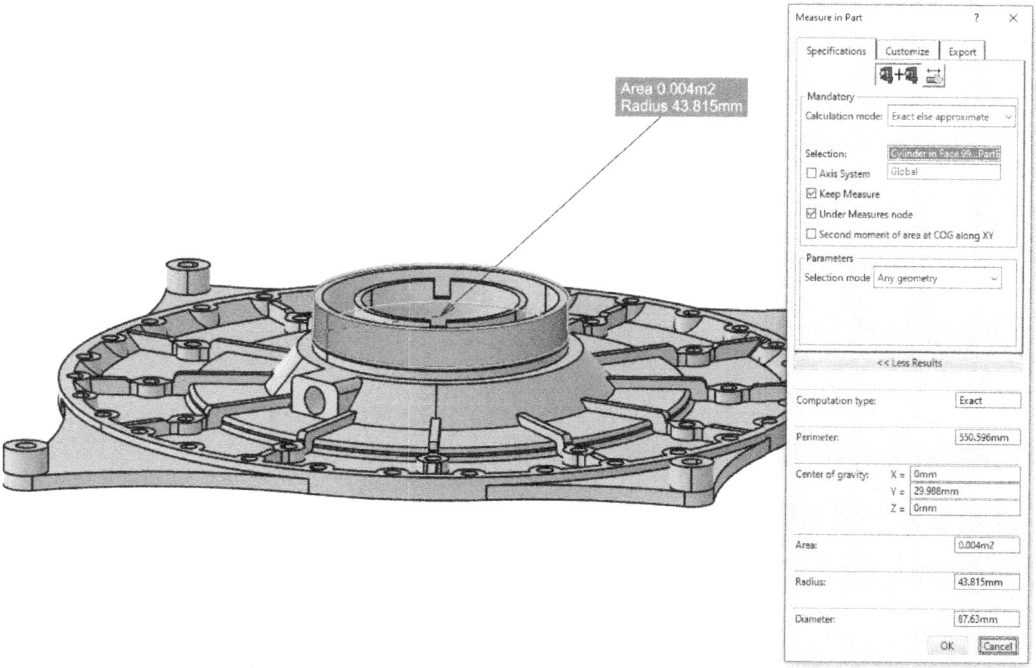

Figure 3–2

The measure item results can be customized for the selected item by selecting the *Customize* tab. The Measure Item Customization dialog box opens as shown in Figure 3–3.

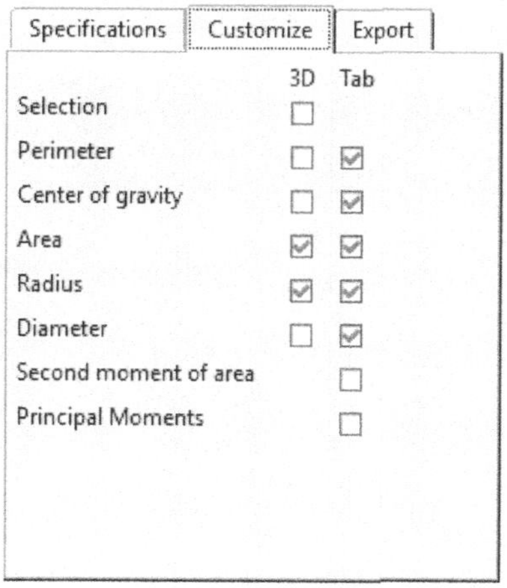

Figure 3–3

You can use the Measure in Part dialog box to create single measures or multiple measures. To create multiple measures, click 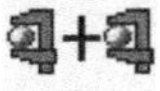 as shown in Figure 3–4.

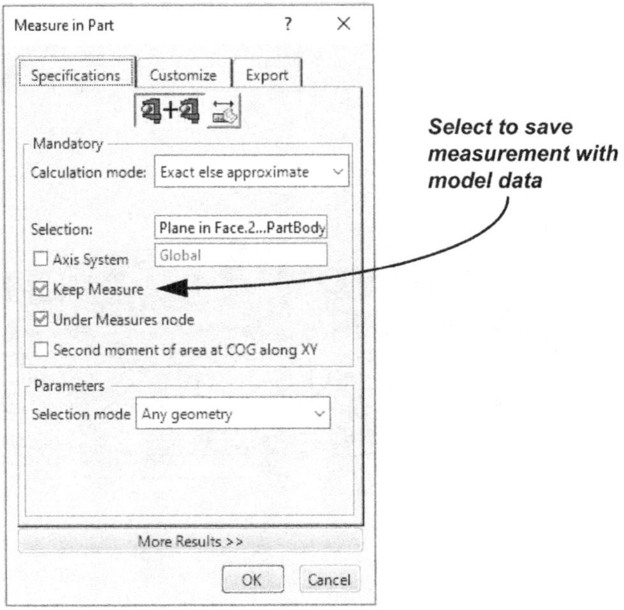

Figure 3–4

The measurement is then added to the specification tree, as shown in Figure 3–5.

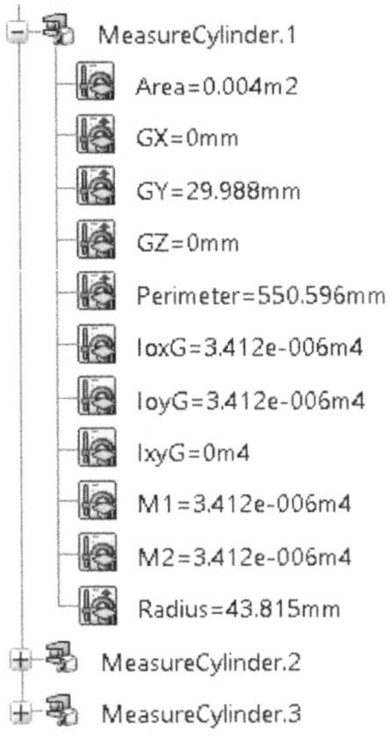

Figure 3–5

3.2 Updating Measurements

If modifications are made in the model that result in a change to a measured value (e.g., geometry change),  displays next to the measurement in the specification tree, indicating that the measured value is not updated.

To update the value, right-click on the measurement name and select **Local update**, as shown in Figure 3–6.

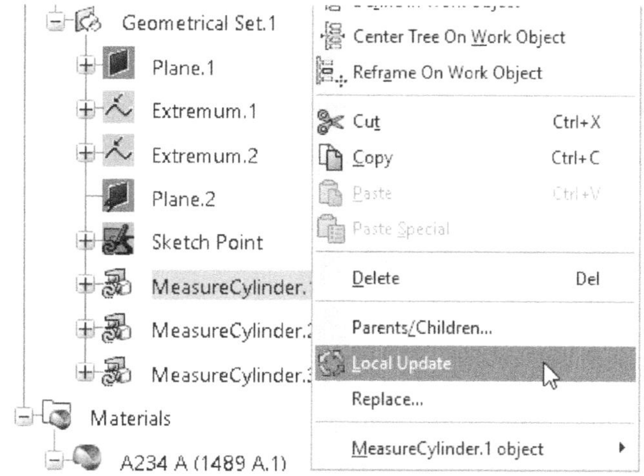

Figure 3–6

To automate the update of these measurements, enable the automatic update options by clicking **Me** > **Preferences** > **Common Preferences** > **Parameters, Measures, and Units** > **Measures** > **Measure Tools** > **Associativity** section, as shown in Figure 3–7.

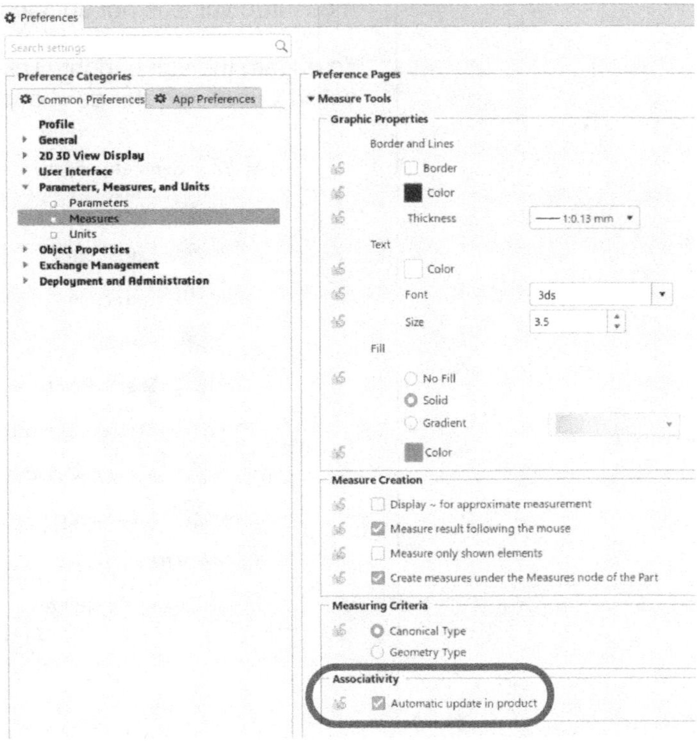

Figure 3–7

3.3 Measuring Between Items

Click (Measure Between) in the *Tools* section of the Action Bar to open the Measure Between In Part dialog box, as shown in Figure 3–8.

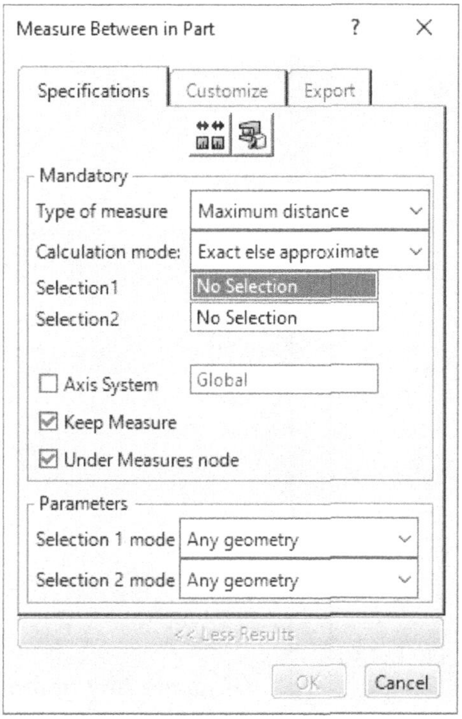

Figure 3–8

Measure Between in Part Geometry Selection

The **Measure Between in Part** tool is a two-click measurement tool that enables you to measure between two selected items of the same or mixed types. You can select from the specification tree or on the screen. The different selectable item types for the **Measure Between in Part** tool are shown in Figure 3–9.

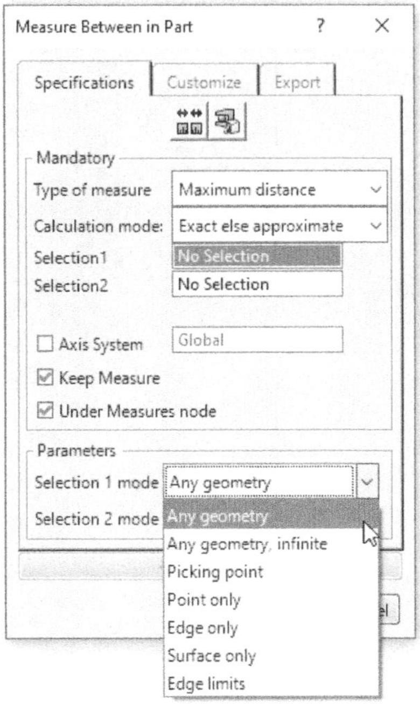

Figure 3–9

Using the **Any geometry** option, the software enables you to measure between geometry of any type. If this causes difficulty in selecting a specific type of element, select a more applicable element in the **Selection 1 mode** and/or **Selection 2 mode** drop-down menus.

The **Any geometry, infinite** option extends the selected plane, curve, or line infinitely to obtain an accurate minimum distance.

The two-click **Measure Between in Part** tool can be used to take measurements, such as the distance between items or angle between items.

An example of a measurement between two selected hole centers is shown in Figure 3–10. The results can be saved and customized using the same method as the **Measure Item** tool.

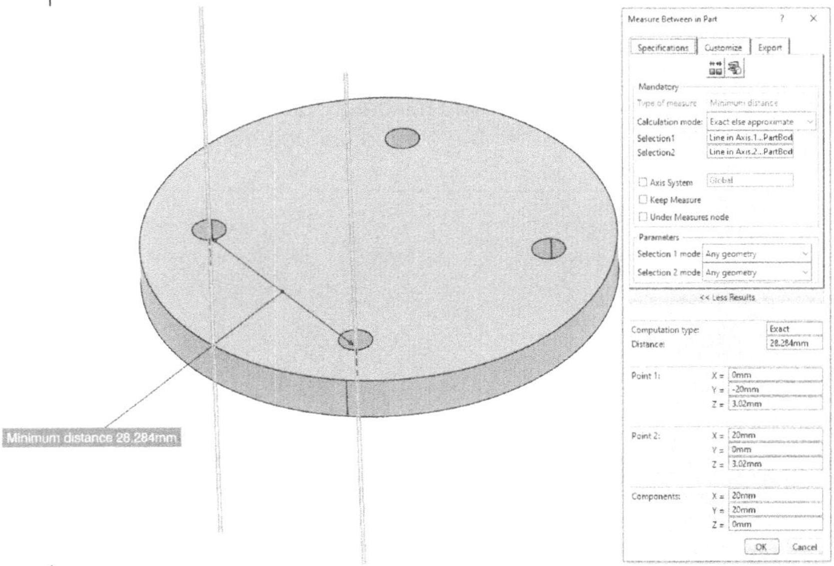

Figure 3–10

When selecting hole and arc centers, you can display an axis by moving the cursor over the approximate center of the hole and arc, as shown in Figure 3–11.

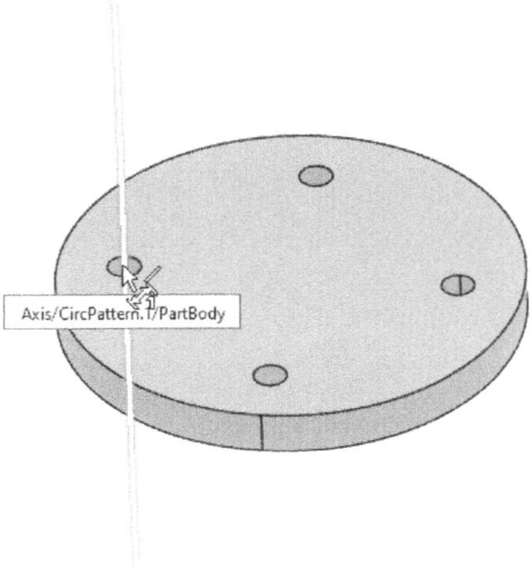

Figure 3–11

Measuring with Reference Elements

In situations where the part geometry is complex, such as models created using surfacing techniques, it is difficult to find planar references to measure between. In this case, reference elements can be constructed to generate an exact measurement reference.

For example, consider the simplified example shown in Figure 3–12. In this case, a Measure Between operation referencing the top and bottom faces can report the minimum and maximum distances. The software can select the location on the curved surface from which the measurement is made.

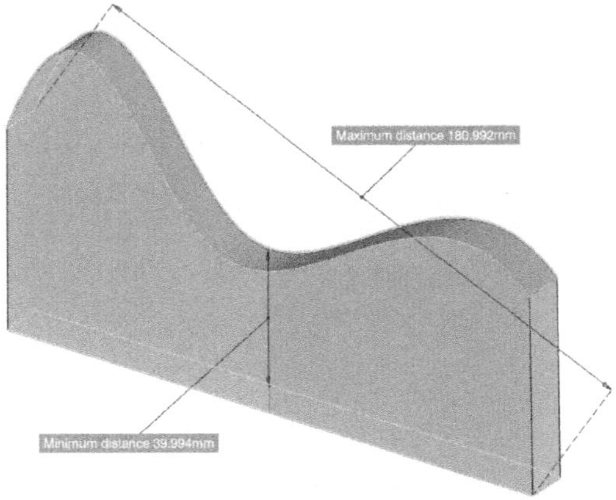

Figure 3–12

To measure the distance between an exact location on the top surface, a reference point can be created to define the location, as shown in Figure 3–13.

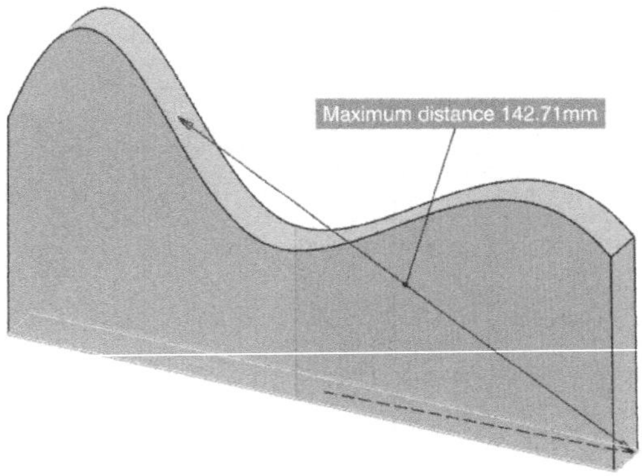

Figure 3–13

To further define the type of measurement, a reference plane can be created. This restricts the measurement direction to be normal to the plane, as shown in Figure 3–14. Another option is to use the **Components** option, accessed by selecting the **Customize** tab. This reports the X, Y, and Z components of a measurement, enabling you to extract the required direction.

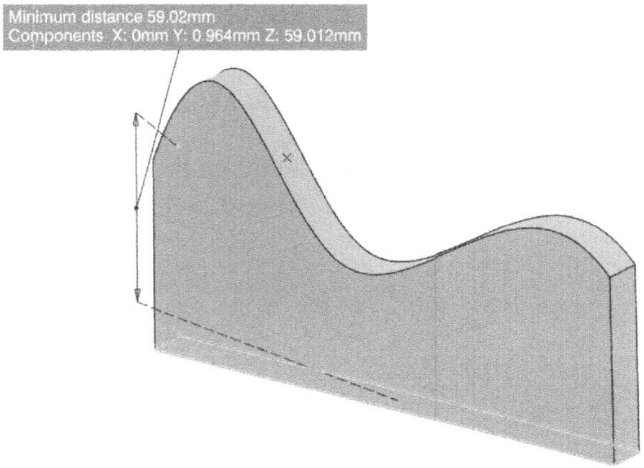

Figure 3–14

3.4 Measuring Inertia

Before measuring the inertia of the model, it is recommended that you first define the model's material properties.

Apply a Material

When you apply a material to a model, the properties of the model (such as density and Young's modulus) are defined. This ensures that accurate inertia values are computed for the model.

Use the following steps to apply a material:

1. Activate the model at the 3D Shape level as shown in Figure 3–15.

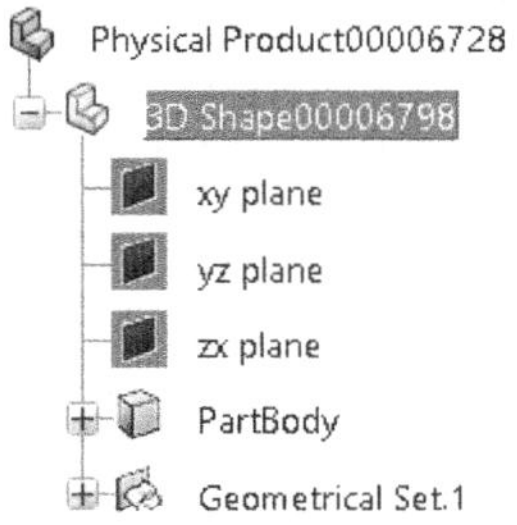

Figure 3–15

2. In the *Tools* section of the Action Bar, click  (Material Browser) to set the material for the model. The Materials dialog box opens as shown in Figure 3–16.

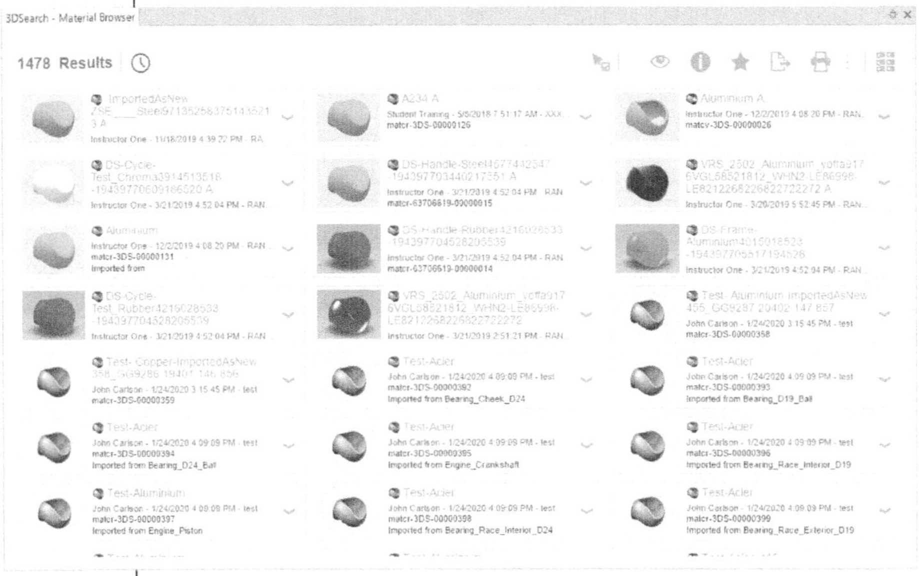

Figure 3–16

3. The view can be changed between Thumbnail, Tile, and Datagrid using the icon in the upper right of the Material browser, as shown in Figure 3–17.

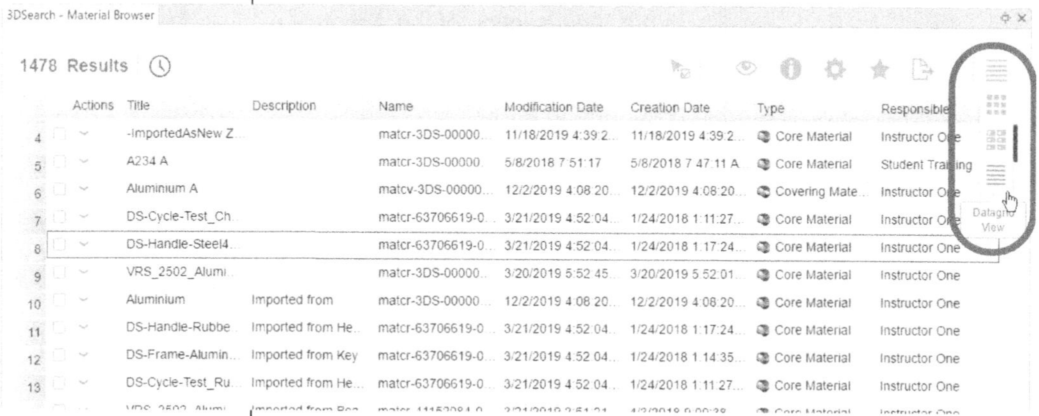

Figure 3–17

4. Select a material in the Materials results dialog box, right-click and select **Apply Material**, then click on the part body.

5. Click (Exit Context Menu). The material is listed in the specification tree, as shown in Figure 3–18. All properties for the selected material are defined for the model to which the material is applied. The properties are also used in the inertia calculations.

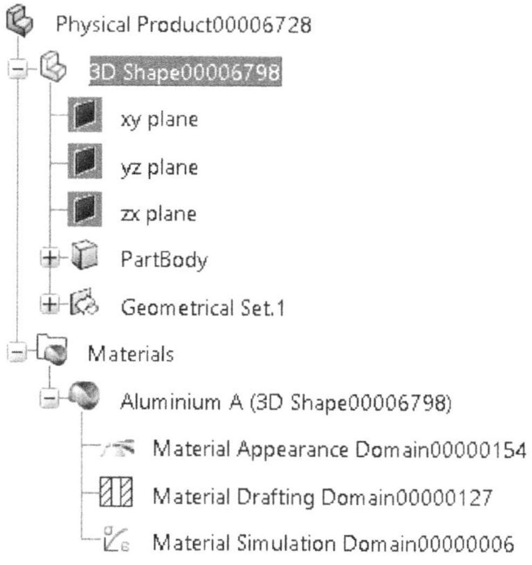

Figure 3–18

Viewing the Material

The model can also be viewed in a custom View mode with the material rendering applied.

In the *View* section of the Action Bar, click  (View Mode), and then select  (Shading With Material) to apply the material rendering to a model.

Changing Material Appearance

After a material is applied, you can change its properties. Double-click the material Rendering domain and the Material Definition: Appearance Domain dialog box opens as shown in Figure 3–19. Here you can edit the appearance by changing the **Transparency, and Sheen**, and so on.

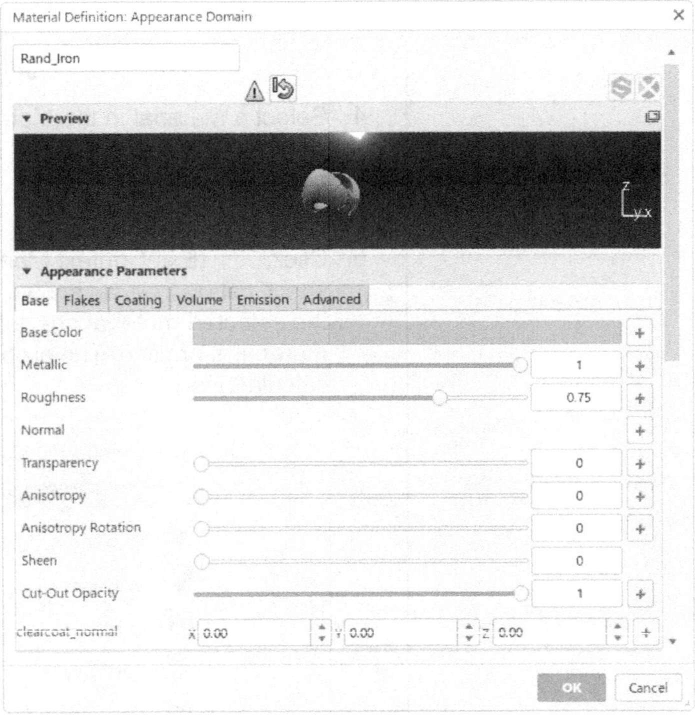

Figure 3–19

Measure Inertia 3D

The inertia of an object is defined as the property by which it retains its present velocity (speed and direction) so long as it is not acted on by an external force. An equivalent definition of inertia is the resistance of an object to a change in its motion.

To compute the model inertia using the model's current material properties, in the *Tools* section of the Action Bar, click

 (Create Inertia Data). You can select 3D entities (such as features or bodies) in the specification tree and measure their inertia. Select the **Volume** option, and the results display in the Measure Inertia dialog box, as shown in Figure 3–20.

Figure 3–20

The dialog box reports the following information:

- Characteristics, such as volume, area, mass, and density.
- The center of gravity relative to the origin of the part.
- Inertia data of the part. (Inertia tabs)

The inertia data of the part can be measured with respect to a variety of elements by selecting one of the tabs described in the table below.

Tab	Meaning
Inertia / G	Measure inertia with respect to the center of gravity of the model.
Inertia / O	Measure inertia with respect to the origin of the model.
Inertia / P	Measure inertia with respect to a selected point.
Inertia / Axis	Measure inertia with respect to a selected axis.
Inertia / Axis System	Measure inertia with respect to a selected axis system.

The *Inertia / G* tab is activated by default. To activate the other four tabs, click **Customization** to open the Customization dialog box shown in Figure 3–21.

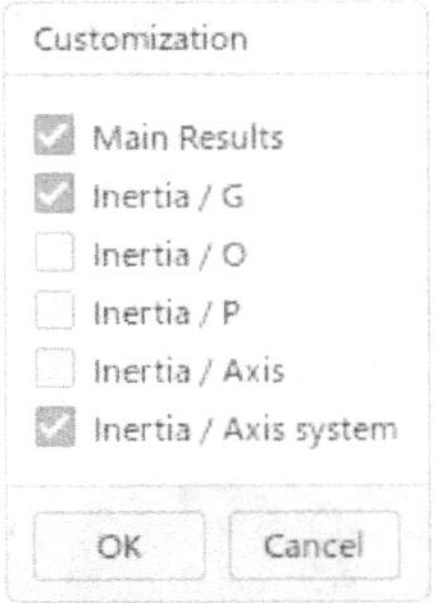

Figure 3–21

Each tab displays a variety of inertia data that is relevant to the measurement reference. For example, the parameters described in the table below are reported for an Inertia / G calculation.

Parameter	Meaning
Iox	Area moment of inertia about the X-axis.
Ioy	Area moment of inertia about the Y-axis.
Ioz	Area moment of inertia about the Z-axis.
Ixy	Mass moment of inertia on the XY plane.
Ixz	Mass moment of inertia on the XZ plane.
Iyz	Mass moment of inertia on the YZ plane.

The **Measure Inertia** tool also enables you to create a point and/or an axis system at the center of gravity in the part. To create geometry, click **Create Geometry** in the Measure Inertia dialog box as shown in Figure 3–22.

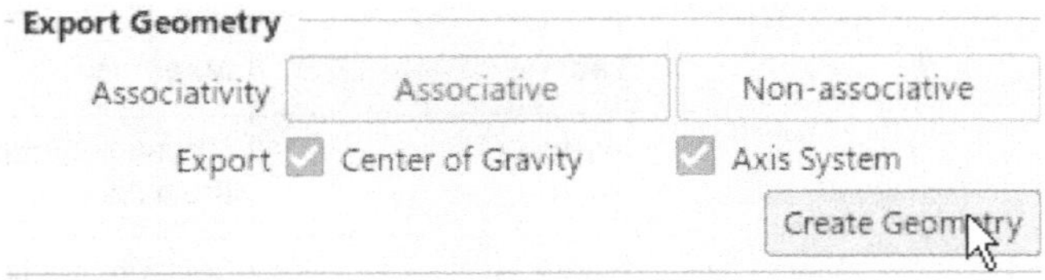

Figure 3–22

An axis system and a point at the center of gravity have been created in Figure 3–23 using the **Create geometry** tool.

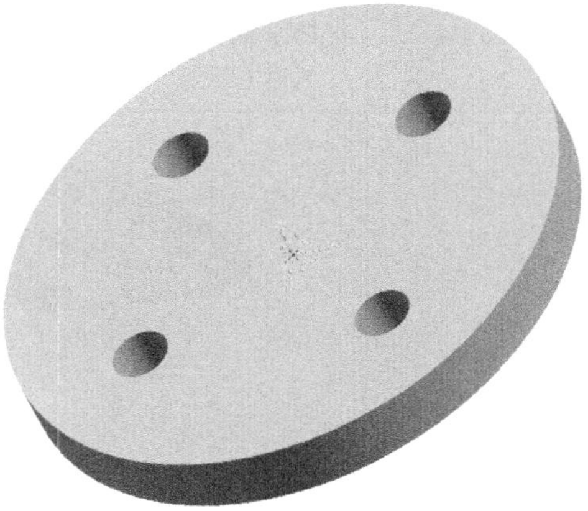

Figure 3–23

Measuring the inertia of a section or surface is useful for rapidly determining the structural properties of complex shapes. With **Surface** selected, you can select solid faces from the model and measure their two-dimensional inertia properties. This tool is identical to its 3D counterpart, except that certain calculations that do not apply to two-dimensional surfaces (mass, density, volume, etc.) are not present. Also, only the *Inertia / G* tab is evaluated when measuring 2D entities.

3.5 Dynamic Sectioning

The Dynamic Sectioning enables you to position a section plane to visualize a 3D section view of a part, as shown in Figure 3–24. The section plan can be dynamically adjusted.

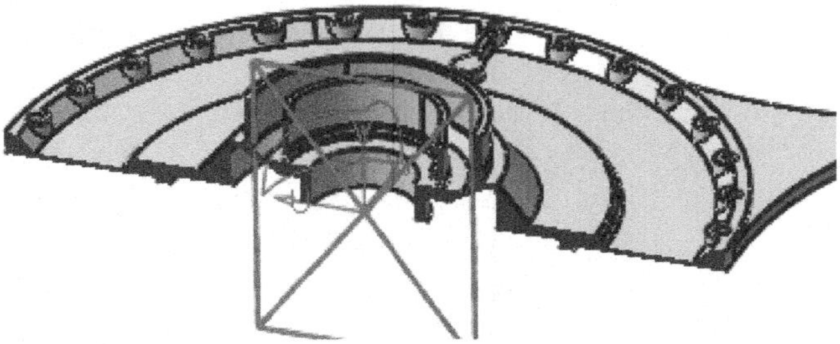

Figure 3–24

To use the Dynamic Sectioning tool, click  (Dynamic Sectioning) from the *Review* section of the Action Bar. A red section plane is automatically displayed on the model.

The location of the section plane can dynamically be modified. To adjust the position, select an edge, surface, plane, or curve in the model. If you are selecting a reference in the model, a purple section plane locater icon displays, as shown in Figure 3–25.

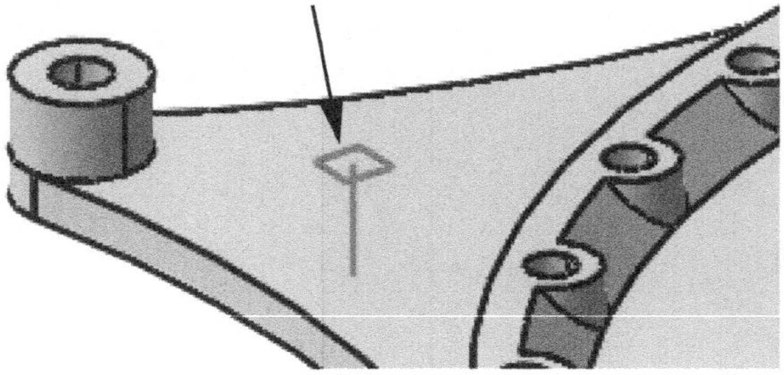

Figure 3–25

To translate the section plane along about the selected reference, hover the cursor over the red section plane, as shown in Figure 3–26. When the green arrow displays, click and drag the plane to the required location. The model is dynamically cut about the section plane as you click and drag.

To rotate the section plane, hover the cursor over one of the red arcs on the section plane compass. Click the arc, and drag the section plane to the required location, as shown in Figure 3–27.

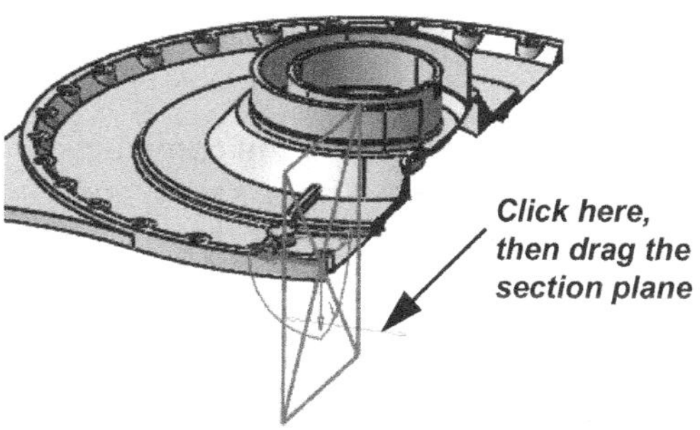

Figure 3–26

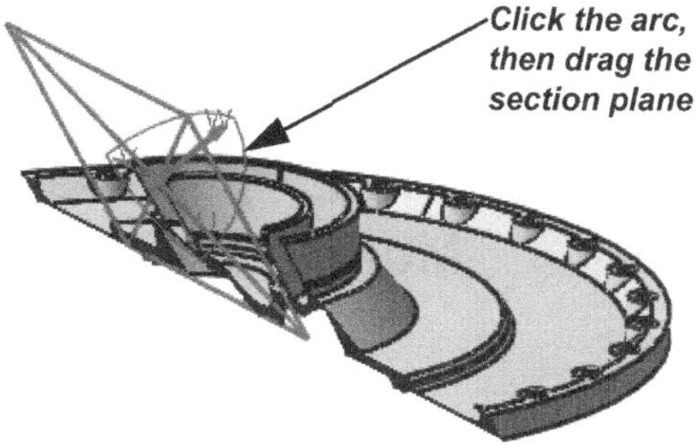

Figure 3–27

The section plane can be adjusted repeatedly. When done using the Dynamic Sectioning tool, deactivate by clicking  (Dynamic Sectioning).

3.6 Feature Investigation

3DEXPERIENCE provides several tools to investigate a model. The investigation tools can be used to determine how a model is constructed. These tools are useful for the following situations:

- If a model is created by someone else.
- If it has been a long time since you worked on the part.
- If the model is complex and you need to modify the feature structure.

Scanning the Model

Scanning the model enables you to review the construction history of a model, one feature at a time. This is very useful when working with models that are created by other users. The **Scan** tool can give you an idea of the model creator's design intent and modeling techniques, by replaying and reviewing the design.

To use the **Scan** tool, in the *Review* section of the Action Bar, click  (Scan or Define In Work Object). The Scan tool opens in the lower left of the 3DEXPERIENCE window. You can leave the tool pinned, or can drag it out to be a stand alone toolbar, as shown in Figure 3–28. Use the control icons to play, step forward, rewind, or stop the model at the current feature creation location.

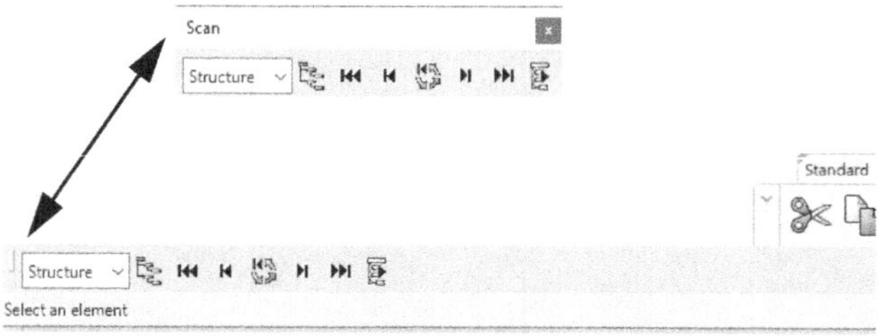

Figure 3–28

By default, the **Structure** option is selected in the Scan tool. With this setting, the software replays the features of the active body based on the feature order displayed in the specification tree. Features in other bodies or geometrical sets are not replayed.

If the **Update** option is selected, the software replays the features in the model in the order in which they are updated, as shown in Figure 3–29.

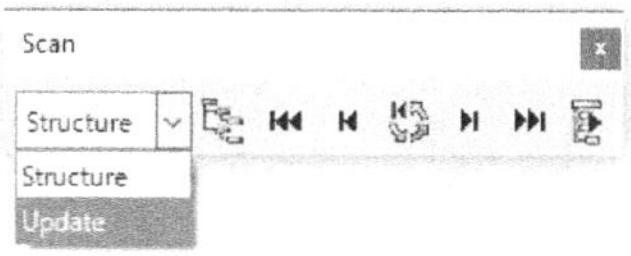

Figure 3–29

For example, consider the specification tree shown in Figure 3–30. The part was created by first adding a reference plane that was used as a support for Sketch.1. The scan order, based on the **Structure** or **Update** option, is shown in the table below.

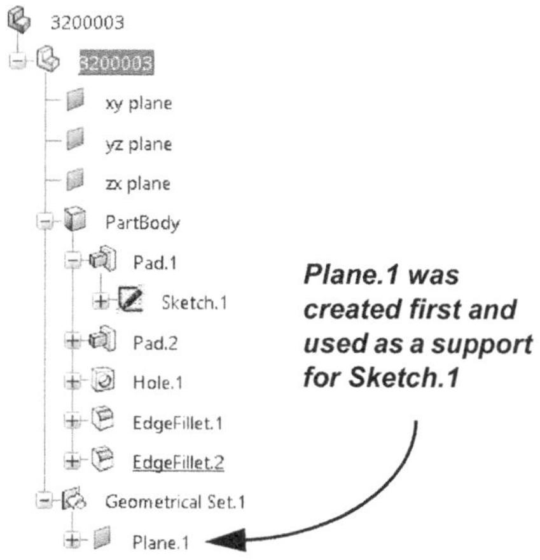

Figure 3–30

#	Structure	Update
1	Pad.1	Plane.1
2	Pad.2	Sketch.1
3	Hole.1	Pad.1
4	EdgeFillet.1	Hole.1
5	EdgeFillet.2	Pad.2
6	End	Hole.1
7		EdgeFillet.1
8		EdgeFillet.2
9		End

Practice 3a Take Measurements

Practice Objectives

- Review the feature creation history.
- Assign a material to the part.
- Determine the mass, volume, and surface area of the part.

In this practice, you will use the Scan tool to view the model's creation history. You will also assign a material to the part, take measurements of the part, and analyze some of its properties, such as mass and volume.

Task 1 - Import the part called Support_Info and review how it is modeled.

1. Import **Support_Info.3dxml**.
2. Right-click **Support** in the specification tree and select **Open**.
3. Set the view orientation to  (* iso).
4. Set the display to  (Shading With Edges) by using the  (View Modes) command. The part displays as shown in Figure 3–31.

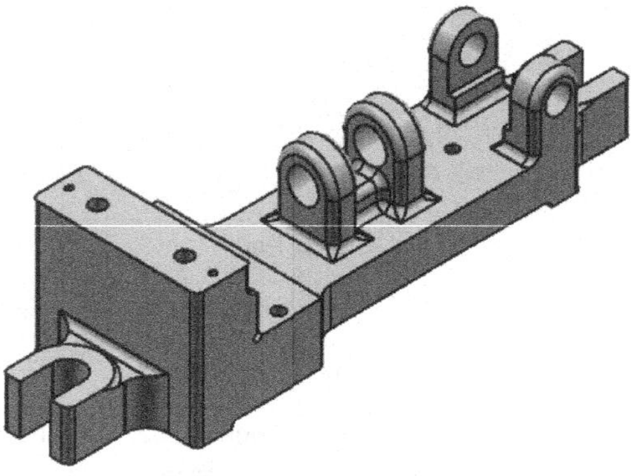

Figure 3–31

5. Note the feature order in the specification tree to review how the model is created.

Task 2 - Scan the model.

Design Considerations

Scanning the model is another way of reviewing its creation history. This is often a helpful tool if you did not create the model, but need to update it. The **Scan** tool enables you to review the creation process and grasp the original designer's design intent.

1. In the *Review* section of the Action Bar, click (Scan or Define In Work Object) to activate the **Scan** tool.
2. In the lower left of the 3DEXPERIENCE window, click (First) to reset the model to the first feature created. The model displays as shown in Figure 3–32. A Pad is the first feature created for the model.

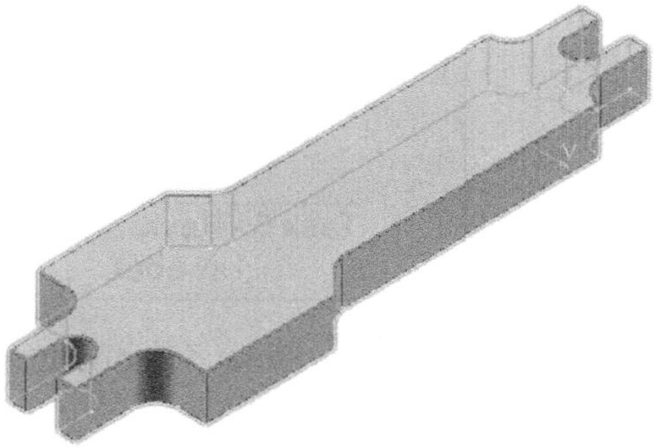

Figure 3–32

3. Click (Next) and note the addition of a second Pad feature.

4. Click (Play Update) and the software will automatically play the addition of the remaining features, as shown in Figure 3–33.

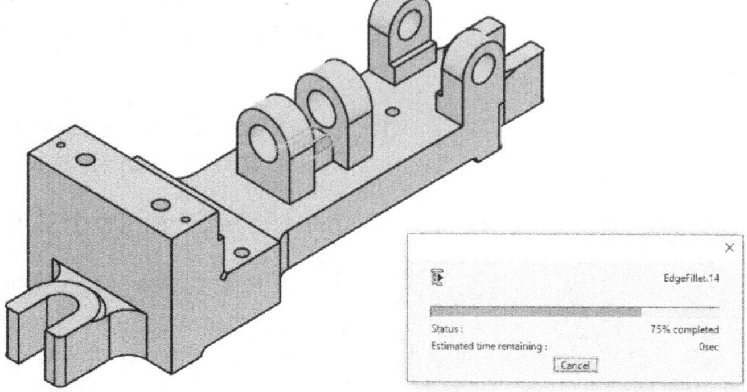

Figure 3–33

5. In the *Review* section of the Action Bar, click (Scan or Define In Work Object) to close the scan tool.

Task 3 - Review some of the parent/child relationships in the model.

1. Expand PartBody in the specification tree to display the features under PartBody.

2. A design change requires that the Shaft support of Pad.6 be modified. As a precaution before making modifications, it is a good idea to review the child features that rely on Pad.6 as a parent. Select the **Pad.6** feature in the specification tree, right-click and select **Parents/Children**. The Parents and Children dialog box opens as shown in Figure 3–34.

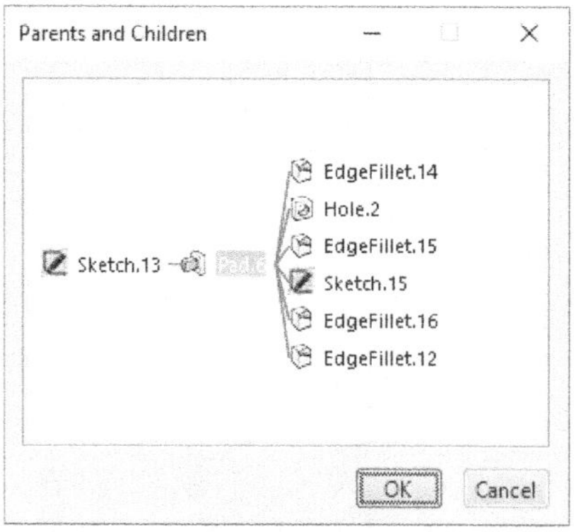

Figure 3–34

All of the items listed on the right side of Pad.6 are child features that reference Pad.6. Modifications to Pad.6 might result in modifications or failures with the child features. The parent feature (Sketch.13) is listed on the left side of Pad.6.

3. Double-click on various items in the dialog box to display further levels of the parent/child relations.
4. Click **OK** to close the Parents and Children dialog box.

Task 4 - Import a Material Library.

1. In the Top Bar, click (Add) **Import**.
2. In the *Format* drop-down list, select **3DXML with authoring (*.3dxml)**.
3. Change the path to **C:\Program Files\Dassault Systemes\B424_Cloud_Content\win_b64\resources\materials** as shown in Figure 3–35.
4. Select **DS Standard.3dxml** and change the Duplication String from to **RAND_** as shown in Figure 3–35.

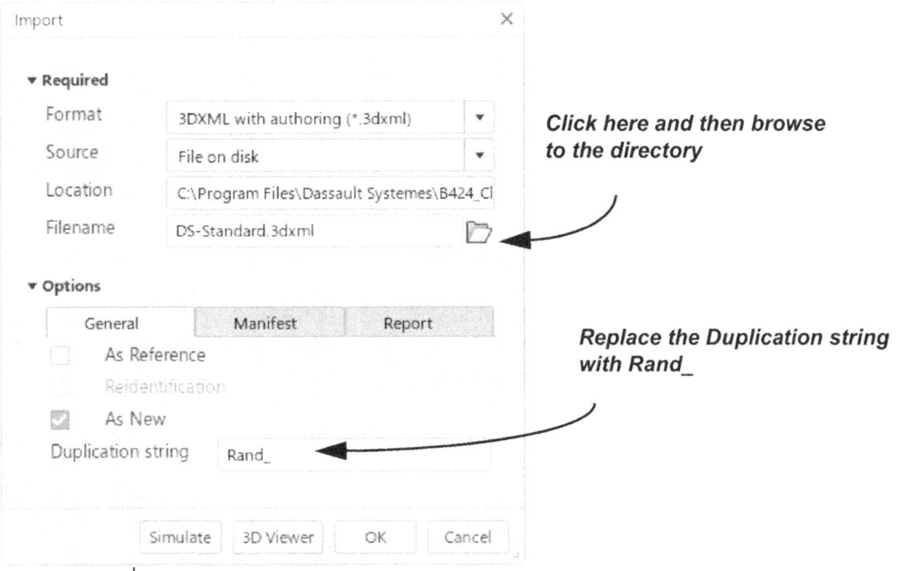

Figure 3–35

5. Click **OK**, and the Material Library will import and become available for use in the next task.
6. Click **OK** in the Operation Report dialog box.

Task 5 - Assign iron as the model material before you calculate inertia.

1. In the *Tools* section of the Action Bar, click (Material Browser) to open the material library.
2. Select **Rand_Iron** in the Material Browser window.
3. Right-click on the material and select **Apply**.
4. Close the Material Browser and select the **Support** 3D Part.
5. Click (Close Context Toolbar).
6. Note the Iron material listed in the specification tree, as shown in Figure 3–36.

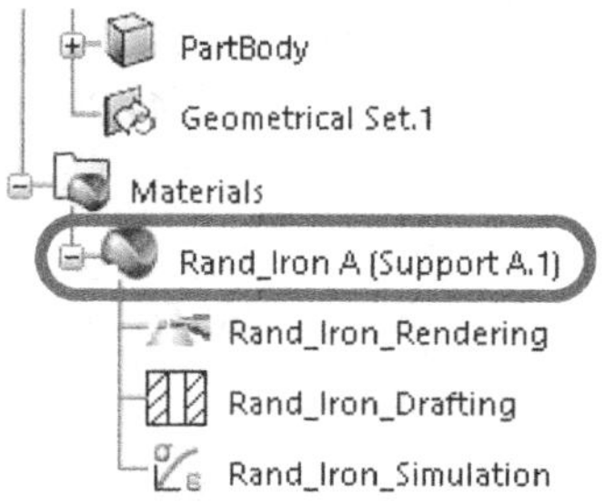

Figure 3–36

Task 6 - Display the model with iron material.

1. In the *View* section of the Action Bar, click (View Modes) then select (Shading With Material). The model is rendered with the material applied to it, as shown in Figure 3–37.

Figure 3–37

Task 7 - View inertia results using the iron material properties.

1. Select the part body in the specification tree, and in the Tools section of the Action Bar, click (Measure Inertia Data) to measure the model inertia. The resulting data displays in the Measure Inertia dialog box as shown in Figure 3–38.

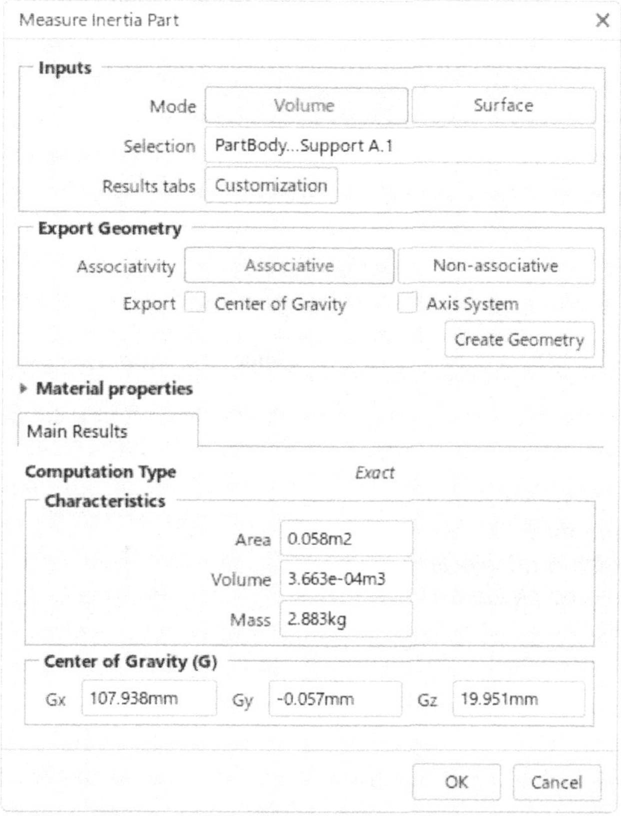

Figure 3–38

2. Note the surface Area value. This might be important if the part is powder-coated or plated.

3. Note the Volume value. This might be important in calculating the material cost of molded or cast parts.

4. Leave the Measure Inertia dialog box open.

Task 8 - Measure inertia with respect to an axis system.

1. If the *Inertia / Axis System* tab is not displayed in the Measure Inertia dialog box, click **Customization** and enable the **Inertia / G** and **Inertia / Axis system** options (if not selected) as shown in Figure 3–39.

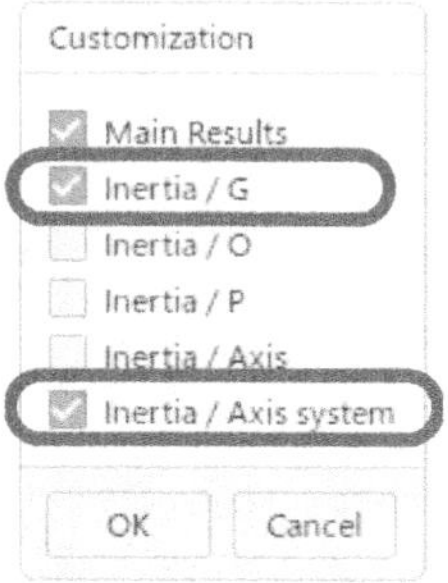

Figure 3–39

2. Click **OK**.
3. Select the *Inertia / Axis System* tab.
4. Select the **Select Axis System** option highlighted in Figure 3–40 and select **Axis System.1** as the axis system.

*Note the **Select Axis System** option is immediately deselected when you click the axis system.*

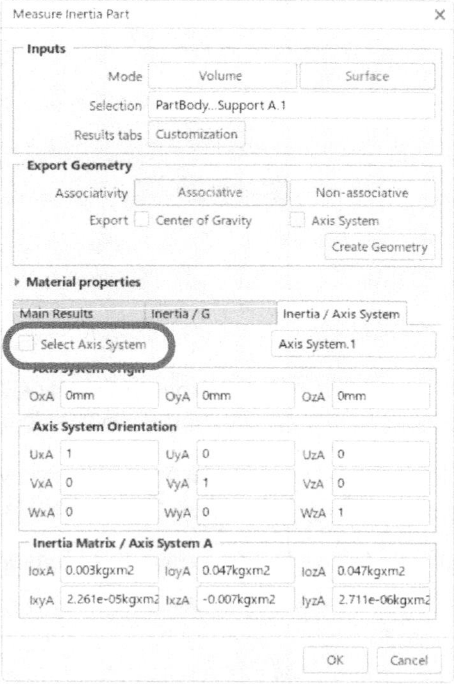

Figure 3–40

5. Note how the values of the Inertia Matrix are different than the values measured in the *Inertia / G* tab (select the PartBody to calculate).

6. Close the dialog box.

7. Change the View mode back to (Shading With Edges) using the (View Modes) command.

Task 9 - Take a series of one-click measurements.

1. In the *Tools* section of the Action Bar, click (Measure Item) to make some one-click measurements.

*If the units for the area calculation are incorrect, select **Preferences > General>Parameters and Measure**, select the Units tab and set the Area units to square meter.*

2. Select the cylindrical surface shown in Figure 3–41. Note that both the area and radius are displayed.

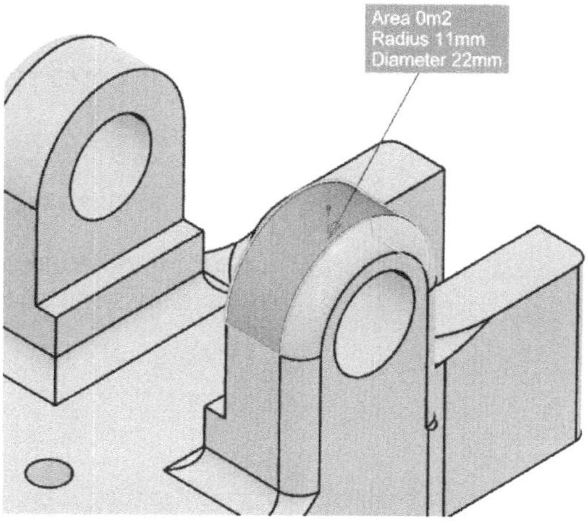

Figure 3–41

Design Considerations

Note that you obtain an area of $0m^2$. This is because the area of the cylindrical surface is relatively small. You can determine the correct area by changing the number of decimal places displayed for measurement.

3. Select **Me** > **Preferences** > **Common Preferences**> **Parameters, Measure, and Units**> *Units* section.

4. Select **Area** in the *Magnitudes* field.

Decimal places cannot be set globally. You must set the number of decimal places for each type of unit individually.

5. Change the value in the *Decimal places for read/write numbers* field to **7**, as shown in Figure 3–42.

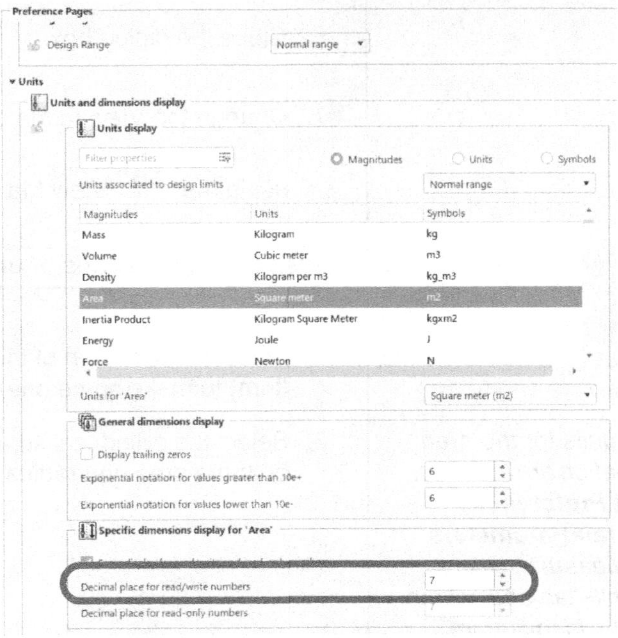

Figure 3–42

6. Click **OK** to close the Options dialog box.
7. Repeat the measurement of the cylindrical surface. The results display as shown in Figure 3–43.

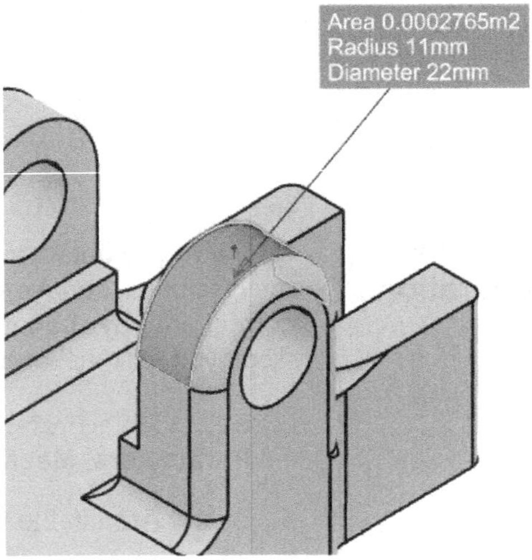

Figure 3–43

8. Take additional one-click measure item measurements for different items in the model, including flat surfaces, the part body, and a vertex.

9. Close the Measure Item dialog box.

Task 10 - Take a series of measure between measurements.

1. Click  (Measure Between) to take some Measure Between measurements.

2. In the *Type of Measure* drop-down list, select **Minimum distance**.

3. Select the flat face and hole axis to measure between, as shown in Figure 3–44.

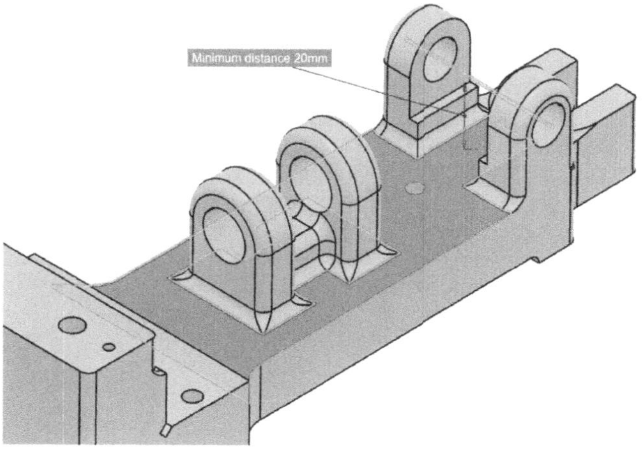

Figure 3–44

4. Note that the Angle dimension is calculated in the dialog box but not on the model. This dimension is not required.

5. Select the *Customize* tab to customize the results.

6. Clear the **Angle** option in the *Tab* column in the Measure Between Customization dialog box.

7. Click **OK**.

8. Repeat Step 3 for a different flat face and hole axis. Note that only the distance is measured and displayed in both the dialog box and on the model.

9. Practice making additional measurements using Measure Between.
10. Hide the parameters that you have just created.
11. Save the model and close the tab.

Practice 3b Measuring with Reference Geometry

Practice Objective

- Create reference geometry to perform measure operations.

In this practice, you will determine the maximum width, height, and length of the model. To do this, you will develop reference geometry, such as points and planes, to assist in your measurements.

Task 1 - Import GameController and take a measurement.

1. Import **GameController.3dxml**.
2. Right-click **GameController** and select **Open**.The model displays as shown in Figure 3–45.

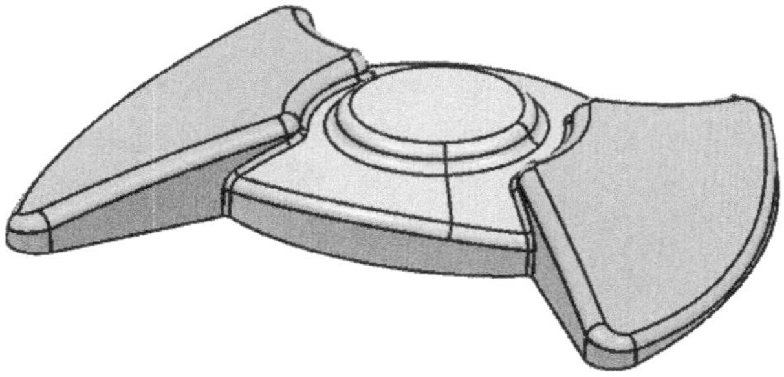

Figure 3–45

3. In the *Tools* section of the Action Bar, click  (Measure Between) and set the *Type of measure* to **Maximum distance** and ensure *Selection 1 and 2 mode* are set to **Any geometry**.

4. Measure between the two arc edges on the bottom of the model, as shown in Figure 3–46, to obtain the overall height of the model.

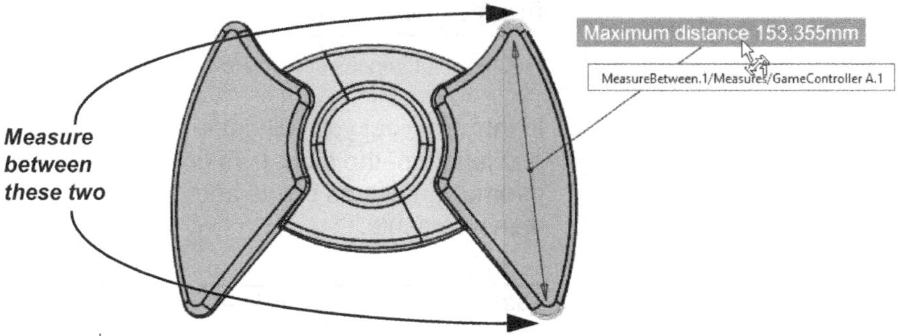

Figure 3–46

The software reports the distance between the centers of the two arcs, as shown in Figure 3–47. To obtain the overall height of the part, additional reference geometry must be developed.

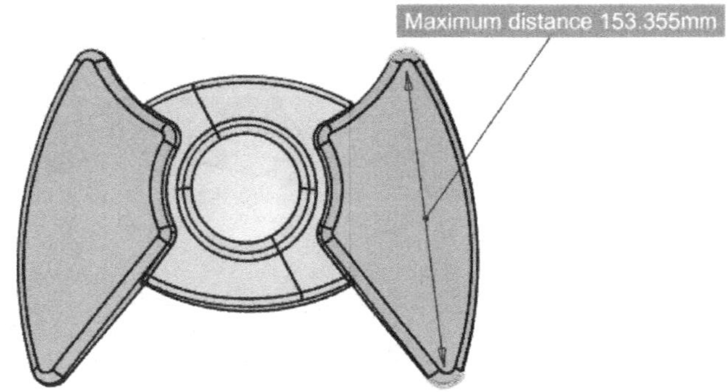

Figure 3–47

5. Cancel the measurement.

Task 2 - Create reference geometry.

In this task, you will build reference points that mark the extremities of the two arc edges that you previously measured. The **Tangent on curve** option is used in this case, as it forces the system to locate the outermost point of the selected curve when viewed from the selected plane.

1. Create a reference point using the following parameters:
   - Point Type: **Tangent on curve**
   - Curve: **Select the arc edge** as shown in Figure 3–48.
   - Direction: **ZX plane**

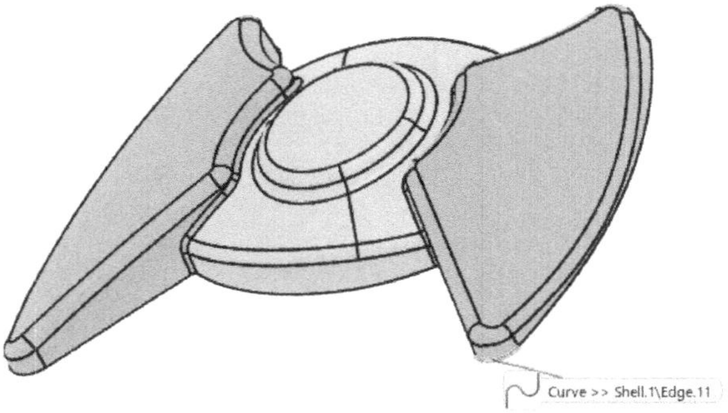

Figure 3–48

2. The resulting point displays as shown in Figure 3–49.

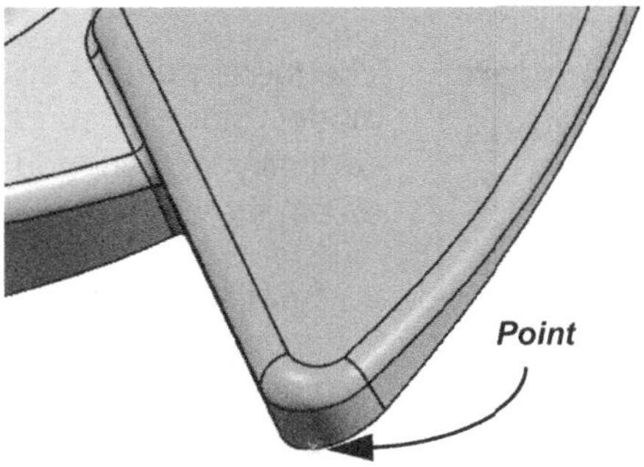

Figure 3–49

3. Repeat this process to create a point on the top arc edge. The point displays as shown in Figure 3–50.

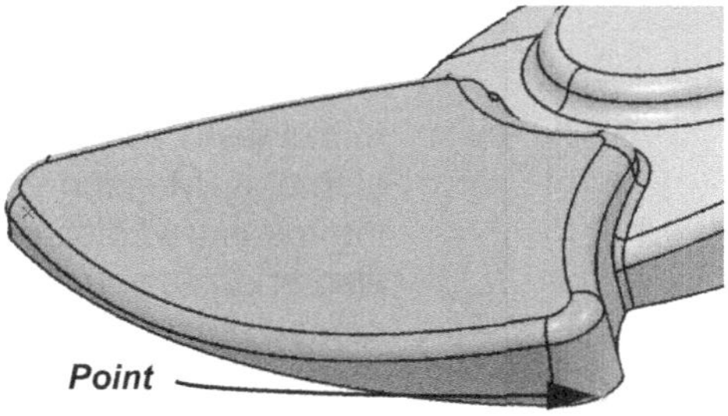

Figure 3–50

Task 3 - Take a measurement between points.

1. Repeat the **Measure Between** operation, selecting the two points that you created. The resulting measurement displays as shown in Figure 3–51.

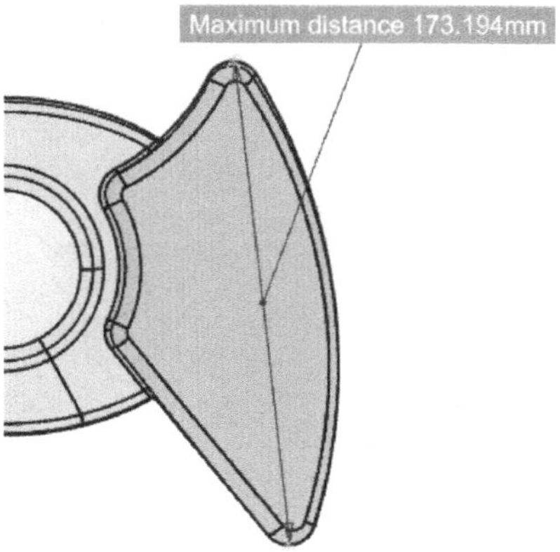

Figure 3–51

Design Considerations

The measurement still does not display the true height of the model. Since it cannot be guaranteed that the two points are vertically aligned, you can use the **Measure Between** tool to obtain the components of the measured distance.

2. Select the *Customize* tab and enable the **Components** option in both the *3D* and *Tab* columns. The dialog box updates to display the X, Y, and Z components of the measurement. The true height of the model is approximately 171.96mm.

3. Cancel the measurement.

Task 4 - Use reference planes to display distance in one direction.

In this task, you will build reference planes through the point elements. Measuring between two reference planes ensures that the measured distance is in the exact required direction. This also enables you to keep only the required component(s) of a measurement and display it on the model.

1. Create a reference plane using the following options:

   - Plane type: **Parallel through point**
   - Reference: **yz plane**
   - Point: **Point.1**

   The completed reference plane displays as shown in Figure 3–52.

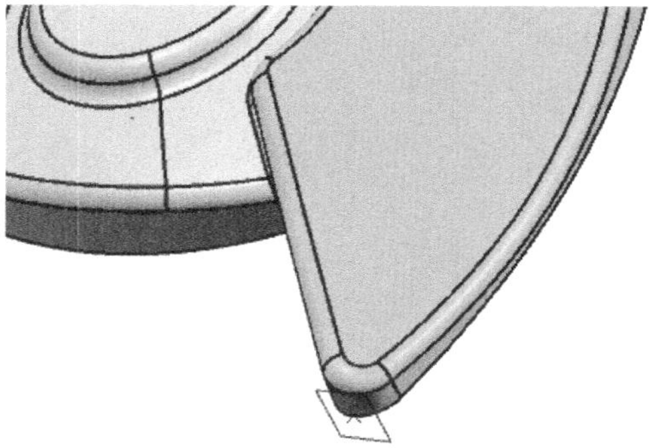

Figure 3–52

2. Create a second reference plane that is parallel to the yz plane and through Point.2. The model displays as shown in Figure 3–53.

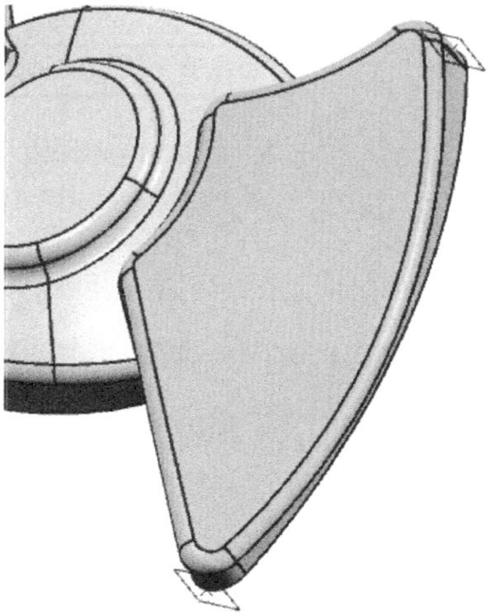

Figure 3–53

You can turn off the Component information in the Customize tab.

3. Measure between the two reference planes just created. The model displays as shown in Figure 3–54.

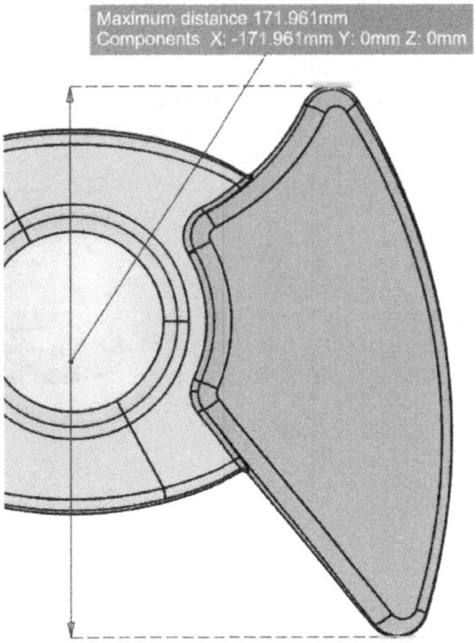

Figure 3–54

4. Click **OK** in the Measure Between in Part dialog box.

Task 5 - (Optional) Take additional measurements.

1. If time permits, use the techniques described in this exercise to determine the true width and depth of the model. The measured values should equal:
   - Width = **241.62mm**
   - Depth = **30.28mm**
2. Save the model and close the tab.

Chapter Review Questions

1. Which of the following items can be measured using the **Measure Item** tool? (Select all that apply).
   a. Point
   b. Edge
   c. Two planes
   d. Flat Surface
2. Measurements are always stored with the model data.
   a. True
   b. False
3. Measurement data is stored in the Results branch of the specification tree.
   a. True
   b. False
4. In Figure 3–55, the icon indicates that the measurement has not been updated.

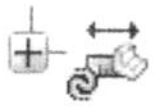

Figure 3–55

   a. True
   b. False
5. When material is applied to a model, the properties (density, etc.) are defined which permits accurate inertial values.
   a. True
   b. False
6. The **Create Geometry** tool enables you to create an axis system and a point at the center of gravity.
   a. True
   b. False

Answers: 1abd, 4b, 3b,4a, 5a, 6a

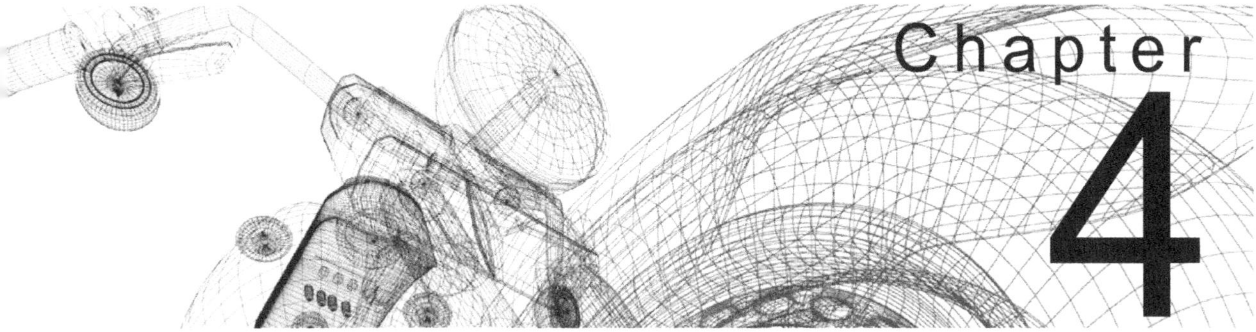

Chapter 4

Assembly Design

This chapter covers how to activate the Assembly Design app and access assembly-specific options. This chapter also guides you through the process of creating an assembly and describes the available assembly constraints.

Learning Objectives in This Chapter

- Learn about the Assembly Design app interface.
- Create an assembly and add components to it.
- Understand product properties and assembly product structure.
- Use the compass to move components.
- Automatically snap objects to the compass.
- Understand the various constraints available for parametrically locating components.

4.1 Assembly Design App

*The terms **Product** and **Assembly** can be used interchangeably.*

In the Part Design app, features are created in the model to build the final part. In the Assembly apps, components can be added to a product file to create an assembly.There are two apps for working with Assemblies:

- (Product Structure): This app is for the creation and manipulation of the Product Structure. It is primarily used for Top-Down Design planning purposes, rather than for assembly design purposes.

- (Assembly Design): This app is for the design of assemblies in cooperation with the Part Design and Drafting apps. This is the app you would typically be using.

Components can be added to a product using either the Product Structure or the Assembly Design apps:

- In the compass shown in Figure 4–1, click **3D**. Then select (Assembly Design). Fill in the applicable information in the Physical Product dialog box.

Figure 4–1

- Alternatively, select (Add)>**Physical Product in the Top Bar**. Fill in the applicable information in the Physical Product dialog box.

In either case, the Physical Product dialog box displays as shown in Figure 4–2.

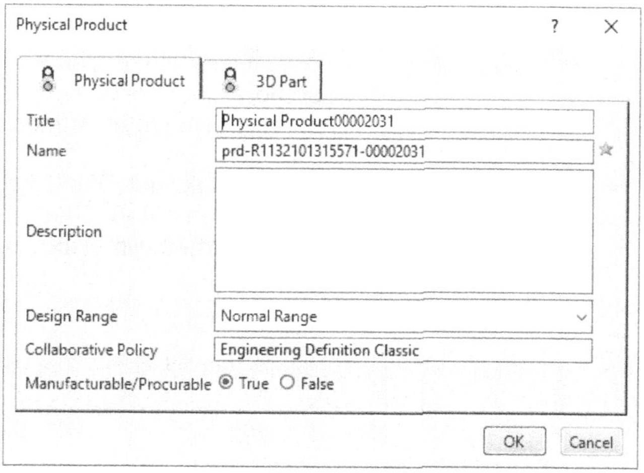

Figure 4–2

The *3D Part* tab, shown in Figure 4–3, enables you to also create a new part model as the first component in the assembly.

3D Shape is the form of the part and the features that make up the shape. A 3D Part has the form information and the location of the geometry in the assembly.

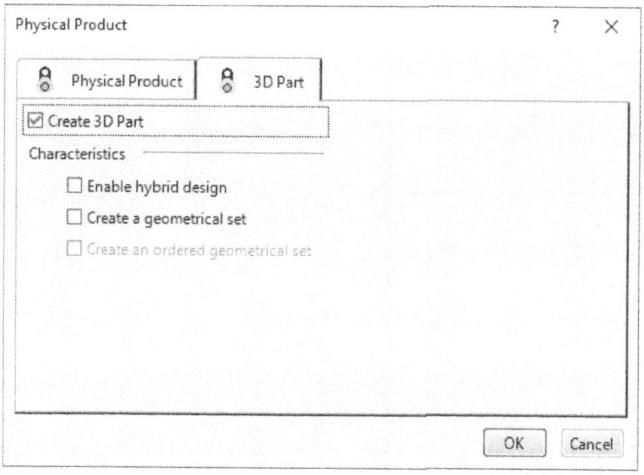

Figure 4–3

Commonly Used Tools

The *Assembly* section of the Action Bar is shown in Figure 4–4.

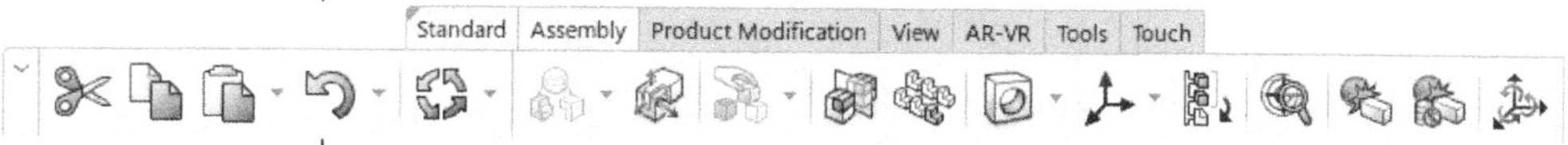

Figure 4–4

The (Engineering Connection) option controls the relative position of components in the assembly.

The (Update) option updates the position of components as assembly Engineering Connections are applied or if Engineering Connections have been modified.

In the *Tools* section of the Action Bar are the Measure tools, shown in Figure 4–5. These commands enable various analyses to be performed within the assembly.

Figure 4–5

4.2 Create an Assembly

Use the following steps to create a new assembly:

1. Create a new product file by activating the Assembly Design app.
2. Modify any product properties (i.e., Title, Version Comments, or Description).
3. Add components to the assembly using the Assembly Tools.
4. Position components using the compass and/or using Engineering Connections.
5. Add assembly features to the model or modify parts within the context of the assembly.
6. Analyze and extract any critical information from the assembly.

Product Properties

When a new product file is created, the system assigns an automatically-generated Name, which uniquely identifies the product within the engineering database. You can change the Title and add a Description, as well as set other options, as shown in Figure 4–6.

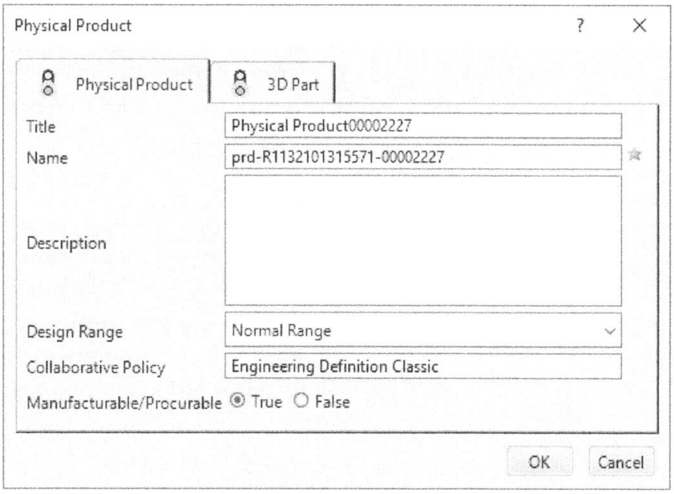

Figure 4–6

Adding Components

A component is an object that is added to an assembly. The following components can be added to an assembly for product design purposes.

- Product
- 3D Part
- 3D Shape

Components can be added to the assembly in the following ways:

- Select the *3D Part* tab in the Physical Product dialog box and enable **Create 3D Part**.This will create a new part assembled to the assembly.
- Select the assembly in the specification tree and use the right-click menu.
- Use the icons in the *Product Edition* section of the Action Bar.

The following table describes some of the icons found in the *Product Edition* section of the Action Bar:

Icon	Option	Description
	**New Product**	Creates a new subassembly within the top-level assembly with its own Product file.
	**New 3D Part**	Creates a new 3D Part within the top-level assembly containing a 3D Shape.
	**New 3D Shape**	Creates a new 3D Shape within the top-level assembly without the creation of a 3D Part.
	**Existing Product**	Adds a product to the assembly whose file already exists within the engineering database.

When using the **Existing Product** option, multiple objects can be added to the assembly at the same time by pressing <Ctrl> or <Shift> while selecting objects.

Product Structure

The product structure of an assembly consists of the top level assembly (Product), components (3D Parts), and subassemblies (Products) as shown in Figure 4–7.

The active level in the product structure is highlighted in blue in the specification tree. When performing actions on a top level or subassembly (such as **Inserting Components**), the active level of the product structure is affected by the actions performed.

To activate a subassembly, double-click on it in the specification tree.

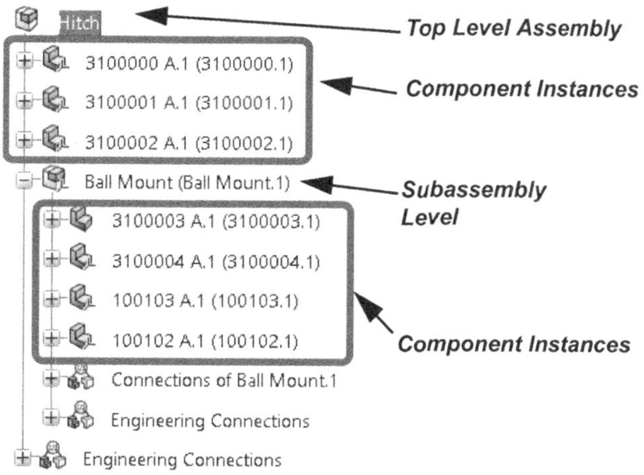

Figure 4–7

Once components have been added to the assembly, they display in the specification tree. The part name and the instance name in parenthesis are listed.

4.3 Engineering Connections and Constraints

Engineering Connections parametrically control the location and orientation between components using the **Constraints** and **Interferences** tools.

Constraints are specified to locate components parametrically with respect to existing components. Any references made to other components when constraining creates parent/child relationships.

Constraints are created using the Engineering Connections Definition dialog box.

The constraint definition can be streamlined using the predefined templates as follows:

1. Expand the *Connection Type* drop-down menu as shown in Figure 4–8.

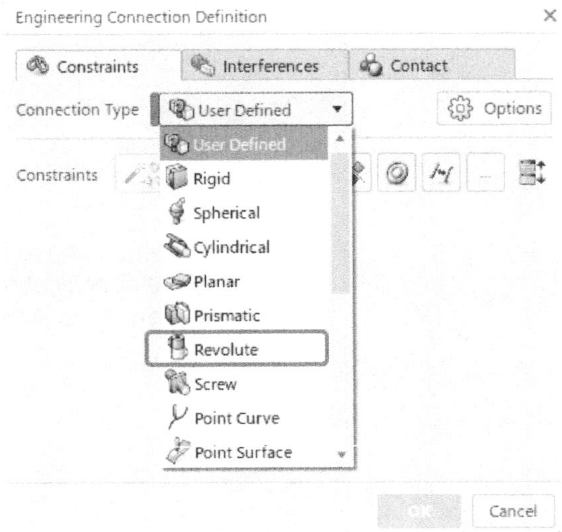

Figure 4–8

2. The available Engineering Connection templates are described in the table below.

Name	Icon	Description
User-Defined		A combination of constraints, which is incompatible with the predefined engineering connection types.
Rigid		*Welds* components together.
Spherical		Point-Point constraint enabling free rotation about the common points.
Cylindrical		Axis-Axis/Line-Line constraint permitting relative motion along the constrained entities.
Planar		Plane-Plane constraint permitting sliding and rotation relative to the constrained entities.
Prismatic		A constraint group permitting relative translation along a single degree of freedom.
Revolute		A constraint group permitting one degree of rotational freedom.
Screw		A constraint group that creates a relation between a translational and a rotational degree of freedom between constrained entities. (i.e. Bolt & Nut)
PointCurve		A constraint permitting a point to be constrained to a linear or non-linear curve.
PointSurface		A constraint permitting a point to be constrained to planar or non-planar curve.
Gear		A Coupling Engineering connection that links two engineering connections containing an angle constraint each.
Rack		A Coupling Engineering connection that links two engineering connections containing an offset constraint and an angle constraint.
Cable		A Coupling Engineering connection that links two engineering connections containing an offset constraint each.
Universal		A constraint that allows for two relative rotations between components along a shared point.

Name	Icon	Description
Roll Curve		Allows two curves that are constrained to maintain contact at a single point. Translation of one curve effects an equivalent translation on the other curve. (i.e Wheel rolling down a path)
Slide Curve		Allows for two curves to be constrained to maintain contact with each other at a single point. Translation of curves is independent as long as contact at point is maintained. (i.e Cam and Follower)
Fix		Fastens a component to its current position in the assembly space. It has no other constraints to components.
Free		
Symmetry		A constraint relating two axis systems, in which symmetry can be specified along either the X,Y or Z axis.
Projection		A constraint typically used for positioning of a Spot Fastener Instance.

Constraints are controlled by three factors:

- Type
- Options
- Mode

Constraint Type

Constraint Type controls the geometric relationship behavior with the most commonly used Constraints.

Constraint Types can be inserted from the Engineering Connections Definition dialog box as shown in Figure 4–9.

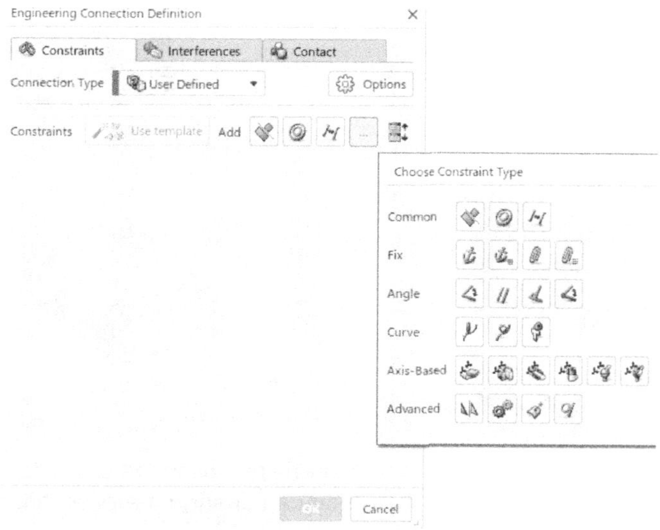

Figure 4–9

Coincidence

Once additional components have been added to the assembly, how they are constrained depends on their geometry. Coincidence can be used to align points, axes and planes. For example, the T-brace shown in Figure 4–10 is positioned over the mounting block using the coincidence constraint and selecting the axis of the holes.

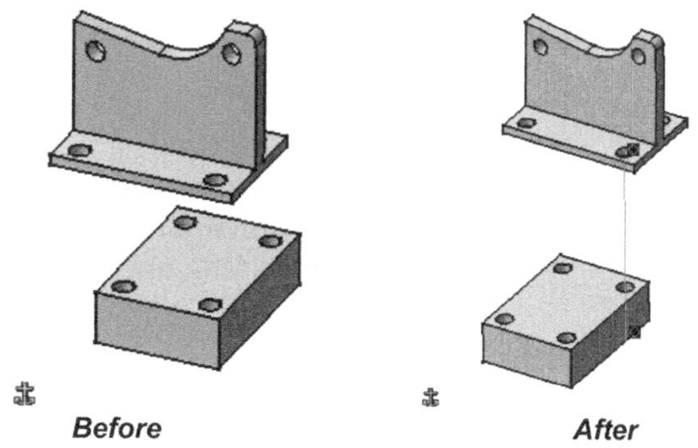

Figure 4–10

The T-brace can be further constrained using the coincidence constraint and selecting planar surfaces by selecting an appropriate Alignment option, as shown in Figure 4–11.

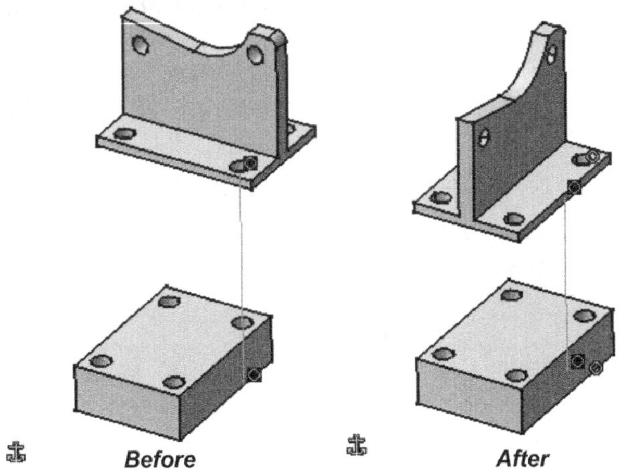

Figure 4–11

When specifying the coincidence constraint with planar surfaces, you can change the orientation of the surfaces, as shown in Figure 4–12.

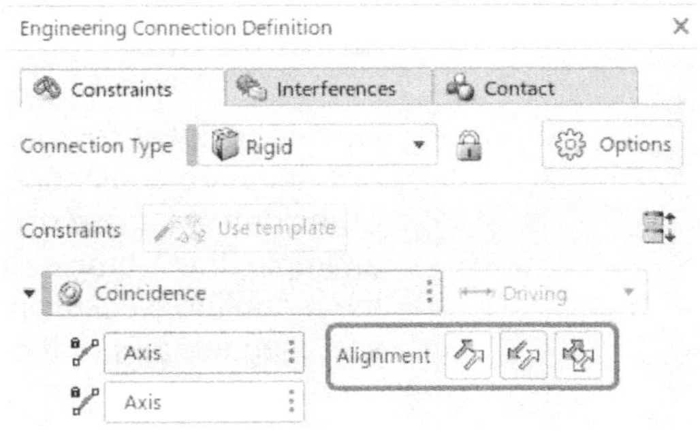

Figure 4–12

Contact

Contact mates two surfaces. The T-brace shown in Figure 4–13 is fully constrained after mating the top surface of the mounting block with the underside surface of the T-brace.

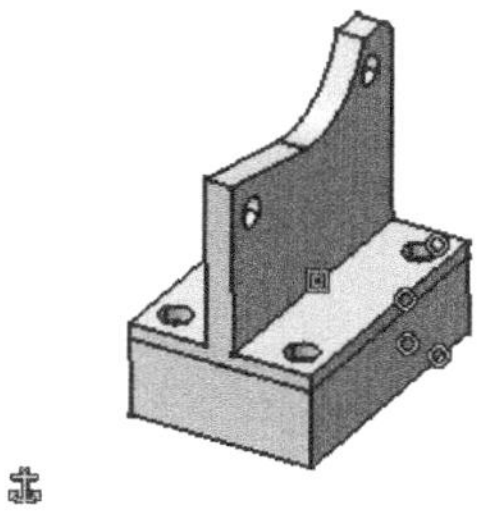

Figure 4–13

Offset

Offset behaves like contact or coincidence with planar surfaces, without the selections being coplanar. The selections are parallel with a specified offset distance. The bolt shown in Figure 4–14 is offset from the T-brace to permit space for future washer placement. Similar to coincidence, the direction of orientation can be specified.

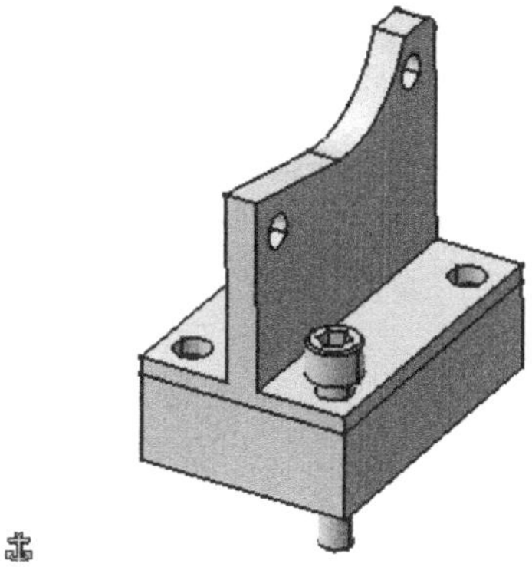

Figure 4–14

Angle

The Angle Constraint contains four sub-types:

- **Angle:** Enables selection of two lines or planes controlled by an angle dimension between entities.
- **Parallelism:** Enables selection of two lines or planes controlled by a 0 or 180 degree relationship between entities.
- **Perpendicularity:** Enables selection of two lines or planes controlled by a 90 degree relationship between entities.

- **Hinge:** Enables selection of two lines or planes controlled by an angle dimension between entities and the selection of the hinge axis.

In the example shown in Figure 4–15, the finger is assembled with a coincidence constraint. Note the intersecting geometry.

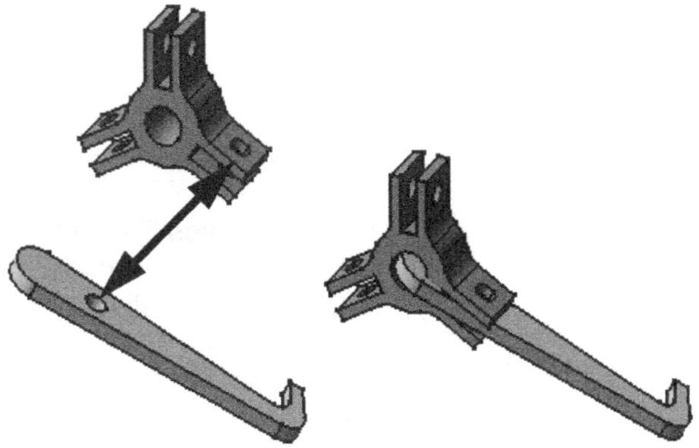

Figure 4–15

The angle constraint is used to indicate the correct orientation of components. The example shown in Figure 4–15 indicates that interference exists. The finger component is under-constrained. Therefore, a parallel or angle constraint must be added. The parallel and angle options are shown in Figure 4–16.

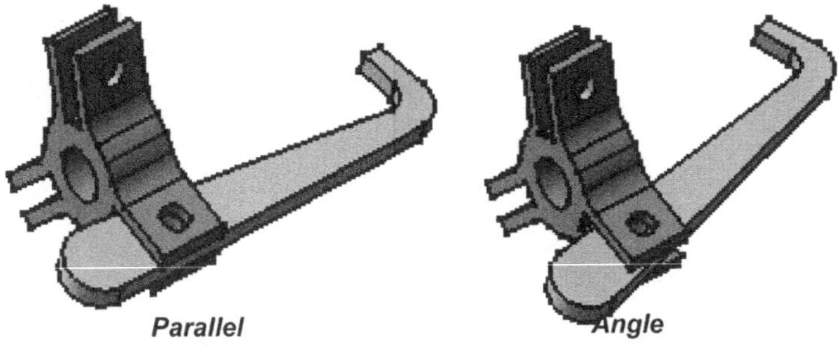

Figure 4–16

Fix Component

In CATIA, the base component is usually constrained to be fixed. This essentially creates a zero position of reference. Once constrained to be fixed, the *Engineering Connections* section displays in the specification tree, as shown in Figure 4–17.

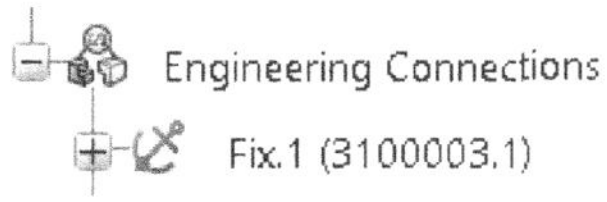

Figure 4–17

Fix Together

Fix together is normally used to fix any remaining degrees of freedom from an under-constrained component. The components behave as a single body in space.

When moving components assembled with a fix together constraint, press <Shift> while using the robot. This forces 3DEXPERIENCE to obey the assembly Engineering Connections during the move. If a component is moved without pressing <Shift>, the fix together constraint updates based on the new locations.

Constraint Options

Constraint Options are only activated when the orientation of the selected elements is available for the constraint type.

Plane geometry orientation options include plane normal vector relationship options:

- **Undefined:** Plane orientation is undefined and can be modified during update.
- **Same Orientation:** Plane orientations are the same (aligned).
- **Opposite Orientation:** Plane orientations are opposite (mated).

Line geometry orientation options include line vector relationship options:

- **Undefined:** Line orientation is undefined and can be modified during update.
- **Parallelism:** Lines are parallel but line vectors are not oriented.
- **Same Orientation:** Line vector orientations are the same.
- **Opposite Orientation:** Line vectors orientations are opposite.

Hinge constraint orientation options include the four quadrants of angular representation:

- Direct angle
- Angle + 180deg
- 180deg - Angle
- 360deg - Angle

Axis System orientation options include the axes of the cartesian coordinate system:

- X axis
- Y axis
- Z axis

Constraint Mode

The Constraint Mode controls measurement behavior that is associated with a constraint. The three Constraint Modes available are:

- **Driving:** Constraint definition value is applied to the product during update.
- **Measurement:** Constraint value is a result of the constraint definitions and any other constraints in the product during update.
- **Controlled:** Permits the constraint to be restricted between upper and lower bounds for use in kinematics.

Change Type

You can change the type of the constraint by selecting it in the Engineering Connection Definition dialog box and selecting the replacement constraint in the flyout, as shown in Figure 4–18.

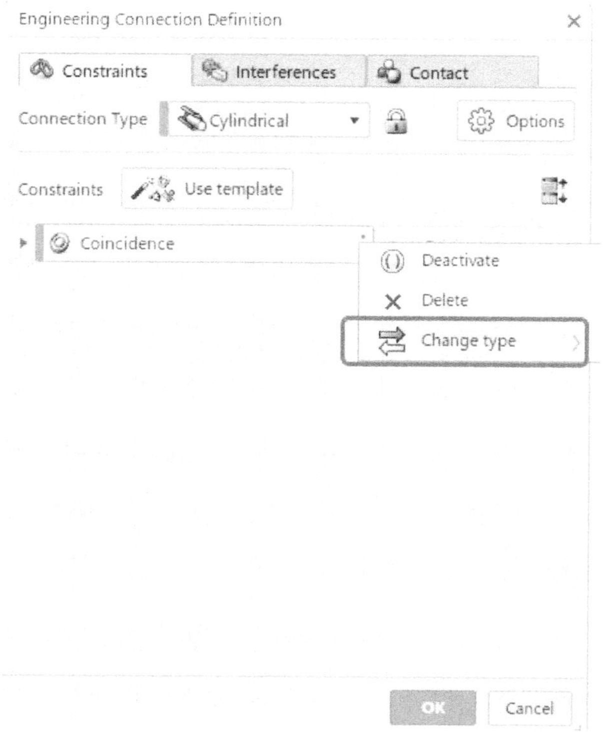

Figure 4–18

Assembly Considerations

When modeling parts, consider which feature form best captures the design intent of the base feature. When working with assemblies, consider which component is best suited for use as the base component.

Also consider the active level of the product structure. If the top level of the structure is active (highlighted in blue), then the constraint you are creating is going to be grouped with the top level assembly Engineering Connections.

If you want to create an Engineering Connection specific to the components in a subassembly, double-click on the subassembly level in the specification tree to activate it. When you create the Engineering Connection, it is grouped with the subassembly Engineering Connections. The product structure, top level assembly Engineering Connections, and subassembly Engineering Connections are shown in Figure 4–19.

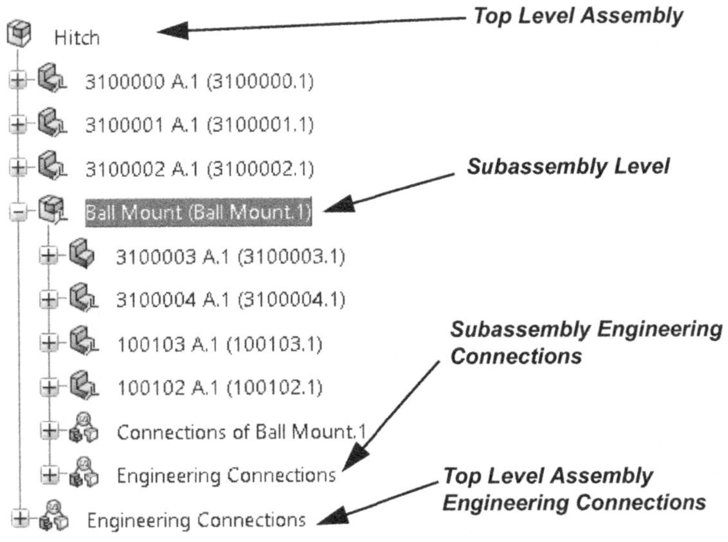

Figure 4–19

4.4 Use the Robot

Once existing components have been added to the assembly, the components are displayed in the default position and orientation. The robot is used to move components within the main window.

To move a selected component, place the cursor over the center dot as shown in Figure 4–20. Press the left mouse button to move the robot.

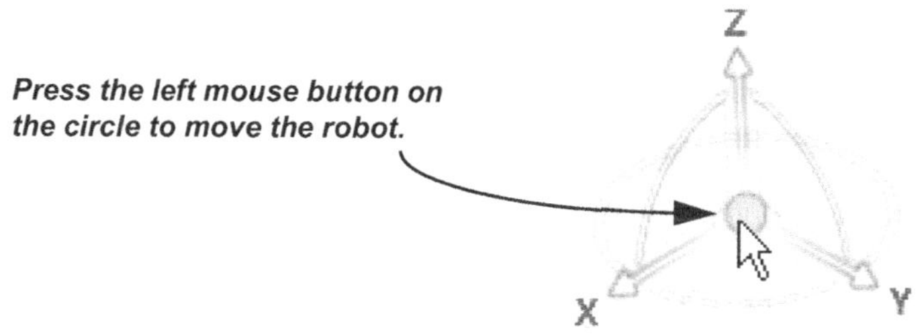

Figure 4–20

Drag the robot to the component to be moved. The robot snaps and reorients to geometry belonging to the component, as shown in Figure 4–21. When the orientation is correct, release the left mouse button to place the robot.

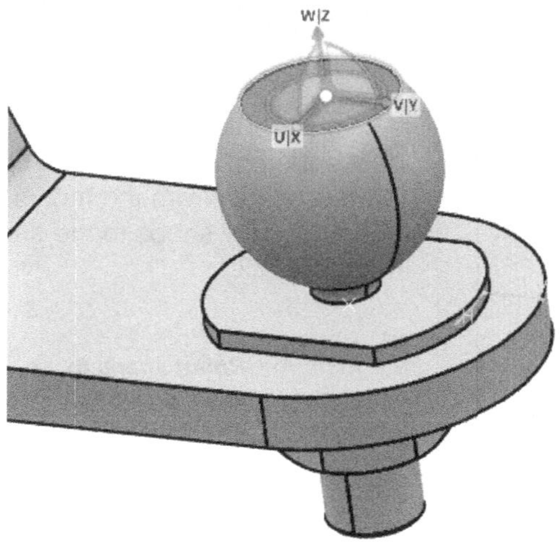

Figure 4–21

Once the robot has snapped to a component, the robot turns orange. If it does not turn orange:

1. Verify that the active model in the specification tree is an assembly.
2. Select the component in the model or specification tree to activate movement of the selected component.

You can activate any component for movement; it does not need to be the component to which the robot is snapped. You can also activate multiple components by selecting them while pressing <Ctrl>.

Automatic Snap

You can automatically snap the robot to a selected object by right-clicking and selecting **Snap Automatically to Selected Object**, as shown in Figure 4–22.

Turn off this option once you have finished moving components.

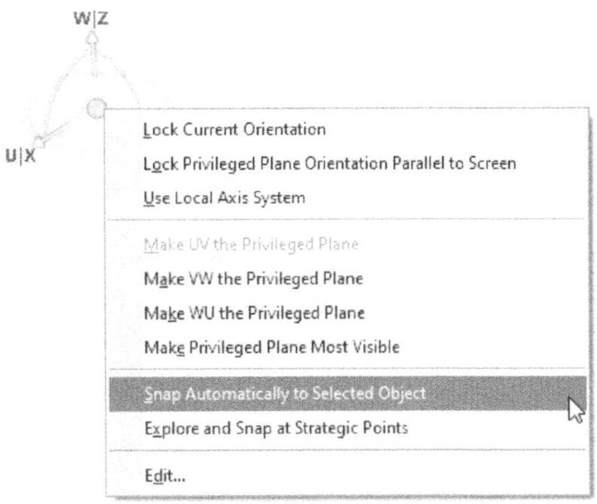

Figure 4–22

Once the option has been activated, select the component you want to move from the model or specification tree. The robot automatically snaps to the selected component, as shown in Figure 4–23.

The system automatically selects the orientation of the robot based on the origin of the selected component.

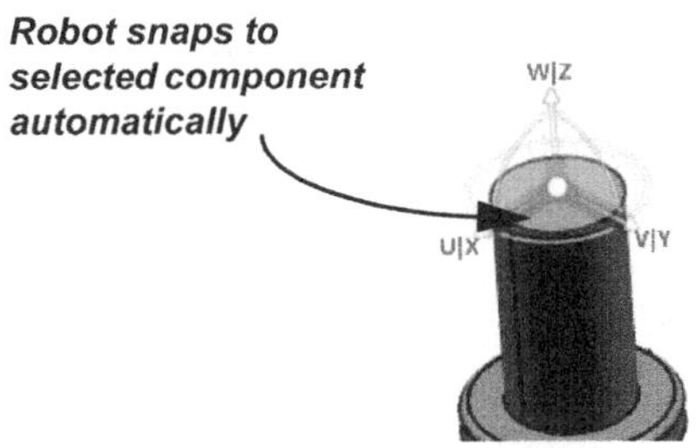

Figure 4–23

Once the robot has been activated on the component, only robot movements control the selected component(s).

If you want to move components while accounting for the placement constraints, hold down <Shift> while pressing the left mouse button. Note that more than one component might move, depending on how the constraints are defined.

More precise movements of a component can be achieved by right-clicking on the robot and selecting **Edit**. The Parameters for Robot Manipulation dialog box, shown in Figure 4–24, enables you to enter exact translation or rotation increment values for precise movements.

*It is recommended that you restore any changed values to 0 once you have completed the **Move** operation. This ensures that further operations do not snap to the previous increment values.*

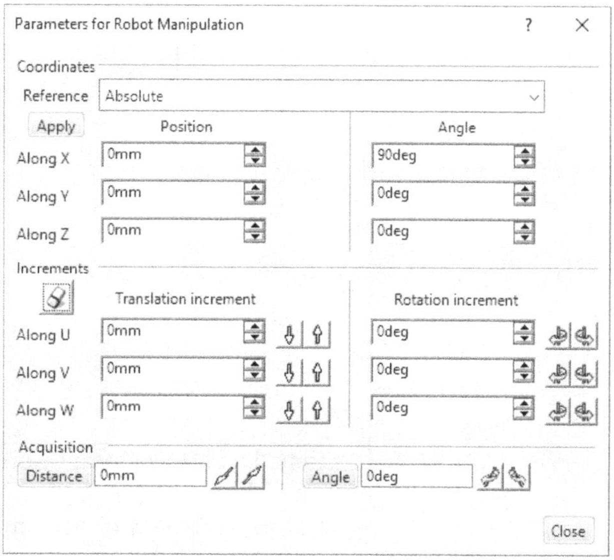

Figure 4–24

Once the component has been moved to the correct location, complete the movement by selecting another component to move or clicking anywhere on the screen to deactivate the robot control of the component. The robot returns to its default color and controls the entire assembly. To return the robot to its default position, right-click and select **Display > Reset Robot**, or drag the robot away from the model and move it anywhere in the background of the screen.

Practice 4a Creating Assemblies I

Practice Objectives

- Change product properties.
- Move components with the robot.
- Apply assembly Engineering Connections.

In this practice, you will create a new ball mount assembly, as shown in Figure 4–25. You will use constraints to assemble the four components of the assembly. The ball mount assembly that you create is a subassembly of a larger assembly.

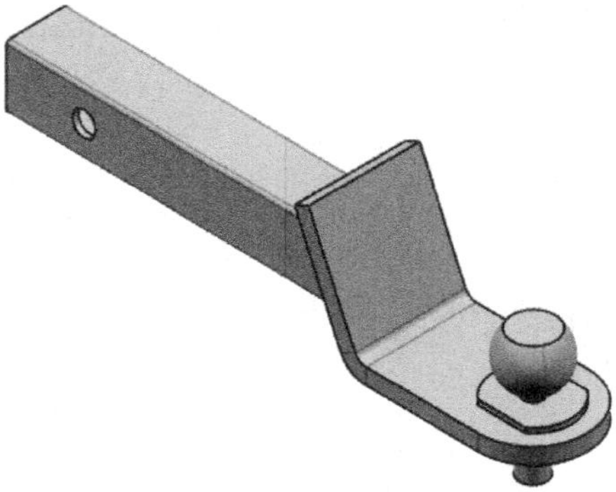

Figure 4–25

Task 1 - Import Components.

1. Import **Creating_Assemblies_I.3dxml**. A folder is imported containing the models needed for this practice. If you expand the folder, it will display as shown in Figure 4–26.

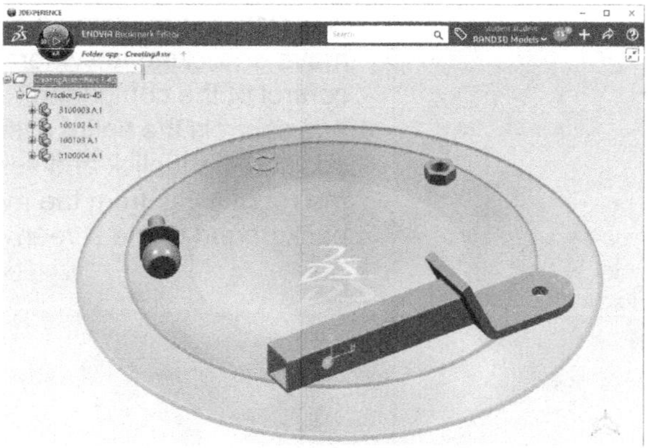

Figure 4–26

Task 2 - Create a new Product file.

1. **In the Top Bar**, select (Add) **> Physical Product**.
2. In the Physical Product dialog box, type ***Your_Initials*_Ball Mount** in the *Title* field.
3. In the *Description* field, type **Ball Mount for Hitch**.
4. Click **OK**.

Task 3 - Assemble the first component and fix it.

1. Ensure that you are in the Assembly Design app.
2. Right-click on the top level assembly (Ball Mount) in the specification tree and select **Insert** > **Existing Product**, as shown in Figure 4–27.

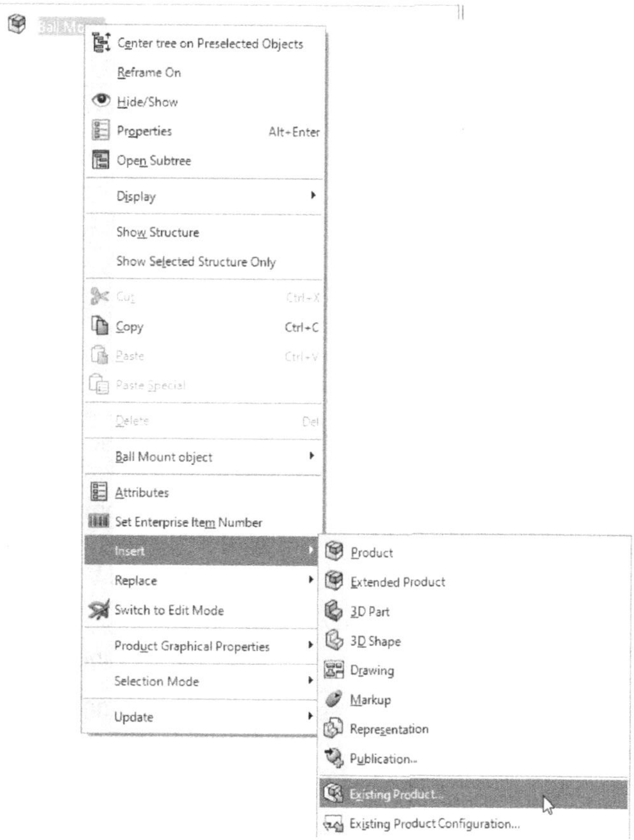

Figure 4–27

3. Select the *Folder app - CreatingAssemblies_I* tab and select **3100003** in the specification tree.

4. The system returns you to the *Ball Mount* assembly tab.Click on the screen to temporarily place the component. The component needs to be fixed.

5. Select the component, on screen or in the specification tree, and select  (Fix) from the context toolbar.

6. This component is now fixed. Note the *Engineering Connections* section in the specification tree, as shown in Figure 4–28.

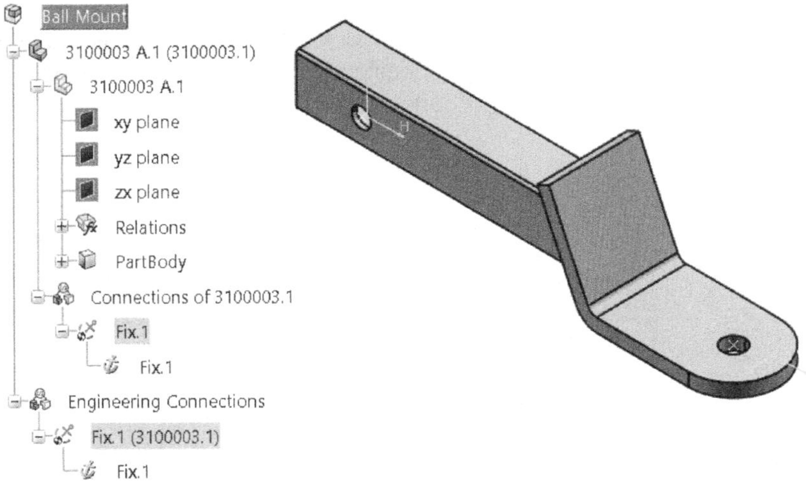

Figure 4–28

Task 4 - Add the second component in a free position.

1. Bring another component into the assembly. Select **Ball Mount** in the specification tree, right-click and select **Insert>Existing Product**.

2. Select the *Folder app - CreatingAssemblies_I* tab and select **3100004** in the specification tree.

3. Note that the **3100004 (Ball)** part is brought into the assembly and placed in the default position, so it intersects the **3100003** component.

4. To view the **3100004 (Ball)** geometry, the part needs to be moved away from the fixed assembly. Drag the **U** axis of the robot on the **Ball** part as shown in Figure 4–29.

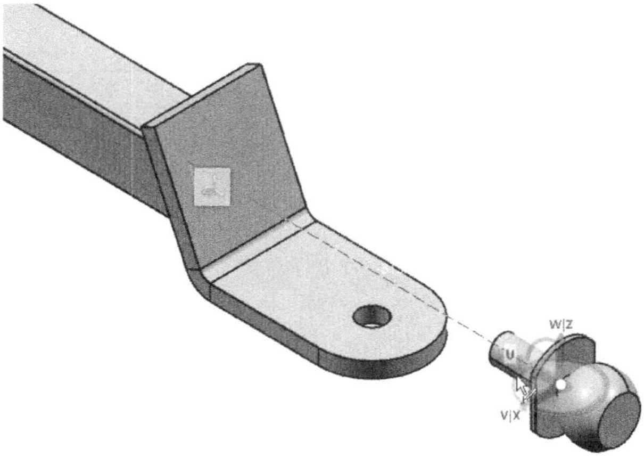

Figure 4–29

Task 5 - Constrain the 3100004 (Ball) part.

1. Click on the screen to temporarily place the component.
2. In the *Assembly* section of the Action Bar, click  (Engineering Connection).
3. In the Engineering Connection Definition dialog box that opens, select Coincidence constraint, as shown in Figure 4–30.

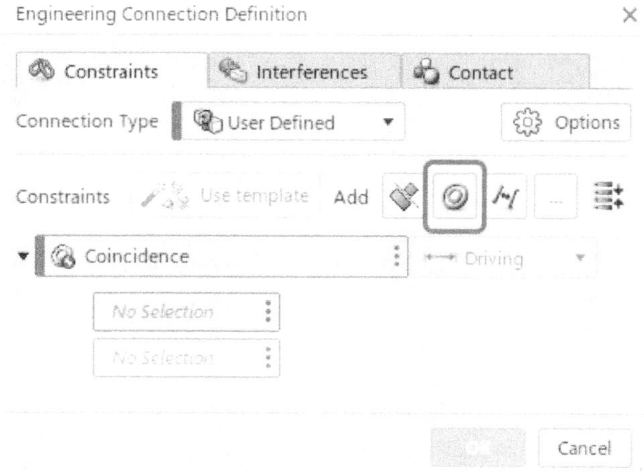

Figure 4–30

4. Select the axis of the Ball stem by selecting the cylindrical surface, as shown in Figure 4–31. You might need to zoom into the part.

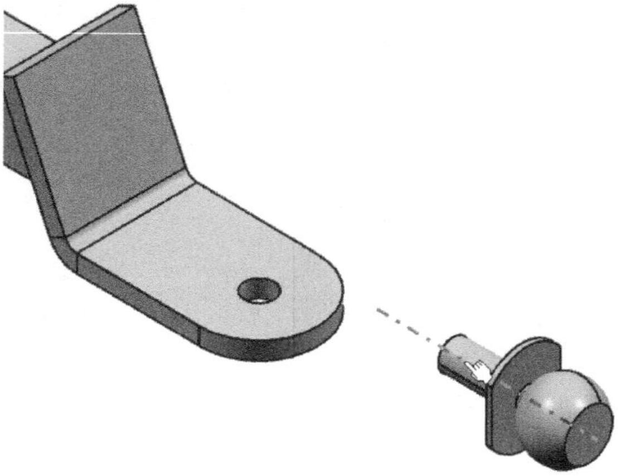

Figure 4–31

5. Select the axis on the base part by selecting the inner cylindrical surface of the hole, as shown in Figure 4–32.

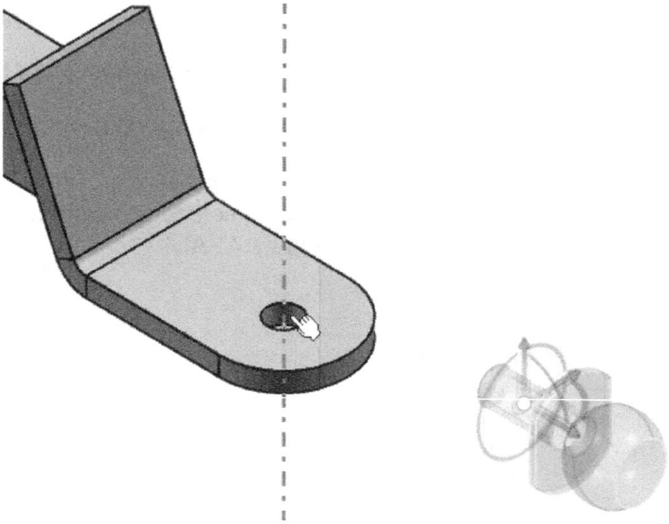

Figure 4–32

6. Part **3100004** is now partially constrained. The assembly updates the position of all of the components. The assembly displays similar to Figure 4–33.

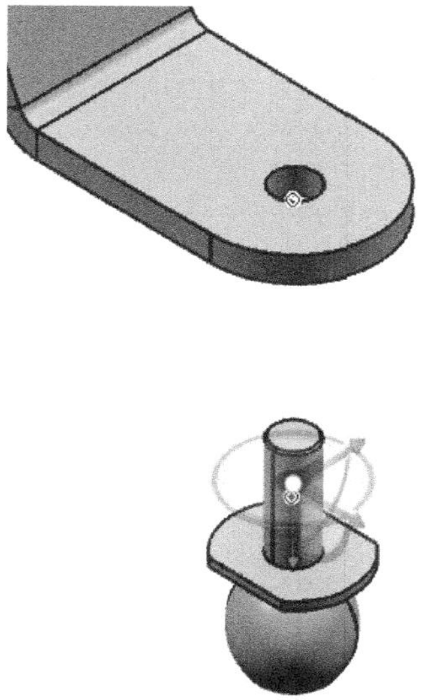

Figure 4–33

7. To control the orientation of the axial Vectors, select  (Opposite) as shown in Figure 4–34.

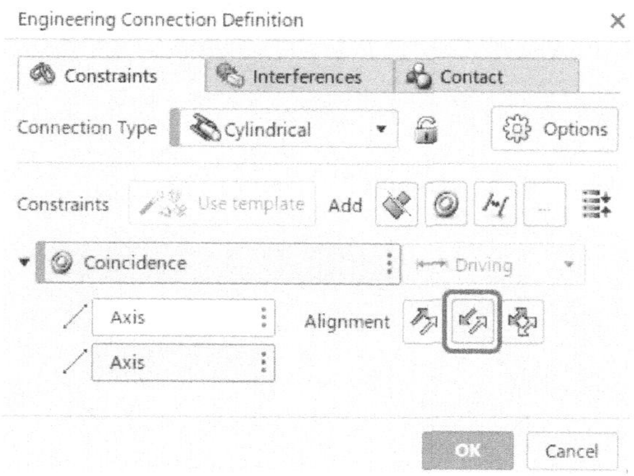

Figure 4–34

8. The assembly updates the position of all of the components. The assembly displays similar to Figure 4–35.

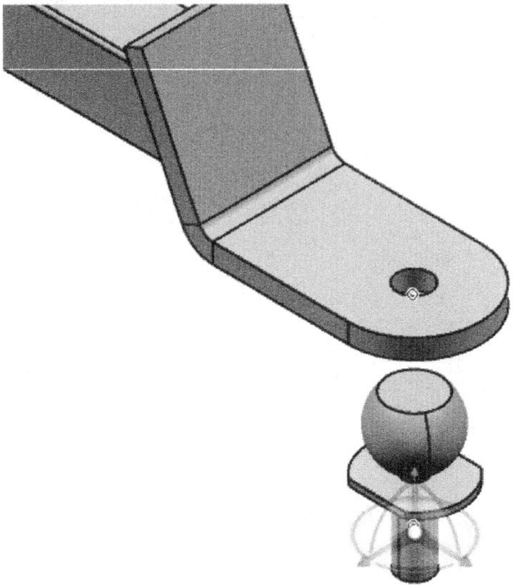

Figure 4–35

Design Considerations

The **Ball** (Part **3100004**) is only constrained along its axis. Therefore, it can still be translated and rotated on its axis.

9. To lock the position of the Ball along the coincident axis, in the Engineering Connection dialog box, click the Contact constraint icon, as shown in Figure 4–36.

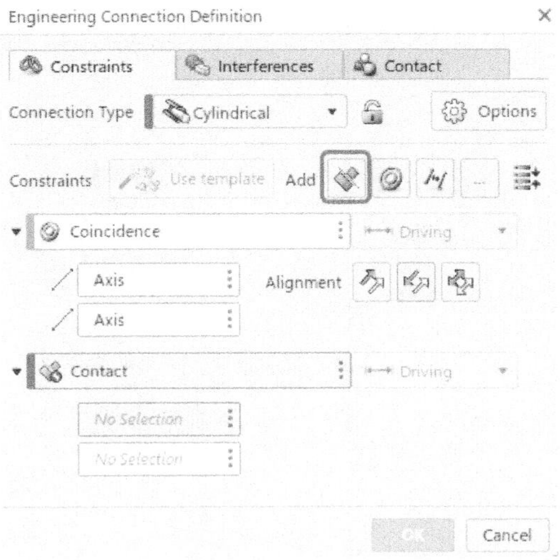

Figure 4–36

10. Select the mating surface of the slide, as shown in Figure 4–37.

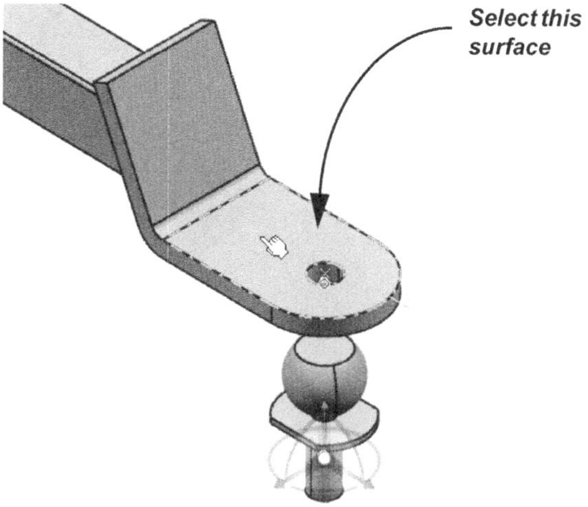

Figure 4–37

11. Select the underside surface of the **Ball**, as shown in Figure 4–38.

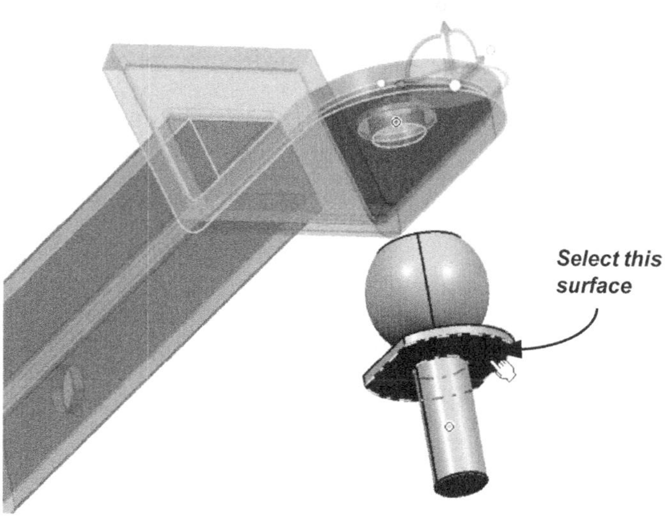

Figure 4–38

12. The position of the components updates, as shown in Figure 4–39.

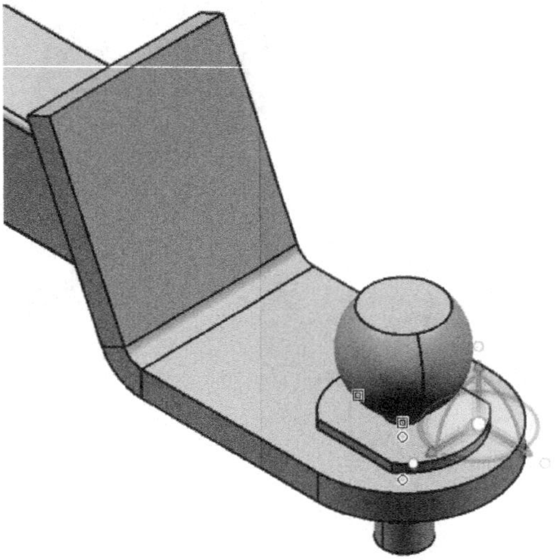

Figure 4–39

13. The **Ball** can still rotate about the coincident axis. Add an angle constraint to the still open Engineering Connection dialog box to fully constrain the ball by clicking the Show all possible constraints icon, and then the Parallelism icon, as shown in Figure 4–40.

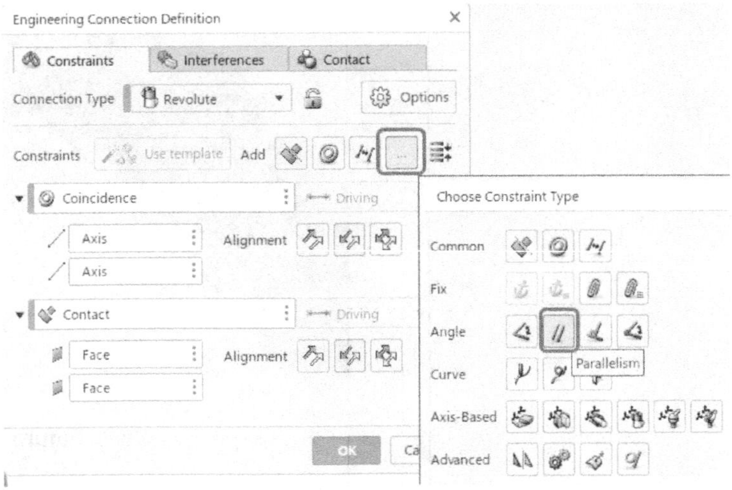

Figure 4–40

14. Select the two surfaces shown in Figure 4–41.

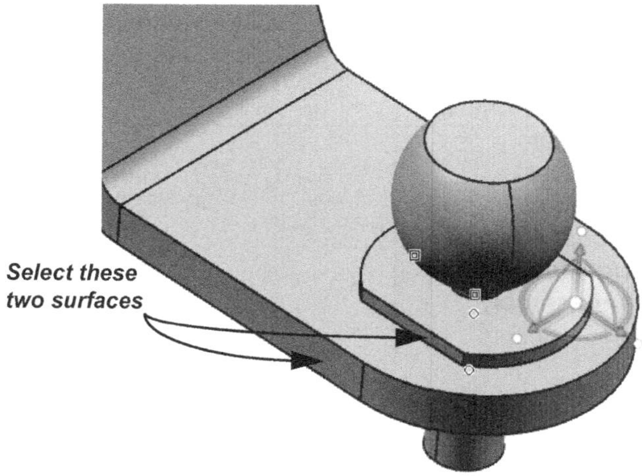

Figure 4–41

15. To control the orientation of the planes' Normal Vectors, select  (Same), as shown in Figure 4–42.

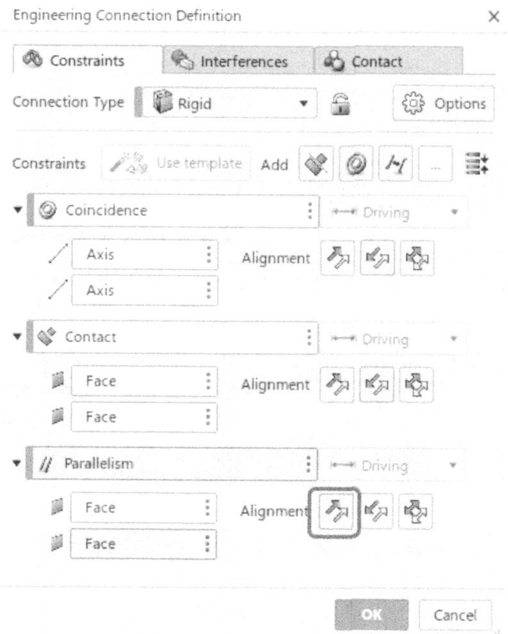

Figure 4–42

16. Click **OK** to finalize the Constraints and close the Engineering Connection Definition dialog box.

17. A dialog box reporting *Undefined Interference Specifications* will open. Click **No** to omit creation of the Interference specification, as shown in Figure 4–43.

*To avoid seeing this warning, disable Check interferences at validation under **Me>Preferences>App Preferences>3D Modeling>Mechanical System>Assembly Design**.*

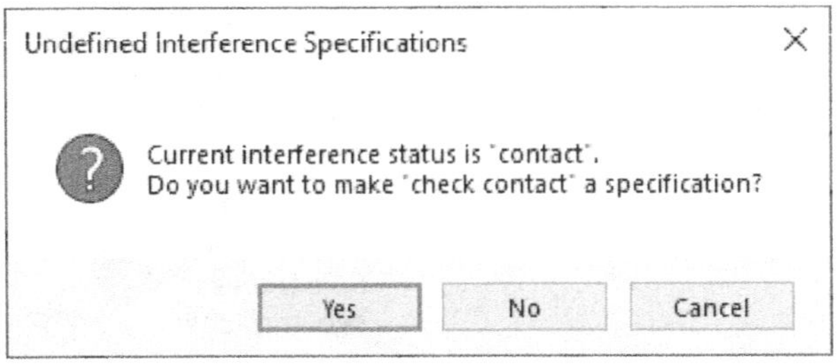

Figure 4–43

18. The **Ball** component is now fully constrained, and displays as shown in Figure 4–44.

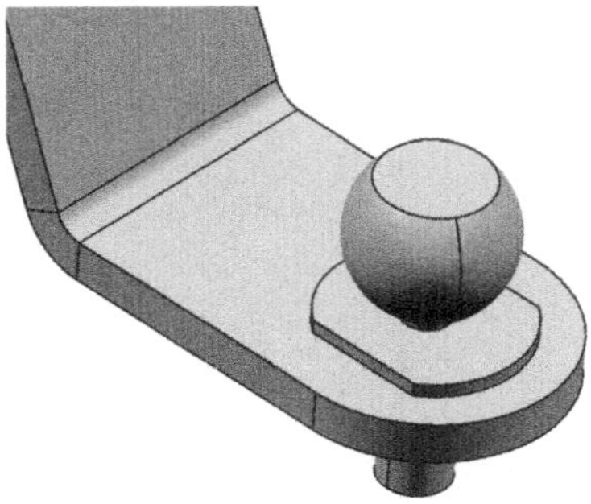

Figure 4–44

Task 6 - Assemble the washer.

1. Right-click on Ball Mount and selecting **Insert > Existing Product**.
2. Select the *Folder app - CreatingAssemblies_I* tab and select **100103** in the specification tree.
3. The system switches back to the *Ball Mount* tab.

4. Use the robot axes to move the washer to a position clear of the Product (as shown in Figure 4–45), then click on the screen to temporarily locate the washer.

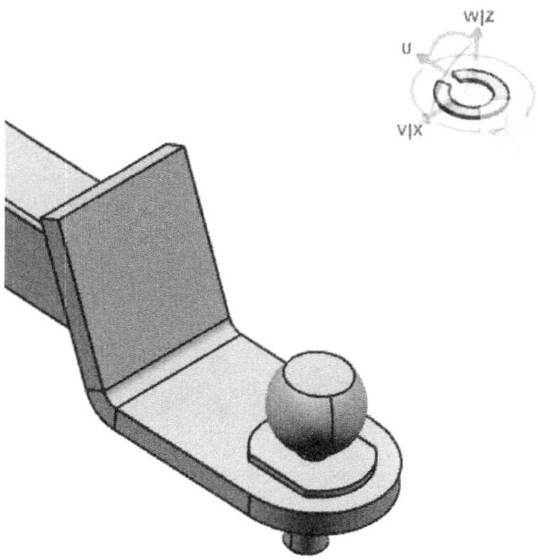

Figure 4–45

5. In the *Assembly* section of the Action Bar, click  (Engineering Connection).

6. In the Engineering Connection Definition dialog box, click  (Coincidence).

7. Click **Options** and, in the *Movable component* drop-down list, select **Second**, as shown in Figure 4–46, to enable part **100103** to be positioned relative to the product.

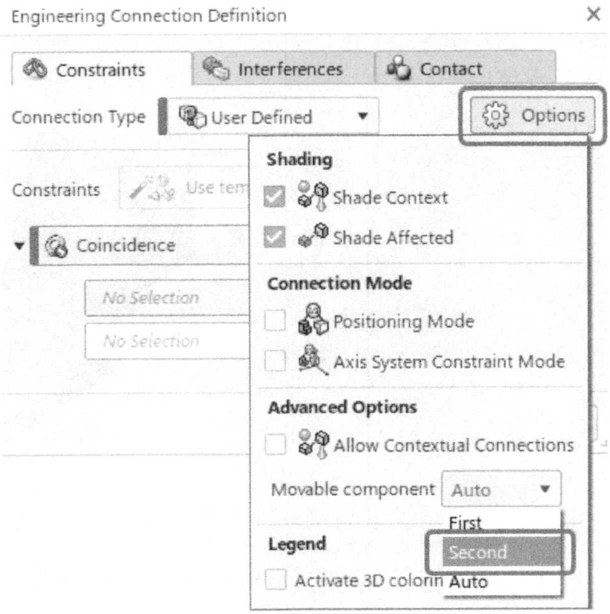

Figure 4–46

8. Select the axis of the ball first, then zoom in and select the axis of the washer. Selecting the cylindrical surface will select the axis.

9. Click **OK** to finalize the Constraint and close the Engineering Connection dialog box.

10. Click **No** to omit creation of the Interference specification.

11. Click  (Engineering Connection).

12. In the Engineering Connection dialog box, select  (Contact) to create a Contact Constraint.

13. Select the surface of the washer and the underside surface of the slide, as shown in Figure 4–47.

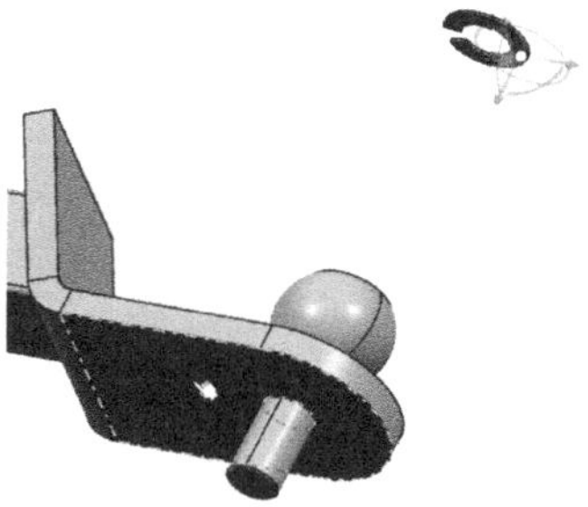

Figure 4–47

14. Click **OK** to finalize the Constraint and close the Engineering Connection Definition dialog box.

15. Click **No** to omit the creation of the Interference specification.

16. To update the position of the components, click  (Update).

17. The washer still has a degree of freedom to rotate about the coincident axis. Double-click on the 3rd Engineering Connection in the specification tree to re-open it.

18. Select **User Defined** as the *Connection type*. Click (Show all possible constraints) and select  (Parallelism), as shown in Figure 4–48.

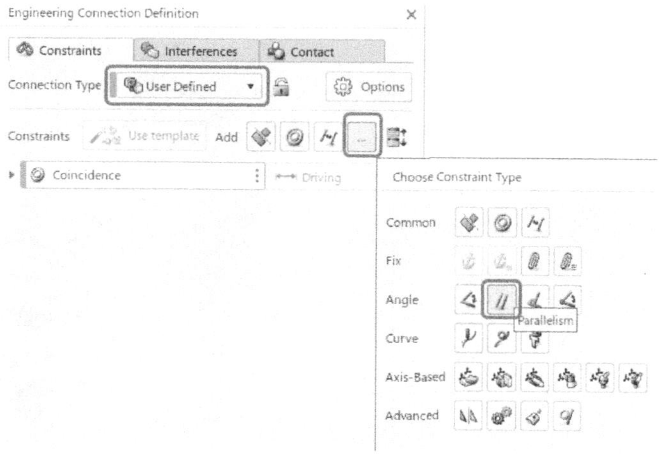

Figure 4–48

19. Select the two surfaces shown in Figure 4–49.

Figure 4–49

20. Click **OK** to close the dialog box.
21. Update the assembly, if necessary.

Task 7 - Add the nut (100102) component.

1. Insert **100102** (**Nut**) into **Ball Mount** by right-clicking on Ball Mount and selecting **Insert > Existing Product**.
2. Select the *Folder app - CreatingAssemblies_I* tab and select **100102** in the specification tree.
3. The system switches back to the *Ball Mount* tab.
4. Use the robot to place the new component in open space, as shown in Figure 4–50.

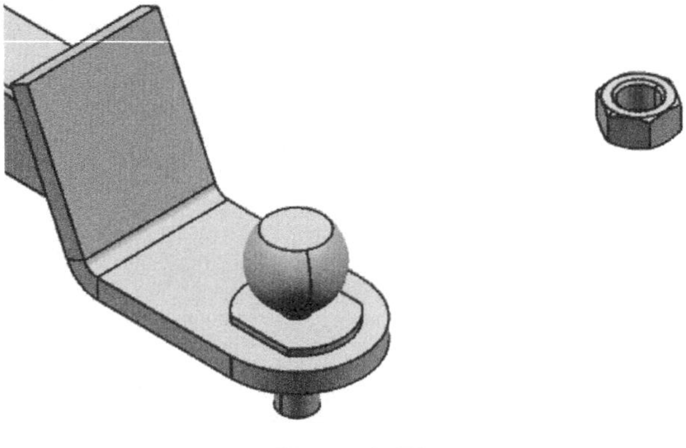

Figure 4–50

5. Click (Engineering Connection).
6. In the Engineering Connection dialog box, select **Options > Movable components > First**.
7. In the Engineering Connection Definition dialog box, select (Coincidence). Select the axis of the nut first, then the axis of the ball, as shown in Figure 4–51.

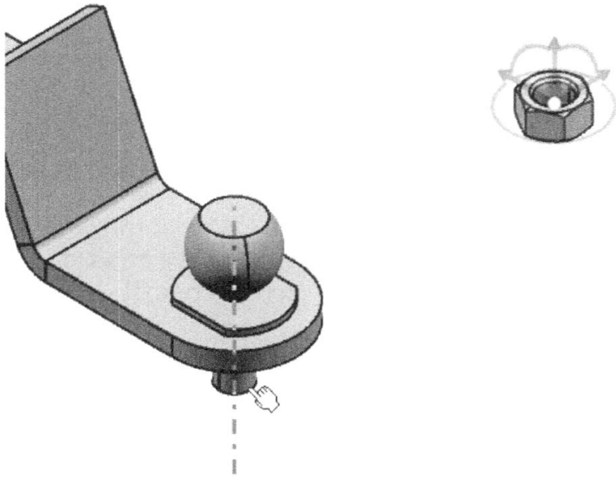

Figure 4–51

8. Click **OK** to finalize the Constraint and close the Engineering Connection dialog box.
9. Click **No** to omit the creation of the Interference specification.
10. Click (Engineering Connection).
11. Select (Contact) to create a Contact Constraint.

12. Select the flat surface of the nut and the surface of the washer, and the position updates as shown in Figure 4–52.

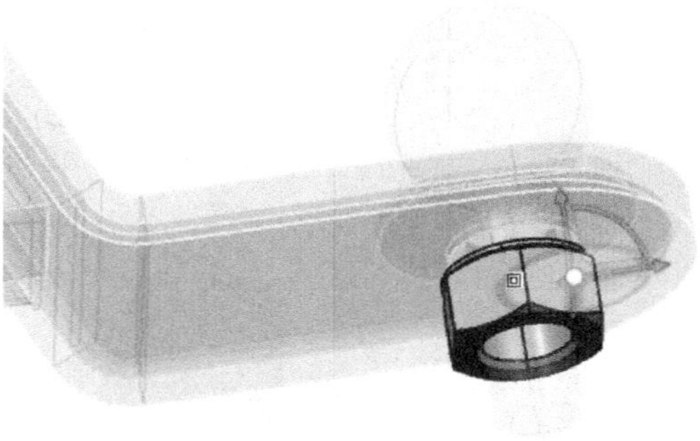

Figure 4–52

13. The nut still has a degree of freedom to rotate about the coincident axis. In the Engineering Connection dialog box, select  (Show all possible constraints) and select  (Fix together) and select both the nut and the washer parts to fix them together.
14. Click **OK** to finalize the Constraint and close the Engineering Connection dialog box.
15. Click **No** to omit the creation of the Interference specification.
16. Save the assembly and close all tabs.

Practice 4b Creating Assemblies II

Practice Objectives

- Apply Engineering Connections.
- Insert a subassembly.

In this practice, you will create the assembly shown in Figure 4–53. This assembly will consist of various parts and the subassembly that you created in a previous practice.

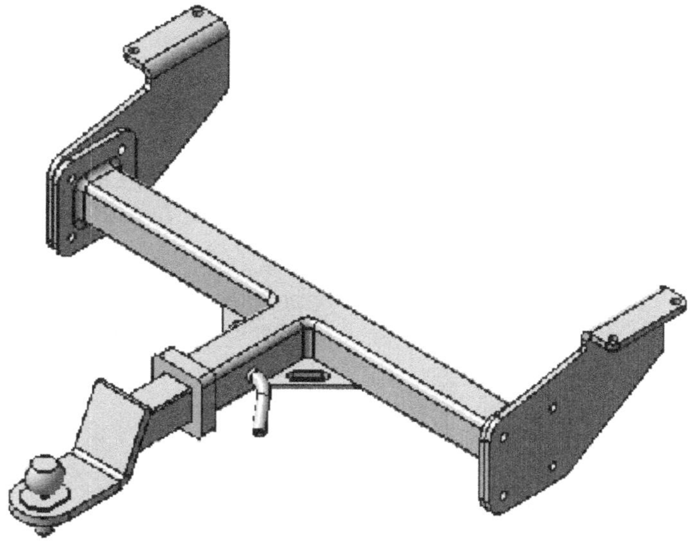

Figure 4–53

Task 1 - Create a new Product file.

1. Import **Creating_Assemblies_II.3dxml**.
2. **In the Top Bar**, select  (Add)>**Physical Product**.
3. In the Physical Product dialog box, type ***Your_Initials*_Hitch** in the *Title* field.
4. In the *Description* field, type **Main Hitch Assembly**.
5. Click **OK**.

Task 2 - Assemble the first component and fix it.

1. Right-click on the top level assembly (Hitch) in the specification tree and select **Insert > Existing Product**.
2. Select the *Folder app - Creating_Assemblies_II* tab and select **310000** in the specification tree.
3. Select **310000** in the specification tree and click (Fix) from the context toolbar.
4. This component is now fixed. Note the *Engineering Connections* section in the specification tree.

Task 3 - Assemble the braces.

1. Insert the **3100001** component into **Hitch** using the same method as in Task 2, steps 1 to 3.
2. Use the robot to drag and rotate the model into the approximate orientation shown in Figure 4–54, Use the arrows to drag translation and the arcs to drag rotation.

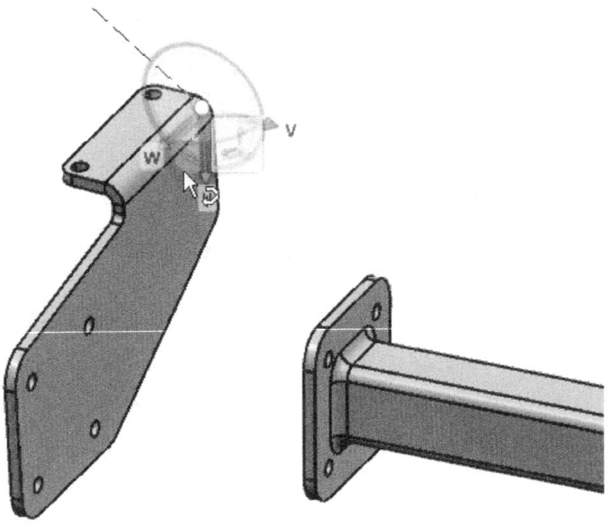

Figure 4–54

3. Click on the screen to temporarily place the component.

4. Create an (Engineering Connection) and insert a (Coincidence) constraint between the axes, as shown in Figure 4–55. The assembly updates automatically.

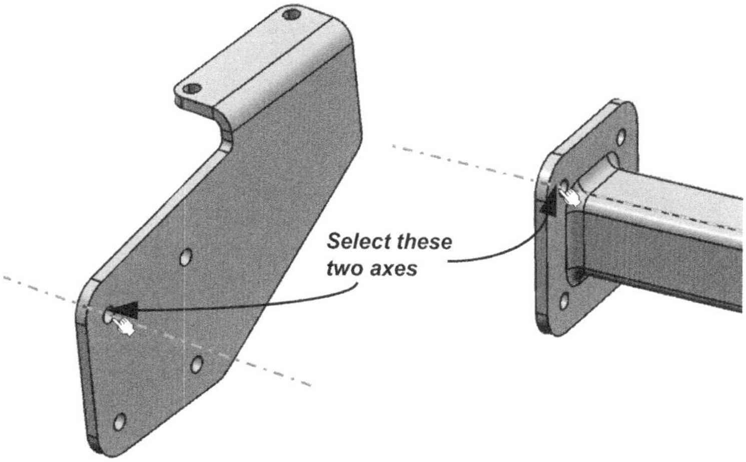

Figure 4–55

5. Within the same Engineering Connection, insert a (Contact) constraint between the surfaces shown in Figure 4–56.

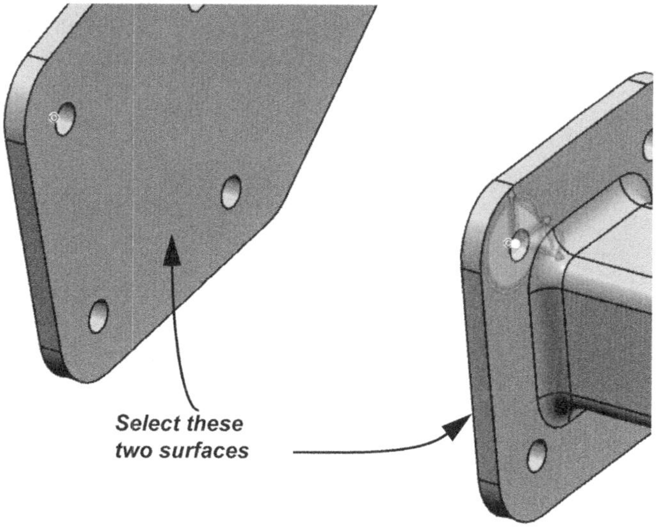

Figure 4–56

6. The assembly updates automatically. Within the same Engineering Connection, select (Show all possible constraints) and select (Parallelism) constraint option between the surfaces shown in Figure 4–57. The assembly updates automatically.

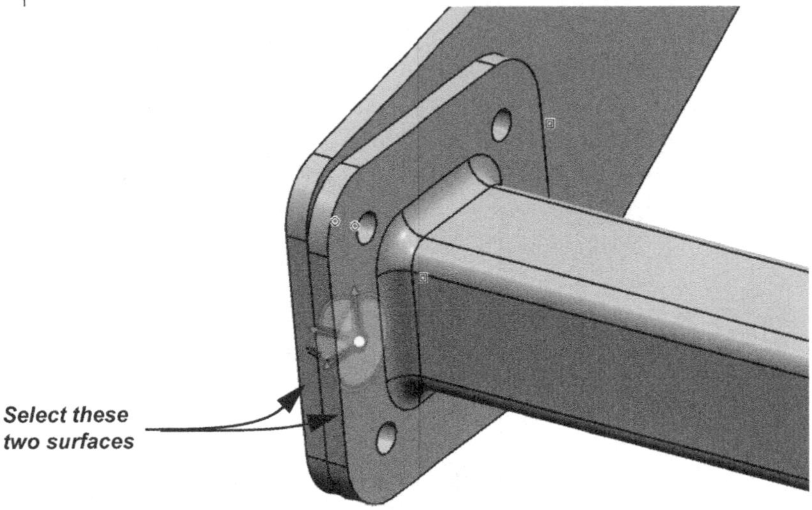

Figure 4–57

7. Select **OK** and **No** to complete the Engineering Connection.
8. Assemble **3100002** using Steps 1-7 described in this Task. The assembly displays as shown in Figure 4–58.

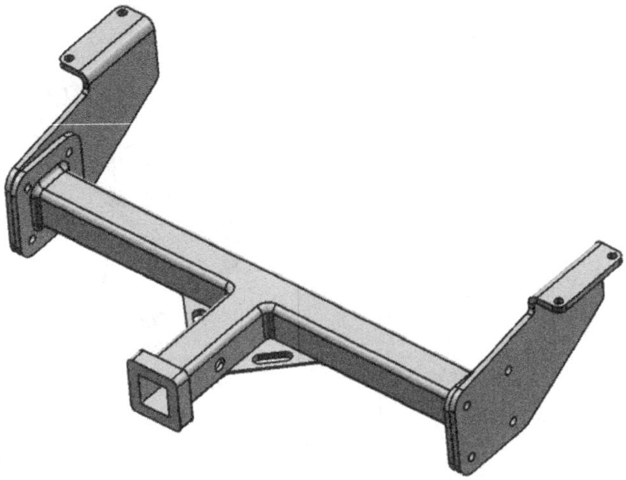

Figure 4–58

Task 4 - Assemble the Ball_Mount subassembly.

1. Insert the **65100010** assembly into **Hitch** by right-clicking on Hitch and selecting **Insert > Existing Product**.

2. Select the *Folder app - Creating_Assemblies_II* tab and select **65100010**.

3. Drag the **Ball_Mount** assembly away from the model and use the robot to manipulate the sub-assembly into a similar position as shown in Figure 4–59. Click to drop it into the product.

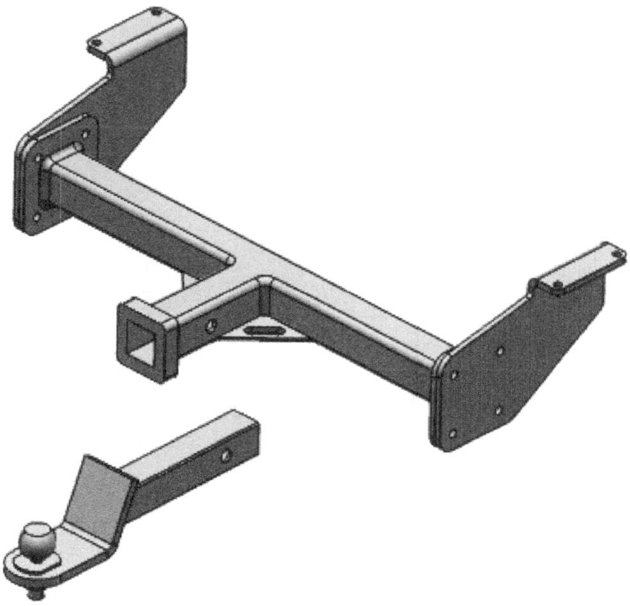

Figure 4–59

4. Select  (Engineering Connection). With the Engineering Connection Definition dialog box open, insert a  (Coincidence) constraint between the axes as shown in Figure 4–60. The assembly updates automatically.

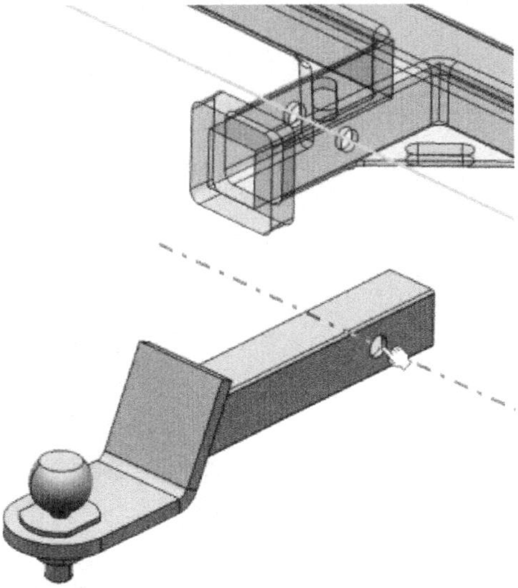

Figure 4–60

5. **65100010** is now partially constrained. Insert an  (Offset) constraint to position along the axis by offsetting two surfaces.

6. Select the surface on the **Slide** and on the **T-Support**, as shown in Figure 4–61.

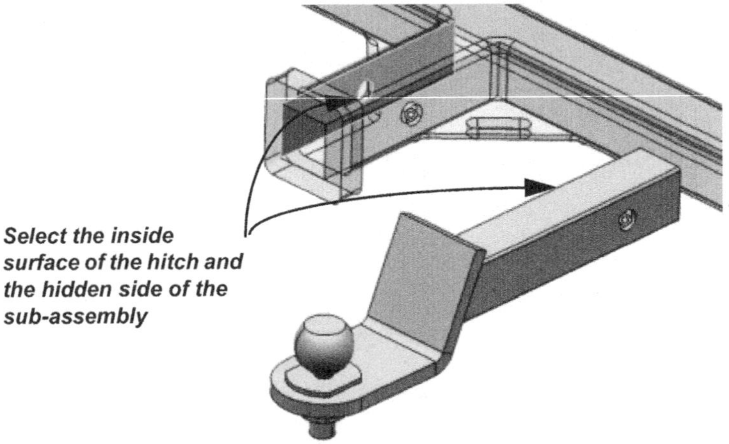

Figure 4–61

7. Within the Engineering Connection Definition dialog box, ensure that *Alignment* is set to  (Opposite) for each reference and enter a *Distance value* of [0.4] as shown in Figure 4–62.

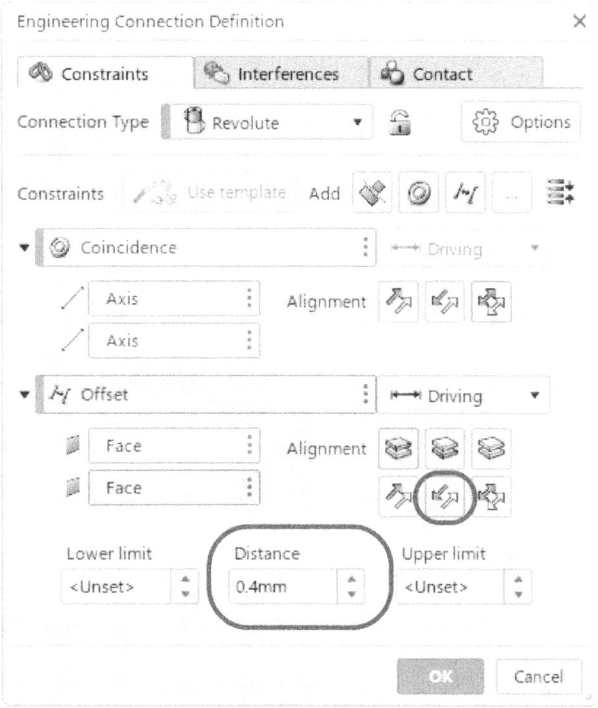

Figure 4–62

8. Insert an Angle Constraint using the (Show all possible constraints) icon. Click (Parallelism) and reference the surfaces shown in Figure 4–63.

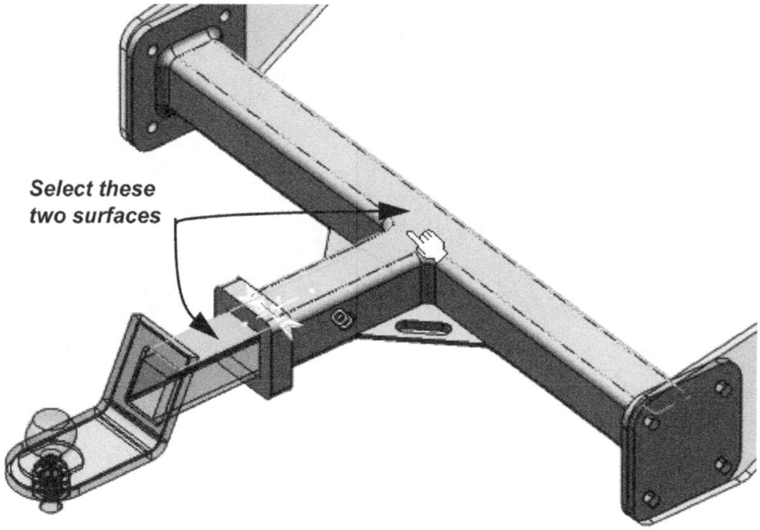

Figure 4–63

9. Click **OK** to finalize the Constraint and close the Engineering Connection Definition dialog box.

10. Click **OK** to omit the creation of the Interference specification. Update the assembly. The model displays as shown in Figure 4–64.

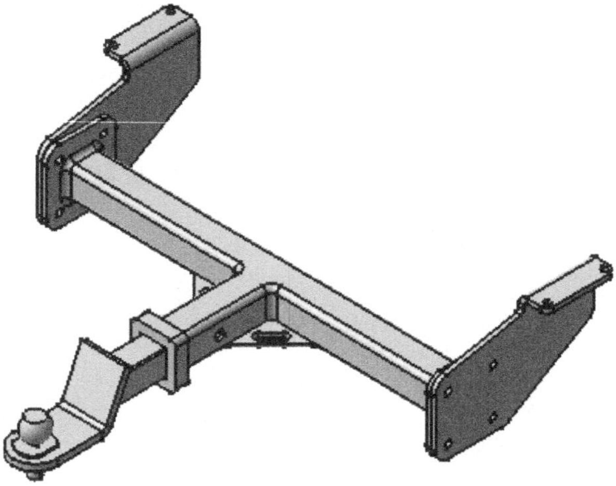

Figure 4–64

Task 5 - Assemble the pin.

1. Insert **3100005** into **65000011** by right-clicking on **Hitch** and selecting **Insert > Existing Product**.

2. Drag the pin away from the model and use the robot to manipulate the component into a similar position as shown in Figure 4–65. Click to drop it into the product.

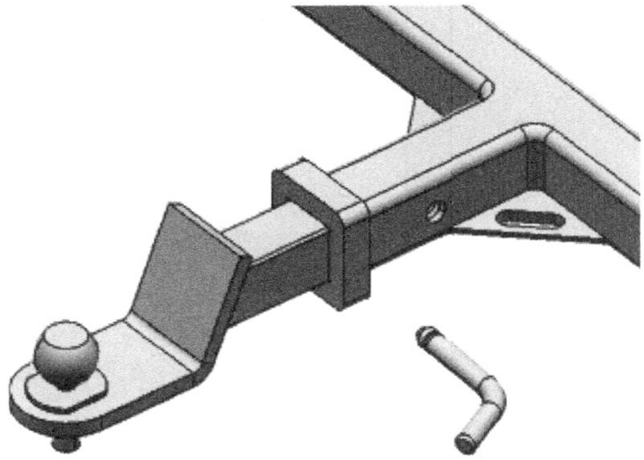

Figure 4–65

3. Select  (Engineering Connection) and insert a  (Coincidence) constraint between the hole of the **T-Support** and the axis of the **Pin**, as shown in Figure 4–66.

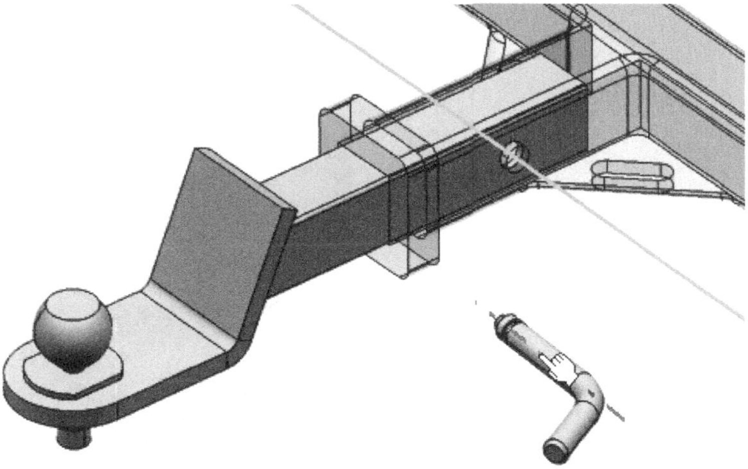

Figure 4–66

4. In the active Engineering Connection Definition dialog box, insert an  (Offset) constraint and select the face of the Pin shown in Figure 4–67.

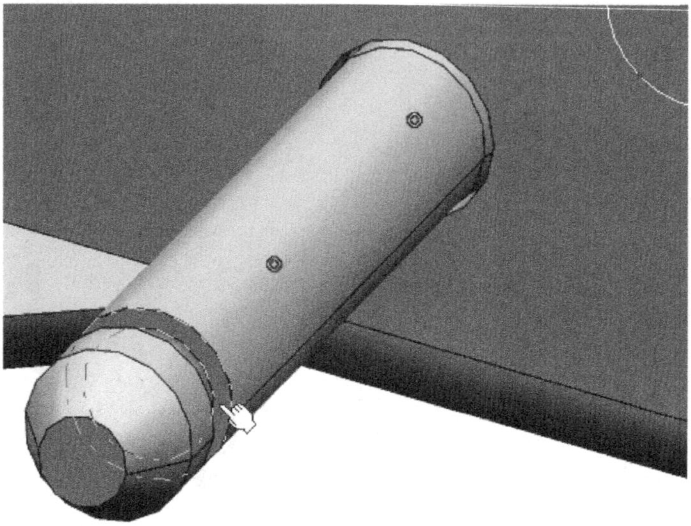

Figure 4–67

5. Select the face of **T-Support** as shown in Figure 4–68.

   Ensure that the *alignment* is set to  (Same) and enter an *offset value* of [0].

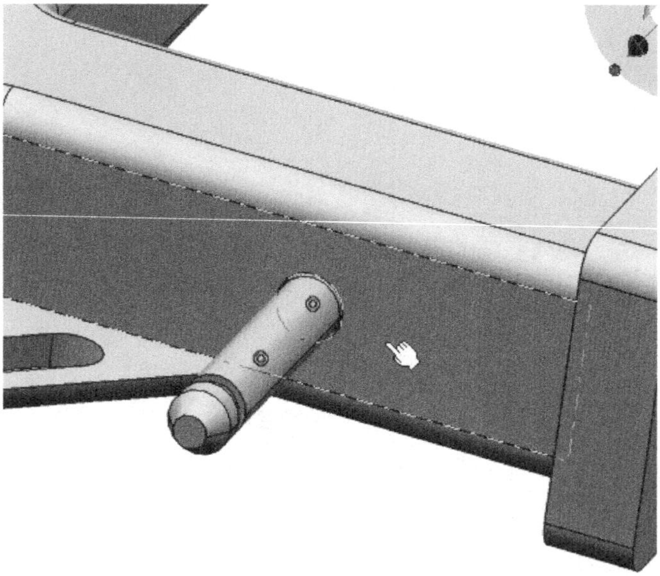

Figure 4–68

6. Select **OK** and  (Update) the assembly. The model displays as shown in Figure 4–69.

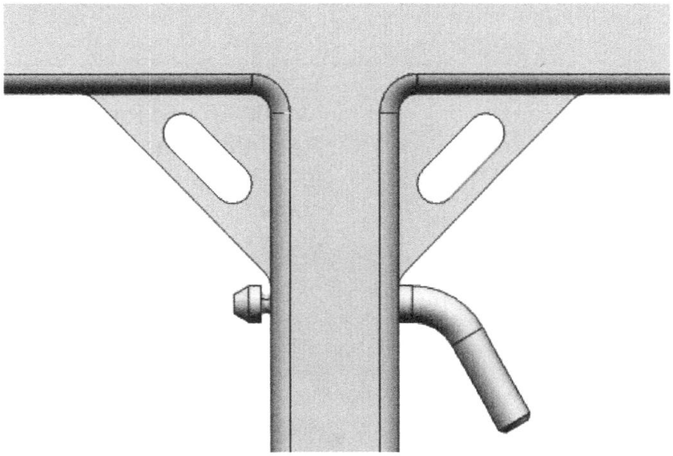

Figure 4–69

Task 6 - Assemble the Retaining Pin (3100006).

1. In this task, you will position the **Retaining Pin** model in the assembly and then constrain its location by fixing it to the **Pin** model.

2. Insert **3100006** into **65000011** by right-clicking on **Hitch** and selecting **Insert > Existing Product**.

3. Drag the retaining pin away from the model and use the robot to manipulate the component into a similar position as shown in Figure 4–70. Click to drop it into the product.

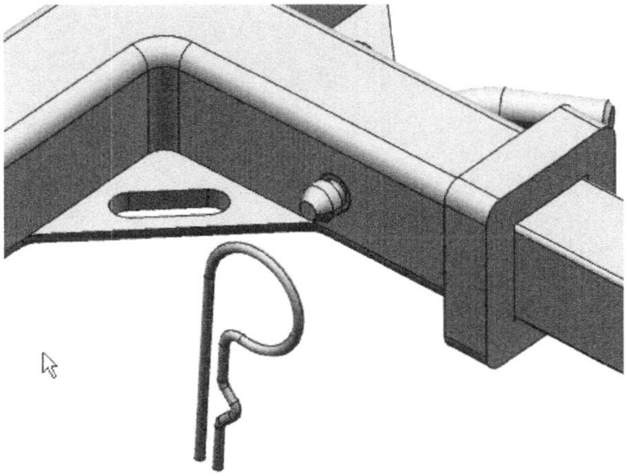

Figure 4–70

Design Considerations

Note the curved geometry of the **Retaining Pin**. Few references can be selected from the model to position it relative to the **T-Support** and **Pin**. For this reason, reference elements have been added to the model that will assist during constraint creation.

4. Show the **RefGeom** geometrical set under **Retaining Pin** (**3100006**) and **Pin** (**3100005**) in the specification tree. The **Retaining Pin** model contains two reference planes and a reference point, as shown in Figure 4–71. The **Pin** model contains a reference plane located at the center of the groove.

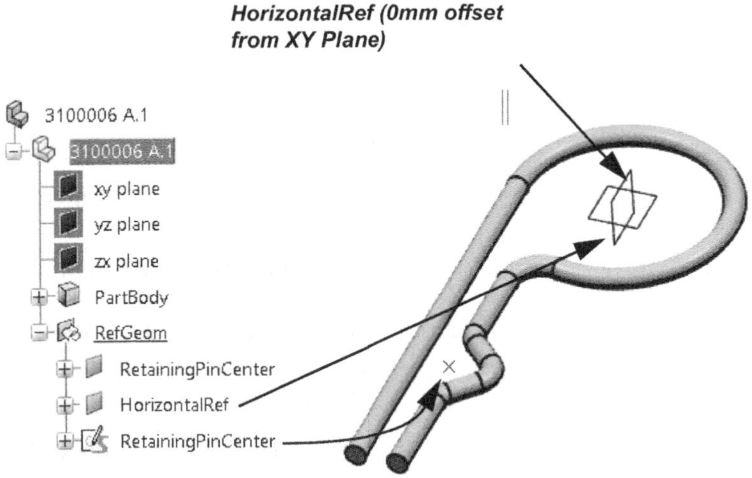

Figure 4–71

5. Using two Engineering Connections, insert the constraints listed in the table below using Figure 4–72 as a guide. The parallelism constraint will require its own Engineering Connection due to referencing the **T-Support**. Modify the vectors of the parallelism constraint to match the **Retaining Pin** orientation as shown in Figure 4–72.

No.	Constraint	Reference 1	Reference 2
1	(Coincident)	Axis of Pin	RetainingPinCenter (sketched point) of Retaining Pin
2	(Offset) (0mm)	GrooveCenter (plane) of Pin	RetainingPinCenter (plane) of Retaining Pin
3	(Parallelism)	Face of T-Support	HorizontalRef (plane) of Retaining Pin

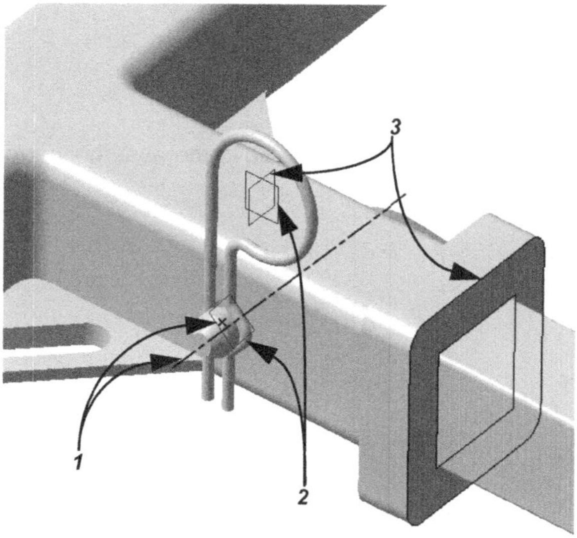

Figure 4–72

6. Update the assembly and hide RefGeom from **Retaining Pin**. The completed model displays as shown in Figure 4–73.

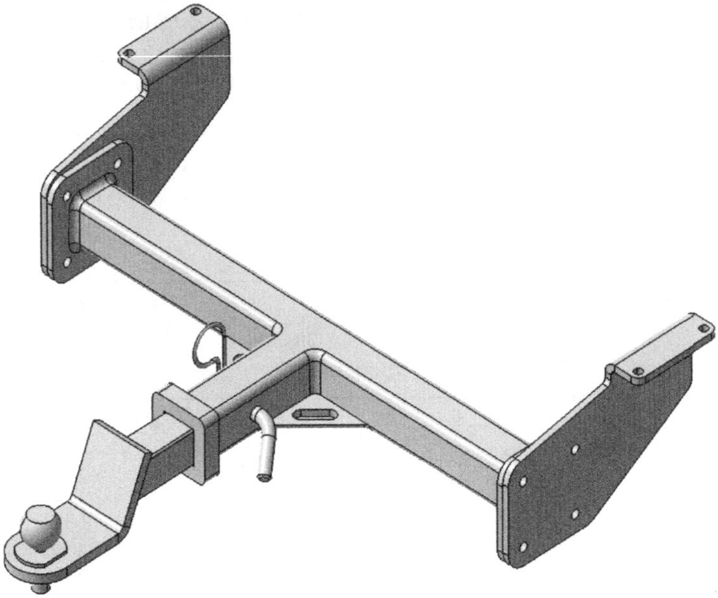

Figure 4–73

7. Save the assembly and close all tabs.

Practice 4c Creating Assemblies III

Practice Objectives

- Create a new product.
- Apply Engineering Constraints.

In this practice, you will create the assembly shown in Figure 4–74.

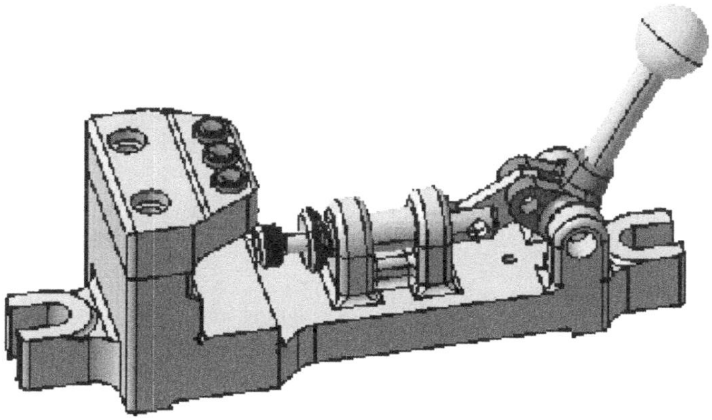

Figure 4–74

Task 1 - Import Components.

1. Import **Bore_Device_Create.3dxml**.
2. In the specification tree, right-click **Bore_Device_Assembly** and select **Open**.
3. In the *View* section of the Action Bar, click  (Fit All In).

4. The assembly displays as shown in Figure 4–75. Note that the components are placed in the assembly but have not been constrained.

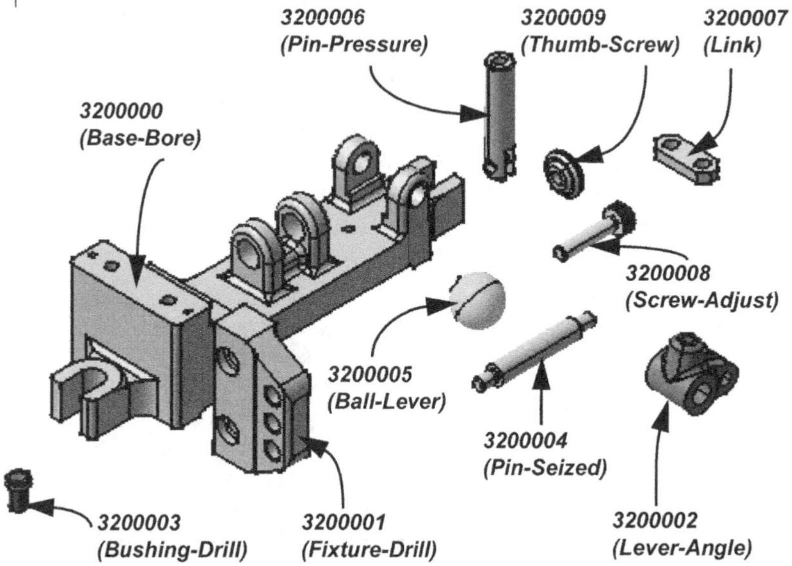

Figure 4–75

Task 2 - Assemble the components.

1. Select the **Base-Bore(3200000)** part and select (Fix) using the context menu that displays, as shown in Figure 4–76.

Figure 4–76

2. Assemble the **Drill Fixture(3200001)**, to the base shown in Figure 4–77. Instead of using the  (Engineering Connection) command, preselect the references of the components you want to constrain. Then, select the Constraints from the Context menu that displays. Use  (Coincidence),  (Contact), and  (Parallel) constraints to Assemble the **Drill Fixture**.

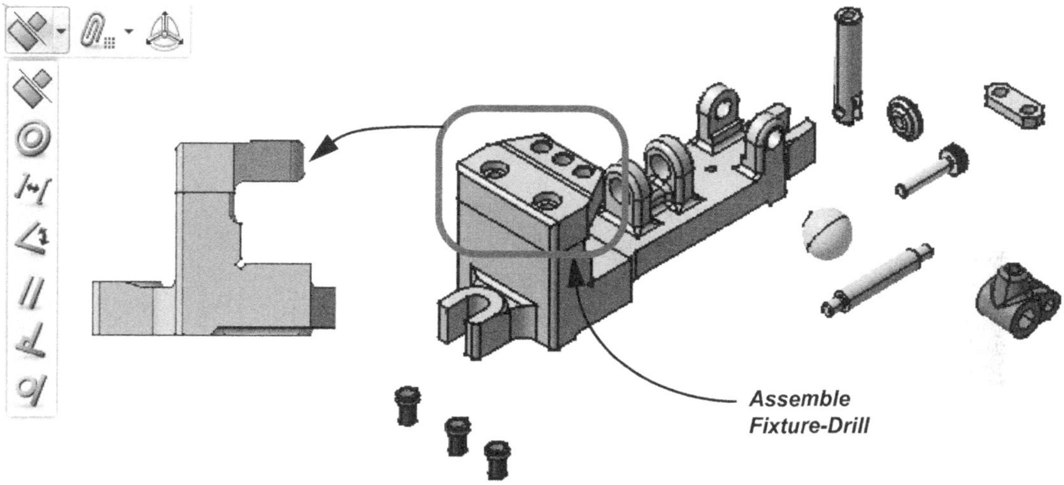

Figure 4–77

3. Assemble the three drill bushings into the drill fixture.

4. Assemble the **Ball-Lever 3200005**, **Pin-Seized 3200004**, and **Lever-Angle 3200002**, as shown in Figure 4–78.

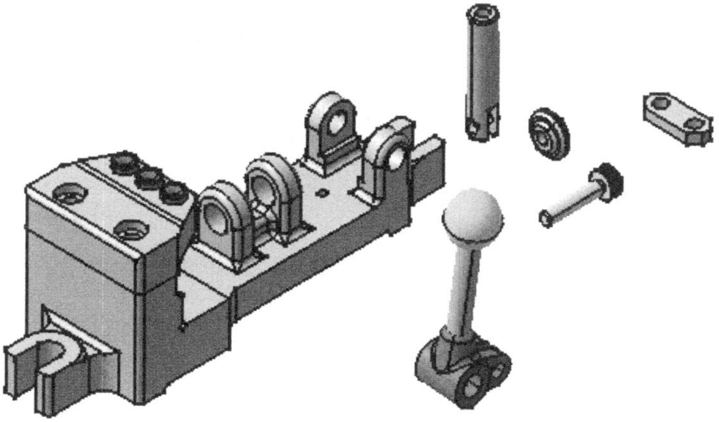

Figure 4–78

5. Assemble **Lever-Angle-3200002**, **Link-3200007**, and **Pin-Pressure 3200006**, as shown in Figure 4–79.

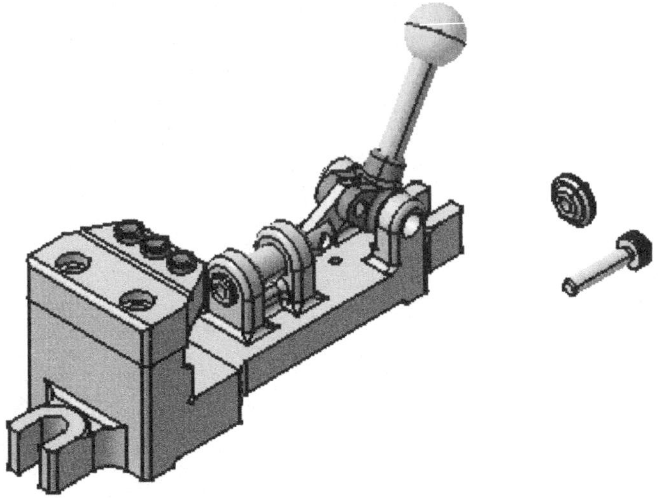

Figure 4–79

6. Assemble the remaining components, as shown in Figure 4–80.

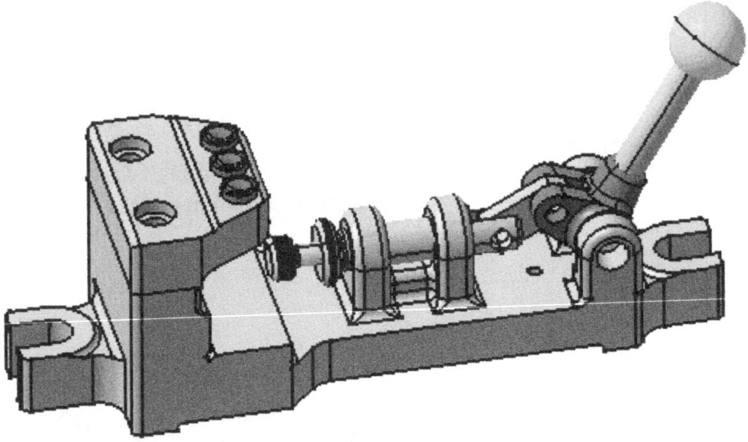

Figure 4–80

7. Save the file and close the assembly.

Chapter Review Questions

1. Parent/child relationships cannot exist between the components in an assembly.
   a. True
   b. False
2. What types of components can be added to a product? (Select all that apply.)
   a. Parts
   b. Products
   c. Drawings
3. Multiple components can be added to an assembly at the same time.
   a. True
   b. False
4. Which constraint can be used to constrain a component so that two surfaces are mated but you maintain the flexibility of entering an offset value if the design intent changes?
   a.  (Contact)
   b.  (Offset)
   c.  (Coincidence)
   d.  (Angle)

5. Which of the assemblies shown in Figure 4–81 could have used the coincidence constraint to constrain surfaces C and 2 and surfaces A and 3? (Select all that apply.)

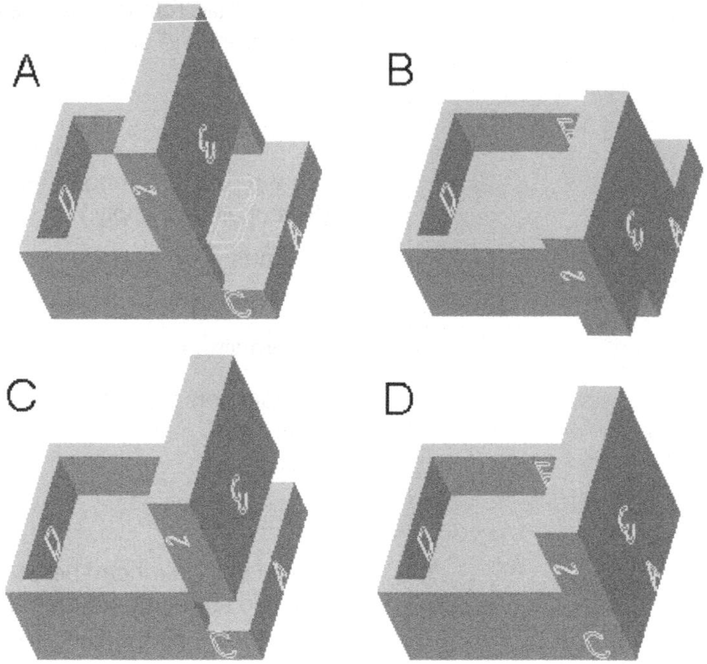

Figure 4–81

   a. A
   b. B
   c. C
   d. D

6. Once a constraint is created, the only way to change it to another type is to delete it and recreate it.

   a. True
   b. False

7. How can you force CATIA to obey the assembly constraints while moving components using the compass?
    a. Press and hold <Ctrl> while using the compass.
    b. Press and hold the middle mouse button while using the compass.
    c. Press and hold <Shift> while using the compass.
    d. Constraints cannot be obeyed when using the compass to move components.

Answers: 1b, 2ab, 3a, 4b, 5cd, 6b, 7c

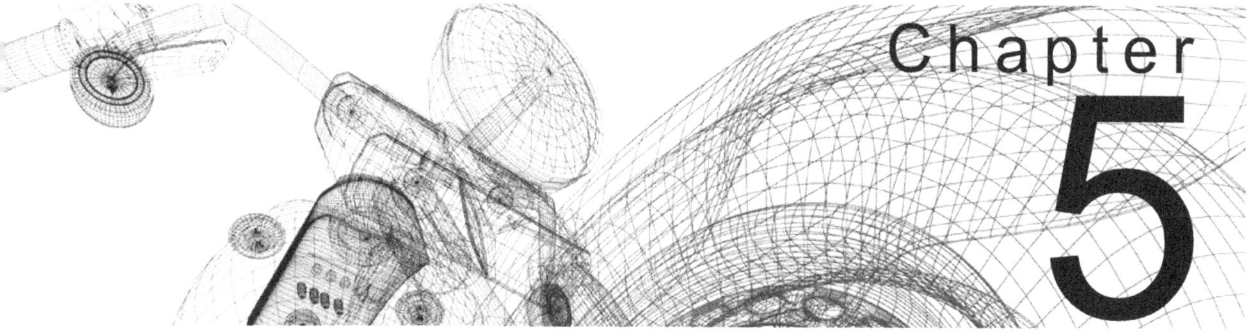

Assembly Information

This chapter covers the techniques that you can use to obtain information about an assembly. The Measure tools enable you to take measurements of the assembly in the same way that you take measurements of parts. The Clash and Clearance Analysis tool enables you to determine whether any interference is present in the assembly.

Learning Objectives in This Chapter

- Use the measurement options for assembly components.
- Understand how the Clipping Tool works within a Product.
- Determine whether interference exists in an assembly.
- Find how to determine Weight Definition and Weight Distribution.

5.1 Measurements

CATIA provides tools to extract important information from your assembly model. The *Tools* section of the Action Bar enables you to perform the following functions:

- Measure the distance between items on different parts.
- Measure the distance between items on a single part.
- Measure the mass properties of the assembly.
- Section the assembly to view internal components

These functions can be accessed using the options shown in Figure 5–1.

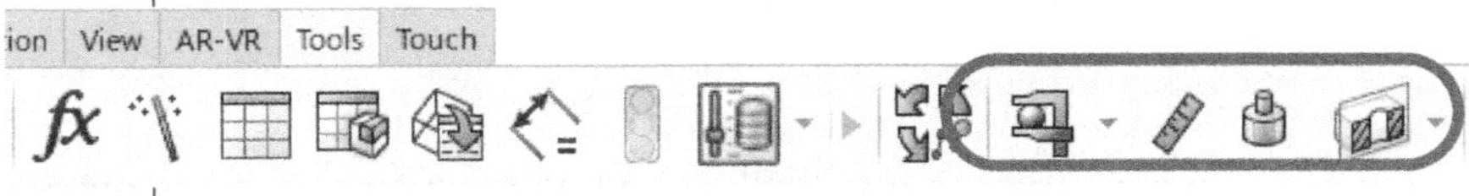

Figure 5–1

Component Materials

To assist in the generation of relevant mass properties measurements, materials can be applied to the components of an assembly at the 3D Part level within the Assembly Design app.

Use the following steps to accomplish this:

1. In the *Tools* section of the Action Bar, click  (Material Browser) to open the Materials catalog.
2. Select the material from the Materials dialog box, as shown in Figure 5–2.

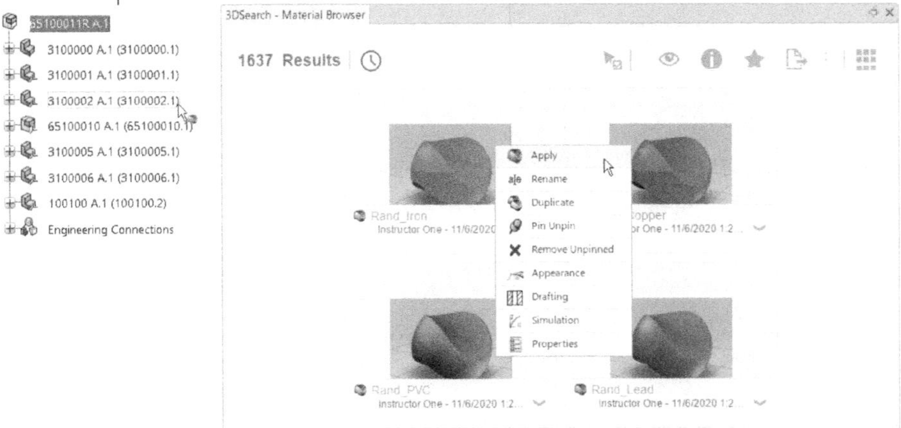

Figure 5–2

3. From the specification tree, select the specific component(s) to which the material be applied.

4. Click (Exit Context Menu).

When this is done, the system considers each component's material property when performing measure inertia calculations.

5.2 Clipping Tool

The  (Clipping Tool) command enables you to create temporary cut sections in one or more components. You can use this tool to perform the following tasks:

- Examine assembly components' positions.
- View complex 2D cross-sections.
- Verify the internal design considerations of a part.
- View internal clash conditions.

General Steps

Use the following general steps when using the Clipping Tool.

1. Activate the **Clipping Tool** command.
2. Select the clipping plane to access the context toolbar.
3. Use the context toolbar to customize settings.
4. Complete the clipping operation.

Step 1 - Activate the Clipping Tool command.

The  (Clipping Tool) icon can be found in the *Tools* section of the Action Bar. Selecting this icon will toggle the Clipping Tool on/off. The clipping plane cuts through all components in an assembly by default, as shown in Figure 5–3.

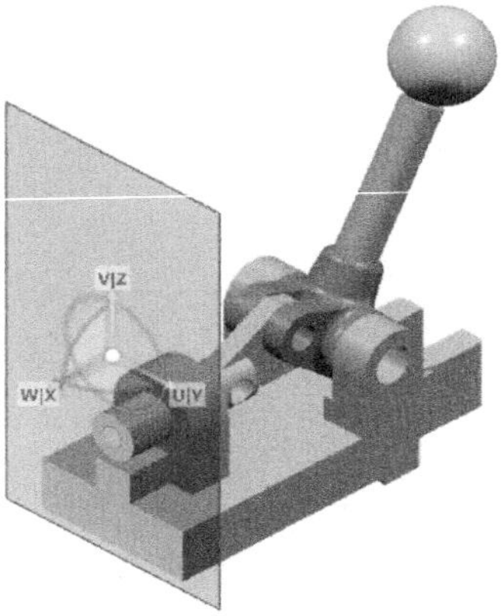

Figure 5–3

The first time you select the Clipping Tool, the clipping plane displays and you are in an edit mode. However, if you select the Clipping Tool more than once, it will only toggle the display of the section on/off without putting you into the edit mode. To be able to edit the section after the initial creation, select

by expanding the arrow next to  (Clipping Tool), as shown on the left in Figure 5–4. Edit Clipping can also be found by selecting the  (Clipping Tool) then right-clicking in the background and selecting **Clipping>Edit Clipping**, as shown on the right in Figure 5–4.

Figure 5–4

Step 2 - Select the clipping plane to access the context toolbar.

Once you see the clipping plane display, selecting it will display the context toolbar, as shown in Figure 5–5. These options allow you to be able to completely customize the Clipping Tool settings.

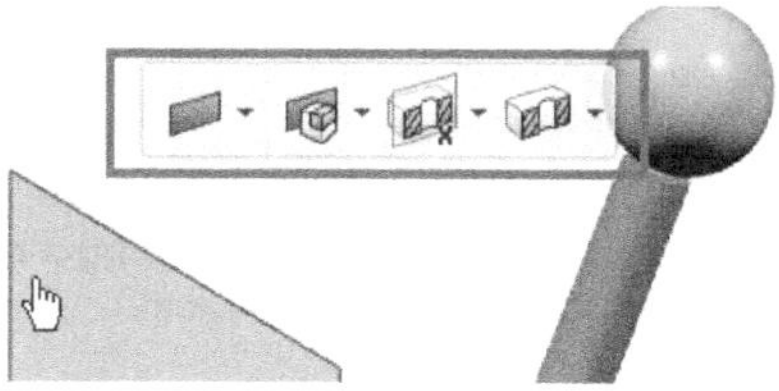

Figure 5–5

There are four different groups of icons within the context toolbar. The icons that are displayed before expanding the groups are the current display settings in the clipping.

Step 3 - Use the context toolbar to customize settings.

The context toolbar has many options for customizing how the Clipping Tool works. Below is a table listing all of the options found within the Clipping Tool. Also note that while many of these commands will reposition the primary clipping plane, you can also click and drag it into a custom position as needed.

Clipping Tool Options

Icon	Name	Definition	Example
	**Display a Plane**	Region of interest is displayed as a single plane.	
	**Display a Slice**	Region of interest is sliced by two parallel planes. Material is kept between those planes.	
	**Display a Box**	Region of interest is displayed as a box.	
	**Define Clipping using Objects selections**	Allows selection of multiple components to define the location of the region of interest.	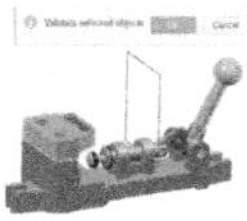
	**Reset Clipping**	Resets primary clipping plane to default location.	
	**Position clipping along X-axis**	Primary clipping plane is placed normal to the X-axis.	
	**Position clipping along Y-axis**	Primary clipping plane is placed normal to the Y-axis.	

	Position clipping along Z-axis	Primary clipping plane is placed normal to the Z-axis.	
	Specify the position of the clipping precisely	Allows position of clipping plane to be placed based on selection of other surfaces.	
	Invert Clipping	Flip which side of the section is displayed or cut.	
	Activate Clipping	Visually cuts the solid, showing 3D geometry on one side of the cut.	
	De-activate Clipping	Visually shows both 3D geometry and the region of interest without cutting any away.	
	Only Contour	Only shows the outline of the section. No solid geometry displayed.	

Step 4 - Complete the clipping operation.

Once you have completed customizing the look of the section using the context toolbar, click in the background to finish the command. The clipping view is displayed on the model. As mentioned in Step 1, you can select **Edit Clipping** if you need to modify the look.

There are other options available for editing the look that are not found in the context toolbar. While the clipping view is being displayed, right-click and select **Clipping**. Under this option, you will find the **Clipping Position** and **Cut / Uncut** tools.

Clipping Position

This tool enables you to adjust the size and location of the primary clipping plane numerically. Type in the values based on robot directions U, V, and W, as shown in Figure 5–6.

Figure 5–6

Cut and Uncut

The  (Cut / Uncut) command is only available while the clipping display is applied. It enables you to pick and choose which components are being sectioned, and is only usable when working with a Product. You can select elements to cut and elements not to cut within the Cut Elements window. An example cutting the larger parts and excluding everything else is shown in Figure 5–7.

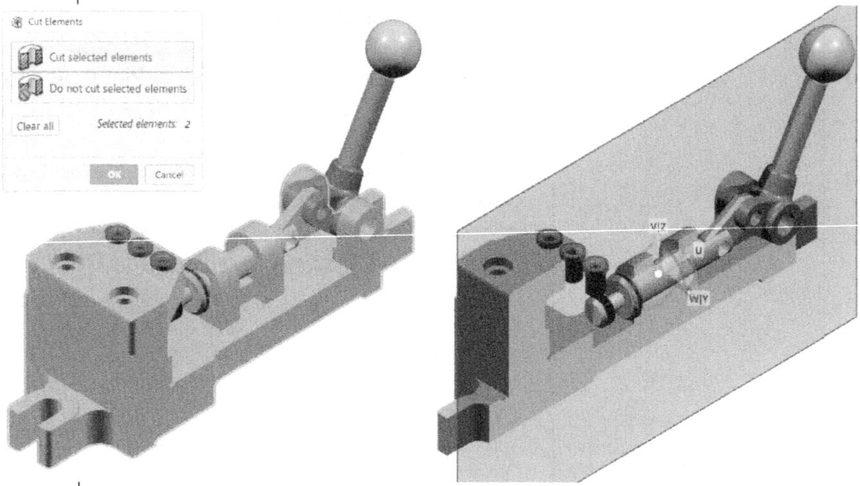

Figure 5–7

5.3 Interference

When creating an assembly, the system permits interference between components. There are three tools that are used to evaluate an assembly for interference and related conditions:

- Engineering Connection Interference Checks
- Interference Check App
- Non Persistent Inference Check

Engineering Connection Interference Check

During the definition of Engineering Connections, the *Interference* tab provides the ability to define a check for clash/contact/clearance conditions between the related components as the Engineering Connection is created. The *Interference* tab displays in the Engineering Connection dialog box as shown in Figure 5–8.

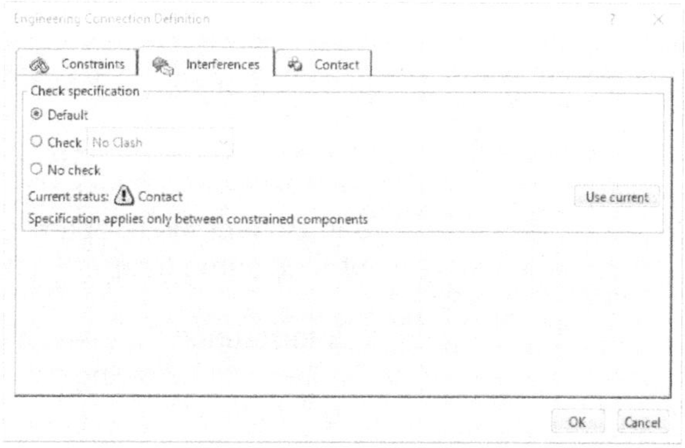

Figure 5–8

If the Check Specification value is set to **Default**, the Undefined Interference message box is triggered as shown in Figure 5–9. This enables a warning to be generated if downstream modifications result in the Engineering Connection components violating the check specification condition.

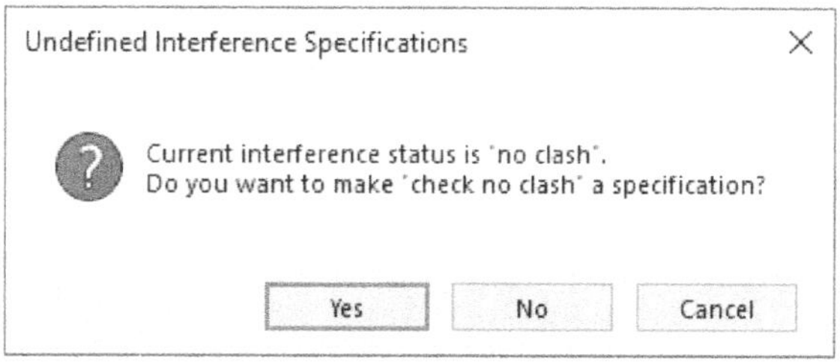

Figure 5–9

Interference Check App

The Interference Check App enables the analysis of conditions including clash, contact and clearance between two or more components.

The Interference Check App is used to determine whether interference exists, and if so, the degree of interference. By using Interference Check App, a Simulation object is created within the system allowing for interference information and additional markup information to be saved for later use.

To access the Interference Check app, click **Roles, Apps & Solutions portfolio** in the compass, as shown in Figure 5–10.

Figure 5–10

In the list of apps, click  (Interference Check). An alternative to selecting on the App from the list is to select  (Create Interference Simulation) from the *Assembly* section of the Action Bar. Both of these options will create a Simulation and put you into the same Interferences Check app.

A Interference Simulation window will display as shown in Figure 5–11, allowing you to fill out any custom specifications you require for your simulation. Select **OK** when finished.

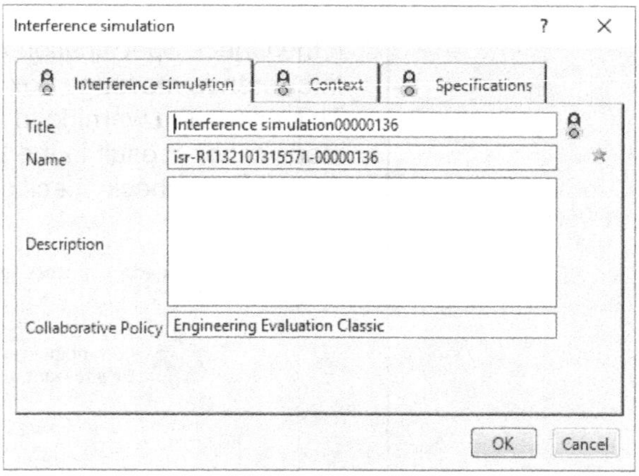

Figure 5–11

In the *Interference* section of the Action Bar, click (Analyze Interference). To see the results of this analysis, click , at the bottom center of screen. The results expand and display as shown in Figure 5–12.

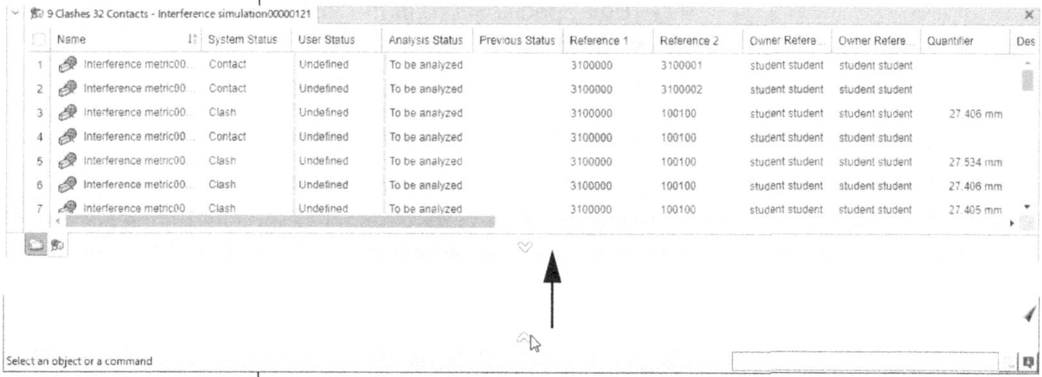

Figure 5–12

If any conflicts occur, you can select and view the result as shown in Figure 5–13. The pair of interfering components is visible and all other components are displayed in a transparent state. Transparency can be adjusted by dragging the Context transparency slider.

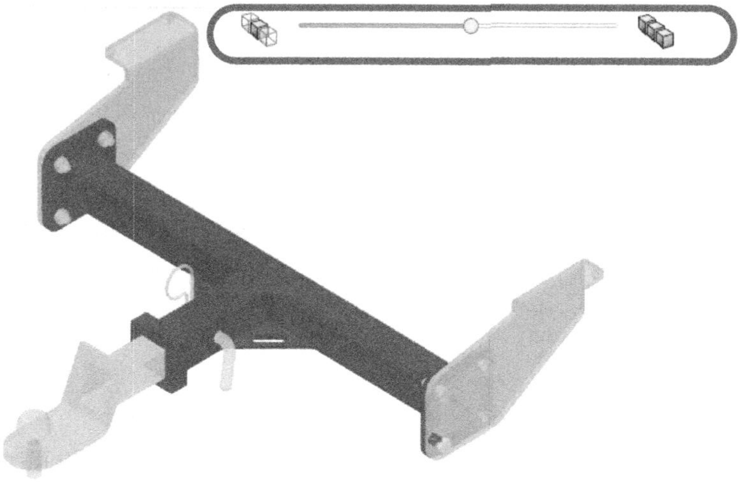

Figure 5–13

By default, Interference Analysis checks between all components for **Clash and Contact** (and **Clearance** if selected). The scope of the analysis might be restricted through the options available in the *Specification* tab as shown in Figure 5–14.

To access the Interference Simulation Definition dialog box, click  (Edit Specification) in the *Interference Analysis* section of the Action Bar.

- **Inside Groups:** Checks components selected to belong to Group1 for Contact/Clash/Clearance between them.
- **Groups against groups:** Checks components selected to belong to Group1 for Contact/Clash/Clearance between each other. The selected components belong to Group2.
- **Groups against context:** Checks components selected to belong to Group1 for Contact/Clash/Clearance against the rest of the product.

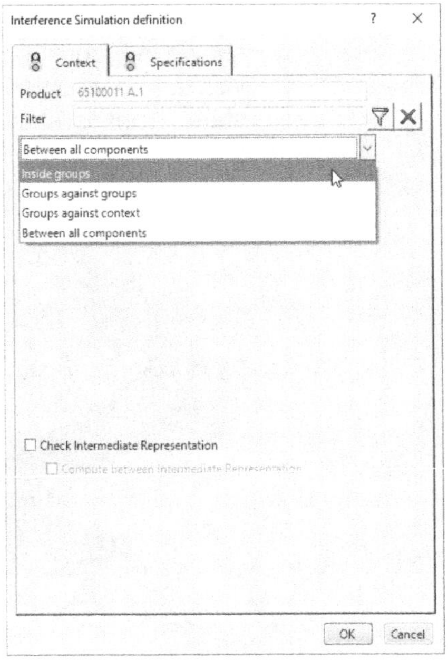

Figure 5–14

Non Persistent Interference Simulation

This is similar to the previously talked about Interference Check App, however the results are displayed within the Assembly and no Simulation object is created. This means that the results are temporary and cannot be saved.

(Non Persistent Interference Simulation) is found in the *Assembly* section of the Action Bar. When selected, a Light Interference Simulation Definition window will display as shown in Figure 5–15, allowing the user to define all of the criteria for the interference check right away.

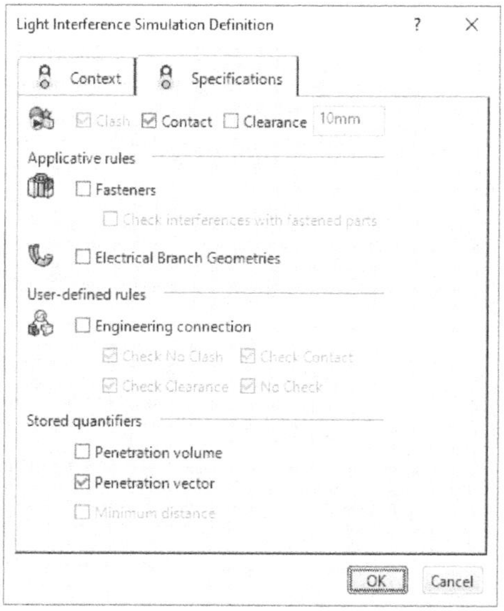

Figure 5–15

Once all of the criteria is defined and the **OK** command is selected, the results of the Interference will display at the bottom of the assembly window similar to how they look in a simulation, as shown in Figure 5–16. A major difference is that while these results can be minimized and expanded, once you hit the (close) icon in the corner, the results are deleted and cannot be retrieved again. A new (Non Persistent Interference Simulation) would need to be run.

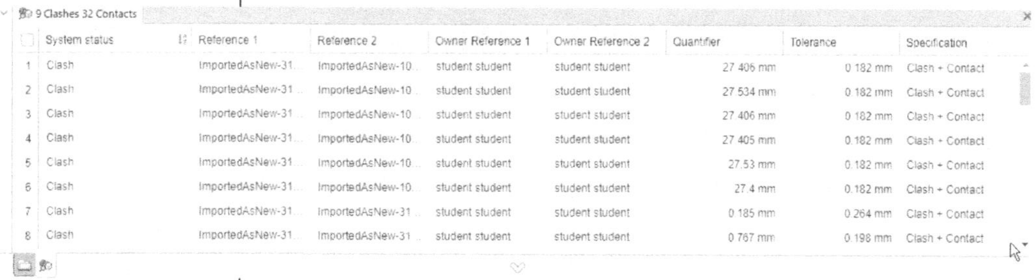

9 Clashes 32 Contacts

	System status	Reference 1	Reference 2	Owner Reference 1	Owner Reference 2	Quantifier	Tolerance	Specification
1	Clash	ImportedAsNew-31...	ImportedAsNew-10...	student student	student student	27.406 mm	0.182 mm	Clash + Contact
2	Clash	ImportedAsNew-31...	ImportedAsNew-10...	student student	student student	27.534 mm	0.182 mm	Clash + Contact
3	Clash	ImportedAsNew-31...	ImportedAsNew-10...	student student	student student	27.406 mm	0.182 mm	Clash + Contact
4	Clash	ImportedAsNew-31...	ImportedAsNew-10...	student student	student student	27.405 mm	0.182 mm	Clash + Contact
5	Clash	ImportedAsNew-31...	ImportedAsNew-10...	student student	student student	27.53 mm	0.182 mm	Clash + Contact
6	Clash	ImportedAsNew-31...	ImportedAsNew-10...	student student	student student	27.4 mm	0.182 mm	Clash + Contact
7	Clash	ImportedAsNew-31...	ImportedAsNew-31...	student student	student student	0.185 mm	0.264 mm	Clash + Contact
8	Clash	ImportedAsNew-31...	ImportedAsNew-31...	student student	student student	0.767 mm	0.198 mm	Clash + Contact

Figure 5–16

5.4 Weight Definition

The **Weight Definition** tool is used to check, calculate, or declare the weight of a part based on its geometry and/or material. This tool is part of the B.I. Essentials tools.

The B.I. Essentials tools are accessed by clicking

 (B.I. Essentials) in the *Tools* tab of the Action Bar. The B.I Essentials dialog box is displayed. In the *Choose information to reveal* drop-down list, select **Weight Definition**, as shown in Figure 5–17.

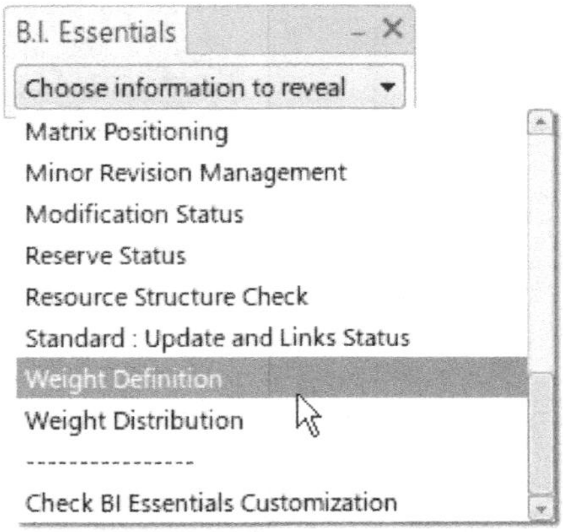

Figure 5–17

The Weight Definition tool uses color coding to indicate the status of each component, as shown in Figure 5–18.

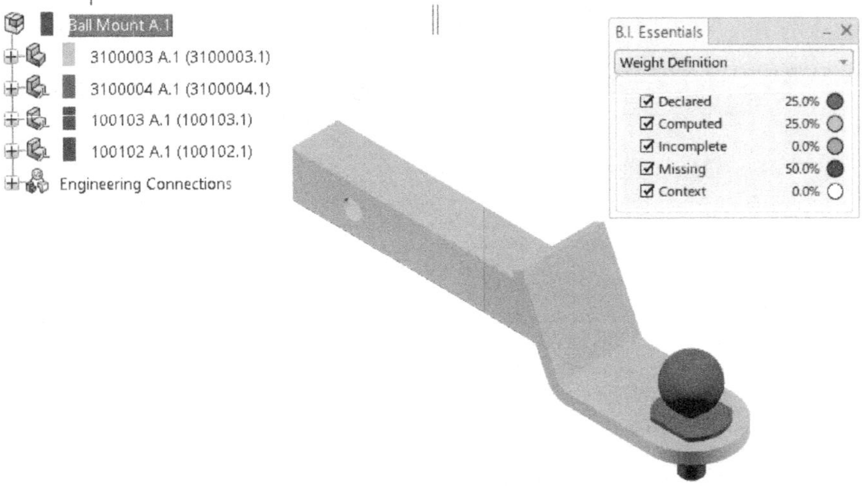

Figure 5–18

The color coding is broken into 5 categories:

- Declared (Blue) - Weight is declared manually through the Weight Definition tool.
- Computed (Green) - Weight is computed automatically using the geometry and material properties.
- Incomplete (Orange) - Weight is partially defined.
- Missing (Red) - No weight is assigned or calculated.
- Context (Transparent White) - The assembly as a whole, or elements not taken into account for the weight computation.

The B.I. Essentials dialog box indicates the percentage of components falling into each category. You can select any (or multiple) category in the B.I. Essentials dialog box and the system will remove any components in that category from display, setting the color to transparent, as shown in Figure 5–19.

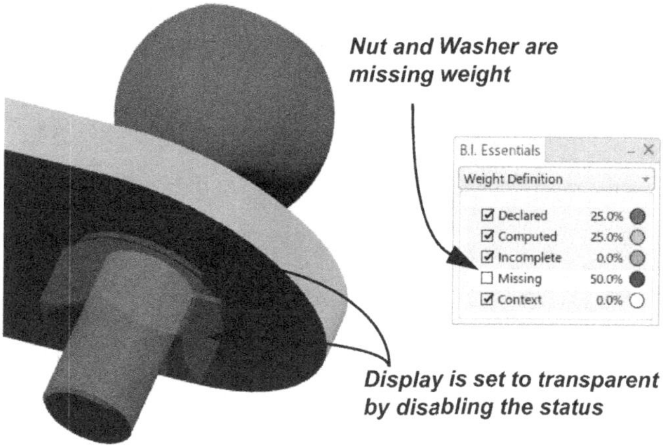

Figure 5–19

Weight Attributes Table

Clicking a component opens a set of hyperlinks on the screen related to declaring or computing the weight. The links displayed depend on the current status of the component. For example, if a component already has a calculated weight, the links are as shown in Figure 5–20.

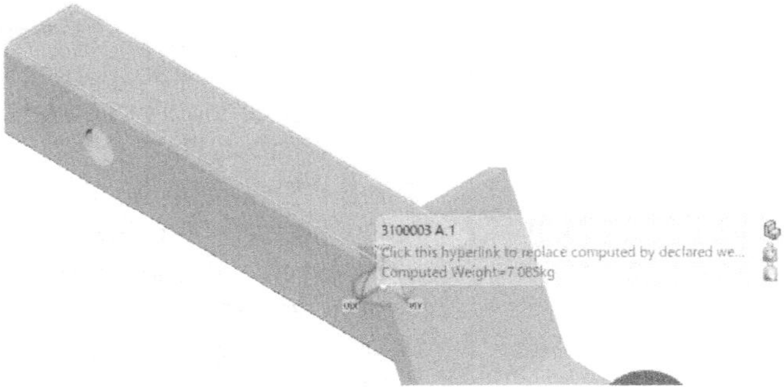

Figure 5–20

Clicking the links will open the Weight Attributes table for the component, as shown in Figure 5–21.

#	Attribute	Value
1	Weight	0.5kg
2	Weight Tolerance (±)	0.05kg
3	CoG along X	1.776e-015mm
4	CoG along Y	154.05mm
5	CoG along Z	-32.3mm
6	CoG Tolerance (±)	10mm
7	Moment Ixx / G	0kgxm2
8	Moment Iyy / G	0kgxm2
9	Moment Izz / G	0kgxm2
10	Product of Inertia Ixy / G	0kgxm2
11	Product of Inertia Ixz / G	0kgxm2
12	Product of Inertia Iyz / G	0kgxm2
13	Comment	

Figure 5–21

The weight will be listed in the *Weight* field. For components that do not have a calculated weight, you can declare a weight. This is particularly useful for purchased parts, where you may want to use the manufacturer's declared weight, rather than calculating it from your model.

5.5 Weight Distribution

To calculate the weight distribution, access the B.I. Essentials tools by clicking (B.I. Essentials) in the *Tools* tab of the Action Bar. From the B.I Essentials dialog box, select **Weight Distribution**, as shown in Figure 5–22.

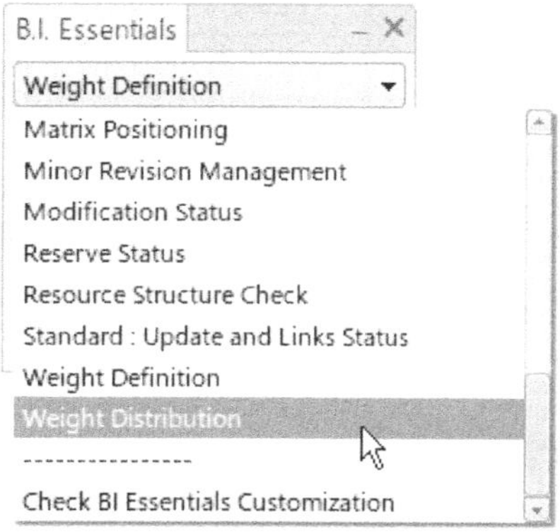

Figure 5–22

The Weight Distribution tool uses color coding to review components according to their weight, as shown in Figure 5–23.

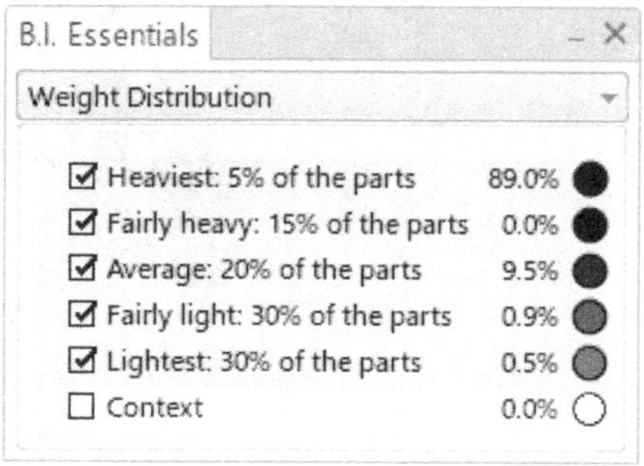

Figure 5–23

The Weight Distribution tool provides insights into your model weight so you can make informed decisions about adjusting components or materials.

Practice 5a Assembly Information

Practice Objectives

- Extract measurements from the assembly.
- Calculate interference.

Task 1 - Import the Hitch assembly.

1. Import the **Hitch_Complete.3dxml** assembly from the *Hitch* folder. If prompted with an Import 3D XML window referencing legacy Flexible or Graphic Property data, click **OK**. This will not affect our exercise.
2. Click **OK** to the Operations report.
3. Right-click **65100011** and select **Open**.
4. In the *View* section of the Action Bar, click  (Fit All In).
5. Fit the model to the display area and activate the Isometric view. The assembly displays as shown in Figure 5–24.

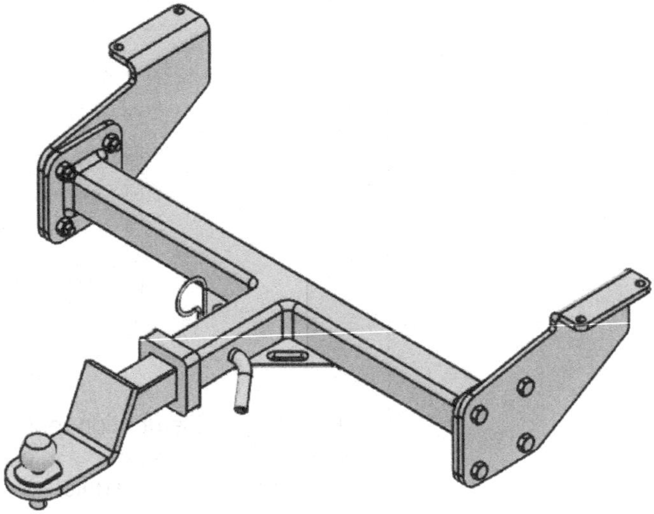

Figure 5–24

Task 2 - Check for interference.

1. Click (Non Persistent Interference Simulation) in the *Assembly* section of the Action Bar.

2. When the Light Interference Simulation Definition window displays, ensure that both Clash and Contact have a check mark, as shown in Figure 5–25.

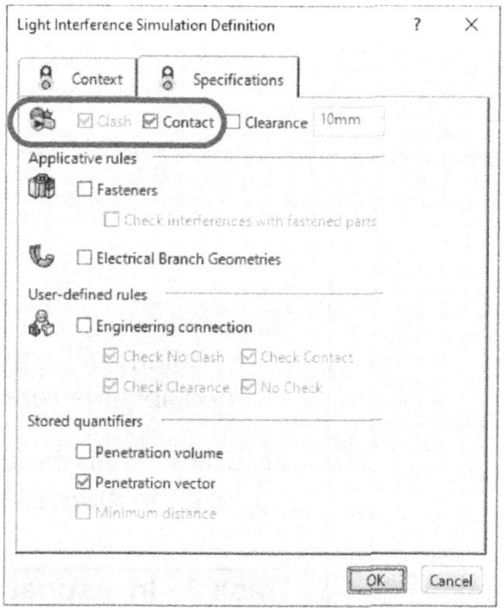

Figure 5–25

3. Click **OK** in the Light Interference Simulation Definition dialog box.

4. Click at the bottom center of the screen, if required. The results of the Interference Analysis are shown in Figure 5–26.

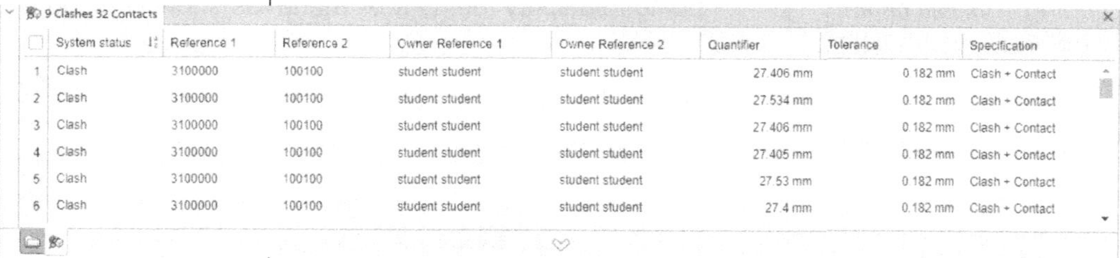
9 Clashes 32 Contacts

	System status	Reference 1	Reference 2	Owner Reference 1	Owner Reference 2	Quantifier	Tolerance	Specification
1	Clash	3100000	100100	student student	student student	27.406 mm	0.182 mm	Clash + Contact
2	Clash	3100000	100100	student student	student student	27.534 mm	0.182 mm	Clash + Contact
3	Clash	3100000	100100	student student	student student	27.406 mm	0.182 mm	Clash + Contact
4	Clash	3100000	100100	student student	student student	27.405 mm	0.182 mm	Clash + Contact
5	Clash	3100000	100100	student student	student student	27.53 mm	0.182 mm	Clash + Contact
6	Clash	3100000	100100	student student	student student	27.4 mm	0.182 mm	Clash + Contact

Figure 5–26

5. Note the detected clash conditions listed in the *System Status* column.

6. Select the first row where clash is indicated. The model zooms in to display the location of the clash on the model. The clash is between the **T-Support** and the **Bolt** as shown in Figure 5–27.

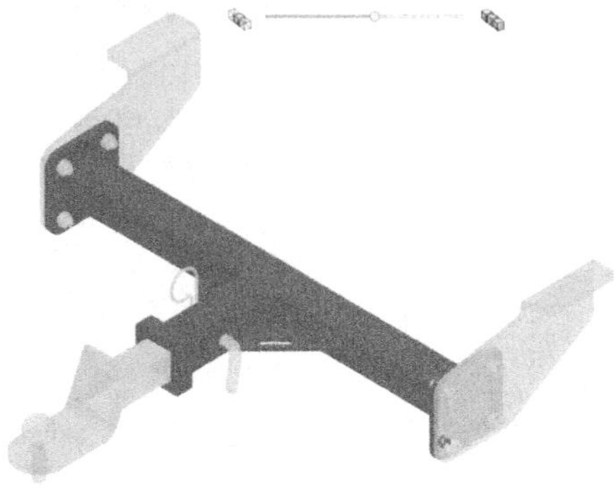

Figure 5–27

7. Continue to review the other clashes in the model. There is a problem with the placement of some of the bolts, and possibly the retaining pin, and the **Ball_Mount** product.

8. Click ✕ in the upper right of the table to close the panel and exit the analysis.

Task 3 - Investigate the cause of the clash with measurements and sectioning.

1. In the *Tools* section of the Action Bar, click (Clipping Tool) to investigate the location of the first clash.

If you accidentally select in the background, the Clipping Tool will finish. To get back into editing the Clipping Tool, select (Edit Clipping) from the Action Bar.

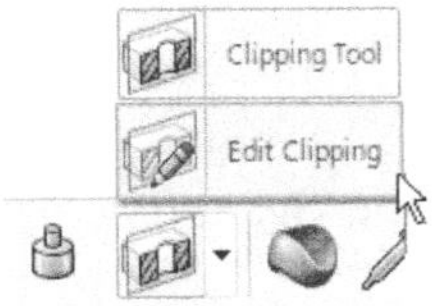

2. Once the Clipping Tool has been activated, a gray rectangle indicating a clipping plane will display. Select the clipping plane to display the context menu, as shown in Figure 5–28.

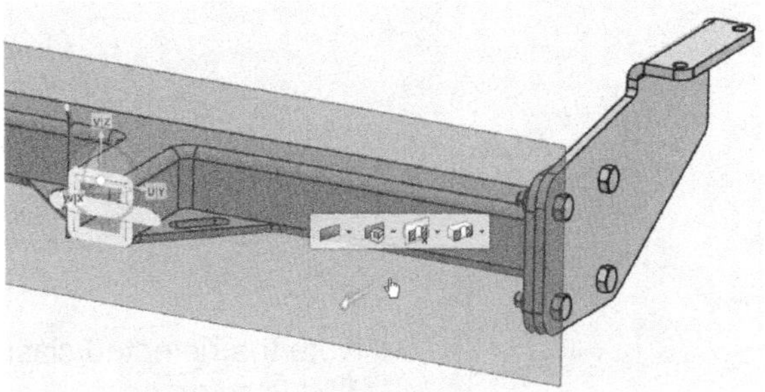

Figure 5–28

3. In the context toolbar, click (Specify Position) Select the center axis of each bolt as shown in Figure 5–29. Turn the model as needed to be able to easily select those references.

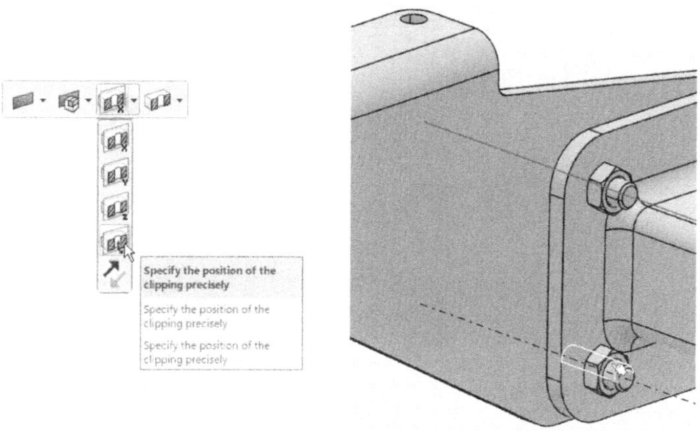

Figure 5–29

4. Zoom in and rotate if necessary on the bottom bolt clash location to examine the reason for the clash, as shown in Figure 5–30. Selecting (Back) from the *View* section will help with this as well.

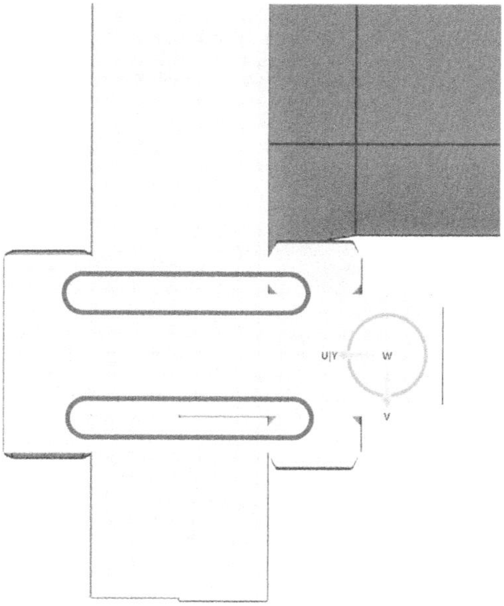

Figure 5–30

5. It maybe difficult to see the interference with half of the model still showing and all the parts the same color. Select on the Clipping Plane to get the context menu to display and select (Only Contour), as shown in Figure 5–31. The upper portion of the intersection should display interference and the lower portion of the intersection should display clearance zoom in as needed.

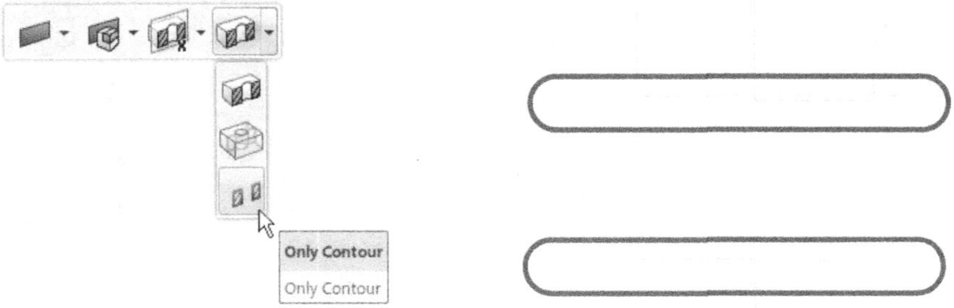

Figure 5–31

6. Select in the white background to complete the **Clipping Tool** command.

7. The assembly will remain sectioned to deactivate the section select (Clipping Tool) in the *Tools* section of the Action Bar again to toggle it off.

8. Click (Measure Item) from the *Tools* section to investigate further.

9. Select the edge of the support as shown in Figure 5–32. Its value is **89.2mm**.

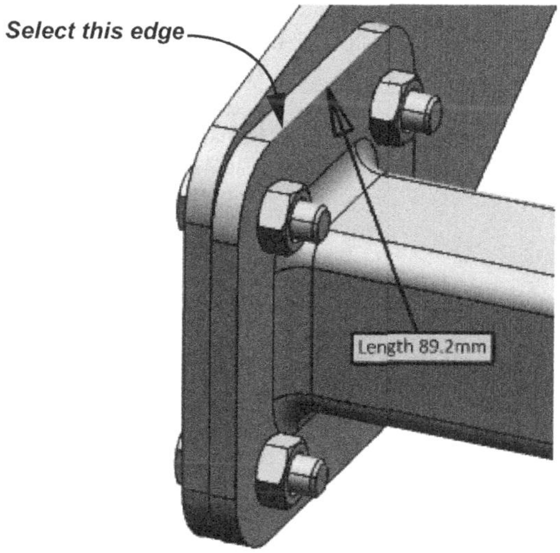

Figure 5–32

10. Select the edge shown in Figure 5–33. Its value is also **89.2mm**. These dimensions are used for the increment of the hole pattern.

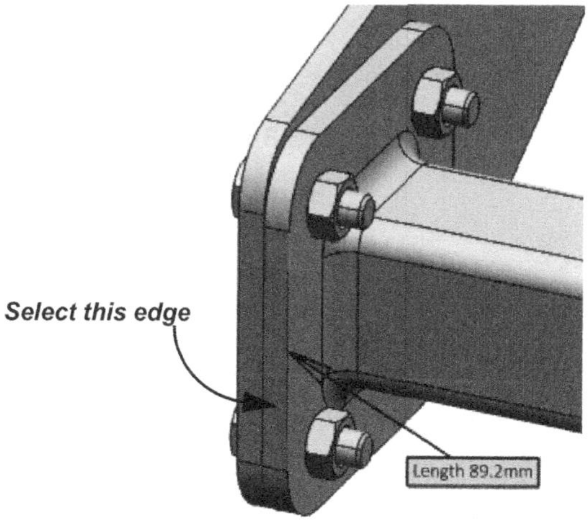

Figure 5–33

11. Click **OK** in the Measure Items window to close the window.

12. Verify that the dimensional increment of RectPattern.1 and RectPattern.2 for part **3100000** is **89.2mm** in both directions. You can do this by double-clicking on part **3100000**, then double-clicking on the patterns.

13. When done, make sure that Product 65100011 is active by double-clicking on it at the top of the tree. It should turn blue.

14. Click  (Measure Between) in the *Tools* section of the Action Bar.

15. Measure between the spacing of the holes in the brace, as shown in Figure 5–34. Here, you can select the axis of the bolts because they are aligned with the holes.

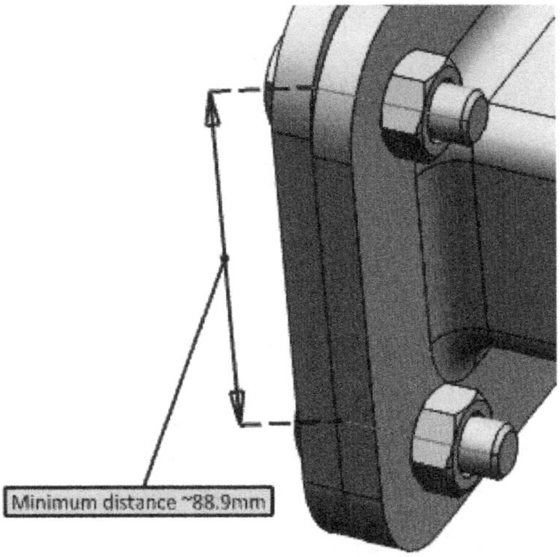

Figure 5–34

16. Note that the hole spacing for this pattern is **88.9** and not **89.2**, which is the dimension used by the pattern.

17. Modify the spacing of RectPattern.1 in both the **3100001** and **3100002** parts to [**89.2**]. And select  (Exit Assembly Feature Specification app) after each part modification.

18. Update the assembly. Verify that the top-level assembly is active by double-clicking on **65100011** in the specification tree.

19. Check for clash again. There should not be any clash involving the bolts.

20. Click  (Measure Inertia) and investigate the mass properties.

21. Save the assembly and close the tab.

Practice 5b

Weight Calculations

Practice Objectives

- Assign material.
- Calculate weight.
- Assign weight.
- Analyze the weight distribution.

In this practice, you will assign material to a model to calculate its weight. You will also assign weight using the B.I Essentials tool, and will analyze the overall weight distribution.

Task 1 - Import the part called Support_Info and review how it is modeled.

1. Import **Ball_Mount_Weight.3dxml**.
2. Right-click Ball Mount and select **Open**.
3. Set the view orientation to (* iso), and if necessary, click (Fit All In). The part displays as shown in Figure 5–35.

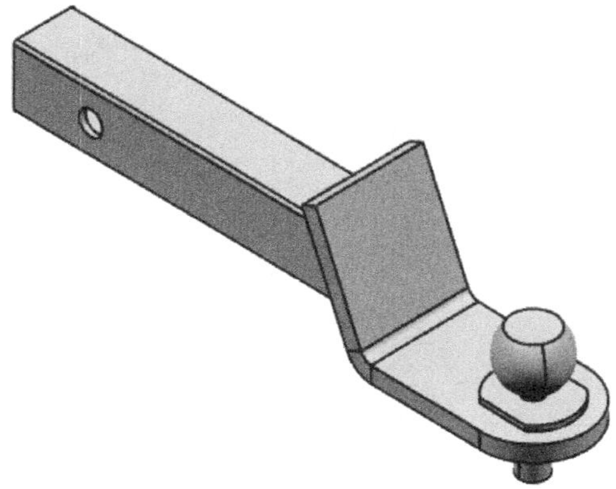

Figure 5–35

Task 2 - Review the weight of the assembly components.

1. In the *Tools* section of the Action Bar, click (B.I. Essentials).

2. In the *Choose information to reveal* drop-down list, select **Weight Definition**, as shown in Figure 5–36.

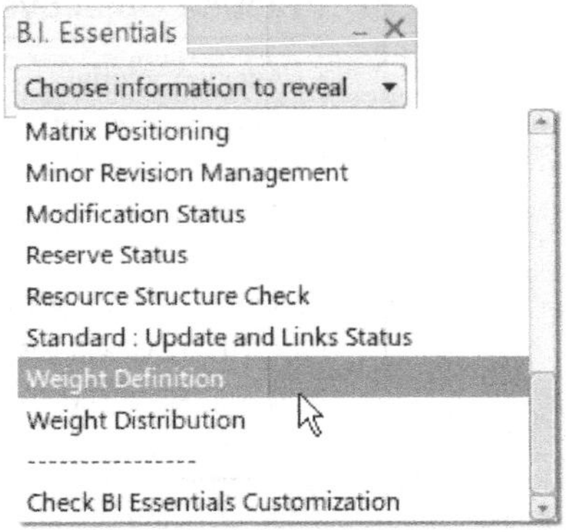

Figure 5–36

3. The model, B.I. Essentials dialog box, and specification tree, all update to show the components with weight assigned, calculated, and so on, as shown in Figure 5–37.

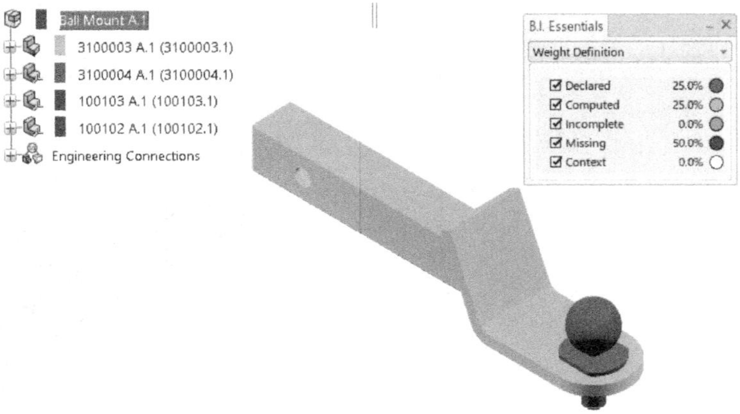

Figure 5–37

4. Select the ball part and note it has an assigned weight of 0.5kg, as shown in Figure 5–38.

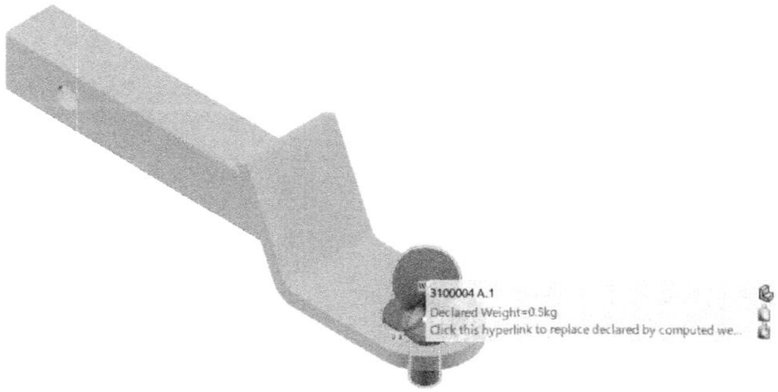

Figure 5–38

Task 3 - Assign a material to the ball part, then calculate the weight.

1. In the *Tools* section of the Action Bar, click  (Material Browser) to open the material library.
2. Select **MaterialSteel** in the Material Browser window.
3. Right-click and select **Apply**.
4. Select **3100004** in the specification tree.
5. Click  (Close Context Toolbar).
6. With the ball part still selected and the BI box open, click **Click this link to replace declared weight with computed**.

7. In the Weight Table, click (Update) as shown in Figure 5–39.

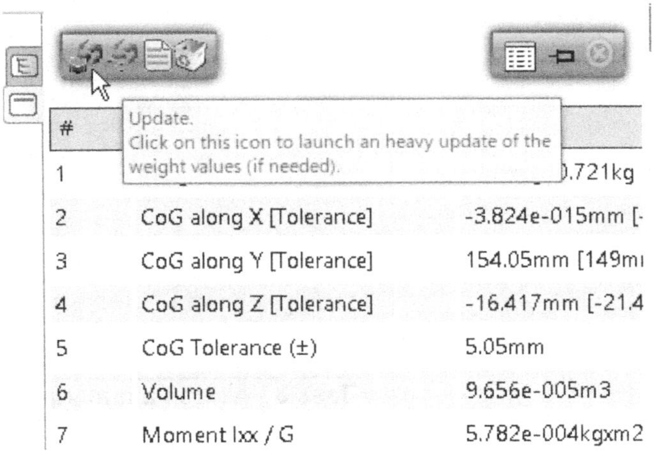

Figure 5–39

8. Close the Weight Table and click on the screen.

9. Note that there are now only two Missing weights, as shown in Figure 5–40.

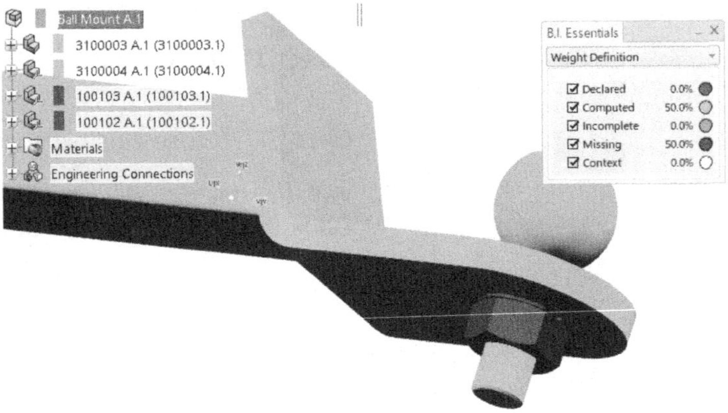

Figure 5–40

Task 4 - Assign weight for the nut and washer.

1. Select the washer on the screen.
2. Click the link shown in Figure 5–41.

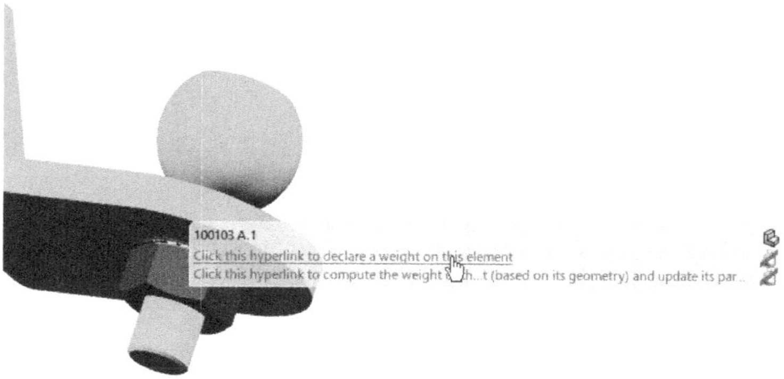

Figure 5–41

3. In the Weight Table, enter **.0075kg** for the weight, and in the *Comments* field, enter **Weight entered from supplier catalog**.
4. Close the Weight Table.
5. Select the nut and use the same process followed for the washer, but enter a weight of **0.1kg**.
6. Close the Weight Table and click on the screen. Note that there are no longer any Missing weights, as shown in Figure 5–42.

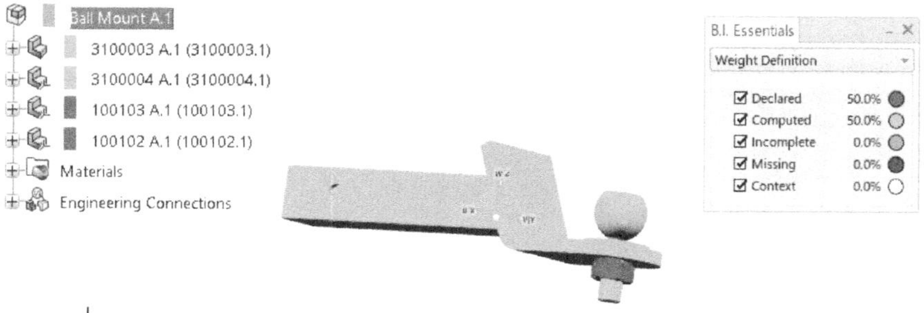

Figure 5–42

Task 5 - Review the Weight Distribution.

1. In the B.I. Essentials dialog box, in the *Weight Definition* drop-down list, select **Weight Distribution** as shown in Figure 5–43.

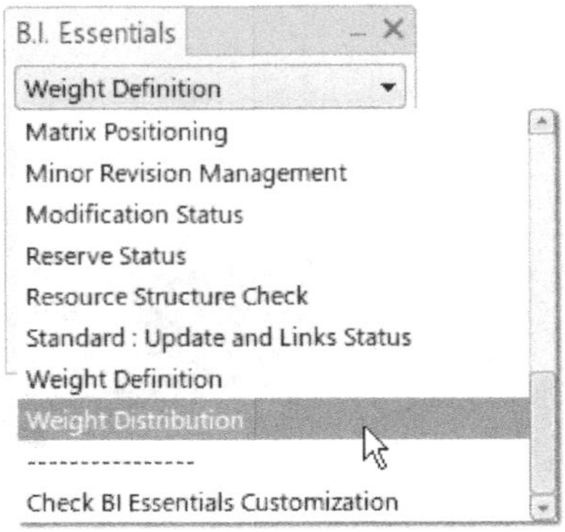

Figure 5–43

2. The model and B.I. Essentials dialog box display as shown in Figure 5–44.

As you would expect, the majority of the weight of this product (88.8%) comes from the sider component.

Figure 5–44

3. Save the assembly and close all tabs.

Chapter Review Questions

1. You must be in the Part Design to apply material to a component.
   a. True
   b. False
2. Material can be applied to the entire assembly or individual components, if required.
   a. True
   b. False
3. In the Check Clash dialog box, clicking **OK** runs the analysis and closes the dialog box while clicking **Apply** keeps the dialog box open, enabling you to review the results of the analysis.
   a. True
   b. False
4. What types of analysis can be reviewed in the Check Clash dialog box? (Select all that apply.)
   a. Clash
   b. Contact
   c. Clearance
5. A Bill of Material report can be exported out of CATIA to either an HTML or an Excel file.
   a. True
   b. False
6. In the Check Clash dialog box, a negative number in the *Value* column indicates ____________________.
   a. Contact
   b. Clearance
   c. Clash.
   d. None of the above.

Answers: 1a, 2a, 3a, 4abc, 5a, 6c

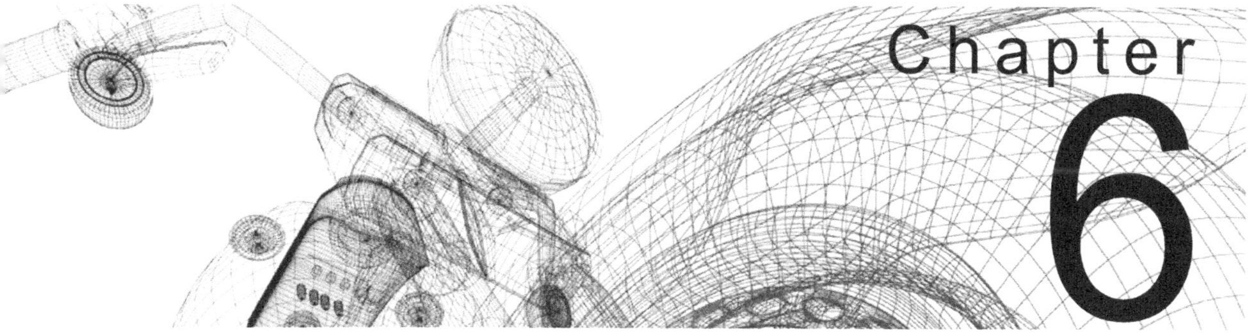

Chapter 6

Design Review I

The Design Review app allows for the creation of review objects, intended for the capturing and sharing of measurements, markups, sections and viewpoints.Once analysis information has been captured, it can be communicated to designers or manufacturers using model annotations called Markers. These markers enable you to display critical information about the part or assembly directly on the 3D geometry.

Learning Objectives in This Chapter

- Learn how to switch to the Design Review app.
- How to create a Design Review object.
- Learn how to create different types of Markers.
- Learn how to create Slides.

6.1 Design Review Process

General Steps

Use the following general steps to add annotations to a model:

1. Create a Design Review.
2. Set the position and orientation.
3. Create a text marker.
4. Create a hyperlink marker.
5. Create a Slide.

Step 1 - Create a Design Review

The Design Review app allows for creation of a Review object within an assembly or part model. This Review object is made up of Markups that can be further broken down into Markers and Slides. The Review object allows for a Designer or Reviewer to add information collaboratively and directly to the model from within 3DEXPERIENCE so that problems can be addressed quickly by everyone involved in the life-cycle of the design.

Creating the Design Review

To create a Design Review, first open the Assembly or Part model that contains the review. Once open, switch to the Design Review app using the Compass as shown in Figure 6–1 .

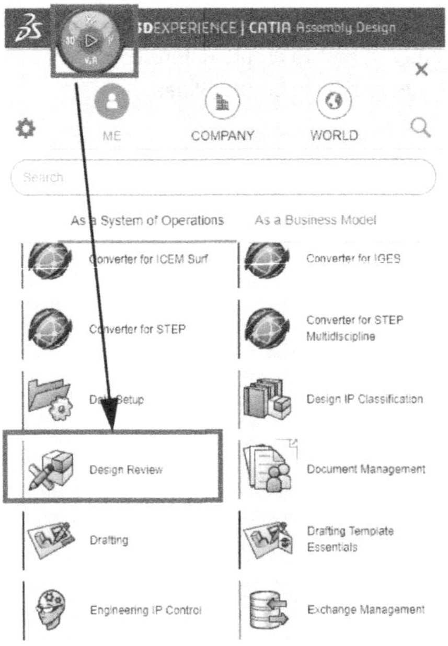

Figure 6–1

Once the Design Review app is selected, a Review window will open. The Review window consists of three different tabs *Review, Context,* and *Markup*. Within the *Review* and *Markup* tabs, the Title and Description can be customized. From the *Context* tab, the model that is linked to the Review can be selected, as shown in Figure 6–2.

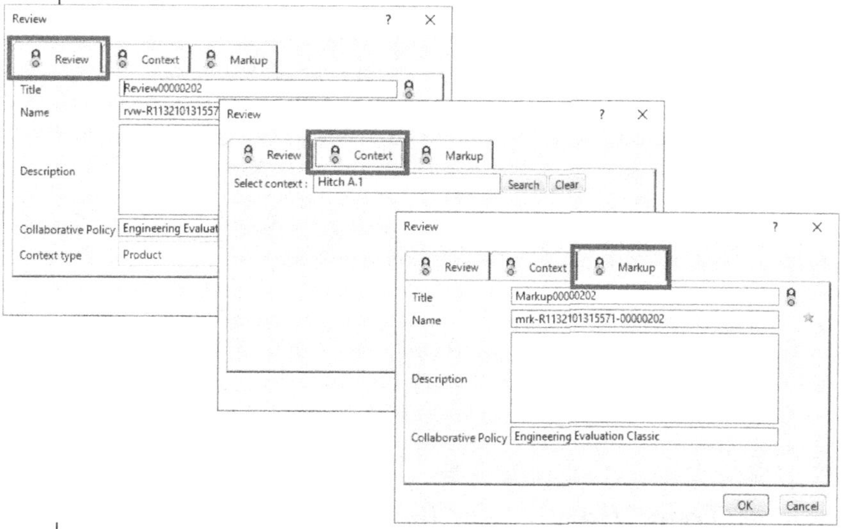

Figure 6–2

Select **OK**. The Review object will be created and placed in the tree of the model. You will now find that the model has completed the switch into the Design Review App, and that a new view display is available.

Review View

The Review View provides a global overview of the review content, guiding you through the reviews and highlights. The Review View allows "see all" and/or filters the views created within the Review object, as shown in Figure 6–3. The *Review View* tab is located in the upper left side of the screen and is displayed as soon as the Design Review object is created.

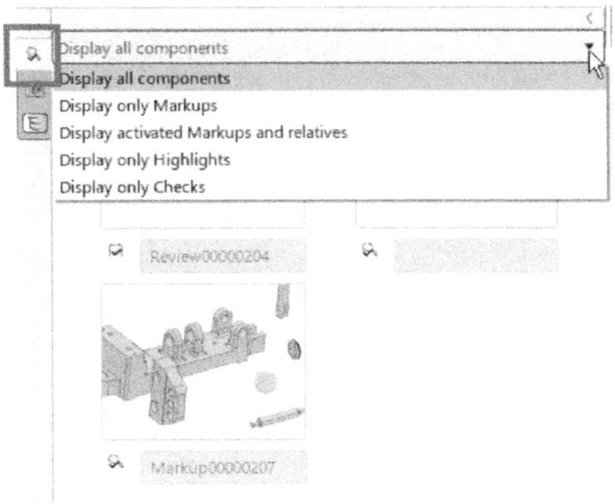

Figure 6–3

Tree View

The Tree view shows the entire specification tree of an assembly while also showing any Review objects that have been created in a separate node at the bottom of the tree. The *Tree* view tab is located on the upper left side of the screen and it displays only when you switch to the Design Review app, as shown in Figure 6–4.

*The Tree view tab can be toggled on/off with the **F3** key.*

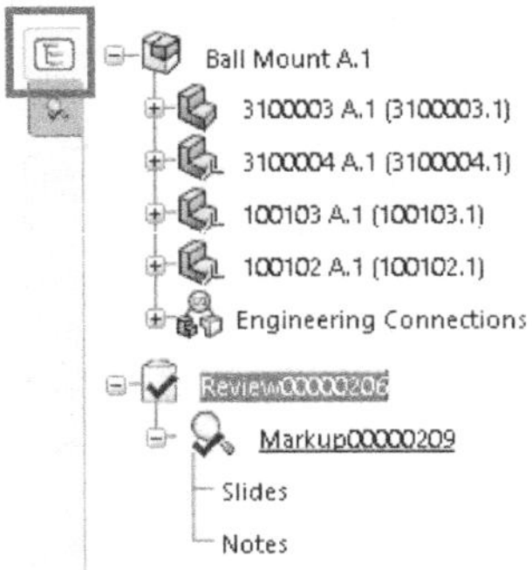

Figure 6–4

Slide View

The Slide View provides a quick way to see the markups for each Review and it also displays the slides created under these markups. The Slide View allows "see all" and/or filters the slides created within the Review object as shown in Figure 6–5. The *Slide View* tab is located on the upper left side of the screen and it displays only after at least one slide has been created.

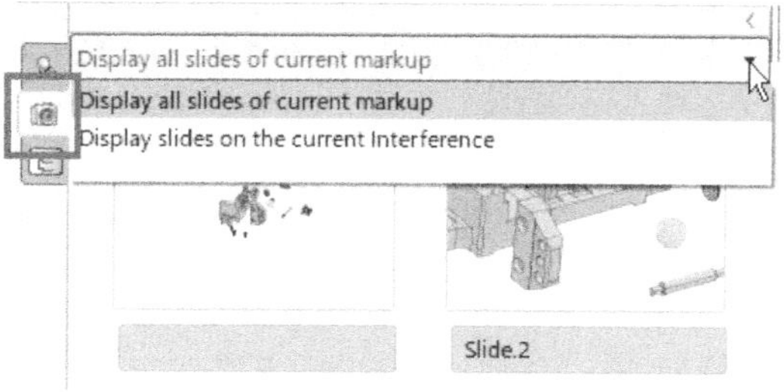

Figure 6–5

Step 2 - Set the position and orientation.

Before you create any Markings or Slides, you should ensure that the orientation of the model is correct. The position and orientation of the model during the creation of the Markings and Slides determine how it will display when a viewer pulls up the slides at a later time. This can be achieved using the Mouse, Robot, or Quick views.

Mouse:

By using the mouse to Rotate (middle mouse + hold left or right button) and Zoom (middle mouse + click and let go left or right button), you can freely orient the model to view the most relevant area of the model. However, note that it may be difficult to orient the model precisely using this method. For example, when trying to get an exact view of the side, you will likely get a slightly skewed view.

Robot:

The Robot feature found in the lower right side of the screen allows you to spin the model into different 90° orientations depending on what area of the Robot you select on. If you click on the X,Y, or Z arrow direction, the model will spin normal to those respective directions. If you select on either the XY, YZ, and ZX planes represented by arcs or circles on the Robot, the first time it is selected, the model will spin parallel to that plan, but if it is selected twice, it will flip 180° to that direction. Figure 6–6 shows the YZ plane being selected on the Robot.

Figure 6–6

Quick Views:

The Quick views can be found in the *View* section of the Action Bar. All of them can be displayed by selecting the flyout arrow next to the (*iso) icon. These include *iso, *back, *top, *right...etc. views and are one of the fastest ways to spin the model into a standard orientation. Figure 6–7 shows all the quick views available within the *View* section.

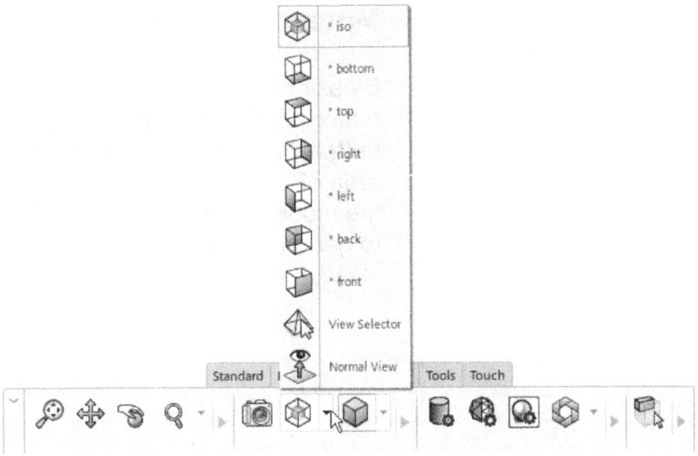

Figure 6–7

Step 3 - Create a text marker.

You can create different types of Markings within a Markup, all of which will display in the *Notes* section of the active Review. This section is specifically about creating a text marker/ annotation.

The leader arrow will not show until the text edit window is finished.

From the *Review* section of the Action Bar, expand the flyout next to the (Label) icon and select the (Text) command. By default the ***Text*** command places customizable text with a leader arrow and a border on the screen so that it is always parallel to the screen. You will have the option to select either on a component or in the background to locate the text. The text editing window displays next to your selection as shown in Figure 6–8.

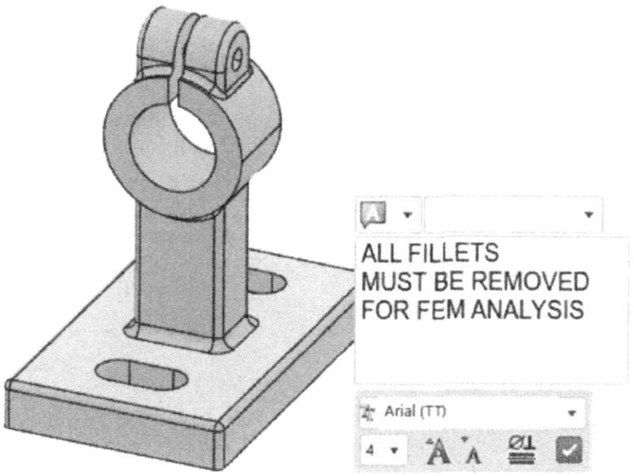

Figure 6–8

Enter the text that you want displayed in the main window. You also have multiple options to customize how this text will look. Below is a list of the customizations:

Option	Icon	Description
Text Marker Type		Displays five recently used text marker categories and allows insertion of different emoticons before the text.
Text Template	<Enter text>	Inserts a variable that can auto populate things like Part Name, Current User, Date, and Time.
Font	Arial (TT)	Customize what font will be used for the text.

Text Size		Increase or decrease the text size by either selecting the drop-down arrow or by selecting the large or small A.
Insert Symbol		Allows for standard drafting symbols to be inserted into the text window.
OK		Selecting the **OK** icon completes and closes the text edit window.

Select the (OK) icon when you have completed customizing the text value. The finished text will look something like Figure 6–9.

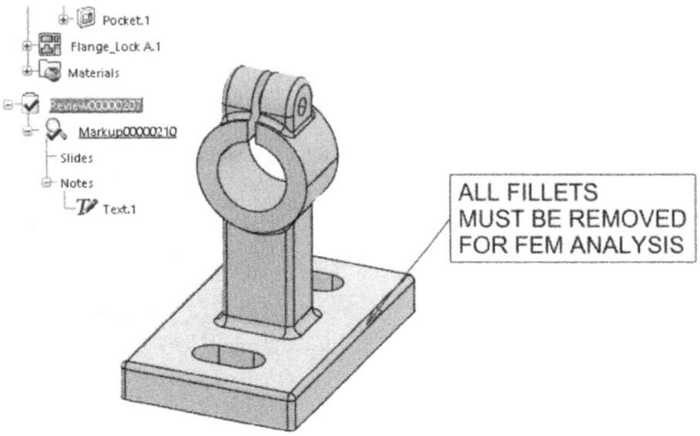

Figure 6–9

Editing Text

Once completed, the text can be relocated by left-clicking and dragging the text window to another location. To edit the text value, the edit window can be opened again by double-clicking on the text marker on the screen or in the tree. The text marker can also be customized using the context menu as shown in Figure 6–10. The context menu displays once you select the text either in the tree or on the model.

Figure 6–10

The context menu allows for customization of the leader line, style, graphical, and hide/show properties, as required. Additional leader lines can be created by right-clicking on the text marker and selecting **Add Leader**. Leaders can also be removed by selecting the leader, right-clicking on the dot it points to, and then clicking **Remove Leader** as shown in Figure 6–11.

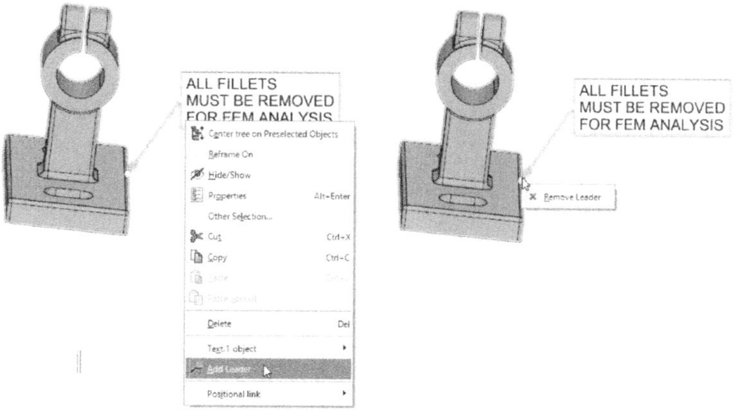

Figure 6–11

When the (Graphical Properties) icon is selected from the context menu, a Graphical Properties window displays as shown in Figure 6–12. This window allows detailed customization of fill, edges, and text. Color and transparency can also be changed.

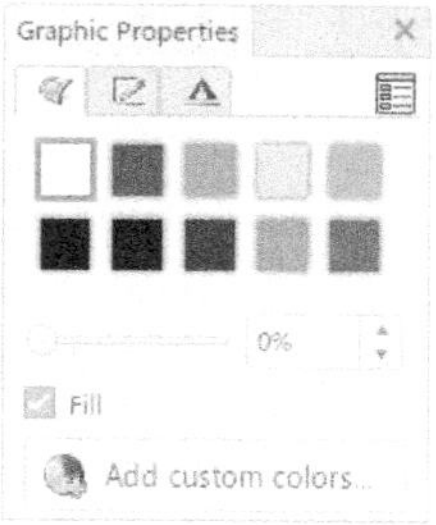

Figure 6–12

The general properties of the text marker are controlled using the Properties window (shown in Figure 6–13) and it can be accessed either by selecting  (Properties) from the Graphical Properties window, or by right-clicking on the text marker and selecting **Properties**. The Properties window allows you to set the various text properties such as color, font type, font size, shadow, border options, fill options etc. Many of these options could have been modified individually in other areas of the context menu, but this window provides the added convenience of modifying all the options in one place.

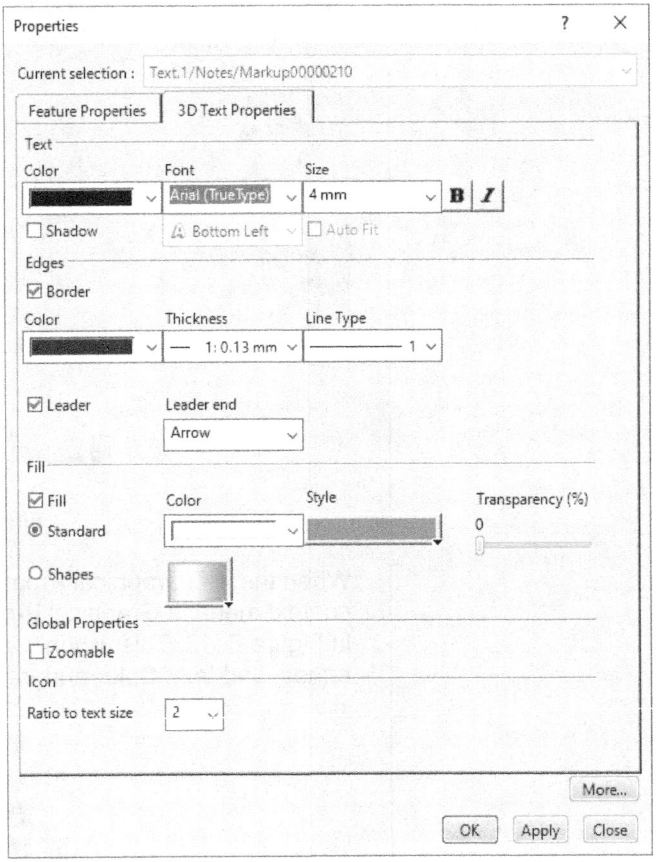

Figure 6–13

Step 4 - Create a hyperlink marker.

A hyperlink marker enables you to create a link to a document or a web page. You can quickly open a related spreadsheet, presentation, or web site from the CATIA document using the hyperlink. An example is shown in Figure 6–14.

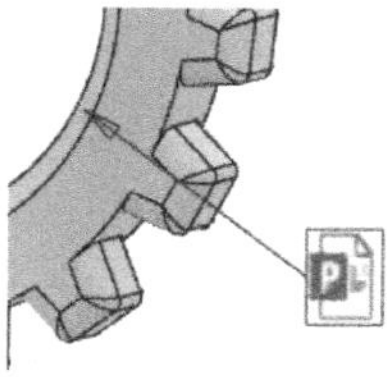

Figure 6–14

How To: Create a Hyperlink

1. Select the  (Hyperlink) icon from the *Review* section of the Action Bar.
2. Select the location on the model that you want the leader arrow of the Hyperlink to point to, and the Hyperlink Panel displays as shown in Figure 6–15.

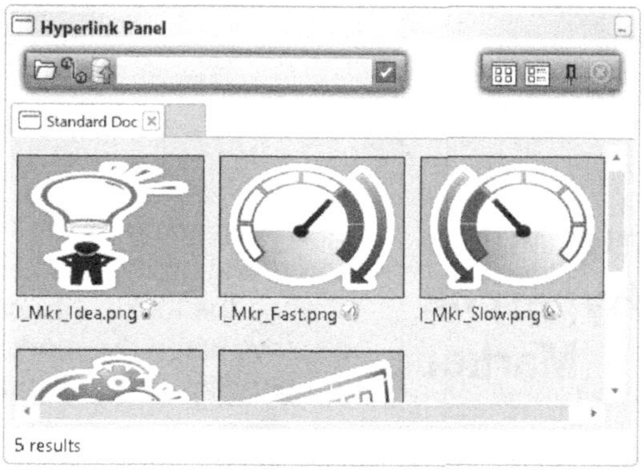

Figure 6–15

3. Within the Hyperlink Panel, there are different options for linking a document to a hyperlink. Select the required option and navigate to the document.

Option	Icon	Description
Browse Document		Allows for the search of a local document and imports it.

Import Document as Link		Saves the document as a link, when it is already saved in the Database.
Import Document as DOC and save it		Imports the document in a DOC formate and saves it.
Text Input Field		Allows for a website's URL or location to be typed in manually.
OK		Select when finished.

4. Once you have completed setting the options in the Hyperlink Panel, select  (OK) to create the Hyperlink.The Hyperlink marker displays in the *Notes* node in the specification tree, as shown in Figure 6–16.

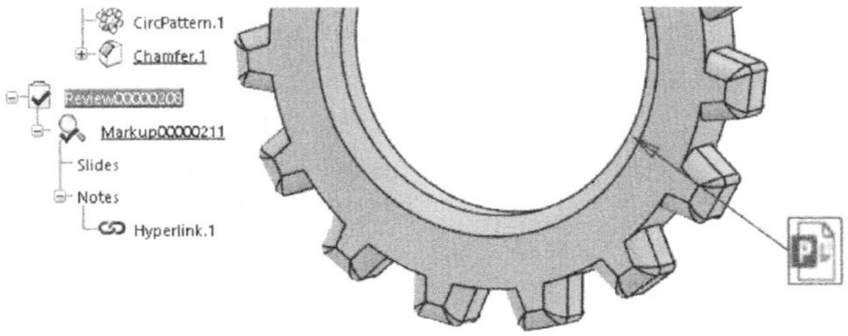

Figure 6–16

Working with a Hyperlink Marker

Like most markers, the hyperlink can also be moved by selecting and dragging the marker to a new location. If you need to change the looks, you can either use the context menu that displays when the marker is selected (as shown in Figure 6–17) or right-click and select **Properties**.

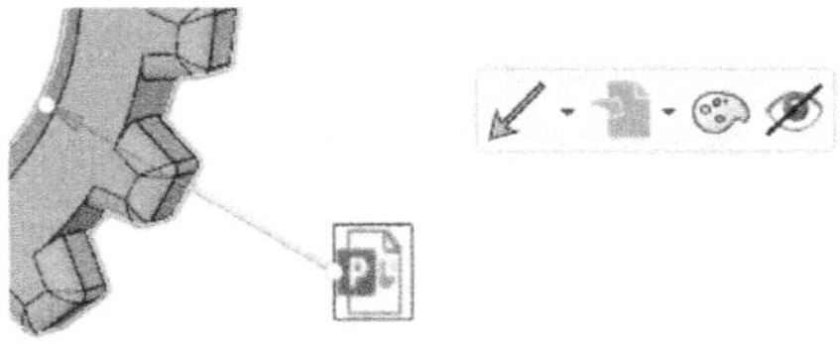

Figure 6–17

To open the document that is linked, right-click on the Hyperlink, then select *** object > Go To Hyperlink**. This will open the document in a separate window.

Step 5 - Create a Slide.

A Slide captures the current viewpoint and current state of the model, allowing for it to be recalled by anyone who might need to see that arrangement of information at any time. Numerous slides maybe created to study variants of mock ups of an assembly with components moved into various positions. For example, consider an assembly of landing gear. One slide might be created to show the landing gear fully extended. Another slide could be created with it completely retracted. There might even be more slides for different stages that the parts move through as the doors open. Finally a slide might exist for an exploded view of all of the parts for better understanding of how the components go together. These slides, once created, would be added to the Design Review like the one shown in Figure 6–18. Slides can capture information such as position, orientation, color, markers and hide/show attributes that might be different from slide to slide.

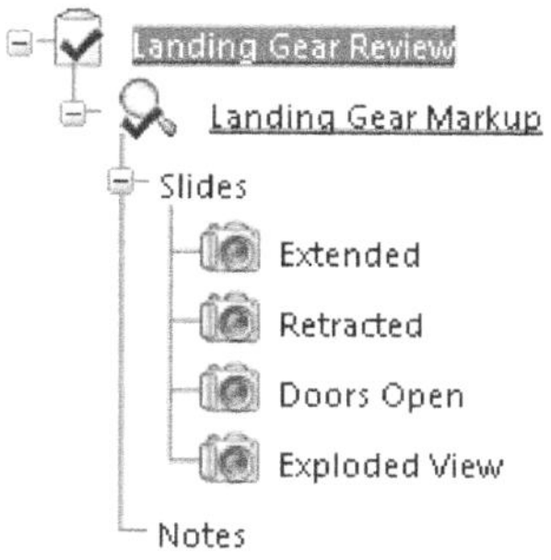

Figure 6–18

General Steps

How To: Create a Slide

1. Before a slide can be created, follow the general steps 1-4 (discussed previously in this chapter and also listed below) to display the information that should be captured.
    1. Create or open an existing Design Review.
    2. Move the components and orient the camera the way you want it to be displayed in the capture.
    3. Add Markers (Text, Hyperlink, Images, Rectangles, Circles, etc.) that you want included in the Slide.
    4. Change the Graphical properties or hide/show properties of anything you want to be different in the slide.

2. Click (Slide) from the *Review* section of the Action Bar and **Slide.1** will be created.
3. If this is the first slide created in the Design Review, then the (Slide View) tab will display in the upper left corner. From here, renaming the views can easily be done by selecting on the name. Return to *Tree* view by selecting its tab (Tree View) in the upper left.
4. If this isn't the first slide, then subsequent slides will just be added to the *Slides* node of the tree as shown in Figure 6–19.

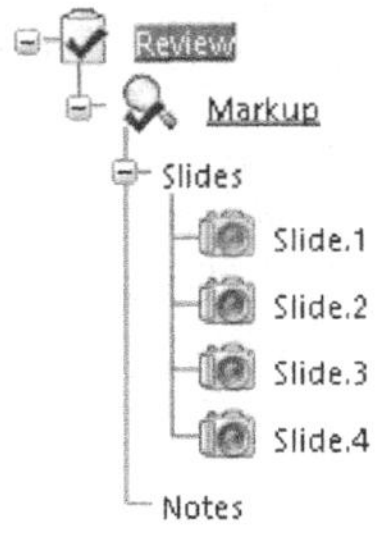

Figure 6–19

5. From the *Tree* view, if a slide needs to be renamed for better identification, simply right-click on the name in the tree and select **Properties**.
6. To view the slides from the *Tree* view, double-click on the slide you wish to view, and the display will change.
7. To view the slides from the *Slides* view, thumbnails of each slide will already be displayed and selecting on the thumbnail once will change the display in the main window to the selected slide, as shown in Figure 6–20.

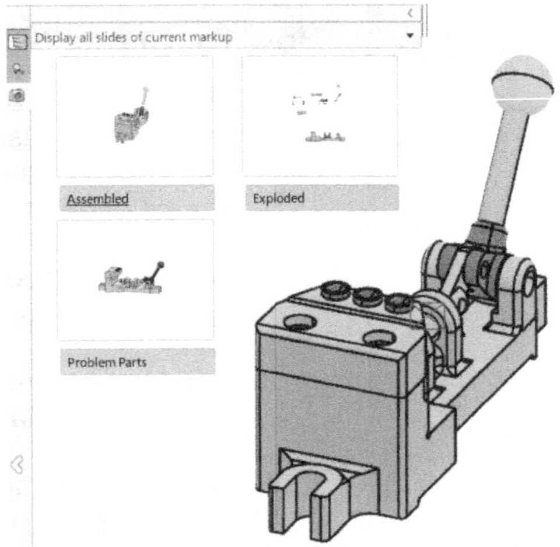

Figure 6–20

Replying to a Slide

Because a Design Review is a way of communicating information to other users about a specific model, someone who views the Design Review may want to use the same tool box of functionality to reply. The (Reply) command can be accessed by expanding the (Review) flyout in the *Review* section of the Action Bar or by hovering over a slide in the *Slide View*. Reply will create a new Markup under the existing Markup (as shown in Figure 6–21) allowing the user to create their own markings and customizations, starting from where other users left off.

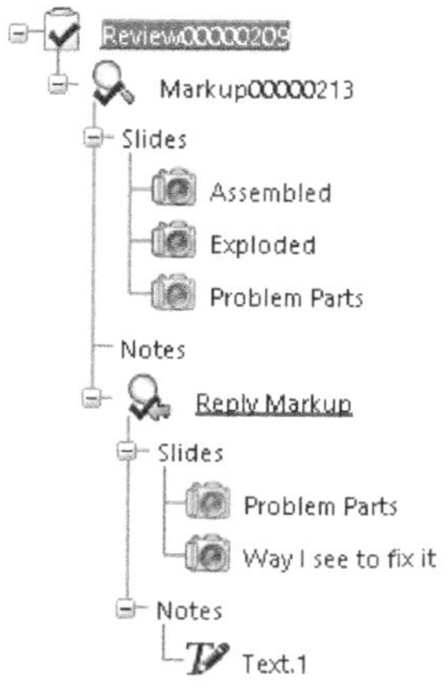

Figure 6–21

6.2 Markers

This section provides an overview of the different Marker tools available in the Design Review app. The annotation/marker tools are located in the *Review* section of the Action Bar shown in Figure 6–22.

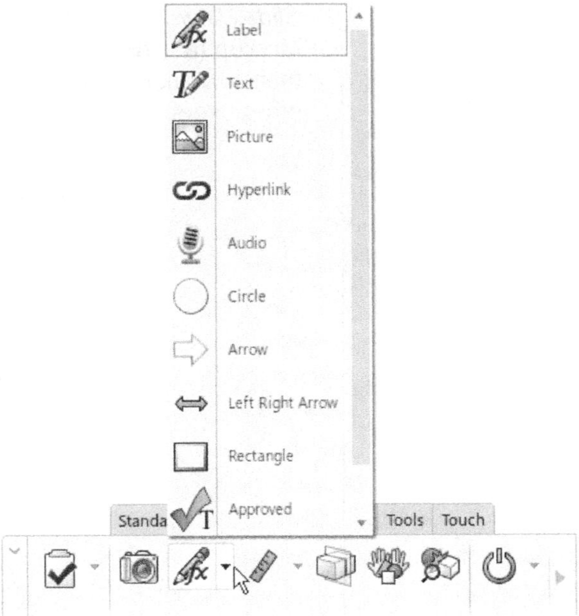

Figure 6–22

The following describes the Marker icons found under the Label flyout. While these Markers are not the only ones available in the Design Review app, they will scale more easily with zooming in and out of the model, and maintain their orientation to the camera when rotating the model than the 2D versions will.

Option	Icon	Description
Label		Creates label with a leader listing the parts Title and Instance Title values.
Text		Creates a customizable text marker with a leader that is capable of auto populating ID, position, user-name, data and time.
Picture		Inserts a picture marker.

Hyperlink		Creates a marking that is linked to another document or web-page.
Audio		Creates an audio marker for associated audio recordings.
Circle		Creates a circle marker.
Arrow		Creates a single direction arrow marker.
Left Right Arrow		Creates a bidirectional arrow marker.
Rectangle		Creates a rectangle Marker.
Approved		Creates an approved text window with user-name-date and time included.
Rejected		Creates a rejected text window with user-name-date and time included.

Practice 6a Create and Manage Reviews

Practice Objectives

- Create a Review Object.
- Create Markers/Annotations of different types.
- Manage 3D annotations.

In this practice, you will add an annotation to the front wheel assembly to help the designer locate the problem areas so that they can be resolved quickly.

Task 1 - Open the assembly.

1. Import with your initials and open **FrontWheelClash.3DXML**. The assembly displays as shown in Figure 6–23.

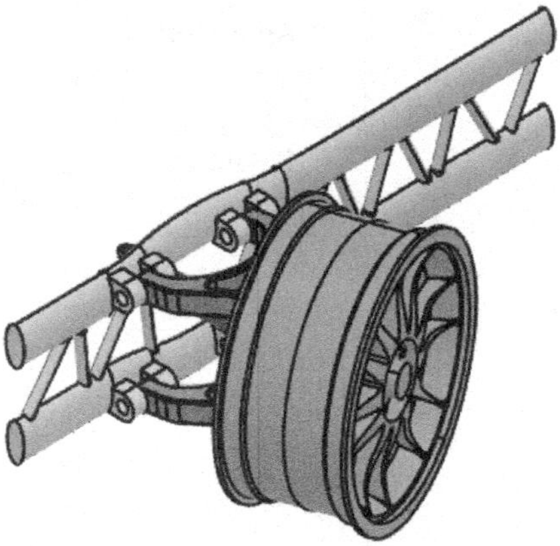

Figure 6–23

2. Ensure that the Design Review app is active. To access the app, in the *Compass* drop-down list, select **Design Review** as shown in Figure 6–24.

Figure 6–24

Task 2 - Create a Review.

In order to be able to document markers/annotations for a CAD object—be it a Physical Product, 3D Part, or a Drawing—a Review must be created first.

1. In the Design Review app, click the  (Review) command. A new Review window will display as shown in Figure 6–25.

   The *Title* of both the review and markup can be customized from their respective tabs.

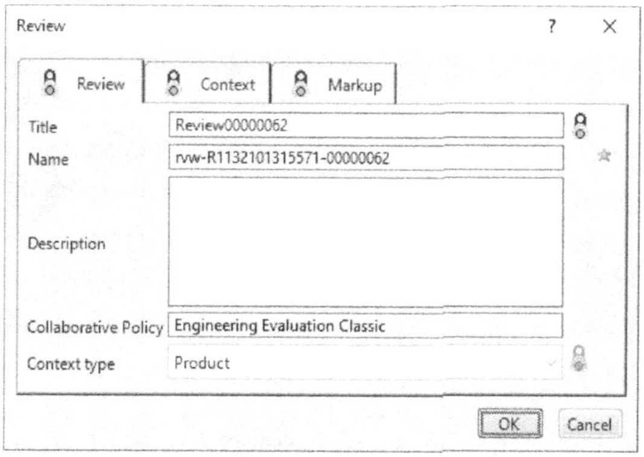

Figure 6–25

2. From the *Review* tab, set the *Title* to **##_Front_Wheel_Review**. Replace ## with your initials as shown in Figure 6–26.

3. From the *Markup* tab, set the *Title* to **##_Front_Wheel_Markup**. Replace ## with your initials as shown in Figure 6–26.

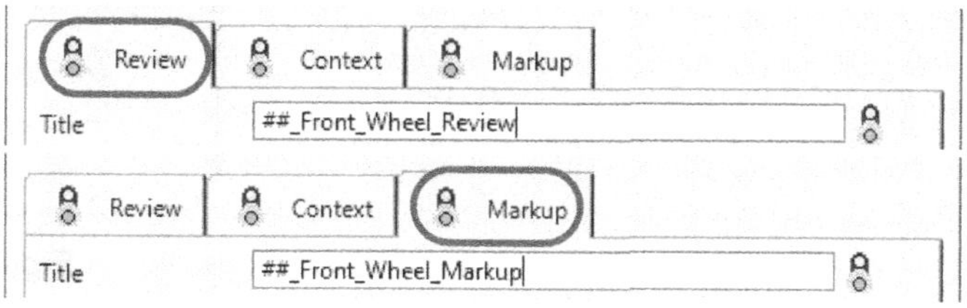

Figure 6–26

4. Select **OK** to complete the review window. The model will switch into *Review View* display as shown in Figure 6–27.

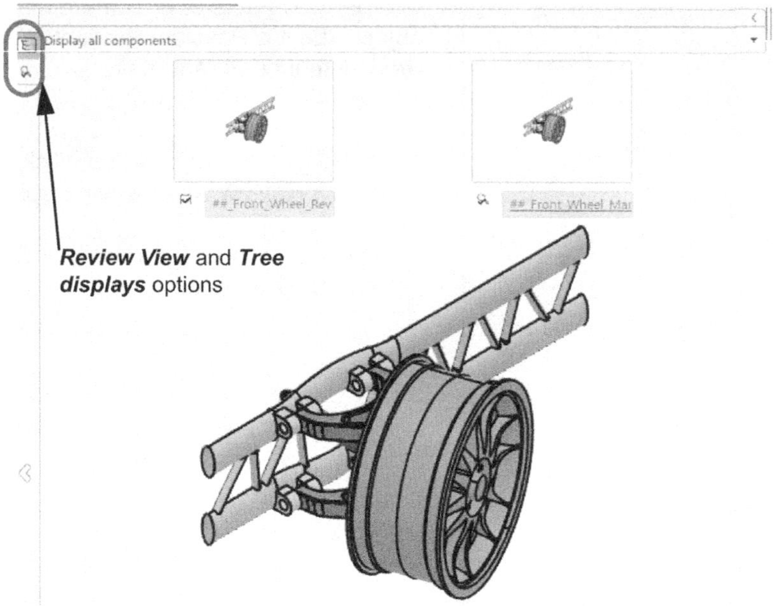

Figure 6–27

5. Select the (Tree) icon in the upper left corner of the screen. This will switch you into a view that allows you to see the tree of the model and the Review object that has been inserted into it, as shown in Figure 6–28.

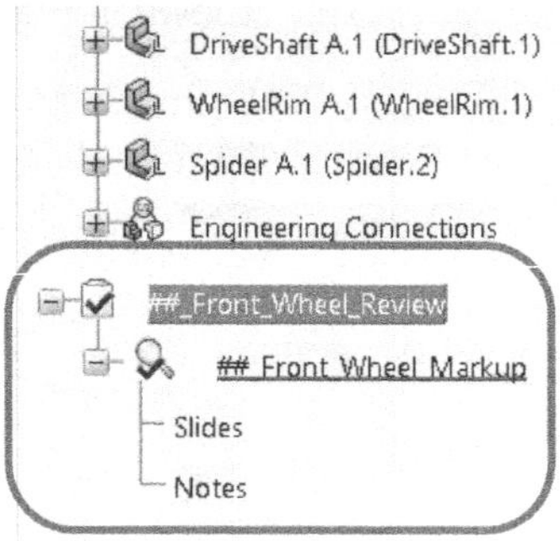

Figure 6–28

Task 3 - Create an annotation.

Annotations must be created to note the areas the designer needs to review.

1. In the *Review* section of the Action Bar, click the (Text) icon.
2. Select the top of the ball on the Mount component as shown in Figure 6–29, to place the note.

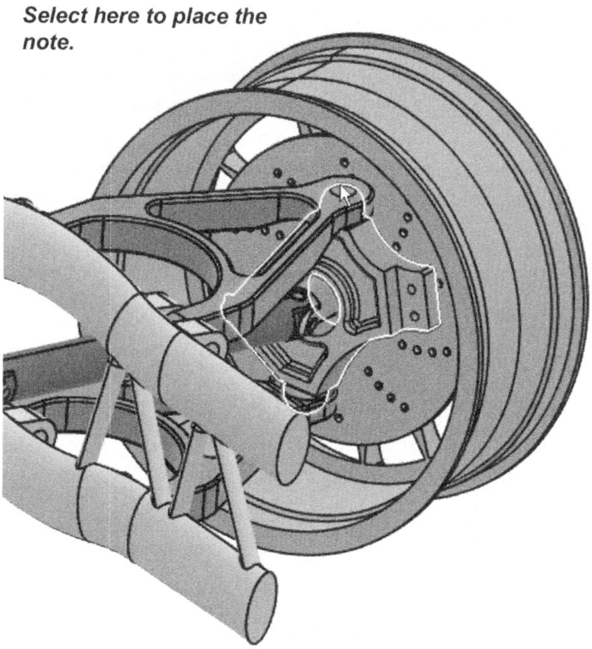

Figure 6–29

3. Enter the text shown in Figure 6–30 using the Text dialog box.

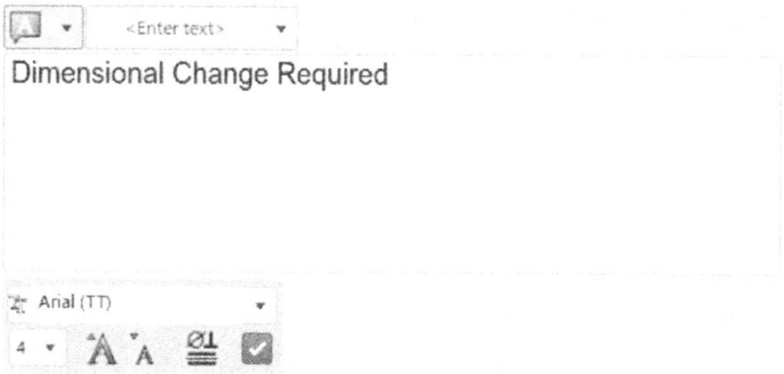

Figure 6–30

4. Click (OK) to place the text.
5. Hover the cursor over the note, hold the left mouse button, and drag the note to the location shown in Figure 6–31.

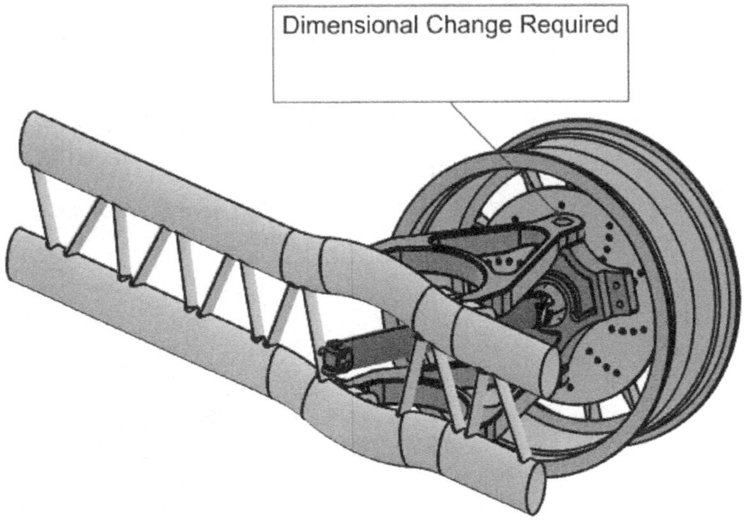

Figure 6–31

6. Click in the background to complete the text location modification.
7. With the model orientated as shown in Figure 6–31, select (Slide) from the Action Bar. This will create **Slide.1** and switch the display to *Slide View.*
8. Select **Slide.1** text in the upper left corner and rename it **First Change Slide**.
9. Select the (Tree) icon in the upper left corner of the screen to switch you into a view that allows you to see the tree of the model. Notice the *Slide* and *Note* nodes listed in the tree as shown in Figure 6–32

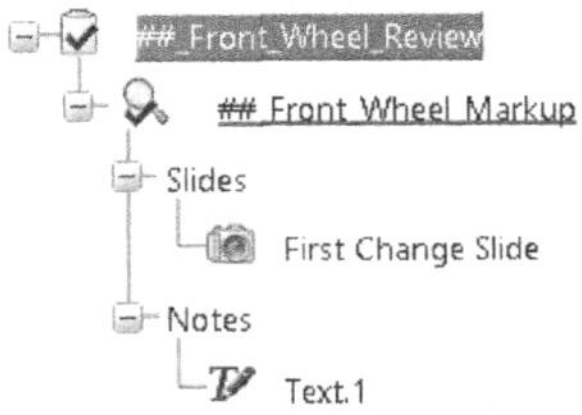

Figure 6–32

Task 4 - Create additional annotations.

1. To better view the problem areas, hide the **WheelRim** component by selecting it in the specification tree, right-clicking and selecting **Hide/Show**.

2. Create a second (Text) annotation and locate it on the top arm, as shown in Figure 6–33.

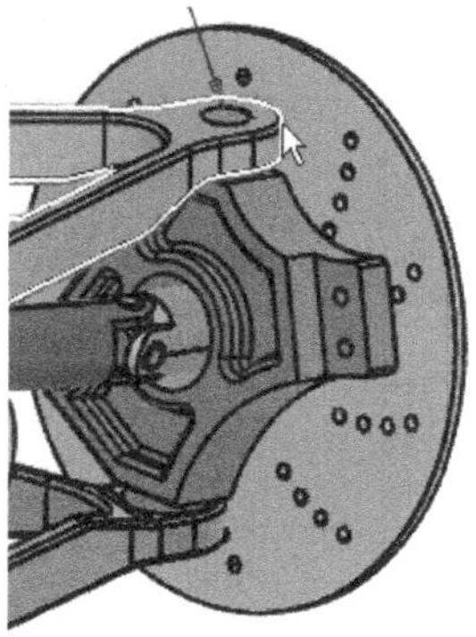

Figure 6–33

3. Enter the note, as shown in Figure 6–34.

Figure 6–34

4. Click (OK) to complete the note and drag it to the location shown in Figure 6–35.

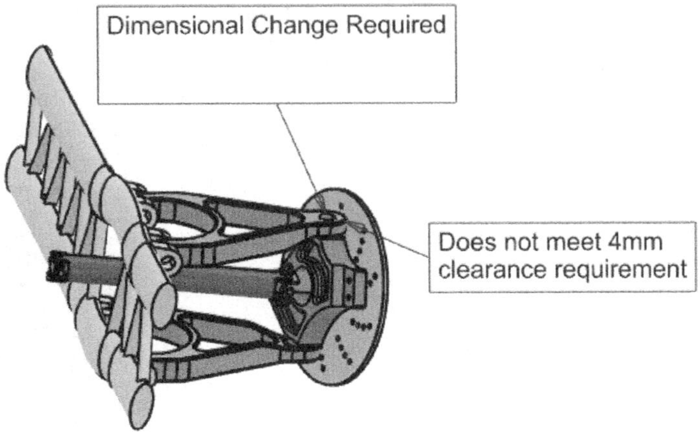

Figure 6–35

Task 5 - Add a link to the second note.

1. In the specification tree, right-click on **Text.2** and select **Add Leader** as shown in Figure 6–36.

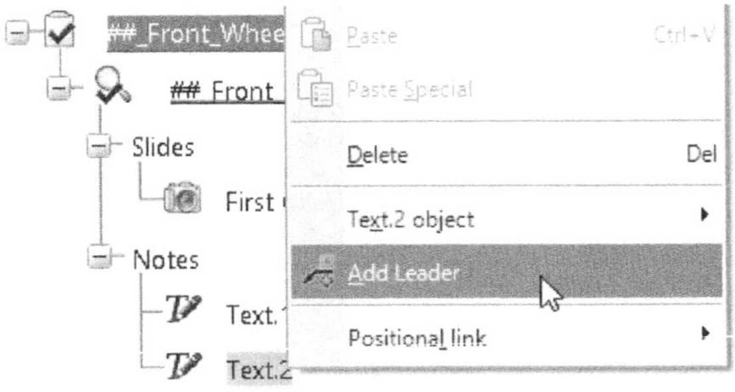

Figure 6–36

2. Select the hub so that a second leader is created, as shown in Figure 6–37.

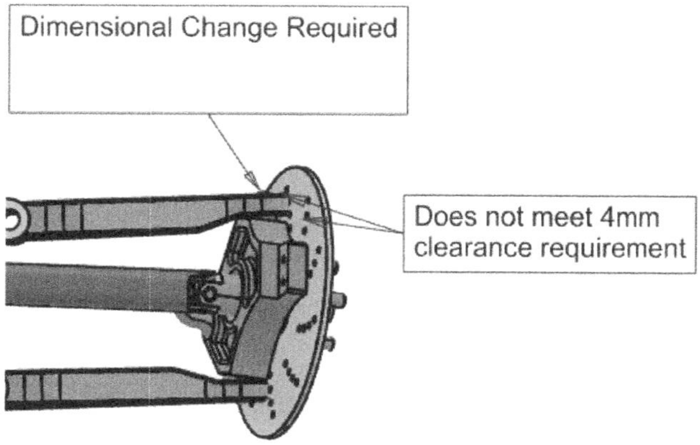

Figure 6–37

3. Select  (Slide) from the Action Bar. This will create **Slide.1** (again).
4. From the tree, right-click on **Slide.1** and select **Properties**.
5. Change **Slide.1** *Feature name* to **Second Change Slide.**

Task 6 - Review the Slides.

1. Double-click on **First Change Slide** from the tree, and select **Yes** to the windows displaying the warning, "Any changes will be lost". The model will turn back into the position it was located in when the slide was originally created with **Text.1** and the WheelRim showing.

   Note: Do not be concerned about changes being lost because all the changes you have made up to this point has been recorded in the **Second Change Slide**.

2. Double-click on **Second Change Slide** from the tree. Again the model's orientation changes into the same position it was in when the slide was first created with both notes showing and WheelRim hidden.

Task 7 - Modify the notes.

1. Select **Text.1** from the tree and the context menu will display.
2. Change the style to T (Light). You will notice the border around the text disappear.
3. Select **Text.2** from the display window, the context menu will display as well.
4. Change the style to T (Light) as you did in step 2. Complete the notes.
5. Create two more text notes to indicate two additional areas the designer needs to look at, as shown in Figure 6–38. Also, change the style to T (Light) for each.

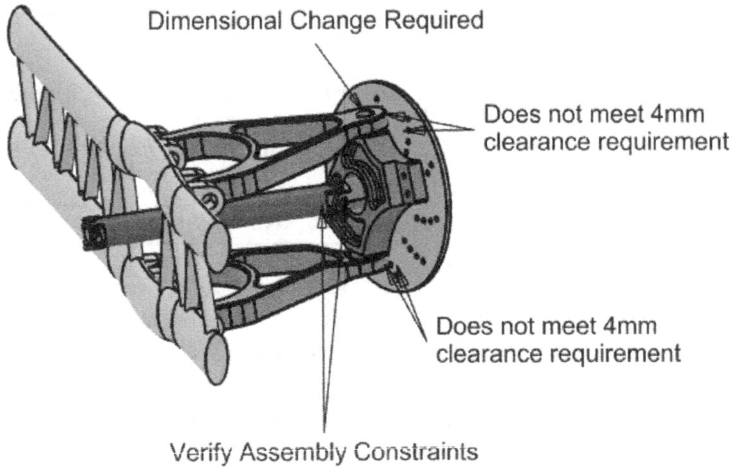

Figure 6–38

6. Select  (Slide) from the Action Bar. This will create **Slide.1** (again). Through its properties, rename the slide as **Third Change Slide**.
7. Manipulate the model to note how the annotations move with the assembly.
8. Save and close the model.

Practice 6b

Annotation Slides

Practice Objectives

- Create Slides.
- Manage Markup/Annotations.
- Viewing and Updating Slides.

In this practice, you will create slides to indicate problems on a bore assembly.

Task 1 - Import and open the assembly.

1. Import with your initials and open **Bore Device.3dxml**. The assembly displays as shown in Figure 6–39.

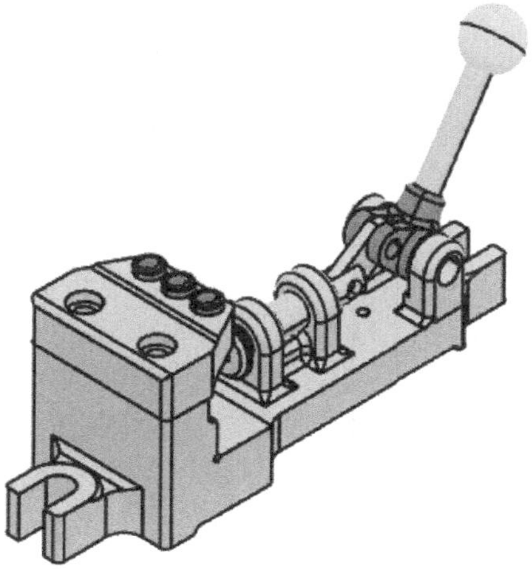

Figure 6–39

2. Once open, you will find that the Assembly is in the Assembly Design app. Switch to the Design Review app by selecting the Compass, then picking **Design Review** from My Apps list, as shown in Figure 6–40.

Figure 6–40

Task 2 - Create a Review Object.

1. The *Review* dialog box displays automatically when switching to the Design Review App. A Review node will need to be added to the tree before any markings or annotations can be created. Enter **###_Bore Device Review** in the *Title field* of the *Review* tab, as shown in Figure 6–41, where ### represents your initials and makes the title unique.

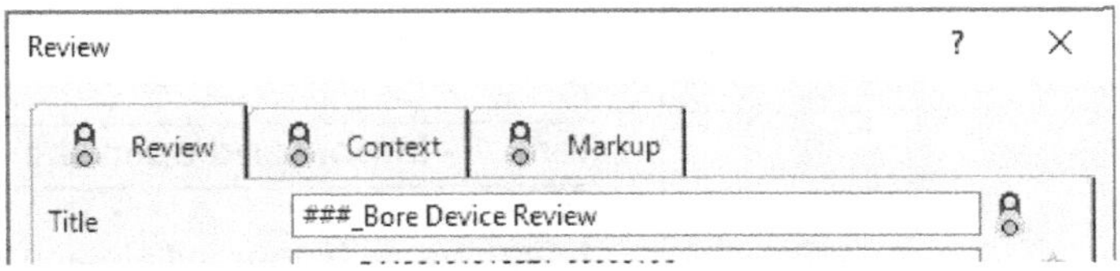

Figure 6–41

2. Select the *Markup* tab in the *Review* dialog box.

3. Enter **###_Bore Device Markup** in the *Title field,* as shown in Figure 6–42, where ### represents your initials and makes the title unique.

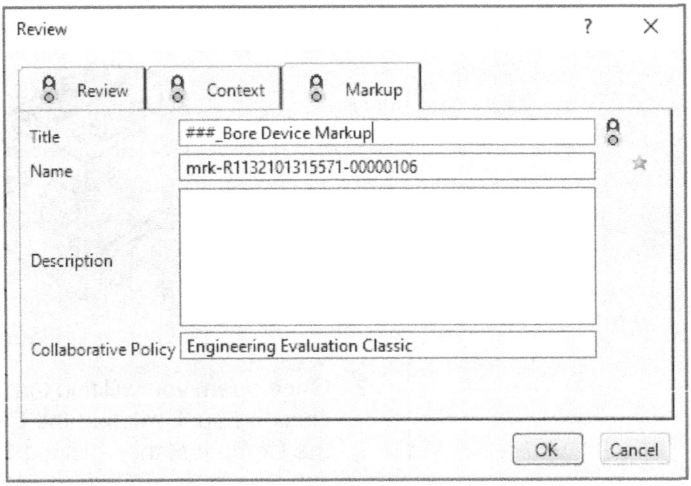

Figure 6–42

4. Select **OK** to the Review dialog box. The assembly will complete the switch to the Design Review app and will display everything in what is called the *Review View*, as shown in Figure 6–43.

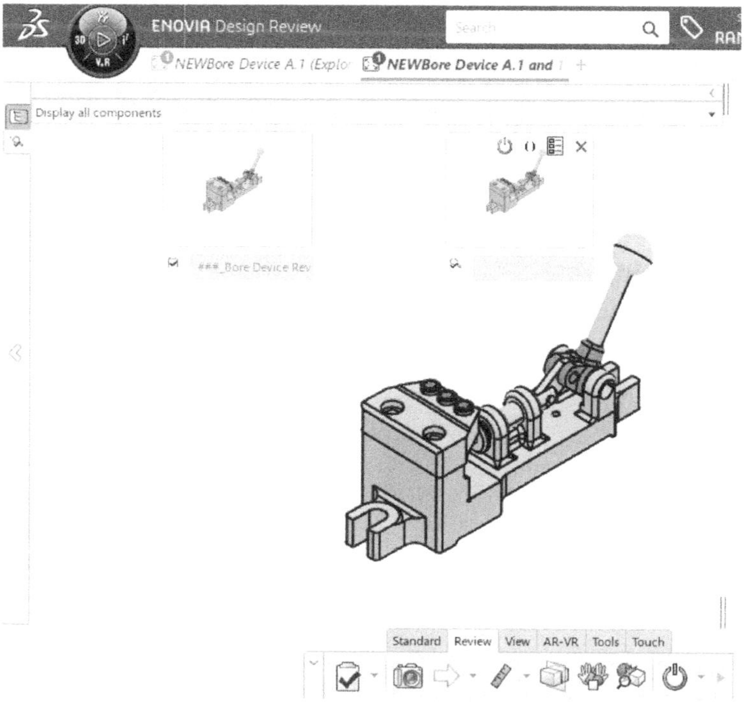

Figure 6–43

If these tabs can't be seen, look for and select the icon on the left side of the screen to display the tabs.

5. On the left side of the screen, you should see two tabs (Review View) and (Tree). The *Review View* allows you to quickly filter markups and annotations once they are created. The *Tree* tab provides the best tools for creating new slides.

   Select (Tree) tab and expand the newly created Review object at the bottom of the tree. It should look as shown in Figure 6–44.

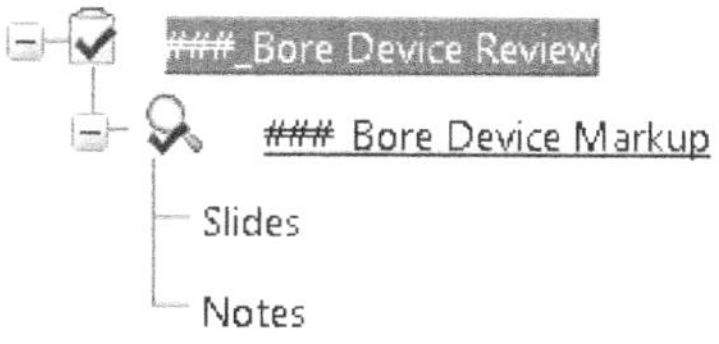

Figure 6–44

Task 3 - Create the first Slide.

Although it is not a requirement, having a "Default" or "All Parts" slide offers a quick way to reset back to a standard view of the model without any annotations or markings. This will be handy when you have multiple slides.

1. With the assembly position as shown in Figure 6–45, select the (Slide) icon from the *Review* section of the Action Bar.

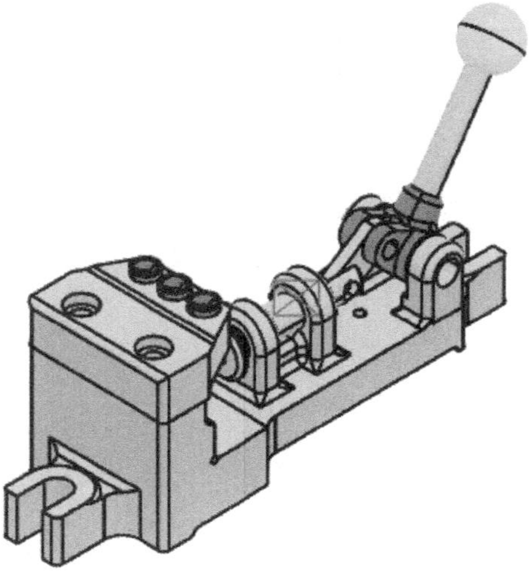

Figure 6–45

2. This will create Slide.1 and switch the view to what is called *Slide View*. Switch back to the *Tree* view by selecting (Tree) in the upper left corner of the screen.
3. Right-click **Slide.1** from the tree and select **Properties.**
4. Set the *Feature Name* to **All Parts**, as shown in Figure 6–46.

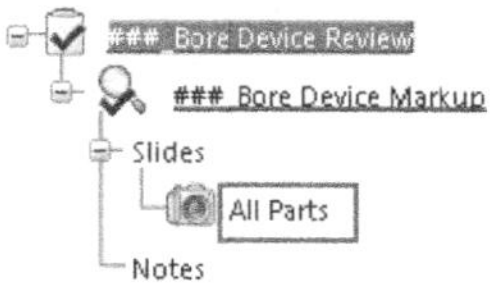

Figure 6–46

Task 4 - Compute and Analyze Interference.

1. In the *Review* section of the Action Bar, expand the Action Bar by selecting the (Expand) icon.

2. Select (Compute Interferences) from the *Review* section of the Action Bar. A *Local Interference Simulation Definition* window will display as shown in Figure 6–47.

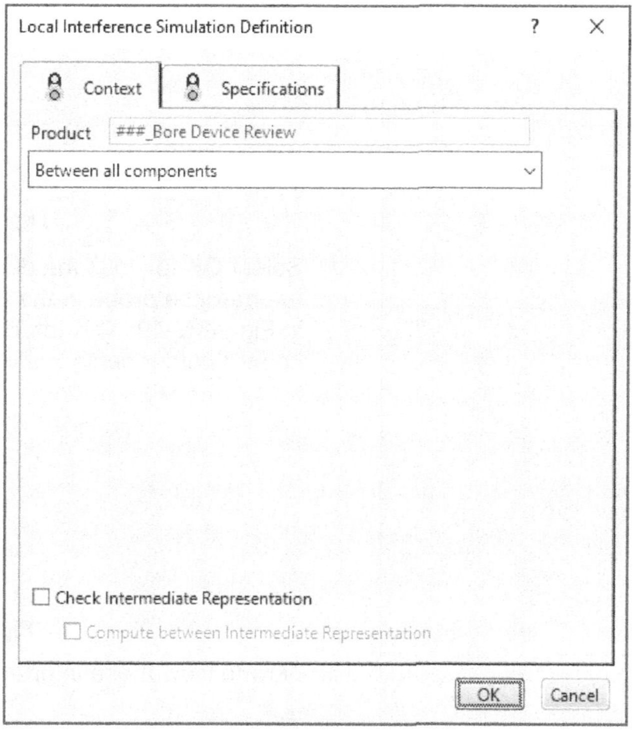

Figure 6–47

3. Ensure that **Between all components** is selected in the *Context* tab, and that **Clash** and **Contact** options are selected in the *Specifications* tab as shown in Figure 6–48.

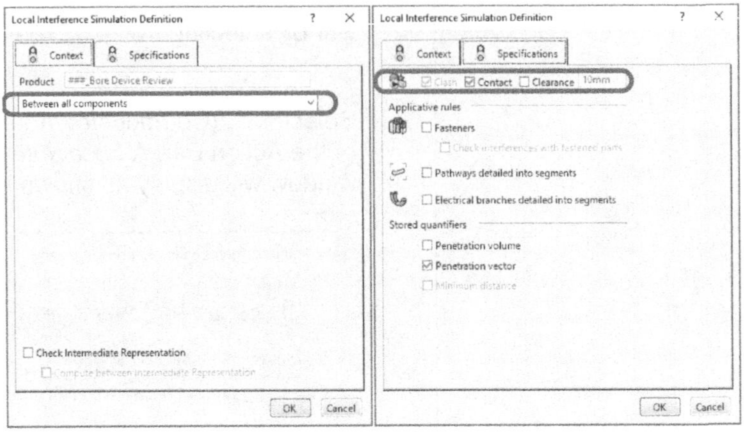

Figure 6–48

4. Select **OK** to close the dialog box. This will create the new Interference probe in the *Notes* section of the tree as shown in Figure 6–49. This Interference probe will allow CATIA to know if components are interfering with each other or not.

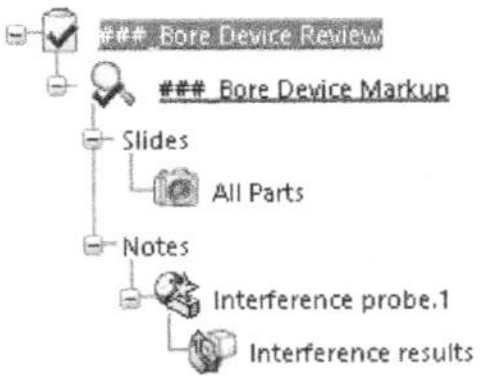

Figure 6–49

5. Now to view those interferences yourself, select  (Analyze Interferences) from the *Review* section of the Action Bar. The results table shows at the bottom of the screen as shown in Figure 6–50.

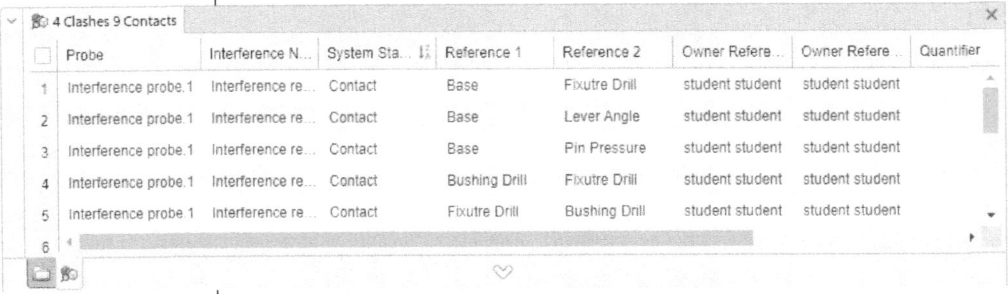
4 Clashes 9 Contacts

	Probe	Interference N...	System Sta...	Reference 1	Reference 2	Owner Refere...	Owner Refere...	Quantifier
1	Interference probe.1	Interference re...	Contact	Base	Fixutre Drill	student student	student student	
2	Interference probe.1	Interference re...	Contact	Base	Lever Angle	student student	student student	
3	Interference probe.1	Interference re...	Contact	Base	Pin Pressure	student student	student student	
4	Interference probe.1	Interference re...	Contact	Bushing Drill	Fixutre Drill	student student	student student	
5	Interference probe.1	Interference re...	Contact	Fixutre Drill	Bushing Drill	student student	student student	
6								

Figure 6–50

6. Scroll through the results and you will notice that 4 total Classes and 9 Contacts exist within the Assembly. Select the column title **System Status** as shown in Figure 6–51. This will reorganize the results so clashes are listed first.

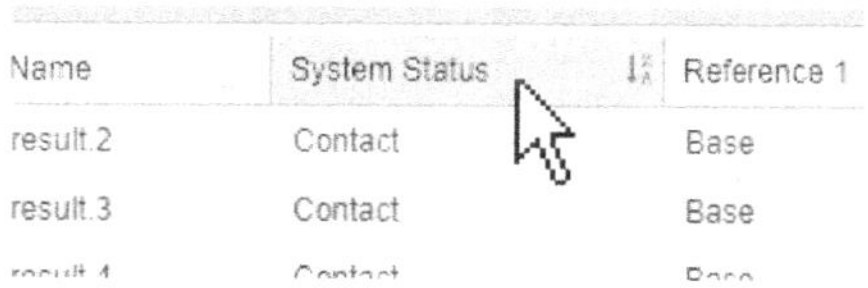

Figure 6–51

7. Select each of the four listed clash items to better understand where issues may exist. The camera will move to show you each condition as displayed in Figure 6–52.

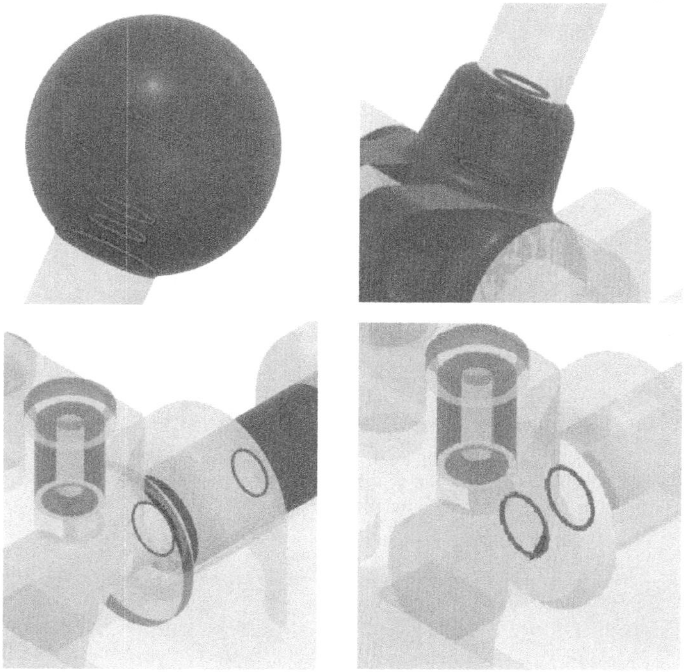

Figure 6–52

8. Once you understand where each of the clashes are, close the results window by selecting the ✕ icon in the upper right corner of the results window.

Task 5 - Create a Volume Cut using Sectioning.

1. In the *Review* section of the Action Bar, select (Sectioning). A section plane and context menu will display on top of it.

2. From the context menu, hover the cursor over the (Move to W position) and a drop-down list will display.

3. Select the (Move to U position) and the display should display as shown in Figure 6–53.

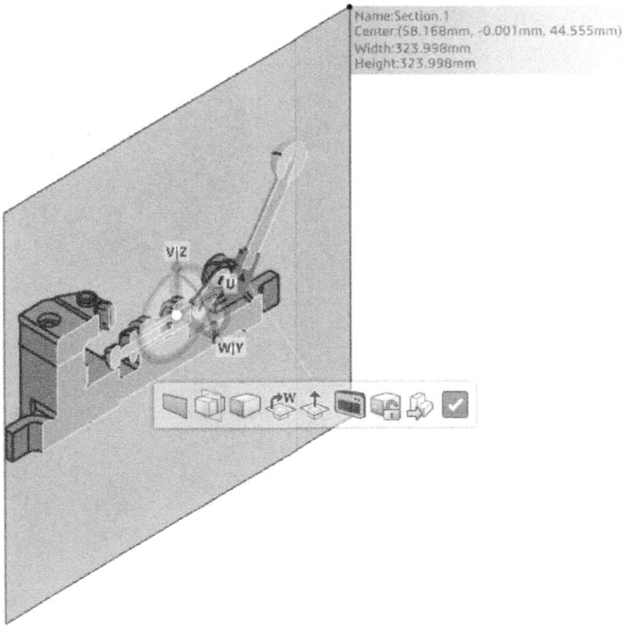

Figure 6–53

4. From the context menu, hover the cursor over the (Display contour and plane of section) and a drop-down list will display.

5. Select the (Display only the contour and context of section) and the display updates as shown in Figure 6–54.

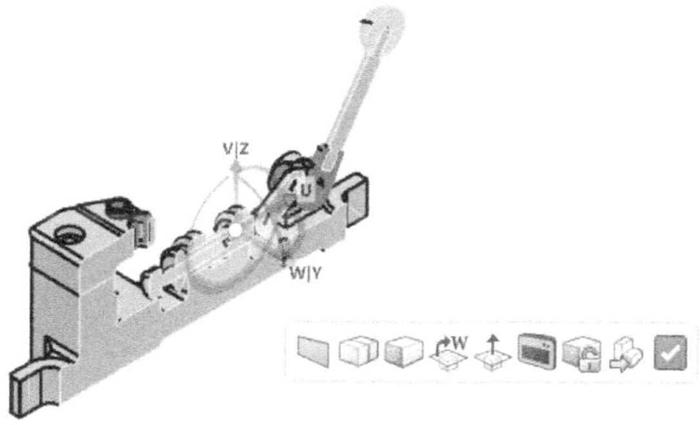

Figure 6–54

6. From the context menu, select (Validate the Section) to complete the operation. The model should look like Figure 6–55.

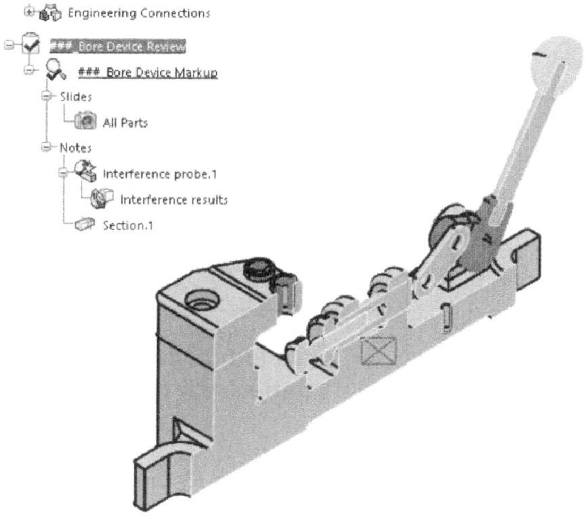

Figure 6–55

Task 6 - Set up orientation for a new slide.

A slide is just a capture of the model's viewpoint and current state that can be recalled at a later time. Before slides are created, you want to ensure that the model is oriented correctly.

1. From the *View* section of the Action Bar, select the expand arrow next to (*iso) view, and then click the (*Right) view from the fly out.

2. Use your mouse to zoom in on the model so that it fits similarly to that shown in Figure 6–56.

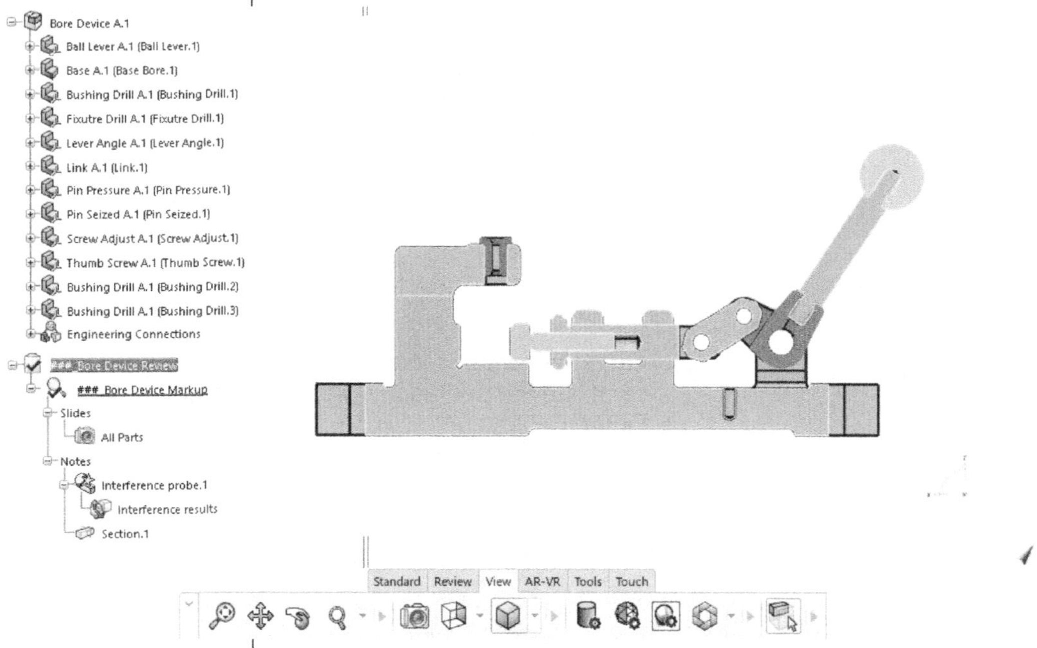

Figure 6–56

Task 7 - Create a circle.

This annotation will note the interference detected inside the Interference probe.

Circle can be found under the (Text) flyout in the Action Bar.

1. In the *Review* section of the Action Bar, click the (Circle) icon. Locate the cursor as shown in Figure 6–57, to locate the center of the circle.

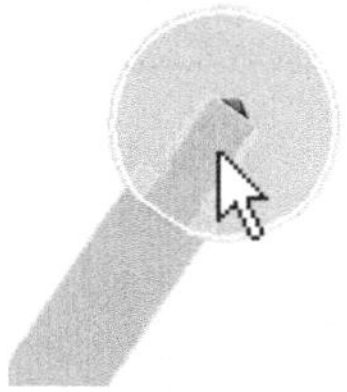

Figure 6–57

2. Click and hold the left mouse button and drag outward to create the circle as shown in Figure 6–58. Release the left mouse button to place the circle.

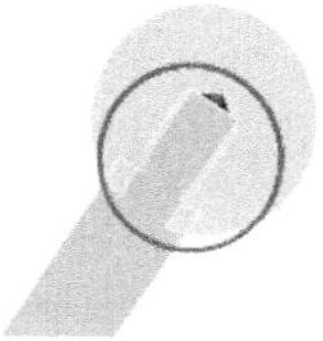

Figure 6–58

Task 8 - Add text with arrow.

1. Click (Text) in the *Review* section of the Action Bar.
2. Click the upper left side of the newly created circle as shown in Figure 6–59. The arrow points to this location.

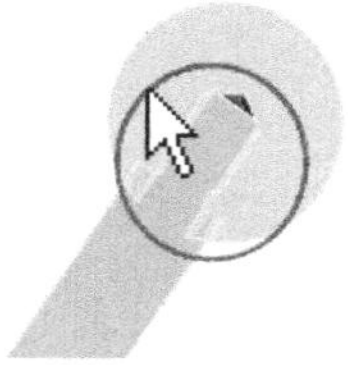

Figure 6–59

3. Enter the text as shown in Figure 6–60.

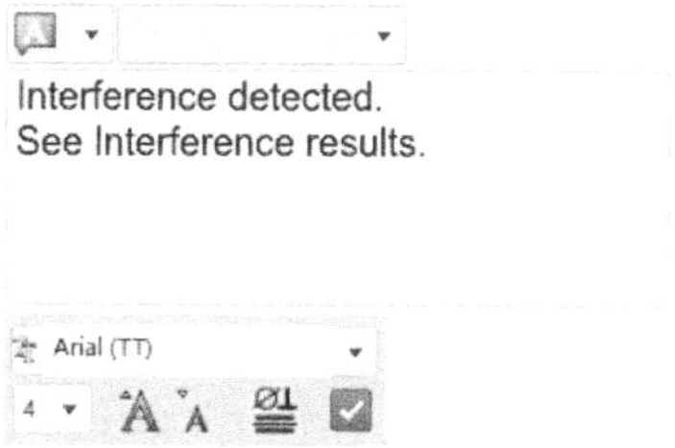

Figure 6–60

4. In the Text Properties toolbar, change the size of the text to **6** as shown in Figure 6–61. Note: Double-click on the text box to display the window again if it closed too soon.

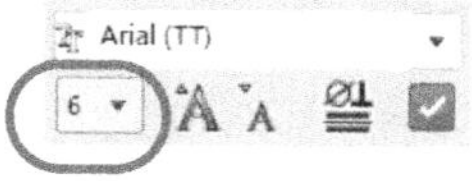

Figure 6–61

5. Click (OK) to place the text.

6. Left-click on the text and, while holding the left mouse button, drag the text to the location shown in Figure 6–62, if required.

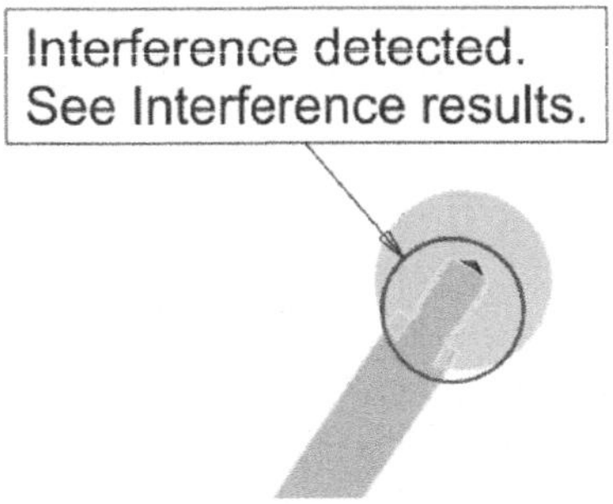

Figure 6–62

Task 9 - Create another circle and modify properties.

1. Click the (Circle) in the *Review* section of the Action Bar.
2. Click and hold the left mouse button and drag outward to create the circle as shown in Figure 6–63. Release the left mouse button to place the circle. Note: After the circle is created, adjustments can be made by clicking and dragging the circle to different locations.

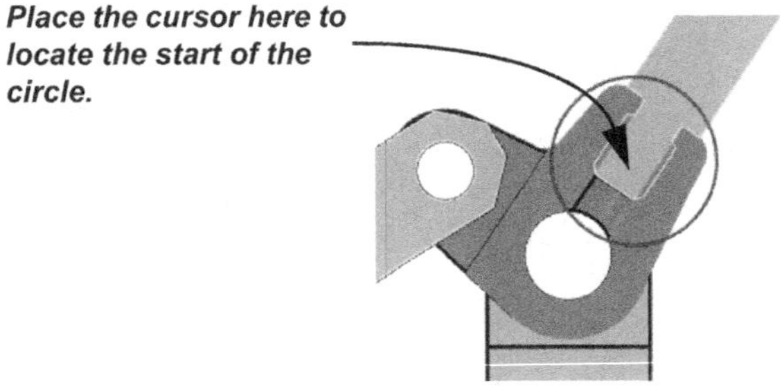

Figure 6–63

3. With the circle still selected, from the context menu, select (Graphic Properties) the Graphic Properties window displays as shown in Figure 6–64.

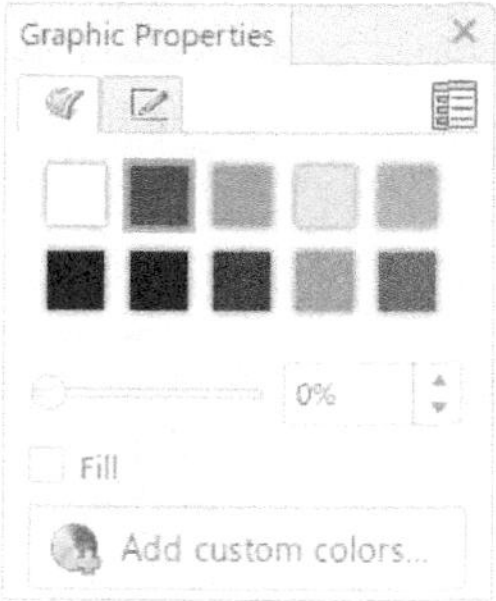

Figure 6–64

4. Select the (Edges) tab from the top of the window.
5. Change the color to (Orange) and Thickness to **4**.
6. Close the Graphic Properties window.
7. Right-click on the text window that was created earlier, and select **Add Leader** in the drop-down list.
8. Now select just above the Circle as shown in Figure 6–65 to create a second arrow.

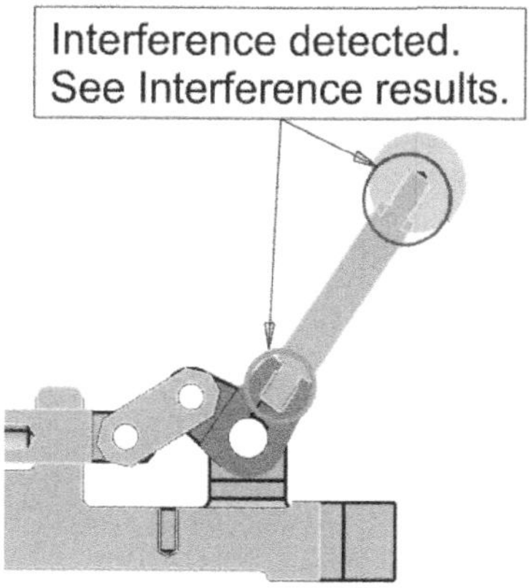

Figure 6–65

Task 10 - Change properties on annotations.

1. Select the **Text.1** object so that it highlights. The context menu will display as shown in Figure 6–66.

Figure 6–66

2. Select the drop-down arrow next to T (Default) and select T (Warning) in the drop-down list.
3. Right-click on one of the leader arrows and select **Properties**.
4. Within the *3D Text Properties* tab, change the color of the edges to **orange** and the thickness to **3** as shown in Figure 6–67.

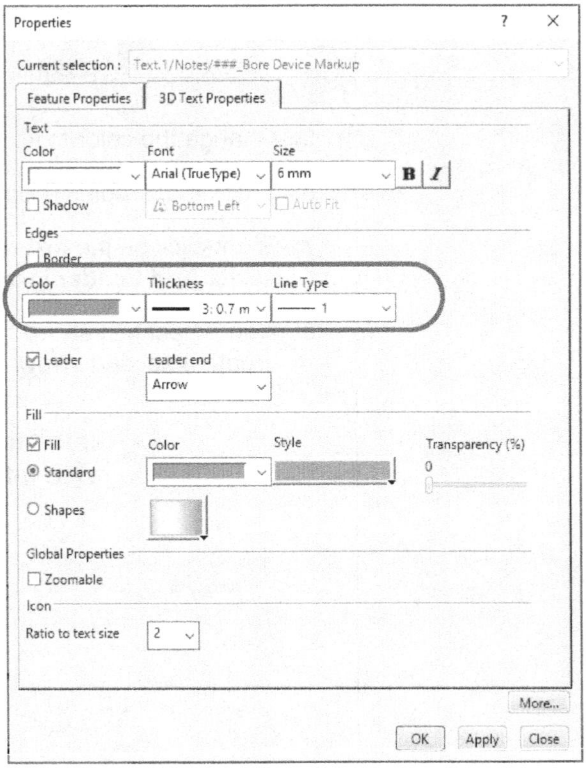

Figure 6–67

5. Click **OK** to close the Properties dialog box and update the arrows.
6. Right-click on **Circle.1** and select **Properties**.

7. Change the Color to **orange**, Linetype to **3**,and the Thickness to **4**, as shown in Figure 6–68.

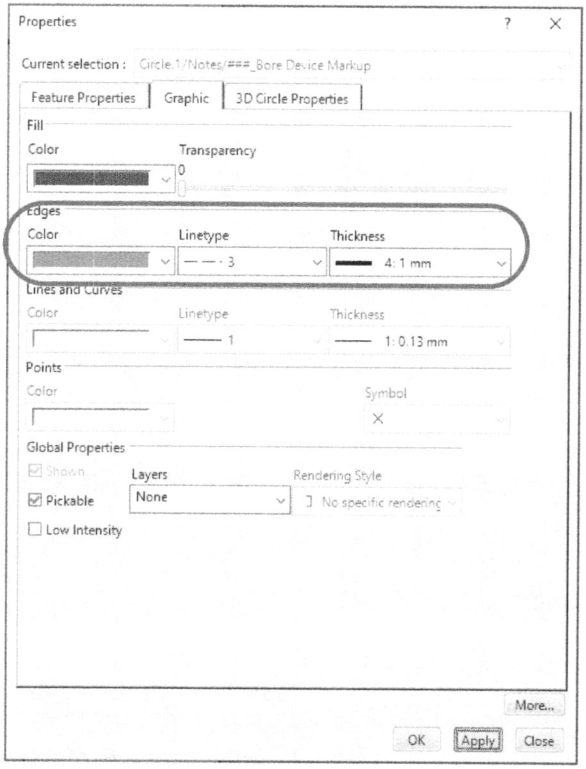

Figure 6–68

8. Select **OK** in the Properties dialog box. The annotations update as shown in Figure 6–69.

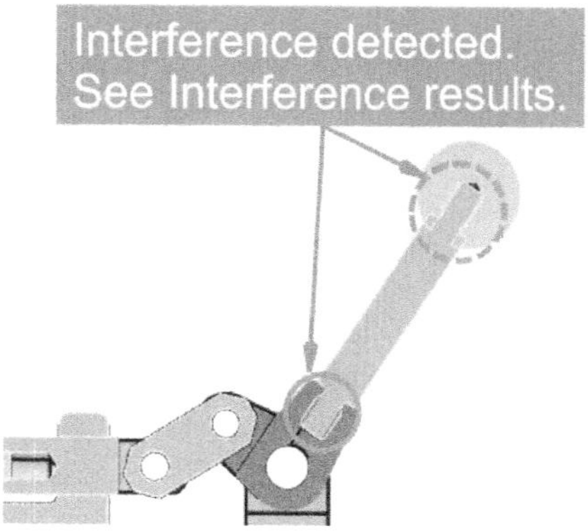

Figure 6–69

Task 11 - Create a Slide.

1. Orient the assembly such that you can see all the markups as shown in Figure 6–70, and select the  (Slide) icon.

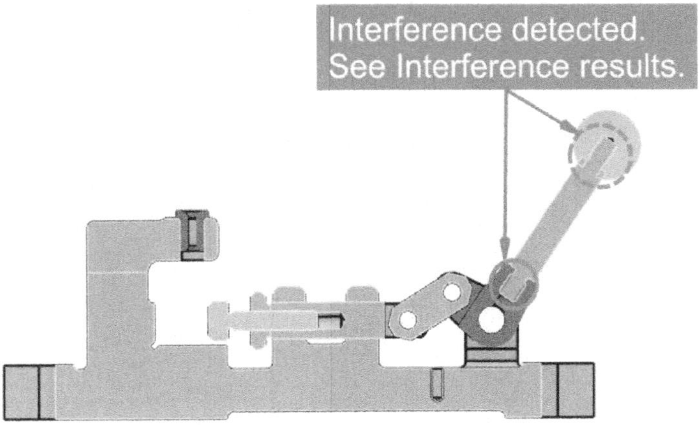

Figure 6–70

2. This will create **Slide.1** and add it to the specification tree.

Task 12 - Add Band Analysis to the Action Bar.

1. Select **Me > Preferences> Customize** and the customize window will display as shown in Figure 6–71.

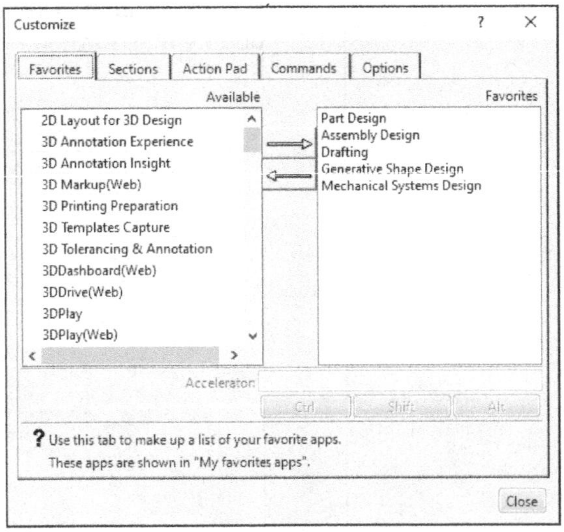

Figure 6–71

2. Select the *Sections* tab, and with *Review* highlighted, select **Add commands....**

3. Enter **Band Analysis** in the top field of the command list and press <ENTER>. This will find the  (Band Analysis) command for you and filter everything else out.

4. Select  (Band Analysis) from the list and select **OK**.

5. Close the Customize window. You will now see that  (Band Analysis) has been added to the *Review* section of the Action Bar as shown in Figure 6–72.

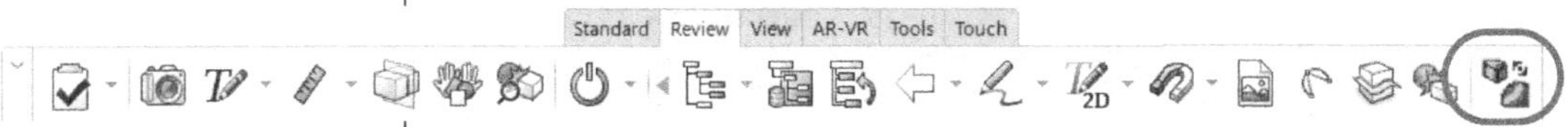

Figure 6–72

Task 13 - Hide current annotations/markings for a new Slide.

In order to create a new slide without showing previous markings, you can either hide the marking individually, or because you created an All Parts slide without any markings earlier, you can use that instead.

1. Double-click on **All Parts** slide from the tree. Alternatively, you can right-click on it and select **Apply Slide**.

2. The model switches back to a view and display that you started with, with all current markings hidden.

Task 14 - Create Band Analysis results.

1. Click the  (* Right) view icon in the *View* section of the Action Bar.

2. Select  (Band Analysis) that you recently placed on the Action Bar, and the Band Analysis window will display.

3. Within the Band Analysis window, set the values to those shown in Figure 6–73.

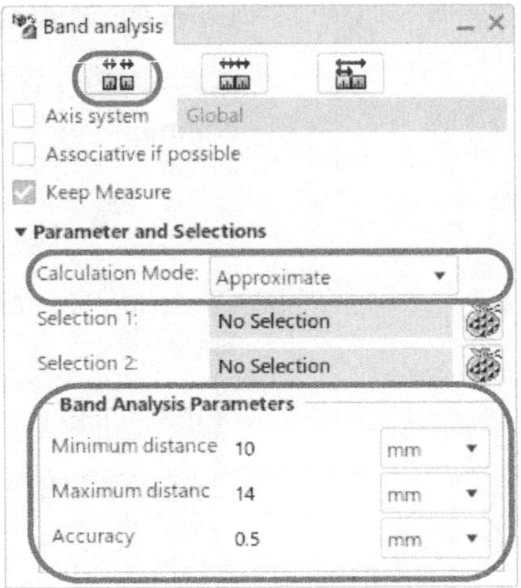

Figure 6–73

4. Now select on the **Lever Angle** and **Pin Pressure** parts as shown in Figure 6–74.

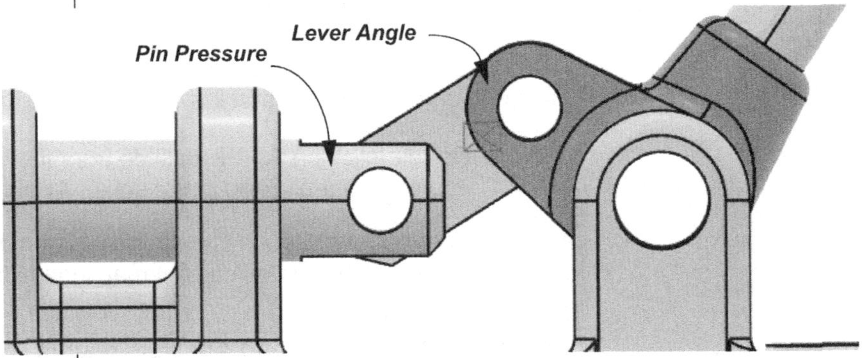

Figure 6–74

5. The Band Analysis should display on the model as shown in Figure 6–75. You may need to click and drag the text box into the location shown.

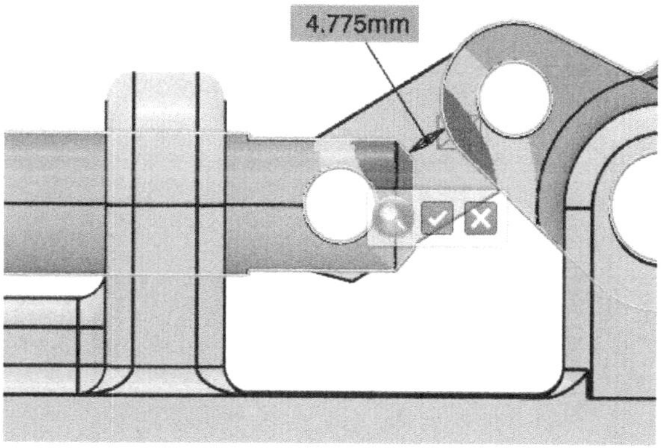

Figure 6–75

6. If the Band Analysis does not display as shown in Figure 6–75, hover your cursor over the icon in the context menu and ensure that the settings match those in Figure 6–76. Toggle the settings to match.

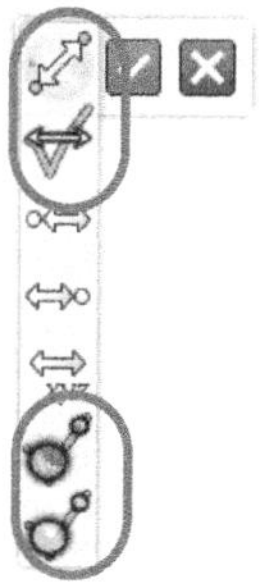

Figure 6–76

7. Select (Validate the Measure) once complete.

Task 15 - Create a Slide for Band Analysis results.

When the band analysis was run for this model, it detected that the minimum distance was not obtained. In this task, you will create another slide to note this to the designer.

1. Click the (* Left) view icon in the *View* section of the Action Bar.
2. Create a rectangle around the link by selecting (Rectangle) in the *Review* section of the Action Bar.

3. Then select on the Link part, as shown in Figure 6–77.

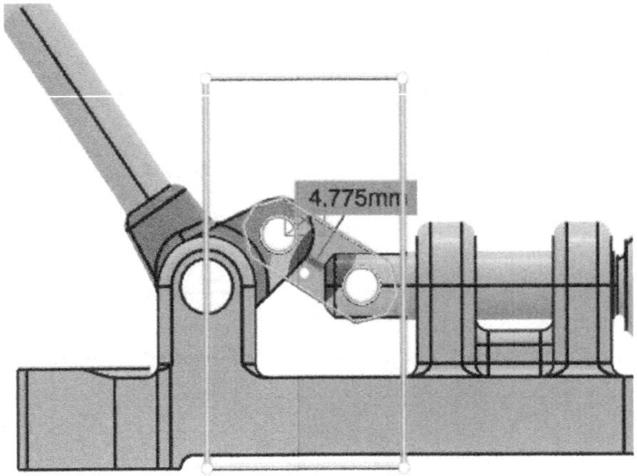

Figure 6–77

4. Create text with the leader arrow as shown in Figure 6–78.

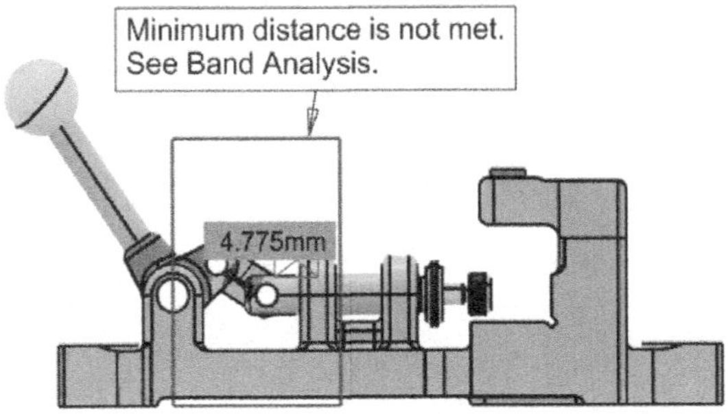

Figure 6–78

5. Using the Properties dialog box, change the properties of the annotations to:

Leave the rest of the properties at their defaults.

Rectangle:

- *Linetype:* **3**
- *Thickness:* **3**

Text:

- *Text Color:* **Red**
- Edges Color: **Red**
- Edges *Thickness:* **2**
- Remove the check mark next to **Border**.

The assembly displays as shown in Figure 6–79.

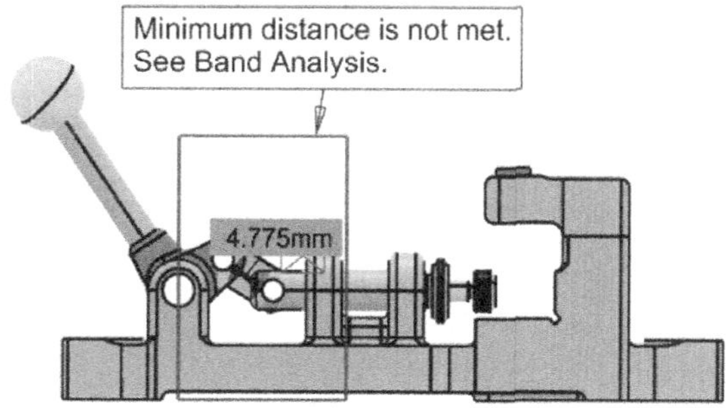

Figure 6–79

6. Select  (Slide) in the *Review* section of the Action Bar, to create **Slide.2.**

7. Rename Slides.

*The **Slides** branch is in the **Markup** branch of the specification tree.*

  - In the **Slides** branch of the specification tree, right-click on **Slide.1** and select **Properties**.
  - Change the name of the view to **Interference Comments**.
  - Change the name of *Slide.2* to **Band Analysis Comments** using the technique used to change the name of **Slide.1**. The specification tree displays as shown in Figure 6–80.

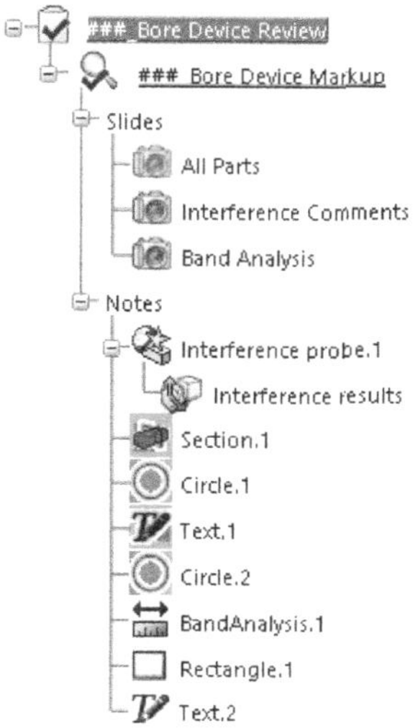

Figure 6–80

Task 16 - View the Slides.

1. In the specification tree, double-click on the **Interference Comments** slide and the display updates to show its annotations as shown in Figure 6–81. Select **Yes** to any warning messages about changes being lost.

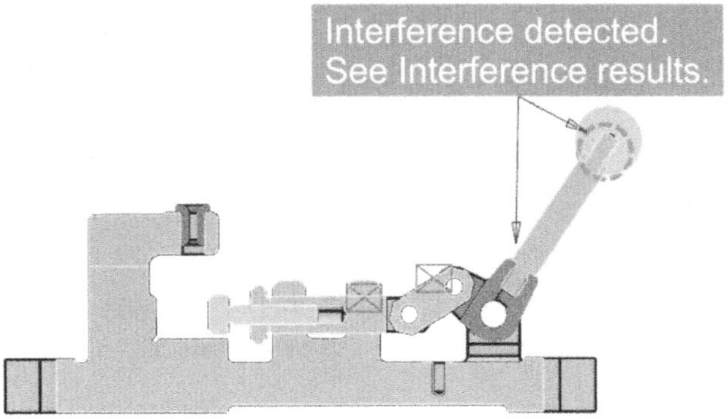

Figure 6–81

2. Double-Click on the **Band Analysis Comments** slide and the display updates to show its annotations, as shown in Figure 6–82.

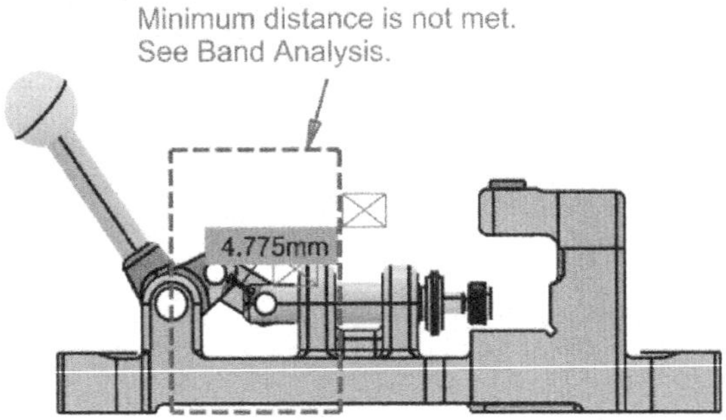

Figure 6–82

3. Notice that Markups in the *Notes* section of the specification tree is hidden automatically based on the state they were in when the slide was created. If changes are needed, modify the notes that are displayed, and then, right-click on the name of a slide in the specification tree, and select  (Update Slide) from the drop-down list.

4. Save and close the model.

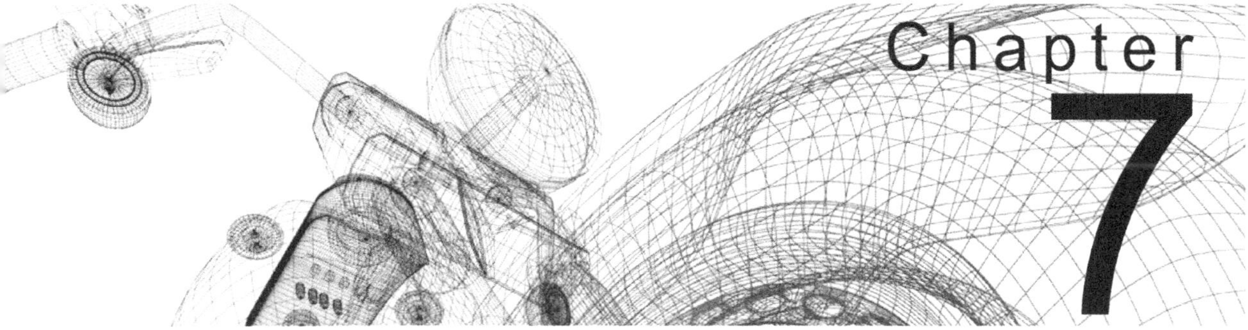

Design Review II

This chapter details what is possible when creating a Review. It also discusses the many tools that the Design Review app has that helps in sharing information about a model's design.

Learning Objectives in This Chapter

- How to use the **Explode** command.
- Use the 3D Compare.
- Create volume cuts using Sectioning.
- Understand how to update a Slide.

7.1 Explode

Exploded views enable you to quickly visualize a group of constrained components separately. While this can always be done manually using the Robot or (Manipulate) command, Explode automates the process with a quick and easy to use interface.

To explode an assembly, in the *Review* section of the Action Bar, expand the secondary area and select the flyout next to (Cumulative Snap), and then click the (Explode) icon. The Explode dialog box opens, as shown in Figure 7–1.

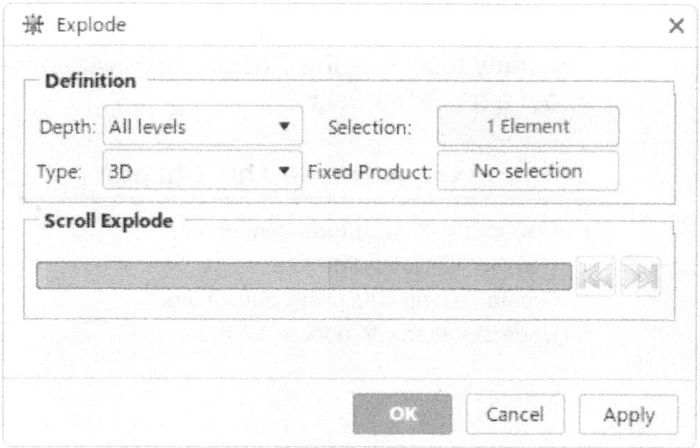

Figure 7–1

The options for the Explode dialog box are described as follows:

Option		Description
Depth		Determines which components in the assembly are exploded.
	All levels	Explodes all levels of the assembly.
	First level	Explodes all first-level components of the assembly. In this case, subassembly components are not exploded.
Type		Determines the exploded placement of the components.
	3D	Places components in a 3D arrangement with respect to the position of the unexploded assembly.
	2D	Explodes components to positions within the 2D plane of the current view. Use named views to determine the 2D explode plane.
	Constrained	Explodes components with respect to the constraints used to contextually place them in the assembly.
Selection		Specifies the product to explode. The active assembly is automatically selected. If multiple levels of the assembly are selected, the assembly explodes in stages.
Fixed Product		Select one component to remain fixed during the explode. If the depth is set to **All levels**, you can select a part. If the depth is set to **First level**, you can select a subassembly.

The components in a 3D explode can be positioned anywhere in 3D space, while the components of the 2D explode can only move within a 2D plane. This plane is always parallel to the screen and is therefore specified by orienting the model. The difference between 3D and 2D explode types is shown in Figure 7–2.

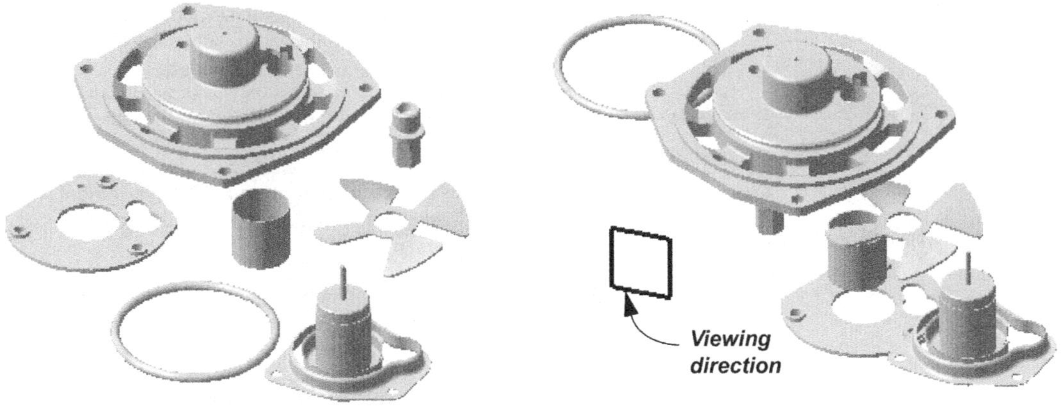

Type set to 3D

Type set to 2D

Figure 7–2

Once the model is exploded, the positions of individual components can be moved using the Robot. You can then position the components to display how the assembly is put together. An example is shown in Figure 7–3.

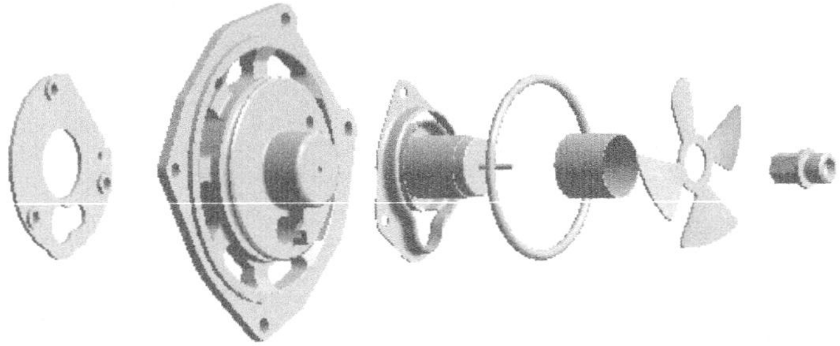

Figure 7–3

The distance between the components can also be customized after the explosion is applied. To do this, in the Explode dialog box, select the slider and drag it from side to side as shown in Figure 7–4. If you drag it all the way to the left, the components will reassemble.

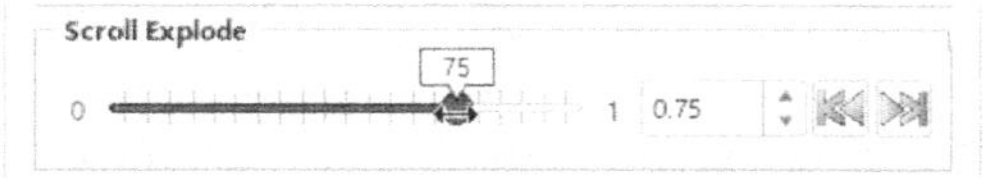

Figure 7–4

To reset the components back to the constraint positions, select  (Reset Products) in the *Review* section of the Action Bar.

The  (Reset All) icon will work as well but will also turn off any markups that are currently displayed.

7.2 3D Compare

The 3D Compare tool detects differences between two 3D objects or two version of a product. It is useful for comparing the same product at different stages in a design or for identifying differences in a design after changes are made.

General Steps

Use the following general steps to compare products:

1. Select the first object.
2. Activate the 3D Compare and select the second object.
3. View results and optionally customize settings.

Step 1 - Select the first object.

To compare two parts or products, you must first start with the original object that you are comparing. This can be done by opening and selecting the object you wish to be the first object. If no object is selected, the root of the existing product will be used as the first object.

Click the (3D Compare) icon from the *Review* section of the Action Bar. The **3D Compare** command will bring up a 3DSearch window allowing you to search for the second object as shown in Figure 7–5.

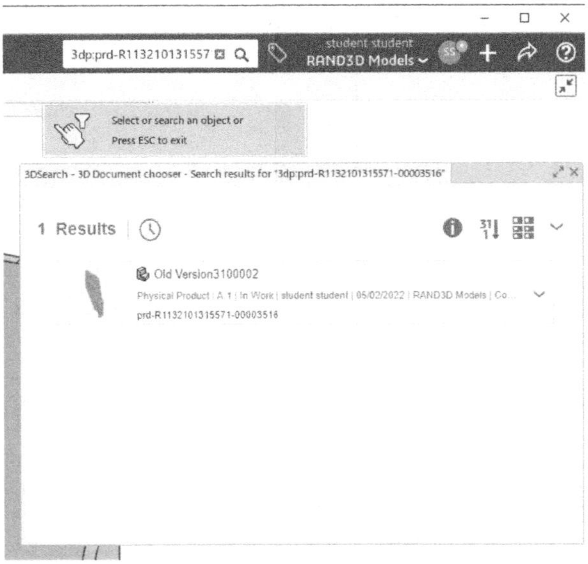

Figure 7–5

Once the search window is open:

If a physical product was selected as the first object, then its revisions are shown in the search results by default. Otherwise, there are two options for defining the second object to compare.

1. Select the object from the tree or from another tab that is already open.
2. Search for the object within the search box in the top bar, then select the required object from the results.

Step 2 - View results and optionally customize settings.

Once the second object is selected, the results are displayed in the 3D area. These results include a Compare.x window, colors indicating old, new, and common areas of the models, and separate panels showing the Old and New versions of the original models. This can be seen in Figure 7–6.

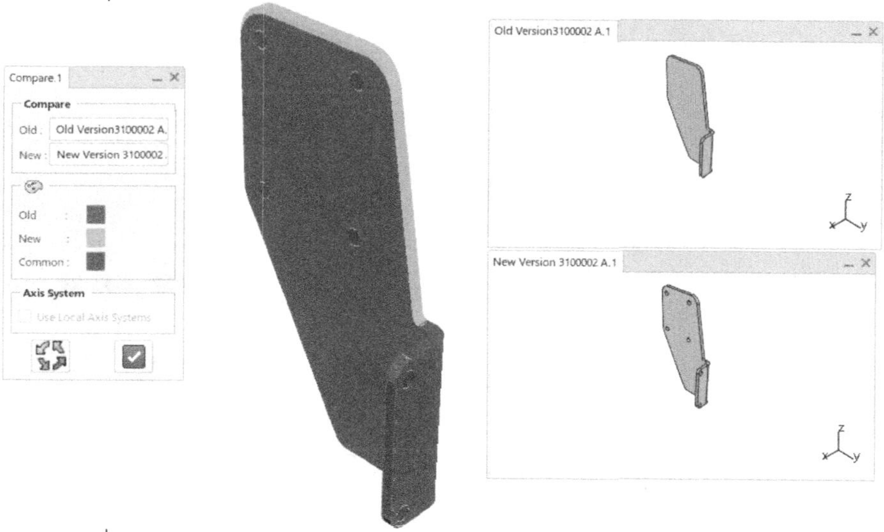

Figure 7–6

Colors

The colors indicate what has changed and what hasn't within the two objects. By default the colors results are in red, green, and blue, and the meanings of which are described below.

- Red indicates geometry that are in the old version but not in the new version.
- Green indicates geometry that are in the new version but not the old version.
- Blue indicates geometry that are common to both the new and old versions.

While those colors are the defaults, they all can be customized by double-clicking the color within the Compare.x window. Doing so will bring up a window that allows for *Color Wheel*, *Custom Color Palette*, and *Sliders* to change the color that it represents as shown in Figure 7–7.

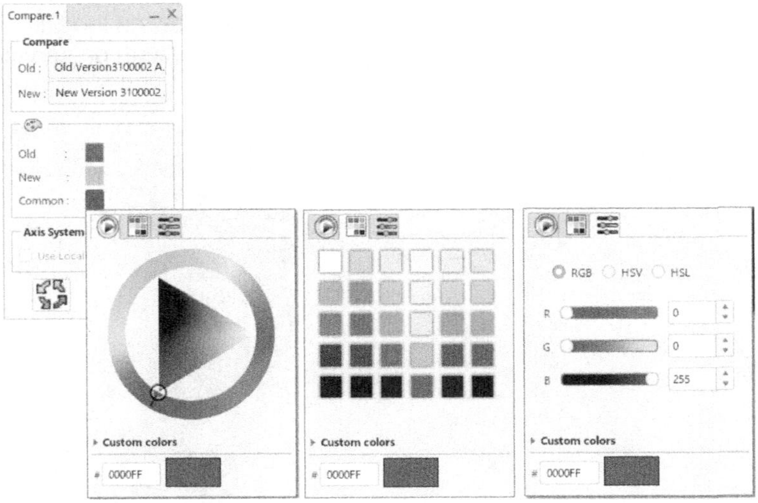

Figure 7–7

Optionally: The Compare.x window has a **Use Local Axis Systems** option. This option becomes available only if you had selected both objects before selecting the  (3D Compare) icon.

When the **Use Local Axis System** option is selected, the comparison results will display with respect to the absolute axis system of the selected objects instead of their local axis systems.

Updating and Displaying Results

When changes are made to the 3D Compare that might include Markers, Measures, or Slides, the (Recompute Compare) icon found in the Compare.x window must be selected to update what is being displayed. When the (OK) button is selected, Compare.x is added to the *Notes* section of the tree but all other visual indicators of the 3D Compare disappear. To see the windows and colors of the results again, double-click on Compare.x in the tree as shown in Figure 7–8. Markers and Measures can be made visible while Compare.x is still displayed, and slides can be created in this state so results can be easily retrieved by double-clicking on those Slides.

Figure 7–8

7.3 Sectioning

The **Sectioning** tool in the *Review* section of the Action Bar, enables the creation of volume cuts to investigate the internal information of a part or assembly. Sections will be created and stored in the Notes branch of a Review.

To use the **Section** tool:

1. Click  (Sectioning).
2. The Section result is manipulated through the Robot and the Section context menu, as shown in Figure 7–9.

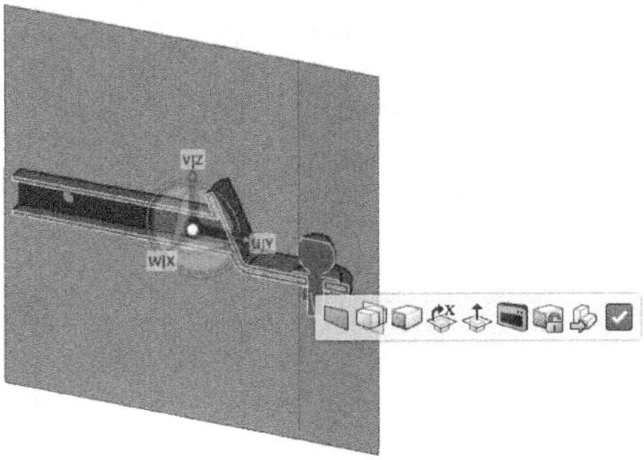

Figure 7–9

3. Click  (Validate Section) in the Section context menu.

A variety of tools for configuring the Section definition are located in the Section context menu. Descriptions for some of the common options are found in the following tables.

Icon	Option	Description
	**Display a Plane**	Section created as cut by single plane.
	**Display a Slice**	Section created as cut by two parallel planes.
	**Display a Box**	Section created as cut by a bounding.

Icon	Option	Description
	Display Contour & Plane	Section result displays Section contour and cutting plane(s).
	Display Contour & Grid	Section result displays Section contour and size grid.
	Display Contour	Section result displays Section contour.

Icon	Option	Description
	Front Cut	Volume cut removes component information in front of the section limit.
	Hide Cut	No volume cut removes component information.
	Back Cut	Volume cut removes component information behind the section limit.
	Always Show Cut	Always display the volume cut.
	Contour Only	Only the contour is visible, and volume cut is applied to both sides.

Icon	Option	Description
	X Position	Section plane oriented on X plane.
	Y Position	Section plane oriented on Y plane.
	Z Position	Section plane oriented on Z plane.
	Specify Position	Section plane oriented according to selected reference (1 plane, 2 linear entities, or 3 points/vertices).
	Select Geometry	Specify the position of the section plane.
	Define Home Position	Define the current section plane position as the HOME position.
	Move to Section Plane	Move to the section plane.

7.4 Updating a Slide

When slides are created, they take a snap shot of the current display and orientation of the model they are capturing. If changes to the slide are required, start by applying the slide you wish to change. This will give you the current representation of the slide. Now you can make changes to the slide, which can include but not limited to:

- Adding new Markups
- Adding new Measures
- Hiding currently displayed Marks or Measures
- Changing the position of individual components or creating a exploded view of all of the components
- Changing the graphical attributes of the components being displayed
- Adding new components

Once those changes are completed, in the specifications tree, right-click on the Slide that you wish to update. From the drop-down menu, select **Update Slide**, as shown in Figure 7–10. This will take a new snapshot of the model with its current display and orientation.

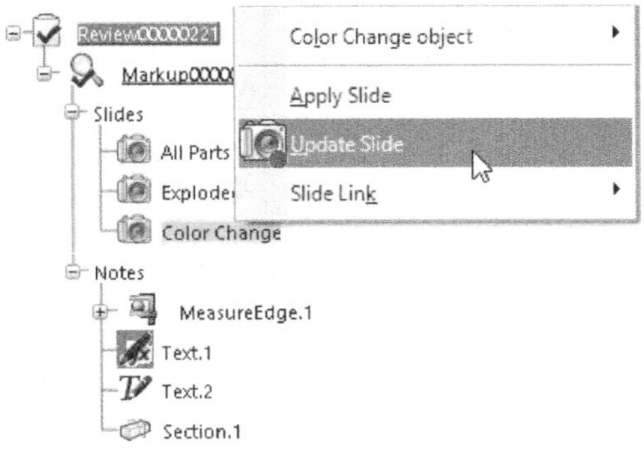

Figure 7–10

Another alternative to this would be to select (Slide View) from the upper left side of the screen. With all the slides listed in thumbnail form, hover over the slide you wish to update. The (Update Slide) icon will appear in the corner and can be selected.

Practice 7a

Creating Exploded Views

Practice Objectives

- Explode an assembly.
- Create Slides.

In this practice, you will create various slides and apply them to the assembly to facilitate assembly of additional components.

Task 1 - Create a Design Review.

1. Import with your initials, and open **Fan_b.3dxml**. The assembly displays as shown in Figure 7–11.

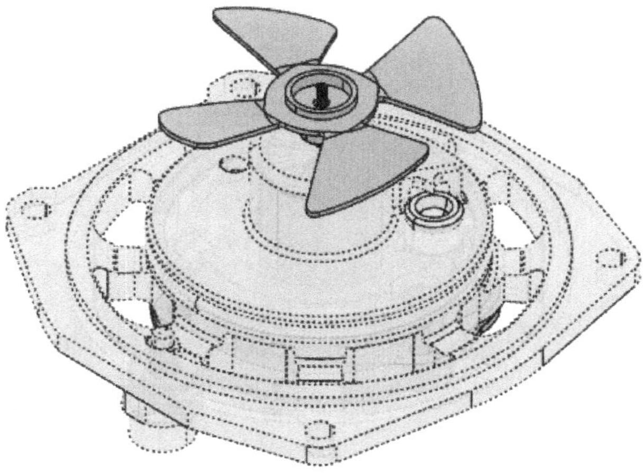

Figure 7–11

2. Switch to the Design Review app by selecting the compass in the upper left corner, and then select  Design Review from the drop down list.

3. A Review window will appear automatically. In the *Review* tab, set the Title to **### Fan Review** where ### represents your initials, as shown in Figure 7–12.

4. Select the *Markup* tab.

5. Set the Title to **### Fan Markup** where ### represents your initials, as shown in Figure 7–12.

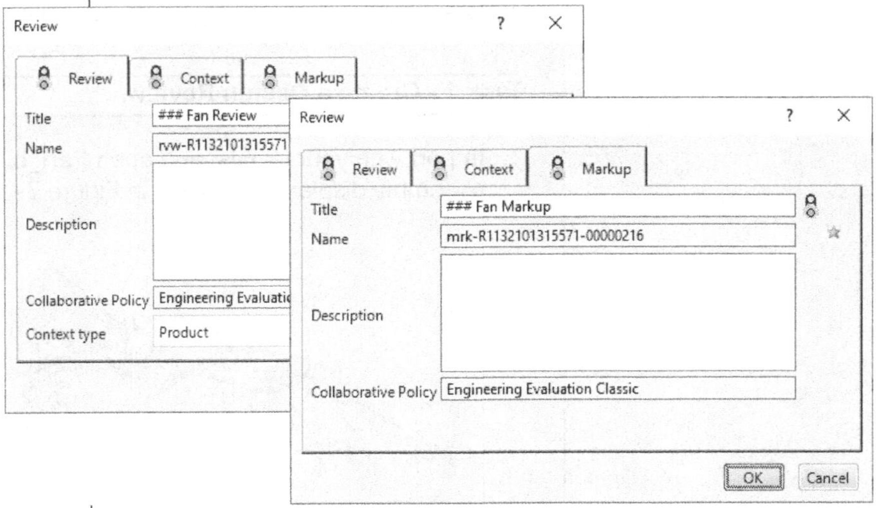

Figure 7–12

6. Select **OK** to finish the Review, and complete the switch to the Design Review app. The specification tree will disappear and the *Review View* tab will be displayed instead.

Task 2 - Create the first Slide.

1. Switch back to *Tree* view by selecting the (Tree) tab in the upper left corner. The specification tree will now be displayed.

2. Expand ### Fan Markup at the bottom of the tree to be able to see the Slides and Notes nodes. The specification tree should look as shown in Figure 7–13.

Figure 7–13

To zoom with the mouse, hold the middle mouse button + click and let go of the left or right mouse button.

3. Use the mouse to zoom in on the assembly so that it fully fills the screen.
4. Click (Slide) from the *Review* section of the Action Bar.
5. The *Slide View* tab is now displayed and **Slide.1** is created. Select the name **Slide.1** and rename it **All Parts**.
6. Switch back to the *Tree* view by selecting the (Tree) tab in the upper left corner. The specification tree will now be displayed.
7. Expand the *Slides* node of the specification tree to see the **All Parts** slide.

Figure 7–14

Task 3 - Create an Exploded View Slide.

1. Expand the secondary area of the *Review* section, then under the (Cumulative Snap) flyout, click the (Explode) icon. The Explode window will appear.

2. Select **First level** from the Depth drop-down list, as shown in Figure 7–15.

3. Now select **Fan** from the tree as the selection, as shown in Figure 7–15.

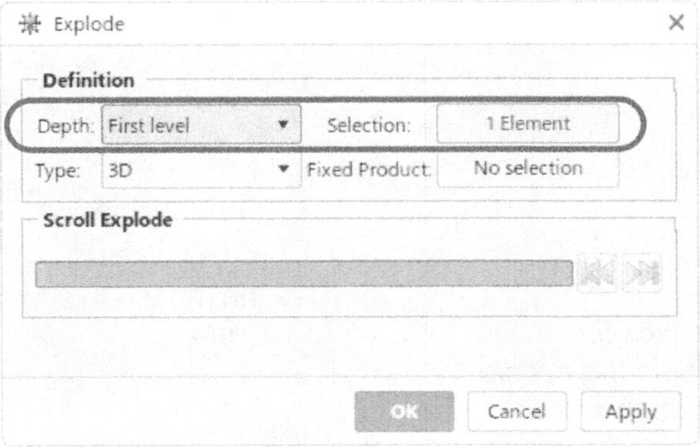

Figure 7–15

4. Click **OK** in the Explode dialog box. The assembly updates, as shown in Figure 7–16.

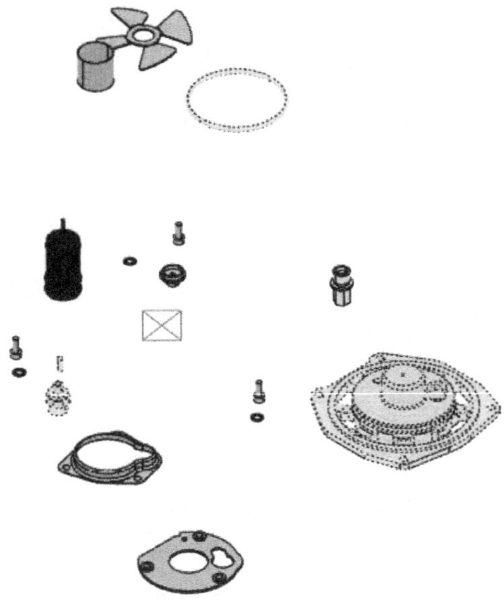

Figure 7–16

5. Click the  (Slide) icon to capture the positions of the components and the view of the camera.

6. Right-click on **Slide.1** from the tree and select **Properties**.
7. Set the Feature Name to **Exploded**, then select **OK.**

Task 4 - Apply the Slides.

1. Right-click on the **All Parts** slide and select **Apply Slide**, as shown in Figure 7–17.

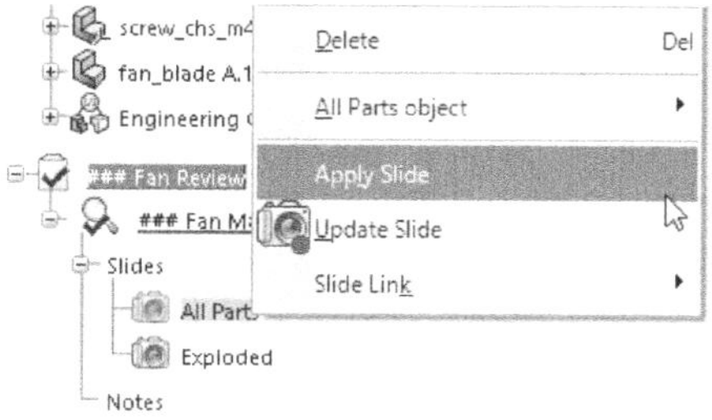

Figure 7–17

You should notice that all the parts move back into the fully assembled position.

2. Another method for applying a slide is to double-click on it. Double-click on the **Exploded** slide from the tree. You should see the components separate from one another.

3. Click (Reset All) to unexplode the assembly. Note: *Reset All* will also turn off the display of any notes if there were any displayed.

Task 5 - Create a Slide.

1. Right-click on the yoke component and select **Hide/Show** to hide the component, as shown in Figure 7–18.

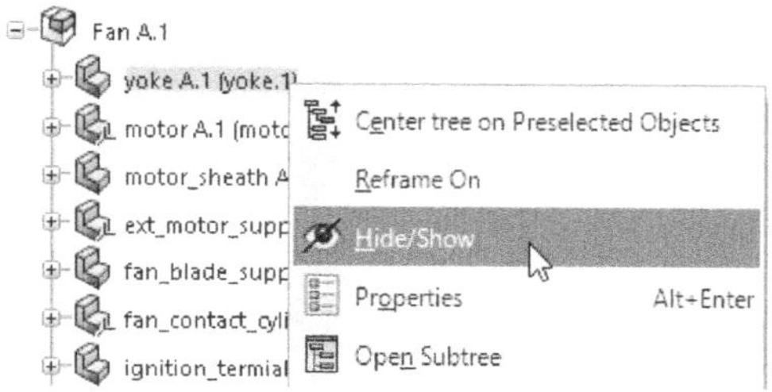

Figure 7–18

2. If required, zoom in on the model so the assembly takes up the entire screen.

3. Click the  (Slide) icon to capture the displayed components and the view of the camera. The assembly displays, as shown in Figure 7–19.

Figure 7–19

4. Right-click on **Slide.1** and select **Properties**.
5. Set the *Feature Name* to **Yoke Removed** and select **OK**.

Task 6 - Update a Slide.

1. Double-click on the **All Parts** slide to apply it to the assembly.
2. Now double-click the **Yoke Removed** slide to compare its display to that of All Parts.

   It is now decided that the fan blade covers up too much detail in the Yoke Removed slide. You will change the transparency of the fan blade and add that change to the Yoke Removed slide.

3. With the Yoke Removed slide applied last, right-click on the **fan_blade** component from the tree and select **Properties**.

4. In the Properties window, select the *Graphic* tab, and drag the Transparency slider to **150** as shown in Figure 7–20.

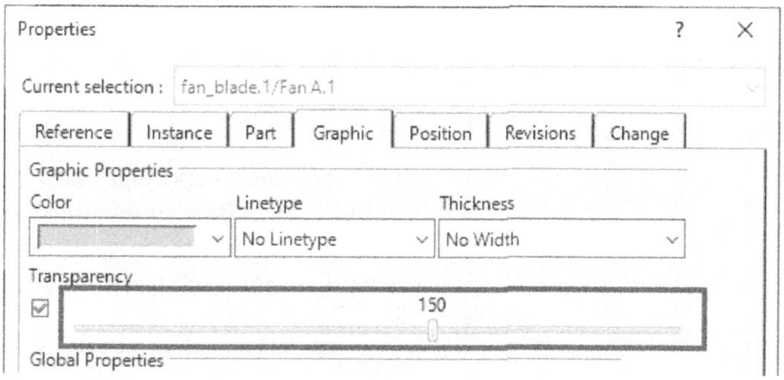

Figure 7–20

5. Select **OK** to apply the change to the component. The assembly displays as shown in Figure 7–21.

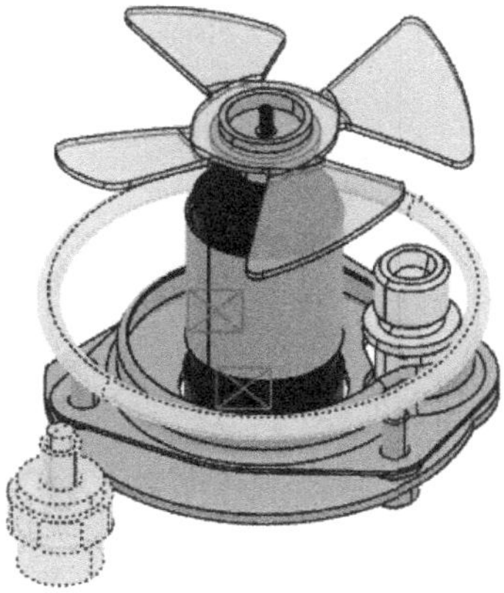

Figure 7–21

While this did change the current settings of the fan_blade component, the change still needs to be recorded in the Yoke Removed slide.

6. Right-click on the **Yoke Removed** slide from the tree, and select **Update Slide**. This will document the change to fan_blade within the Yoke Removed slide.
7. Confirm the changes worked by double clicking both **All Parts** and **Yoke Removed** from the tree. The assembly should update correctly for both.
8. Save and close the assembly.

Practice 7b 3D Compare

Practice Objectives

- Set up a 3D Compare.
- Create a Slide.

In this practice, you will compare two versions of the same part to check for differences between the versions. A diffuser vane has been adjusted since its first revision. You will use the 3D Compare tool to determine where the changes have occurred.

Task 1 - Import and Open.

To compare two parts, they must first exist in 3DExperience. In this task, you will import both part models.

1. Select (New)>**Import** from the upper right side of the 3DEXPERIENCE window, and the Import window is displayed.
2. Select (Browse), then navigate to and select **DiffuserVane_01.3dxml**.
3. Select **Open** and then **OK** from the Import window.
4. An *Operation Report* window is displayed. Select **OK** to close this window.

   With this, you have successfully imported the 2410(DiffuserVane_01) part; however, you are exploring this model and do not have it "open" or in the Assembly Design app.
5. Right-click on **2410** in the tree and select **Open**. The part should now be displayed in the Assembly Design app.
6. Repeat steps 1-5 but this time use the file **DiffuserVane_02.3dxml**. This will display part **2411** in a separate tab.

Task 2 - Create a Review.

At this point, you will have 4 different tabs open—two in the Explore app and two in the Assembly Design app. To simplify, close the tabs in the Explore app.

1. At the top of the screen, hover the cursor over the two tabs that have (Explore) in their names and select  (Close) that appears in those tabs as shown in Figure 7–22.

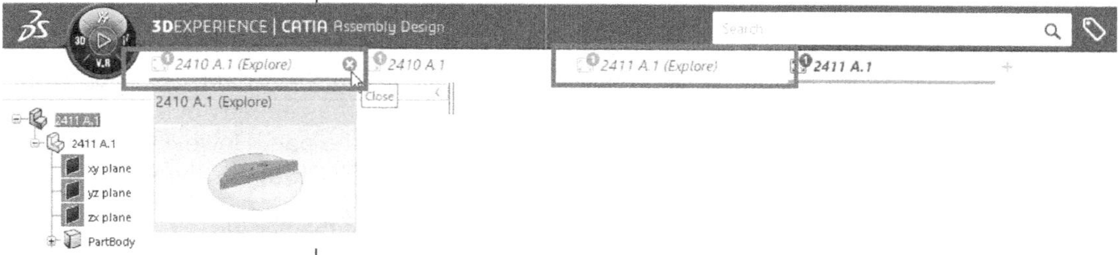

Figure 7–22

This should leave you with only two tabs (*2410* and *2411*).

2. Select the *2410* tab. This is our original part and you will create the Review.
3. In the upper left side of the screen, select the Compass and select  (Design Review) from the drop-down list. The Review window is displayed.
4. In the *Review* tab, set the Title to **###_DiffuserVane_Review** where ### are your initials.
5. In the *Markup* tab, set the Title to **###_DiffuserVane_Markup** where ### are your initials.
6. Select **OK** to create the Review. This will complete the switch to Design Review app.
7. Switch to *Tree* view by selecting  (Tree) in the upper left corner.
8. The specification tree should look like Figure 7–23.

Figure 7–23

Task 3 - Compare the models.

1. In the *Review* section of the Action Bar, select  (3D Compare).

   Note: This will bring up the 3DSearch window. Because the model you will be comparing to has already been opened, you will not need to search for the part. However, it is possible to search 3DEXPERICNCE at this time.

2. Select the *2411* tab at the top of the screen.

3. Select the **2411** part at the top of the specification tree. This will take you back to the *2410* tab window where the results of the 3D Compare are displayed, as shown in Figure 7–24.

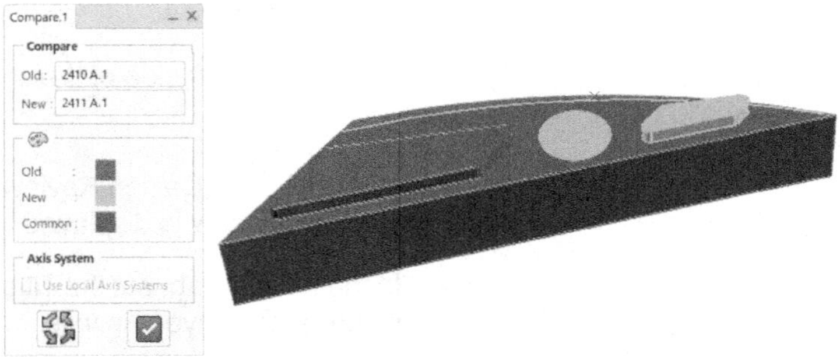

Figure 7–24

The results, displayed in the Compare.1 window, include the following:

- Part numbers of the two parts that were compared
- A color key each for the Old, New, and Common areas of the models

  Along with this, two new windows are displayed with the part numbers listed in them as shown in Figure 7–25. These windows can be adjusted and scaled to size to better understand the parts being compared.

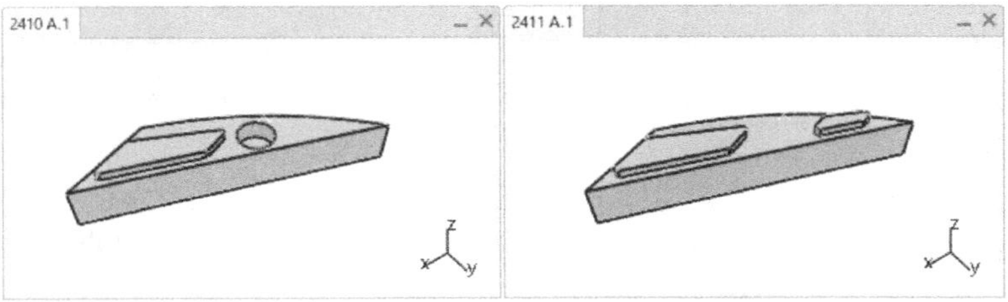

Figure 7–25

Using this information you can tell that from the original model, the hole was filled/removed and an extrusion was added highlighted by the green area of the results. You can also tell that the curve edge of the model has been changed to remove some material, indicated by the red area of the results.

4. Select (OK) to close the Compare.1 window.

Task 4 - Creating a Slide to show Compare results.

When the Compare.1 window closes, all of the information and graphics disappear with it. If you would like to be able to quickly call upon that information, you can create a slide.

1. Double click **Compare.1** from the specification tree. The Compare.1 window displays along with the colors and Part Number preview windows, as shown in Figure 7–26.

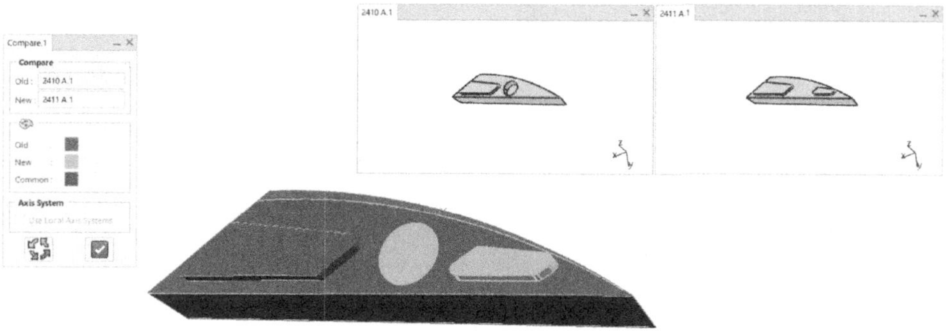

Figure 7–26

2. **Spin** and **Zoom** in on the model to get the best orientation to show the different colors.
3. Select (Slide) to capture this display.
4. Ensure that you are in the *Tree* view tab by selecting (Tree) in the upper left of the screen.
5. Right click on **Slide.1** and select **Properties**.
6. Set *Feature Name* to **Compare 2410 to 2411** and select **OK** to close the properties window.
7. Select (OK) to close the Compare.1 window.

8. Now double-click on **Compare 2410 to 2411** slide to test the slide.

9. Select ☑ (OK) to close the Compare.1 window.

10. Save and close both documents (2410 and 2411).

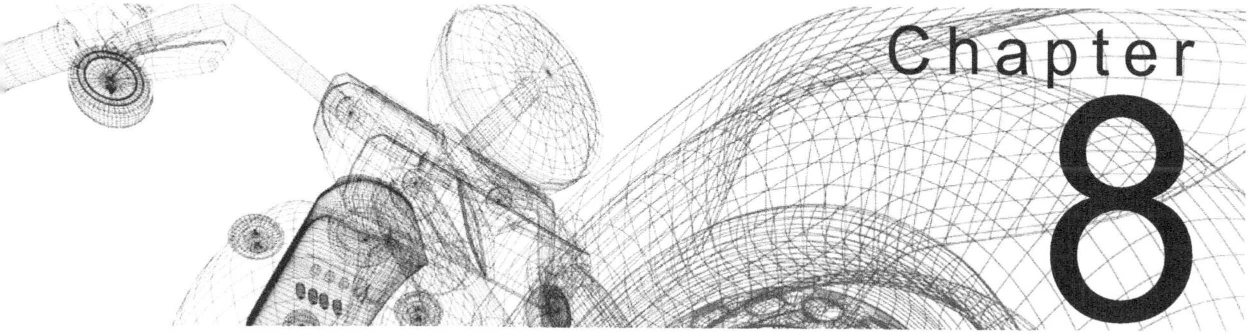

Image Capture

Model images might be required to communicate information about the design to other people. These images can be attached to an e-mail or inserted into product documentation. This chapter also discusses methods of printing images directly from 3DEXPERIENCE.

Learning Objectives in This Chapter

- Capture model images.
- Learn how to print images.

8.1 Capturing Images

CATIA enables you to capture images from the screen in pixel or vector formats. These images can be saved to an album, printed, or copied to a clipboard for use in other applications.

General Steps

Use the following general steps to capture an image:

1. Activate the Capture tool.
2. Select the Capture mode.
3. Define image configuration.
4. Capture the image.
5. Define the output of the image.

Step 1 - Activate the Capture tool.

In the *Tools* section of the Action Bar, select (Capture). Note: You will need to expand a secondary area to see it. The Capture dialog box opens, as shown in Figure 8–1.

Figure 8–1

Step 2 - Select the Capture mode.

Once the Capture dialog box is displayed, the next important step is to define the Capture mode. Selecting the arrow next to (Capture) will display the drop-down list as shown in Figure 8–2.

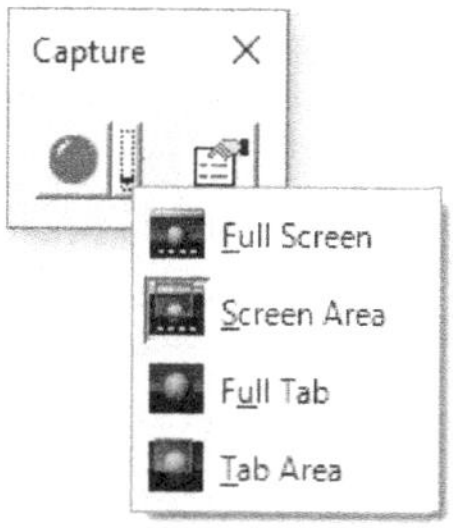

Figure 8–2

The Capture mode option you select from the drop-down list will determine what is included in the image and what configuration options will be available for use.

Option	Description
Full Screen	Entire screen including 3DEXPERIENCE and any other windows that might be open. Rendering configuration options will be disabled.
Screen Area	User define rectangular area including 3DEXPERIENCE and any other windows that might be open in that area. Rendering configuration options will be disabled.
Full Tab	Within 3DEXPERIENCE only, the active tab's window will be captured. Rendering configuration options will be enabled.
Tab Area	User define rectangular area that is only within the 3DEXPERIENCE active tab. Rendering configuration options will be enabled.

Step 3 - Define image configuration.

With the **Capture Configuration** command, additional options can be set to control the output of the image. Click the (Capture Configuration) icon to open the Capture Configuration dialog box.

Once open, you will notice three specific tabs - *General*, *Rendering*, and *Output Preferences*. While all three will always be displayed, the *Rendering* tab can be grayed and inaccessible (as shown in Figure 8–3) based on the Capture mode that was used.

General Tab

The *General* tab shown in Figure 8–3 controls options relevant to both types of image output (pixel and vector).

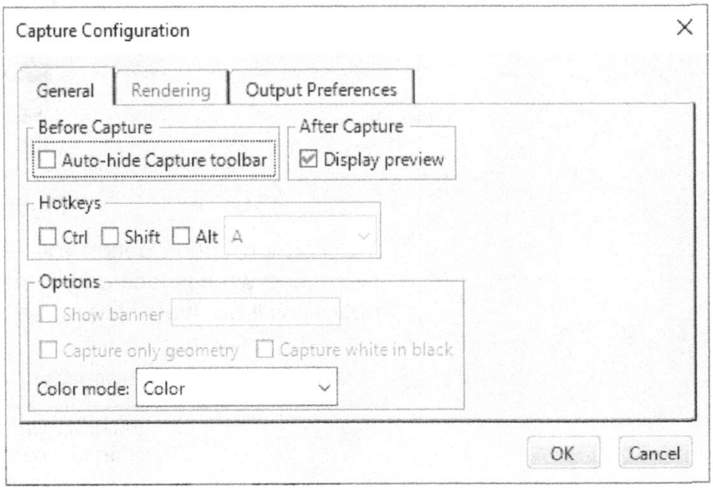

Figure 8–3

Before Capture

Select the **Auto-hide Capture toolbar** option to hide the Capture toolbar from the image that is created.

After Capture

Select the **Display Preview** option so a preview window can display after the capture is complete. This preview window will allow for viewing of the image along with the options to save, print, copying to clipboard, and saving into an album as shown in Figure 8–4.

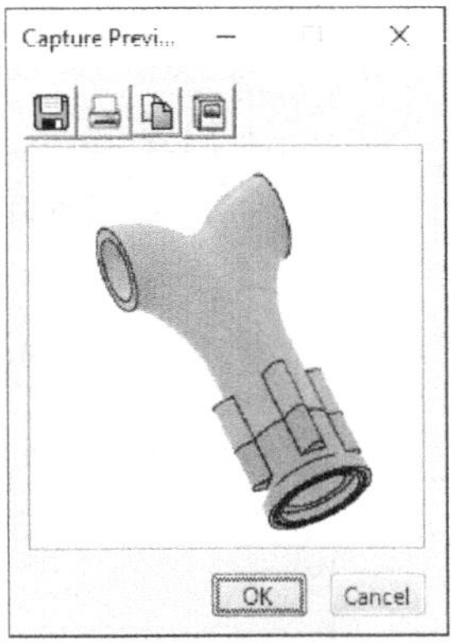

Figure 8–4

Hotkeys

The Hotkeys section allows for the use of custom keyboard shortcuts to activate the **Capture** command. <Ctrl>, <Alt>, or <Shift> can be used along with any other custom key from the keyboard.

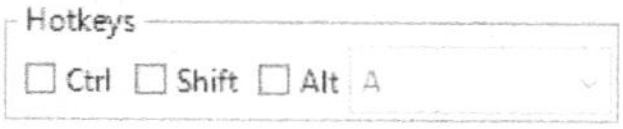

Banner

Select the **Show Banner** option to display a banner at the bottom of the image. By default, this banner displays the name of the model and the date and time when the shot was taken, as shown in Figure 8–5. Use the Banner field to modify the information output in the banner.

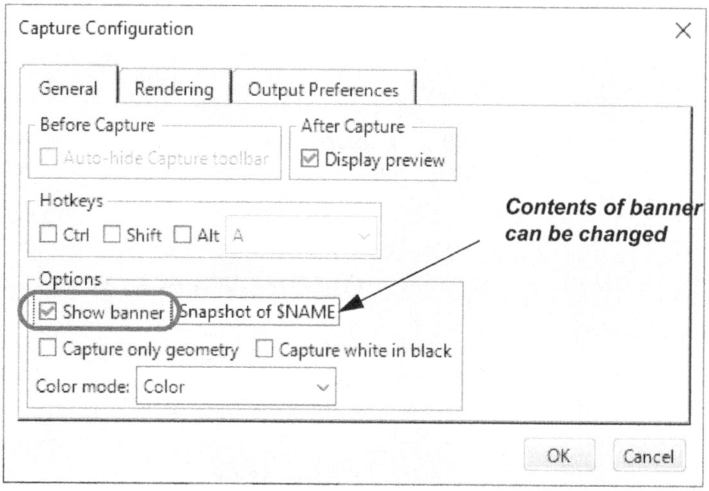

Figure 8–5

Capture Only Geometry

Select the **Capture Only Geometry** option to capture the geometry of the model without the background information, such as the specification tree and compass. For example, the image on the left of Figure 8–6 is taken without having the option selected and the image on the right is taken with the option selected. The **Capture Only Geometry** option cannot be used with vector images.

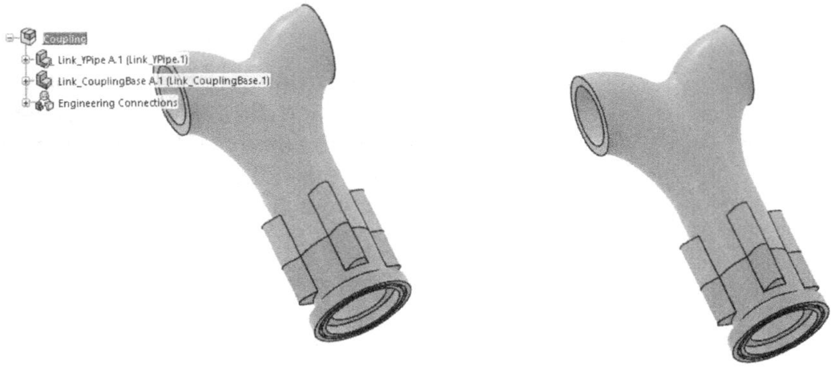

Without Capture Only Geometry option selected

With Capture Only Geometry option selected

Figure 8–6

Capture White in Black

Select the **Capture White in Black** option to change all of the white elements on the screen to black in the image. This is useful if you are creating the image on a white background.

Color Mode

Use the *Color mode* drop-down list to select the appropriate output color, as shown in Figure 8–7. By default, images are output in color, but can be changed to Greyscale or Monochrome.

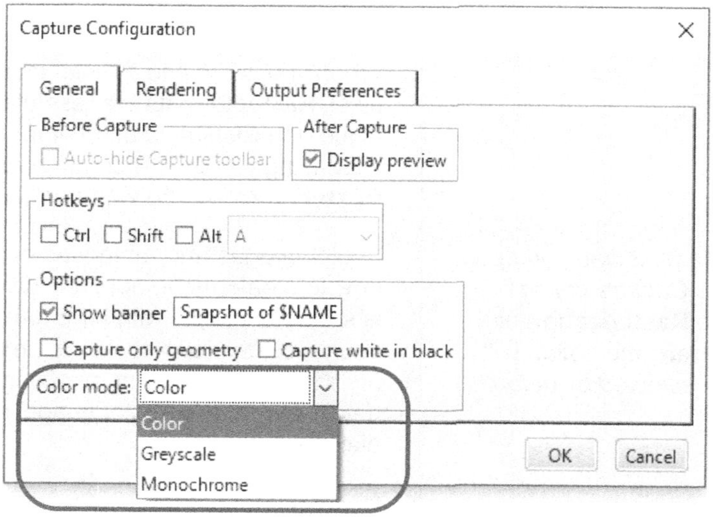

Figure 8–7

Rendering Tab

Within the *Rendering* tab, there are three sub tabs *Active Mode*, *Rasterization Options*, and *Wireframe Options*. Start with the *Active Mode* and select the type of image you want to capture. Based on that selection, you then will be able to select the corresponding **Rasteriztion** or **Wireframe** options to customize settings.

Active Mode

Within the *Active Mode* tab, there are only two options, **Rasteriztion** and **Wireframe**, as shown in Figure 8–8. The selection within the *Active Mode* tab determines what other *Rendering* tabs are applicable for the current image.

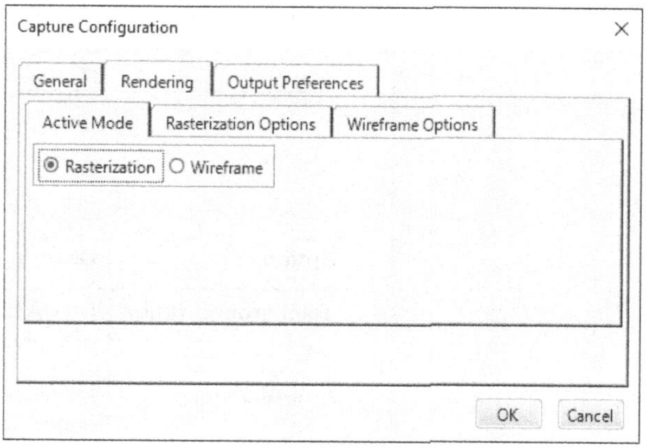

Figure 8–8

Images can be taken in raster or vector formats. A raster image, often called a pixel image, consists of squares of color (pixels). When you zoom into a raster image, you can see each individual pixel. Raster formats are resolution-dependent, meaning that the higher the resolution of the image, the better the quality when increasing its size. To create a raster image, select **Rasterization** in the Capture dialog box.

The next time you open the Capture dialog box, the **Rasterization** or **Wireframe** option *will be selected by default.*

Vector images are comprised of mathematical instructions on how to create the image. It is divided into objects, each of which is stored in the file with information about its position in the image, color, size, etc. Vector images are resolution-independent, enabling it to be resized without losing detail. To create a vector image, select **Wireframe** in the Capture dialog box.

Rasterization Options

Select the *Rasterization Options* tab, as shown in Figure 8–9, to customize options specific to raster images. The options in this tab are described in the table below.

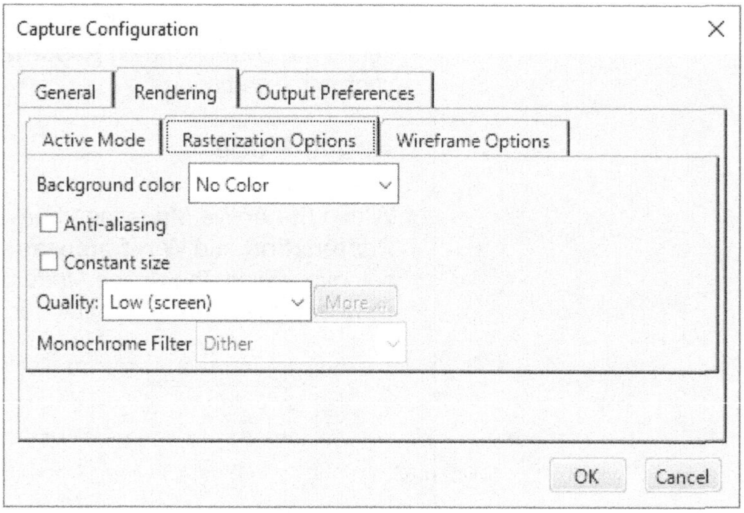

Figure 8–9

Option	Description
Background Color	CATIA background color is replaced with the color of your choice in the image.
Anti-Aliasing	Modifies the appearance of lines to make jagged edges look smoother.

Constant Size	Captures images to a scale of 1:1, no matter the resolution.
Quality	Sets the quality of the output image. Quality can be set to: • Low (screen) - quality matches the screen resolution. • Medium • Highest • Custom - Image pixel and print size can be customized by clicking **More**.
Monochrome Filter	For black and white images, you can set the Monochrome filter to: • Dither - density of dots based on darkness of color. • Threshold- Solid black or white look to image.

Wireframe Options

Select the *Wireframe Options* tab, as shown in Figure 8–10, to customize options specific to vector images. The options in the *Wireframe* tab are described in the table below.

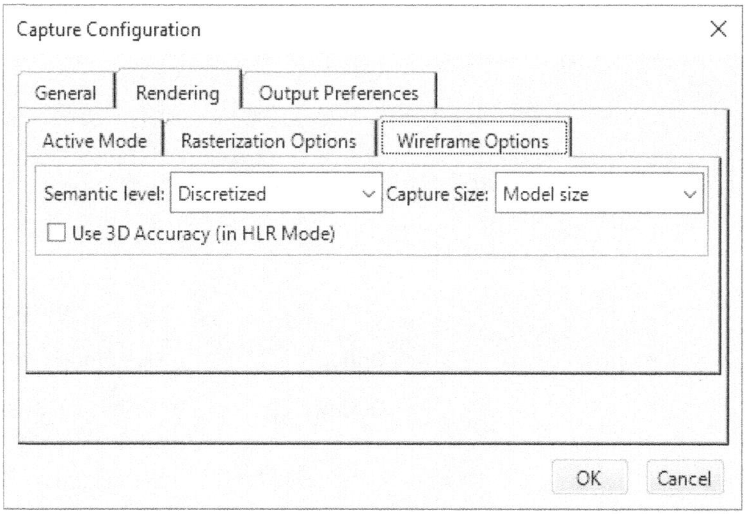

Figure 8–10

Option	Description
Semantic Level	Selects the Rendering mode, which can be: • Discretized • Low • Polyline • Polyline and Conic • Polyline and Spline
Capture Size	The image of the model can be saved as: • Model size • Display size
Use 3D Accuracy (in HLR Mode)	Use 3D Accuracy when the display is in HLR Mode.

Output Preferences Tab

Select the *Output Preferences* tab, as shown in Figure 8–11, to customize options specific to the completed image, and what the end result will be used for. The options in the *Output Preference* tab are described in the table below.

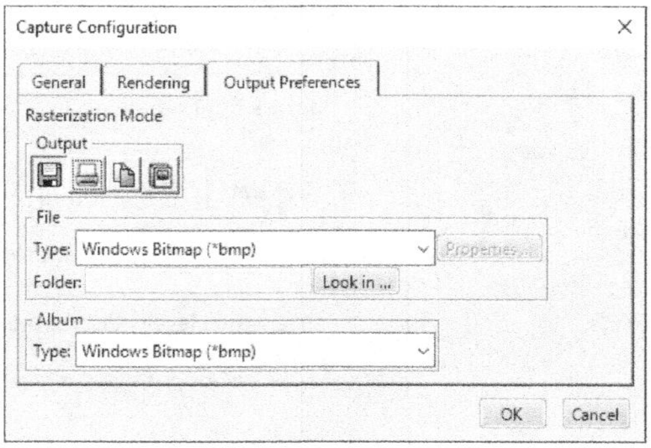

Figure 8–11

Option	Description
Output	Defines the default options for what to do with the image if *Display Preview* is turned off. Any and all of the (Save), (Print), (Copy), and (Album) selections can be used.
File	Defines what type of image will be output if a file is being saved. (.bmp, .jpg, .png, etc...)
Album	Defines preferences for storing the images captured to an album.

Step 1 - Capture the image.

To capture the image, click the  (Capture) icon. If *Full Screen* or *Full Tab* were selected for the Capture mode, then no other input is required. However, if *Screen Area* or *Tab Area* were selected for the Capture mode, then a section will need to be defined for the Capture area. Click on the screen to open the selection box. While holding the left mouse button, drag the cursor to create the selection area. Release the left mouse button to complete the selection box, as shown in Figure 8–12.

Selection box can be resized by dragging the border of the box.

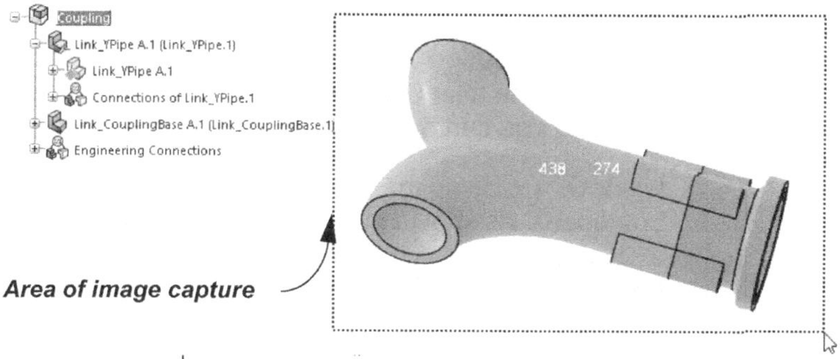

Figure 8–12

If Display was turned on in the Capture configuration options, the Capture Preview dialog box opens displaying the captured image, as shown in Figure 8–13. If not, whatever output options where selected will automatically executed.

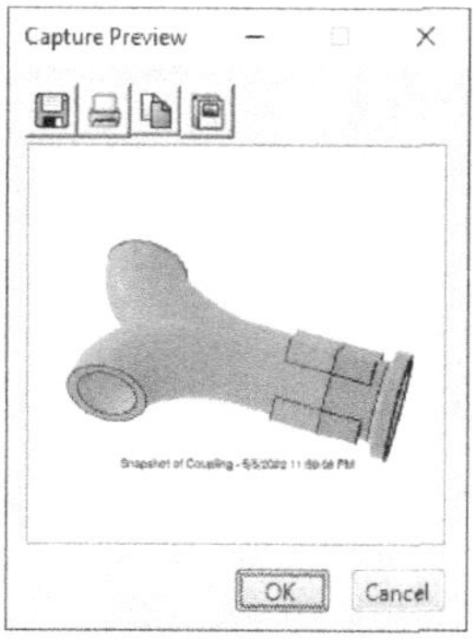

Figure 8–13

Step 2 - Define the output of the image.

You can also open the album by selecting (Album) from the tools section of the Action Bar.

A number of options are available for the output of the image in the Capture Preview dialog box. These options are described as follows:

Icon	Option	Description
	Save As	Saves the capture to the hard drive.
	Print	Opens the Print dialog box to print the image.
	Copy	Copies the image to the clipboard where it can be pasted into another Windows application.
	Album	Stores the image in the album.

Album

The album is used to store images, which are stored on your system in the folder defined by the CATTemp environment variable. You can open the album from the Capture Preview window by clicking the (Open Album) icon. The Album dialog box opens, as shown in Figure 8–14. The options that are available in the dialog box and in the shortcut menu are described in the table below.

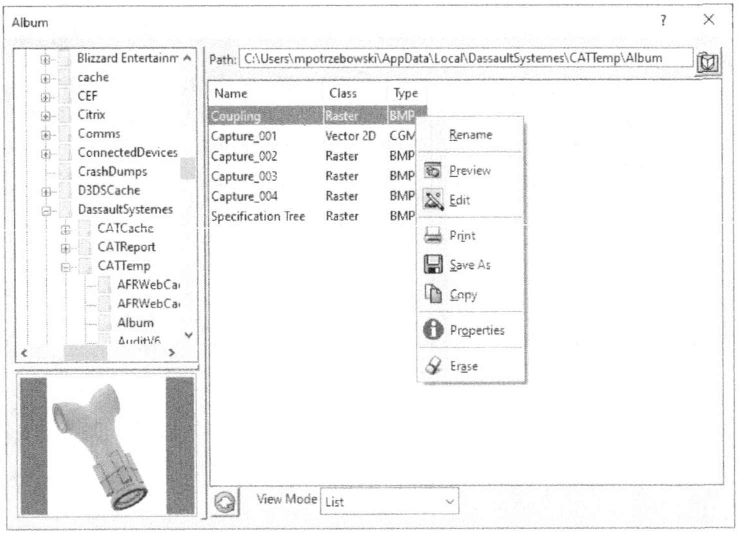

Figure 8–14

Icon	Description
	Changes the file path to the album folder.
	Refreshes the list of files stored in the current Album folder.
	Saves the selected image under another name or in another format.
	Opens the Print dialog box to print the image.
	Opens the selected image in the Print Preview dialog box. Use <Ctrl> to select more than one image to print preview at a time. All images are placed on the same sheet for printing.
	Copies the image to the clipboard where it can be pasted into another Windows application.
	Removes the selected image from the album.
	Opens the Image Information Panel for the selected image.
	Opens the Image Editor panel to modify the image. Not available for vector images.
Rename	Enables you to rename the image.

8.2 Printing Images

Once you have completed and saved your image(s), you can print them.

General Steps

Use the following general steps to print a document:

1. Activate the Print tool.
2. Select the printer.
3. Configure the layout.
4. Print the document.

Step 1 - Activate the Print tool.

Select (Print) or select (Share) **>Print** or **Ctrl+P** to open the Print dialog box shown in Figure 8–15.

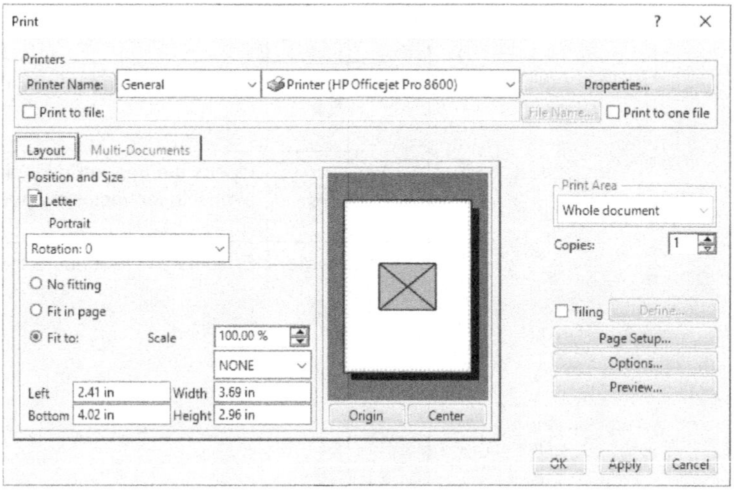

Figure 8–15

Step 2 - Select the printer.

Images can be sent to any printer set up in Windows, or saved to a .PRN file.

Printer

To print to a printer, select it in the *Printer* drop-down list. If required, the properties of the printer can be modified by clicking **Properties**.

File

Prints can be saved to a .PRN file by selecting the **Print To File** option. Click **File Name** to create a print file to which to save the document. Using the Print to File dialog box, navigate to the directory to which you want to save the print, and enter a name for the print in the *File Name* field, as shown in Figure 8–16.

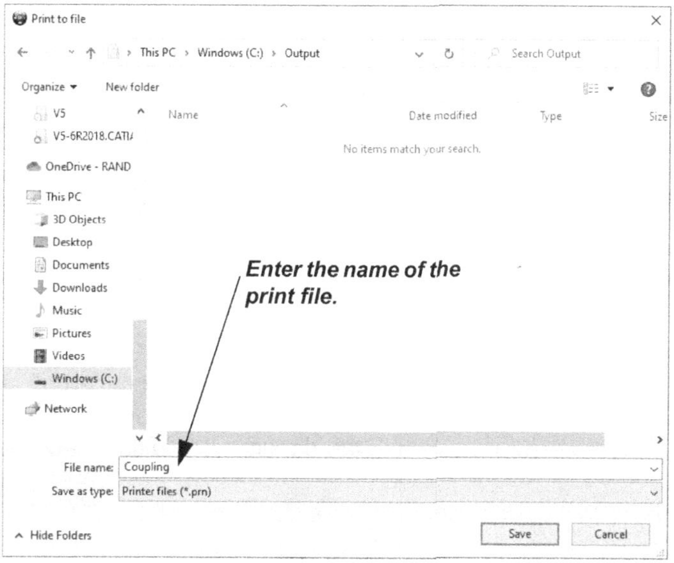

Figure 8–16

Click **Save** to return to the Print dialog box. The *Print to File* field is populated with the path and filename, as shown in Figure 8–17.

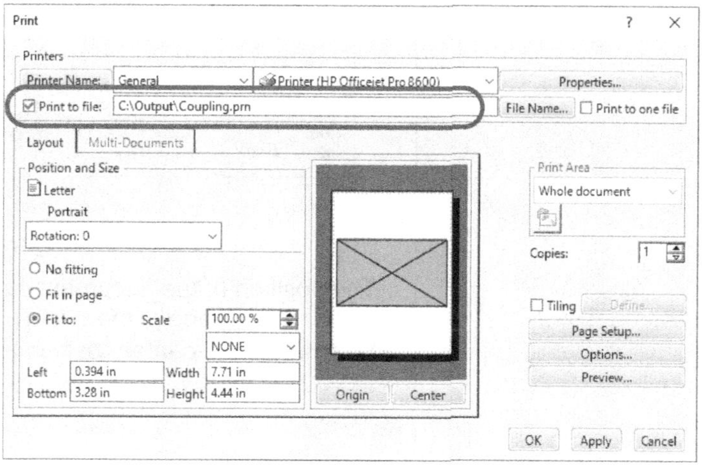

Figure 8–17

Step 3 - Configure the layout.

The layout of the print can be customized to suit your requirements.

Position and Size

The preview window of the Print dialog box indicates how the print displays on the page. If the current position is not correct, you can change it using a number of options.

Documents can be rotated on the sheet using the *Rotation* drop-down list. To change the scale of the document, use the fitting options **Fit in Page** and **Fit to**.

The **Fit in Page** option scales the document to fit the page based on the selected rotation and also centers the document on the page.

Fitting can be customized by selecting **Fit to**, as shown in Figure 8–18. This option enables you to customize the scale of the document and its location on the page.

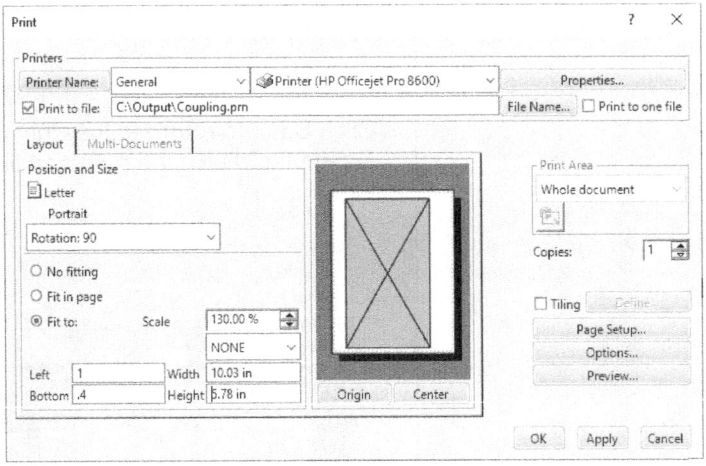

Figure 8–18

The position of the document can also be changed from the center of the page to the origin by clicking **Origin**. An example of both origin and center position is shown in Figure 8–19.

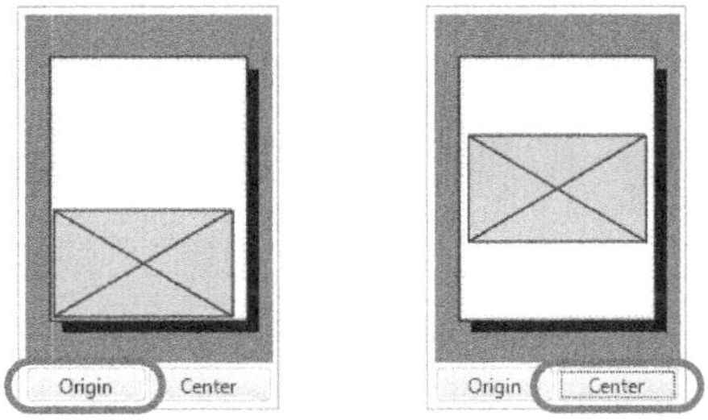

Figure 8–19

You might need to change the paper size to fit the document.

Select the **No Fitting** option to scale the document to a 1:1 scale. Click **Page Setup** to select a new page size, as shown in Figure 8–20.

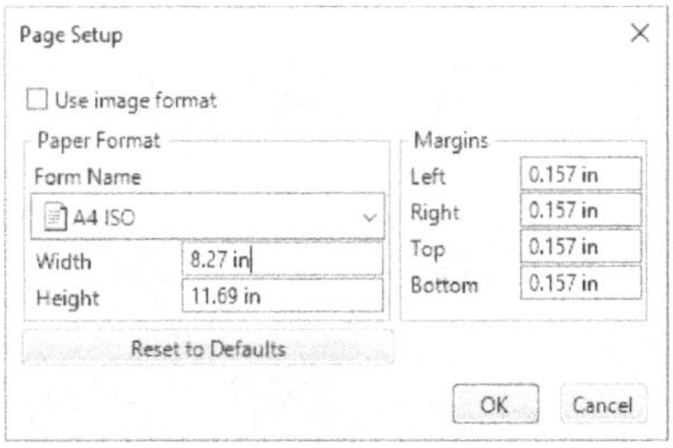

Figure 8–20

Print Area

By default, the **Whole Document** option is selected in the Print Area section. The **Display** option enables you to change what displays on the screen. The **Selection** option enables you to define the area of the document that you want to print. To define the print area, click the icon, left-click in the document to start the box and while holding the left mouse button, drag the cursor. Release the left mouse button to finish, as shown in Figure 8–21.

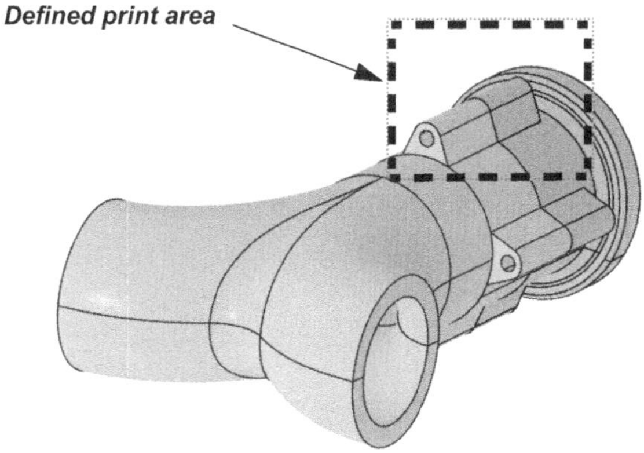

Figure 8–21

Options

Additional options for the print can be configured by clicking **Options** to open the Options dialog box, as shown in Figure 8–22. Using this dialog box, you can adjust the image's color output, add banners and company logos, and customize its quality.

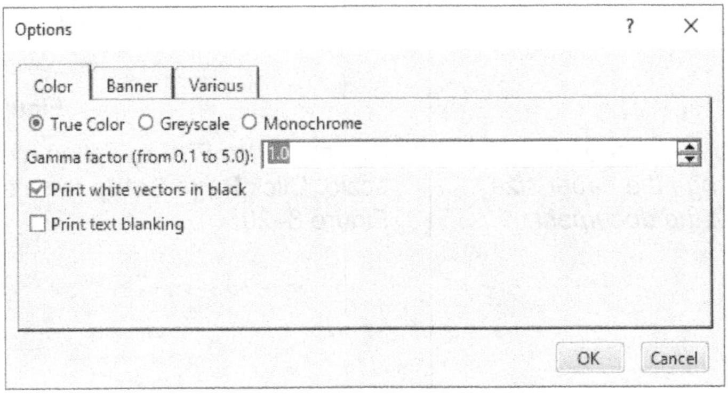

Figure 8–22

Step 4 - Print the document.

Click **OK** to print the image. It is printed to the selected printer with the customized settings.

Practice 8a

Capturing Images-Needs updating

Practice Objectives

- Set up an image capture.
- Capture an image.
- Save an image to an album.
- Copy an image to other documents.

In this practice, you will take screen shots of annotation views, which will be used to document your findings. You will save these images to the album and import them into other documents.

Task 1 - Open the assembly.

1. Import and **Bore Device Complete.3dxml**, then open ###_Bore Device Review. The assembly displays, as shown in Figure 8–23.

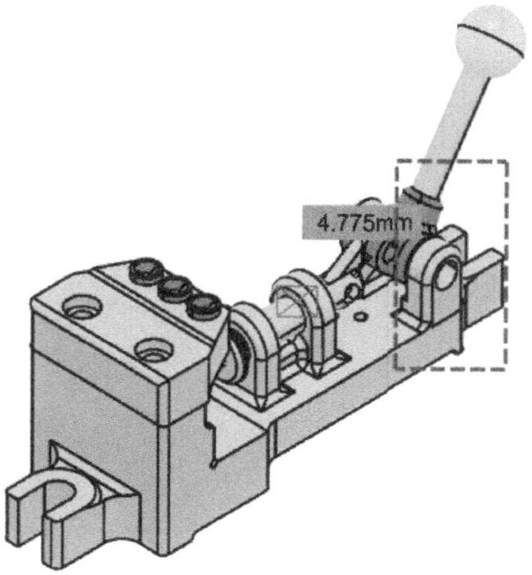

Figure 8–23

2. Ensure that the Design Review app is active.

Task 2 - Capture an image.

1. Within the *Tools* section of the Action Bar, select the (Expand) arrow then select (Capture) to open the Capture dialog box.

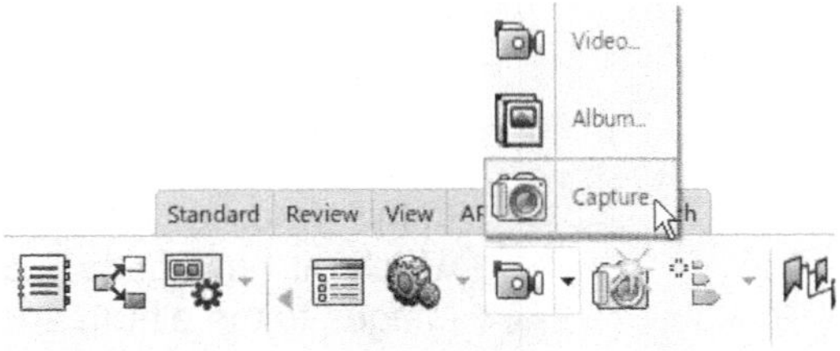

Figure 8–24

2. Select the (Expand) arrow next to Capture and select Full Tab.

3. Click the (Configuration) icon and the Capture Configuration window will display.

4. In the *Rendering* tab, in the *Active Mode* sub tab, ensure that **Rasterization** is selected, as shown in Figure 8–25.

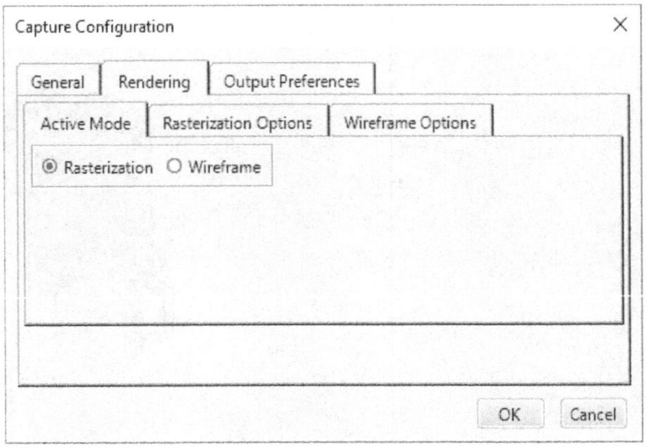

Figure 8–25

5. Select **OK** to close the Configuration window.

6. From the left side of the screen, select the (Tree) tab so that the tree view is displayed and will be part of the image capture.

Your preview might not look exactly like the preview shown.

7. From the tree, in the *Slides* node, double-click on the **Interference Comments** slide so that the model changes to show the notes associated to that slide.

8. Click the (Capture) icon to capture the image. A snapshot of the screen is taken and displayed in the Capture Preview window, as shown in Figure 8–26.

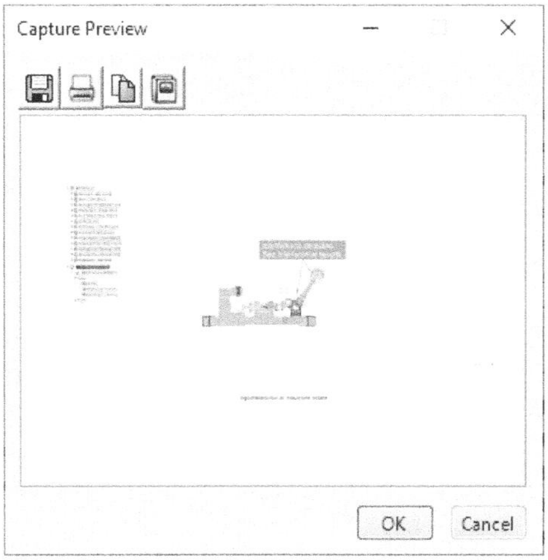

Figure 8–26

This image does not meet the requirements. The background should not have a color, and the robot and specification tree should not be in the view.

9. Click **Cancel** to close the image capture window.

Task 3 - Change the options for the image.

1. Click the (Configuration) icon to change the options of the capture.
2. In the *General* tab, select the **Capture Only Geometry** option to ensure that the specification tree and robot do not display in the image. Select the **Capture White in black** option to ensure that any white geometry displays when the background is changed to white.
3. In the *Rendering* tab, in the *Rasterization Options* sub tab, set the Background color to **White**.
4. Click **OK** to return to the Capture Configuration dialog box.
5. Click the (Capture) icon to recapture the image. The Preview Window displays the new capture, as shown in Figure 8–27.

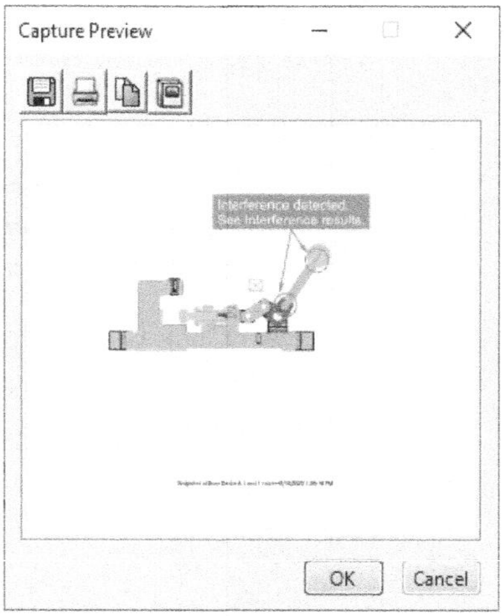

Figure 8–27

Task 4 - Save the image.

1. Click (Save As) in the Capture Preview window to save the file.
2. Enter **Interference Comments** in the *File Name* field and save the file to the Managers and Reviewers training files directory. Leave the file format as **Windows Bitmap**.

3. Click **Save** to save the file to the hard drive.

4. In the Capture Preview window, click the (Album) icon to save the image to the album.

5. Click **Cancel** to exit the preview window and return to the Capture dialog box.

Task 5 - Create another image.

1. From the tree, in the *Slides* node, double-click on the **Band Analysis Comments** slide so that the model changes to show the notes associated to that slide.

2. Click the (Capture) icon to capture the image and the Capture Preview windows displays, as shown in Figure 8–28.

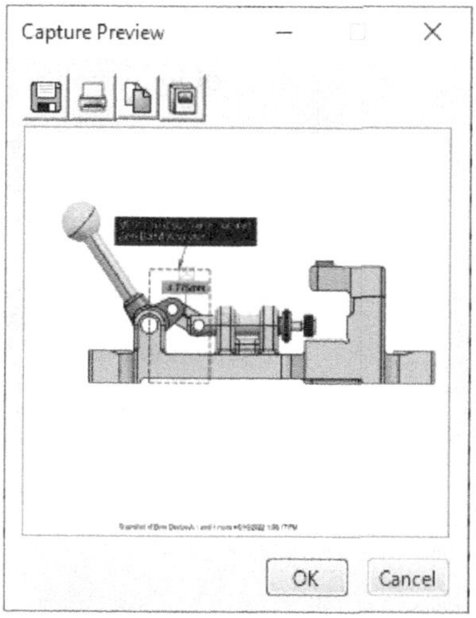

Figure 8–28

In this capture, only the area around the rectangle, including the text, is required. Also the white background around the text should stay white.

3. Click **Cancel** to close the capture.

Task 6 - Change the configuration and select the area for capture.

1. Select (Configuration) icon to change the options of the capture.
2. In the *General* tab, uncheck the box next to **Capture white in Black.**
3. Select **OK** to close the Capture Configuration Window.
4. In the Capture dialog box, select the (Expand) arrow next to Capture and select Tab Area to select the area to be captured.
5. Click the (Capture) icon to begin the Capture process, the cursor will change to a 70 icon to let you select the area of the Capture.
6. Left-click in the top left corner of the box and drag the cursor to the bottom right of the box. Release the left mouse button to create the selection box, as shown in Figure 8–29.

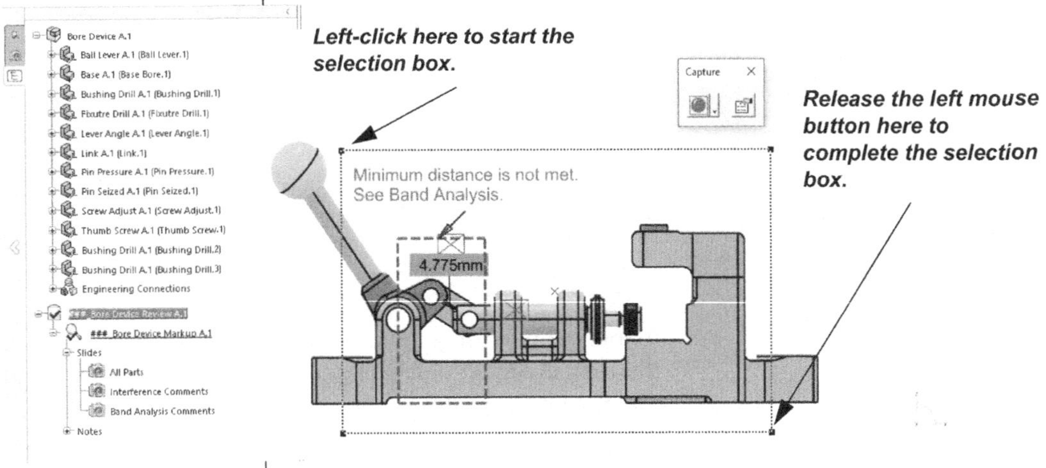

Figure 8–29

7. After releasing the left mouse button, the Capture Preview window displays the results, as shown in Figure 8–30.

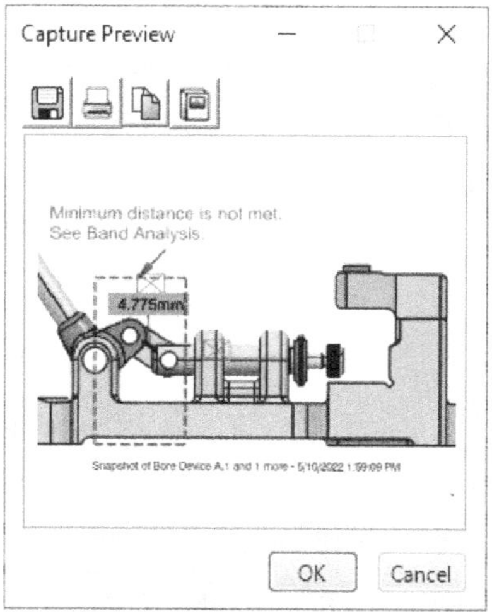

Figure 8–30

Note: If the selection area is wrong, by selecting **Cancel**, the box outline can be changed by dragging the corners. A new updated Capture Preview window will display.

Task 7 - Copy an image and save it to an album.

1. Click  (Copy) to copy the image to the clipboard.
2. Open Windows Paint by selecting **Start>Run...** in Windows.
3. Enter **mspaint** in the *Open* field of the Run dialog box, as shown in Figure 8–31.

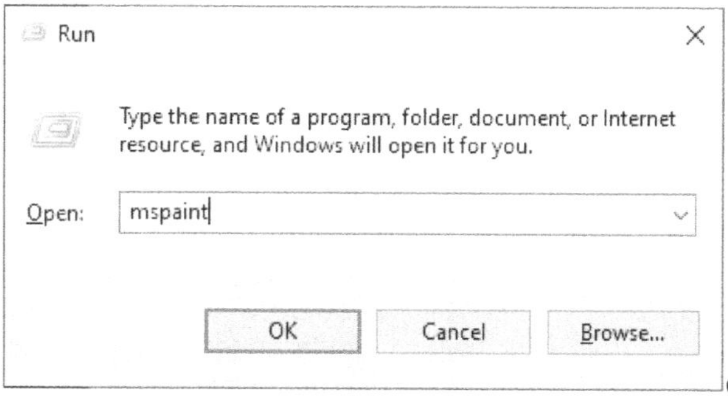

Figure 8–31

4. Click **OK** and the MS Paint application opens.

5. Select Paste (Paste) in the Paint application. The copied image displays, as shown in Figure 8–32. This technique can be used to copy images to most Windows applications.

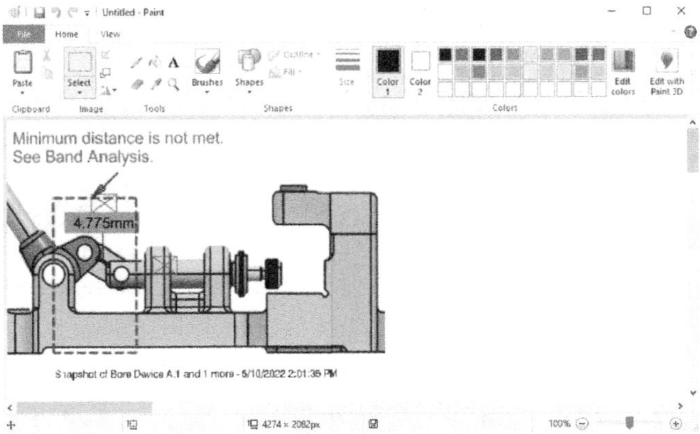

Figure 8–32

6. Close the Paint application. Do not save the image.

7. Click the (Album) icon in the Capture Preview Window to save the image to the album.

8. Cancel the Preview to return to the Capture dialog box.

Task 8 - Take a capture in Wireframe mode.

1. Select (Configuration) icon to change the options of the capture.

2. In the *Rendering* tab, in the *Active Mode* sub tab, select the **Wireframe** option.

3. Click the (Vector Mode) icon to change to Vector mode.

4. Click the (Capture) icon to start the capture process. Select a similar area to the one used in Task 6. Note the difference between the outputs of Wireframe and Rasterization modes.

5. Save the Wireframe image to the album and close the Capture Preview window.

6. Close the Capture window.

Task 9 - View the album.

1. From the *Tools* section of the Action Bar, expand the arrow next to Capture and click the (Album) icon. The Album dialog box opens as shown in Figure 8–33.

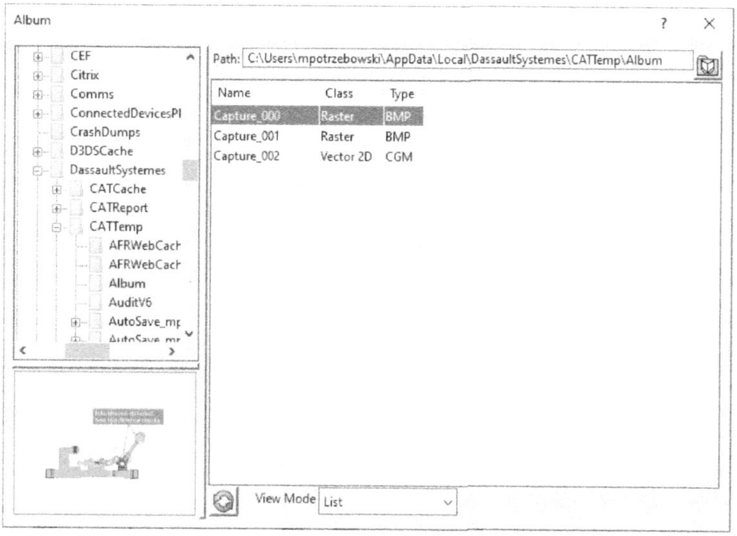

Figure 8–33

2. Right-click on the first image in the album and click the (Properties) icon. View the information obtained from the Properties dialog box. It enables you to determine information such as the size, type, and location of the captured files.
3. Click **OK** to close the dialog box.
4. Right-click on the Vector2D image in the Album. The (Edit) icon is grayed out. Vector images cannot be edited from the Image Editor.
5. Right-click the Vector2D image and click the (Erase) icon.
6. Click **Yes** to confirm the erase, and the Vector2D image is removed from the album. Removing an image from the album also removes it from the hard drive.
7. Click × to close the Album dialog box.
8. Close the file.

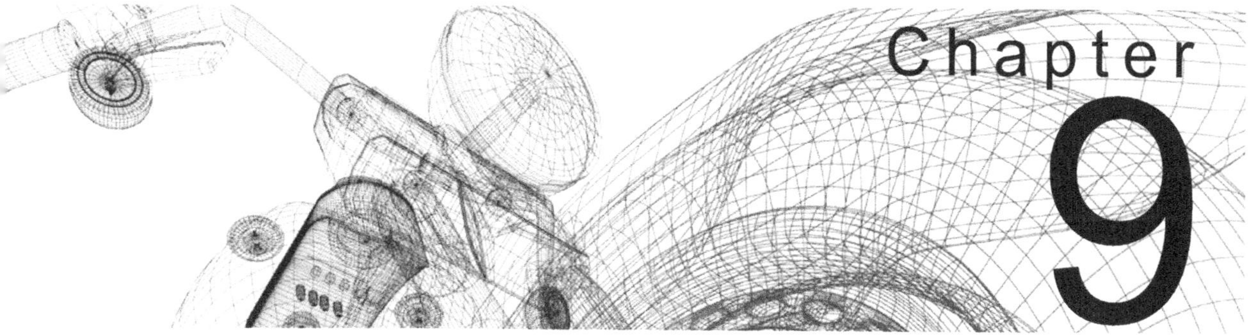

Chapter 9

Drafting App

This chapter introduces the Drafting app by outlining the drawing creation process. You learn how to create, modify, and manipulate drawing views. Once drawing views are placed on a drawing sheet, you must add dimensions and notes to communicate manufacturing information.

Learning Objectives in This Chapter

- Understand the steps required to create a drawing.
- Review the Drafting app interface.
- Add views and create a drawing frame and title block.
- Understand the view orientation compass.
- Review the available view properties.
- Learn how to manipulate views.
- Manually create dimensions and move dimensions.
- Learn how to update a drawing when geometry changes.

9.1 Creating a New Drawing

All drafting view geometry and dimension information comes from the 3D model. The 3D model must be open to create a drawing.

Open the model that is to be included in the new drawing as shown in Figure 9–1.

Figure 9–1

With the 3D Part or the Product Level active, right-click on the 3D Part level in the specification tree and select **Insert > Drawing** as shown in Figure 9–2.

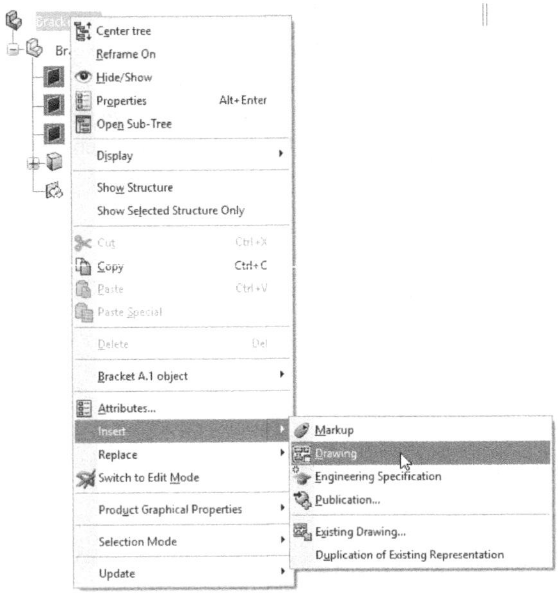

Figure 9–2

Enter the name for the new drawing in the *Drawing* tab in the Drawing/Physical Representation dialog box as shown in Figure 9–3.

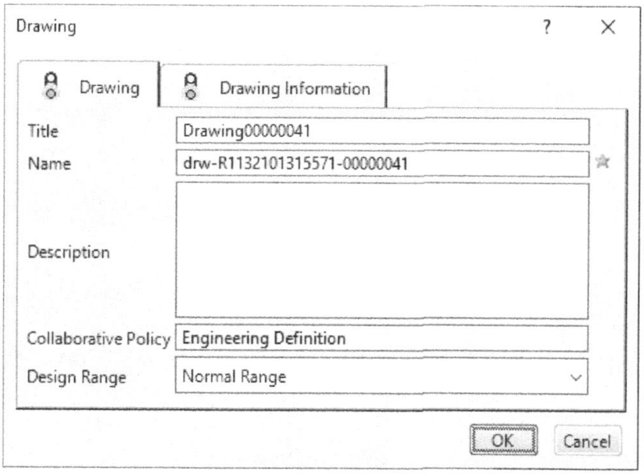

Figure 9–3

Select the *Drawing Information* tab and select the drafting **Standard** and **Sheet Style** options as shown in Figure 9–4.

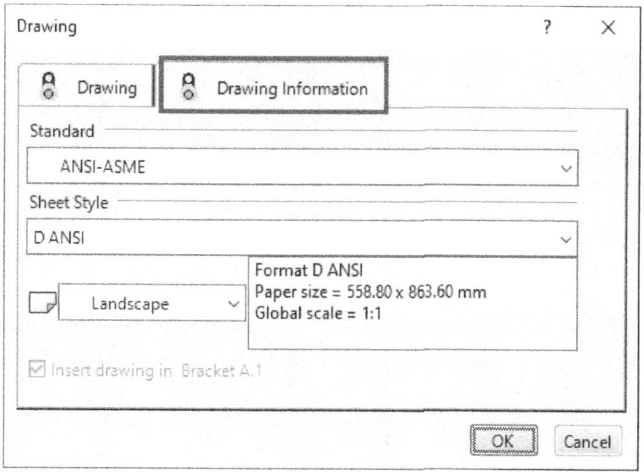

Figure 9–4

Click **OK** to begin with an empty drawing. The Drawing displays in the specification tree as shown in Figure 9–5. Double-click on the Drawing entity in the specification tree to open the drawing.

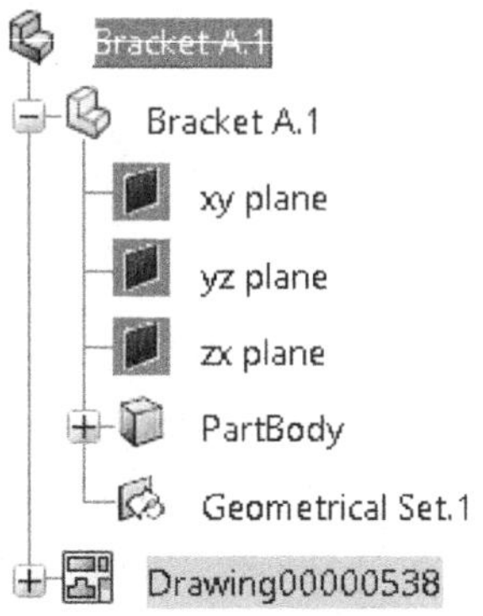

Figure 9–5

9.2 Drafting App Interface

The user interface of the Drafting app is shown in Figure 9–6.

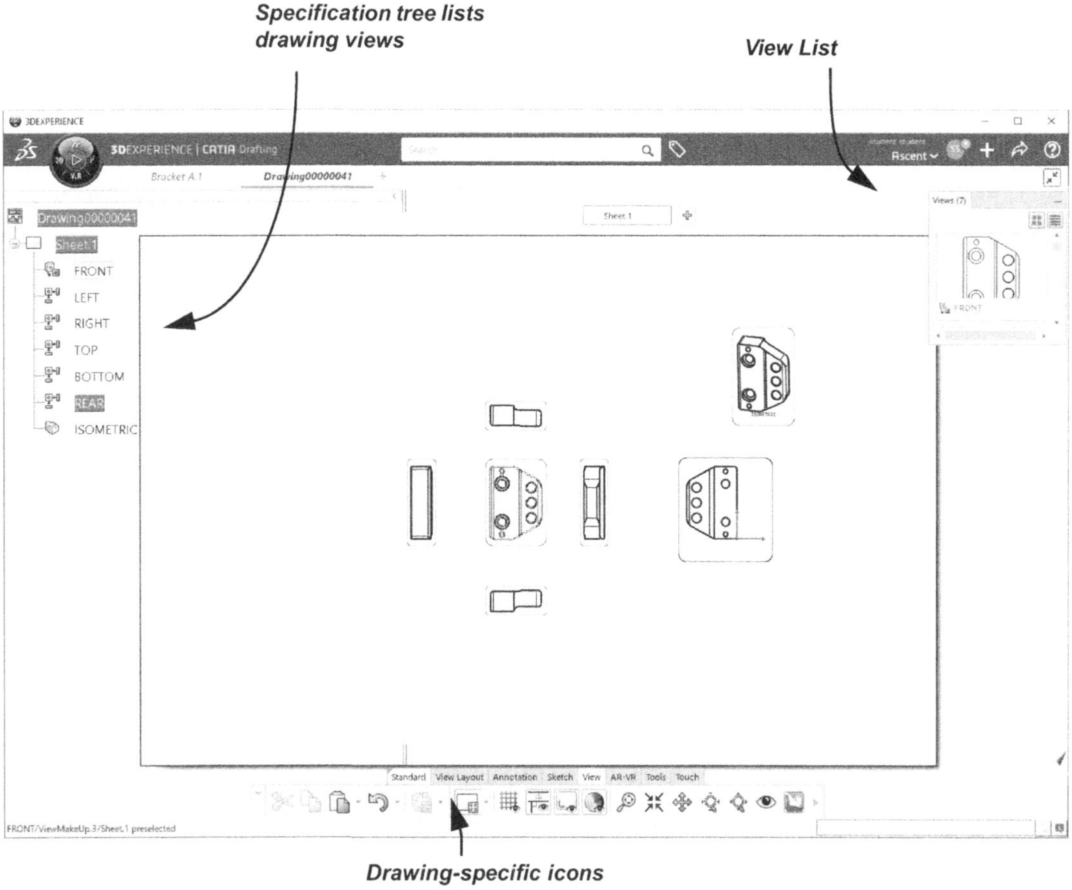

Figure 9–6

9.3 Creating Drawing Frame and Title Block

Title Block

You can assign titles to identify the drawings. Use the following steps to insert a title block:

1. In the *View Layout* section of the Action Bar, click (Page Layout). The Page Layout dialog box opens as shown in Figure 9–7, where you can select the desired Frame, Title Block, and Revision Table.

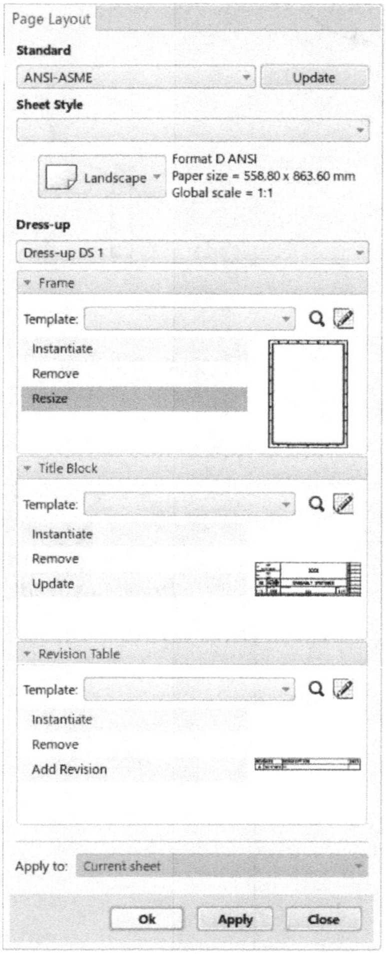

Figure 9–7

2. Click **OK** or **Apply**.

9.4 Adding Views

Views are added to the drawing using the icons in the *View Layout* section of the Action Bar, as shown in Figure 9–8.

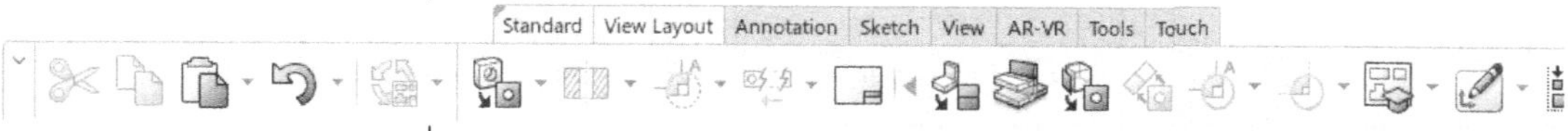

Figure 9–8

The placement and orientation of the first drawing view requires the selection of a reference from the 3D model. To facilitate this selection, you can click between tabs to move from the drawing to part and back, as shown in Figure 9–9.

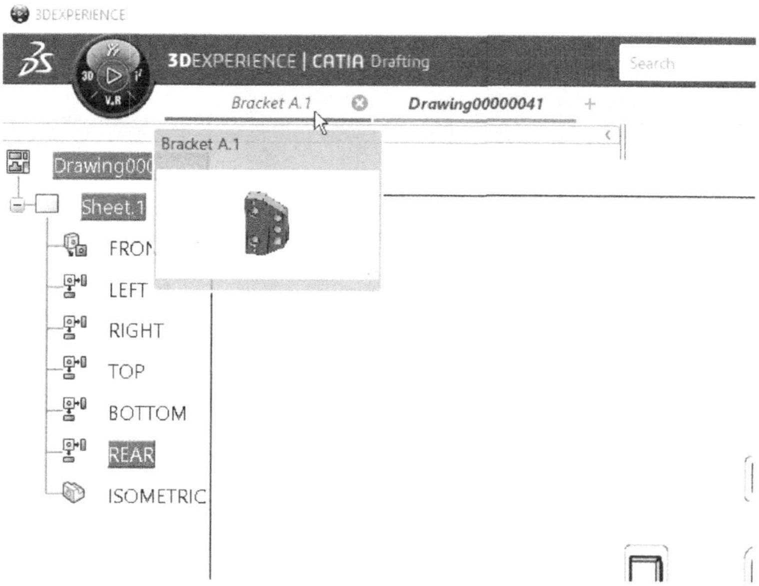

Figure 9–9

The first drawing view can be one of the view types listed in the table below. Select the appropriate icon in the Projections toolbar to initiate the creation of the first view.

View Type	Description
 (Front View)	The front view is also known as the main view. You can use the view compass to orient it. 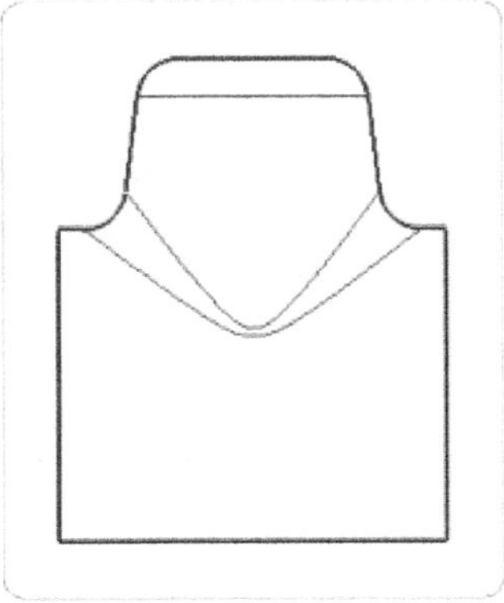
 (Isometric)	An isometric view is used as a reference view, and is typically set at a smaller scale. A reference surface must be selected from the 3D model. You can use the view compass to orient this view. 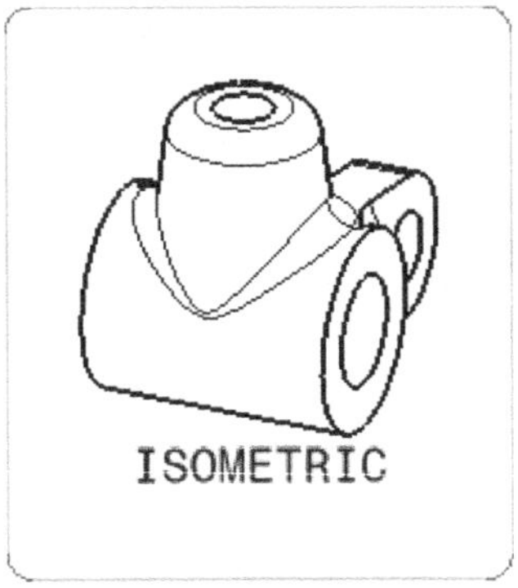

Once a view icon has been clicked, switch to the model window and select a planar surface, face, or reference plane. As you move your cursor over each surface, a preview displays to help you select the proper surface, as shown in Figure 9–10.

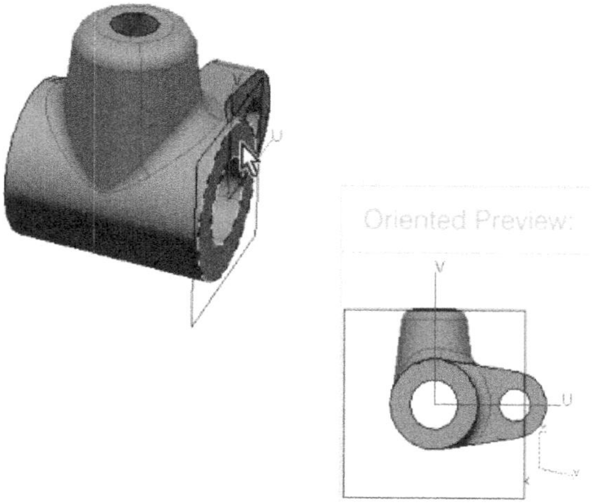

Figure 9–10

Once a reference surface is selected on the 3D model, the view orientation compass displays in the top right corner of the display, as shown in Figure 9–11.

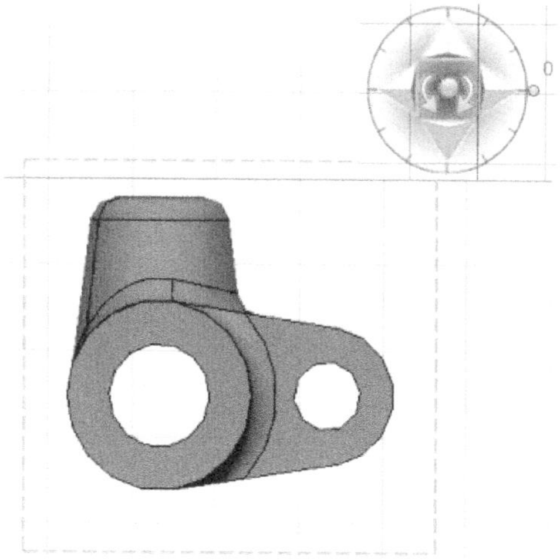

Figure 9–11

View Orientation Compass

The view orientation compass enables you to rotate and flip the front view until the correct orientation displays. The view compass functionality is shown in Figure 9–12.

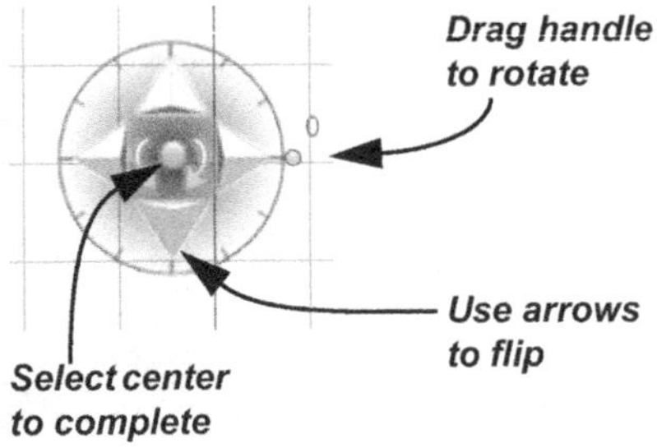

Figure 9–12

Use the right-click menu to change the compass properties, as shown in Figure 9–13 (right-click over the rotate handle).

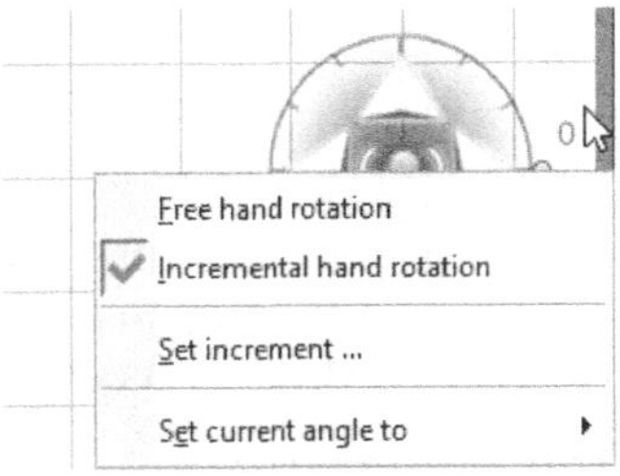

Figure 9–13

When you reach the required view orientation, select the center of the compass or select the active view to complete the view definition. The completed view definition is shown in Figure 9–14.

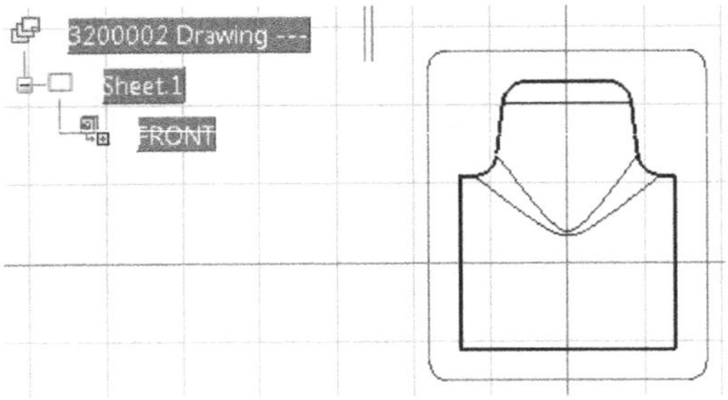

Figure 9–14

The view is added to the sheet in the drawing specification tree. The view displays on the drawing with a red border, indicating that it is the active view. When more than one view is present, a view can be activated by double-clicking on its border.

A variety of view types can be added to complete the drawing. Three of these view types are described in the table below.

View Type	Description
 (Projection)	Projects a view perpendicular from the front view. It creates views, such as top, right, left, and bottom and is placed by selecting a location on the screen. The system applies the proper label (name) based on its position relative to the front view. It maintains the same scale value as its parent view. 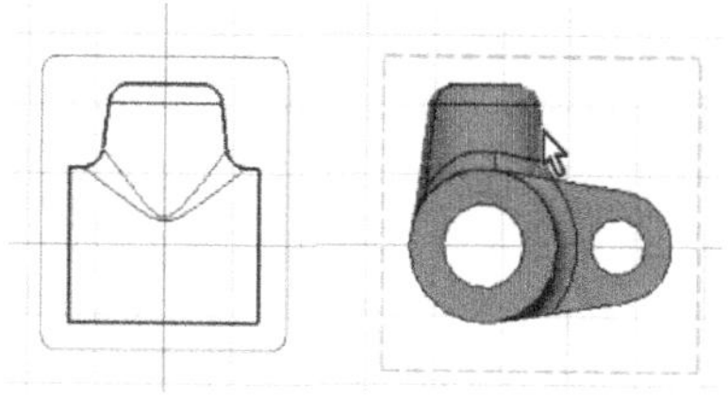
 (Quick Detailed View)	Creates a scaled view focusing on a specific area of an existing view. It is created by sketching a circle on an existing, active view that encloses the geometry to be represented. To complete the view, assign a name, boundary type, and note location. The system automatically assigns a label identifying the scale value and view name of the detailed view. Orientation of this view corresponds to its parent view. 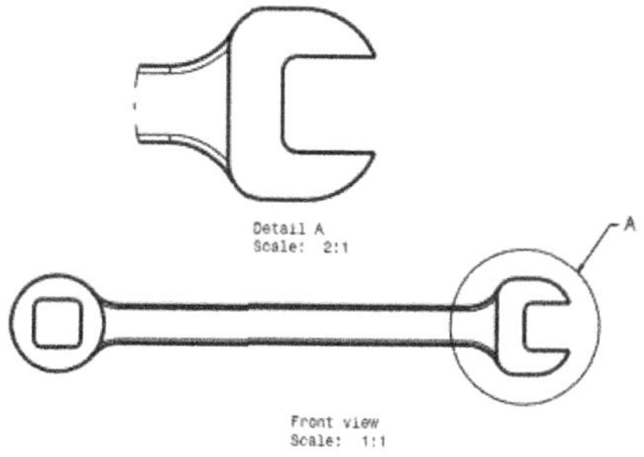

View Type	Description
(Offset Section View)	The offset section view creates a section that displays all of the edges that are behind the cutting plane. You can create this view as planar or as a sketched cutting plane. 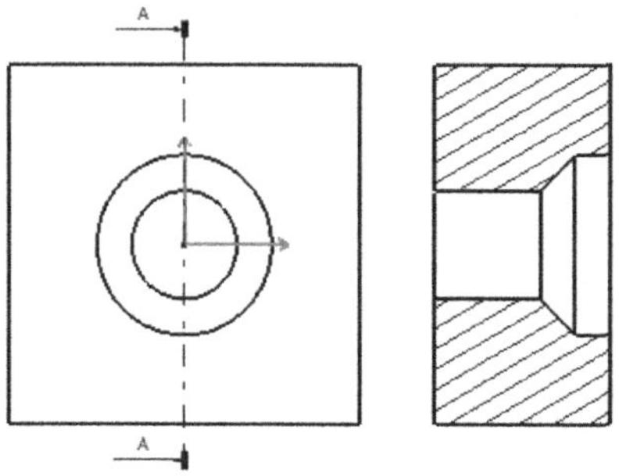 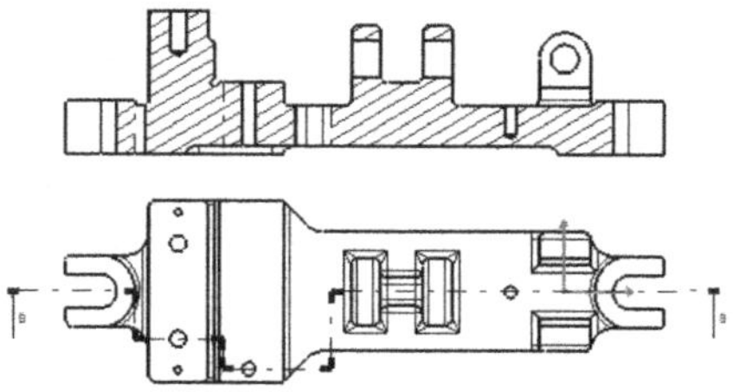

9.5 View Properties

View properties include scale and orientation, view name, frame display, hidden line display, and fillet display. The Properties dialog box is shown in Figure 9–15.

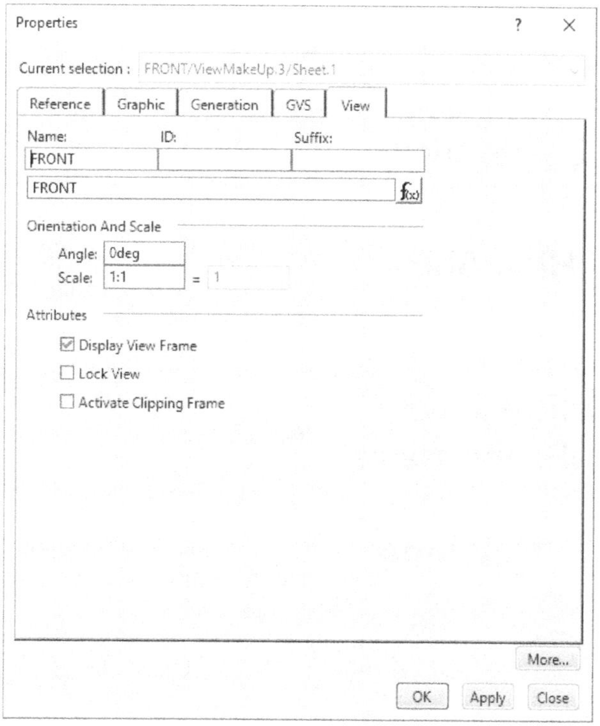

Figure 9–15

You can display your views in various ways, as shown in Figure 9–16.

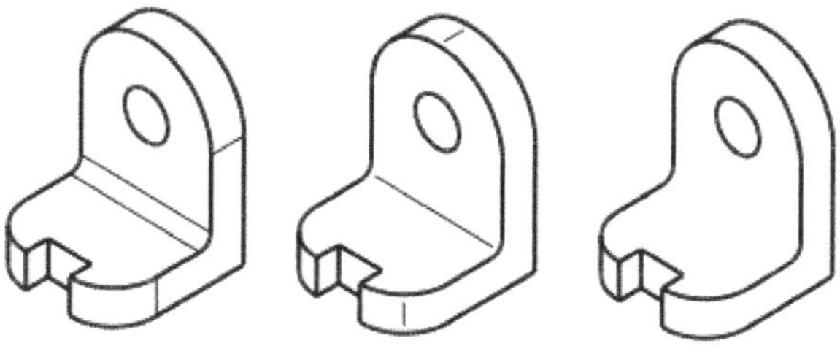

Figure 9–16

Moving Views

You can move a view within the same sheet or to another sheet. To move a view within the same sheet, select the dashed line frame of the view and drag it to the required location.

Standard windows shortcut keys, Cut (<Ctrl> + <X>) and Paste (<Ctrl> + <V>), can also be used.

To move a view to another sheet, cut and paste it from the display or in the specification tree.

Delete View

To delete a view, select the view from the display or in the specification tree, right-click and select **Delete**.

Hide/Show

You can hide a view to simplify the sheet. To hide a view, select the view from the display or specification tree, right-click and select **Hide/Show**.

Section Arrow Properties

To modify section arrows, select the arrows, right-click and select **Properties**.

Hatching

To modify section hatching, select the section view from the display, right-click and select **Properties**.

9.6 Manually Creating Dimensions

Use the **Dimensions** flyout in the Annotations toolbar, as shown in Figure 9–17, to manually create dimensions.

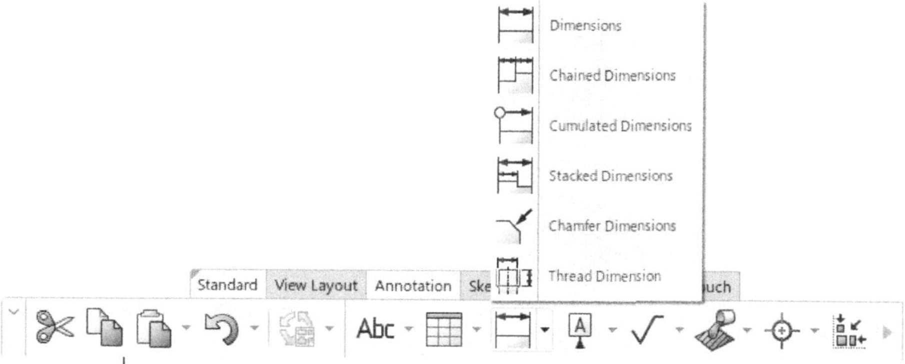

Figure 9–17

Use the following steps to manually create a dimension:

1. Click the icon that resembles the required dimension type.
2. Select entities as dimension references, as shown in Figure 9–18.

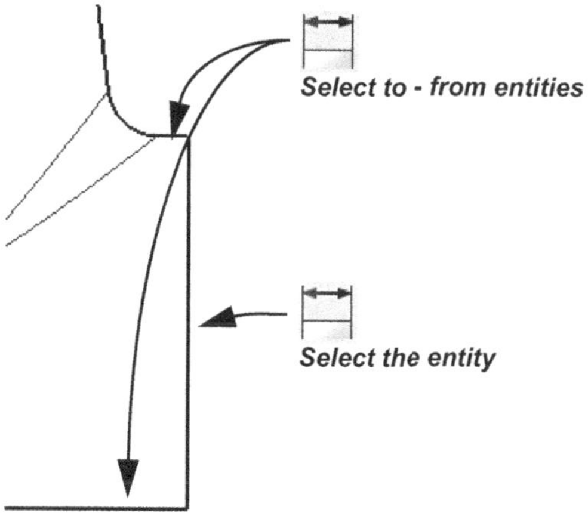

Figure 9–18

3. Place the dimension, as shown in Figure 9–19.

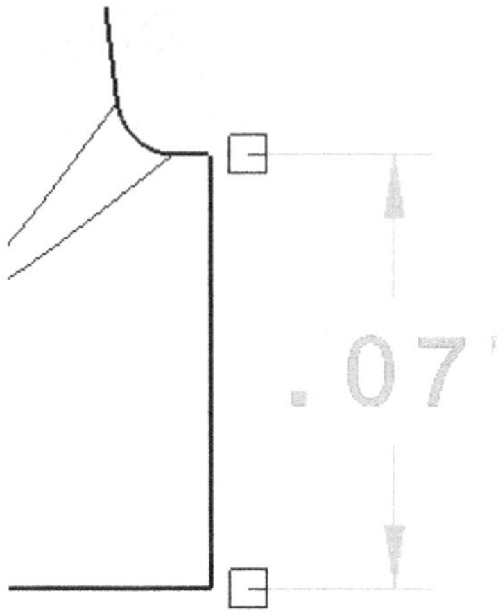

Figure 9–19

Moving Dimensions

You can move dimensions to clean up the display. To move a dimension, use one of the following methods:

- Click and drag on a handle to move both extension lines independently.
- Click and drag on a dimension to move it left, right, up, or down.
- Click on an arrow head to *flip* it.

These methods are shown in Figure 9–20.

Figure 9–20

9.7 Changed Geometry

Updating a Drawing

If a drawing has been created from a 3D model and the model geometry has changed, the drawing must be updated to reflect the changes.

To update the drawing, click (Update Current Sheet) or press <Ctrl> + <U>.

A grayed out indicates that the 3D model has not changed, and that the model does not need to be updated.

Links to 3D Models

If a drawing is open and the 3D model it references is not open, the drawing cannot be updated. To open the referenced model, right-click on a drawing view and select Open 3D data. The 3D Part/Product opens in a new window.

Practice 9a Create a Drawing

Practice Objectives

- Create a new drawing.
- Place views using the View Wizard.
- Manipulate the views in various ways.

In this practice, you will use a part to create a new drawing. The drawing will consist of two sheets and multiple views. One of the sheets displays as shown in Figure 9–21.

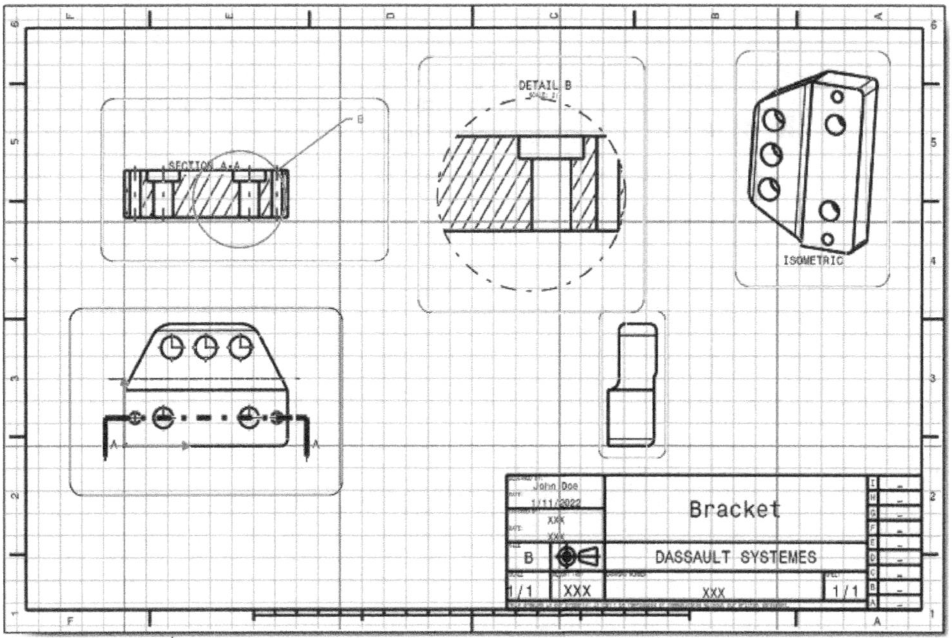

Figure 9–21

Task 1 - Import the part Bracket.

1. Import **Bracket.3dxml**.

2. Right-click on Bracket in the specification tree and select **Open**. The model displays as shown in Figure 9–22.

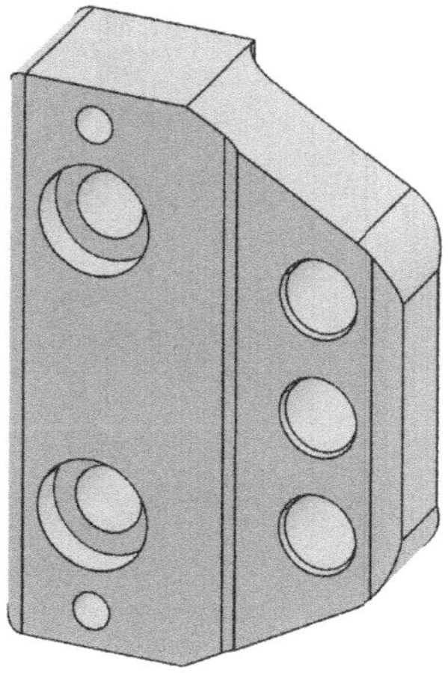

Figure 9–22

Task 2 - Insert a Drawing in the 3D Part.

1. Double-click on the 3D Part level of the specification tree. The specification tree should display as shown in Figure 9–23.

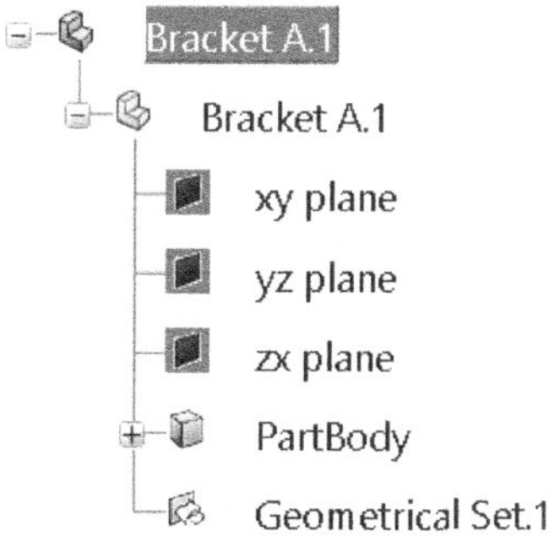

Figure 9–23

2. Right-click on the top line of the specification tree and browse to **Insert > Drawing** in the contextual menu as shown in Figure 9–24.

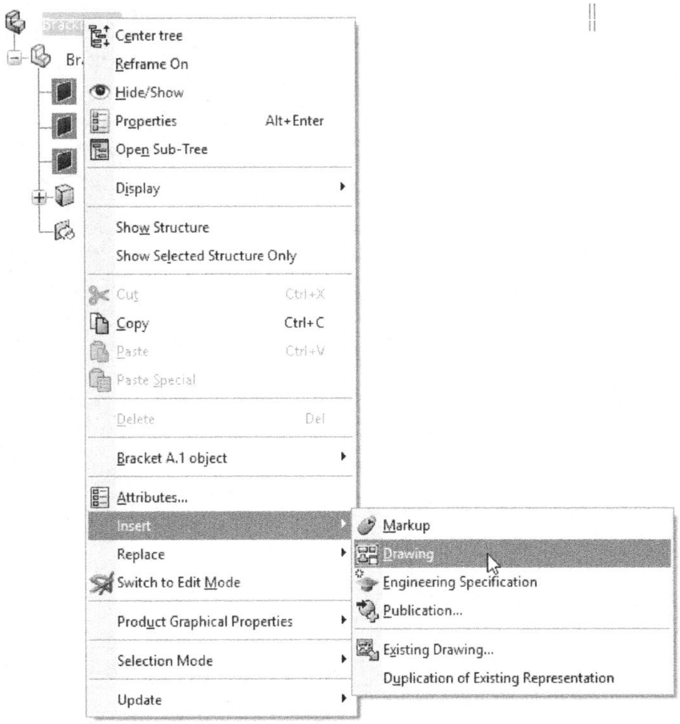

Figure 9–24

3. Enter the name ***Your_Initials*_Bracket** in the Drawing dialog box, as shown in Figure 9–25.

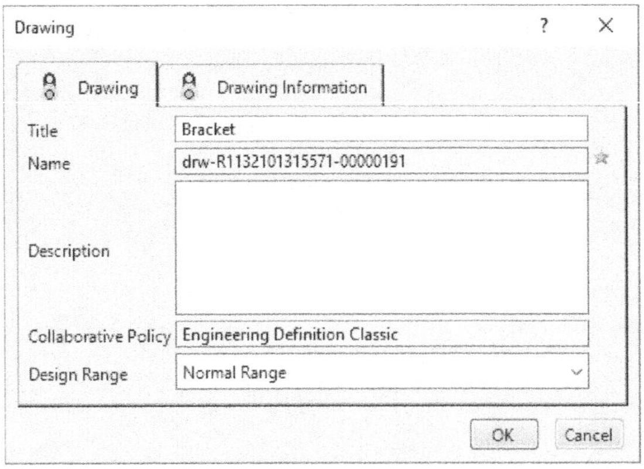

Figure 9–25

4. Select the *Drawing Information* tab.

5. Select the following options so the dialog box updates as shown in Figure 9–26:
    - Standard: **ANSI-ASME**
    - Format: **B ANSI**
    - Orientation: **Landscape**

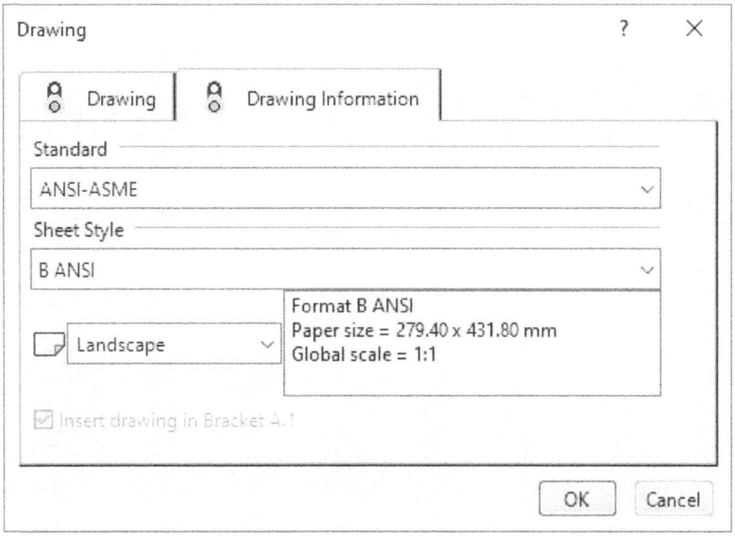

Figure 9–26

6. Click **OK** to finalize drawing creation.

Task 3 - Create a front view.

1. Double-click on the drawing name in the specification tree, to open the drawing.
2. In the *View Layout* section of the Action Bar, click (Front View).
3. Select the *Bracket* part tab. You must now orient the view by selecting a face from the model. Select anywhere in the **Bracket** window and hover over the faces of the model. An Orientation Preview window displays the resulting view orientation.

4. Turn the model and select the face shown in Figure 9–27. This surface is selected to face the front of the screen in the front view.

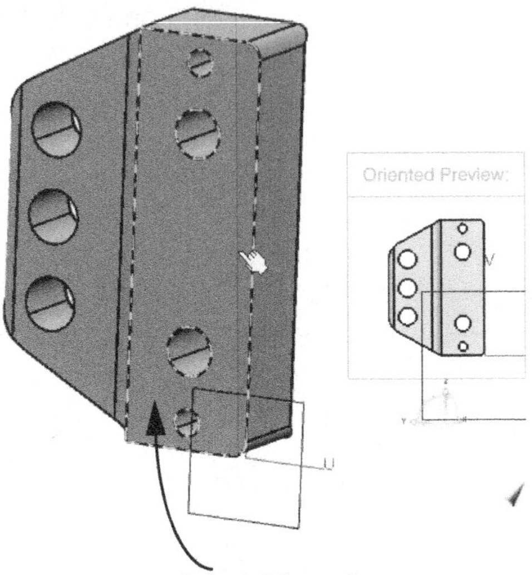

Figure 9–27

5. The display automatically toggles back to the drawing sheet. A compass displays in the top right corner of the display. Use the cursor to drag the green handle to the 270° location. The front view is oriented as shown in Figure 9–28.

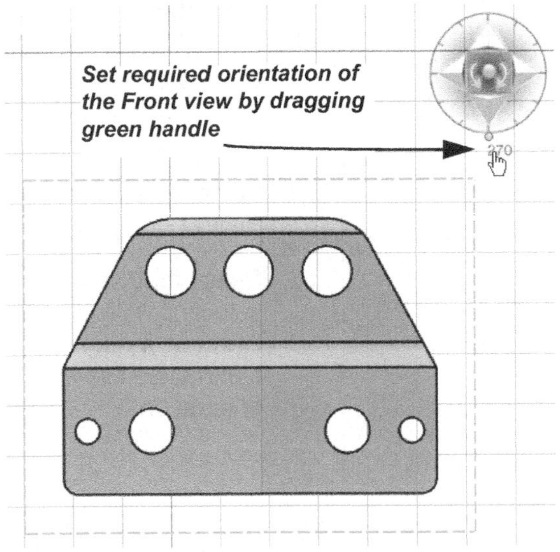

Figure 9–28

At any time the grid can be toggled on/off by selecting  *(Display Grid) icon in the View section of the Action Bar.*

6. Click anywhere in the drawing to complete the orientation. Maximize the drawing window. The drawing sheet is shown in Figure 9–29.

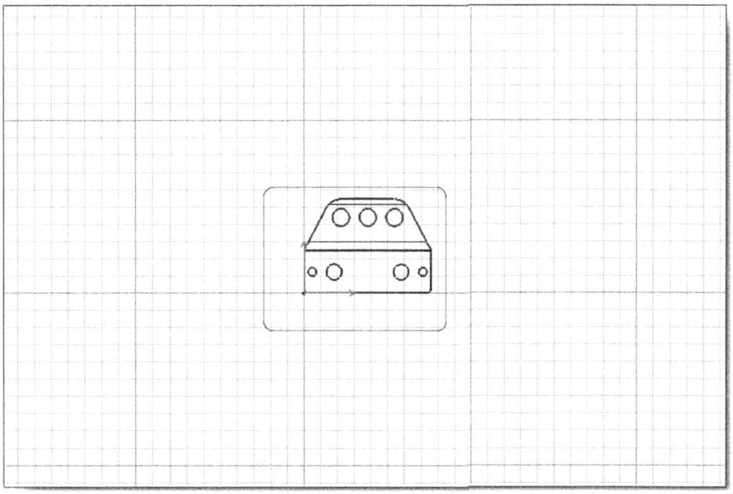

Figure 9–29

Task 4 - Create an isometric view.

1. In the *View Layout* section of the Action Bar, click  (Isometric) in the **Front View** flyout.
2. Activate the *Bracket* tab and select a face on the model. The system orients the Isometric view using the current model orientation. Therefore, the face selected is not important. The system places the view on the drawing and the orientation compass displays.

3. Select the dashed green border of the view and drag it to the top right corner of the drawing, as shown in Figure 9–30.

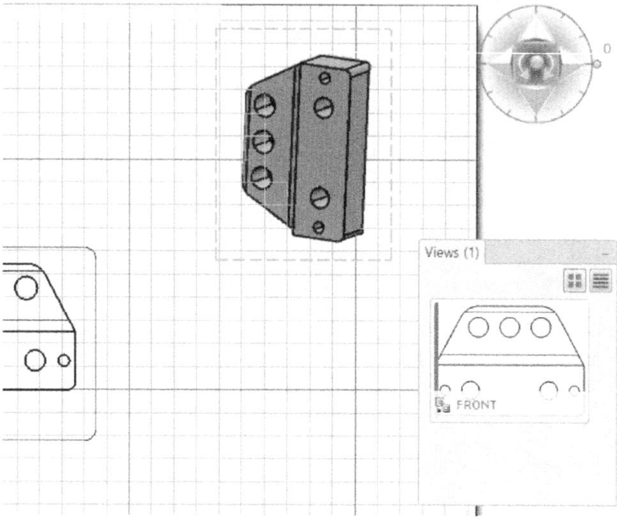

Figure 9–30

4. Select anywhere on the drawing to complete the creation of the view.

Design Considerations

The border of the front view is currently red, while the border of the isometric view is blue. The red border indicates that it is the active view. Any view operations are always performed on the active view. As well, the creation of a section or projection view will reference the active view. Double-click on the view border to activate a view.

Task 5 - Create a projection view.

In this task, you will project a view from the front view. The front view must be active.

1. Ensure that the front view is active.

2. Click  (Projection).

3. Position the cursor around the front view. Four possible projections can be created, as shown in Figure 9–31.

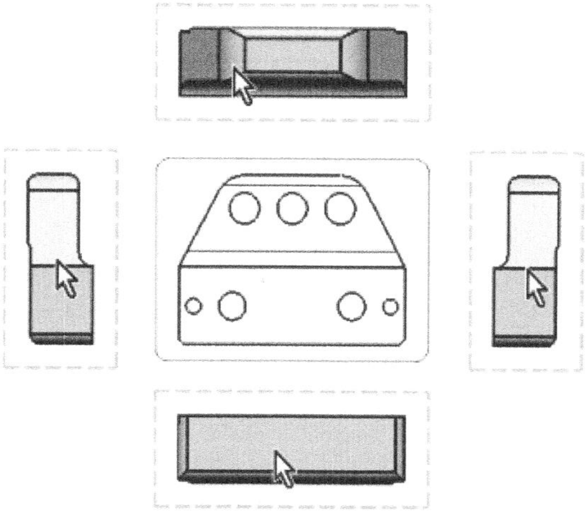

Figure 9–31

4. Create the projection to the right of the front view. The drawing view displays as shown in Figure 9–32.

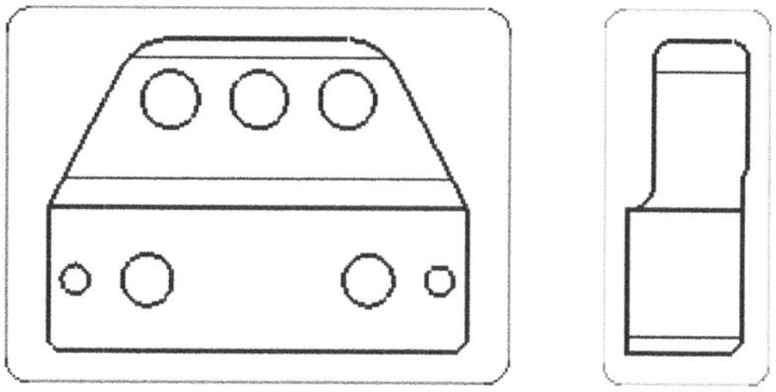

Figure 9–32

Task 6 - Move the views.

1. Select the view frame of the front view and drag it to the bottom left corner of the sheet.
2. Experiment by moving the right view. Move the Isometric view as well and note the differences between the linked and unlinked views.

Design Considerations

The projected right view is a child of the front view, so it maintains an aligned position with it. The isometric view can be moved independent of the front view.

Task 7 - Change the properties of a view.

1. Right-click on the FRONT view in the specification tree and select **Properties**.
2. Select **Center Line** and **Axis** in the *Dress-up* area in the *Generation* tab in the Properties dialog box, as shown in Figure 9–33.

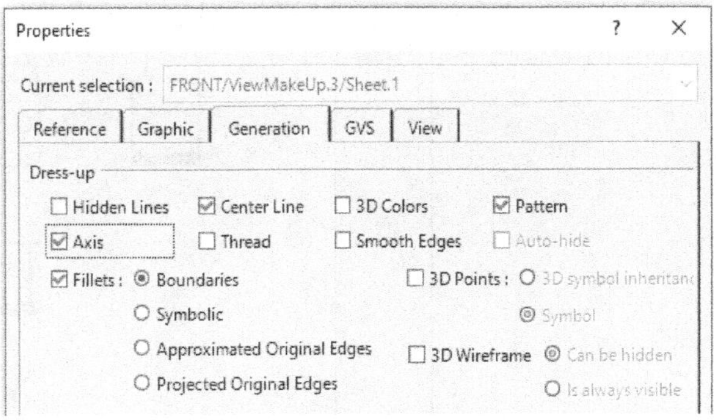

Figure 9–33

3. Click **OK**.

Task 8 - Create a section view.

1. Zoom in on the front view.
2. Click (Offset Section View) in the Views toolbar.
3. Sketch a line that starts to the left of the view, as shown in Figure 9–34. Enable the system to assume an alignment with the axis of the Hole feature.

To align the start of the section line with the hole, try positioning the cursor over the hole to create a coincidence constraint before starting the creation of the line.

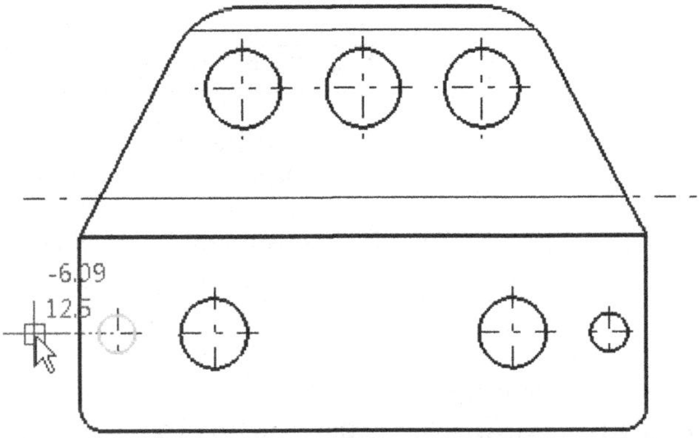

Figure 9–34

4. Move the cursor to the right of the front view and select a location approximately one grid square space to the right of the view, as shown in Figure 9–35.

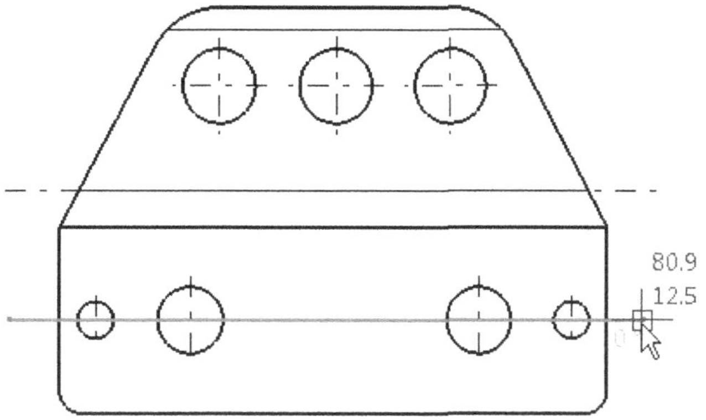

Figure 9–35

5. Double-click to complete the x-section definition.

6. Select a location above the front view. The view displays as shown in Figure 9–36.

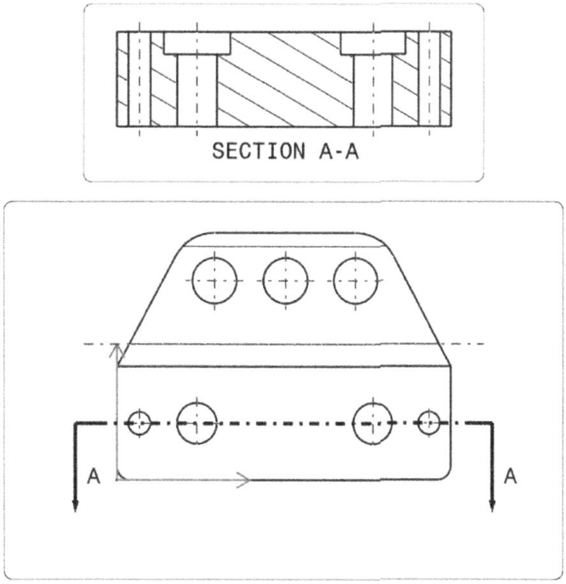

Figure 9–36

7. If the section view call out arrows are pointing in the wrong direction, right-click on the arrow and select **Callout (Section View).x object > Definition** as shown in Figure 9–37.

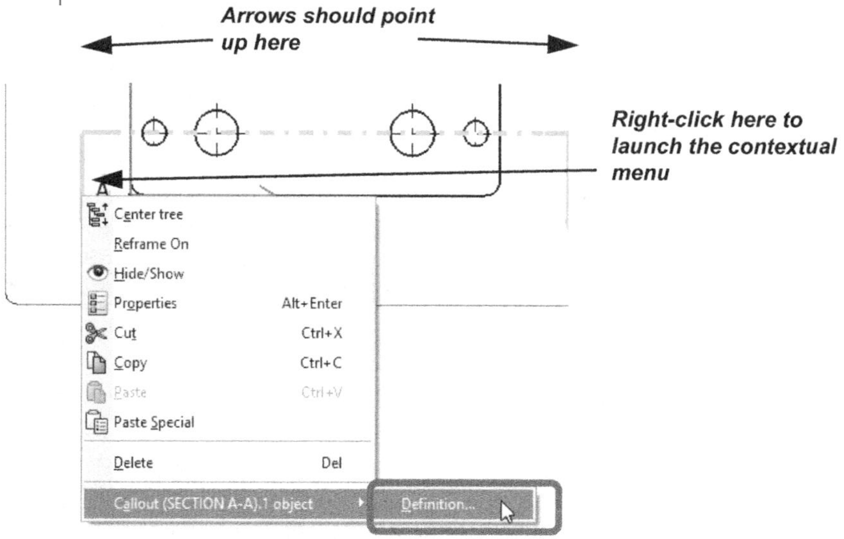

Figure 9–37

8. The Profile Edition mode is displayed. From the Edit/ Replace toolbar, click (Reverse View Direction).
9. Click on the screen to complete the action.

Task 9 - Add a detail view.

1. Zoom in on the section view.
2. Double-click on the frame of the section view to make it active. The border turns red and the name of the view in the view tree indicates that this view is the active view.
3. In the *View Layout* section of the Action Bar, click to expand it, then click (Quick Detail View).

4. Click a location on the right side of the counterbored hole feature and click again to create a circle callout, as shown in Figure 9–38.

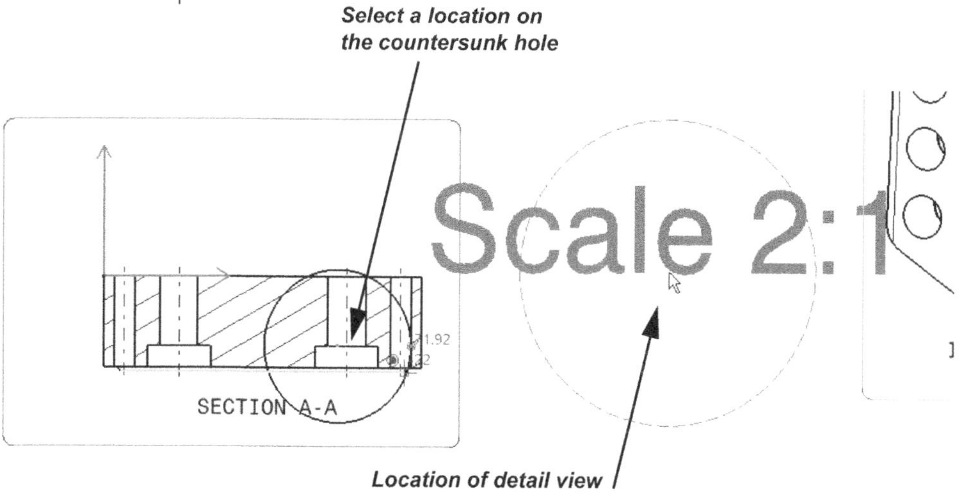

Figure 9–38

If the axis is not visible, right-click and select ***Properties*** *and then select the* ***Axis*** *option in the View tab in the Properties dialog box.*

5. Select a point to the right of the section view to define a location for the detail view. The complete detail view containing the callout is shown in Figure 9–39.

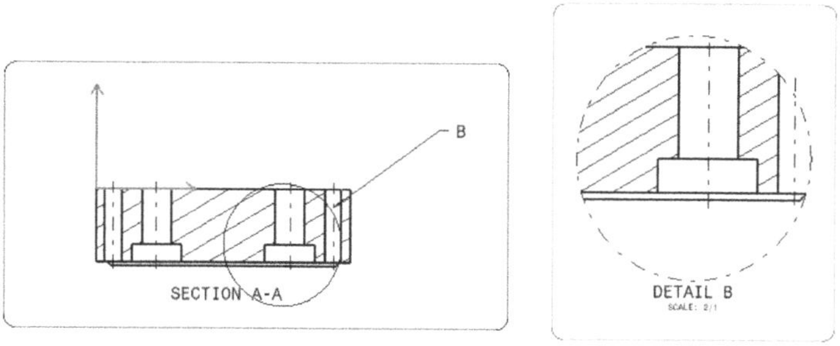

Figure 9–39

6. Right-click on the arrows in the front view, right-click and select **Callout (Section View).x object > Definition.**
7. Click (Reverse View Direction) in the context toolbar.
8. Click on the screen and note that the circle defining the section view has moved.
9. Double-click the section circle to activate it.

10. Move and resize the section circle as shown in Figure 9–40.

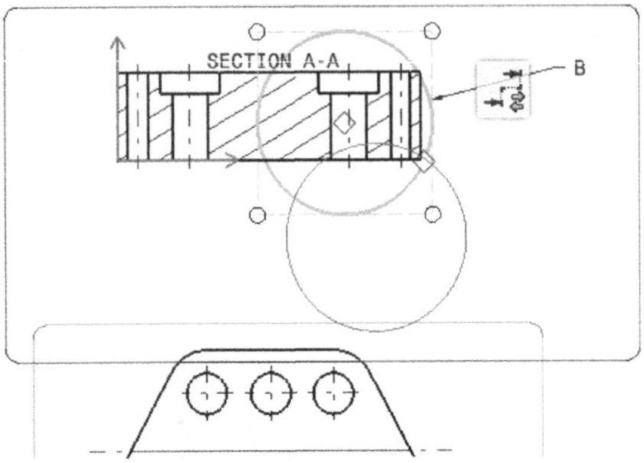

Figure 9–40

11. Click on the screen to complete the edit.

12. Move the section view to an appropriate location.

Task 10 - Insert a frame and title block.

1. In the *View Layout* section of the Action Bar, click (Page Layout). In the *Dress-up* drop-down list, select **Drawing Titleblock Sample 1**, as shown in Figure 9–41.

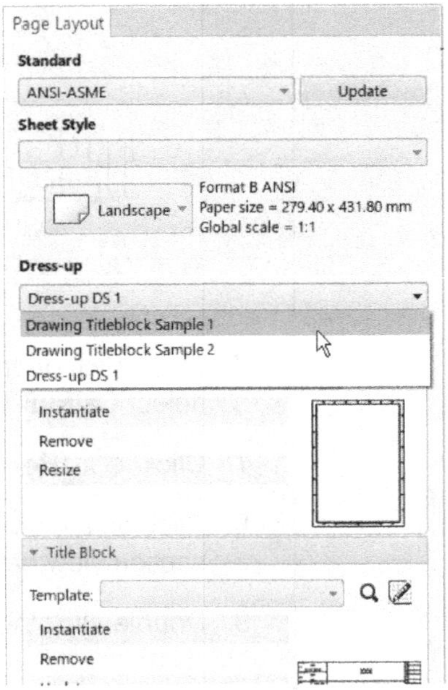

Figure 9–41

2. In the Frame and Title Block area, click **Create**.
3. Click **Apply**. The frame and title block are displayed. Close the Insert Frame and Title Block dialog box.
4. Save the drawing.
5. Do not close the tab. The drawing is used in the next exercise.

Practice 9b

Annotate a Drawing

Practice Objective

- Create and manipulate dimensions.

In this practice, you will add dimensions to a drawing. You will modify these dimensions and explore their various properties. The end result is shown in Figure 9–42.

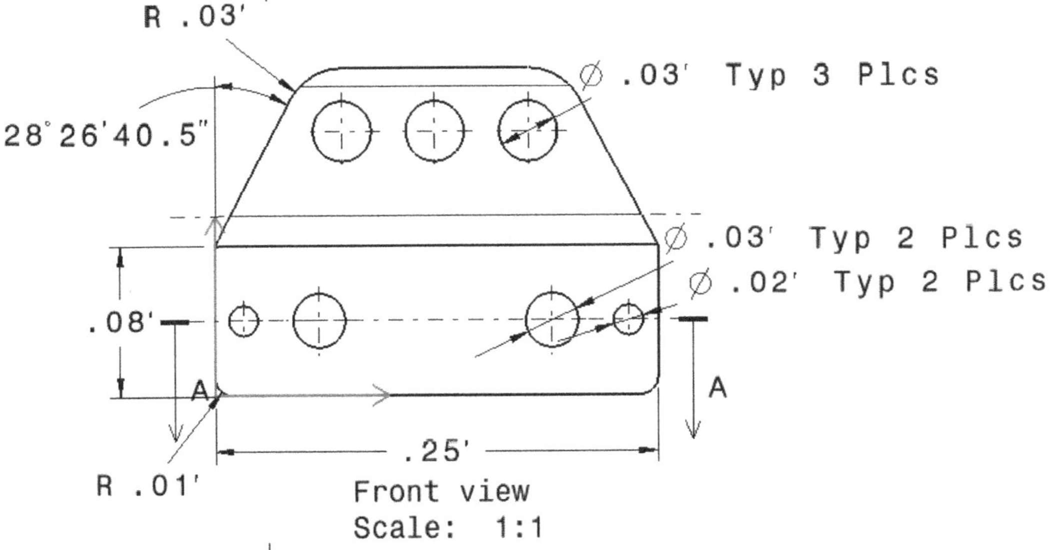

Figure 9–42

Task 1 - Import the Bracket Drawing.

1. Either continue using the drawing from the previous exercise or import **Bracket_Views.3dxml** and open the drawing.
2. Activate the front view.
3. Hide all of the views except the front view.
4. If the grid is displayed and you want to toggle it off, select (Display Grid) in the *View* section of the Action Bar.

Task 2 - Generate manual dimensions.

1. Zoom in on the front view and, in the *Annotation* section of the Action Bar, click (Dimension).

2. Select the edge shown in Figure 9–43. The system creates a linear dimension for the edge.

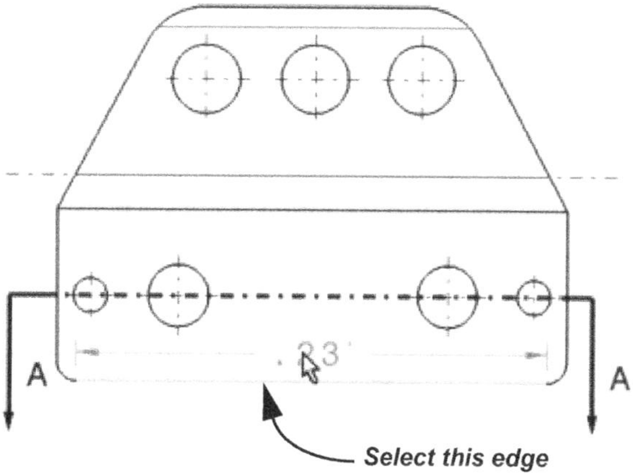

Figure 9–43

3. Select a second reference for the dimension, as shown in Figure 9–44. The system displays a length dimension between the two references.

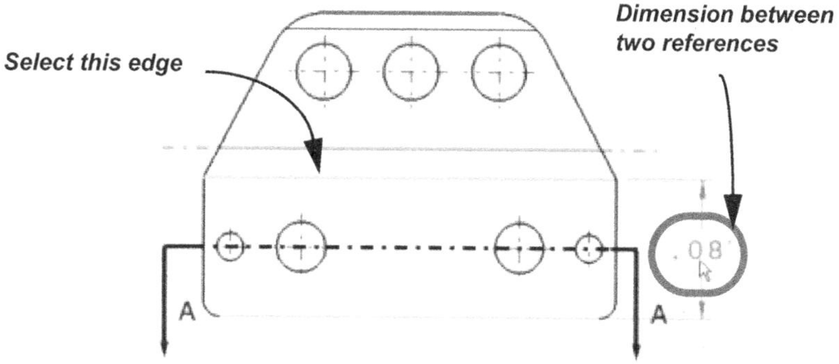

Figure 9–44

4. Press the left mouse button to complete the reference selection and place the dimension. The dimension highlights in blue and can now be moved.

5. Move the dimension to the side, as shown in Figure 9–45.

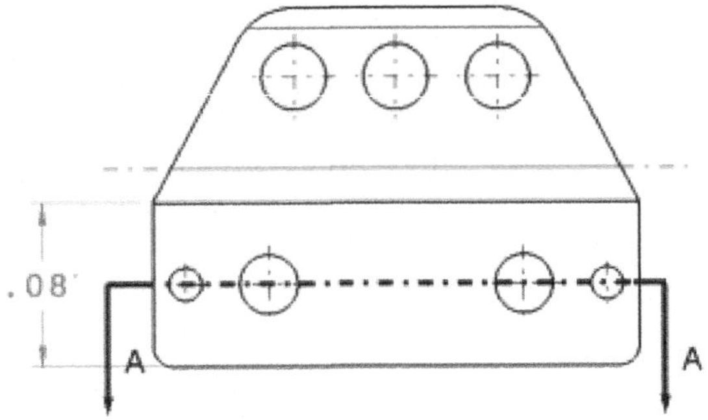

Figure 9–45

6. Create the horizontal dimension shown in Figure 9–46.

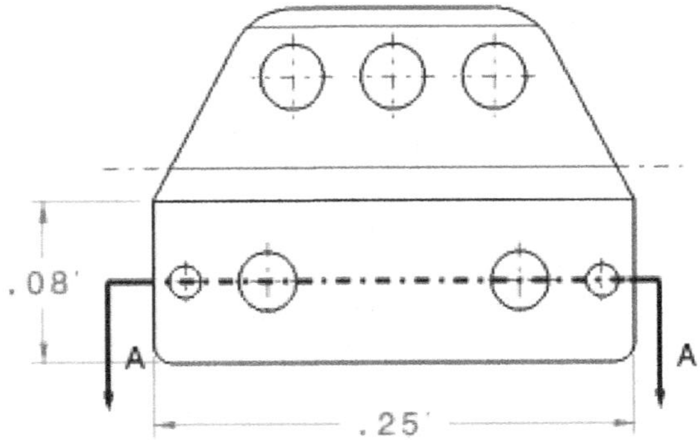

Figure 9–46

7. Select the circle as shown in Figure 9–47, and place the diameter dimension.

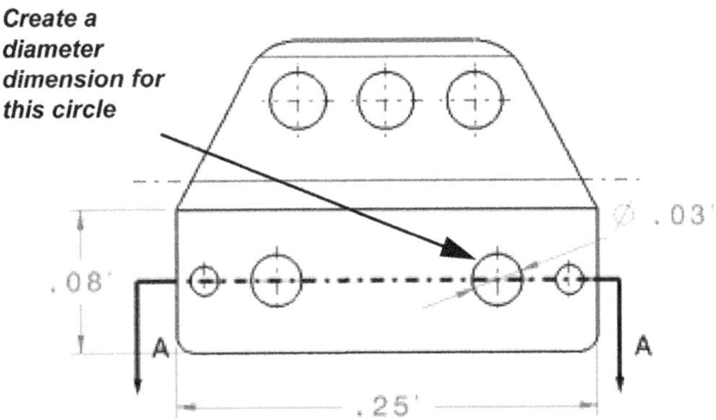

Figure 9–47

8. Create the other four dimensions as shown in Figure 9–48.

   Note: After selecting an arc/circle to place a dimension, it will give you either a Radius/Diameter. If what it gives you is incorrect, right-click immediately after selecting arc/circle and select either **Diameter Center/Radius Center** to switch.

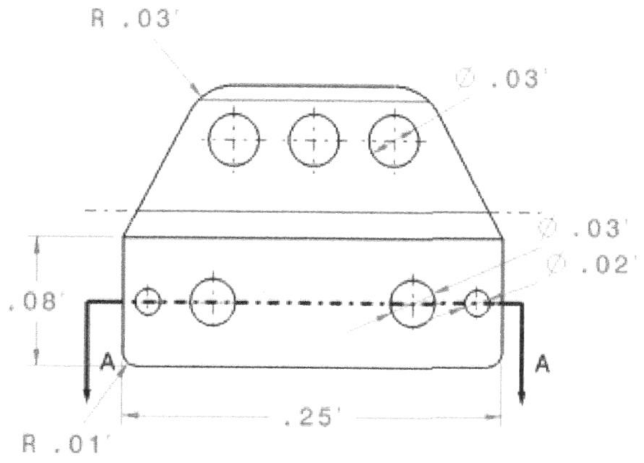

Figure 9–48

Task 3 - Manipulate dimensions.

1. Select the **.03'** diameter dimension on the right Hole feature, as shown in Figure 9–49.

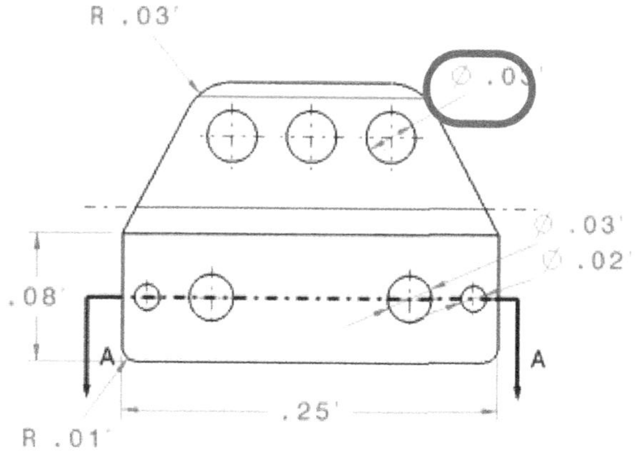

Figure 9–49

2. Right-click and select **Properties**.
3. Select the *Dimension Texts* tab in the Properties dialog box.

4. Enter **Typ 3 Plcs** in the suffix text field, as shown in Figure 9–50.

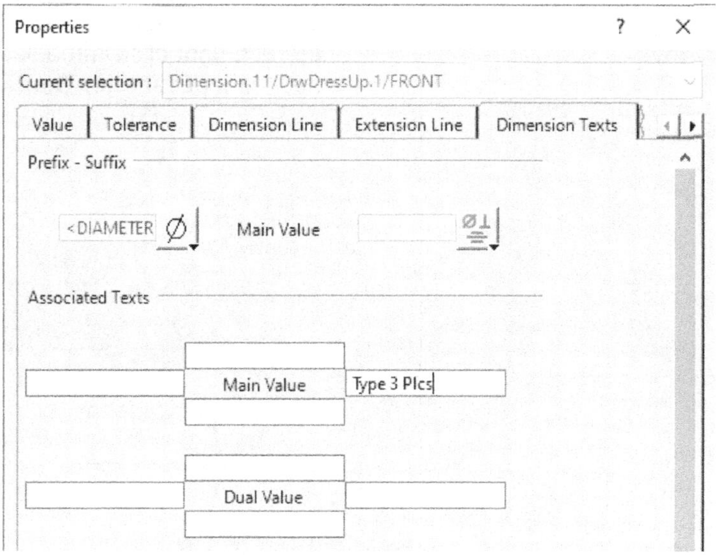

Figure 9–50

5. Click **Apply** and click **OK**. The dimension updates with the changes, as shown in Figure 9–51.

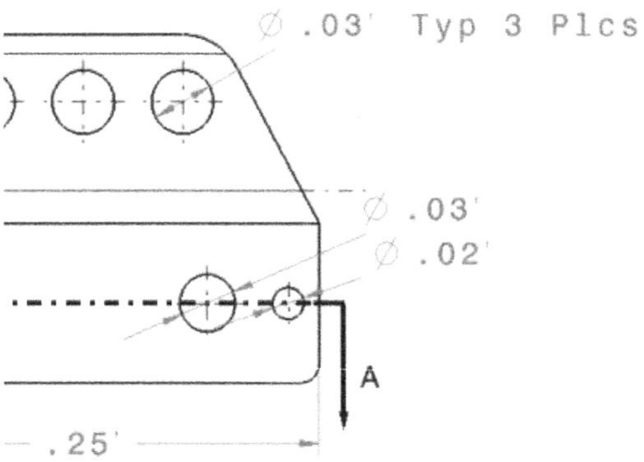

Figure 9–51

6. Select the **.03'** and **.02'** diameter dimensions (hold down <Ctrl> to select both) and add the suffix dimension text, as shown in Figure 9–52.

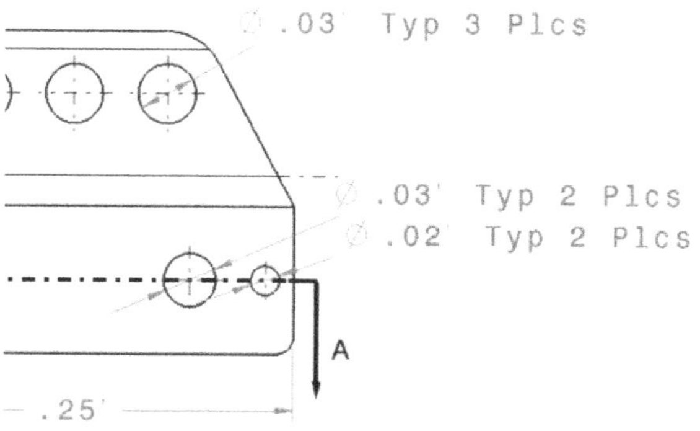

Figure 9–52

Task 4 - Create an angle dimension on the Front view.

1. Click  (Dimension) (click the flyout arrow if it is not visible) and select the two entities shown in Figure 9–53.

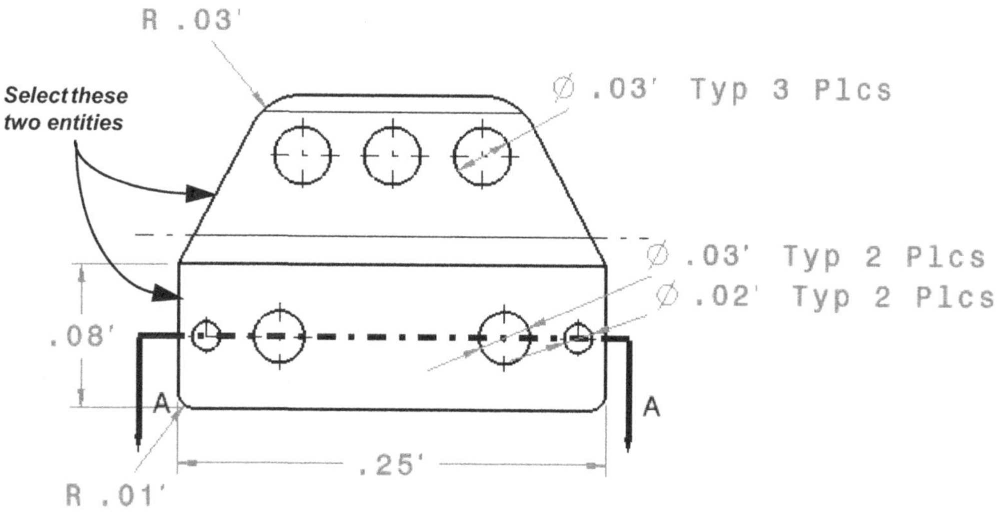

Figure 9–53

Depending on where your cursor is located, you might need to select a different angle sector to get the result shown in Figure 9–55.

2. Define how the angled dimension is generated. While moving the dimension into position, right-click and select **Angle Sector > Sector 2**, as shown in Figure 9–54.

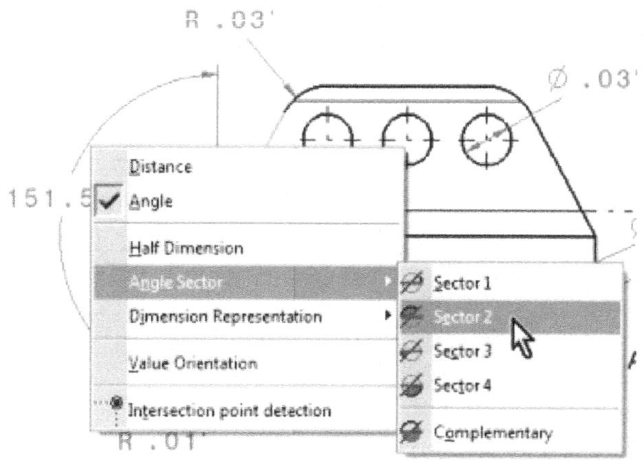

Figure 9–54

3. Click to place the dimension. It displays as shown in Figure 9–55.

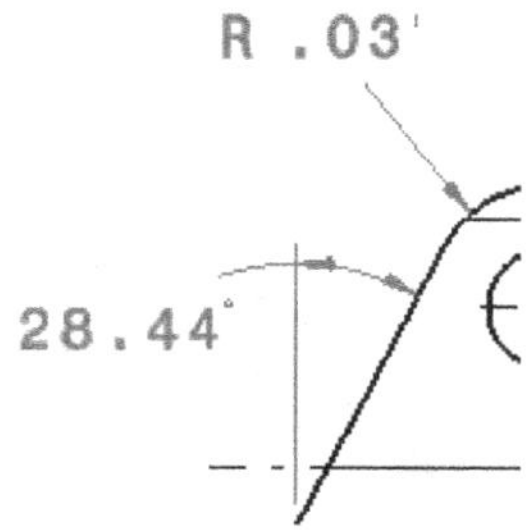

Figure 9–55

4. Modify the format of the angle dimension by right-clicking on it and selecting **Properties**.

5. Select the *Value* tab in the Properties dialog box. Modify the value in the *Display* field to **3 factors** and the value in the *Precision* field to **0.1** as shown in Figure 9–56.

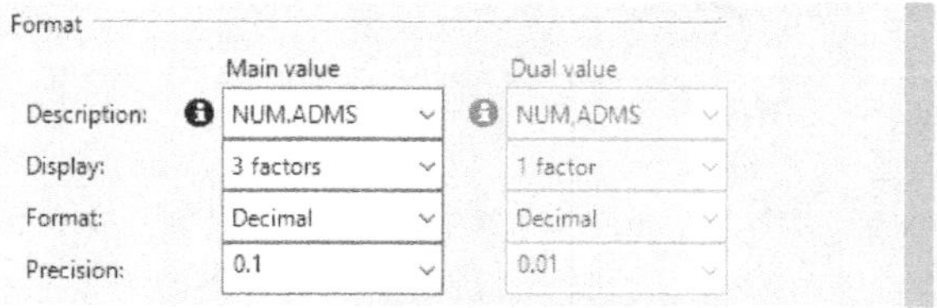

Figure 9–56

6. Apply the changes and close the Properties dialog box. The dimension displays as shown in Figure 9–57.

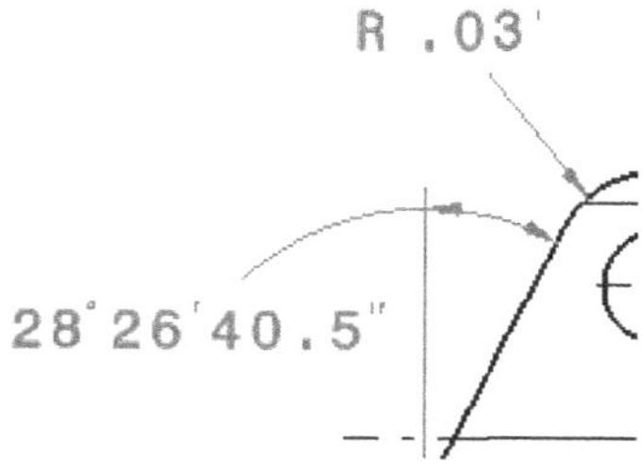

Figure 9–57

7. The completed drawing is shown in Figure 9–58. Save the drawing and close the window.

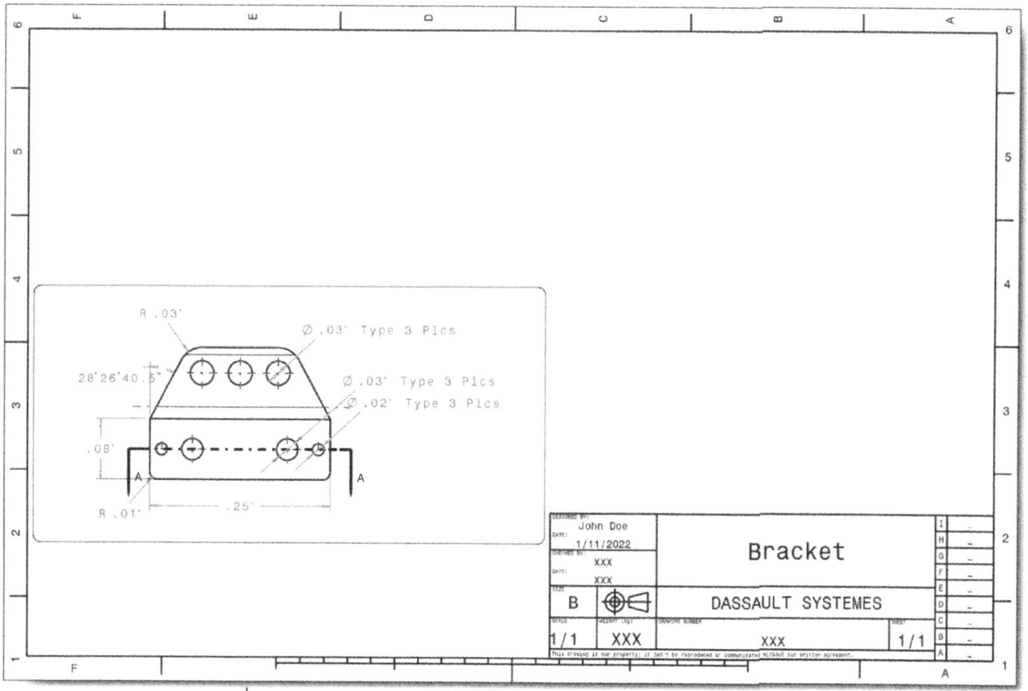

Figure 9–58

Practice 9c (Optional) Piston

Practice Objective

- Create more complex geometry without instructions.

Create a new part titled **Piston**. Refer to the drawing shown in Figure 9–59 for dimension values.

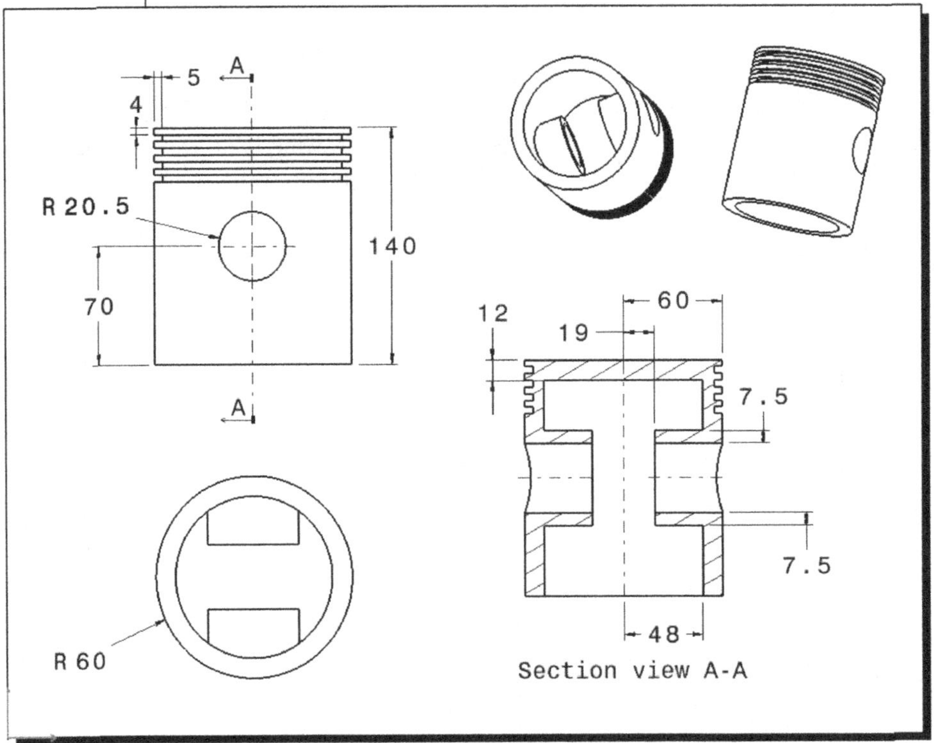

Figure 9–59

Practice 9d (Optional) Flange

Practice Objective

- Duplicate features without instructions.

Create a new part titled **Flange**. Refer to the drawing shown in Figure 9–60 for dimension values.

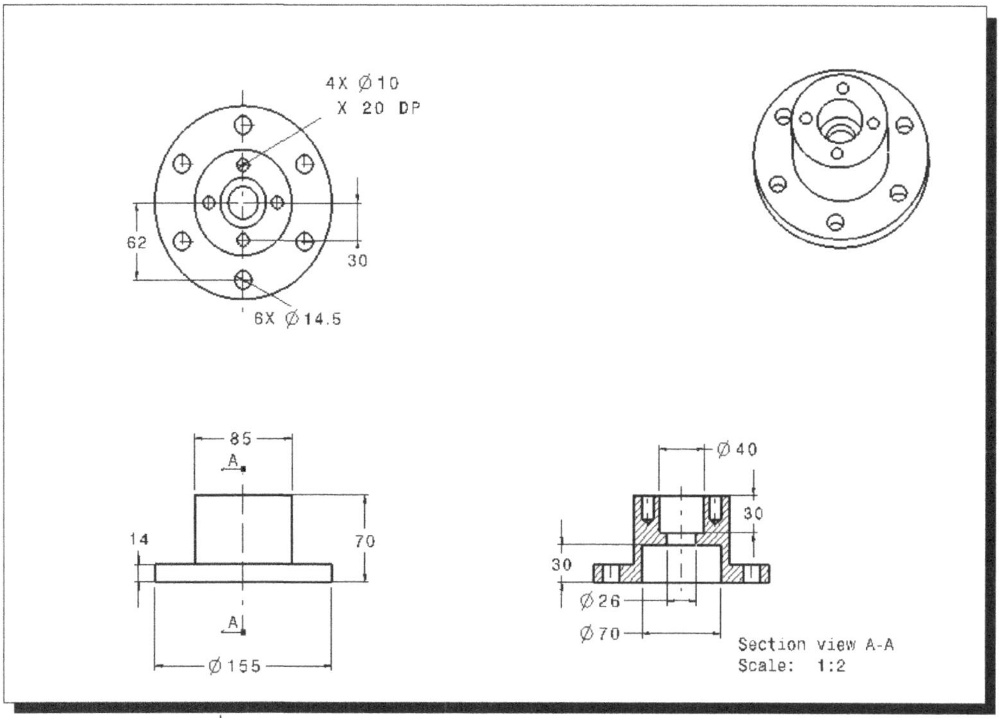

Figure 9–60

Chapter Review Questions

1. Which of the following view types can be the first view in a drawing?
   a. Offset Section view
   b. Projection view
   c. Front view
   d. Detail view
2. When you delete a parent view, dependent views are automatically deleted.
   a. True
   b. False
3. An isometric view is placed in the drawing at the same orientation as in the model. This orientation can be changed inside the drawing using the compass before the view has been placed.
   a. True
   b. False
4. The only way to tell which view on a drawing is active is that is has a red border.
   a. True
   b. False
5. Dimensions created in a drawing update when changes are made to the model.
   a. True
   b. False
6. You cannot hide a drawing view.
   a. True
   b. False
7. Changes in the 3D model automatically display in the drawing.
   a. True
   b. False

Answers: 1c, 2b, 3a, 4b, 5b, 6a, 7b

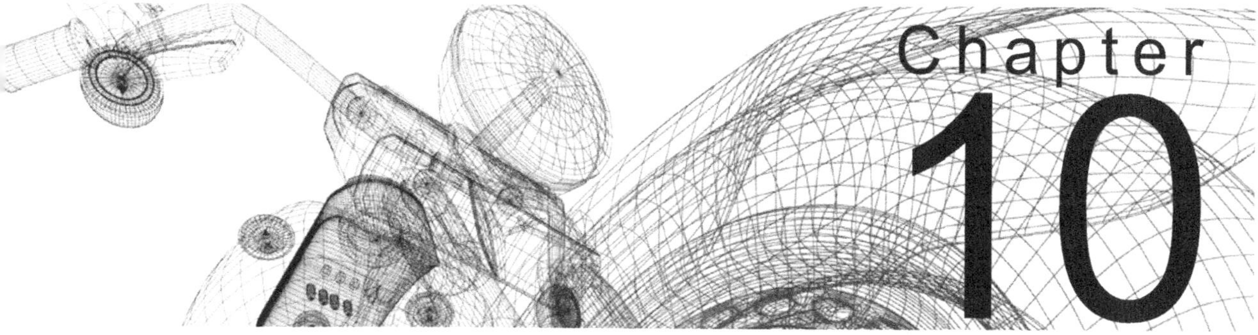

Creating Sketches

In this chapter, you learn how sketches are used to create features. You also learn some of the basic capabilities of the Sketch app, which enables you to create sketch-based features. Then, you use reference planes and surfaces to orient and sketch the profile of your first feature.

Learning Objectives in This Chapter

- Understand the basics of sketched features.
- Review the general steps for creating a new part.
- Understand the use of default and reference planes for sketching.
- Review the basic tools that you can use to create entities in sketches.
- Create a sketch for the model profile.
- Understand several operations for editing sketches.
- Learn various tips and techniques for working with sketches.
- Understand how features and sketches display in the specification tree.

10.1 Getting Started on Sketching Features

2D sketches are used to create 3D features. A sketch plane is selected and used to create a sketched feature, as shown in Figure 10–1.

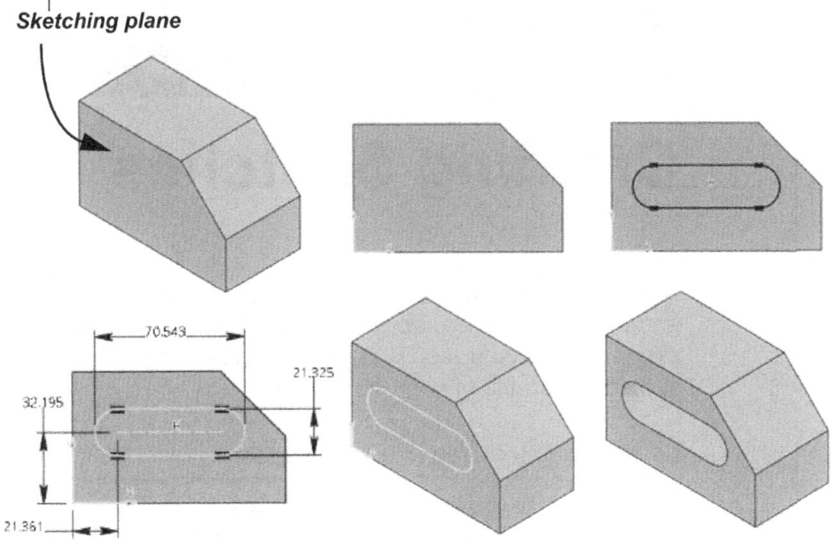

Figure 10–1

How To: Create a Sketched Feature

1. Select a sketch plane and enter the Sketch app. The plane you select is initially oriented parallel to the screen. The Y-axis faces the top of the screen and the X-axis faces the right side of the screen.
2. Sketch the required profile or cross-section.
3. Create constraints/dimensions to define the size and location of the sketch.
4. Exit the Sketch app.
5. Use the sketch to create a solid feature, such as a Pad or Pocket.

10.2 Creating a New 3D Part

The 3DEXPERIENCE Part Design modeling engine is the same as CATIA V5, which ensures file compatibility so V5 data will be able to transfer to 3DEXPERIENCE without any issue. Because of this, most of the modeling commands are very similar and the overall approach to modeling is quite familiar, with a few differences.

Creating a New Part

There are three main ways to create a new 3D part:

1. Use the Compass.
2. Click Add from the Top Bar.
3. Add to an assembly (design in context).

Using the Compass to Create a New Part

The compass is used to access the various apps available in the 3DEXPERIENCE platform. Use the following steps to create a new model.

1. Click the outer ring of the compass, as shown in Figure 10–2.

Figure 10–2

2. Select the app that you would like to use, such as Part Design or Assembly Design, as shown in Figure 10–3.

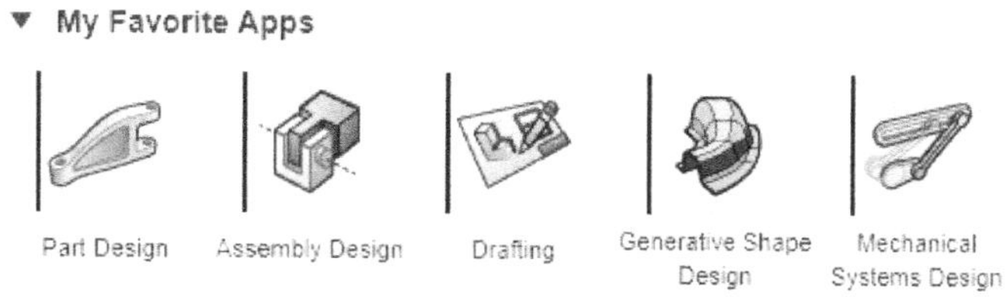

Figure 10–3

3. A part file is created when entering the app, as shown in Figure 10–4.

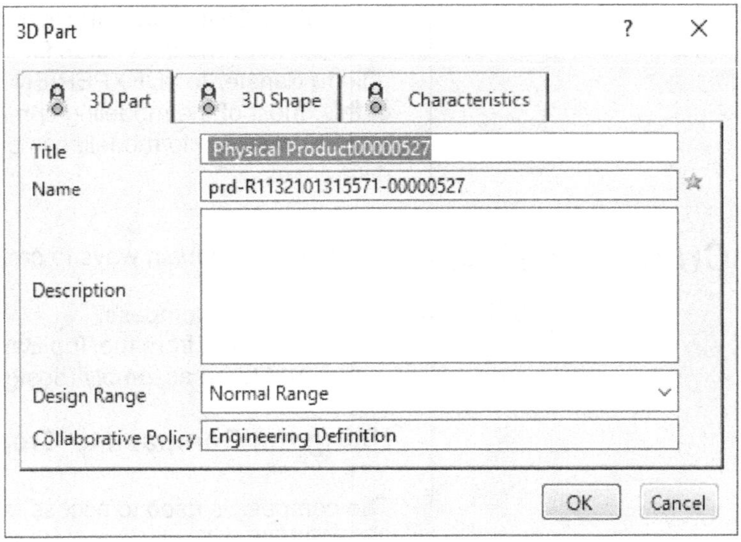

Figure 10–4

Using the Add Command

By clicking the  (Add) drop-down, you can select to create Physical Products, Parts, and Drawings directly, as shown in Figure 10–5.

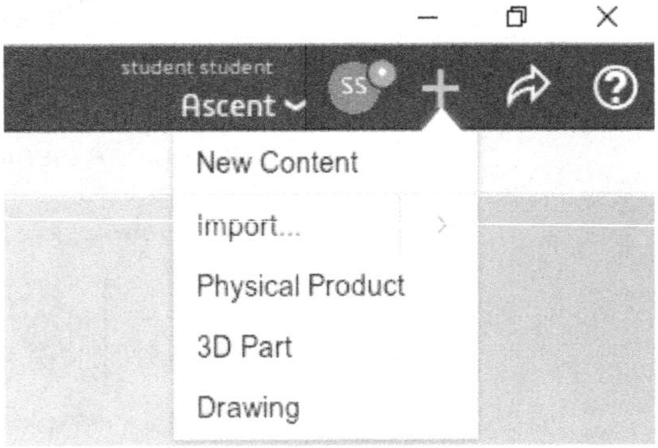

Figure 10–5

Or, by clicking Content, all other 3DEXPERIENCE platform objects can be created, as shown in Figure 10–6.

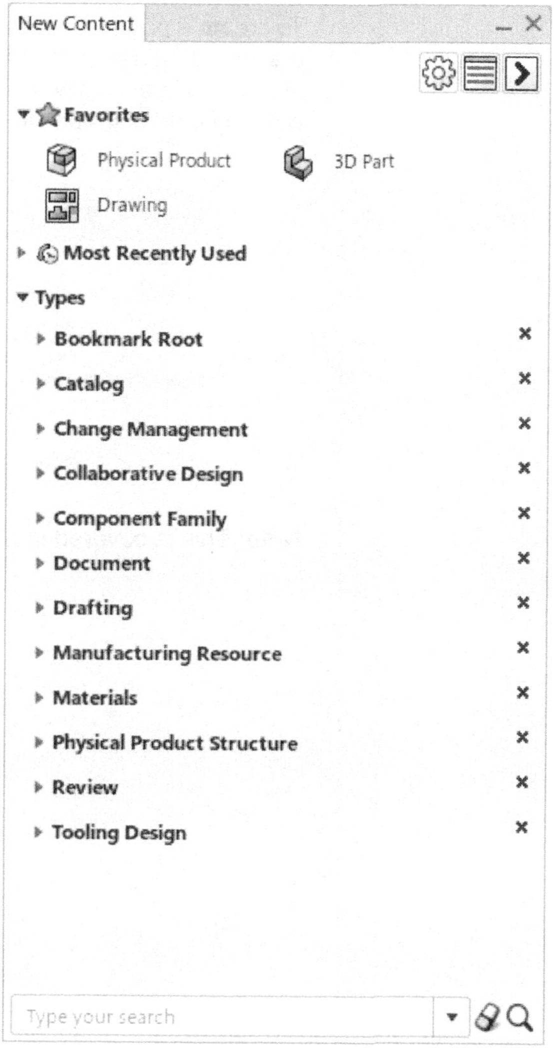

Figure 10–6

Build a New Part in an Assembly (Design in Context)

To create a part in an assembly, right-click the Product and select **Insert** > **3D Part**, as shown in Figure 10–7. Keep in mind that a 3D Part is specifically a 3D shape that contains a product that will only hold a shape file.

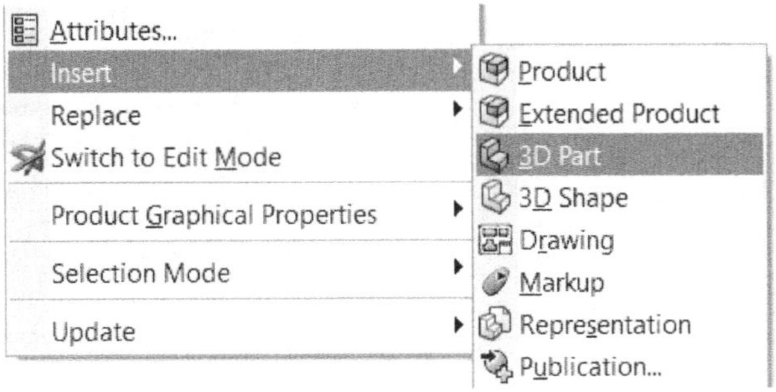

Figure 10–7

Note: This is covered in detail in a later section.

10.3 New Part Dialog

The 3D Part dialog box has three tabs. There are two titles, one for the 3D Part and one for the 3D Shape, as shown in Figure 10–8.

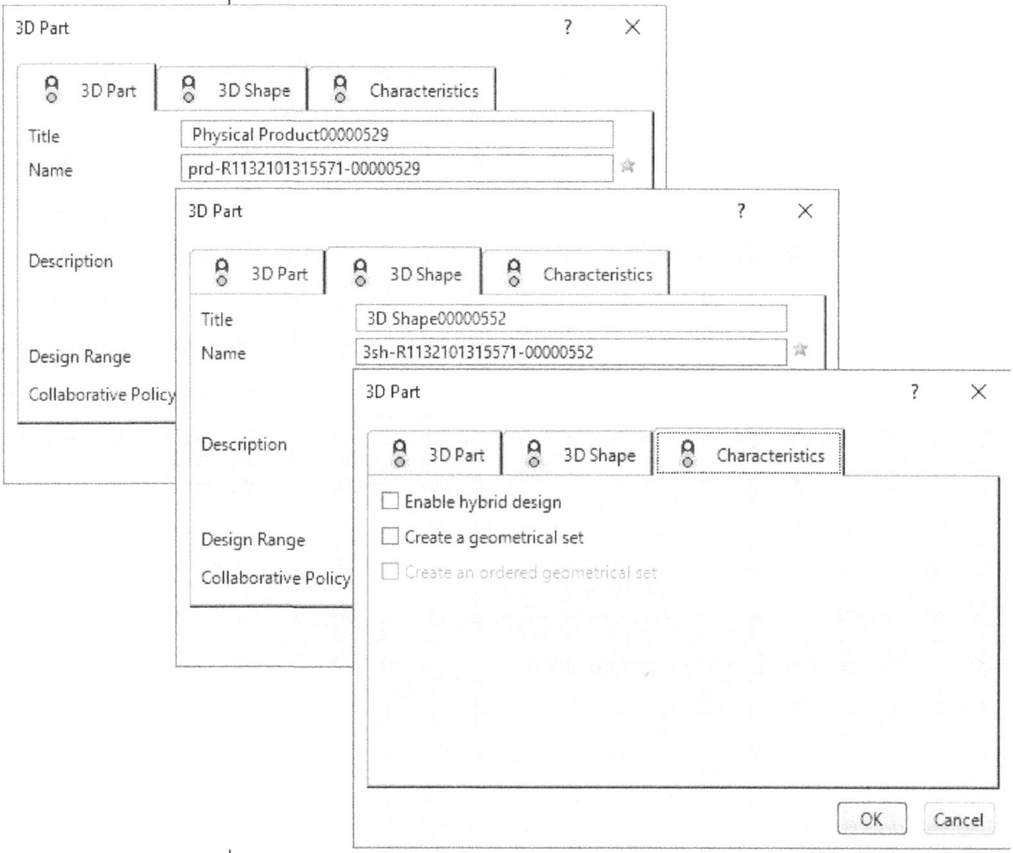

Figure 10–8

There is also a Characteristics tab, allowing you to select additional options for creating the part.

The titles for a part are shown in Figure 10–9. The 3D Part is a container that will contain reference information (such as position in an assembly, reviews, or drawing) for that part. The 3D shape will be the 3D model and contain 3D features, such as Pads, Pockets, Extrudes, Joins, etc.

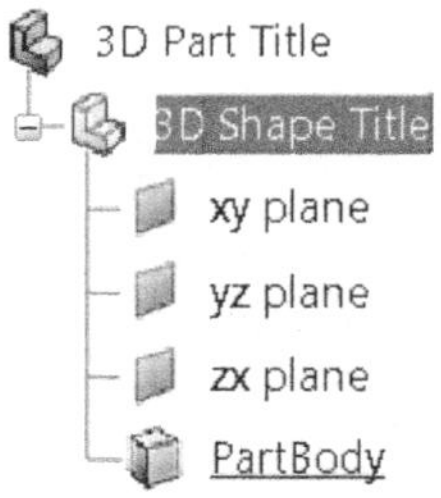

Figure 10–9

The following options can be configured for the new part:

Parameter	Description
Enter part Title field	Enter a name for the part model. This name is automatically assigned to the Part Number of the new file.
Enter part *Description* field	Optional description of the model.
Enable hybrid design option	Hybrid design uses a special type of body, called a hybrid body. It can contain both wireframe/surface and solid features. This enables direct integration of the surface and part design environments into a single body. For current purposes, the hybrid design environment is disabled.
Create a geometrical set option	When the hybrid design environment is disabled, a geometrical set is used to store wireframe and surface elements, as well as sketched elements. A geometrical set is automatically added to the new part file when this option is selected.
Create an ordered geometrical set option	When the hybrid design environment is enabled, an ordered geometrical set can be used to group together wireframe or surface geometry with order preserved.

Click **OK** when the part parameters have been specified. The model is created with three default reference planes that can be used as sketching planes, as shown in Figure 10–10.

If the New Part dialog box is not displaying when you create a new part, it can be turned on by selecting the **(Add)> New Content>** **(Tools)** and enabling **Set attributes at creation for all types.**

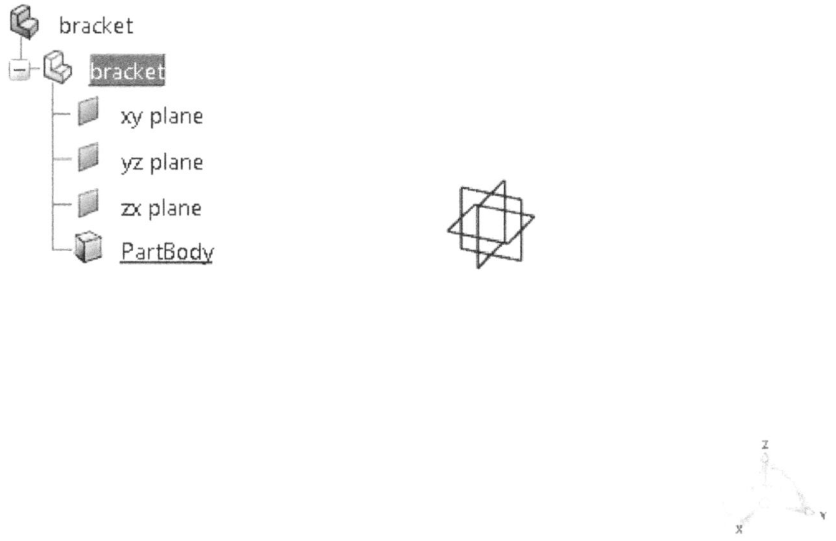

Figure 10–10

10.4 Sketch Planes

A new part always starts with three default reference planes. The model and specification tree display is shown in Figure 10–11. The planes are automatically named to match the directions of the coordinate system that they are parallel to, such as the XY plane.

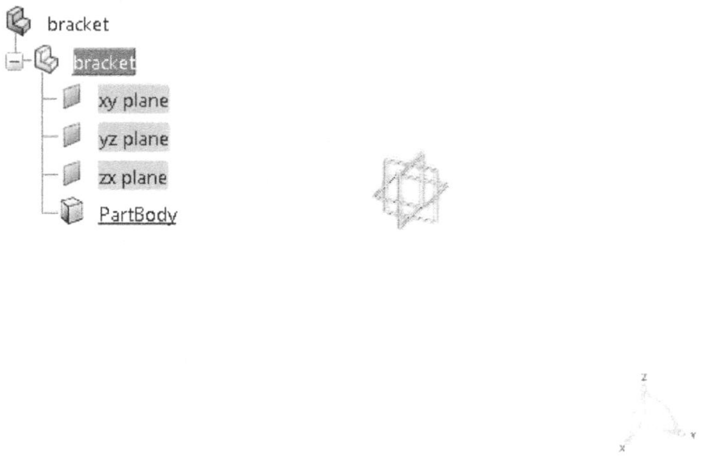

Figure 10–11

Reference Planes

For better visualization, highlight each plane by placing the cursor over a reference plane in the specification tree or on the screen.

All CATIA parts contain default reference planes as the first three features. The default reference planes remain the same size relative to screen, regardless of model size or zoom level, as shown in Figure 10–12.

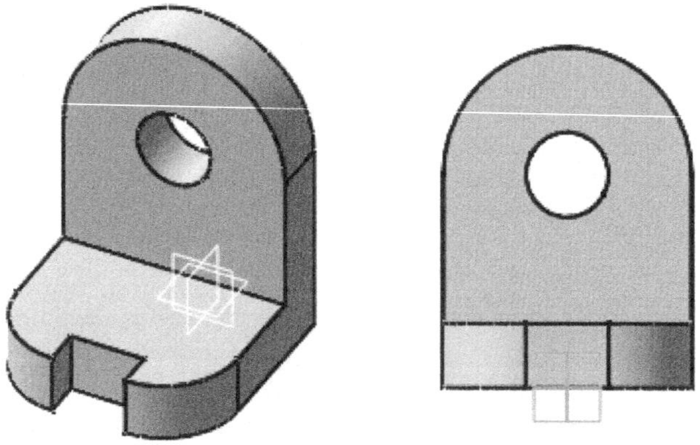

Figure 10–12

Default reference planes are useful for creating a new model because they provide a planar reference to place the first sketch. Figure 10–13 shows three shaded rectangular surfaces to help visualize the reference planes orientation.

Planes cannot be displayed as shaded. This is for illustration only.

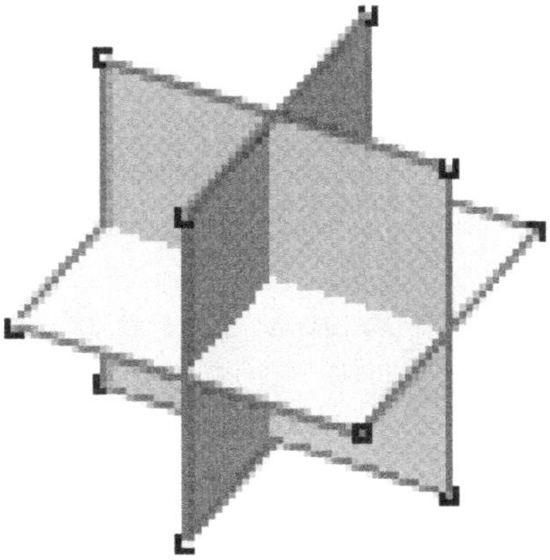

Figure 10–13

Selecting a Plane for Sketching

Selecting one plane over another impacts the Quick Views and the default orientation of the model. The YZ plane is considered the front of the part, as shown in Figure 10–14. However, this does not mean that you always sketch on the YZ plane.

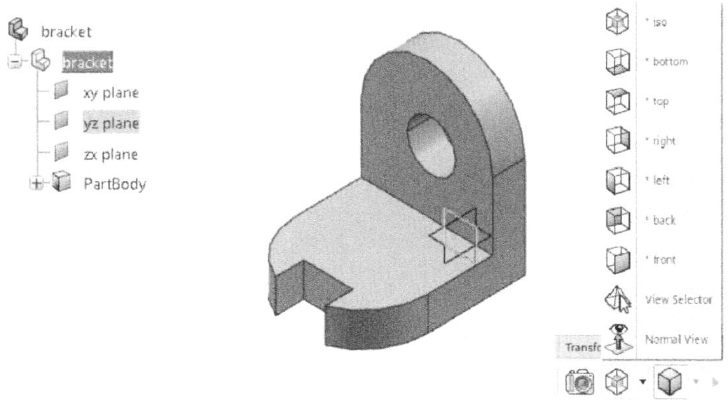

Figure 10–14

Sketch a front profile on the YZ plane, a side profile on the ZX plane, and a top profile on the XY plane.

The sketch of the bracket part is two lines at right angles, sketched on the ZX plane.

Consider the following example. The possible default orientations of a cylinder when one of the default planes is selected, as shown in Figure 10–15.

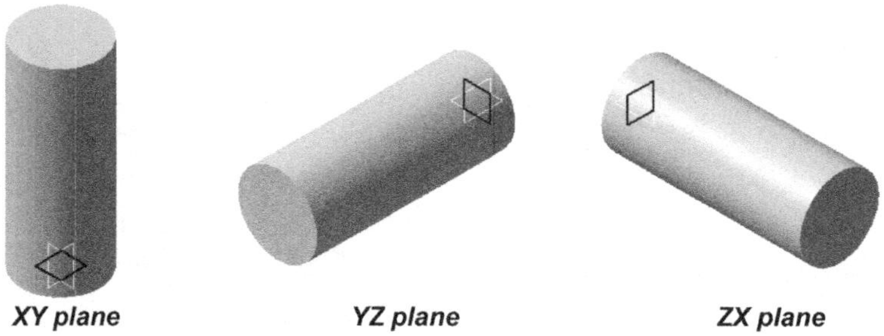

Figure 10–15

10.5 Sketch Application

How To: Create a Sketch

1. Select an appropriate sketching plane and click (Sketch) from the context toolbar.
2. Create your sketch.
3. Click (Exit App) to complete the sketch.

Sketcher Grid

When you first enter the Sketch app, the following objects display, as shown in Figure 10–16:

- Sketcher grid over your sketch plane
- Three default reference planes
- Horizontal and Vertical axes
- Robot
- Specification tree

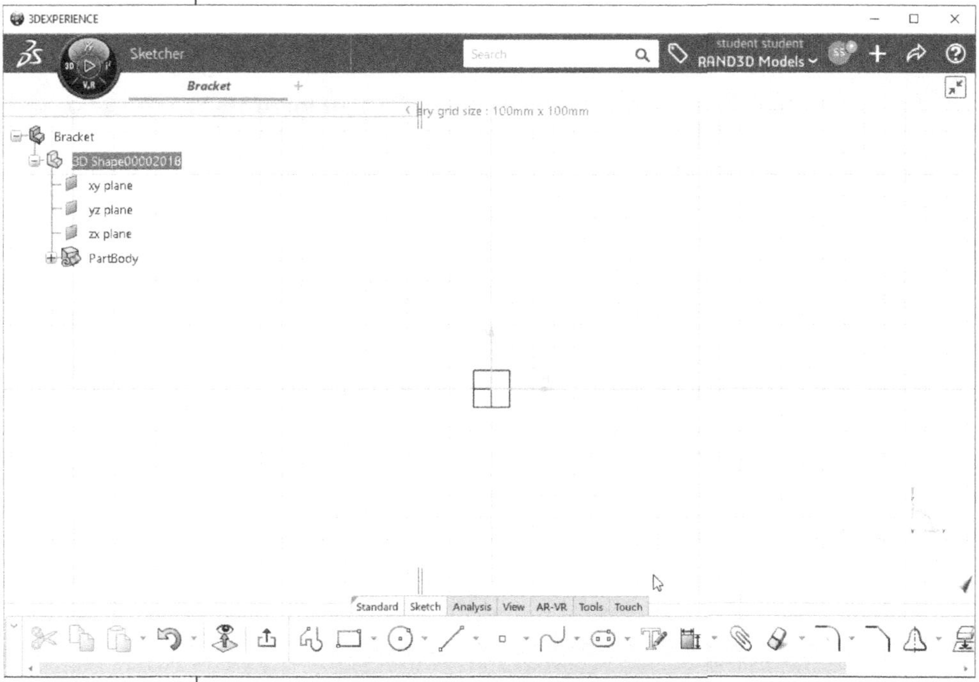

Figure 10–16

(Grid) is also available in the View section of the Action Bar. (Snap to Point) is available in the Sketch section.

To use the sketcher grid, right-click and select **Display>Action Pad** to display the Action Pad, shown in Figure 10–17. You can set the following options:

- Enable/disable the grid: (Grid)
- Enable/disable the snap function: (Snap to Point)

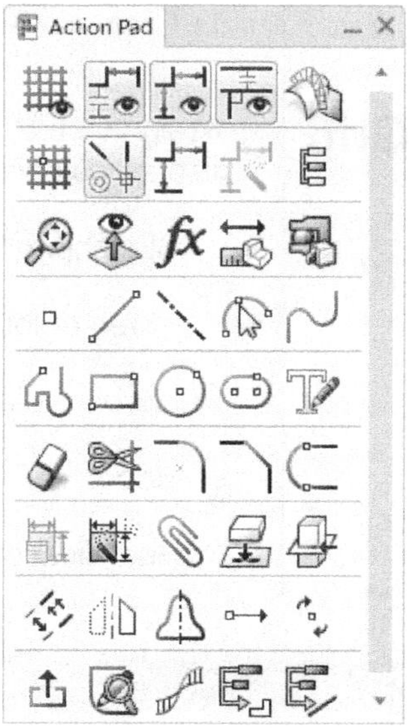

Figure 10–17

10.6 Basic Shapes

Other sketch tools are available. These are covered in a different chapter.

Once inside the Sketch app, the feature's profile (or cross-section) must be sketched. The most commonly used tools for sketching are described as follows.

Icon	Sequence	Description
 (Line)		Select the start and end points of the line.
 (Bi-Tangent Line)		Select two arcs or circles for the line to be tangent to.
 (Line Normal To Curve)		Select a location on a curve, or a point on a curve. Then select the end point of the line.
 (Rectangle)		Select the location for two diagonal corners of the rectangle.
 (Arc)		Select the start point of the arc, end point of the arc, and then another point for the arc to pass through.
 (Circle)		Select the center of the circle and a point on its perimeter to define the diameter.
 (Elongated Hole)		Select the center of each arc, and then select a location on the profile to define the diameter.

 (Corner)	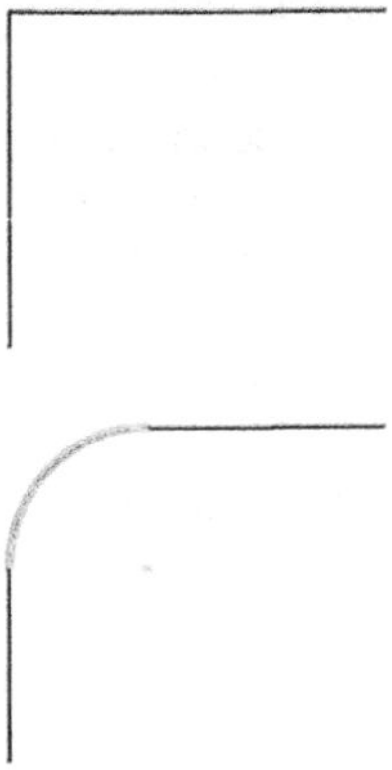	Select the two lines the corner is tangent to, and then drag the corner out to the required size.
 (Chamfer)	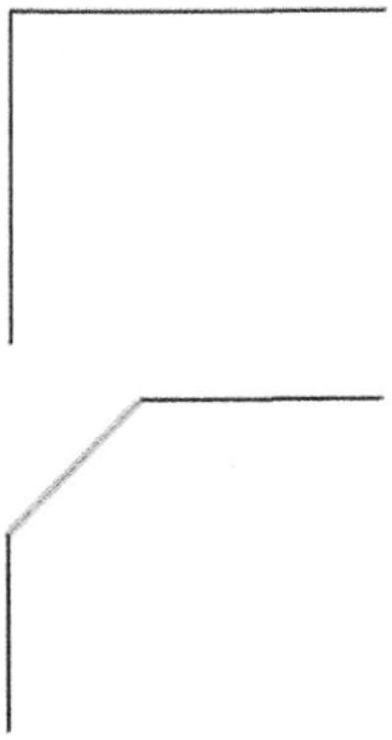	Select the two lines the chamfer contacts, and then drag the chamfer out to the required size.
 (Axis)		Select the start and end points of the axis.

Manual Definition

With many sketch tools, you can use another toolbar called the Tools Palette that contains additional functions for that specific type of geometry. Some of these options are described as follows:

Option	Description
Lines	Manually enter the coordinates of the start point, end point, line length, and angle into the Sketch Tools toolbar.

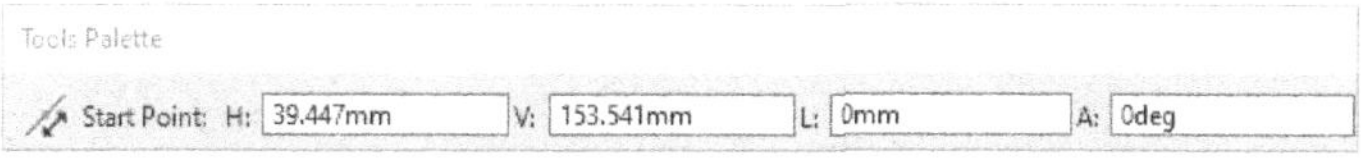

Rectangle	Manually enter the coordinates of the first point, the coordinates of the second point, and the height and width of the rectangle.
Circle	Manually enter the coordinates for the circle's center and specify its radius.
Corner	Specify how to trim the existing lines when the corner is completed.

10.7 Profile Sketching

To create a connected series of lines and arcs, use (Profile). Sketch a series of connected lines, then when you have formed a closed loop, the profile automatically terminates, as shown in Figure 10–18. You can also terminate the profile with an open loop by double-clicking the left mouse button at the end of the last line, as shown in Figure 10–19.

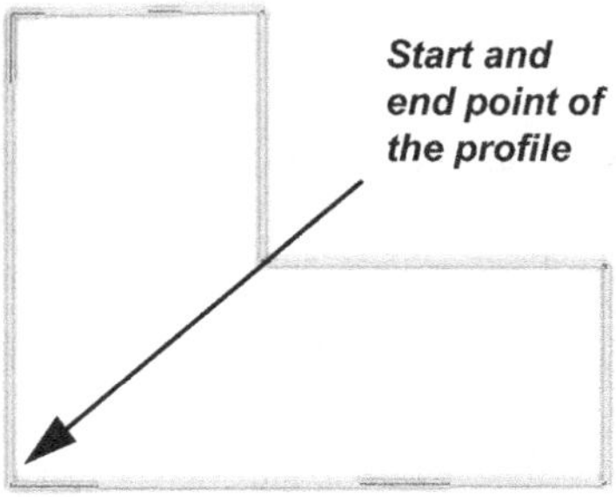

Figure 10–18

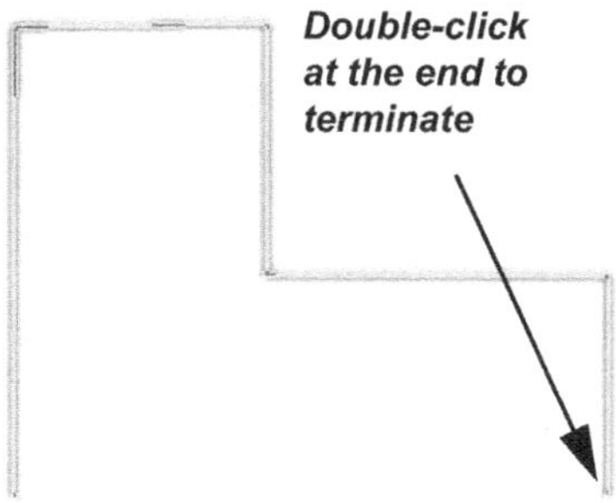

Figure 10–19

You can toggle from sketching a line to sketching a tangent arc (as shown in Figure 10–20) or three-point arc (as shown in Figure 10–21), by using the temporary icons in the Sketch tools toolbar. You return to sketching a line after you finish the arc.

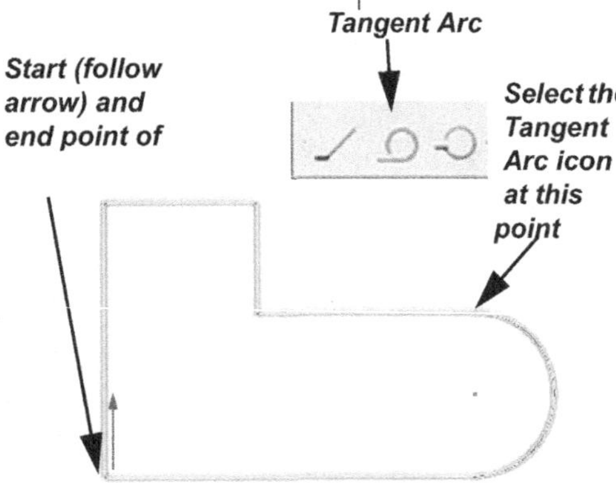

Figure 10–20

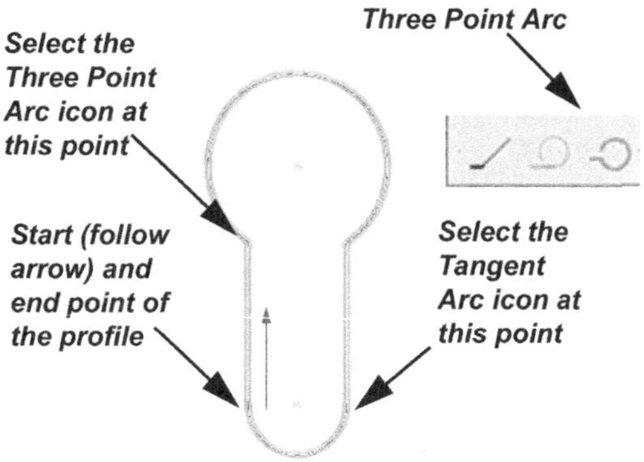

Figure 10–21

10.8 Sketcher Editing Operations

Quick Trim

(Quick Trim) deletes the selected portion of a feature. The software automatically breaks the element at its intersections with other sketched elements.

- The **Quick Trim** method is used to remove the arc segment between two vertical lines, as shown in Figure 10–22.

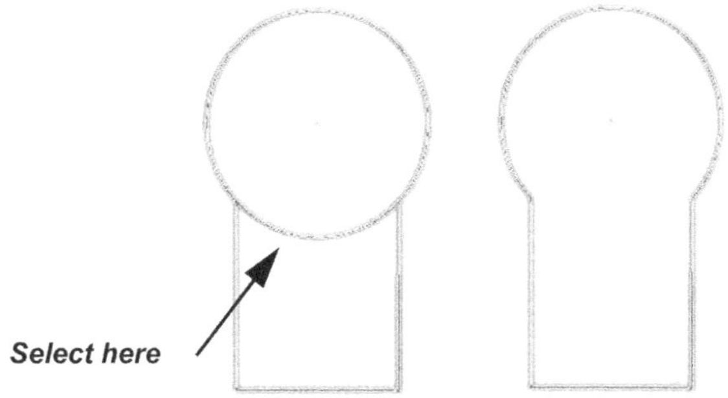

Figure 10–22

Trimming

 (Trim) extends or trims sketched entities to form a closed corner. Select each entity on the side of the intersection that you want to keep. Figure 10–23 shows three examples of trimming and extending line segments.

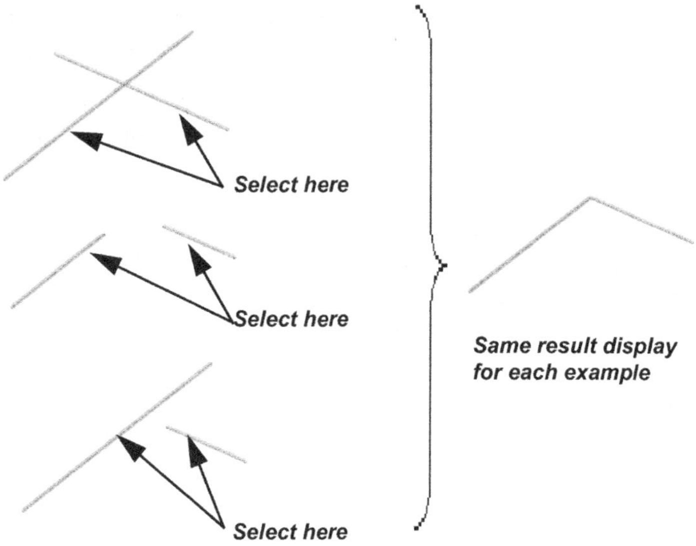

Figure 10–23

You can also choose to trim only the first selected entity by clicking (Trim First Element) in the Tools Palette toolbar that opens after you click (Trim), and selecting the entity to which the first element should be trimmed, as shown in Figure 10–24.

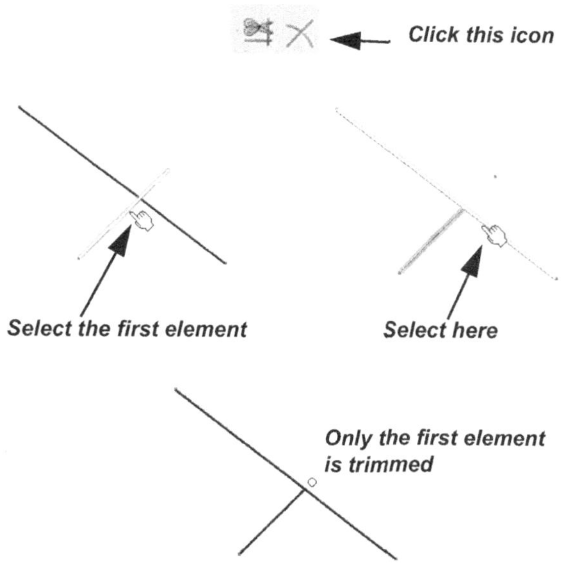

Figure 10–24

Break

(Break) divides a sketched entity at its intersection with another sketched entity. To use the **Break** tool, select the feature you want to divide and select the intersecting feature. The intersection point is projected if the feature does not intersect the first entity.

- The **Break** tool is used to break circles into arcs using an intersecting line, as shown in Figure 10–25. Note that a closed entity, such as the circle, is also divided by an implicit 360° mark.

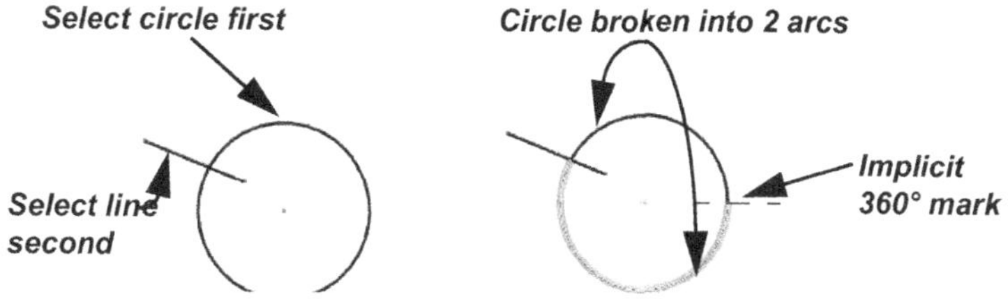

Figure 10–25

Delete and Undo

Pressing <Delete> enables you to remove portions (one or more lines) of a model or the entire sketch (rectangle).

- To completely eliminate a feature you just sketched, you can press <Ctrl>+<Z> or click  (Undo). The keyboard shortcut executes the **Undo** command. CATIA records your previous actions, enabling you to undo multiple times.

  If **Undo** doesn't seem to be working, ensure that you have finished the previous command or hit the **Esc** key to exit the command you are currently using. This should allow **Undo** to be preformed.

10.9 Tips and Techniques

Repeating a Command

When you use any of the geometry creation icons, the command is automatically deactivated once you perform the action. However, by double-clicking on the icon, you can perform that command multiple times.

- Select the icon again to deactivate it. This technique is more efficient than repeatedly selecting the same icon.

Sketching in 3D

Sketching in a 3D orientation can be useful when solid geometry exists and you are sketching on the face of a previously defined feature.

- To return to the planar sketch view, click  (Normal View).

Construction Geometry

You can use construction geometry to help create lines, shapes, and points for your standard geometry. Construction geometry is useful when working with more complex sketches, as shown in Figure 10–26.

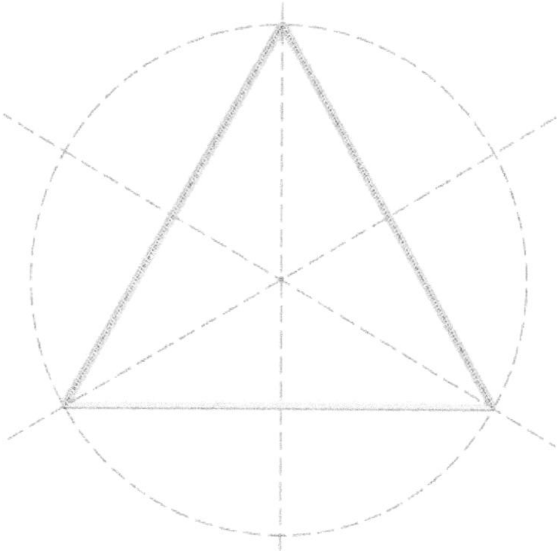

Figure 10–26

You can create construction geometry using one of the following methods:

Do not forget to return to Standard elements when you are done.

- Click 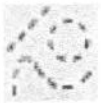 (Construction/Standard Element) in the *Sketch* section of the Action Bar, as shown in Figure 10–27. Any geometry you sketch displays as construction geometry.

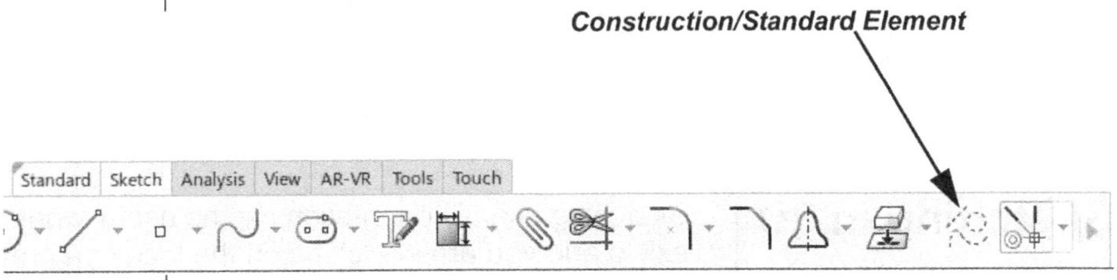

Figure 10–27

- Select the existing standard geometry and click  (Construction/Standard Element) to convert it to construction geometry.

Auto Search

Use the **Auto Search** tool to automatically select all entities that are connected to the selected entity.

- To use the **Auto Search** tool, select a sketched entity that belongs to the profile you want to select and click  (Auto Search), as shown in Figure 10–28. The continuous chain of entities is highlighted for the next operation.

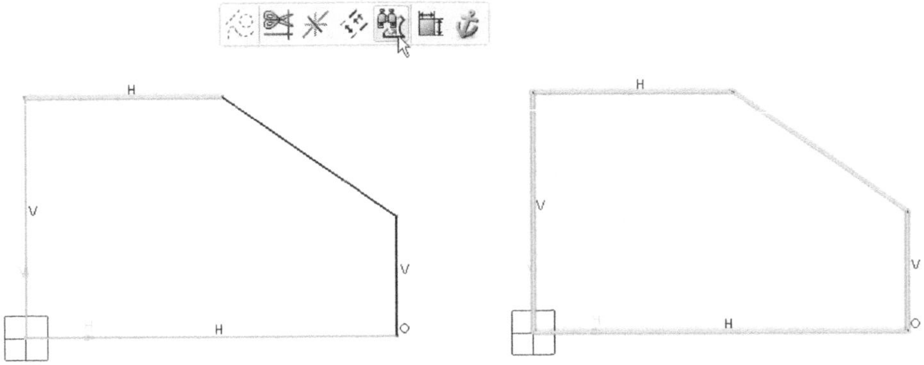

Figure 10–28

- Alternatively, you can select the entity, right-click and select *** object>Auto Search**.

Sketching at Origin

If you select the origin of the sketch during the creation of a profile, CATIA automatically creates an implicit constraint between the vertex of the sketch and the origin. This constraint restricts the vertex of the profile from being moved at a later time, but can be broken by selecting the profile, selecting (Cut) and (Paste) from the Action Bar. This pastes the profile on its original position without the constraint, so you can move it. This only works if the sketched entity has not been referenced by any other features. Any features that reference the entity being cut and pasted fail because the pasted item is considered a new sketched entity and does not maintain the references.

- This type of constraint can be used for a base feature since it is unlikely to move later. However, for other features that should be constrained to the origin, it is recommended to sketch offset from the origin and manually constrain the sketch to it. Figure 10–29 shows a circle that can be manually constrained to the origin using a **Coincident** constraint.

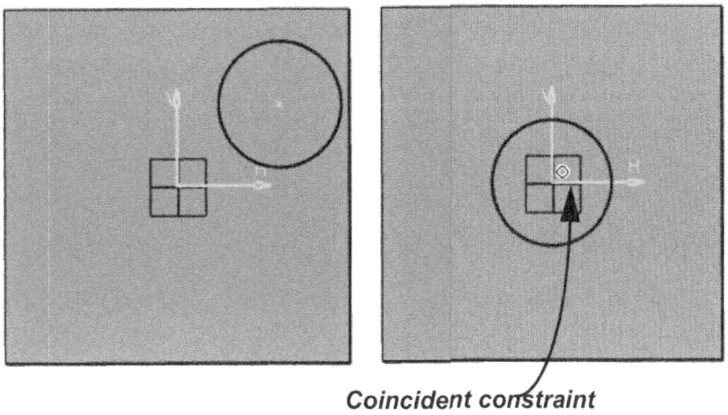

Figure 10–29

10.10 Specification Tree

The features you create are listed in the specification tree in the order in which you create them. Solid geometry features are listed under PartBody, as shown in Figure 10–30.

Sketches are automatically listed under the feature branch that uses them.

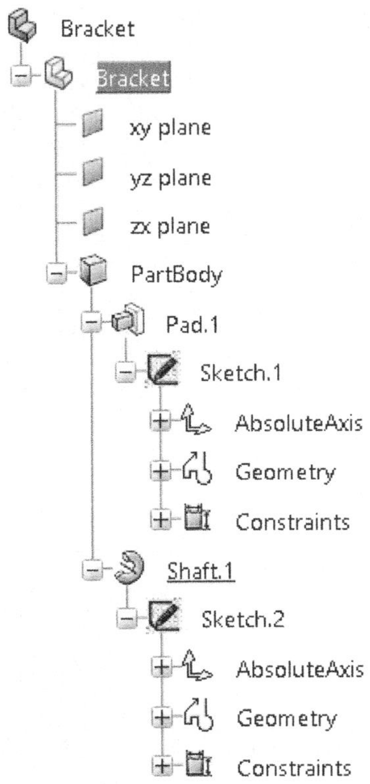

Figure 10–30

- A sketch is automatically hidden once referenced by a solid feature. Right-click on the sketch and select **Hide/Show** to toggle on its display.

Practice 10a Sketching Basic Shapes

Practice Objectives

- Sketch a line, arc, rectangle, circle, and elongated hole.
- Trim overlapping shapes.

In this practice, you will create a sketch as shown in Figure 10–31. You will use various constraints to help constrain the sketch.

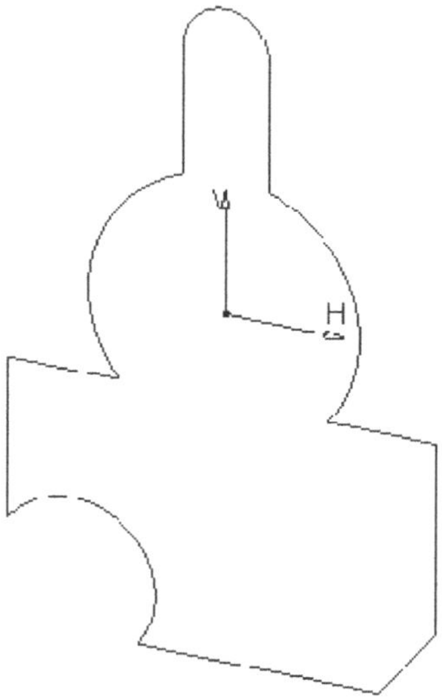

Figure 10–31

Task 1 - Create a new part and set the length units to millimeter.

1. In the Top Bar, click (Add)>**3D Part**.
2. In the 3D Part dialog box, enter ***Your_Initials*_Sketch_1** as the *Title*.
3. Select the *3D Shape* tab and enter **Sketch_1** for the *Title*.
4. Select the *Characteristics* tab and ensure **Enable hybrid modeling** is disabled.
5. Click **OK**.

Task 2 - Select the sketching plane and enter the Sketch app.

1. Select the YZ plane as shown in Figure 10–32.

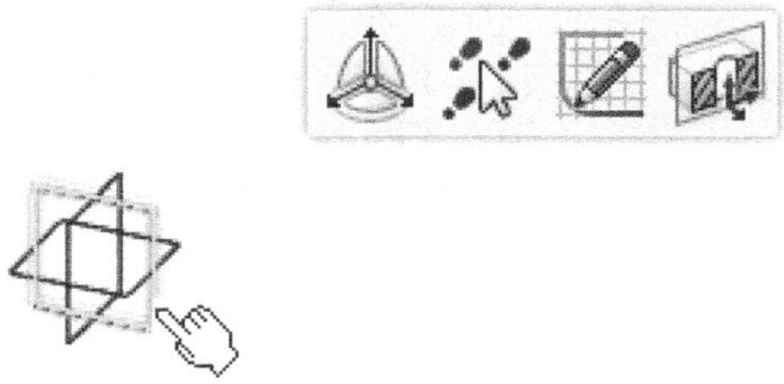

Figure 10–32

2. In the Context toolbar, click (Sketch).
3. The selected reference plane displays parallel to the screen, as shown in Figure 10–33.

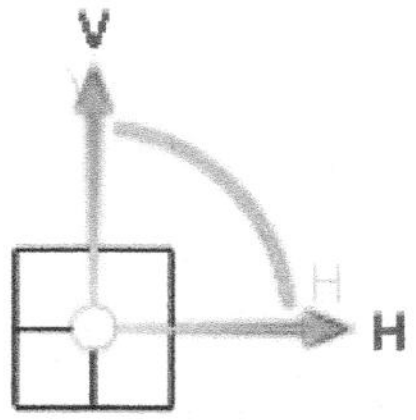

Figure 10–33

Task 3 - Sketch a circle.

Automatic Dimensional Constraints are discussed in more detail in a later chapter.

1. Right-click and select **Display>Action Pad** if the Action Pad is not already displayed.
2. Ensure that (Automatic Dimensional Constraints) is toggled off.
3. If necessary, in the Action Pad, click (Grid) to turn off the grid display.
4. If necessary, in the Action Pad, click (Snap to Point) so you can sketch freely.
5. Click (Circle) to sketch a circle.

6. Place the cursor over the intersection of the horizontal and vertical axes. Select the **0.0**, **0.0** location of the XY axis to define the circle's center point.

7. Move the cursor and select a location to define the radius of the circle. The sketch displays as shown in Figure 10–34.

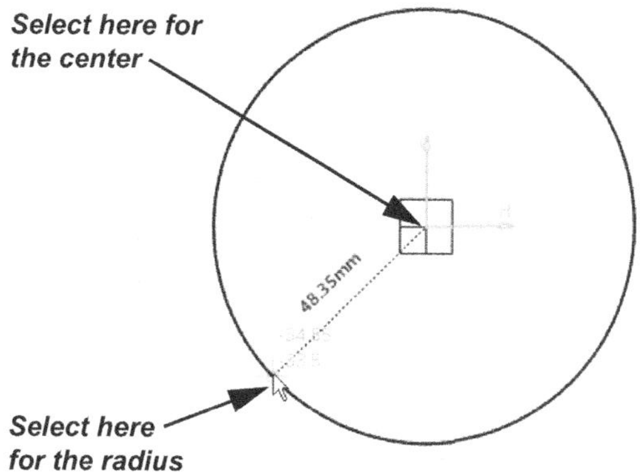

Figure 10–34

Task 4 - Sketch a rectangle that overlaps the circle.

1. Click (Rectangle) to sketch a rectangle.

2. Select the first point of the rectangle and the second point of the rectangle, as shown in Figure 10–35.

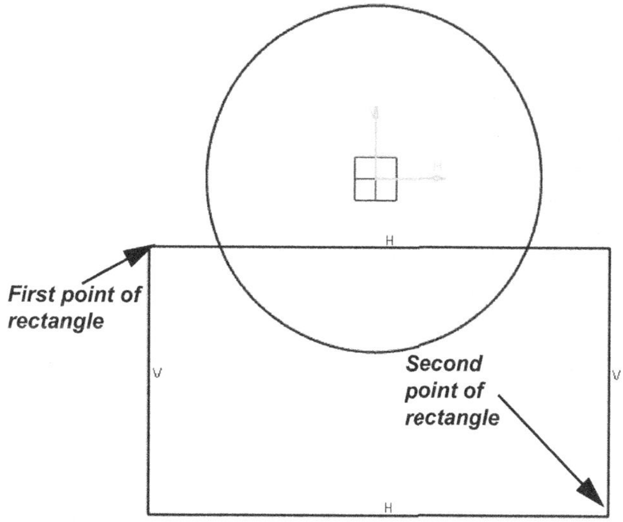

Figure 10–35

Task 5 - Sketch a line.

1. Click  (Line) to sketch a line.
2. Select the locations for the start and end points of the line, as shown in Figure 10–36.

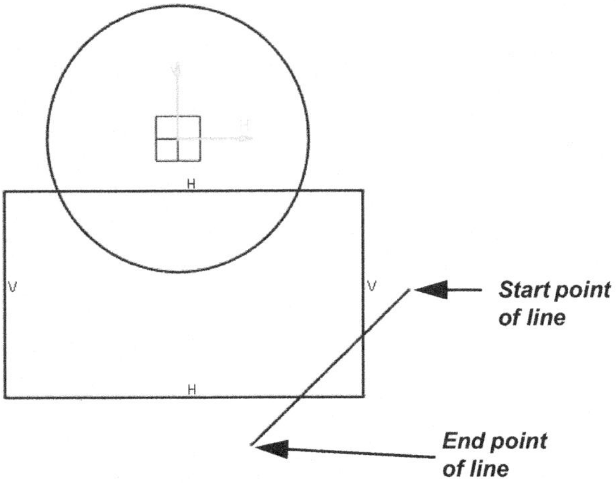

Figure 10–36

Task 6 - Sketch an arc.

1. In the Action Bar, expand the  (Circle) flyout and click  (Three Point Arc) to sketch an arc.

Select the start point of the arc. Note that the lines of the rectangle highlight in blue when the cursor is over them. This color change indicates that the ends of the arc are aligned with that feature.

2. Select the second point that the arc passes through and select the end point of the arc, as shown in Figure 10–37.

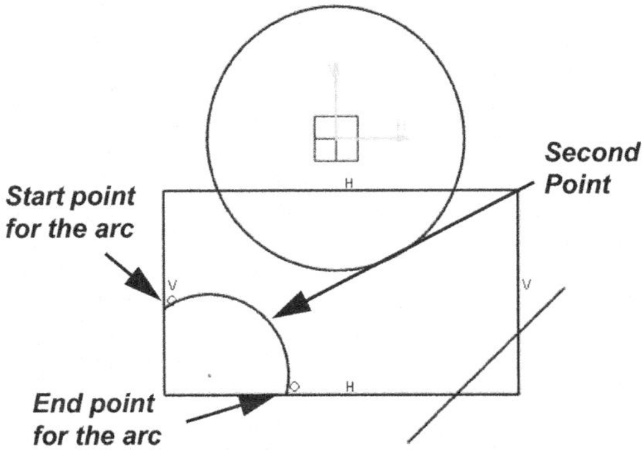

Figure 10–37

Task 7 - Sketch an elongated hole.

1. Click  (Elongated Hole) to sketch an elongated hole.
2. Select the locations for the two arc centers, and a location to define the width of the elongated hole, as shown in Figure 10–38.

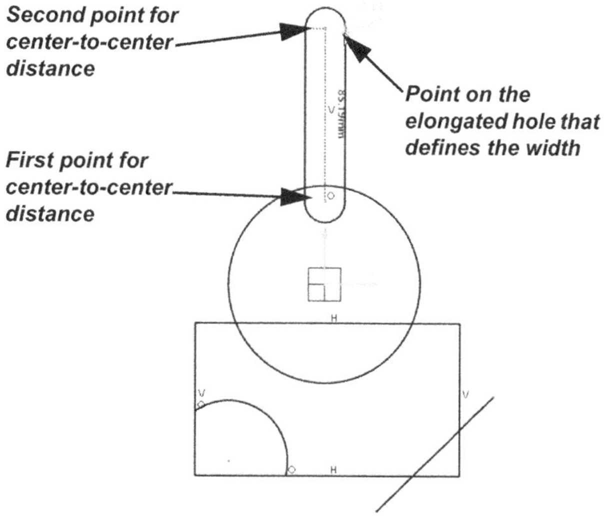

Figure 10–38

Task 8 - Trim the rectangle to the line and the circle.

1. In the Action Bar, expand  (Quick Trim) and click  (Trim) to trim the rectangle.
2. Select the line and the bottom of the rectangle, as shown in Figure 10–39.

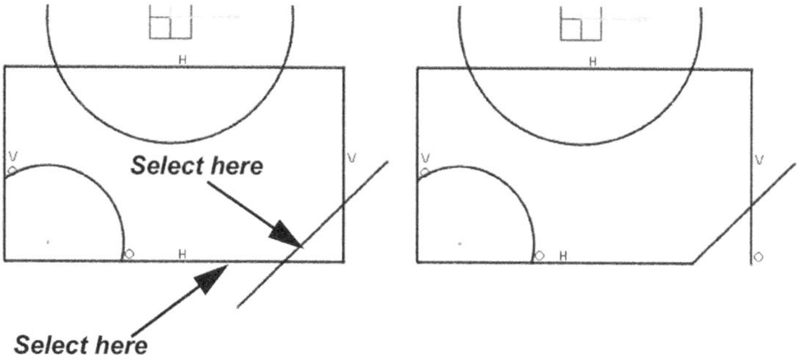

Figure 10–39

3. Note that (Trim) is no longer highlighted. This means you have to click the icon again to perform another trim.

4. Double-click (Trim) so it remains active.

5. Trim the other side of the rectangle and the line by clicking the elements labeled **Trim #2** in Figure 10–40.

6. Trim two more times to trim the arc to the box. The elements to select are labeled **Trim #3** and **Trim #4** in Figure 10–40.

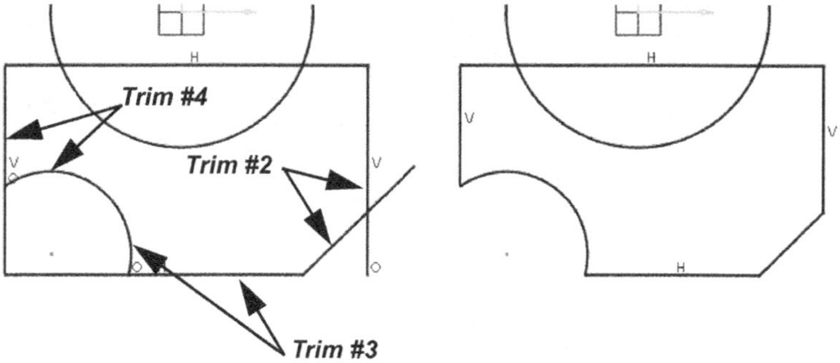

Figure 10–40

Task 9 - Trim the rectangle to the circle and the circle to the elongated hole using the Quick Trim method.

---

1. In the Action Bar, expand (Trim), and click (Quick Trim) to perform a **Quick Trim**.

2. Select the bottom of the circle to delete that segment, as shown in Figure 10–41.

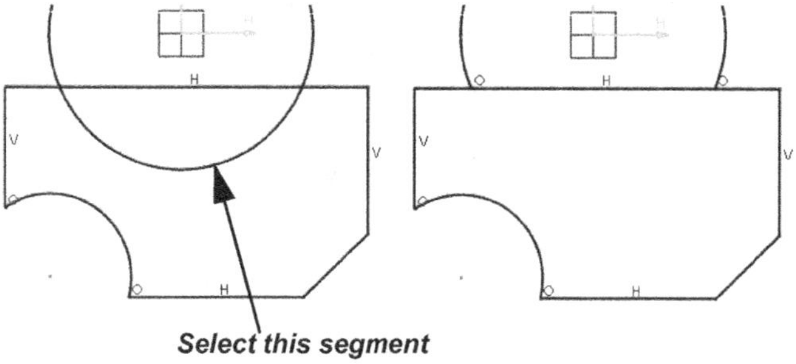

Figure 10–41

3. Double-click (Quick Trim) and trim multiple segments to clean up the sketch, as shown in Figure 10–42.

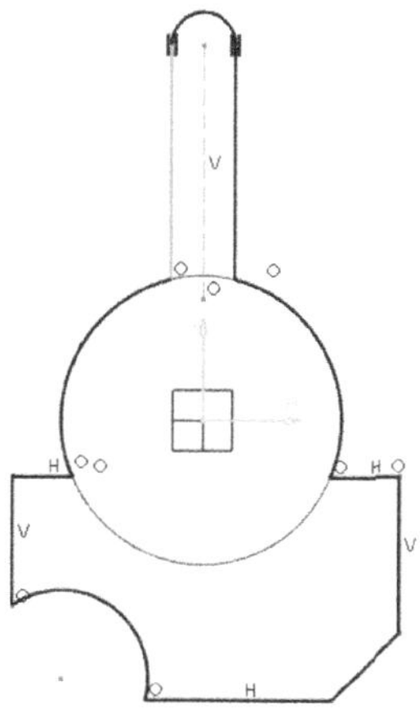

Figure 10–42

Task 10 - Exit the Sketch app and save the part.

1. Click (Exit App) to exit the Sketch app. The sketch displays as shown in Figure 10–43.

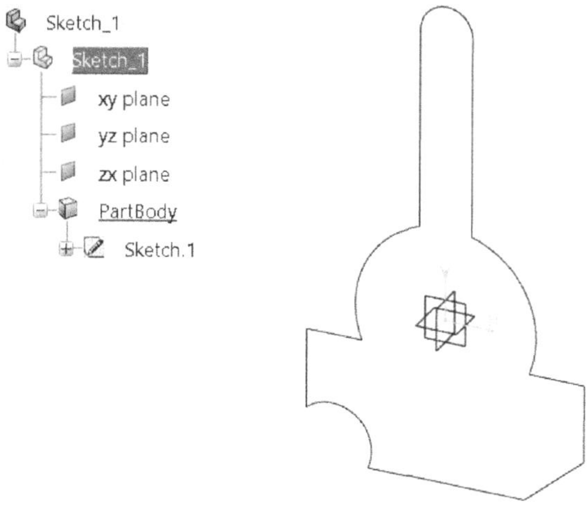

Figure 10–43

2. In the Top Bar,click (Share)>**Save** to save the part.
3. Close the *Sketch_1* tab.

Practice 10b Profile Sketching

Practice Objective

- Use Profile Sketching to create lines and arcs.

In this practice, you will use the profile sketcher to create the sketch shown in Figure 10–44.

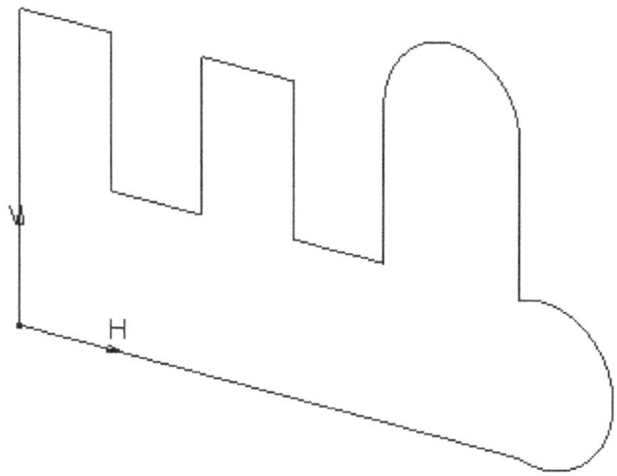

Figure 10–44

Task 1 - Create a new part and begin creating a sketch.

1. In the Top Bar, click  (Add)>**3D Part**.
2. In the 3D Part dialog box, enter ***Your Initials*_Sketch_2** as the *Title*.
3. Select the 3D Shape tab and enter **Sketch_2** for the *Title*.
4. Select the *Characteristics* tab and ensure **Enable hybrid modeling** is disabled.
5. Click **OK**.

6. Select the YZ plane as shown in Figure 10–45.

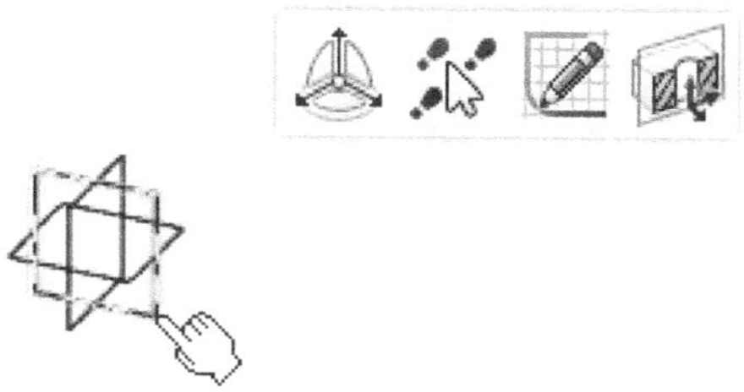

Figure 10–45

7. In the Context toolbar, click (Sketch).

Task 2 - Begin sketching a profile.

1. In the *Sketch* section of the Action Bar, click (Profile).
2. Place the cursor at the intersection of the horizontal and vertical axes, as shown in Figure 10–46. Press the left mouse button to begin sketching.

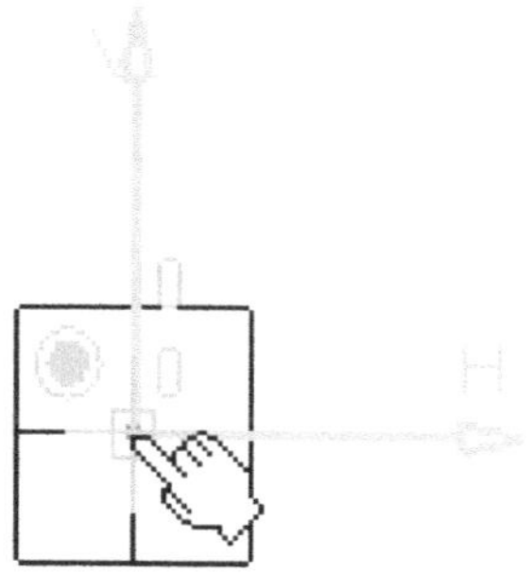

Figure 10–46

3. Sketch the series of connected vertical and horizontal lines, as shown in Figure 10–47. Note that the line turns blue when it is vertical or horizontal. Also note that the software displays a line to indicate when the cursor is coincident with other sketched elements.

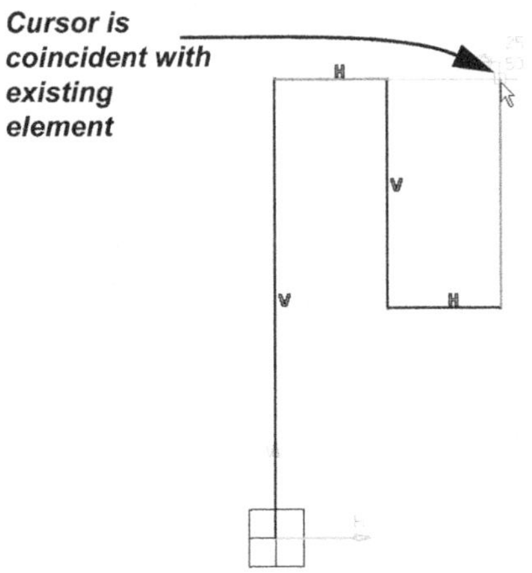

Figure 10–47

4. Continue sketching the profile until the section displays as shown in Figure 10–48. DO NOT end the profile yet.

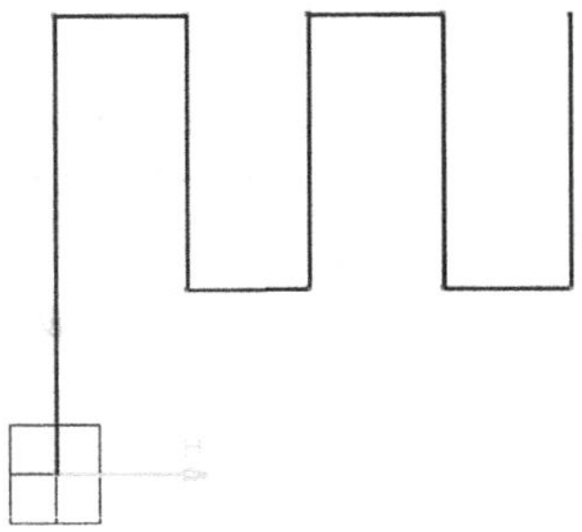

Figure 10–48

5. After selecting the end point of the last vertical line segment, click  (Tangent Arc) in the Tools Palette toolbar, as shown in Figure 10–49.

*The **Profile** tool needs to be active to display the **Tangent Arc** icon in the Tools Palette toolbar.*

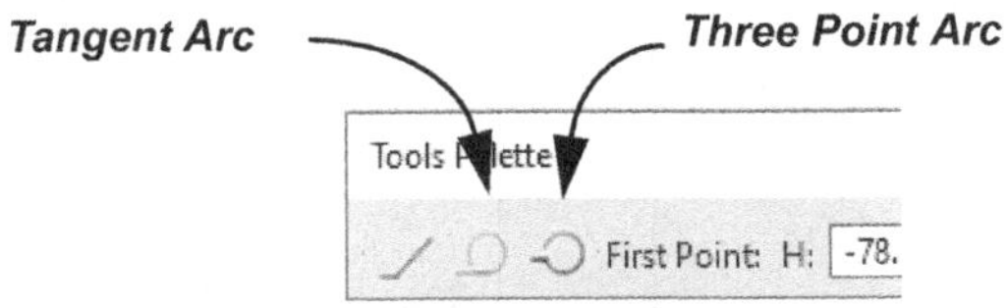

Figure 10–49

The dimensions at the end of the arc on your sketch will be different. You are currently only concerned about the shape.

6. Drag the arc to **180°**, as shown in Figure 10–50. The arc highlights in blue once you reach 180°.

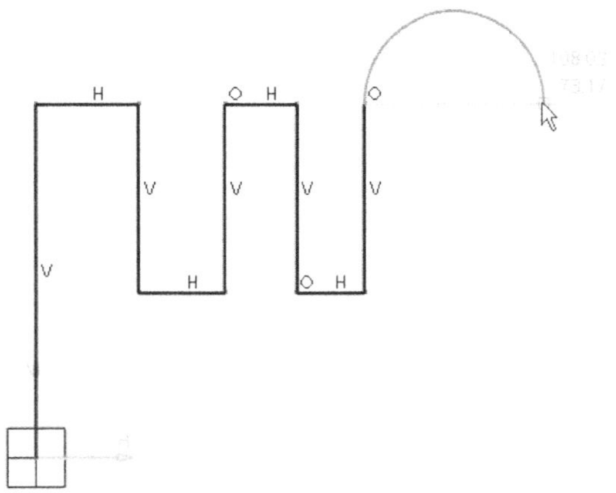

Figure 10–50

7. Draw a vertical line that is coincident with the intermediate horizontal lines, as shown in Figure 10–51.

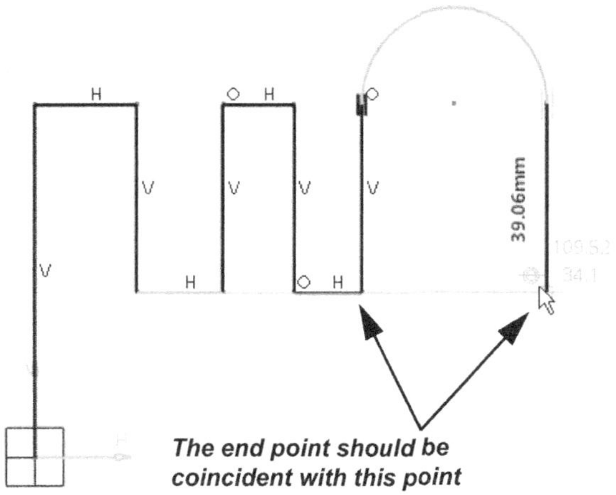

Figure 10–51

8. In the Tools toolbar, click  (Three Point Arc).

9. Sketch the three point arc shown in Figure 10–52. Try to make the end of the arc coincident with the horizontal axis and your last vertical line.

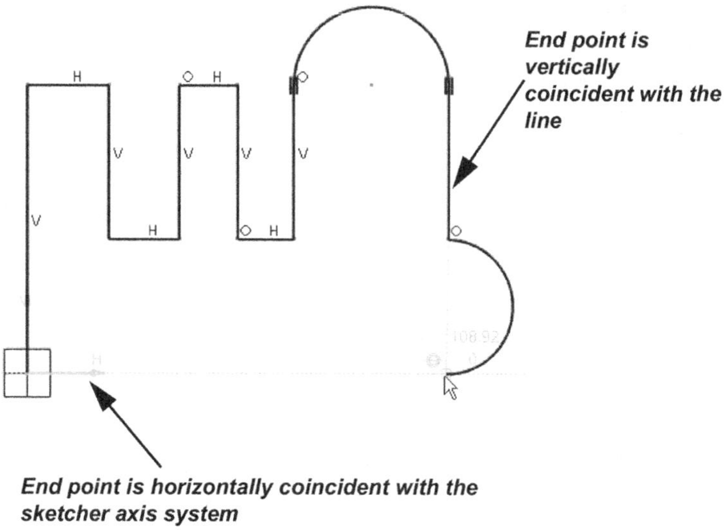

Figure 10–52

10. Drag the last horizontal line and connect it to the start point to close the sketch as shown in Figure 10–53.

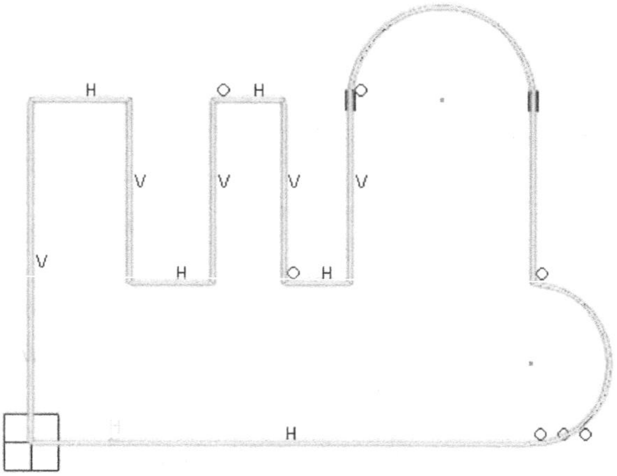

Figure 10–53

Task 3 - Select the profile.

In this task, you will demonstrate the use of the **Auto Search** option by selecting the 13 entities of the sketch.

1. Select any entity in the sketch and click (Auto Search) in the context toolbar. The software highlights the entire profile.
2. Select anywhere on the background to clear the profile.

Task 4 - Exit the Sketch app and save the part.

1. Click (Exit App) to exit the Sketch app.
2. In the Top Bar, click (Share)>**Save** to save the part.
3. Close the *Sketch_2 A.1* tab.

Practice 10c (Optional) Sketcher Practice I

Practice Objective

- Create a sketch without instructions.

Create a new part called **SketchProfile** and sketch the profile shown in Figure 10–54. Use the YZ plane as the support for the sketch. Do not be concerned with the size of the profile; ensure that the same shape is developed.

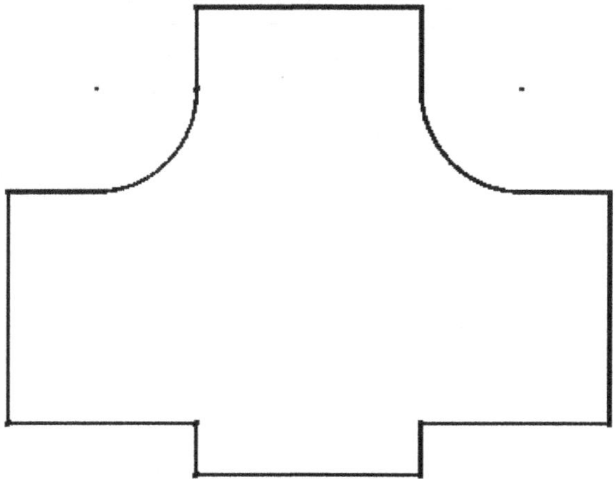

Figure 10–54

Practice 10d (Optional) Sketcher Practice II

Practice Objective

- Create a sketch without instructions.

Create a new part called **OutletProfile** and sketch the profile shown in Figure 10–55. Use the YZ plane as the support for the sketch. Do not be concerned with the size of the profile; ensure that the same shape is developed.

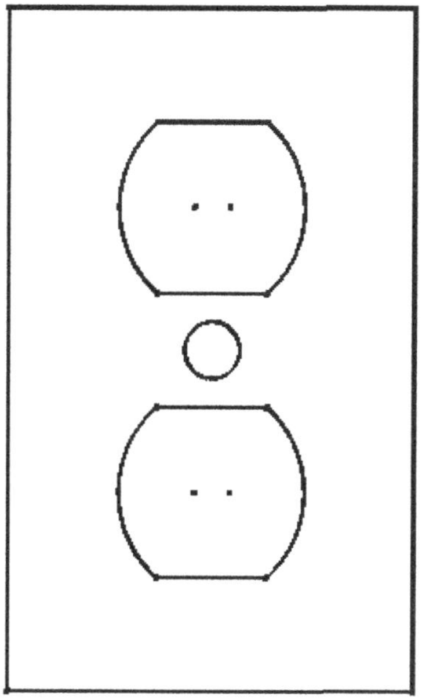

Figure 10–55

Chapter Review Questions

1. What is the process of accessing the Sketch app? (Select all that apply.)
   a. Select an appropriate sketch support and click .
   b. Click  and select an appropriate sketch support.
   c. When a CATIA part is created, the Sketch app is immediately opened.
   d. Select an appropriate sketch support and click .
2. All new parts start with what features?
   a. Pads
   b. Pockets
   c. Surfaces
   d. Default Reference Planes and the Part Body.
3. Which of the following statements best describes the default reference planes?
   a. They are the first solid feature.
   b. They have mass.
   c. They are the foundation of a part.
   d. They are not required and should be deleted.
4. If Figure 10–56 is shown in the Isometric view orientation, what is the sketching plane for the feature?

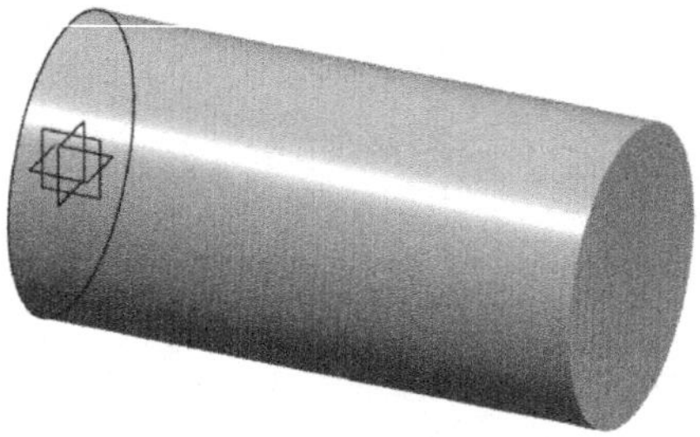

Figure 10–56

   a. XY plane
   b. ZX plane
   c. YZ plane

5. Which of the following icons enables you to sketch construction geometry?

   a. 

   b. 

   c. 

   d. 

6. Sketches are automatically hidden once they are referenced by a solid feature.

   a. True

   b. False

7. Which tool is the most efficient method of creating a series of connected lines and arcs?

   a. 

   b. 

   c. 

   d. 

8. When is a profile terminated? (Select all that apply.)

   a. When you form a closed loop.

   b. When you click  again.

   c. When you double-click.

   d. When you right-click and select **End Profile**.

Answers: 1ab, 2d, 3c, 4b, 5c, 6a, 7b, 8abc

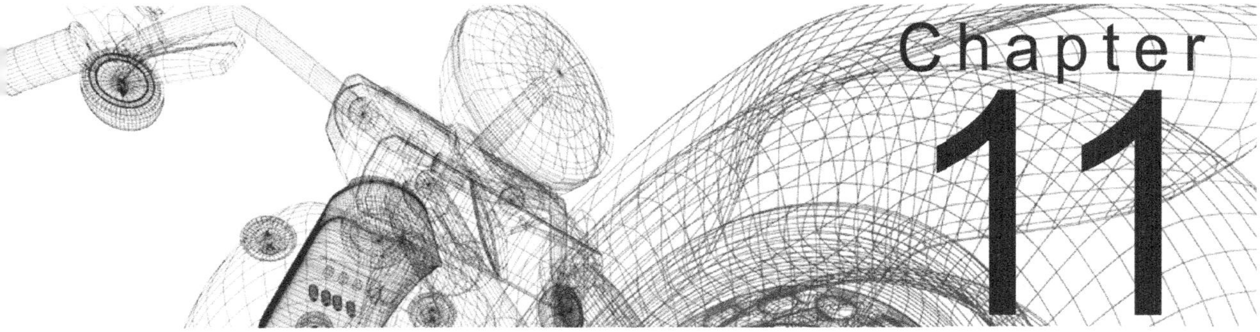

Constraining Sketches

Constraints can be either geometric or dimensional. Geometric Constraints assess a relationship between geometric elements that forces a limitation, whereas dimensional constraints define the size and location of an element. In addition, the Auto Constraint feature creates the missing constraints to make the profile fully constrained.

Learning Objectives in This Chapter

- Understand the difference between Geometric, Dimensional, and Automatic Dimensional Constraints.
- Understand the advantages of using constraints to control sketches.
- Understand the various geometric constraints.
- Work with constraints and learn how to automatically constrain a sketch.
- Use the Edit Multi-Constraint dialog box to edit multiple dimensions before the section updates.
- Understand the system-defined constraint colors for the sketch status.
- Understand the Sketch Analysis dialog box and how to use its various tabs to analyze a sketch.

11.1 Constraints

Constraints define the size and location of a sketch. You can use dimensional and geometrical constraints, as shown in Figure 11–1.

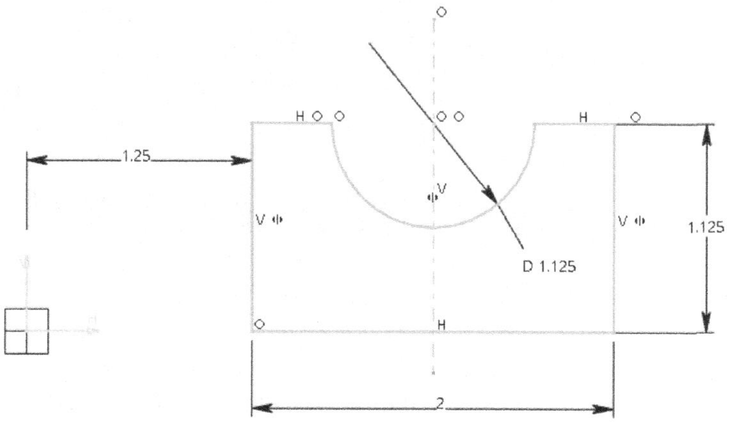

Figure 11–1

The constraints available, along with their icons in the Action Pad, are used to control their display. They are described as follows:

Icon	Constraint	Description
	**Geometrical Constraints**	Relationships between geometric elements that describe how they are oriented.
	**Dimensional Constraints**	Values used to define the size, distance, or angle of an element.
	**Automatic Dimensional Constraints**	Automatically apply the values used to define the size or angle of elements as you sketch.

You can develop sketches that are completely unconstrained or partially unconstrained. Thus, you do not need to place any unnecessary dimensions on a sketch. However, it is recommended that you fully constrain your sketches.

Figure 11–2 shows an example of a partially constrained sketch. Initially, the box is 50 wide. When this dimensional constraint is changed to 100, the software updates one side of the box and leaves the other side in its original state. If the design intent of this sketch is to create a rectangle, the current design of this part requires additional constraints to maintain the geometry over time.

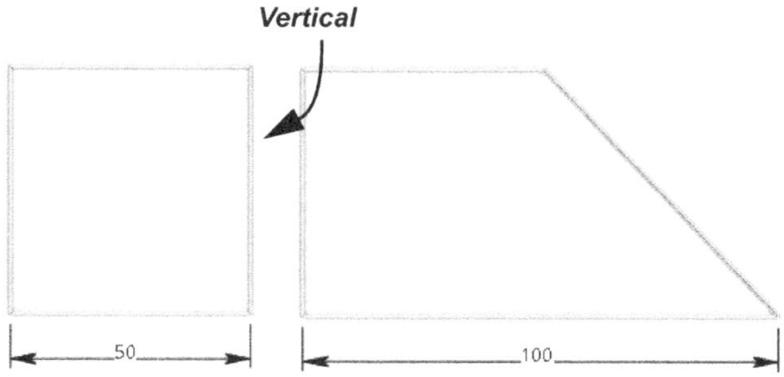

Figure 11–2

Constructing 3D solid models from unconstrained sketches can lead to unpredictable results. Figure 11–3 shows an example of an unconstrained Pocket. If the block is made wider or taller, what happens to the Pocket? Should it remain centered on the block or should it remain the same distance from the right or left side? This unpredictable nature can lead to undesirable shapes and update outcomes.

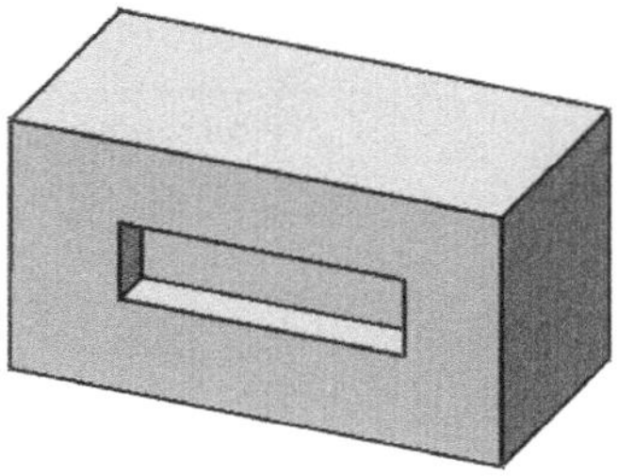

Figure 11–3

Advantages of Using Constraints

Using constraints has the following advantages:

- Dimensional constraints enable you to precisely define the size of your sketch and to quickly and accurately change its size.
- Geometric constraints enable you to incorporate design intent into your sketches, which automates the geometry update process.

11.2 Geometric Constraints

Geometric constraints can be created by selecting entities while  (Constraint) is enabled. As you select entities, the context toolbar displays with constraints applicable to the selected entities. For example, if two lines are selected, the context toolbar provides access to the Dimension, Parallelism Constraint, Perpendicular Constraint and so on, as shown in Figure 11–4.

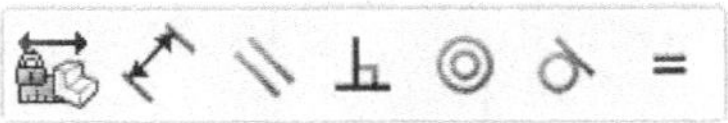

Figure 11–4

The constraints in the context toolbar will vary depending on the type of entity selected.

Geometric constraints consist of a relationship between geometric elements that forces a limitation of some type. For example, you can constrain a line in a sketch to be vertical. With the vertical constraint in place, the line is limited and cannot be at an angle.

The most commonly-used geometric constraints are described as follows:

Constraint	Example	Description
Horizontal 	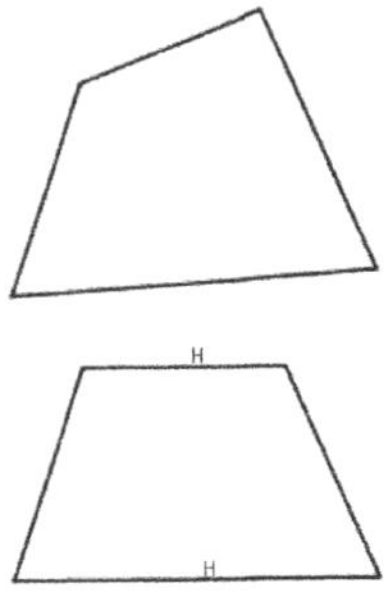	Use <Ctrl> to preselect the lines that are to be horizontal.

Constraint	Example	Description
Vertical 	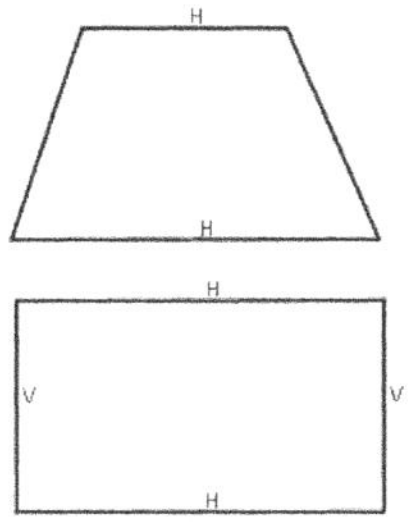	Use <Ctrl> to preselect the lines that are to be vertical.
Parallelism 	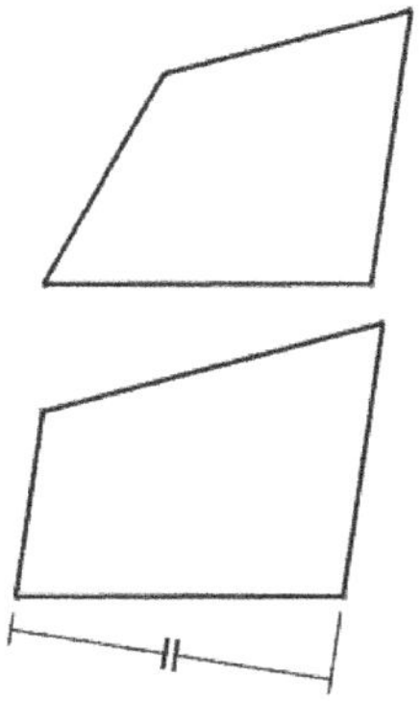	Select the first line to remain fixed, and select the second line to make parallel to the first.
Perpendicular 	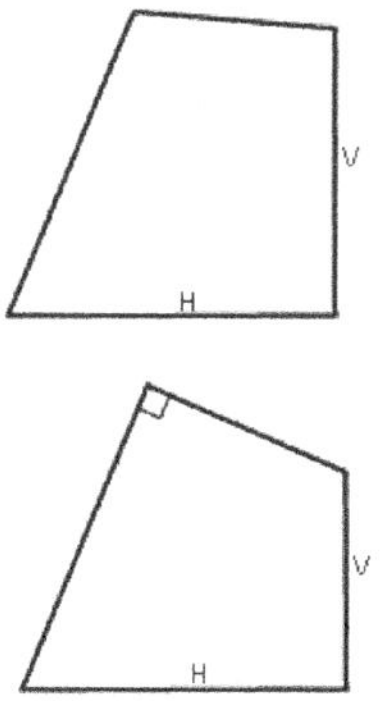	Use <Ctrl> to preselect lines to be perpendicular.

Constraint	Example	Description
Concentricity or Concentric 	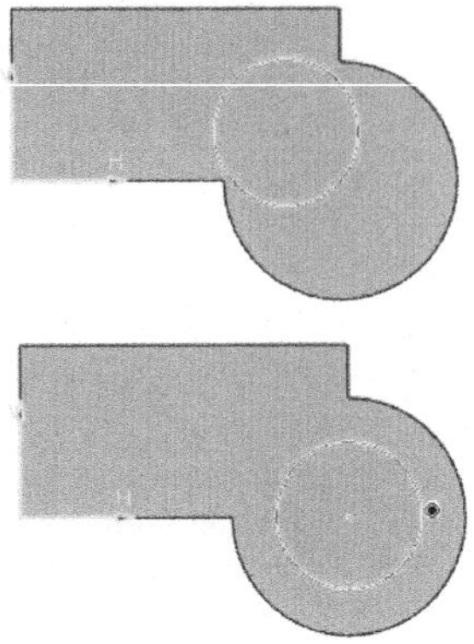	Select a curved edge of a Pad feature and the sketched circle. Concentricity only works with existing geometry.
Tangency 		Use <Ctrl> to preselect the entities to be tangent.
Symmetry 	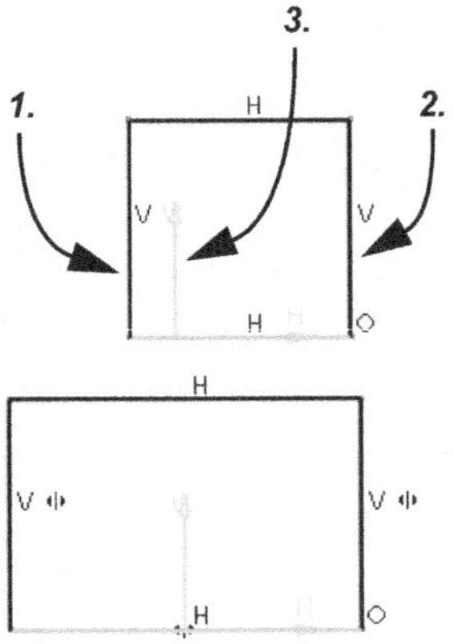	Press and hold <Ctrl> while selecting references in the following order: first symmetric element, second symmetric element, and symmetry reference.

Constraint	Example	Description
Coincidence 	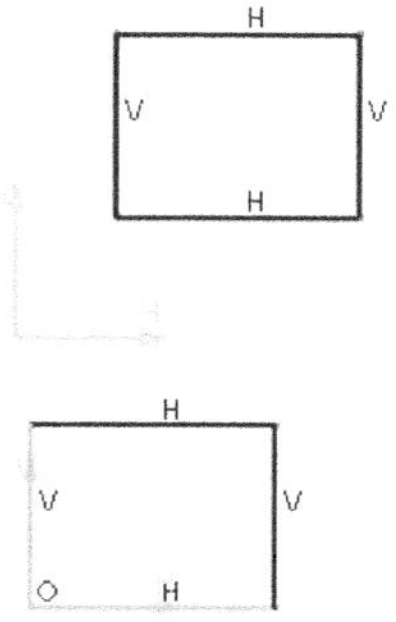 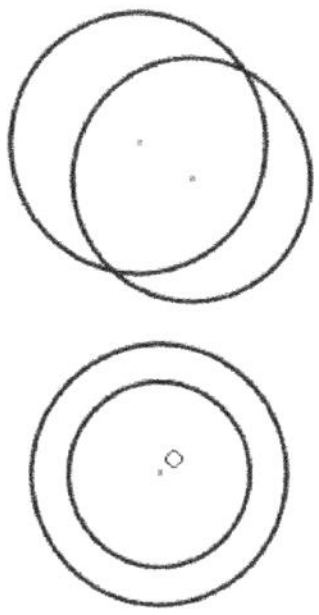	Select end points of entities to be coincident with one another and/or to another point. For circles, you must select the circle centers.
Equal 	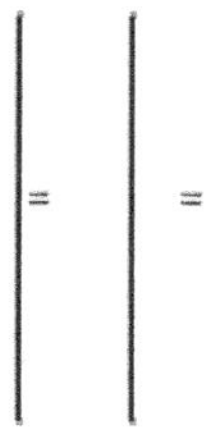	Select two entities to make their length, diameter or radii equal.

Shortcut Menu

The shortcut menu is another method to apply constraints. It provides access to frequently used geometric constraints and operations such as **Horizontal** or **Vertical** constraints for linear elements and **Close** or **Complement** operations for arcs. For example, a slanted line can be vertically constrained by right-clicking and selecting **Line.# object> Vertical**, as shown in Figure 11–5.

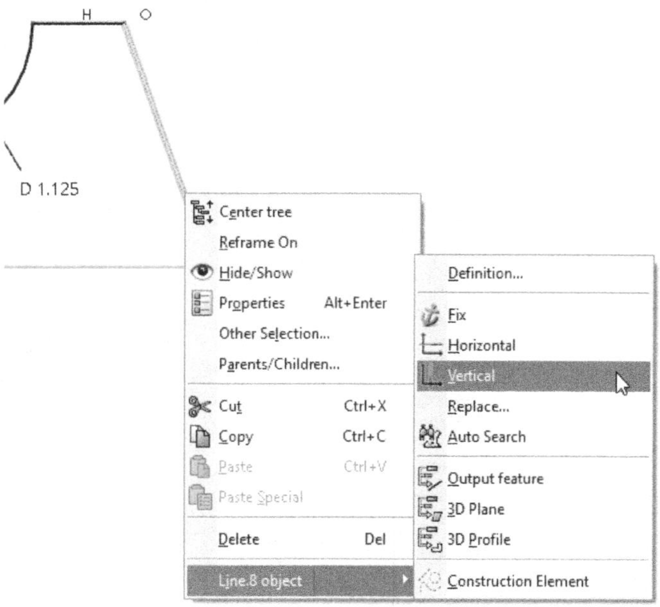

Figure 11–5

Geometric Constraints can also be generated using

 (Constraint) in conjunction with the shortcut menu.

How To: Place Geometric Constraints Using the Shortcut Menu

1. Select one or more geometric entities in your sketch.
2. Select  (Constraint) from the context toolbar or the *Sketch* section of the Action Bar.
3. Instead of clicking to place the dimension that displays, right-click to display the shortcut menu shown in Figure 11–6.

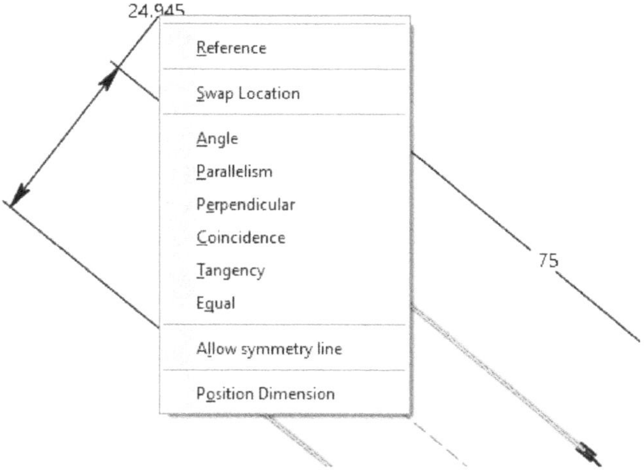

Figure 11–6

4. Select the geometric constraint you want to apply to the selected geometry from the shortcut menu. The geometric constraint is now applied as shown in Figure 11–7.

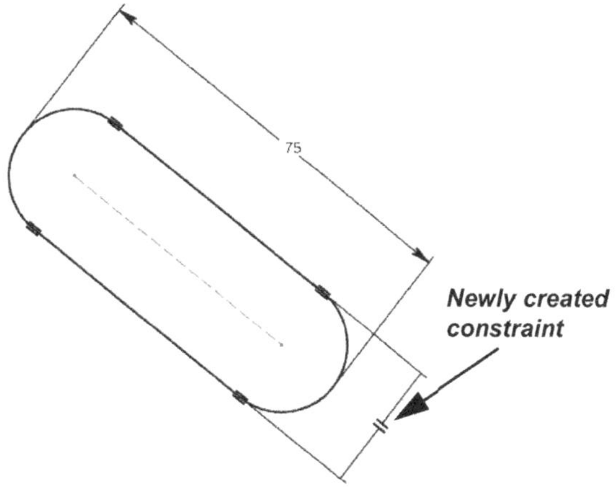

Figure 11–7

Repeat Steps 2 to 4 to place more geometric constraints.

Constraints Defined in Dialog Box

Another method for applying constraints is to use the  (Constraints Defined in Dialog Box) option. This option displays a dialog box that shows the available constraints for the selected entities. Here you can select the constraints you want to enable.

How To: Apply a Constraint with the Constraint Definition Dialog Box

1. Use <Ctrl> to preselect the elements in the correct sequence.
2. Click (Constraints Defined in Dialog Box).
3. Select the required constraint in the Constraint Definition dialog box shown in Figure 11–8.

Only the constraints that are valid for the elements you selected are available.

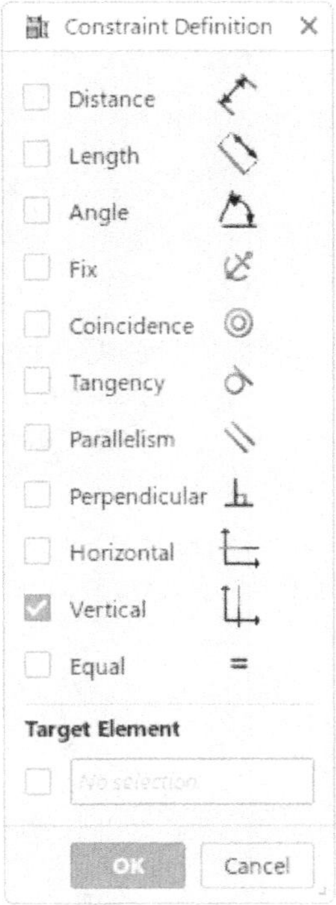

Figure 11–8

4. Click **OK**.

Note that you can apply constraints between entities using the **Target Element** option. Enable **Target Element**, click in the *Target Element* field and select an element from the sketch. The selected element will drive the resulting constraints.

Three lines were selected in Figure 11–9, and the top line, **Line.3**, is used as the Target Element. When the **Distance** constraint is selected, the dimensions for the distance between the lines, are added, using **Line.3** as the baseline.

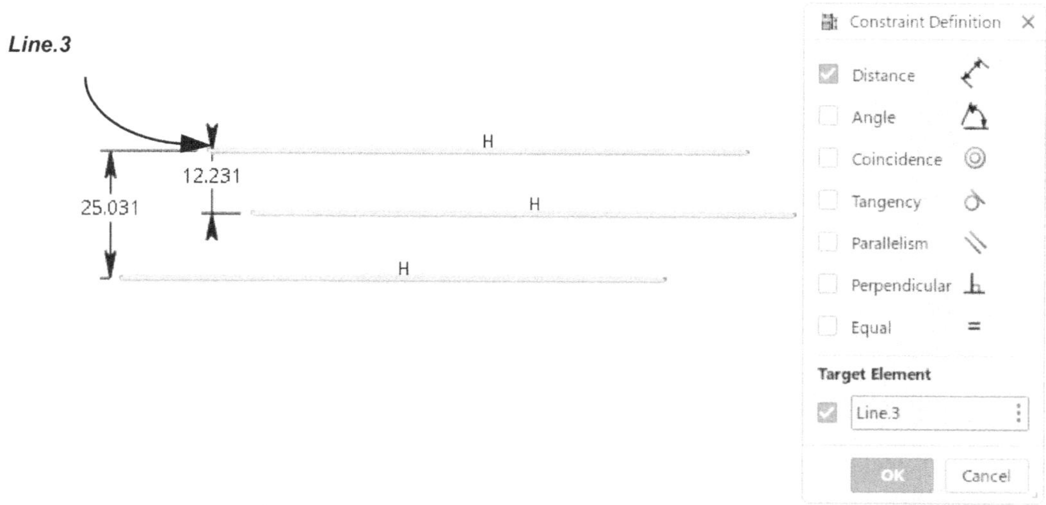

Figure 11–9

Deleting Constraints

Use one of the following methods to remove a constraint:

- Select the constraint symbol on the screen to highlight it, and press <Delete>.
- Select the constraint in the specification tree and press <Delete>.

Centering a Sketch

To center a sketch on a part, sketch an axis and use the **Symmetry** constraint to constrain the axis to the middle of the part. Use <Ctrl> to multi-select the two edges of the part, and then an axis. In the context toolbar, click (Fast Symmetry), and the selected entities are set to be centered around the vertical axis, as shown in Figure 11–10.

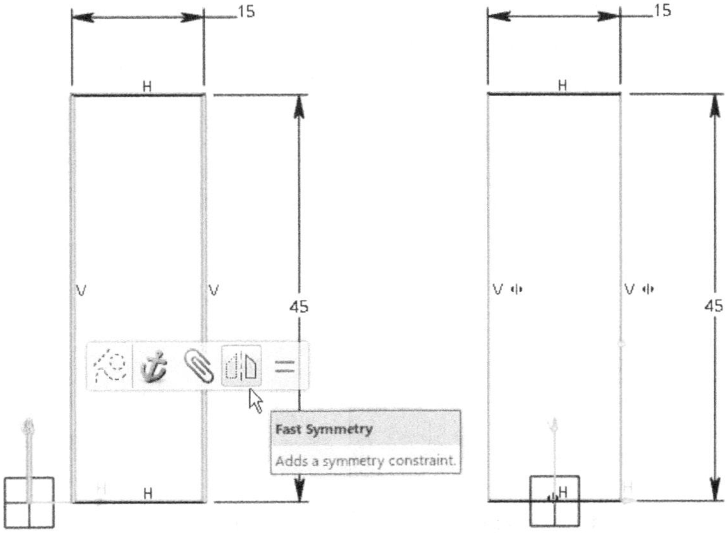

Figure 11–10

Group Constraint

The **Group** constraint constrains selected sketched elements together so that they can be moved as one entity.

How To: Group Elements Together

1. Select the entities to add by drawing a selection box around them, or by multi-selecting with <Ctrl>.
2. Click (Group). The Group Definition dialog box opens as shown in Figure 11–11.
3. Click **OK**. The sketch elements can be dynamically moved using the cursor, as shown in Figure 11–12.

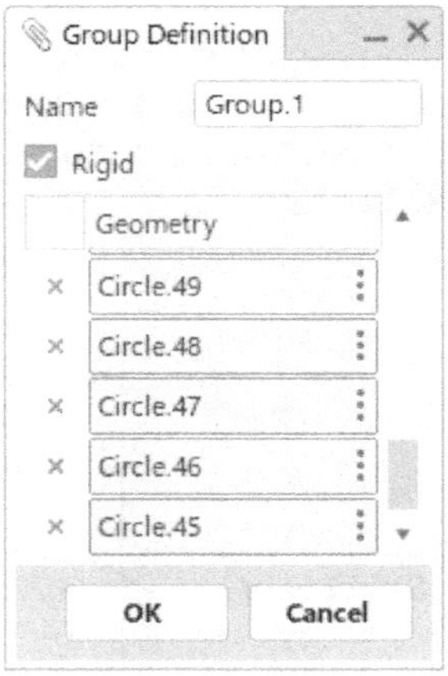

Figure 11–11

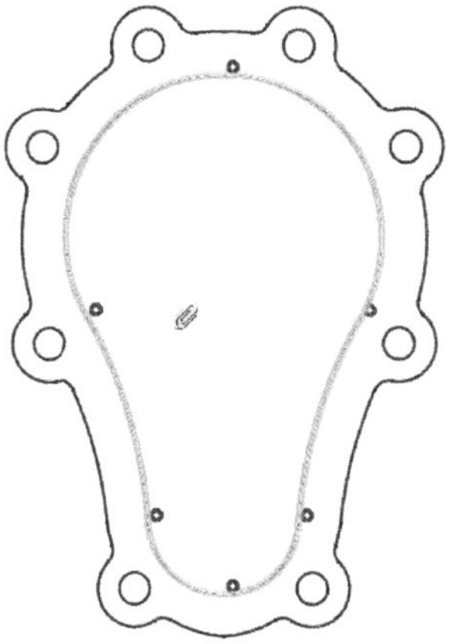

Figure 11–12

11.3 Dimensional Constraints

Dimensional constraints define an element's size and location. In most cases, you need to create several dimensions. Double-click on 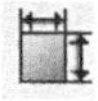 (Constraint) to create as many dimensions as you require without having to click the icon every time.

The following topics describe how to create various dimension types.

Line Length Dimension

To dimension a line, select the line to be dimensioned and drag the dimension to the required location, as shown in Figure 11–13.

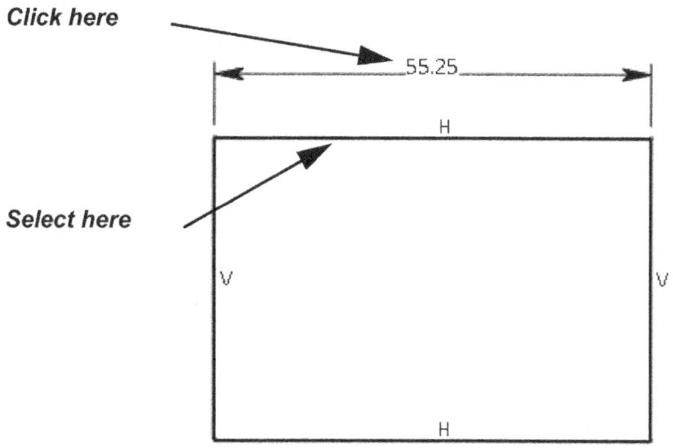

Figure 11–13

Distance between Parallel Lines

To dimension the distance between parallel lines, select the first line. A length dimension displays. Select the second line. The distance between the two lines displays. Click to place the dimension. An example is shown in Figure 11–14.

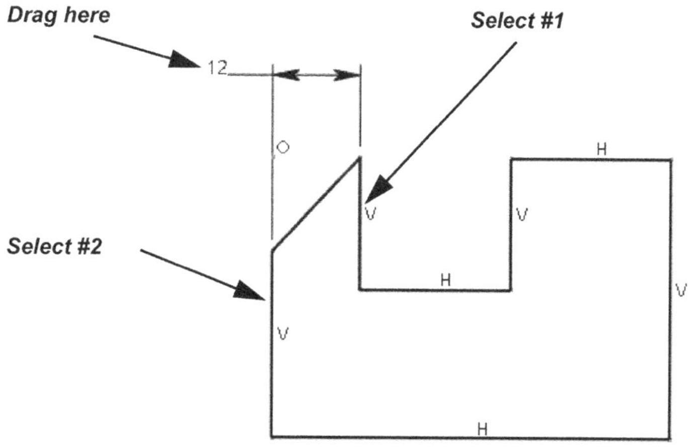

Figure 11–14

Arc Radius

To create an arc radius dimension, sketch a corner and the dimension is automatically created. To manually create an arc radius dimension, select the arc and click a location on the screen to place the dimension, as shown in Figure 11–15.

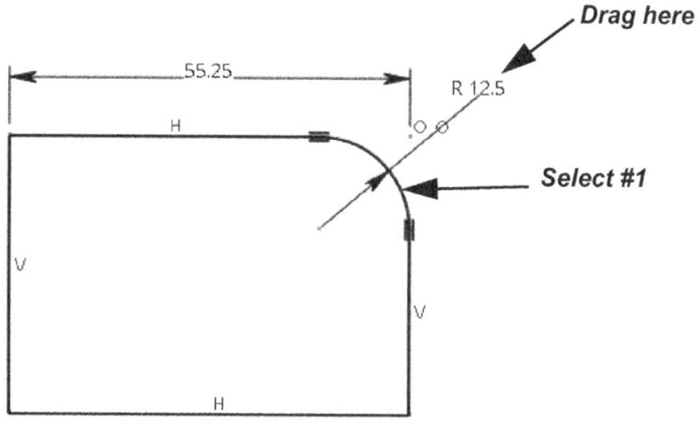

Figure 11–15

Arc Diameter

To dimension an arc as a diameter, you can use one of the following methods:

- A radius dimension displays by default when you select the arc. Before placing the dimension, click  (Diameter Constraint) in the context toolbar, or right-click and select **Diameter**, as shown in Figure 11–16.

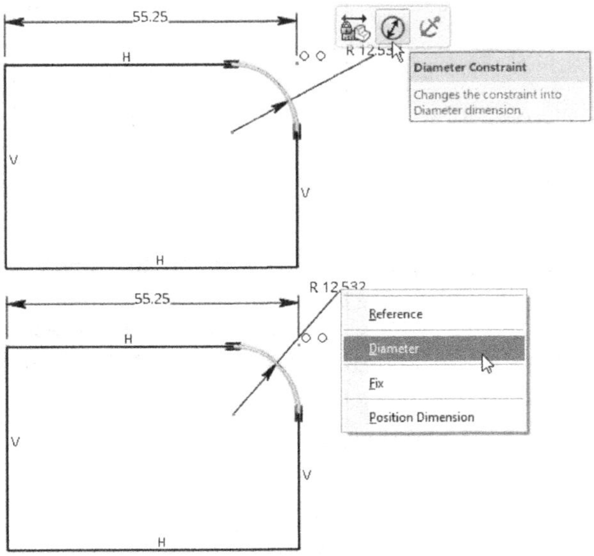

Figure 11–16

- Convert an existing arc radius dimension into a diameter dimension by double-clicking on the radius dimension. The Radius dialog box opens. In the *Dimension* drop-down list, select **Diameter** and click **OK** to complete the change, as shown in Figure 11–17.

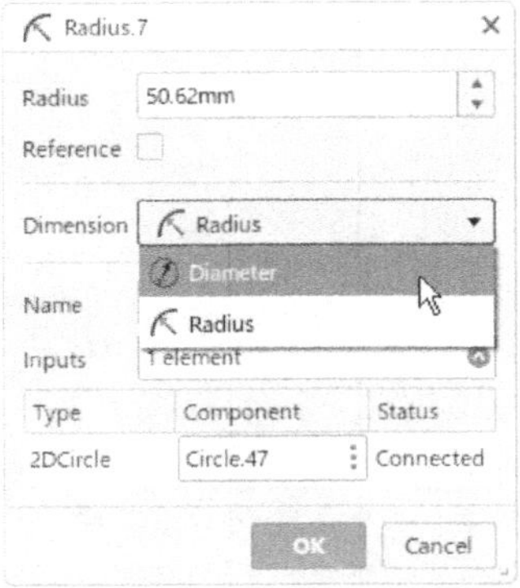

Figure 11–17

Revolved Diameter

The revolved diameter can only be created using an axis and not a construction line.

When creating sketches for revolved features, only half of the profile is sketched. It is then revolved about the centerline. To create this dimension, select a line element and an axis. By default, a dimension representing the distance between the two parallel elements displays. Before placing the dimension, right-click and select **Diameter**, as shown in Figure 11–18.

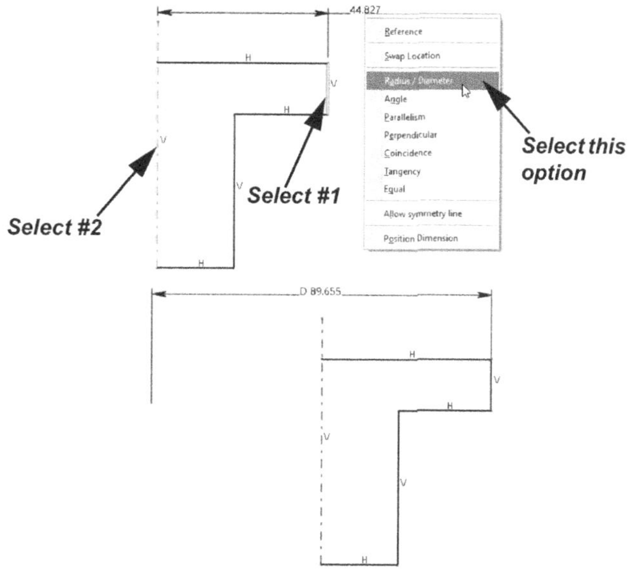

Figure 11–18

Angle Dimension

To create an angle dimension, select two non-parallel lines and an angle dimension displays. The dimension location determines how the angle dimension displays. The result of placing an angle dimension in four different locations is shown in Figure 11–19.

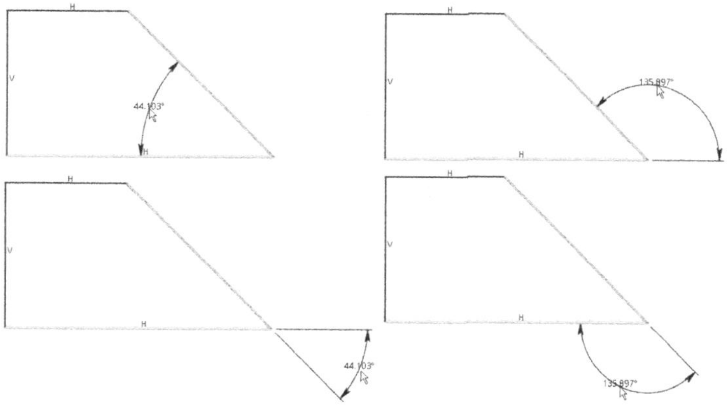

Figure 11–19

Point-to-Point Dimension

Point-to-point dimensions can be created between any two of the following elements:

- Center of an arc or circle
- End of a straight line
- Construction point

By default, the dimension displays as the absolute distance between the points. Before placing the dimension, use the shortcut menu to display the dimension as the horizontal or vertical distance between the points. These dimension options are shown in Figure 11–20.

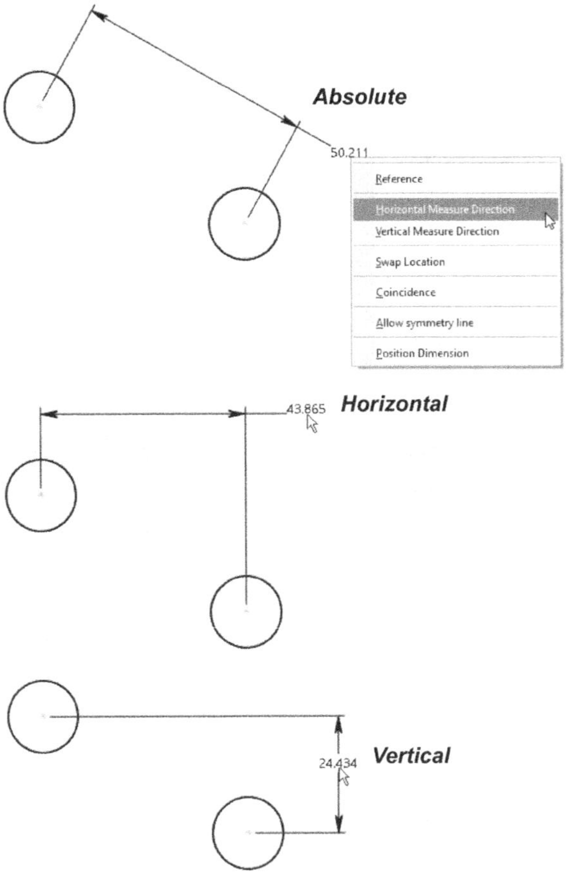

Figure 11–20

Line-to-Arc Tangent

You can also dimension to the arc center by selecting on the point.

To create a line-to-arc tangent dimension, select the line as the first element to dimension from. The line length dimension displays. Ignore this dimension and select the arc. The arc tangent dimension displays as shown in Figure 11–21.

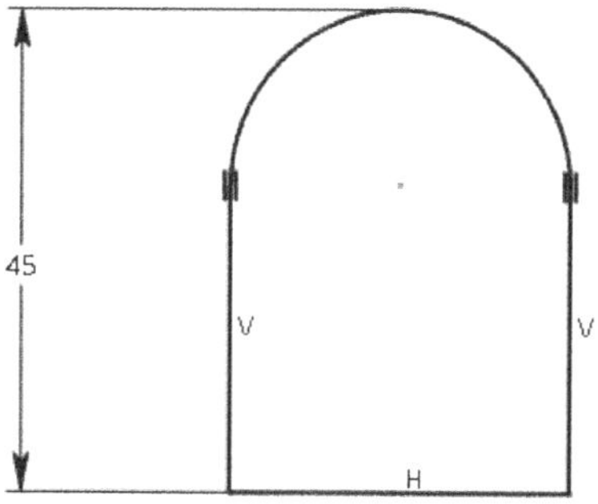

Figure 11–21

Arc Tangent-to-Arc Tangent

Select each of the arcs and drag the dimension to the required location. By default, the dimension displays as the absolute distance between the arc tangents, as shown in Figure 11–22.

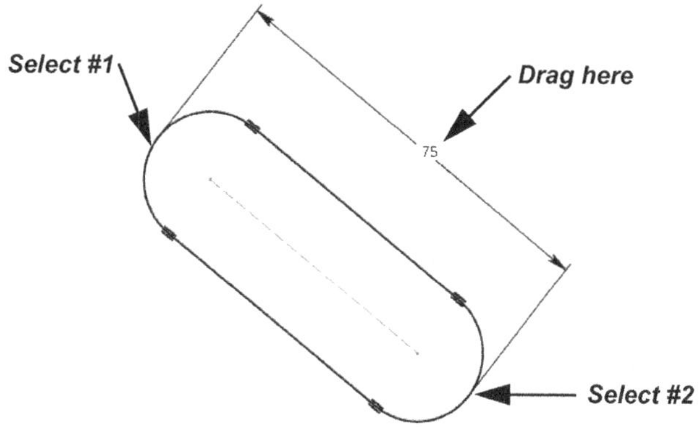

Figure 11–22

Before placing the dimension, you can use the shortcut menu to display the dimension as the horizontal or vertical distance between the arcs.

11.4 Automatic Dimensional Constraints

By default, in the *Sketch* section of the Action Bar, the  (Automatic Dimensional Constraints) is enabled, as shown in Figure 11–23.

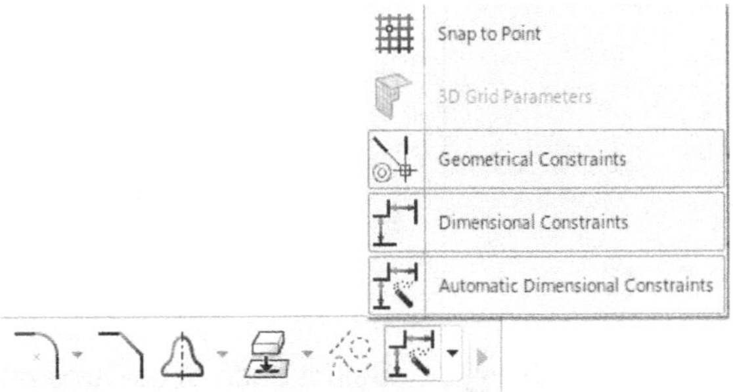

Figure 11–23

With this option enabled, the system automatically adds dimensional constraints as you sketch geometry.

In Figure 11–24, as soon as the rectangle is sketched, the system automatically determined the required dimensions to constrain it and applied them accordingly.

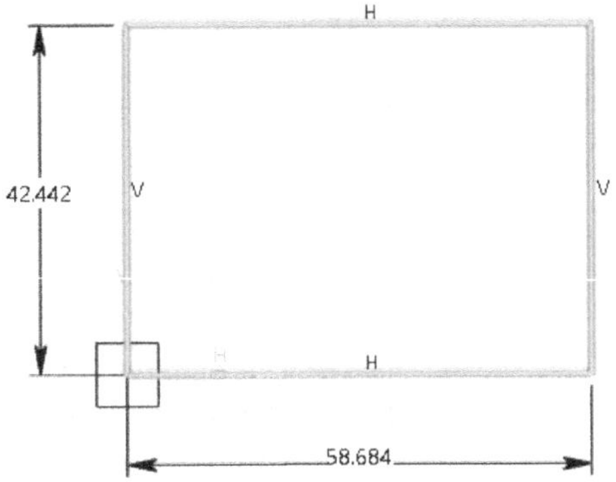

Figure 11–24

You can edit the dimensions to finalize them, as required. Automatic dimensional constraints are only applied to rectangles, circles, arcs and ellipses, and will only be added to define the size of an element, not its location relative to other elements.

11.5 Edit Multi-Constraint Dialog Box

The Edit Multi-Constraint dialog box enables you to modify the value of more than one dimension before updating the section. This is useful when modifying all dimensions of an oversized section. Typically, you would have to select the order of modification carefully to ensure that the modified dimension does not cause the section to fail. Using the **Edit Multi-Constraint** tool, you can modify all dimension values, and then preview and accept the changes.

The **Multi-Constraint** tool is found in the Constraint toolbar shown in Figure 11–25.

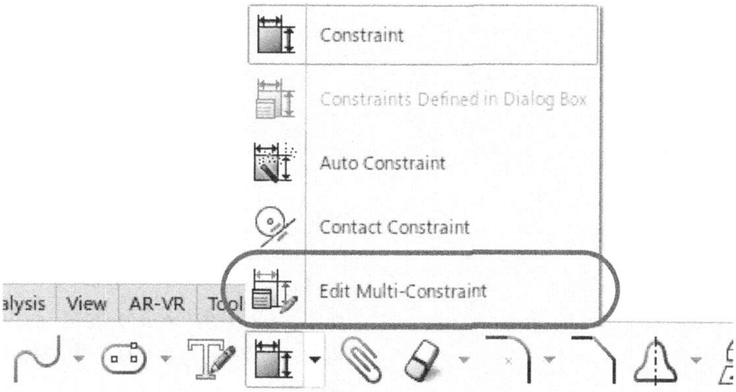

Figure 11–25

How To: Modify Dimensions Using the Edit Multi-Constraint tool

1. Click (Edit Multi Constraint) in the Action Bar.
2. The Edit Multi-Constraint dialog box opens. The software displays the constraint name, initial value, current value, and the maximum and minimum tolerances for each dimension in the section as shown in Figure 11–26.

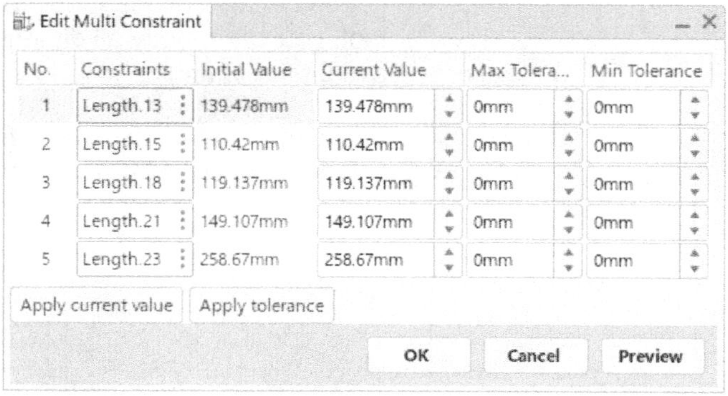

Figure 11–26

3. Select the dimension from the list or directly from the model. The corresponding dimension highlights in light blue on the section.
4. In the *Current value* field, enter a new value. The dimension highlights in cyan to indicate that the initial value has been modified.
5. Once all dimensions have been modified, click **Preview** to preview the changes to the section.
6. Click **OK** to complete the changes. If an error occurs, click **Restore Initial Value** to undo the modification to the selected dimension.

Tips and techniques

- You can modify or restore multiple dimensions by using <Ctrl> to select them.
- Maximum and minimum tolerances can be added to any dimension by selecting it and entering the tolerance in the appropriate field.
- You can right-click in the *Current value* field in the Edit Multi-Constraint dialog box to access standard constraint editing options, as shown in Figure 11–27.

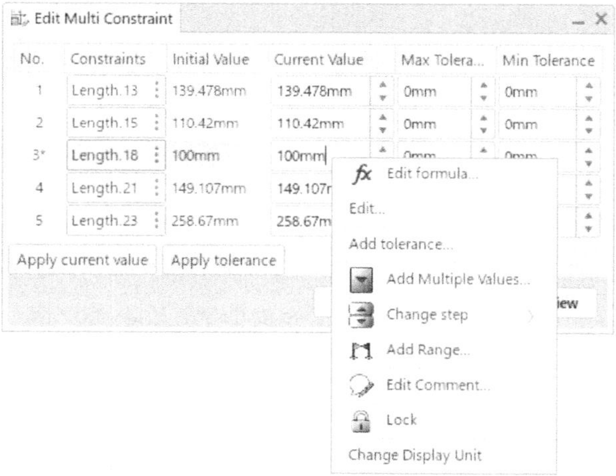

Figure 11–27

- For large, complex sections, click **Preview** frequently to update and test the section. If an error occurs, it is likely a dimension that was modified after the last preview.
- Selecting dimensions before clicking  (Edit Multi Constraint) only adds those dimensions to the Edit Multi-Constraint dialog box.

11.6 Constraint Colors

To fully constrain your sketches, you must define the size and location of the sketch. For the first sketch on a new part, you must constrain the sketch to the horizontal and vertical axes, as shown in Figure 11–28.

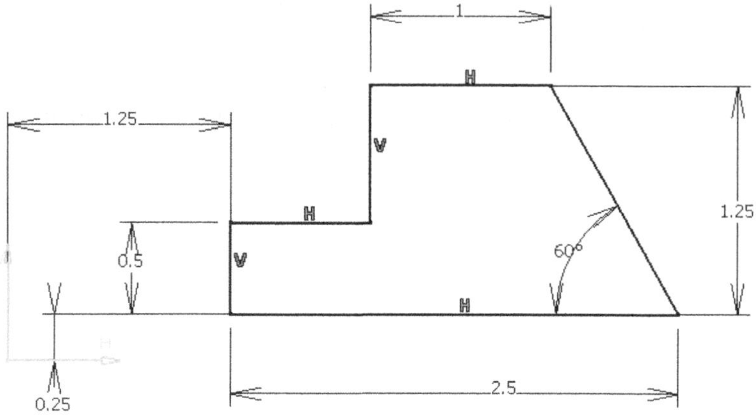

Figure 11–28

The software uses colors on the elements of your sketch to visually indicate the constraint status. These colors are described as follows:

Color	Definition	Description
Black	Under constrained	Some degrees of freedom still remain for the element.
Green	Constrained	The geometry is completely fixed and cannot be moved without altering a dimensional value.
Purple	Over constrained	Too many dimensions or geometric constraints are on the element.
Red	Inconsistent	The sketch cannot be solved with the current combination of constraints and values.
Brown	Not changed	Geometry that is dependent on over-defined or inconsistent elements and is not up to date.

11.7 Sketch Analysis

Once the sketch is created and constrained, you can analyze the sketch by clicking  (Sketch Analysis) in the *Analysis* section of the Action Bar. The Sketch Analysis dialog box opens as shown in Figure 11–29.

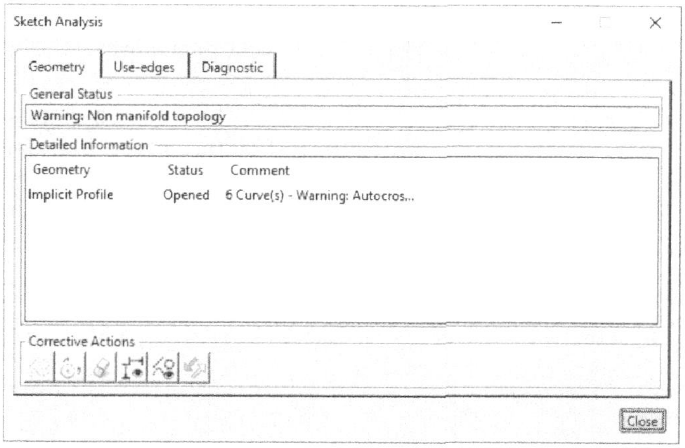

Figure 11–29

The following are examples of the types of analyses that can be performed:

- Ensure that the section meets the design intent.
- Ensure that the section is fully constrained.
- Check the status of projections and intersections.
- Perform corrective actions, as required.

Geometry Tab

The *Geometry* tab is used to analyze individual elements of the sketch. It displays the general status of the elements being analyzed. It is used to analyze the sketched elements and determine the status of each element in the model.

The different values available in the *Status* column are described as follows:

Status	Description
Opened	A collection of sketched entities that form an open loop. Open loops can occur when the start and end points of a loop appear to be touching, but actually have a gap between them.

Closed	A collection of sketched entities that form a closed loop.
Isolated	A single sketched entity that is not touching or connected to any other geometry in the section. This could indicate a line which should be converted to a construction line, or a line which should belong to a loop of entities, but has gaps at either end.
Wrong Point	A sketched point is connected to existing geometry. This indicates that the point should be converted to a construction point to be a valid section to create 3D geometry.

The *Geometry* tab also displays detailed information about each selected element type and general comments, as shown in Figure 11–30.

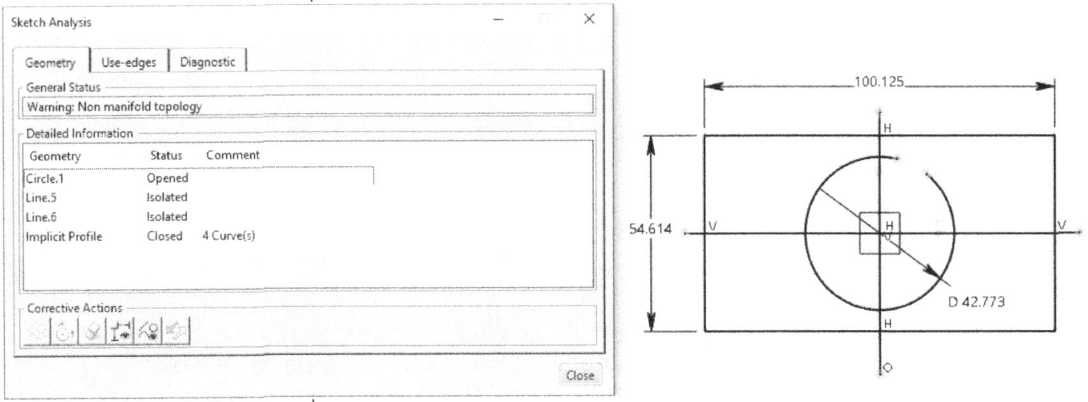

Figure 11–30

If you select an item in the Detailed Information area, the entity highlights on the screen, making it easier to find.

The sketch shown in Figure 11–30 has several problems. The detailed information displays that the circle is not closed (which is not the design intent) and that two line entities in the profile should be construction lines. The icons in the *Corrective Actions* area of the dialog box enable you to correct the problems in your sketch.

These icons are described as follows:

Icon	Description
	Changes the selected entity to a construction entity.
	Closes the open profile.
	Deletes the selected entity from the sketch.
	Toggles the display of constraints on and off in the sketch.
	Toggles the display of construction geometry on and off in the sketch.
	Reverses the orientation of the sketched entity.

The icons in the *Corrective Actions* area correct the problem, as shown in Figure 11–31. **Line.5** and **Line.6** were converted to construction entities using . **Circle.1** was closed using .

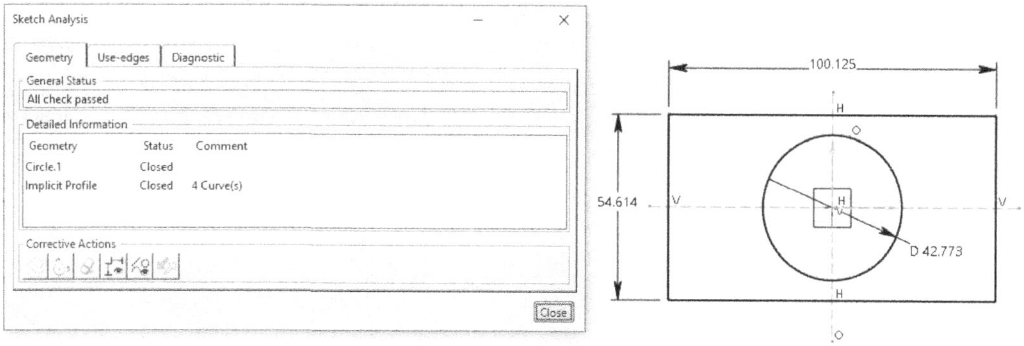

Figure 11–31

Use-edges

The *Use-edges* tab displays the status of all entities that are projected from existing geometry. The contents of this tab are discussed in detail once the concept of projecting 3D geometry has been introduced.

Diagnostic Tab

The *Diagnostic* tab provides a detailed summary of each sketched entity and the solving status of the sketch. A sketched entity can have one of the following three status values:

- **Under-Constrained:** Additional dimensions or constraints must be applied to the sketched entity.
- **Over-Constrained:** Too many dimensions or constraints have been applied to the element.
- **Iso-Constrained:** The entity is fully constrained.

The *Detailed Information* area lists all sketched entities, their current constraint status, and the type of entity (i.e., geometry, constraint, construction geometry, etc.), as shown in Figure 11–32.

You cannot edit the sketch while the tab is open. You must first exit the Sketch Analysis dialog box, solve any constraint issues, and re-open the dialog box to verify.

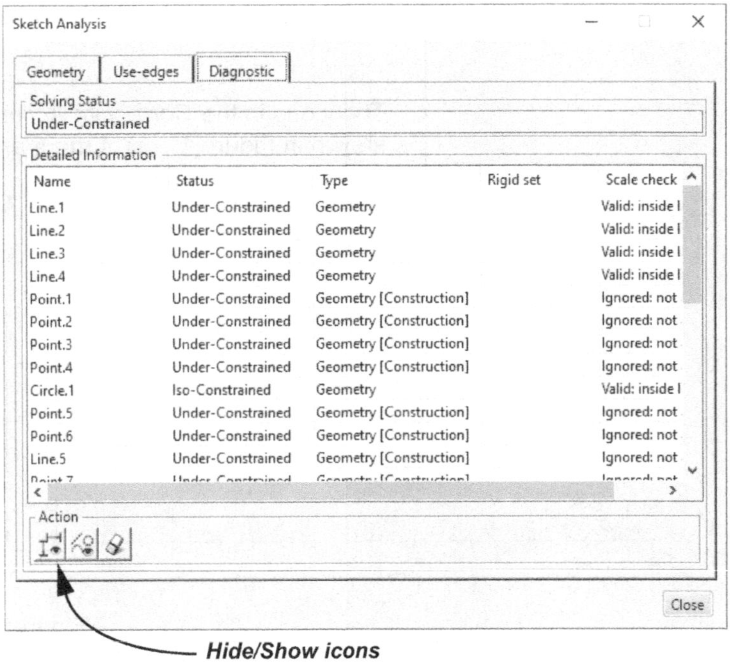

Figure 11–32

The **Hide/Show** icons in the *Action* area can be used to simplify the screen. Select an entity in the *Detailed Information* area and select the appropriate icon to hide or show the entity.

Sketch Solving Status

The Sketch Solving Status dialog box is used to determine the constraint status of the sketch. A sketch can either be under-constrained, over-constrained, or fully constrained (Iso-constrained). If the section is over-constrained or under-constrained, the software highlights the affected entities on the sketch.

Click  (Sketch Solving Status) in the *Analysis* section of the Action Bar to open the Sketch Solving Status dialog box, as shown in Figure 11–33.

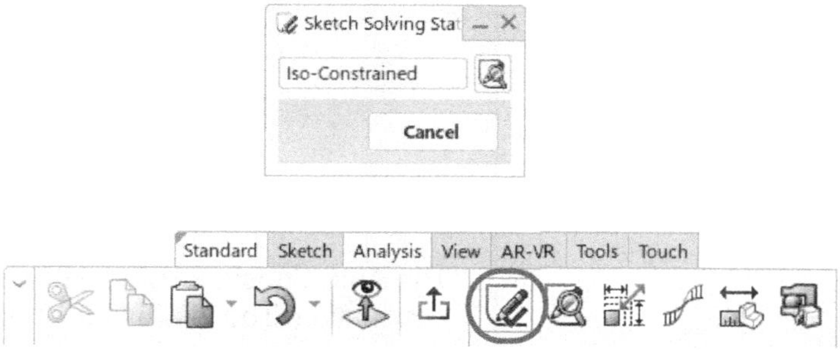

Figure 11–33

You can open the **Sketch Analysis** tool from this dialog box by clicking  (Sketch Analysis).

11.8 Auto Constraint

If you are having trouble eliminating all degrees of freedom, you can use  (Auto Constraint) to fully constrain your sketch. The **Auto Constraint** tool is found in the *Sketch* section of the Action Bar, as shown in Figure 11–34.

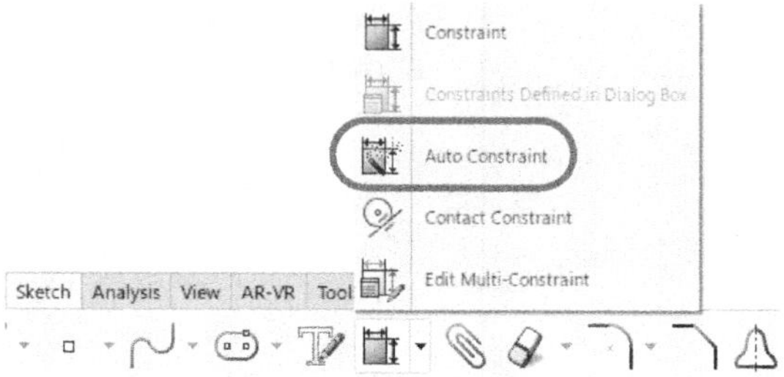

Figure 11–34

The Auto Constraint dialog box requires up to three sets of information. These are described as follows:

Information	Description
Elements to be constrained	These elements of your sketch display in black. When in doubt, select your entire sketch.
Reference elements	These elements are what your sketch is located to. For new sketches, select the horizontal and vertical axes.
Symmetry lines	If you want your sketch to be symmetrical, select the horizontal axis, the vertical axis, or a sketched axis.

The Auto Constraint dialog box opens as shown in Figure 11–35.

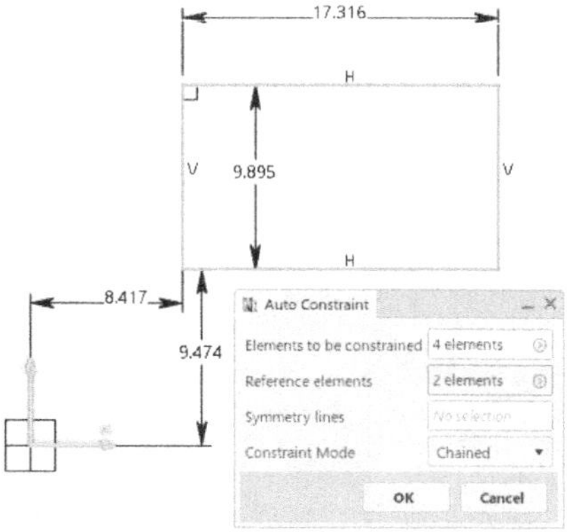

Figure 11–35

Practice 11a Dimensions

Practice Objectives

- Create a sketched profile.
- Create the dimensions required to fully define a sketch.
- Recognize when a sketch is under-constrained or constrained.

In this practice, you will create the sketch shown in Figure 11–36. You will constrain the sketch using geometrical and dimensional constraints. You will also be able recognize whether a sketch is under-constrained or over-constrained.

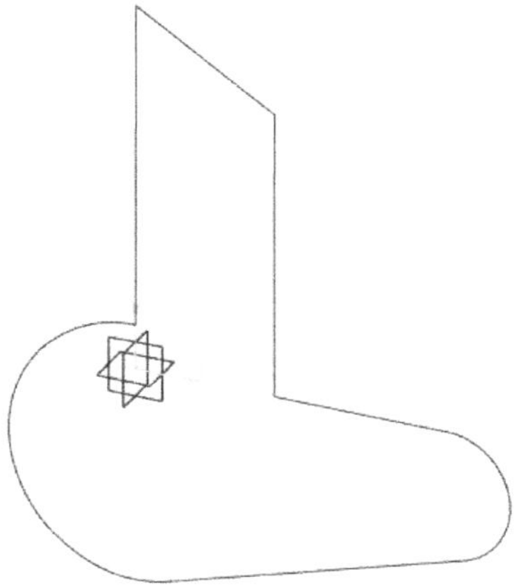

Figure 11–36

Task 1 - Create a new part and begin creating a sketch.

1. In the Top Bar, click  (Add)>**3D Part**.
2. In the 3D Part dialog box, enter **Constraints_1** as the *Title*.
3. Select the *3D Shape* tab and enter **Constraints_1** for the *Title*.
4. Select the *Characteristics* tab and ensure **Enable hybrid modeling** is disabled.
5. Click **OK**.
6. In the specification tree, select the YZ plane.
7. In the Action Bar, click  (Sketch).

Task 2 - Begin sketching the profile.

1. If necessary, right-click and select **Display>Action Pad**.

An activated icon displays with a blue highlight.

2. Verify (Geometrical Constraints) is selected to enable automatic geometric constraints.

3. Ensure (Automatic Dimensional Constraints) is disabled.

4. Sketch the part profile shown in Figure 11–37 using (Profile). Verify that the arcs are tangent in the locations shown.

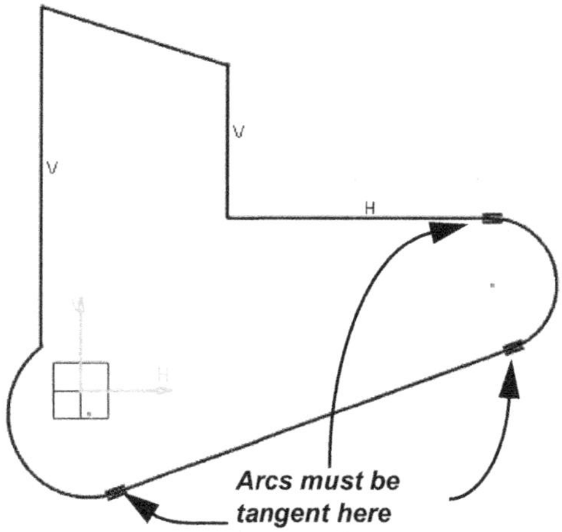

Figure 11–37

Task 3 - Perform a sketch analysis.

1. In the *Analysis* section of the Action Bar, click (Sketch Solving Status). The Sketch Solving Status dialog box opens as shown in Figure 11–38.

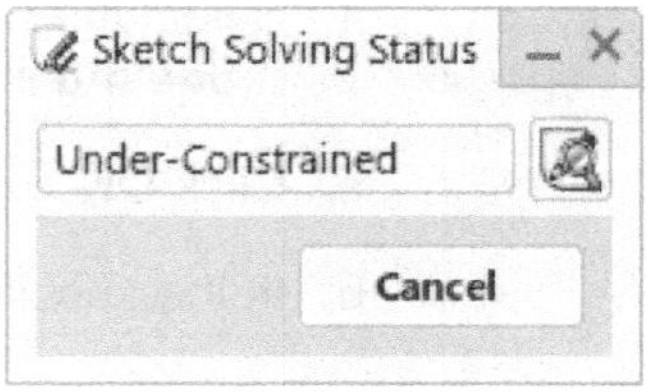

Figure 11–38

Design Considerations

The software reports that the section is under-constrained. Since no dimensions have been applied to the section, all entities are highlighted to indicate that they are under-constrained. You will apply dimensions to the section to constrain it in the part.

2. In the Sketch Solving Status dialog box, click  (Sketch Analysis).
3. Select the *Geometry* tab. The Sketch Analysis dialog box opens as shown in Figure 11–39.

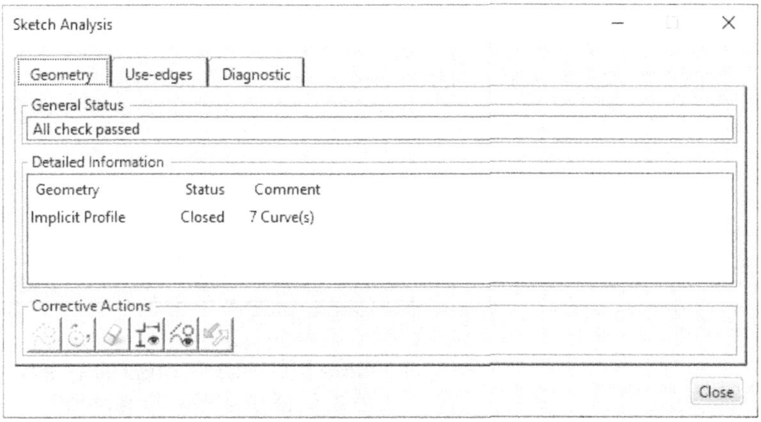

Figure 11–39

4. Verify that the software reports a closed status for the sketch and that only seven curves exist. If you receive a different result, verify that your section has been created correctly.
5. Close the Sketch Analysis dialog box.

Task 4 - Dimension the length of a straight line.

1. In the *Sketch* section of the Action Bar, click  (Constraint) to start constraining.

2. Select the vertical line shown in Figure 11–40. Click the dimension to the left side of the line. Do not modify the default values of your sketch. You will adjust them later.

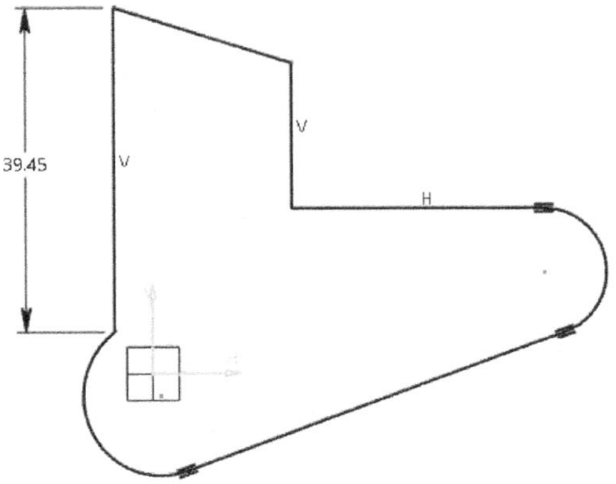

Figure 11–40

Task 5 - Dimension between parallel lines.

1. Note that  (Constraint) is no longer active. Select it again to create another dimension.

2. Select the short vertical line, as shown in Figure 11–41. A length dimension displays. You do not want this dimension. Select the long vertical line, and a dimension displays for the distance between the two lines.

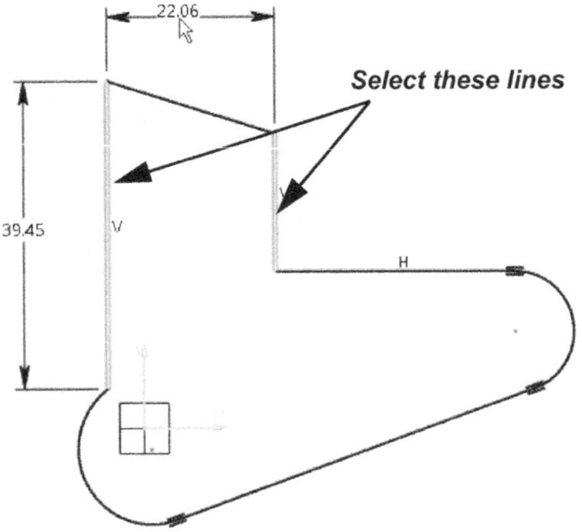

Figure 11–41

Task 6 - Enable continuous dimensioning and dimension the two arcs, one as a radius and one as a diameter.

1. Double-click on (Constraint) to enable continuous dimensioning. The icon remains enabled until you select another action.
2. Select the arc on the left side and click to place the radius dimension outside the sketch, as shown in Figure 11–42.
3. Select the other arc, and click (Diameter Constraint) from the context menu, then click to place the dimension, as shown in Figure 11–42.

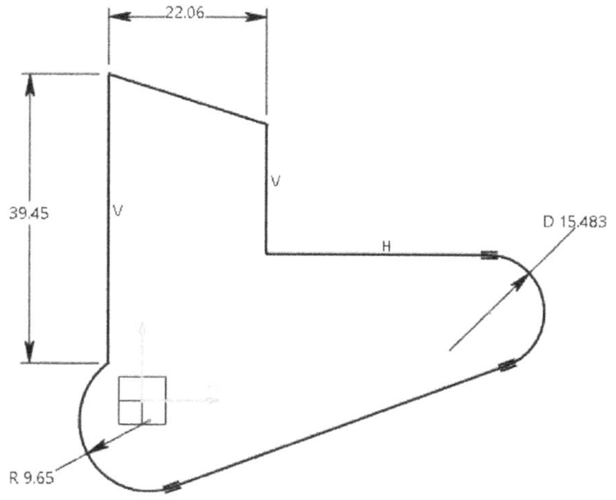

Figure 11–42

Task 7 - Change the radius dimension to a diameter dimension.

1. Click (Constraint) again to terminate dimension creation.
2. Double-click on the radius dimension.
3. In the Radius dialog box, in the *Dimension* drop-down list, select **Diameter**.
4. Click **OK** to complete the change.

Task 8 - Create an angle dimension.

1. Double-click on  (Constraint).
2. Select the slanted line as the first element and the long vertical line as the second element, as shown in Figure 11–43. Before you place the dimension in its final location, move the cursor to other positions to preview the possible angle dimensions.
3. Place the angle dimension as shown in Figure 11–43.

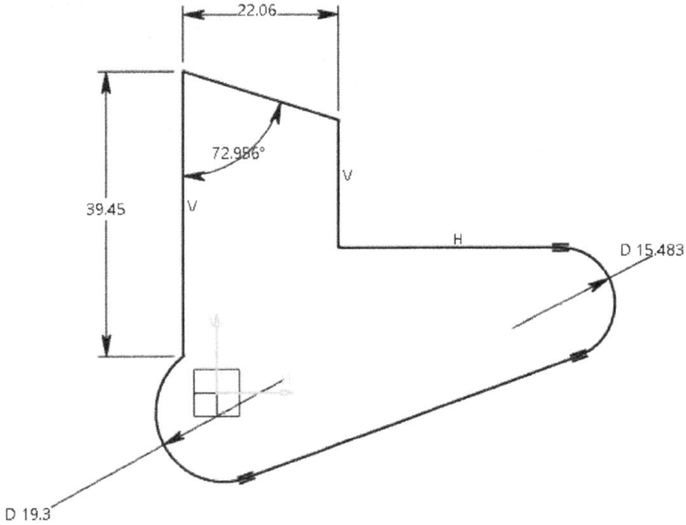

Figure 11–43

Task 9 - Create a horizontal dimension between the two arcs.

1. With  (Constraint) still be active, select each arc to initially create an absolute arc tangent dimension, but do not place the dimension.

2. Right-click and select **Horizontal Measure Direction**. The sketch displays as shown in Figure 11–44. Horizontal Measure Direction is also available in the context toolbar.

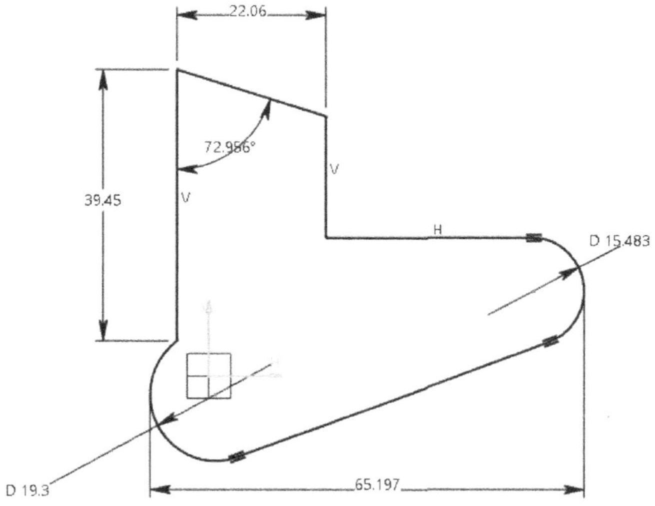

Figure 11–44

Task 10 - Create dimensions to fully constrain the sketch.

1. To finish constraining the shape of the sketch, create the two dimensions circled in Figure 11–45.

The 5.08 dimension is created by selecting the center point of the D51.664 arc and the 104.292 vertical line.

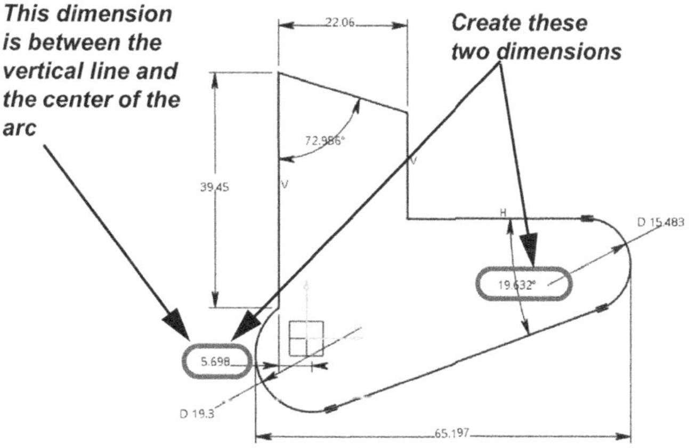

Figure 11–45

2. To constrain the location of the sketch relative to the datum planes, create the two dimensions circled in Figure 11–46. Create each dimension from the line to the horizontal or vertical axis.

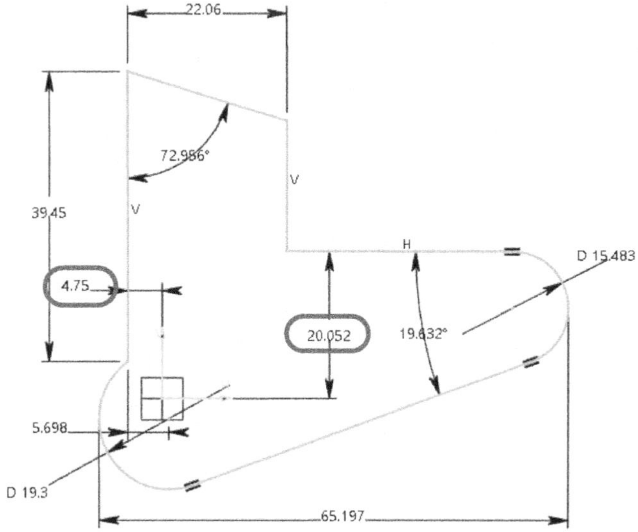

Figure 11–46

3. In the *Analysis* section of the Action Bar, click  (Sketch Solving Status) to open the Sketch Solving Status dialog box, and verify that the section is fully constrained, as shown in Figure 11–47.

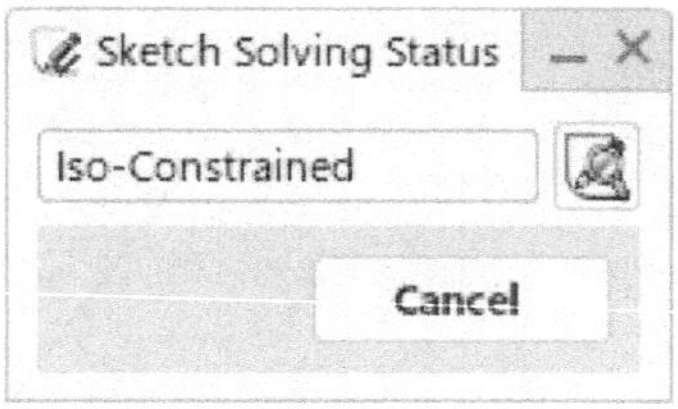

Figure 11–47

4. Click **Cancel** to close the dialog box.

Task 11 - Over-constrain the sketch.

1. Create a dimension for the length of the angled line, as shown in Figure 11–48.

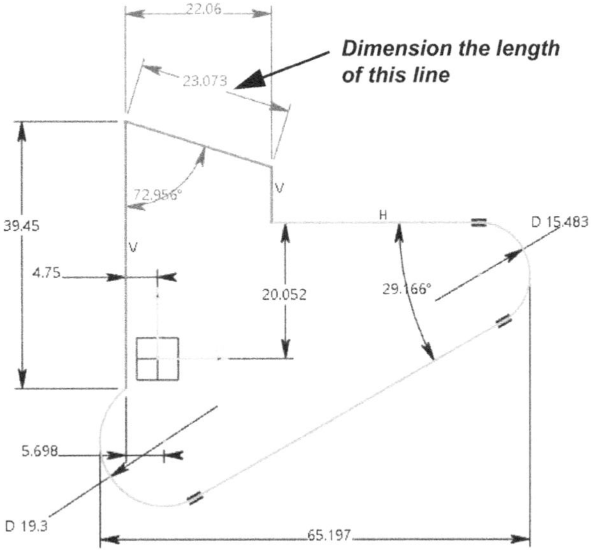

Figure 11–48

The sketch is now over-constrained, as indicated by the purple color of the affected sketch entities.

2. Click  (Sketch Solving Status). The software now reports that the sketch is over-constrained and highlights the three impacted sketch entities in light blue.

3. Close the Sketch Solving Status dialog box.

Remember that your dimensions will have different values.

4. Select the leader line of the **22.06** horizontal dimension, right-click and select **Delete**. If you select on the 22.06 number, it will attempt to change the number and not allow for the same right-click options. The sketch is again fully constrained (it will turn green).

Task 12 - Manipulate the dimensions.

1. Practice moving dimensions, as shown in Figure 11–49. Click the dimension's leader line to select the dimension it will turn light blue. Once selected, click and drag the number to move the dimension along the arrows. Click and drag the leader lines to move the dimension closer or farther from the sketch.

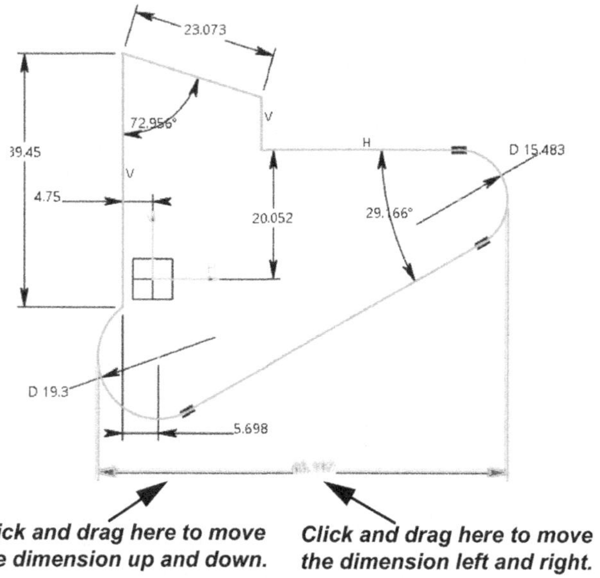

Figure 11–49

Task 13 - Modify the size of the dimensions.

1. Select the **72.956** angle dimension's number.
2. Set the *Angle* = value to **60.00** and press the **Enter** key.

3. Expand the (Constraint) fly-out and click (Edit Multi Constraint), as shown in Figure 11–50.

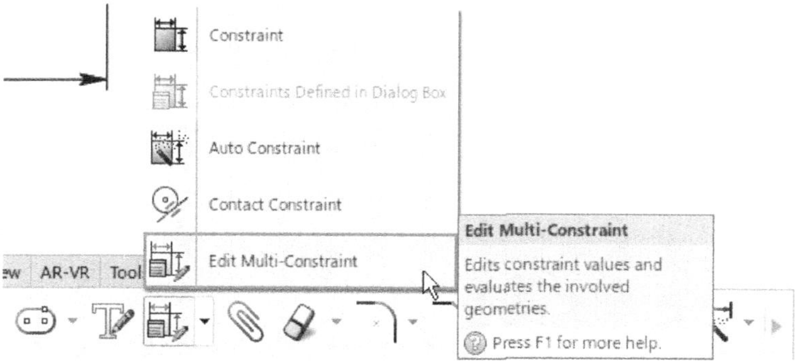

Figure 11–50

4. The Edit Multi-Constraint dialog box opens as shown in Figure 11–51. It contains all constraints in the sketch and their values.

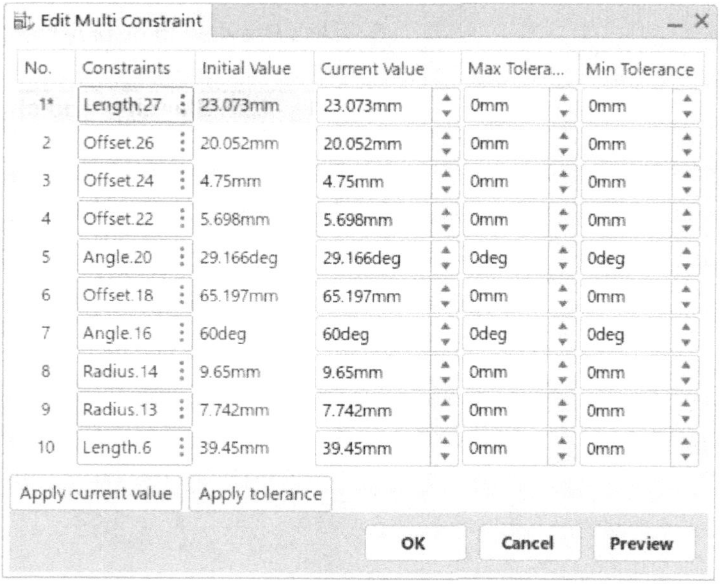

Figure 11–51

The constraint is highlighted in the sketch when you select it in the list.

Design Considerations

Be sure to enter half the diameter for the radius constraints, since both radius and diameter dimensions are represented using a radius.

Note that all entities are green, indicating that the sketch is fully constrained.

5. In the Edit Multi-Constraint dialog box, select each dimension and modify its value in the field below the list to the value shown in Figure 11–52.

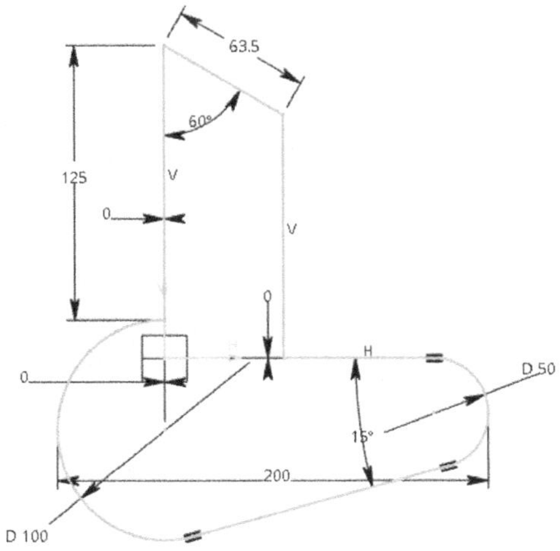

Figure 11–52

6. Click **Preview** to display the changes and then click **OK**.

Task 14 - Exit Sketcher and close the window.

1. Click (Exit App). The sketch displays as shown in Figure 11–53.

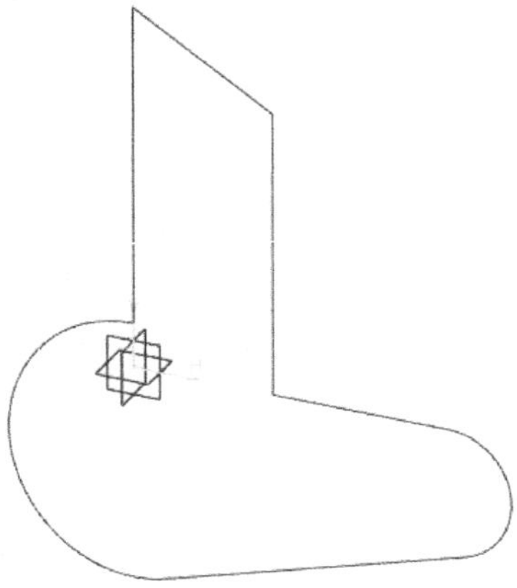

Figure 11–53

2. In the Top Bar, click (Share)>**Save** to save the part.
3. Close the *Constraints_1 A.1* tab.

Practice 11b Constraints

Practice Objective

- Apply a variety of constraints to document the design intent of the sketch.

In this practice, you will create the sketch shown in Figure 11–54. You will gain an understanding of how geometrical constraints interact with one another. This practice will focus on driving the geometry through the use of constraints.

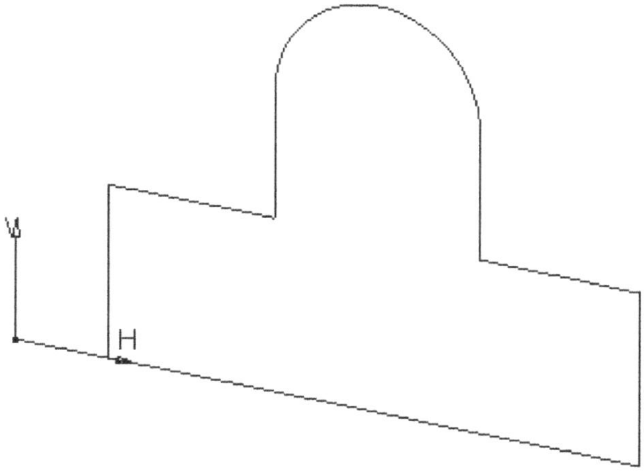

Figure 11–54

Task 1 - Create a new part and begin creating a sketch.

1. In the Top Bar, click (Add)>**3D Part**.
2. In the 3D Part dialog box, enter **Constraints_2** as the *Title*.
3. Select the *3D Shape* tab and enter **Constraints_2** for the *Title*.
4. Select the *Characteristics* tab and ensure **Enable hybrid modeling** is disabled.
5. Click **OK**.
6. In the specification tree, select the YZ plane.
7. In the Action Bar, click (Sketch).

Task 2 - Begin sketching the profile.

1. Ensure that the Sketch Action Bar is available.

2. Ensure that  (Geometrical Constraints) is selected, to enable automatic geometric constraints, as shown in Figure 11–55.

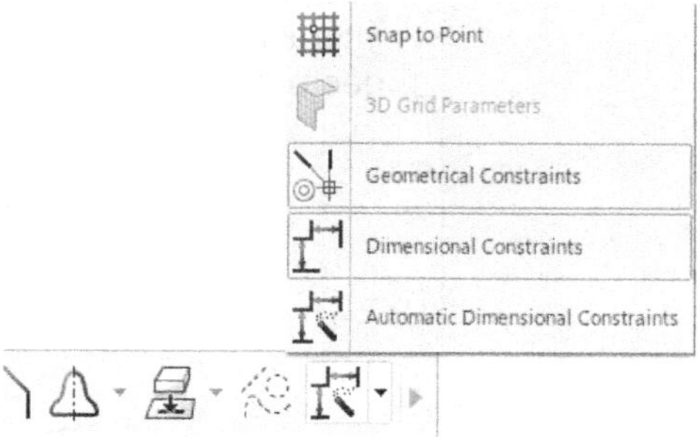

Figure 11–55

3. Sketch the profile and the axis, as shown in Figure 11–56.

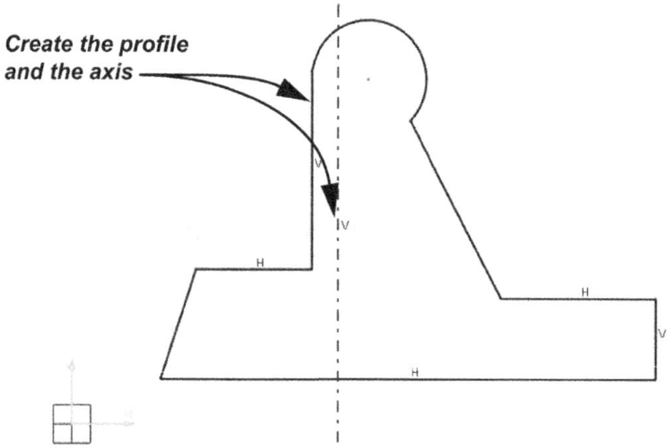

Figure 11–56

4. Use the Sketch Analysis to confirm that the section consists of one close profile that is constructed using 8 curves.

Task 3 - Make a slanted line vertical.

1. Select the slanted line shown in Figure 11–57 and click (Geometrical Constraints) to make the line vertical.

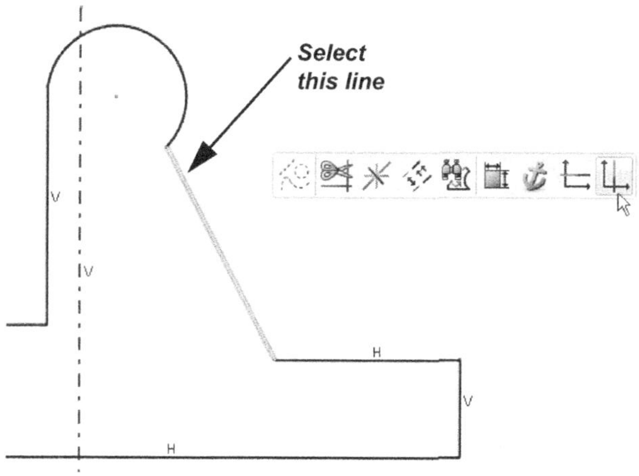

Figure 11–57

2. Click (Undo) to repeat the constraint another way.

3. Right-click on the line and select **Line.# object>Vertical**, as shown in Figure 11–58.

Figure 11–58

Design Considerations

This practice demonstrates the most efficient method of creating a geometric constraint in a sketch. Depending on the scenario, this might involve using a combination of icons and shortcut menu options. In each case, (Constraints Defined in Dialog Box) can be used instead. The corresponding option in the dialog box will be indicated in the margin. For example, the option for the **Horizontal** constraint displays as shown in Figure 11–59.

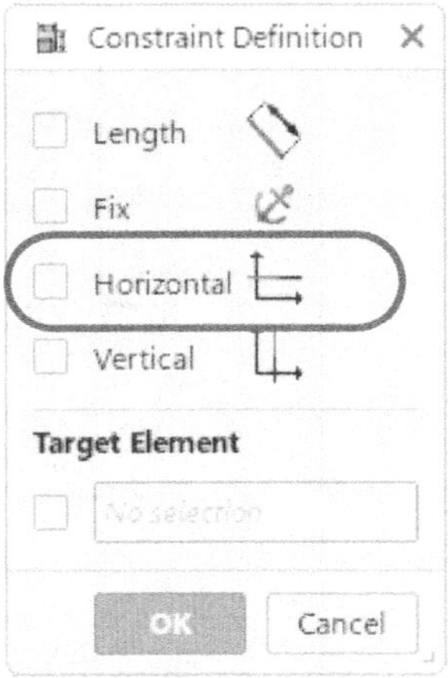

Figure 11–59

Task 4 - Make two lines coincident.

Enabling the Constraint icon also enables the Constraint context toolbar that displays on screen when selecting entities. If the toolbar does not display, verify that the Constraint icon is active.

1. In the Action Bar, double-click on (Constraint) to define a series of constraints. Select the horizontal lines shown in Figure 11–60. This will begin the creation of a dimension between the two entities. Do not place the dimension.

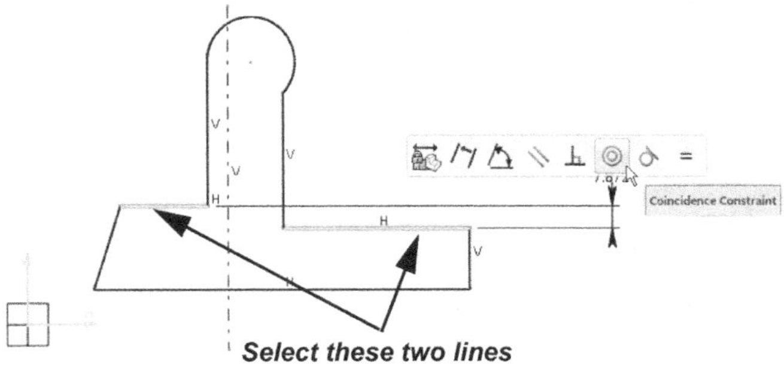

Figure 11–60

2. Click (Coincidence Constraint) in the Constraint toolbar.

Task 5 - Make two lines parallel.

1. Select the vertical lines shown in Figure 11–61.

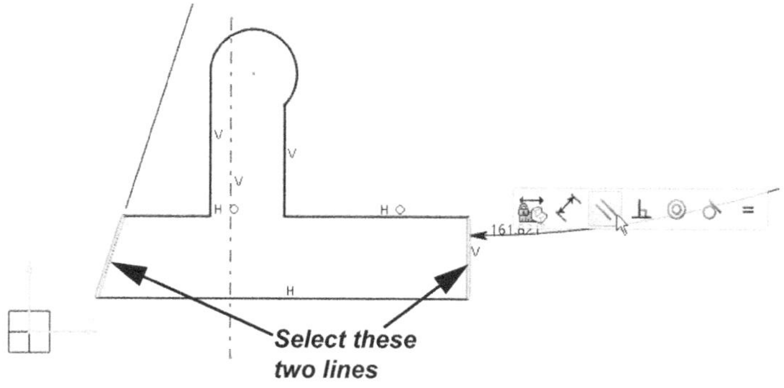

Figure 11–61

2. **Click** (Parallelism Constraint) in the Constraint toolbar.
3. Place the parallel constraint using the left mouse button.

Task 6 - Make the arc tangent to the adjacent lines.

1. Select the arc and one of the adjacent straight lines as shown in Figure 11–62.

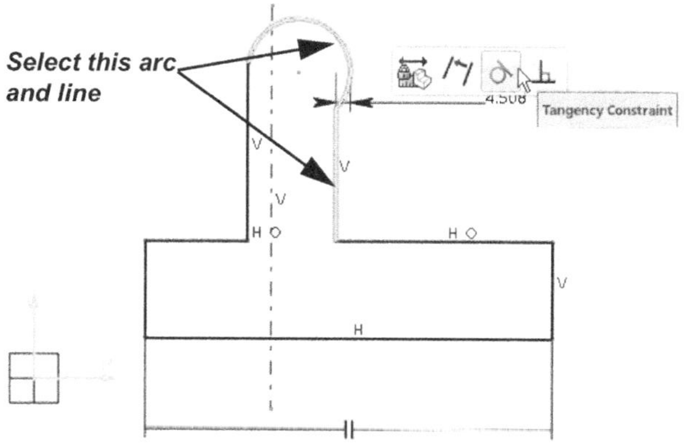

Figure 11–62

2. **Click** (Tangency Constraint) in the Constraint toolbar.
3. Repeat this task for the arc and for the line on the other side.

Task 7 - Make arc center coincident with a sketched axis.

1. Select the sketched axis and the center of the arc shown in Figure 11–63.

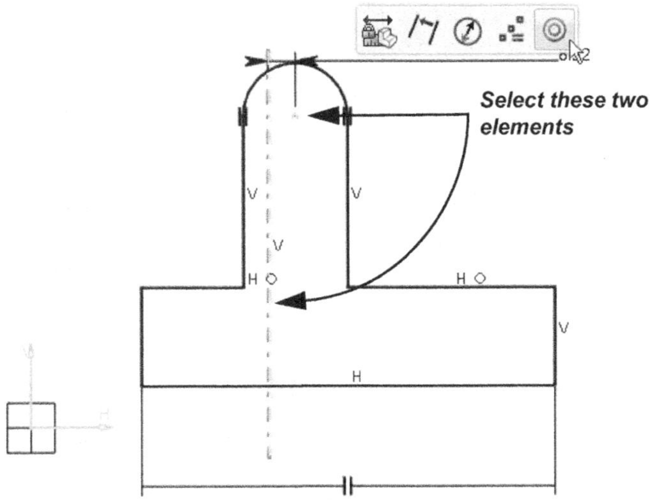

Figure 11–63

2. **Click** (Coincidence Constraint) in the Constraint toolbar.

Task 8 - Make the sketch symmetrical about the sketched axis.

To make two elements symmetrical about an axis, start by selecting the elements to be made symmetrical (in this case, two vertical lines). Once you have identified the symmetry constraint, select the symmetry element (in this case, the vertical axis).

1. Select the two vertical lines shown in Figure 11–64.

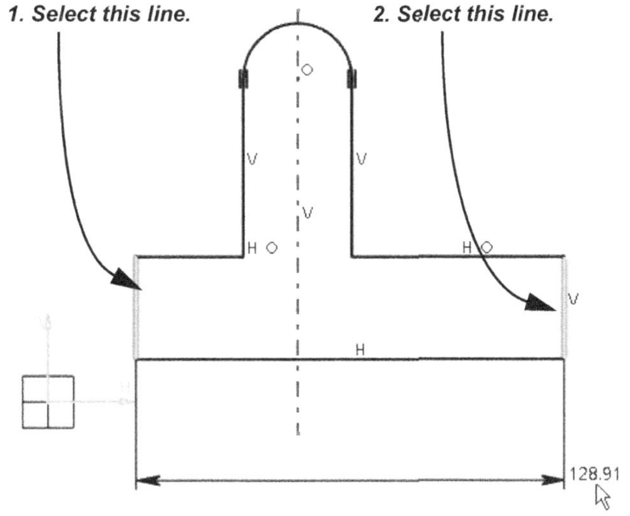

Figure 11–64

2. Right-click and select **Allow Symmetry Line**, as shown in Figure 11–65.

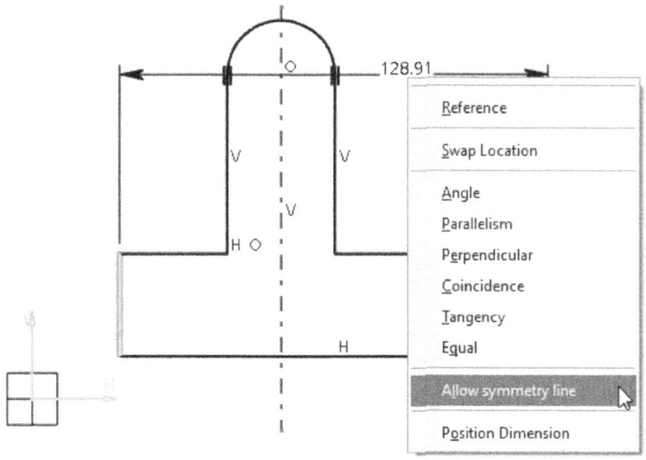

Figure 11–65

3. Select the axis shown in Figure 11–66 to complete the **symmetry** constraint.

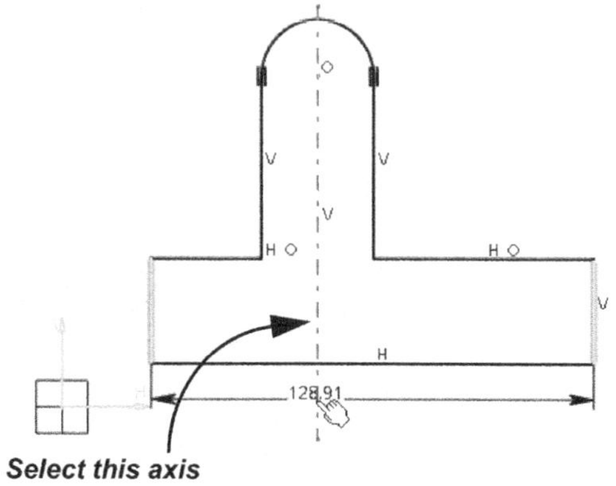

Figure 11–66

Task 9 - Constrain the sketch to the datum planes.

1. Create a (Coincidence Constraint) between the bottom horizontal line and the horizontal axis, as shown in Figure 11–67.

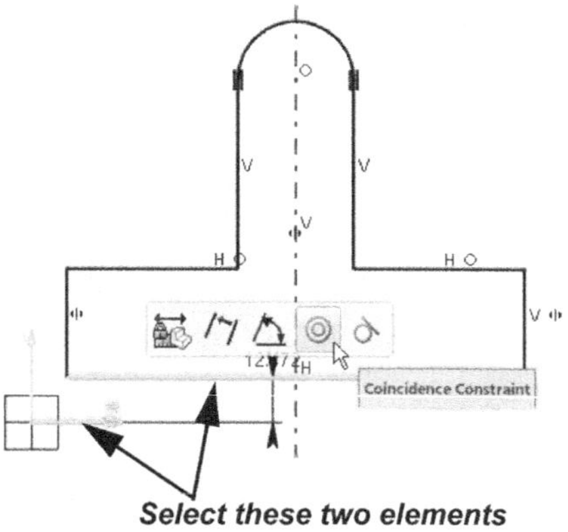

Figure 11–67

2. Click (Constraint) to clear it and to stop creating constraints.

Task 10 - Drag the sketch to test your constraints.

1. Select the vertical line on the far right side of the sketch and drag it left and right. The sketch updates to remain symmetrical.

2. Drag other elements to test your constraints, as shown in Figure 11–68.

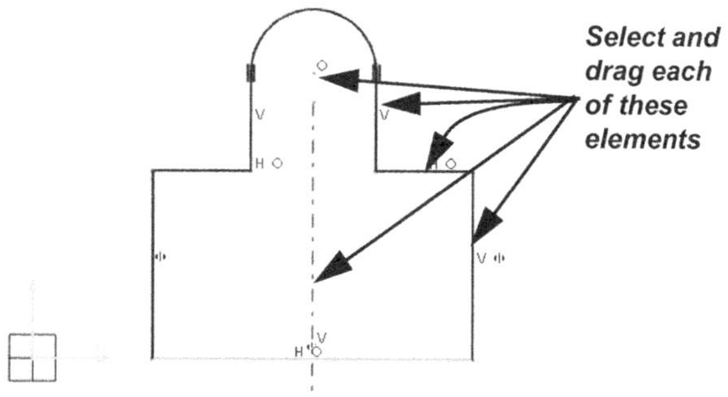

Figure 11–68

Task 11 - Dimension the section.

1. Add the dimensions and constraints shown in Figure 11–69. Adjust the dimension values accordingly.

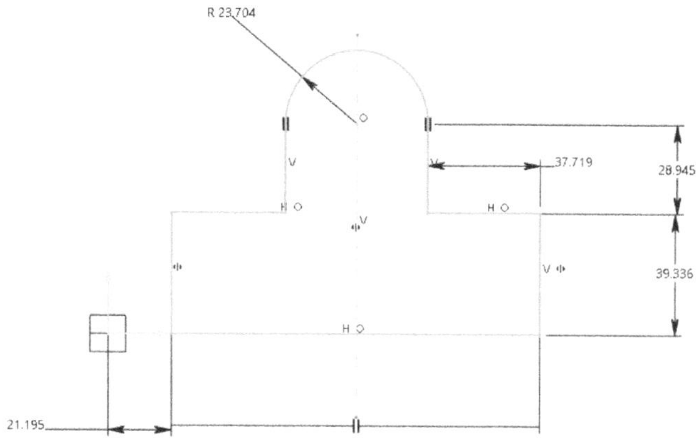

Figure 11–69

Task 12 - Exit the sketch and close the window.

1. Click (Exit App) to exit the Sketch app.
2. In the Top Bar, click (Share)>**Save** to save the part.
3. Close the *Constraints_2 A.1* tab.

Chapter Review Questions

1. You can create an unconstrained sketch.
   a. True
   b. False
2. When a sketch is fully constrained, what color are the sketched entities?
   a. Red
   b. White
   c. Green
   d. Purple
3. What tool can you use to edit more than one constraint at one time?
   a. **Edit**
   b. **Edit Multi-Constraint**
   c. **Modify Constraints**
   d. None of the above.
4. Geometric constraints can be added using which tools? (Select all that apply.)
   a.  (Constraint)
   b.  (Edit Multi Constraint)
   c.  (Constraints Defined in Dialog Box)
   d. The shortcut menu.
5. What sketched entity must be present to create a revolved diameter dimension?
   a. An axis.
   b. A construction line.
   c. A line.
   d. The revolved diameter dimension can be created between any sketched entities.

6. Once created, how can you change a radius dimension to a diameter dimension?
    a. Right-click on the radius dimension and select **Diameter**.
    b. Double-click on the radius dimension and enter twice its value.
    c. Double-click on the radius dimension, and in the *Dimension* drop-down list, select **Diameter**.
    d. None of the above.
7. The **Sketch Analysis** tool can be used to perform corrective actions on sketches.
    a. True
    b. False
8. What displays in the Sketch Solving Status dialog box when a sketch is fully constrained?
    a. Fully Constrained
    b. Iso-Constrained
    c. Constrained
    d. None of the above.
9. How can an under-constrained sketch be identified?
    a. Sketch entities in a fully constrained sketch are, by default, green.
    b. When you use the **Sketch Solving Status** tool it reads Under-Constrained and highlights the affected entities on the sketch
    c. Use the **Sketch Analysis** tool. The *Diagnostic* tab indicates the status of each sketched entities.
    d. All of the above.

10. Select all of the following constraints that were used to sketch the geometry shown in Figure 11–70. (Select all that apply.)

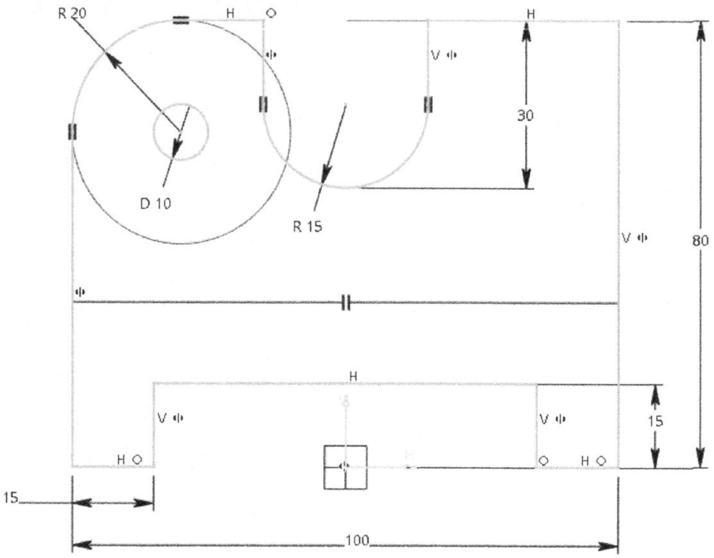

Figure 11–70

a. Tangent
b. Parallelism
c. Coincidence
d. Symmetry
e. Concentricity
f. Perpendicular

Answers: 1a, 2c, 3b, 4acd, 5a, 6c, 7a, 8b, 9d, 10abcde

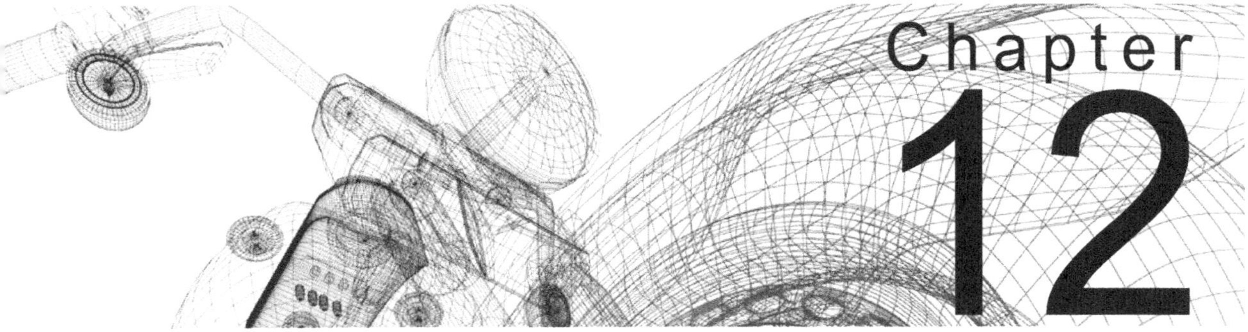

Chapter 12

Pad and Pocket Features

This chapter introduces the creation and modification of Pad and Pocket features, which serve as the foundation of your model. Understanding the various base features and the process of creating them helps you develop robust and flexible models. You learn how to create pads to add material and pockets to remove material. When creating sketches for features, you can have sketches that form a closed loop, or sketches that are open, depending on the existing geometry. You learn how to make changes to sketches.

Learning Objectives in This Chapter

- Use the various base features available.
- Use opened and closed sketches.
- Understand the basic process of creating a pad feature.
- Understand the restrictions on sketches used for pad features.
- Use the various options available for creating pad features.
- Understand the difference between a Pad and a Pocket.
- Understand the Limit options for the depth of Pad features.
- Learn how to use Open profiles.
- Learn about the types of changes that can be made to sketches, and the restrictions on those changes.

12.1 Base Features

When designing a new part, one of your first modeling decisions is to select which feature form to use as the Base feature. The Base feature is the first solid feature created in the model and it provides the foundation on which the entire model is constructed.

You can use one of the following features for your Base feature geometry:

- Pad
- Shaft
- Multi-sections Solid
- Rib

Figure 12–1 shows an example of a Pad feature.

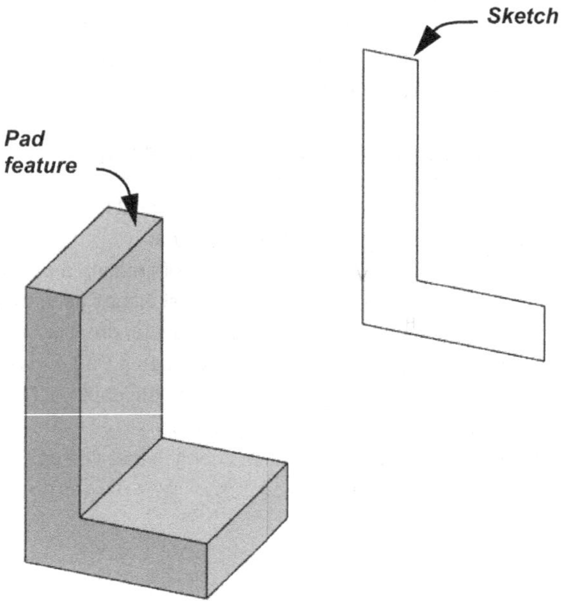

Figure 12–1

12.2 Creating a Pad Feature

With a Pad feature, an existing sketch is extruded a specified distance to define the solid geometry.

How To: Create a Pad Feature

1. Select a profile or surface. The shape of a Pad is determined by the profile that is used to create the feature. Select the sketch. Selected items display in blue by default, as shown in Figure 12–2.

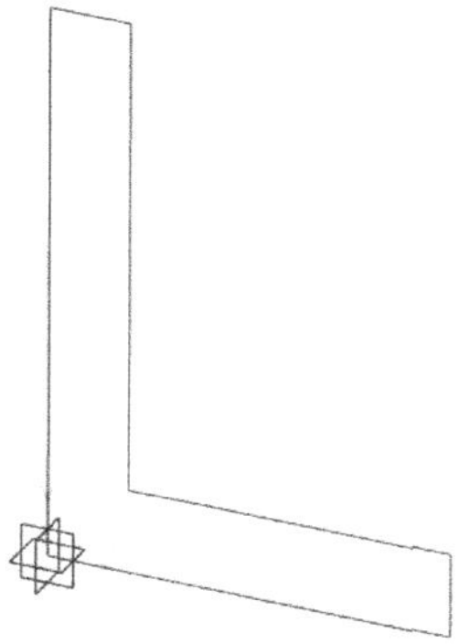

Figure 12–2

2. In the Action Bar, click (Pad). The software initially constructs the Pad feature using the default values, as shown in Figure 12–3. The Pad Definition dialog box opens.

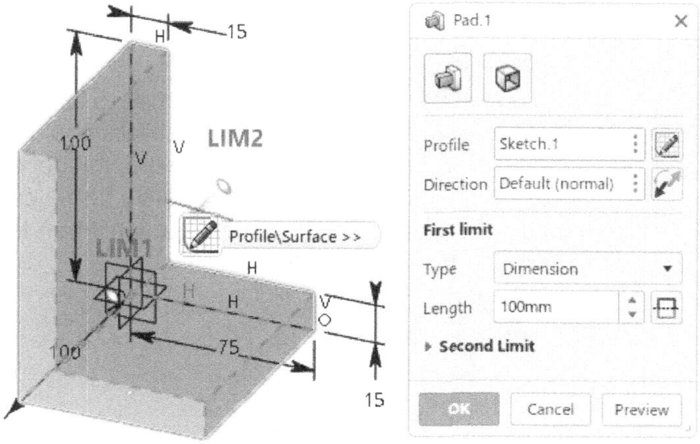

Figure 12–3

Additional limit types for Pad features are discussed later.

3. Specify Pad limit options.

   The distance that the sketch is extruded is known as the limit. The default limit type is dimension, which enables you to manually specify the extrusion distance. To specify the length of the feature, simply enter the distance in the *Length* field.

4. Click **Preview** to examine the geometry before completing the feature.
5. Click **OK** to complete the feature.

Mirrored Extent

You can select  (Mirrored extent) in the Pad Definition dialog box to create geometry on both sides of the sketch, as shown in Figure 12–4.

The total depth of a Mirrored extent Pad feature is twice the length value entered in the Pad Definition dialog box.

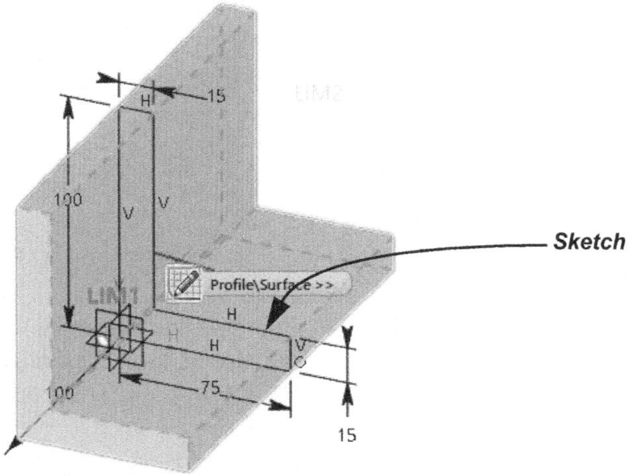

Figure 12–4

It is common practice to start a model with symmetrical geometry. This enables you to capture the design intent from the very beginning. Using this technique, additional features can be easily located relative to the center of the part and automatically remain centered, even when the size of the Base feature is changed.

Second Limit

Click **Second Limit** to fully expand the Pad Definition dialog box, as shown in Figure 12–5. By expanding the dialog box, you have access to options, such as the Type and Length in the Second Limit direction. By changing the value from the default *zero* to a new value, you can create asymmetrical geometry about the sketch. If the values are grayed out, ensure that the

 (Mirrored extent) icon is turned off.

- You can enter a negative value for the First or Second Limit.

As a reference, the software displays an arrow to indicate the direction of the First Limit.

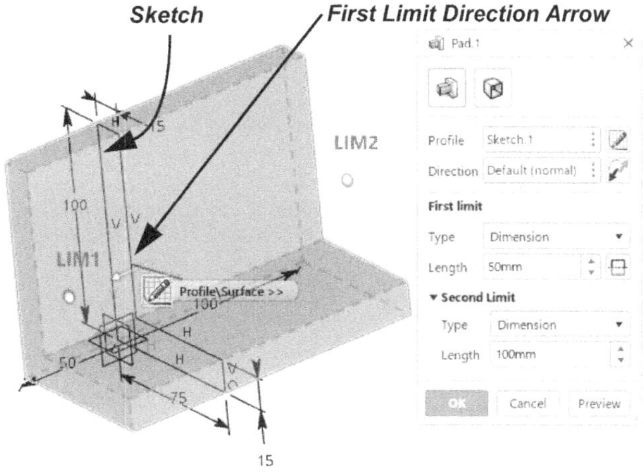

Figure 12–5

Sketch Restrictions for Pad Features

Not every sketch is valid for use with a Pad feature. Comparisons of valid and invalid sketches are described as follows:

Valid Sketch	Invalid Sketch	Description
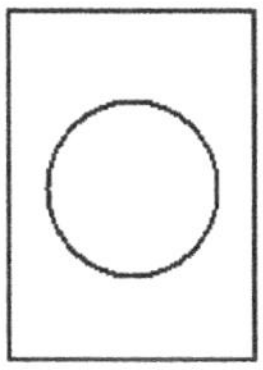	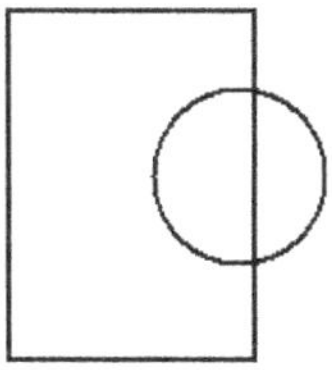	Multiple sections are acceptable, but they cannot intersect each other. You can use the trim function to eliminate the overlap condition.
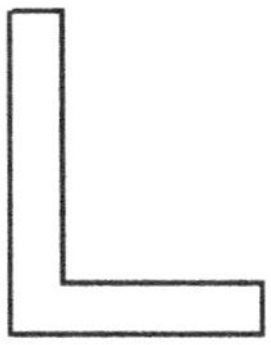		Open sections are not permitted for the first solid feature on the part unless the **Thick** option is used to create the Pad.

- If you try to create a Pad feature with an invalid section, an error message displays and you are not able to create the feature.

12.3 Pad Feature Options

To facilitate sketched feature creation, additional reference planes can be created at specific locations.

As features are added to a model, planar surfaces of existing geometry can be selected as sketching planes, as shown in Figure 12–6.

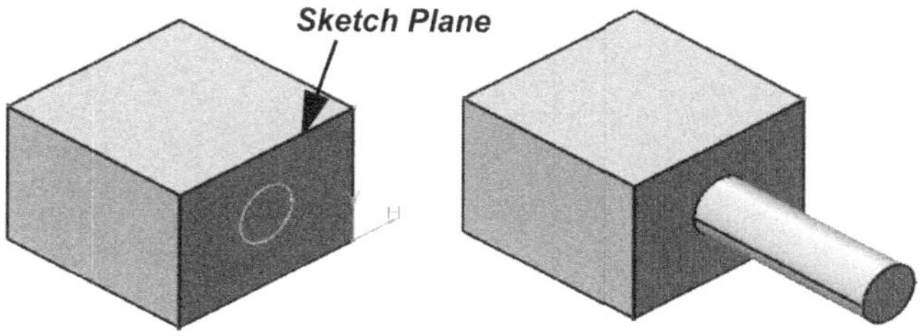

Figure 12–6

The following topics discuss several options available during Pad feature creation that help capture design intent.

Feature Depth Options

There are a number of methods that can be used to define the depth of a Pad feature. These options are shown in Figure 12–7.

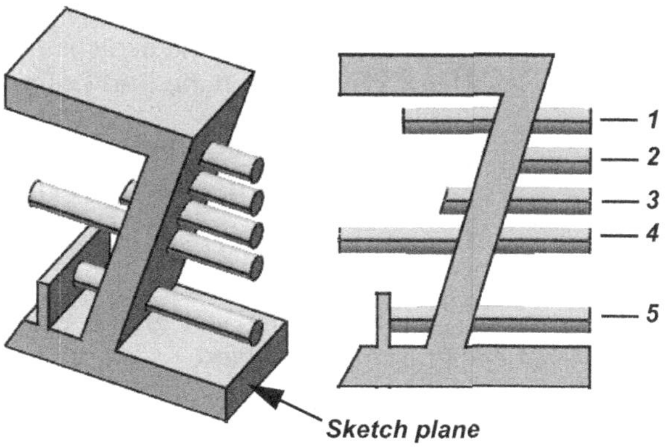

Figure 12–7

The depth options, set in the *Type* drop-down list of the Pad dialog box, are described as follows:

Example	Option	Description
1	**Dimension**	Manually enter length of feature.
2	**Up to next**	Feature extruded to next solid surface that completely intersects sketch. You can use the **Offset** option which enables you to specify a positive or negative distance from that terminating plane.
3	**Up to last, with Offset**	Feature terminates at last solid surface that sketch completely intersects. Offset enables you to specify a positive or negative distance from that terminating plane.
4	**Up to plane**	Feature can be terminated at selected planar surface or reference plane.
5	**Up to surface**	Feature can be terminated at selected planar or non-planar surface that completely intersects sketch.

Second Limit Option

With Pad features, you can extrude the sketch on either side or both sides of the sketching plane. To access this functionality, click **More** in the Pad Definition dialog box.

For example, a circle is sketched on the planar surface of the Pad feature, as shown in Figure 12–8 and Figure 12–9.

- First limit type is **Dimension** with a length value of **20**.
- Second limit type is **Up to surface** and the cylindrical surface is selected.

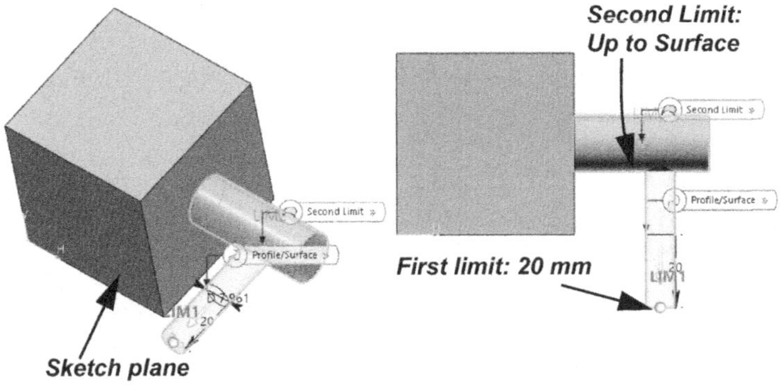

Figure 12–8

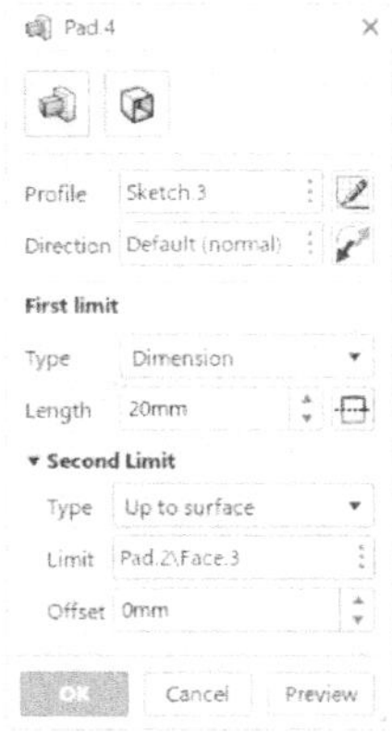

Figure 12–9

In simple cases, where you want to create a pad in one direction and with a dimensional depth, you can select a sketch and click  (Pad) in the context toolbar, as shown in Figure 12–10.

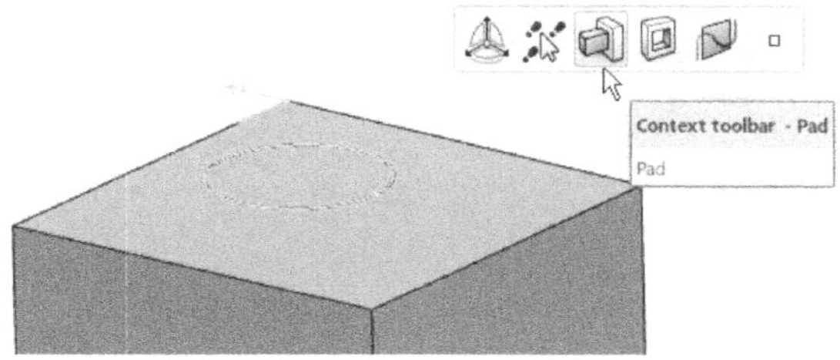

Figure 12–10

The pad immediately previews with a dimension dragger that allows you to drag to increase or decrease the depth dimension, as shown in Figure 12–11. When accessing the tool this way, you do not have access to the additional options found in the Pad Definition dialog box.

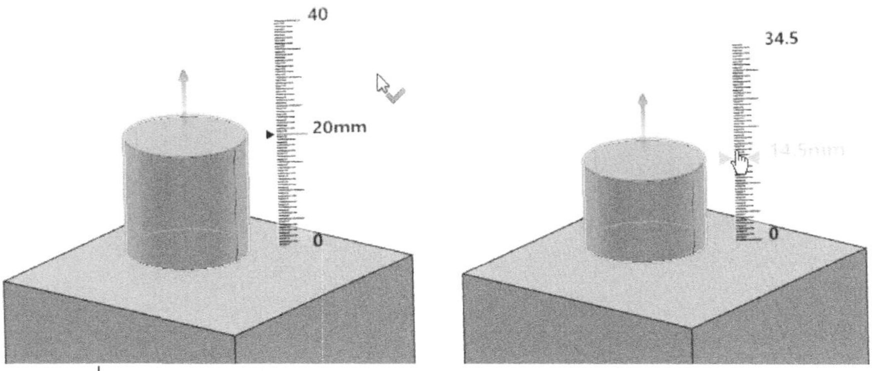

Figure 12–11

After entering the tool, if you realize that you do require the additional options, you do not have to restart the feature. Simply click  (Pad) in the Action Bar, and the Pad Definition dialog box will open.

Non-Normal Direction

By default, Pads are extruded perpendicular (normal) to the sketch plane. You can choose an alternative direction by selecting in the *Direction* field, and then selecting a straight line or edge to define the feature direction.

In the example shown in Figure 12–12, note that the sketch does not extend the entire length of the Pad feature. This sketch is used to define the direction only; the length of the line is not important.

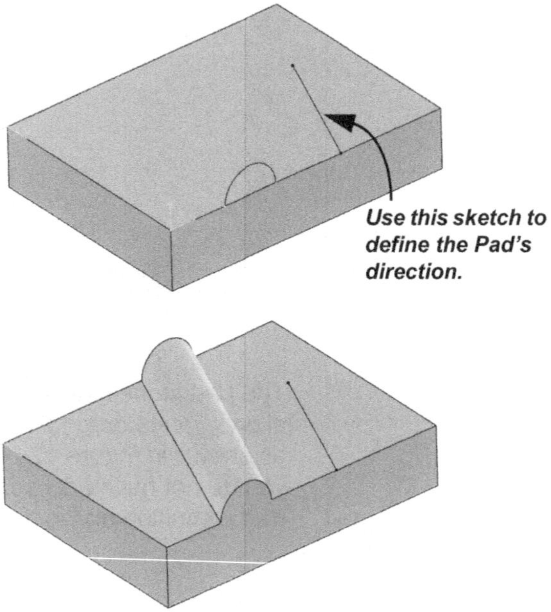

Figure 12–12

Open and Closed Sketches

Using open profiles for feature creation increases update time and introduces instability into the model. A closed profile should be developed whenever possible.

Your profile sketches do not have to form a closed loop. An open profile is acceptable under certain circumstances. However, the open end of the sketch must be bounded by existing geometry. This means the existing geometry must touch the open ends of the sketch at all times. If the Pad shown in Figure 12–13 is lengthened so that it extends off the part, the feature fails.

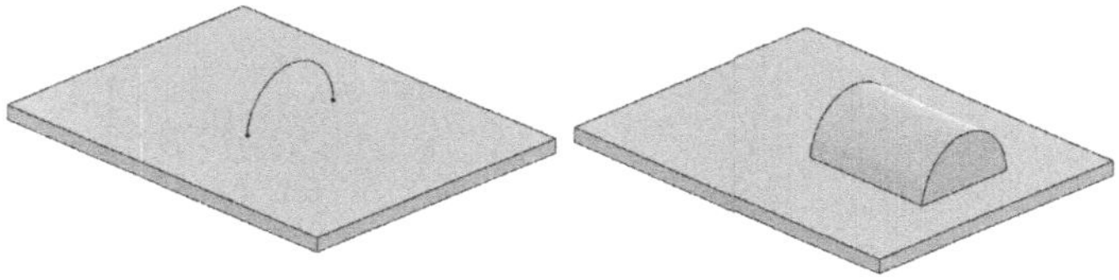

Figure 12–13

12.4 Pocket

A Pocket feature removes material by extruding a profile. It is similar to a Pad feature, except that a Pad adds material and a Pocket removes material, as shown in Figure 12–14.

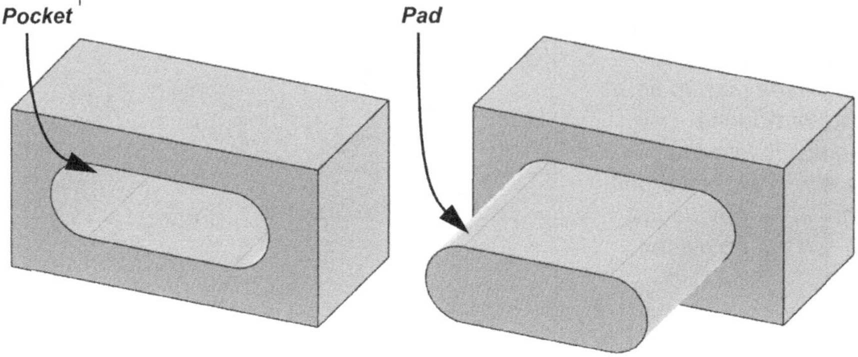

Figure 12–14

Limit Options

Several options are available to control the limits of a Pocket feature. These options are similar to those for the Pad feature, as shown in Figure 12–15.

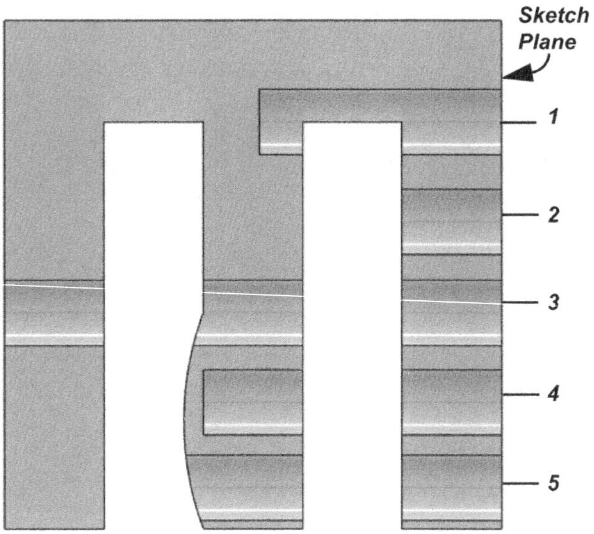

Figure 12–15

The limit options are described as follows:

Example	Option	Description
1	**Dimension**	Manually enter the depth of the Pocket.
2	**Up to next**	Sketch is extruded to the next surface that intersects the entire sketch. You can use the **Offset** option which enables you to specify a positive or negative distance from that terminating plane.
3	**Up to last**	Sketch is extruded through the entire model. You can use the **Offset** option which enables you to specify a positive or negative distance from that terminating plane.
4	**Up to plane**	Sketch is extruded to a specified plane. The sketch does not need to reside on the plane.
5	**Up to surface**	Sketch is extruded to a specified surface. The surface can be planar or non-planar. The surface must intersect the entire sketch.

All of the limit options, except for **Dimension**, have a default offset value of 0. You can change it to a positive value to extend the Pocket beyond the reference or change it to a negative value to pull it back from the reference, as shown in Figure 12–16.

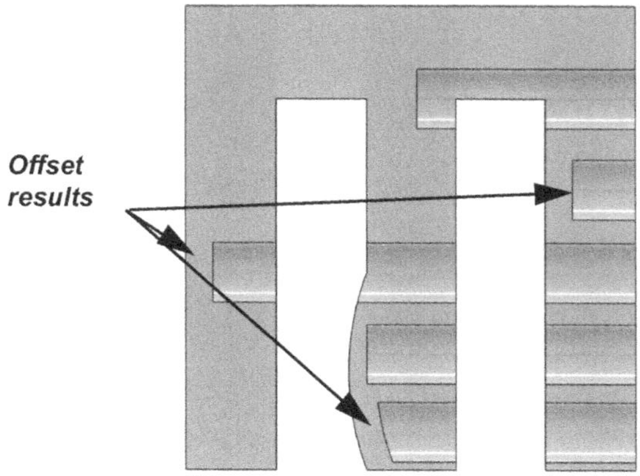

Figure 12–16

Open Profiles

When a Pocket feature uses an open profile sketch, the software only removes material from one side of the sketch to the boundaries of the model. Clicking  (Reverse Side) in the dialog box enables you to remove material on the other side, as shown in Figure 12–17.

If the open ends of the sketch are not coincident with the sides of the part, the software automatically extends them, as shown in Figure 12–18.

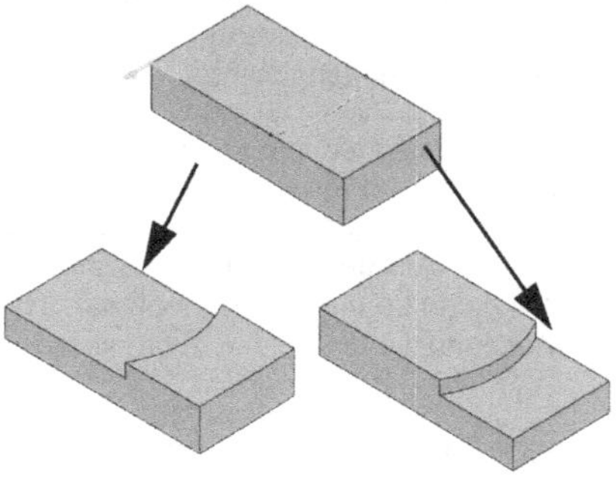

Figure 12–17

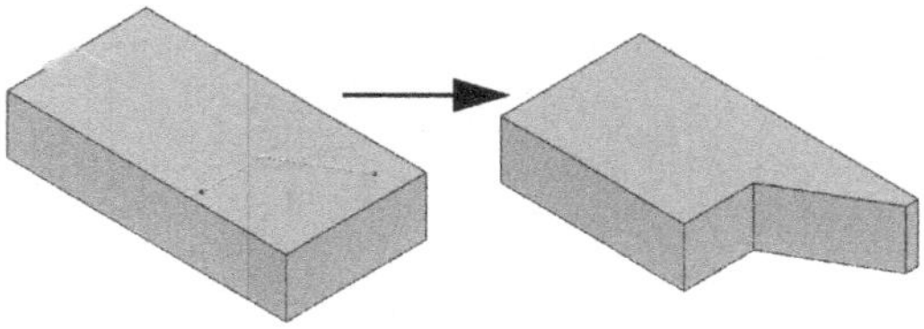

Figure 12–18

- Open profiles are subject to increased update time and introduce instability in the model. Avoid them whenever possible.

Other Feature Options

As is the case with Pads, Pocket features can have a unique second limit; they can be mirrored about the sketch and can be extruded in various ways, as shown in Figure 12–19.

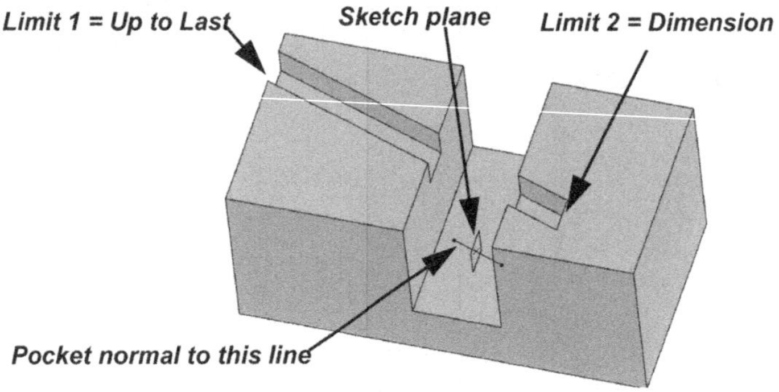

Figure 12–19

The Pocket Definition dialog box is shown in Figure 12–20.

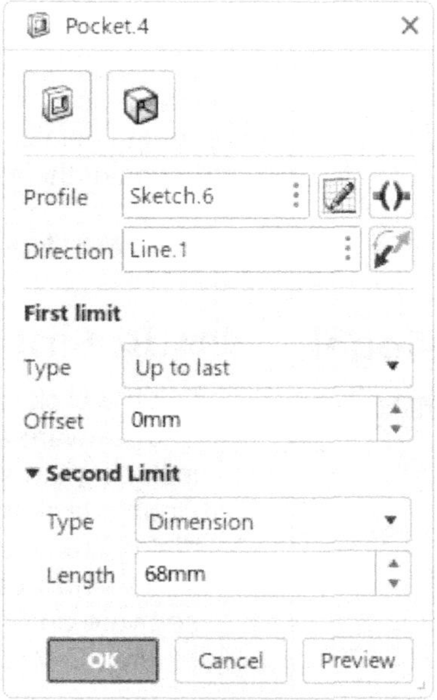

Figure 12–20

12.5 Making Changes to a Sketch

You can easily change the characteristics of a feature, such as the length, sketch dimensions, shape of the sketch, and attributes of the feature (e.g., Mirrored extent).

The following topics discuss these changes in more detail.

Dimensional Changes

How To: Change Dimensions

1. Double-click on a feature on the model to open its dialog box. The software also displays all dimensions of the feature, including the sketch dimensions.
2. Double-click the dimension to open the constraint's definition dialog box.
3. Enter a new value and click **OK** to complete the change. The software automatically updates the geometry, as shown in Figure 12–21.

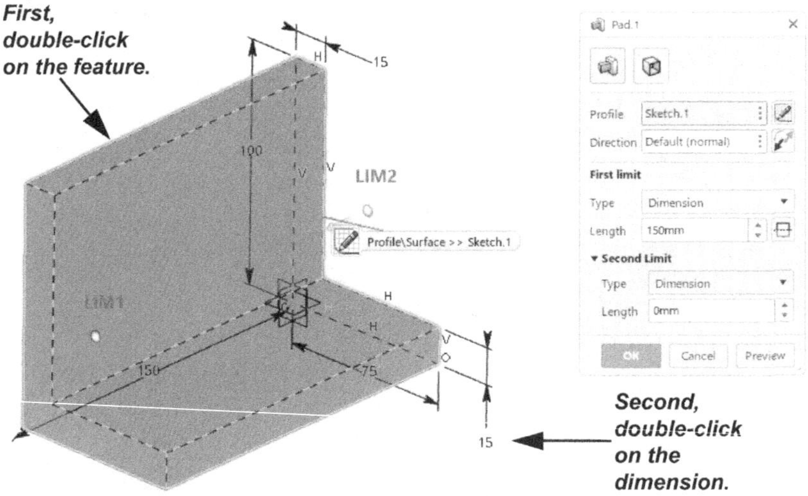

Figure 12–21

Changing the Sketch

The software automatically hides the sketch once you have used it for a Solid feature. To modify the sketch in the Sketch app, you can use one of the following methods:

- Double-click on the sketch in the specification tree. Even if the sketch is hidden from the display, it displays in the Sketch app.
- Click (Sketch) in the dialog box for the feature, as shown in Figure 12–22. You enter the Sketch app, where you can modify the sketch. When you exit Sketcher, you return to editing the feature in the Part Design.

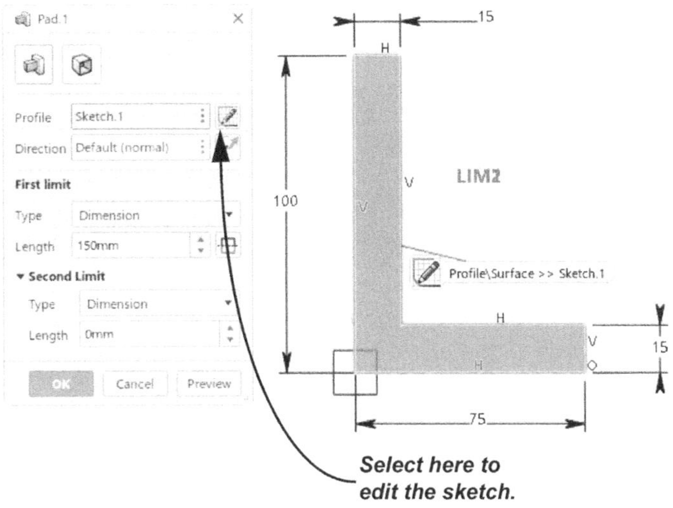

Figure 12–22

Deleting the Feature

Deleting a feature removes the geometry from the model. When a feature is deleted, the sketch remains. This enables you to use the sketch again, as required. Remember that you can use the (Undo) and (Redo) commands from the Action Bar to restore features that are accidentally deleted or changed.

You can delete a Pad or a Pocket feature in one of the following ways:

- Select the feature in the specification tree and press <Delete>.
- Select the feature in the specification tree, right-click and select **Delete**, as shown in Figure 12–23.

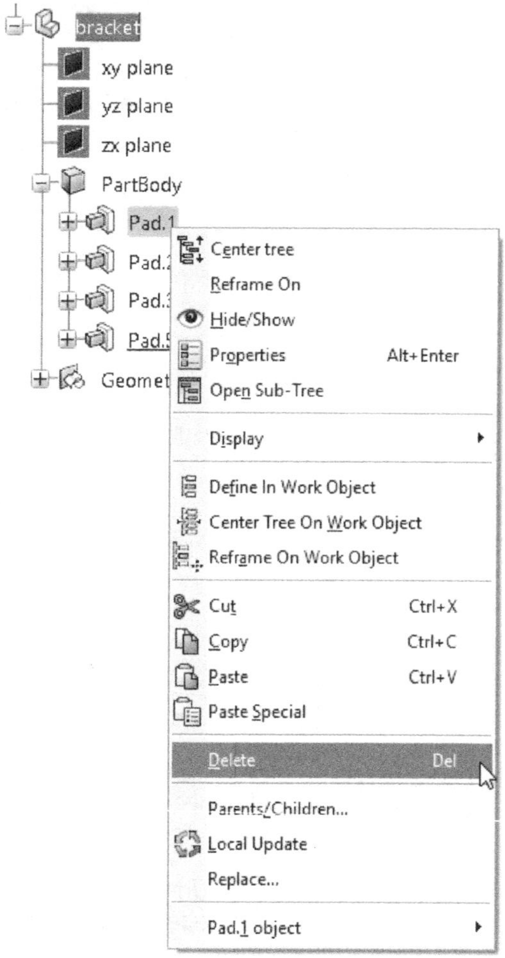

Figure 12–23

Change Restrictions

The only restriction to feature changes is on the feature form. You cannot change a Pad feature into a Pocket feature. You must delete the Pad feature, select the sketch, and then create a Pocket feature.

Practice 12a

Creating and Modifying Pad Features

Practice Objectives

- Create a sketch to create a Pad feature.
- Modify a Pad feature.

In this practice, you will create a Pad feature and modify it using the Pad Definition dialog box. You will create the part shown in Figure 12–24.

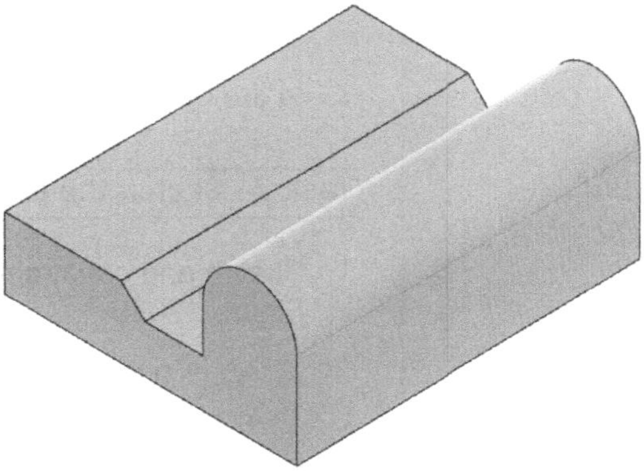

Figure 12–24

Task 1 - Create a new part.

1. In the Top Bar, click  (Add)>**3D Part**.
2. In the 3D Part dialog box, enter ***Your_Initials*_Pad_Sketch** as the *Title*.
3. Select the *3D Shape* tab and enter ***Your_Initials*_Pad_Sketch** as the *Title*.
4. Select the *Characteristics* tab and ensure **Enable hybrid design is disabled**.
5. Click **OK.**

6. Select the YZ plane as shown in Figure 12–25.

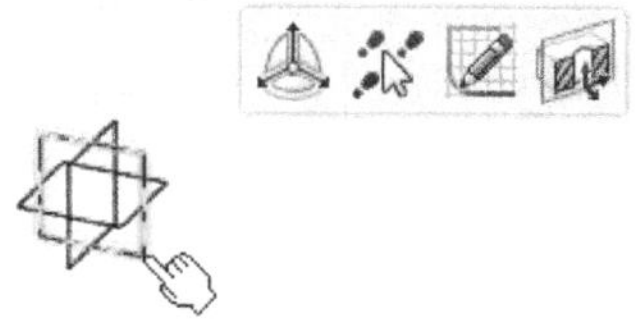

Figure 12–25

7. In the context toolbar, click (Sketch).

Task 2 - Sketch the profile.

1. Sketch and constrain the part profile, as shown in Figure 12–26.

    - 50 (1.969 in)
    - 60 (2.362 in)
    - 25 (4.921 in)
    - 125 (4.921 in)
    - 20 (0.787 in)
    - 45 (1.772 in)

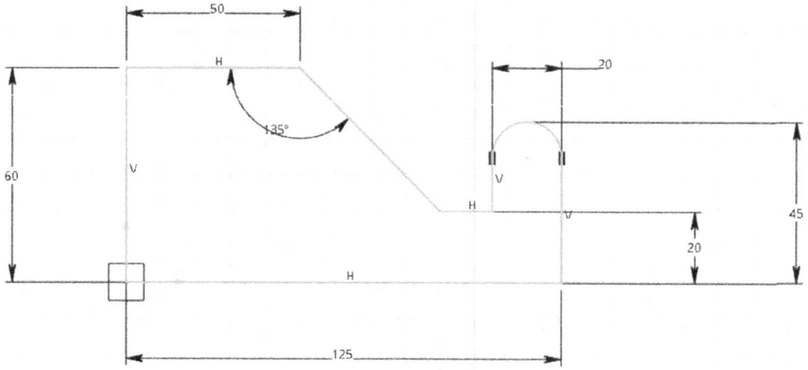

Figure 12–26

2. In the *Sketch* section of the Action Bar, click (Exit App) to exit the Sketch application.

Task 3 - Create a Pad feature from the sketch.

1. With the sketch highlighted, in the *Essentials* section of the Action Bar, click  (Pad).
2. The Pad Definition dialog box opens and the geometry previews, as shown in Figure 12–27.

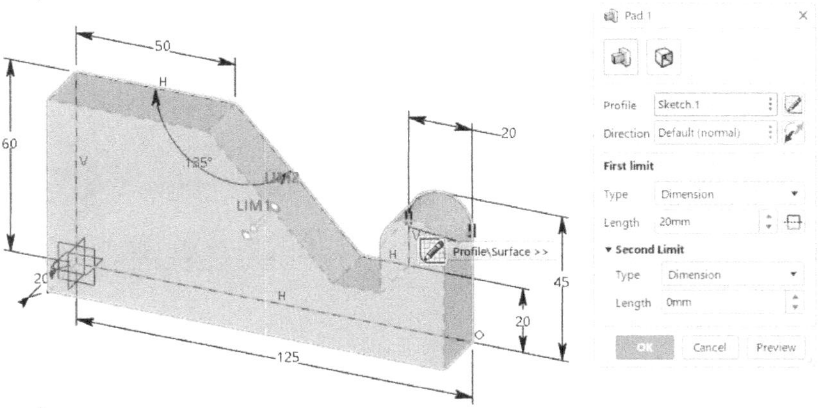

Figure 12–27

3. In the *Length* field, enter **75 (2.953 in)**.
4. Click **OK** to complete the feature. The resulting geometry displays as shown in Figure 12–28.

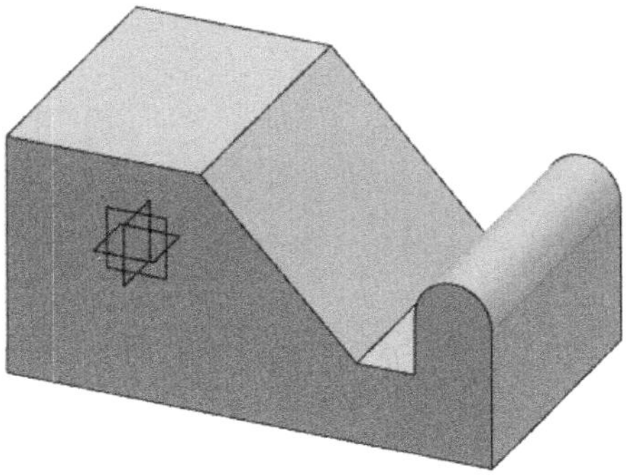

Figure 12–28

Task 4 - Make dimensional changes to the Pad feature.

1. Double-click on any face of the Pad feature. All of the dimensions of the feature are now displayed. The Pad Definition dialog box also opens.

*You can press <Enter> instead of clicking **OK**.*

2. Double-click on the *60* (2.362 in) dimension and change it to **30 (1.181 in),** as shown in Figure 12–29.

3. In the Constraint Definition dialog box, click **OK**.

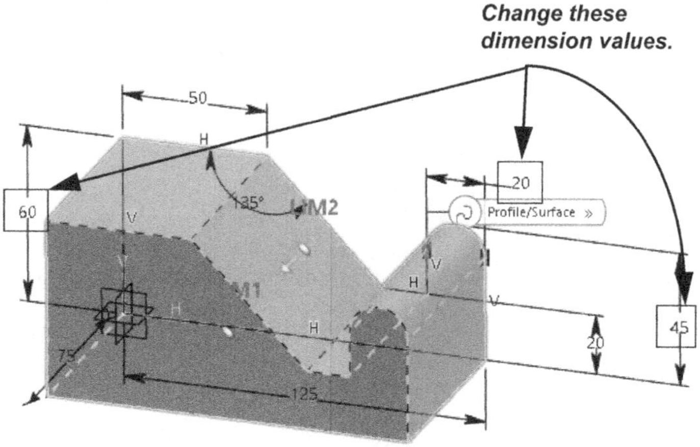

Figure 12–29

4. Repeat this process to change the *20* (0.787 in) dimension to **40 (1.575 in)** and the *45* (1.772 in) dimension to **60 (2.362 in)**.

5. Click **OK** in the Pad Definition dialog box to complete the dimensional changes and update the geometry. The resulting geometry displays as shown in Figure 12–30.

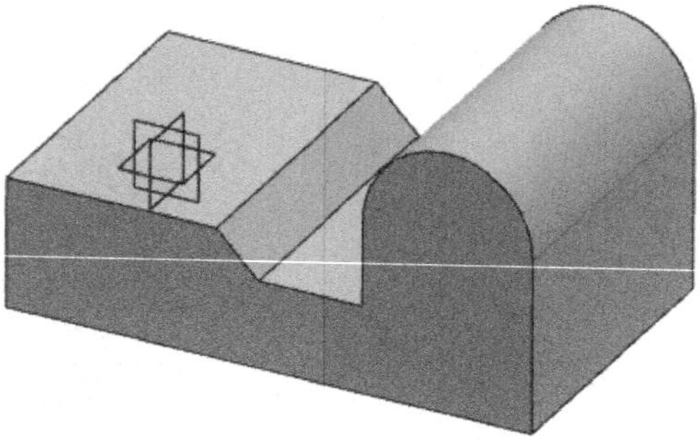

Figure 12–30

Task 5 - Change the attributes of the feature.

1. Double-click on the Pad feature again to open the Pad Definition dialog box.

2. Click (Mirrored extent). The software previews the geometry in wireframe, as shown in Figure 12–31. The geometry is symmetrical about the sketch and has a total length of 150 (5.906 in).

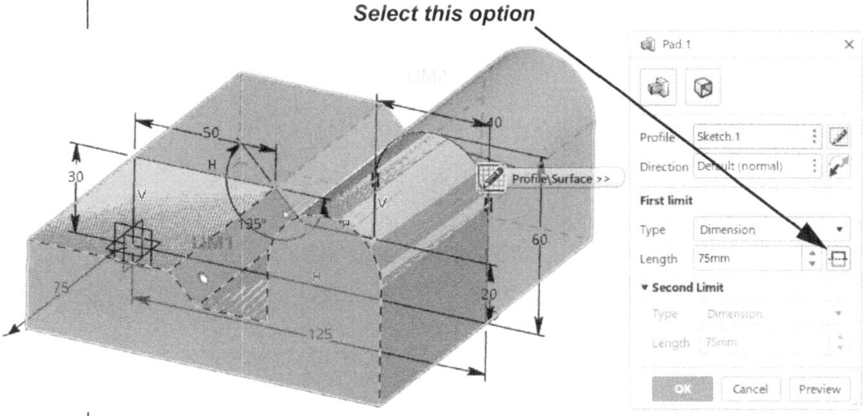

Figure 12–31

3. Clear the (Mirrored extent) icon.

4. Select **Second Limit** if it isn't already expanded. In the *First Limit* area, enter **50 (1.969 in)** for the length.

5. In the *Second Limit* area, enter **100 (3.937 in)** for the length. Click **Preview** and the resulting geometry displays, as shown in Figure 12–32.

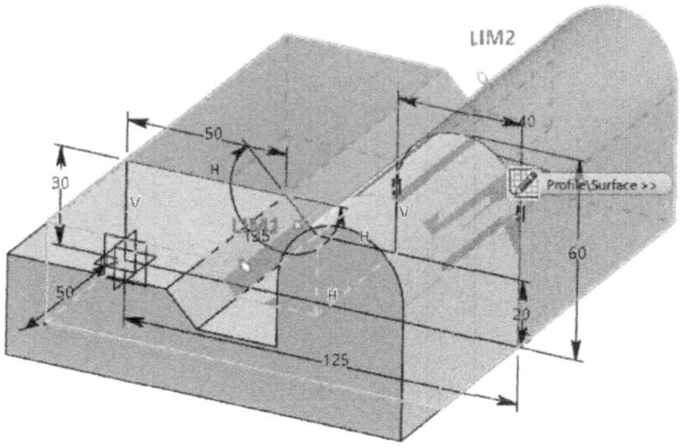

Figure 12–32

6. Click **OK** in the Pad Definition dialog box to complete the change and update the geometry.

Task 6 - Save the part and close the window.

1. In the Top Bar,click (Share)>**Save** to save the part.
2. Close the *Pad_Sketch A.1* tab.

Practice 12b Creating Pocket Features

Practice Objectives

- Create a sketch to create a Pocket feature.
- Modify a Pocket feature.

In this practice, you will create and modify three Pocket features. The first feature will represent a hole with a keyway Groove to accept a Shaft. The second feature will create a cylindrical elongated hole cutout on the flange of the part. The completed model displays as shown in Figure 12–33.

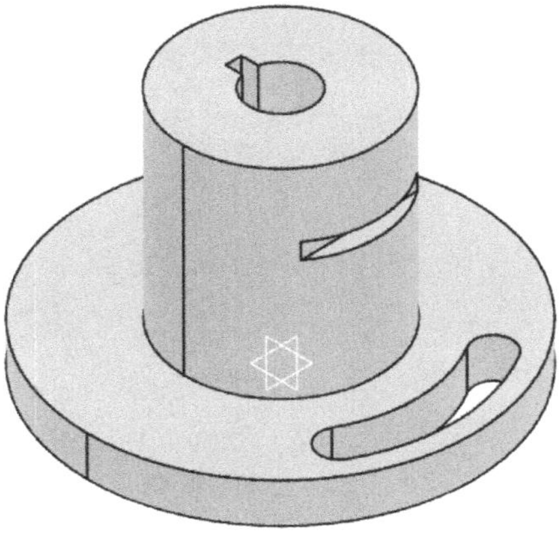

Figure 12–33

Task 1 - Import and Open the model.

1. In the Top Bar, click (Add)>**Import**.
2. In the Import dialog box, click (**Open**).
3. Select **Pockets.3dxml** and click **Open**.
4. Click **OK** in the Import dialog box.
5. Click **OK** in the Import Report dialog box.
6. You are currently in Explore mode. Right-click *Pockets* in the specification tree and select **Open**.

Task 2 - Create a Pocket.

1. Select the top cylindrical face of the model and click  (Sketch) in the Context toolbar, as shown in Figure 12–34.

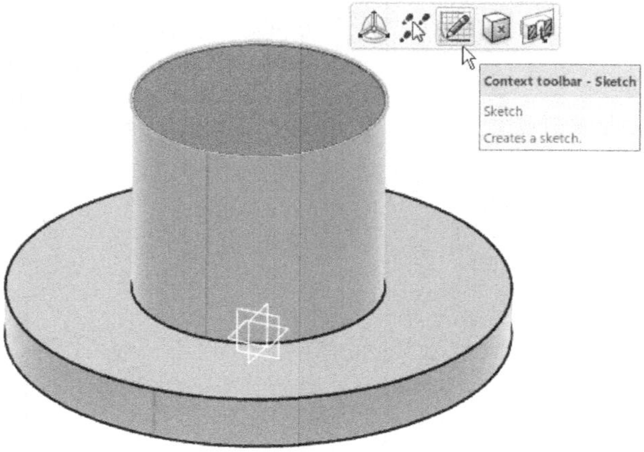

Figure 12–34

2. Sketch the profile as shown in Figure 12–35. Note that the arc is concentric with the cylindrical face and the keyway geometry is symmetrical about the vertical axis.

   - 4 (0.157 in)
   - 8 (0.315 in)
   - 12 (0.472 in)

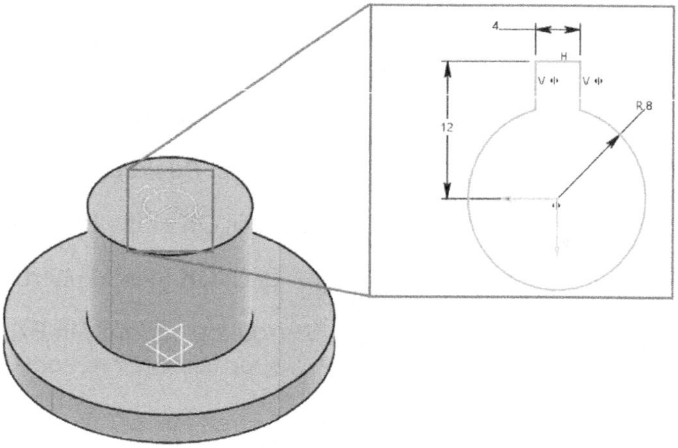

Figure 12–35

3. In the Action Bar, click (Exit App) to complete the sketch.

4. In the *Essentials* section of the Action Bar, click (Pocket) and select the sketch just created, if not already selected. The Pocket Definition dialog box opens as shown in Figure 12–36, indicating a *Depth* of **33 (1.299 in)**.

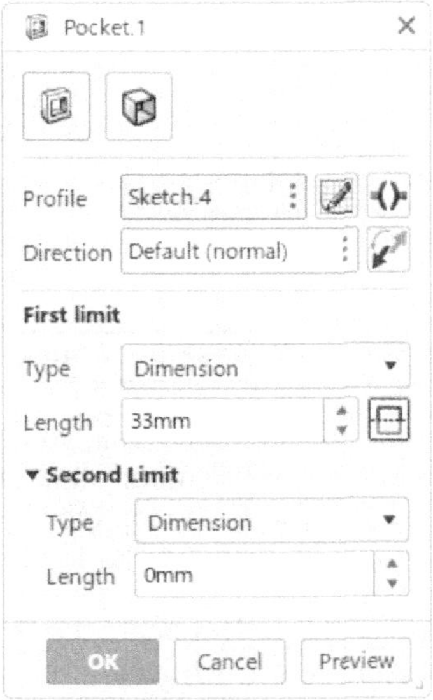

Figure 12–36

5. Verify that the arrow indicating direction points down into the part. Also confirm that the arrow indicating the material side, points toward the inside of the profile, as shown in Figure 12–37.

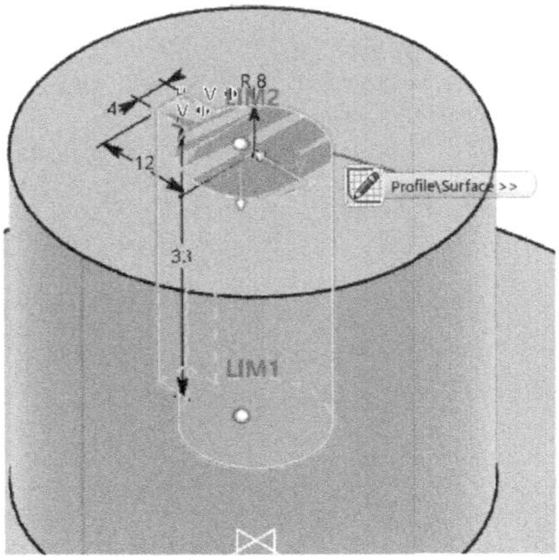

Figure 12–37

6. Enter a depth of **40 (1.575 in)** and click **OK**. The completed Pocket feature displays as shown in Figure 12–38.

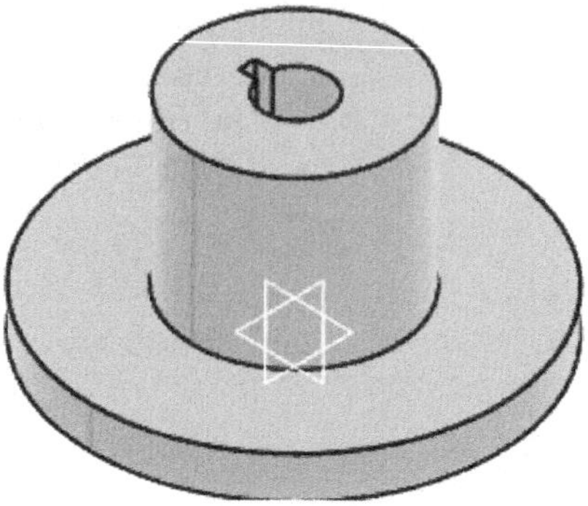

Figure 12–38

Task 3 - Modify the Pocket feature.

In this task, you will carry out a design change on the model. You will modify the depth of the cutout so that it will always extend up to the top face of the flange. This is done by modifying the depth options for the Pocket feature.

1. Locate the Pocket feature in the specification tree and double-click on it to open the Pocket Definition dialog box.

2. In the *First Limit* area, set *Type* to **Up to plane** and select the face as shown in Figure 12–39.

Since the section does not entirely intersect the selected face, the ***Up to surface*** *option cannot be used.*

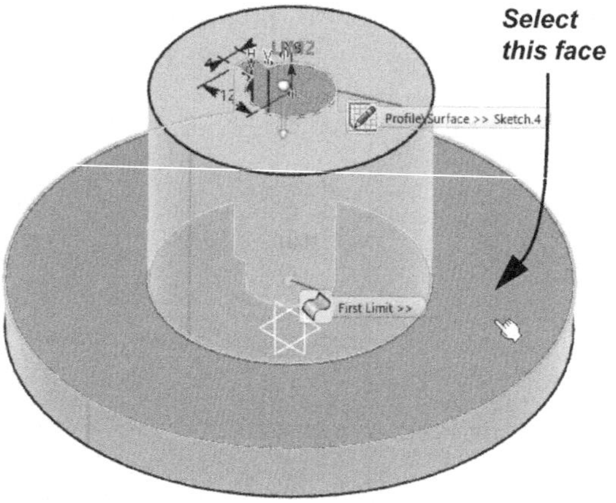

Figure 12–39

3. Click **OK** to complete the modification.

4. Using (ViewModes), select (Shading With Edges and Hidden Edges) to review the depth of the feature.

5. Modify the depth of Pad.1 from *40* (1.575 in) to **50 (1.969 in)**. Review the model to verify that the Pocket feature is reacting correctly (depth should still run to the previously selected surface).

6. Once complete, use (View Modes) to return the model to the (Shading With Sharp and Smooth Edges) display.

Task 4 - Create a second Pocket feature.

1. Select the face of the model as shown in Figure 12–40 and click (Sketch).

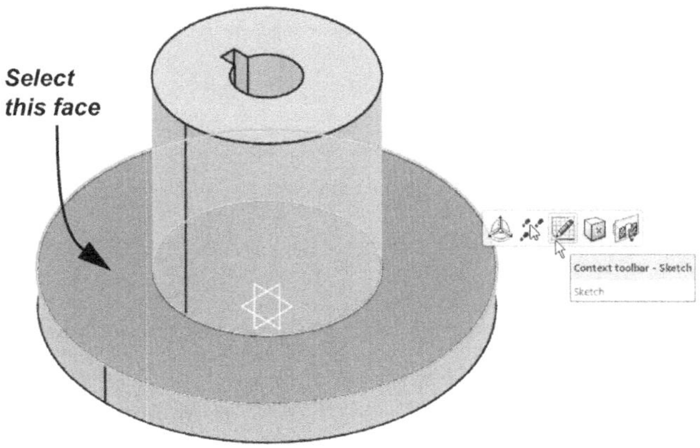

Figure 12–40

2. Sketch the profile as shown in Figure 12–41, using (Cylindrical Elongated Hole). To create the angle dimension, create two construction lines that are symmetrical about the vertical (**V**) axis and pass through the center of each arc.

   - 5 (0.197 in)
   - 40 (1.575 in)

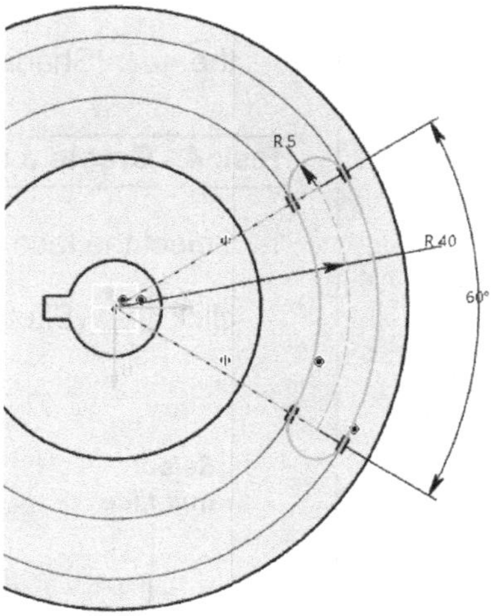

Figure 12–41

3. In the Action Bar, click (Exit App) to complete the sketch.

4. In the *Essentials* section of the Action Bar, click (Pocket) and select the sketch just created if not already selected. Define the depth using the **Up to last** option. The completed feature displays as shown in Figure 12–42.

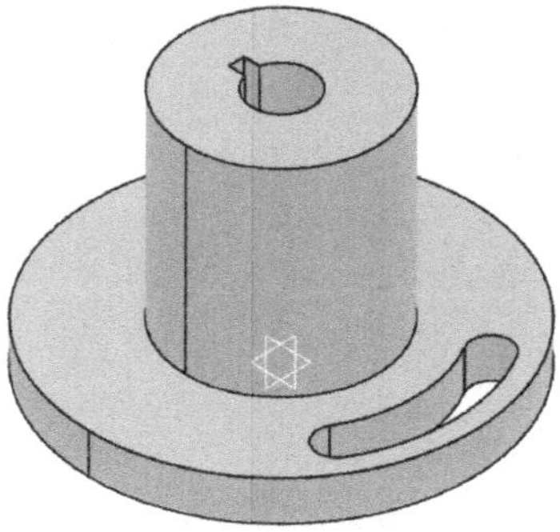

Figure 12–42

Task 5 - Create a Pocket using two limits.

In this task, you will sketch a profile for a Pocket feature on the YZ plane. Then you will create a Pocket feature that cuts material from both sides of the sketch plane.

1. Create a sketch on the YZ plane. Sketch the profile as shown in Figure 12–43.
   - 4 (0.157 in)
   - 10 (0.394 in)
   - 20 (0.787 in
   - 40 (1.575 in)

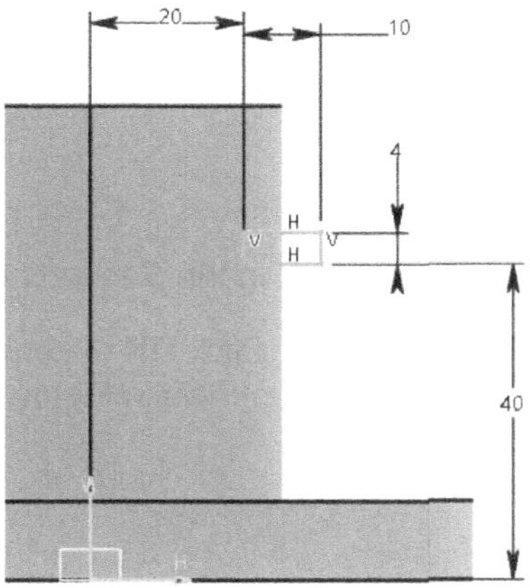

Figure 12–43

2. In the Action Bar, click (Exit App) to complete the sketch.
3. In the *Essentials* section of the Action Bar, click (Pocket) and select the sketch just created if not already selected.
4. Set the *First Limit* type as **Up to last**.

5. Click **Second Limit**. The Pocket Definition dialog box expands as shown in Figure 12–44.

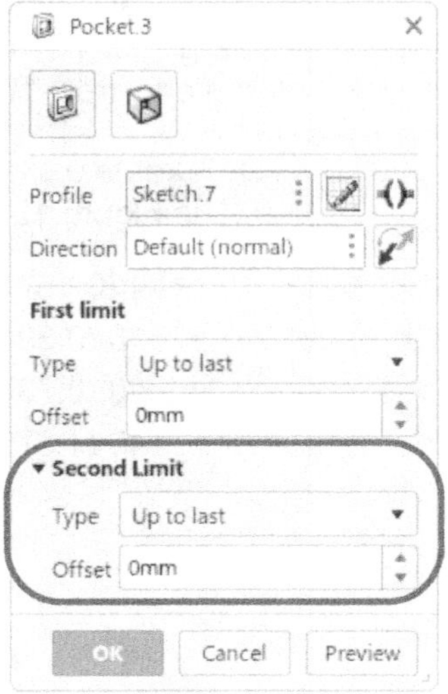

Figure 12–44

6. In the *Second Limit* area, set *Type* to **Up to last**.

7. Click **OK** to complete the feature. The model displays as shown in Figure 12–45.

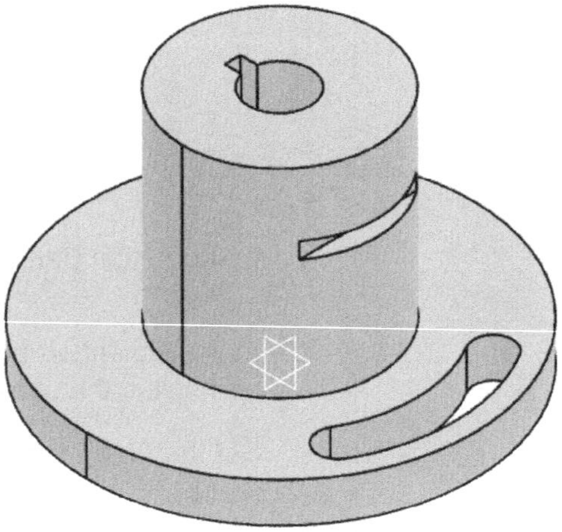

Figure 12–45

8. In the Top Bar, click (Share)>**Save** to save the part.

9. Close the *Pocket A.1* tab.

Practice 12c Working With Open Sketches

Practice Objectives

- Correctly sketch and constrain an open profile.
- Use an open sketch to create a Pad feature.

In this practice, you will add a Rib to a part, as shown in Figure 12–46. You will need to create an open profile sketch and use the Pad feature to create the Rib.

You can also use a stiffener to create the Rib geometry. Stiffeners are described later.

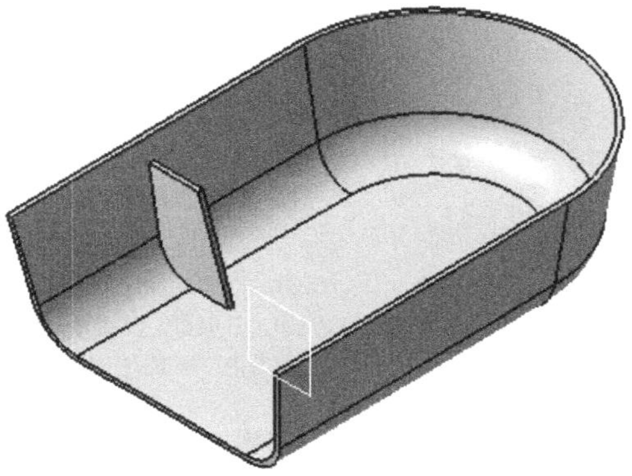

Figure 12–46

Task 1 - Create an open profile on the YZ plane.

1. In the Top Bar, click (Add)>**Import**.
2. In the Import dialog box, click **(Open).**
3. Select **Open_Sketch.3dxml** and click **Open**.
4. Click **OK** in the Import dialog box.
5. Click **OK** in the Import Report dialog box.
6. You are currently in Explore mode. Right-click **Part1** in the specification tree and select **Open**.
7. Select the YZ plane and click (Sketch).

8. Sketch a horizontal and angled line as shown in Figure 12–47.

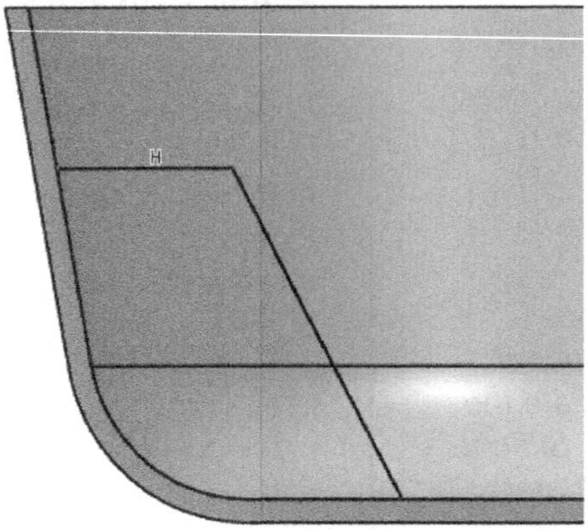

Figure 12–47

Design Considerations

To successfully use an open sketch as a Pad feature, the sketch must be fully constrained to other geometry. This way, CATIA knows how to extrude the open sections of the profile.

9. Press and hold <Ctrl> and select one of the open end points and the adjacent edge of the part, as shown in Figure 12–48.

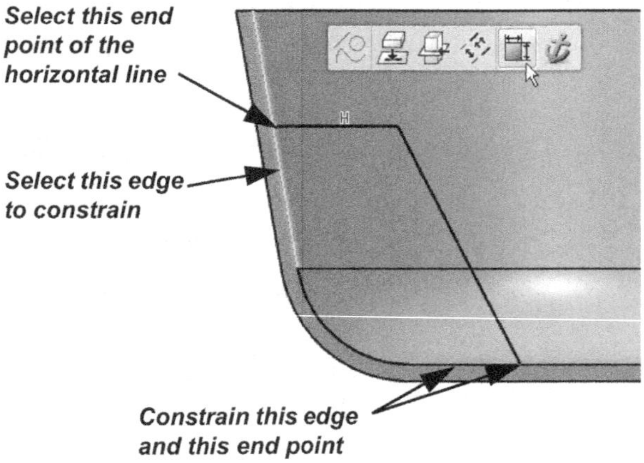

Figure 12–48

10. Click (Coincidence Constraint) in the context toolbar, as shown in Figure 12–49, or right-click and select **Coincidence**.

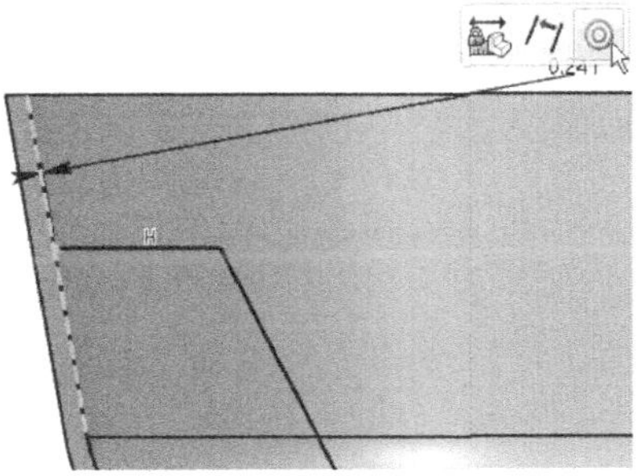

Figure 12–49

11. Repeat the previous three steps for the other open end.

12. Create the **12.5 (0.492 in)**, **32 (1.260 in)**, and **110** dimensions as shown in Figure 12–50.

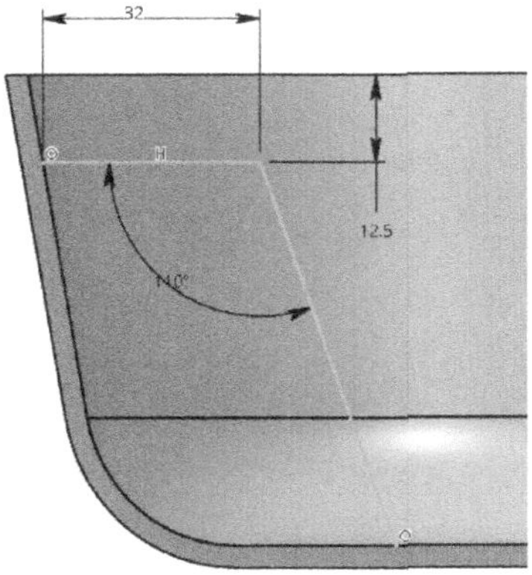

Figure 12–50

13. In the Action Bar, click (Exit App) to complete the sketch. The part displays as shown in Figure 12–51.

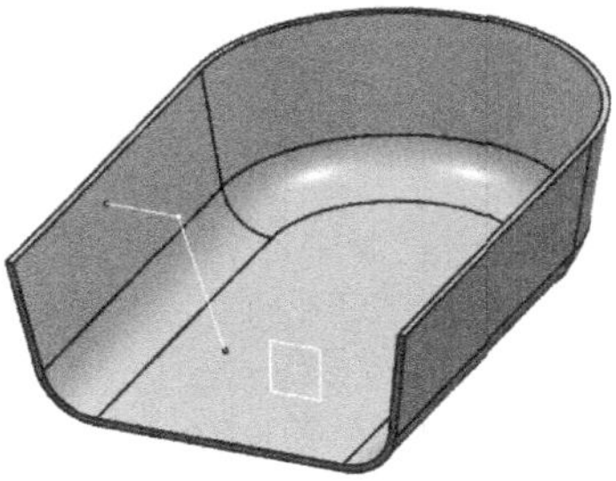

Figure 12–51

Task 2 - Create a Pad feature that represents the Rib's geometry.

1. Select the sketch and, in the *Model* section of the Action Bar, click (Pad).
2. Enter **1.60 (0.063 in)** for the length.
3. Select the (Mirrored extent) option to add material on both sides of the sketch plane.
4. Click **OK** to complete the feature. The part displays as shown in Figure 12–52.

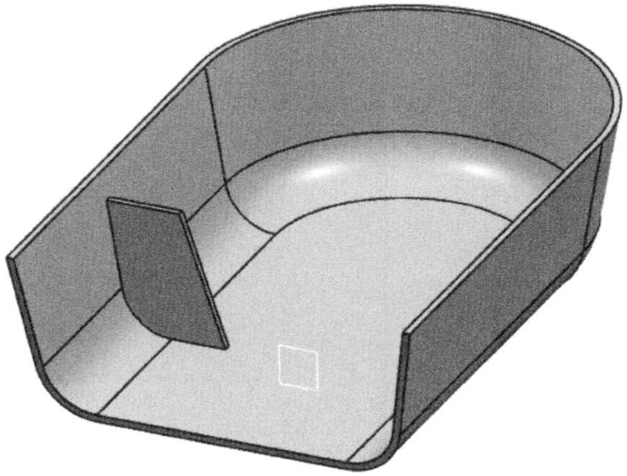

Figure 12–52

5. In the Top Bar, click (Share)>**Save** to save the part.
6. Close the *Part1* tab.

Practice 12d Pad and Pocket

Practice Objective

- Create a Pad feature and a Pocket feature.

In this practice, you will create the model shown in Figure 12–53 using Pad and Pocket features.

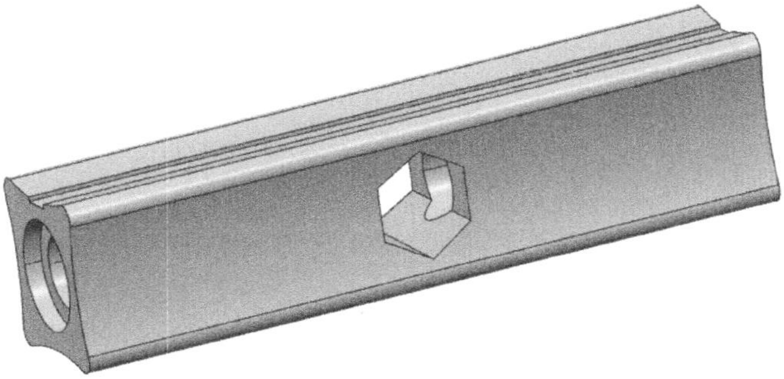

Figure 12–53

Task 1 - Create a Pad feature.

In this task, you will create a Pad feature to define the base feature for the model.

1. Create a new part.
2. In the 3D Part dialog box, enter ***Your_Initials*_Pad_Pocket** as the *Title.*
3. Select the *3D Shape* tab and enter **Pad_Pocket** as the *Title*.
4. Select the *Characteristics* tab and ensure **Enable hybrid design** is disabled.
5. Click **OK.**
6. Select the YZ plane and click  (Sketch).

7. To create the required profile, start by creating two centered rectangle construction squares, using dimensions of **80 (3.150 in)** and **100 (3.937 in)**, as shown in Figure 12–54.

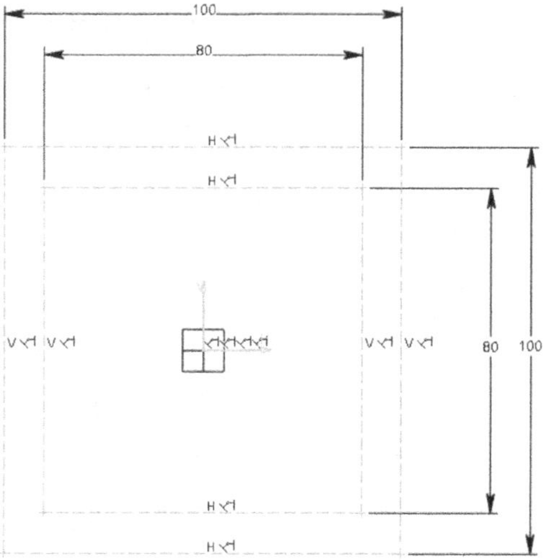

Figure 12–54

8. In the Action Pad, expand the circle flyout and click  (Three Point Arc).

9. Select the three points as shown in Figure 12–55 to create the arc.

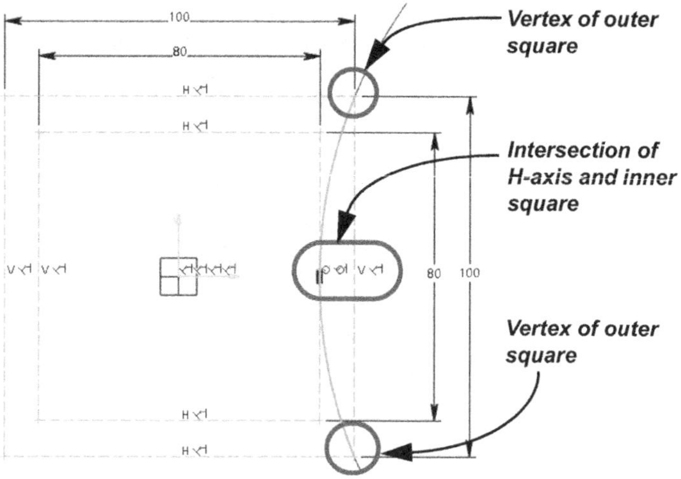

Figure 12–55

10. Create three more arcs using the method described in the previous step. The completed arcs display as shown in Figure 12–56.

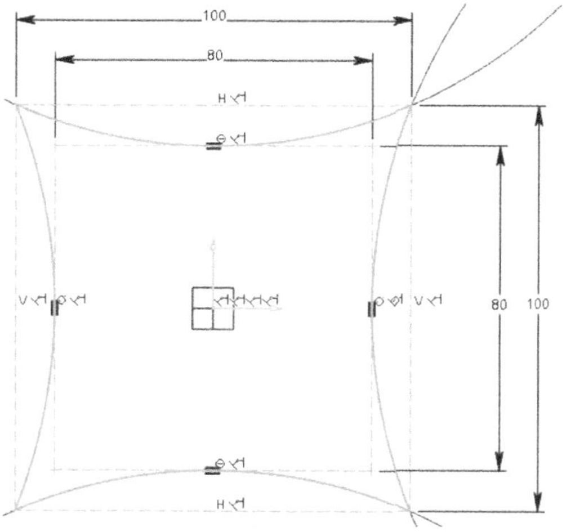

Figure 12–56

11. Select one of the arcs and click (Auto Search).

12. In context toolbar, click (Corner).

13. In the Tools Palette, enter **8 (0.315 in) for the radius**. The completed profile displays as shown in Figure 12–57.

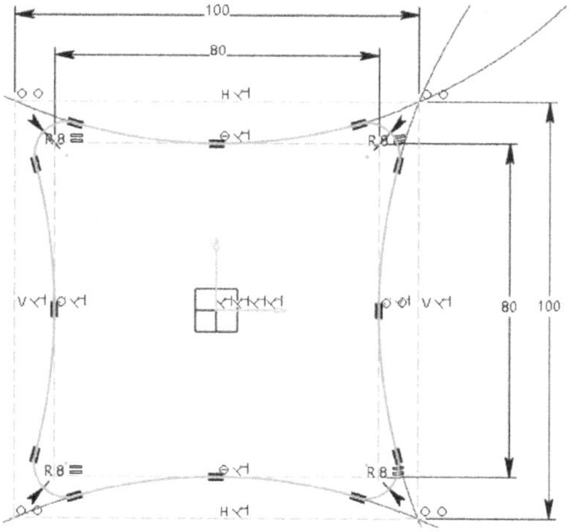

Figure 12–57

14. Exit the Sketch app to complete the sketch.

*If prompted to convert points to construction entities, click **Yes**.*

Task 2 - Create a Pad feature.

1. In the Action Bar, click (Pad) and enter the following properties:
   - *Profile:* **Sketch.1**
   - *Length:* **400mm (15.748 in)**
2. Click **OK**.

Task 3 - Create a Pocket profile.

1. Create a sketch on the face as shown in Figure 12–58.
2. Sketch the **60 (2.362 in)** diameter circular profile as shown in Figure 12–59.

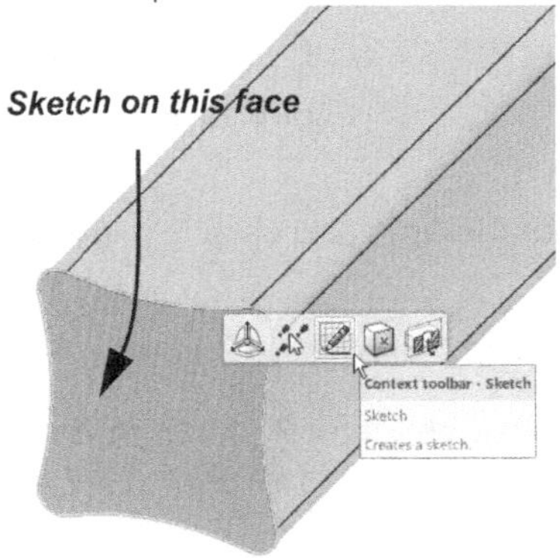

Figure 12–58

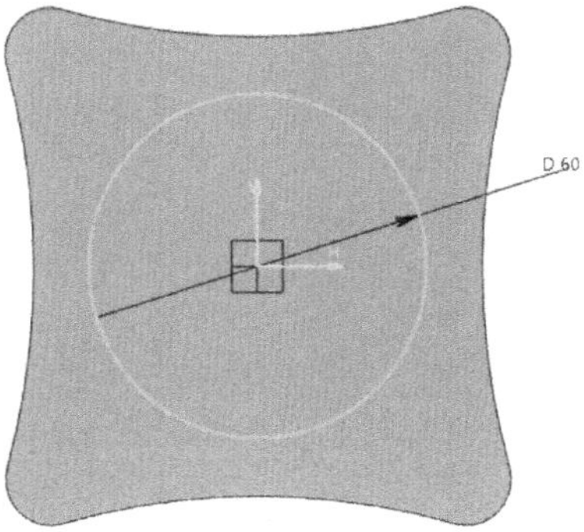

Figure 12–59

3. Exit the Sketch app.

Task 4 - Create a Pocket.

1. Create a Pocket feature using the profile just created. Enter a depth of **10 (0.394 in)**. The completed feature displays as shown in Figure 12–60.

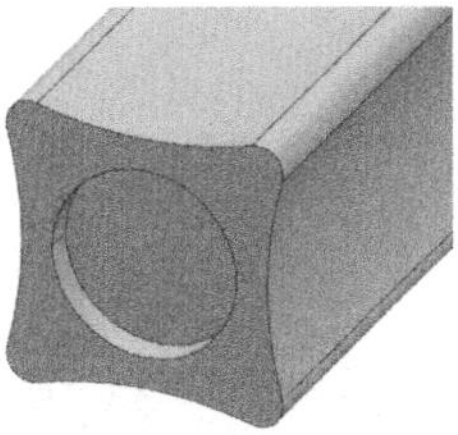

Figure 12–60

Task 5 - Create a through Pocket.

To create this Pocket, you will copy and paste a Sketch. This Sketch will act independently of the original profile.

1. In the specification tree, expand PartBody and Pocket.1, and then select **Sketch.2**. This is the 60mm diameter profile used to create the previous Pocket feature.

2. In the Action Bar, click  (Copy).

3. Select the face as shown in Figure 12–61.

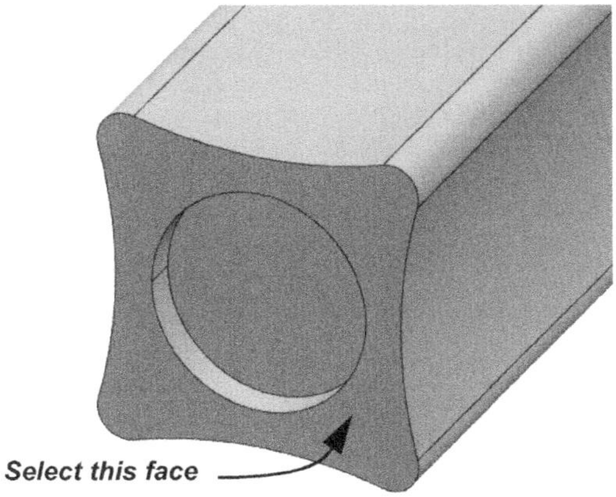

Figure 12–61

4. In the Action Bar, click  (Paste). The profile is pasted onto the part as **Sketch.3**, as shown in Figure 12–62.

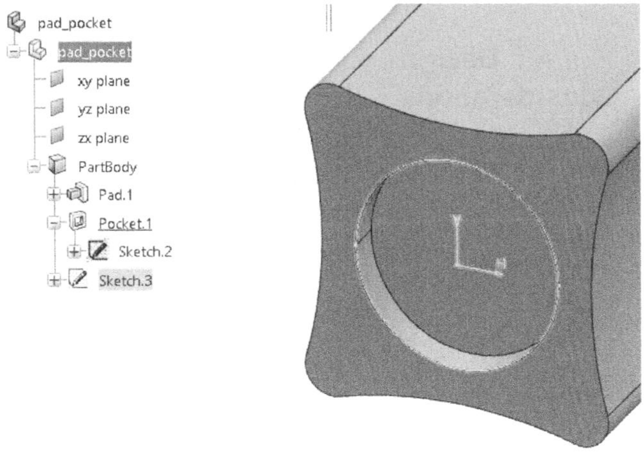

Figure 12–62

5. Double-click **Sketch.3** and change the diameter from *60* (2.362 in) to **40 (1.575 in)**. Do not exit Sketcher.

6. Sketch and dimension a rectangular profile, as shown in Figure 12–63. Verify that the rectangle is symmetrical about the vertical axis.

   - 10 (0.394 in)
   - 20 (0.787 in)
   - 38 (1.496 in)
   - 40 (1.575 in)

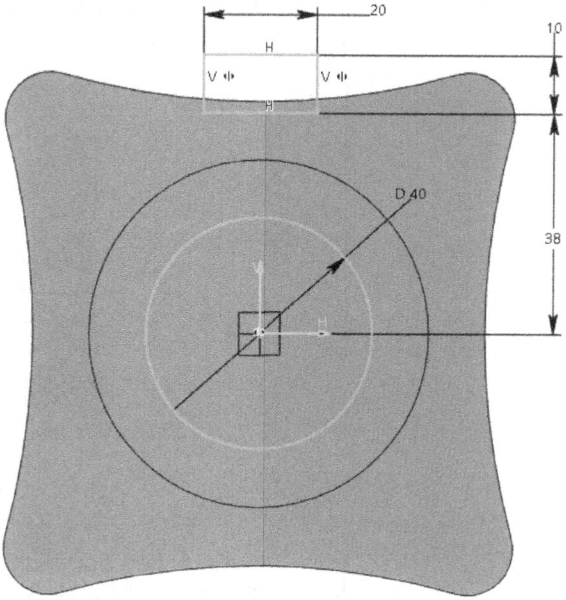

Figure 12–63

Design Considerations

Creating a profile that has more than one closed section has advantages and disadvantages. One advantage is that fewer sketched based features need to be created (in this case, one less sketch and Pocket will be created). However, the disadvantage is that the rectangular Pocket cannot be deactivated without deactivating the circular Pocket. Verify that you structure your model according to your design intent.

7. Create a Pocket feature using **Sketch.3**. Set the *First Limit Type* to **Up to last**. The model displays as shown in Figure 12–64.

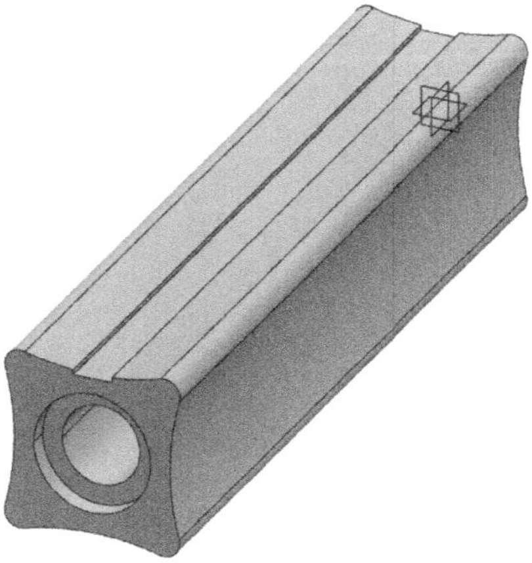

Figure 12–64

Task 6 - Create a Pocket.

1. Create a sketch on the ZX plane. In the Action Bar, expand the (Rectangle) flyout and click (Polygon). Place the sketch and use a dimension of **50 (1.969 in)**, as shown in Figure 12–65.

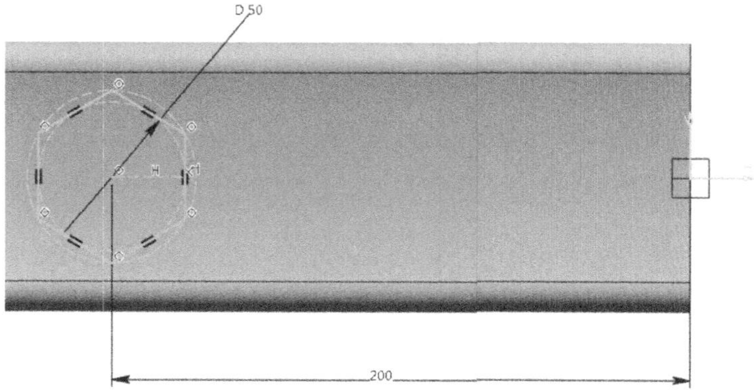

Figure 12–65

2. Create a Pocket feature that removes the hexagonal section from both sides of the sketch plane, using the **Up to last** option.

3. Hide the default reference planes. The completed model displays as shown in Figure 12–66.

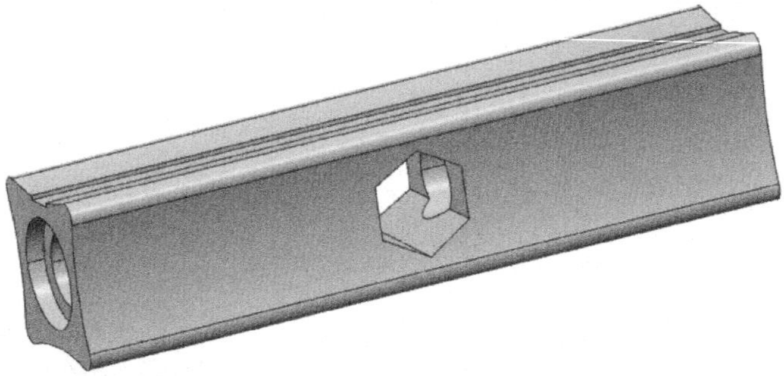

Figure 12–66

4. In the Top Bar, click  (Share)>**Save** to save the part.

5. Close the ***Pad_Pocket*** tab.

Practice 12e (Optional) Additional Pockets

Practice Objective

- Create a Pocket feature.

In this practice, you will create the part shown in Figure 12–67. You will open an existing part and add two Pocket features.

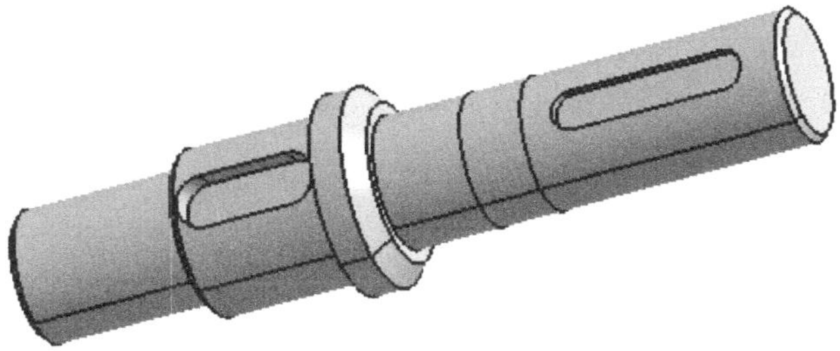

Figure 12–67

1. Import **Shaft.3dxml**.

2. Create the two Pocket features as shown in Figure 12–68. Place them in the approximate locations as shown with appropriate dimensioning schemes.

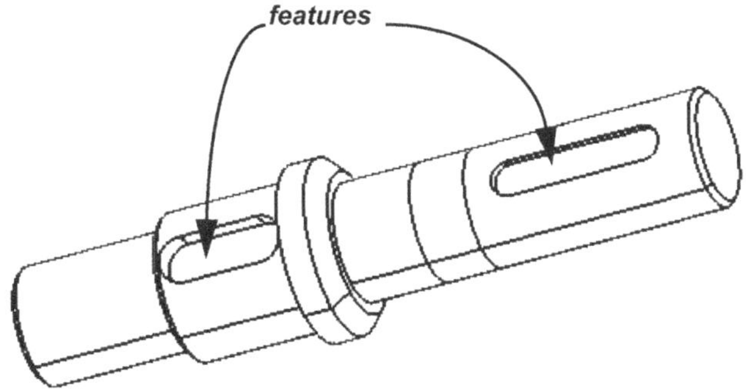

Figure 12–68

3. In the Top Bar, click  (Share)>**Save** to save the part.

4. Close the ***Shaft** A.1* tab.

Practice 12f (Optional) Crank

Practice Objective

- Create a part using pads without any instructions.

1. Create the **Crank.** part shown in Figure 12–69.

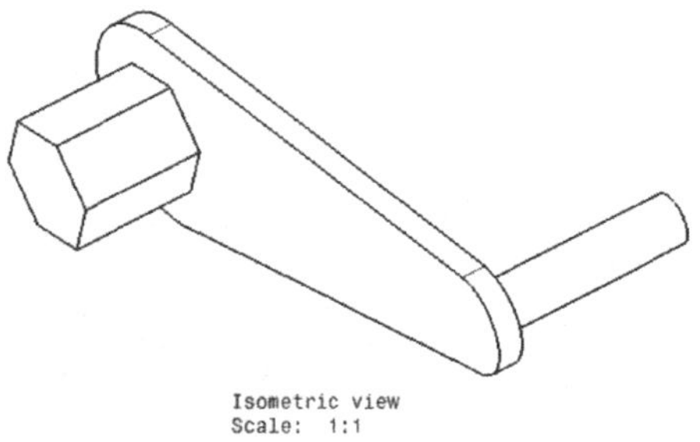

Figure 12–69

Drawing views are shown in Figure 12–69 and Figure 12–70.

- 10 (0.394 in)
- 20 (0.787 in)
- 25 (0.984 in)
- 40 (1.575 in)
- 50 (1.969 in)
- 80 (3.150 in)
- 200 (7.874 in)

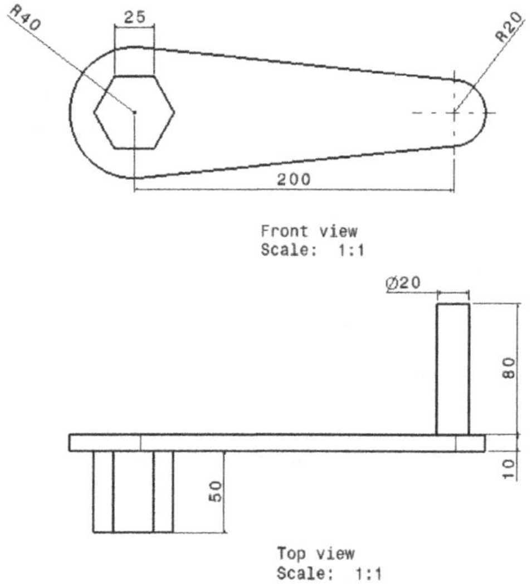

Figure 12–70

Practice 12g (Optional) Cylinder Block

Practice Objective

- Create a base feature and Pocket features without instruction.

1. Create the **CylinderBlock** part model shown in Figure 12–71.

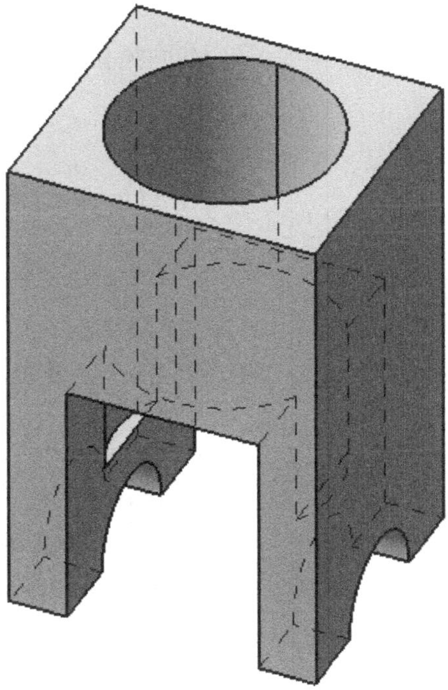

Figure 12–71

Chapter Review Questions

1. What is the general term for the first solid feature in a model?
    a. Foundation feature
    b. Base Feature
    c. Sketch
    d. Reference plane
2. Multiple profiles can be used as a profile for a Pad feature.
    a. True
    b. False
3. A Pad feature can be converted to a Pocket by changing its direction.
    a. True
    b. False
4. What option is used to create a Pad that is symmetrical to the sketch support?
    a. **Symmetric**
    b. **Mirror**
    c. **Mirrored Extent**
    d. None of the above.
5. To use the **Up to Surface** depth option, the terminating surface must completely intersect the feature.
    a. True
    b. False
6. Which of the following are true, related to open sketches?
    a. An open profile can be used as the profile for a Pad when the open end of the sketch is bounded by existing geometry.
    b. Although you can use open profiles, it is good practice to create features using closed profiles wherever possible.
    c. Open profiles increase update time and introduce instability in the model.
    d. All of the above.

7. The sketch shown on the left side of Figure 12–72 is used to create a Pocket feature. What will the Pocket look like? Note the direction arrows in the image on the right side of Figure 12–72.

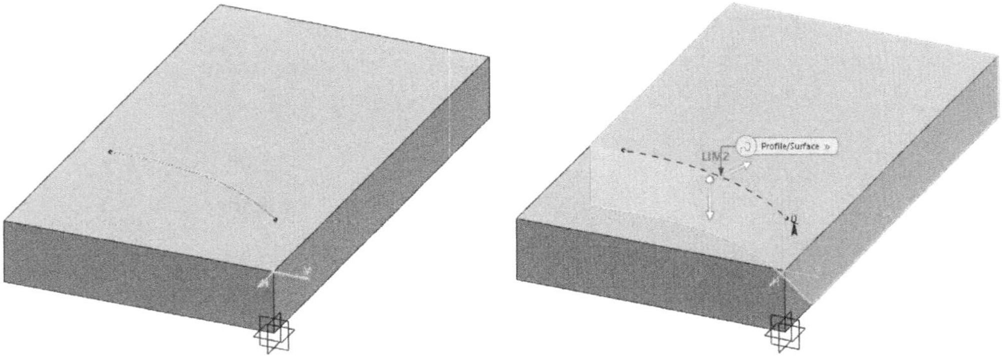

Figure 12–72

a. The Pocket feature would fail (No image).

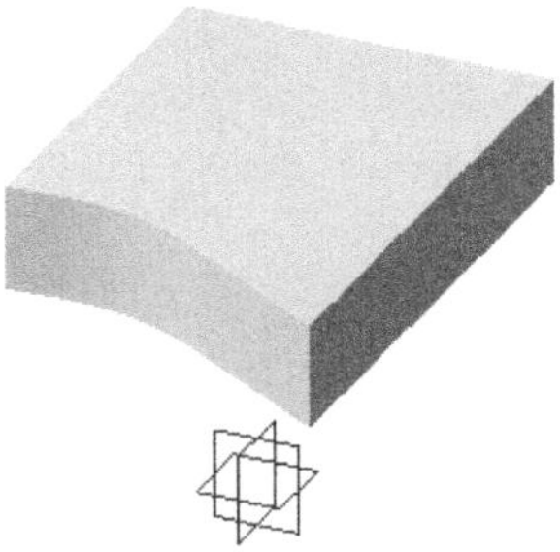

b. Resulting Geometry:

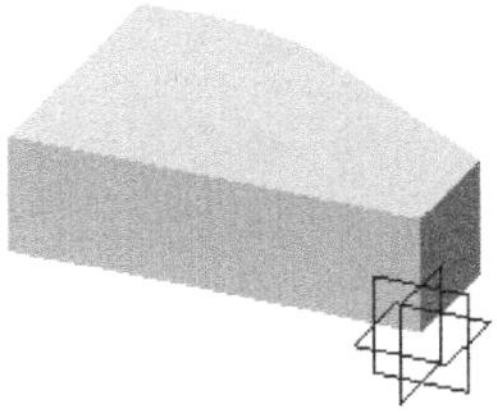

c. Resulting Geometry:

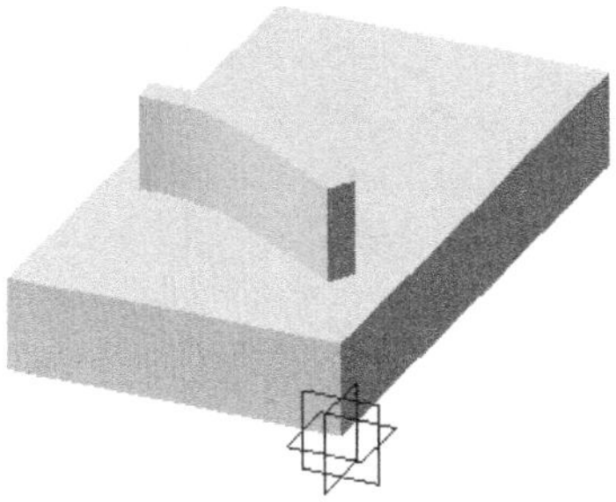

d. Resulting Geometry:

8. In the specification tree shown in Figure 12–73, if you delete **Sketch.1**, **Pad.1** fails because **Sketch.1** is listed under the **Pad.1** branch of the feature tree, meaning **Pad.1** uses **Sketch.1** as its profile.

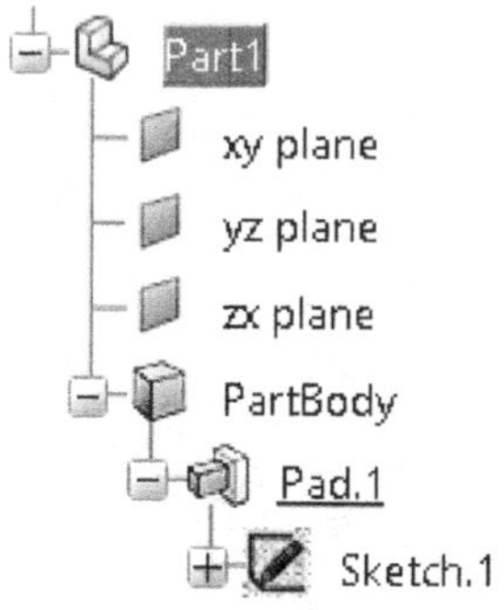

Figure 12–73

   a. True
   b. False

Answers: 1b, 2a, 3b, 4c, 5a, 6d, 7c, 8a

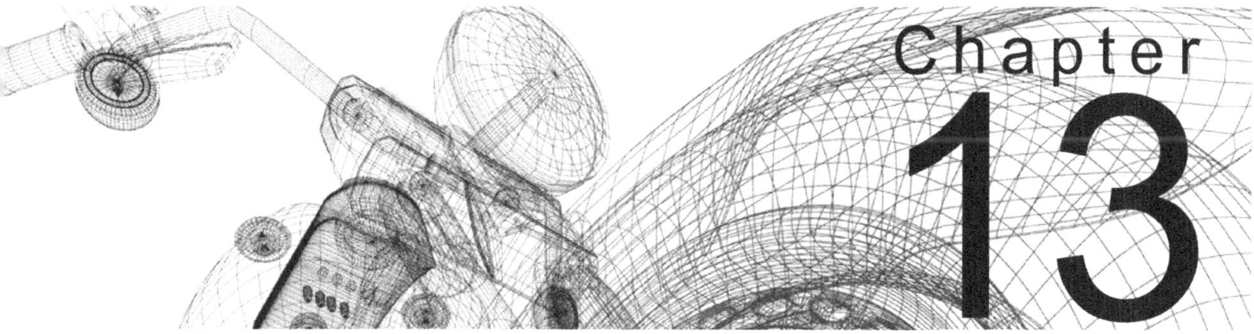

Chapter 13

Shaft and Groove Features

Shafts and Grooves are used to create revolved shapes and are set up similarly to Pads and Pockets. This chapter covers the requirements for sketches used in Shaft features. Additionally, you learn how to create grooves to remove material from the model and how you can create grooves on both planar and cylindrical surfaces.

Learning Objectives in This Chapter

- Learn the steps required to create a shaft feature.
- Understand the restrictions on sketches used for shaft features.
- Learn the steps required to create a groove feature.
- Create grooves on cylinders.

13.1 Shaft Feature

A Shaft feature consists of an existing sketch rotated about an axis. Figure 13–1 shows an example of a section rotated 360° about a sketched axis.

You can also use the vertical axis of the sketch.

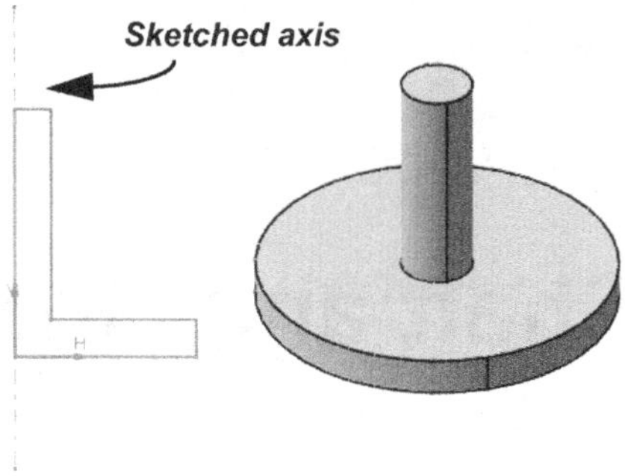

Figure 13–1

General Steps

Use the following general steps to create a Shaft feature:

1. Select a profile.
2. Initiate the creation of a Shaft.
3. Select a rotational axis.
4. Specify **Shaft limit** options.
5. Complete the Shaft feature.

Step 1 - Select a profile.

The shape of a Shaft is determined by the profile that is used to create the feature. An example is shown in Figure 13–2.

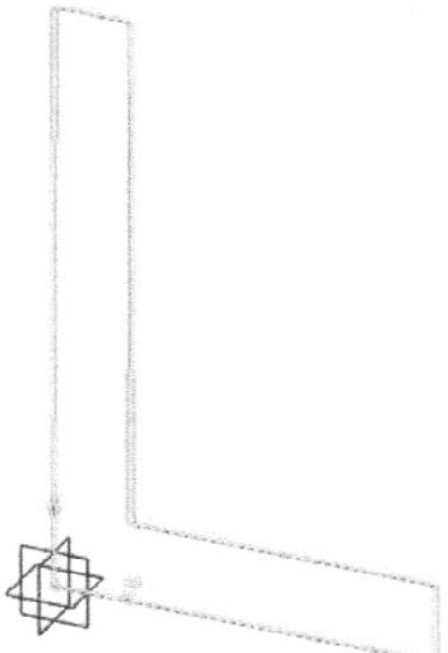

Figure 13–2

Sketch Restrictions

The sketch you select for a Shaft feature requires valid sketch geometry and an axis. The valid and invalid combinations of geometry and axis are described as follows:

Sketch	Shaft Geometry	Description
	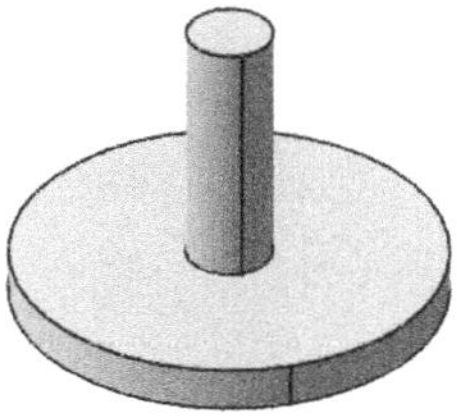	This is a closed sketch with the axis on the edge of the profile.
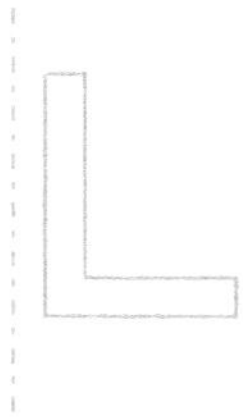	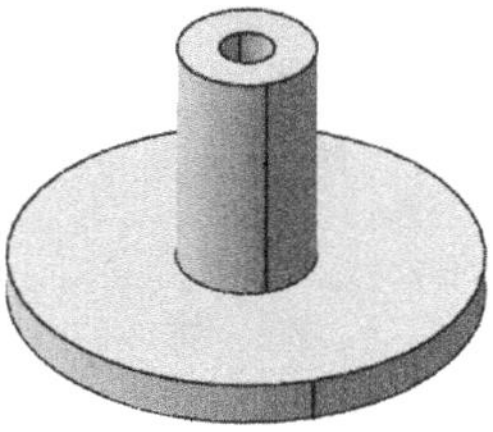	This is a closed sketch with the axis offset from the profile. The result is a hole in the Shaft.
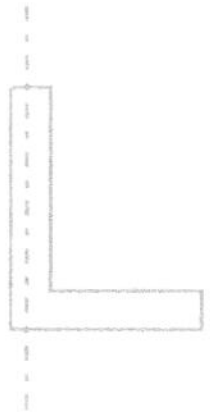	**Invalid**	This is a closed sketch with the axis inside the profile. A Shaft feature cannot sketch geometry on both sides of the axis of rotation, since the geometry would overlap.
	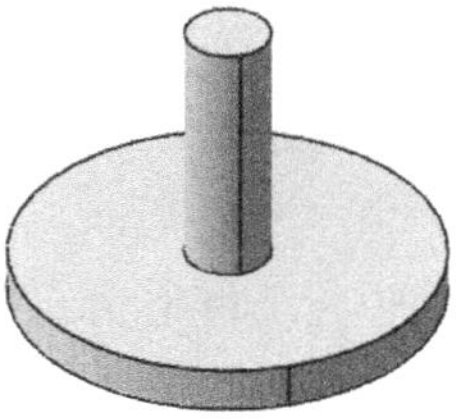	This is an open sketch with the axis coincident with the open ends of the profile. This sketch is valid, because the axis closes the sketch.
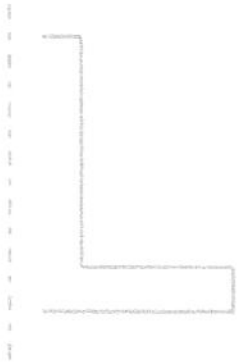	**Invalid**	This is an open sketch with the axis offset from the profile. This sketch is invalid, because no sketched geometry exists that generates a surface on the inside of the hole in the Shaft.

Step 2 - Initiate the creation of a Shaft.

To create a shaft, click (Shaft). The software initially creates the feature using the default values shown in the Shaft Definition dialog box in Figure 13–3.

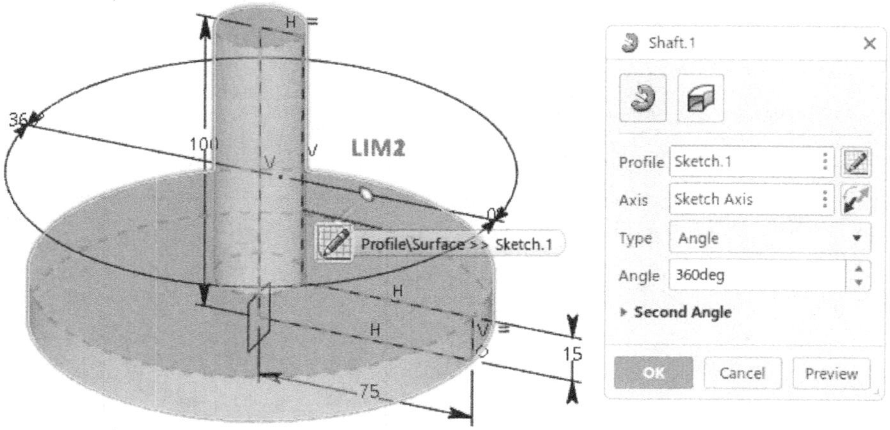

Figure 13–3

Step 3 - Select a rotational axis.

To create the Shaft feature, the rotational axis about which the profile is going to be revolved is required. By default, the software uses the first sketched axis created in the profile. If the sketch does not contain an axis, click (Sketch) in the Shaft Definition dialog box to alter the sketch without leaving the definition of this feature.

- While in the Sketch app, expand the (Line) flyout and click (Axis) to sketch an axis, as shown in Figure 13–4.

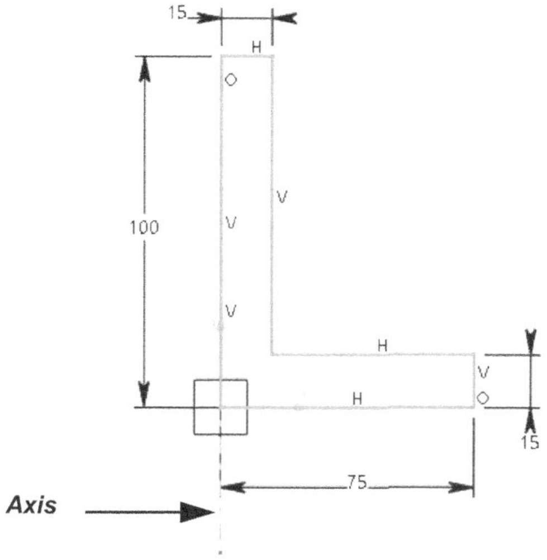

Figure 13–4

- Alternatively, you can select an existing edge, line, or axis. Figure 13–5 shows the selected vertical absolute axis of the sketch.

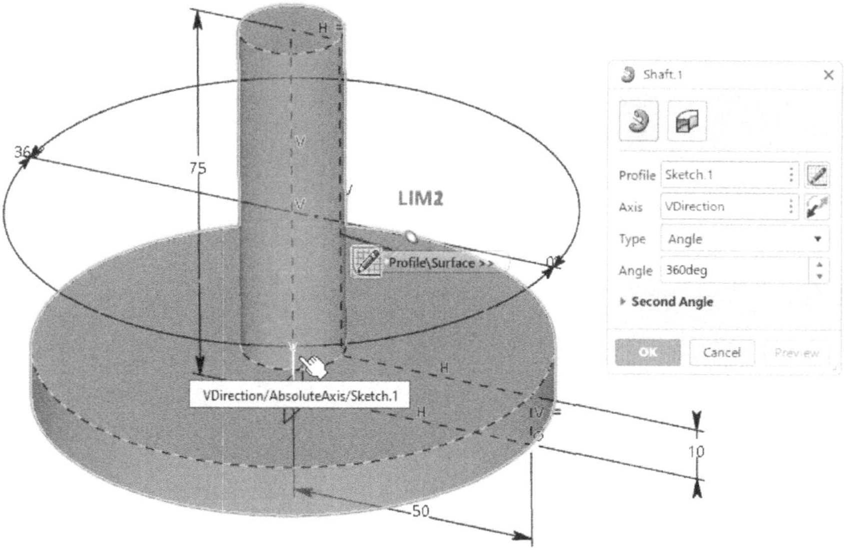

Figure 13–5

Step 4 - Specify Shaft limit options.

The angle that the sketch is rotated through is known as the limit. By default, the sketch is rotated 360° about the axis.
This value can be changed, as required.

Rotation Angle

The default rotation angle is 360°. If you enter a smaller angle, the sketch is rotated in the direction indicated by the first angle direction arrow, as shown in Figure 13–6.

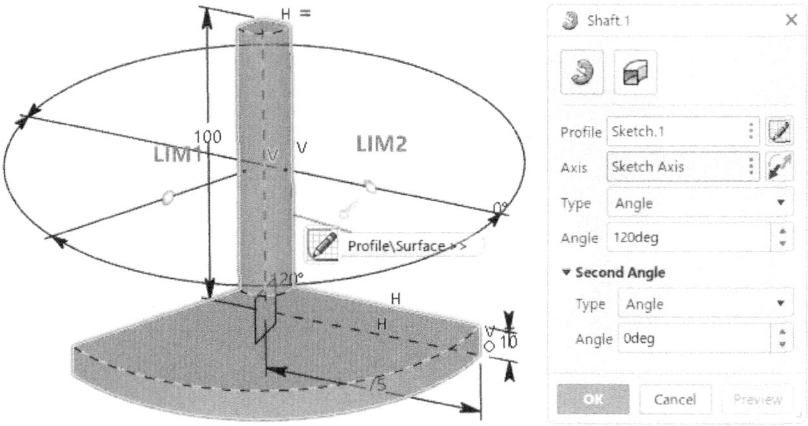

Figure 13–6

Entering a negative first angle value enables you to specify the angle of material to be removed from a 360° Shaft, as shown in Figure 13–7.

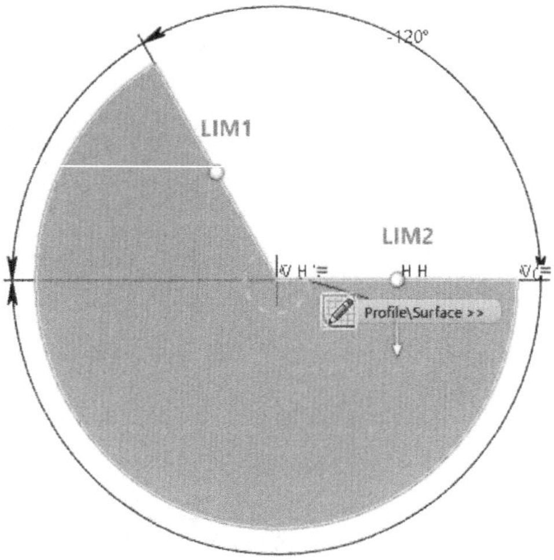

Figure 13–7

The sum of the first and second angles must be greater than zero and no more than 360°.

You can also change the default zero value of the second angle to rotate the sketch to the opposite side, as shown in Figure 13–8.

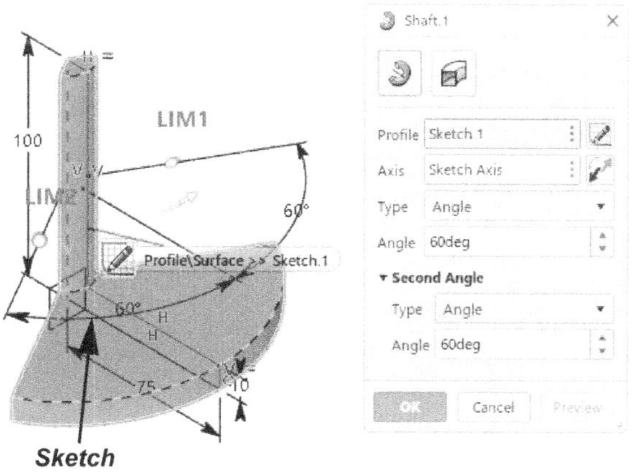

Figure 13–8

- Entering **0** for *Angle* and a value for the *Second angle* enables you to reverse the direction of the Shaft feature.
- Ensure that the sum of the two angles is 360° or less.
- To examine the geometry before you complete the feature, click **Preview**.

In addition to entering the *Angle* and *Second Angle* limits, you can apply any of the following limiting types, which are similar to those used for Pad and Pocket features:

- **Angle**: Creates a feature up to the defined angle value.
- **Up to next**: Creates a feature up to the next intersecting feature.
- **Up to last**: Creates a feature up to the last intersecting feature.
- **Up to plane**: Creates a feature up to the defined plane.
- **Up to surface**: Creates a feature up to the defined surface.

Step 5 - Complete the Shaft feature.

Click **OK** to complete the feature.

13.2 Groove Feature

A Groove feature removes material by rotating a sketch about an axis, as shown in Figure 13–9. It is similar to the Shaft feature, except that material is removed, instead of being added.

- As with the Shaft feature, you can accept the default value of 360° for the first limit and 0 for the second limit value. Figure 13–10 shows a model where the first limit value is changed to 90° and the second limit value is changed to 45°.

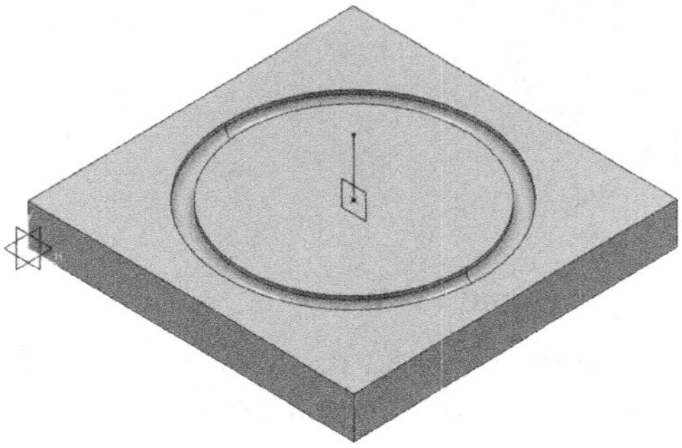

Figure 13–9

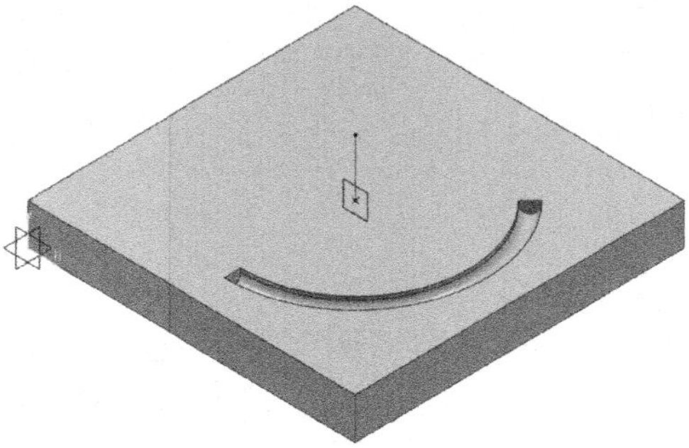

Figure 13–10

In addition to entering the *Angle* and *Second Angle* limits, you can apply any of the following limiting types:

- **Angle**: Creates a feature up to the defined angle value.
- **Up to next**: Creates a feature up to the next intersecting feature.
- **Up to last**: Creates a feature up to the last intersecting feature.
- **Up to plane**: Creates a feature up to the defined plane.
- **Up to surface**: Creates a feature up to the defined surface.

Requirements

To create a Groove feature, you must meet the following requirements:

- You must provide a rotation axis for the sketch. It can be a line, a sketched axis in the profile, or the implicit axis.
- Your profile must only be on one side of the axis.
- The section can be open or closed.

Grooves on Cylinders

To create a Groove feature on a cylindrical feature, a sketch plane must pass through the center of the cylindrical feature. If a suitable plane does not exist, you can use the **Angle/Normal to Plane** option when creating the reference plane. An axis must be selected as a placement reference.

- To select an implicit axis, hold <Shift> and place the cursor over the cylinder to highlight it, as shown in Figure 13–11. You can then select this axis as the rotation axis for the new plane.

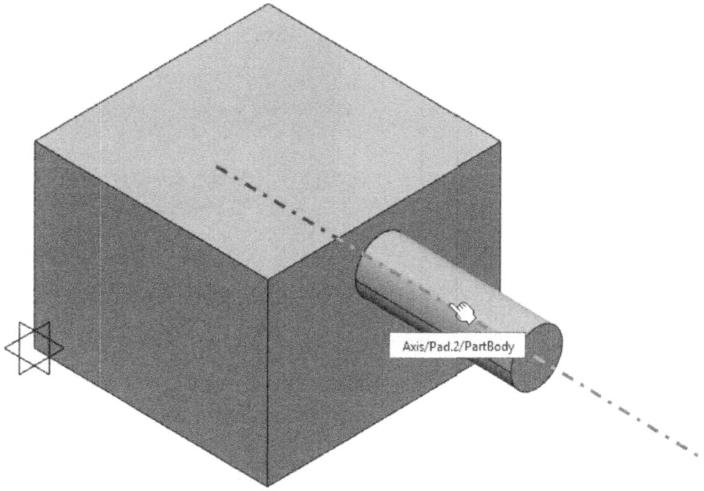

Figure 13–11

Rotation Axis

The implicit axis can be used to define the rotation axis for the Groove feature. This reduces the need to create additional line or sketched axis features.

Silhouette Edges

In some cases, you might need to constrain the sketch so that one or more sketched entities are coincident with the silhouette edge of the cylinder, as shown in Figure 13–12.

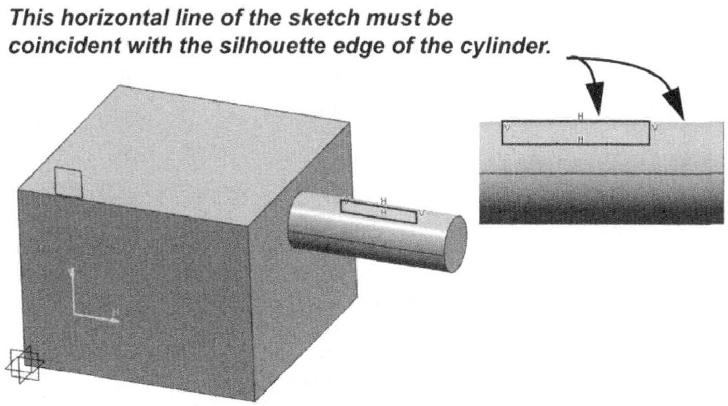

Figure 13–12

You cannot apply a coincidence constraint between the line and the silhouette edge. Therefore, click  (Project 3D Canonical Silhouette Edges) and select the cylinder. This copies the top and bottom edges into the sketch, as shown in Figure 13–13.

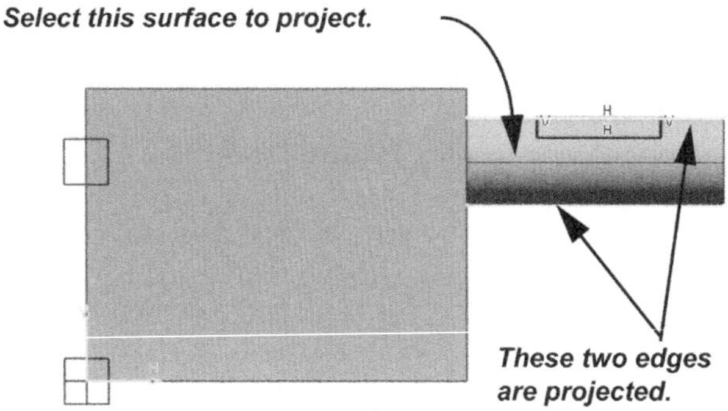

Figure 13–13

Once the silhouette edges are copied into your sketch, they display in yellow, which indicates projected geometry.

To complete your sketch, use one or a combination of the following methods:

- Delete the top or bottom silhouette edge that is not required.
- Convert the silhouette edge to construction geometry, and constrain your sketch to it.
- Leave the silhouette edge as a geometry element.

Dimension the Remaining Material Diameter

If the design intent is to control the diameter of a Groove feature, create a diameter dimension between the bottom of the sketch and the sketched axis, as shown in Figure 13–14.

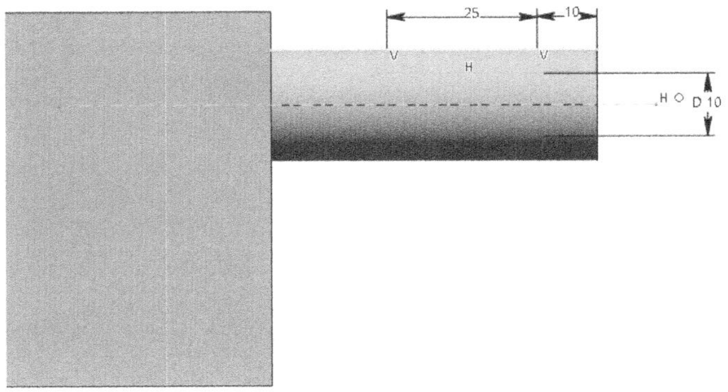

Figure 13–14

Practice 13a Shaft & Groove Features

Practice Objective

- Create a Shaft feature and a Groove feature.

In this practice, you will create the part shown in Figure 13–15. The base feature for the model is created using a Shaft feature by revolving a profile about the Y-axis. A Groove feature is then used to develop the lubrication grooves.

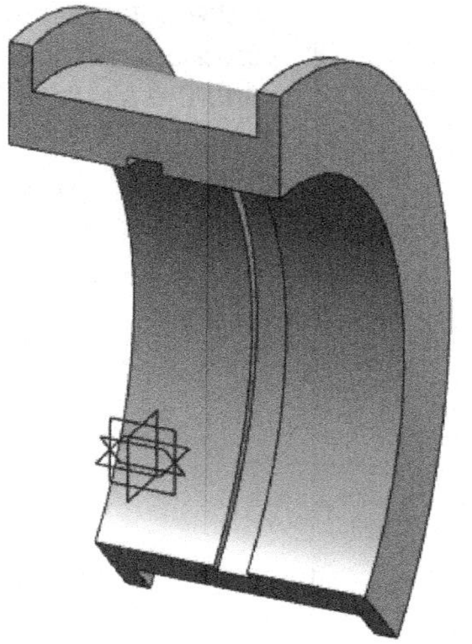

Figure 13–15

Task 1 - Create a new part.

1. In the Top Bar, click  (Add)>**3D Part**.
2. In the 3D Part dialog box, enter **Bearing** as the *Title*.
3. Select the *3D Shape* tab and enter **Bearing** as the *Title*.
4. Select the *Characteristics* tab and ensure that **Enable hybrid** design is disabled.
5. Click **OK**.

Task 2 - Create a sketch.

1. Select the YZ plane as shown in Figure 13–16.

Figure 13–16

2. In the context toolbar, click (Sketch).

3. Sketch the horizontal axis, as shown in Figure 13–17. This will define the rotational axis of the Shaft feature.

Figure 13–17

4. Sketch the profile as shown in Figure 13–18. Verify that the vertical elements are symmetrical about the vertical axis, and that the top horizontal elements are coincident.

   - 2 (0.079 in)
   - 5 (0.197 in)
   - 9 (0.354 in)
   - 24 (0.945 in)
   - 60 (2.362 in)

*To create the diameter dimension, right-click and select **Radius/ Diameter**.*

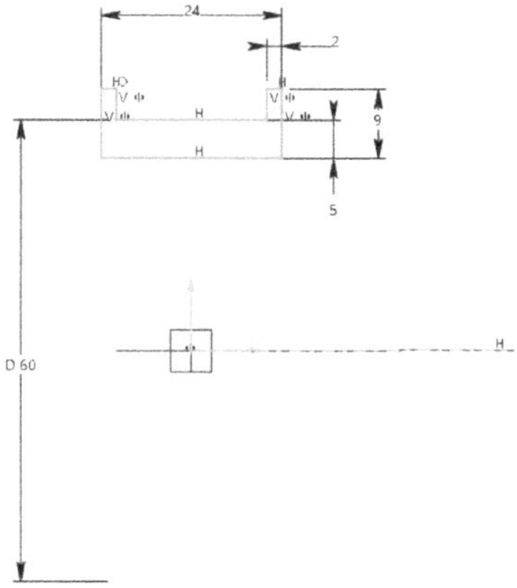

Figure 13–18

5. Click (Exit App) to exit the Sketch app.

Task 3 - Create a datum plane for use later in this practice.

1. In the *Essentials* section of the Action Bar, click  (Plane).
2. In the Plane Definition dialog box, in the *Plane type* drop-down list, select **Angle/Normal to plane**.
3. Right-click in the *Rotation axis* field and select **Insert Wireframe>Y Axis**, as shown in Figure 13–19.

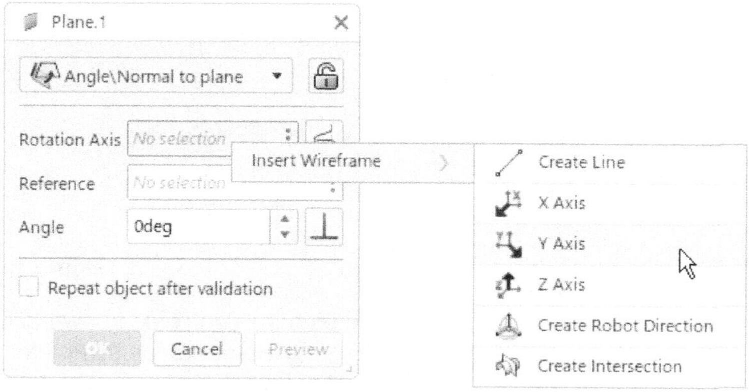

Figure 13–19

4. For the *Reference*, select **yz plane** in the specification tree.
5. Edit the angle to **100**, as shown in Figure 13–20.

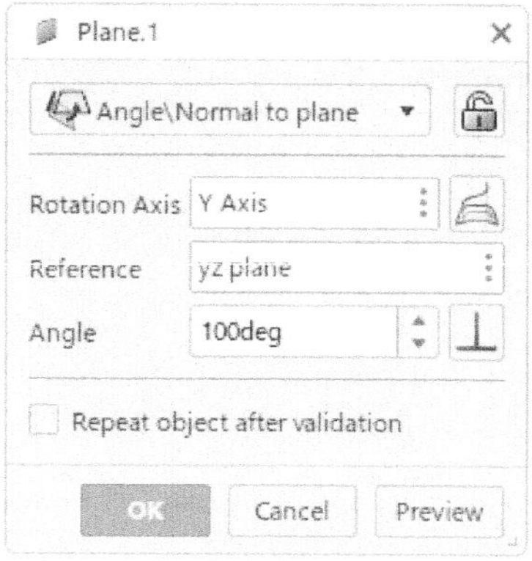

Figure 13–20

6. Click **OK** in the Plane Definition dialog box.

Task 4 - Create a Shaft feature.

Selecting (Shaft) will create a shaft with default settings. You want to access the Shaft Definition dialog box, so select (Shaft) from the Action Bar.

1. Select the sketch and click (Shaft) in the *Essentials* section of the Action Bar. The Shaft Definition dialog box opens as shown in Figure 13–21.

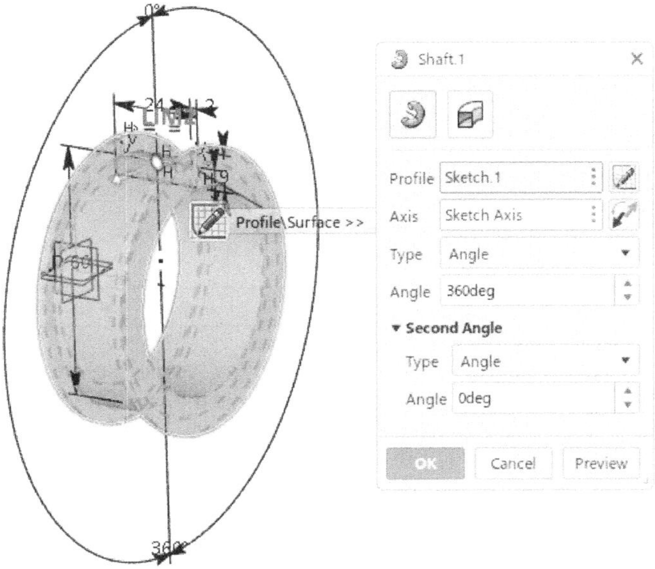

Figure 13–21

2. Enter the following parameters to define the Shaft feature:
   - *Angle:* **180deg**
   - *Second Angle-Angle:* **0deg**
   - Click *(Reverse Direction)*.

3. Click **OK**. The model displays as shown in Figure 13–22.

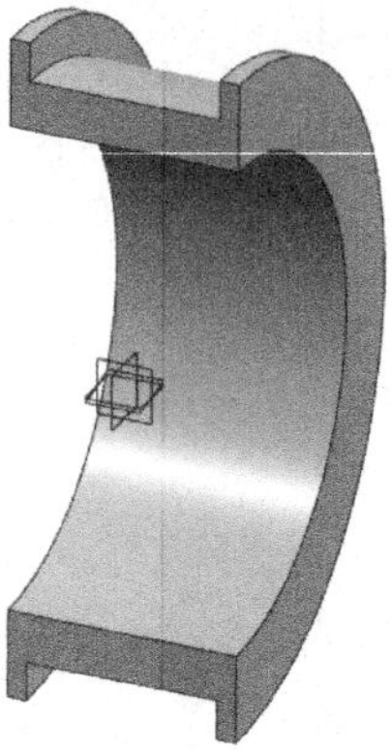

Figure 13–22

Task 5 - Create a Groove feature.

In this task, you will create a feature to represent the lubrication Groove on the inside diameter of the bearing. The completed feature displays as shown in Figure 13–23.

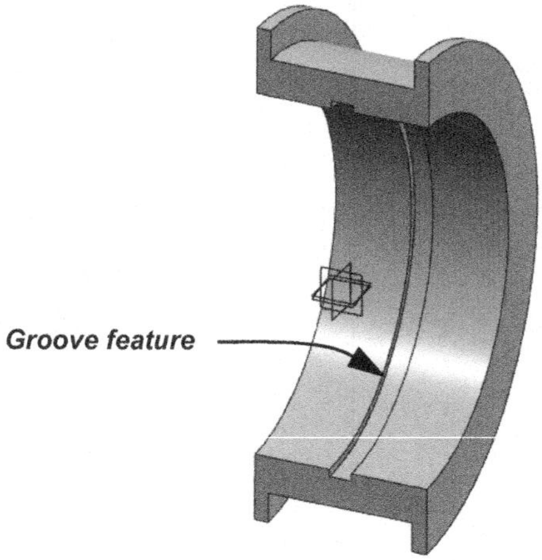

Figure 13–23

1. In the *Essentials* section of the Action Bar, click (Positioned Sketch). Create a positioned sketch on the YZ plane. To define the origin, use the **Middle Point** type and select the edge shown in Figure 13–24.

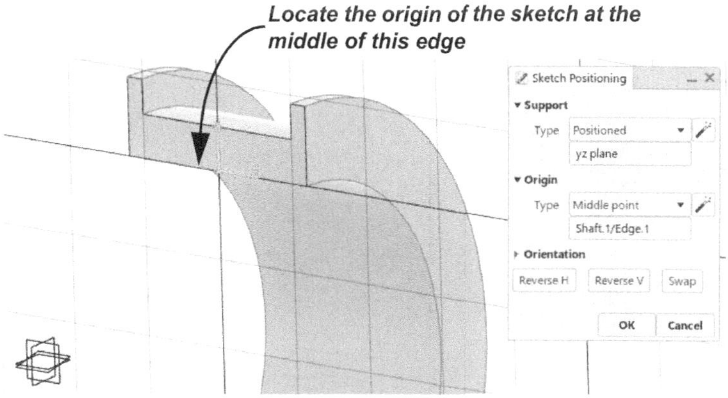

Figure 13–24

2. Click **OK**.

3. Sketch the profile shown in Figure 13–25, using the dimensions of **1 (0.039 in)** and **3 (0.118 in)**. Verify that the profile is symmetrical about the vertical sketch axis.

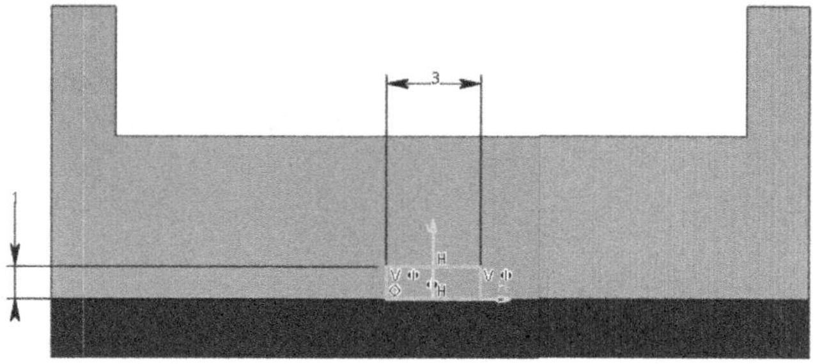

Figure 13–25

4. Click (Exit App).

5. With the sketch preselected, click (Groove) in the *Essentials* section of the Action Bar. The Groove Definition dialog box opens as shown in Figure 13–26.

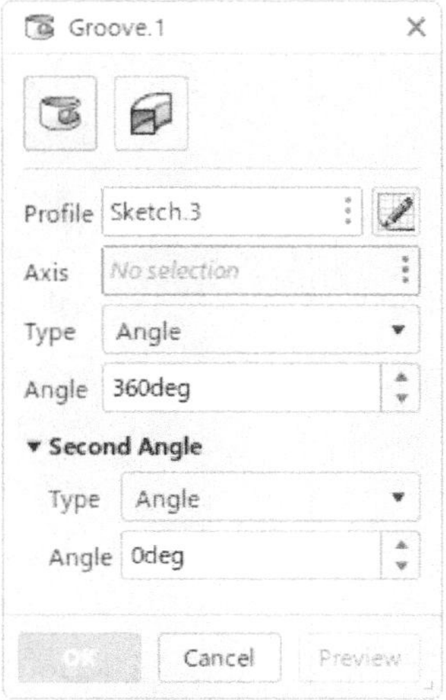

Figure 13–26

Design Considerations

Note how the **OK** and **Preview** buttons are grayed out. An axis was not sketched into the profile used for the Groove, so a rotation axis for the feature is not automatically defined.

6. Select the **Shaft.1** feature to select its axis. The Groove Definition dialog box updates as shown in Figure 13–27.

Figure 13–27

*You might need to click **Reverse Direction** to get the required result.*

7. Modify the options in the Groove Definition dialog box so that the resulting feature displays as shown in Figure 13–28.

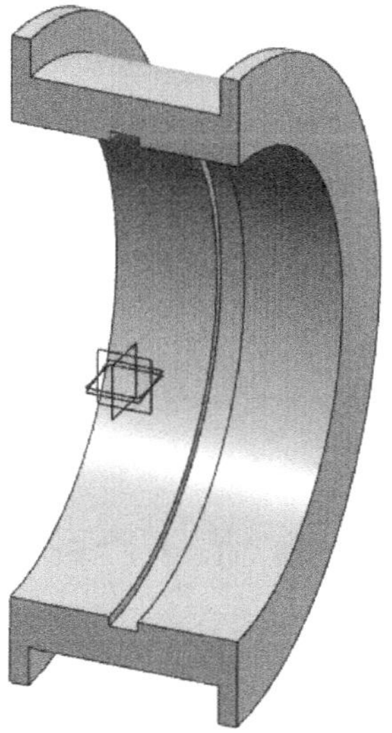

Figure 13–28

Task 6 - Change the shaft to reference the datum plane.

1. In the specification tree, double-click on **Shaft.1**.
2. In the Shaft Definition dialog box, in the *Limit* drop-down list, select **Up to plane**.
3. Select **Plane.1** in the specification tree.
4. Click **OK**.
5. In the Update Diagnosis Shaft.1 dialog box, click **Sub Elements**.

6. In the Sub Elements in Error dialog box, click **OK**. The model updates as shown in Figure 13–29.

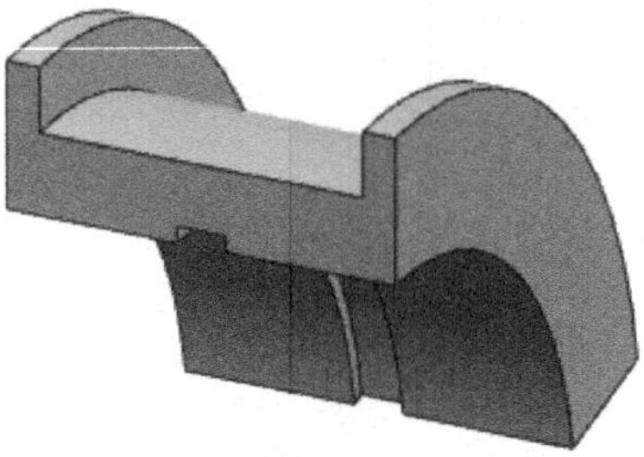

Figure 13–29

Task 7 - Edit the angle of the plane.

1. In the specification tree, double-click **Plane.1**.
2. Edit the *100* angle dimension to **45** and click **OK**.
3. The model updates as shown in Figure 13–30.

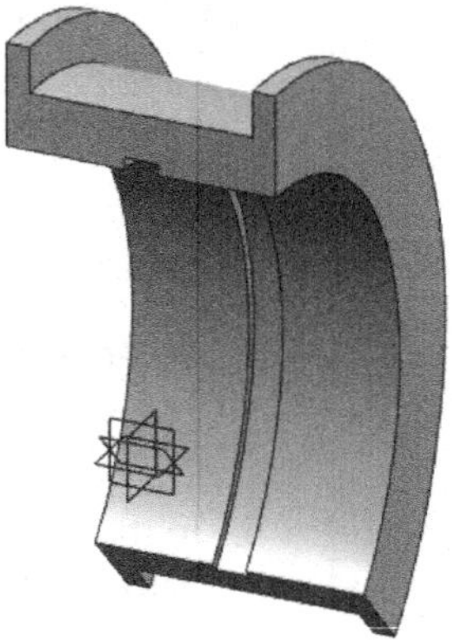

Figure 13–30

4. Save the model and close the tab.

Practice 13b Groove Features

Practice Objectives

- Create a Groove feature.
- Locate revolved sketches to cylindrical geometry.

In this practice, you will create the part shown in Figure 13–31. The part will consist of two Groove features. You will also use silhouette projections to locate a sketch onto cylindrical geometry.

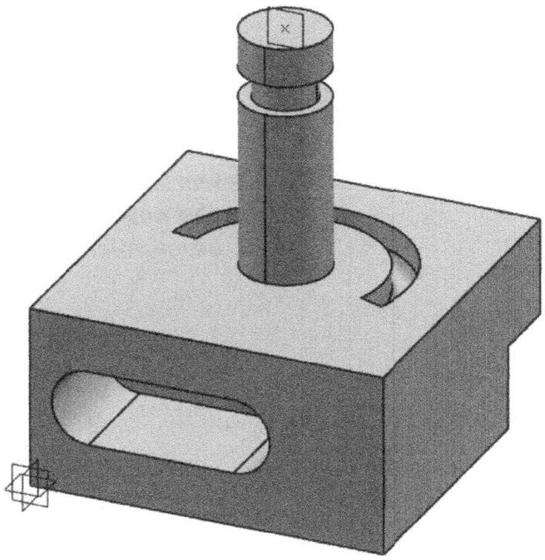

Figure 13–31

Task 1 - Create a point.

Design Considerations

This point will mark the center of the cylinder. It will be used as a reference for a plane, which will be used to create the two profiles in this task.

1. Import **Groove.3dxml**.
2. In the *Groove (Explore)* tab, right-click **Groove** in the specification tree and select **Open**.
3. Click  (Point) in the Reference Elements toolbar.
4. Select **Circle/Sphere/Ellipse center** as the point type.

5. Select the circular edge on the top of the cylinder, as shown in Figure 13–32.

6. Click **OK** to complete the feature.

7. Click  (Plane) and select **Parallel through point** as the plane type.

8. Select the YZ plane as the parallel reference for the new plane, and select the point to locate the plane.

9. Click **OK** to complete the feature. The new point and plane display as shown in Figure 13–32.

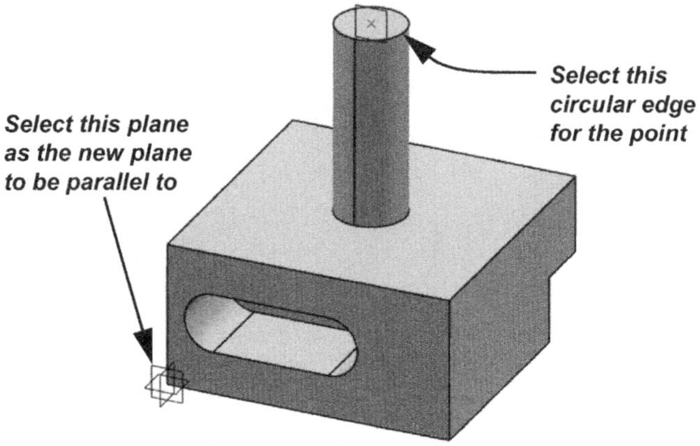

Figure 13–32

Task 2 - Create a sketch to be used for a Groove feature.

1. Create a positioned sketch on the newly created reference plane, using **Point.1** as the origin.

2. Click (Profile) to sketch the shape. Dimension the width and height of the shape, as shown in Figure 13–33.
   - 22.5 (0.886 in)
   - 32 (1.260 in)
   - 95 (3.740 in)

This sketched profile should be closed to avoid feature failure.

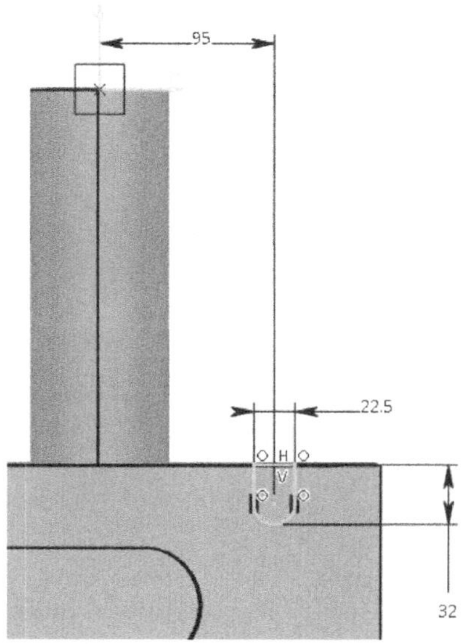

Figure 13–33

3. Constrain the horizontal line of the sketch with the horizontal edge of the part.
4. Dimension the center of the arc to the vertical sketcher axis.
5. When the sketch is fully constrained, click (Exit App).
6. With the sketch still highlighted, click (Groove) to create a Groove feature. The software does not automatically build a preview of the Groove because the sketch does not have an axis. Note that the axis selection box is active.

7. Place the cursor over the cylinder. The implicit axis displays. Select this axis and feature displays as shown in Figure 13–34.

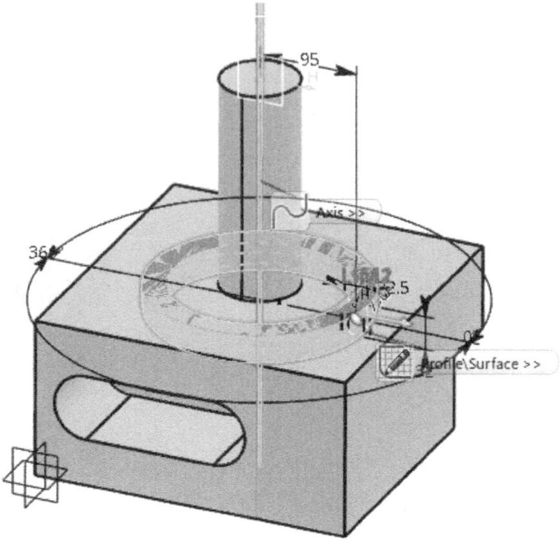

Figure 13–34

8. Set the *Angle* as **90** and set the *Second Angle-Angle* as **150.**

9. Click **Preview**. The part displays as shown in Figure 13–35.

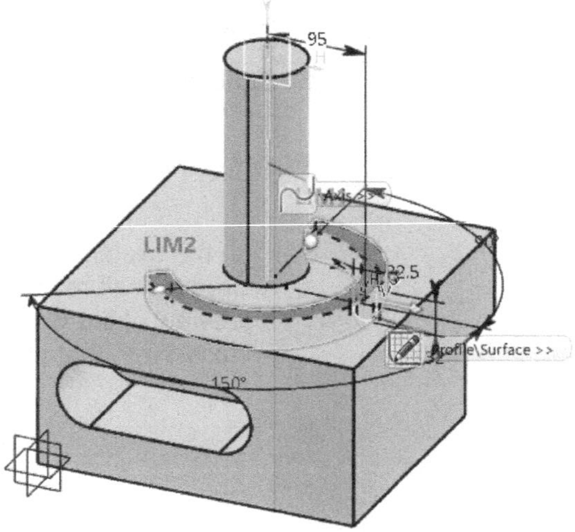

Figure 13–35

10. Select and drag the **LIM1** and **LIM2** tags of the Groove to dynamically modify the rotation angles.

11. When you have set the limits to an angle similar to that shown in Figure 13–36. Click **OK**.

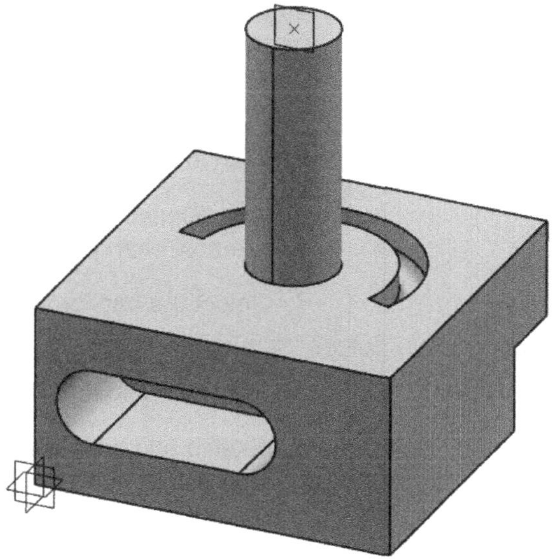

Figure 13–36

Task 3 - Create a sketch for a Groove feature on the cylinder.

1. Create a positioned sketch on the newly created reference plane using **Point.1** as the origin.
2. Select **View>Zoom Area** and zoom into the top of the cylinder by dragging a box around it.
3. Click  (Project 3D Canonical Silhouette Edges).
4. Select the cylinder. The warning message box opens, as shown in Figure 13–37.

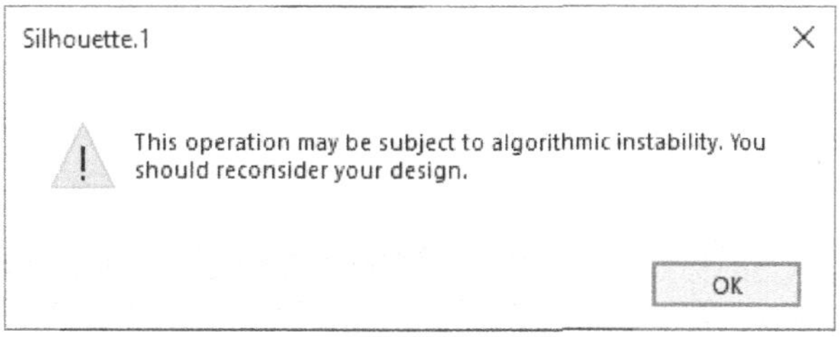

Figure 13–37

Design Considerations

The warning message displays to make you aware that features using silhouette edge projections in a sketch might become unstable. CATIA occasionally loses references to silhouetted edges. Use caution when using this type of projection in your models.

5. Click **OK** and two vertical lines display.
6. With the two silhouette projections selected, click (Construction/Standard Element). The silhouette edges are now changed to construction lines.
7. Select the background area of the display to clear the geometry and click (Construction/Standard Element) to return to Standard Element creation.
8. Sketch and dimension the rectangle as shown in Figure 13–38. Verify that the right vertical edge of the rectangle is coincident with the construction line.
   - 25 (0.984 in)
   - 27 (1.063 in)
   - 32 (1.260 in)

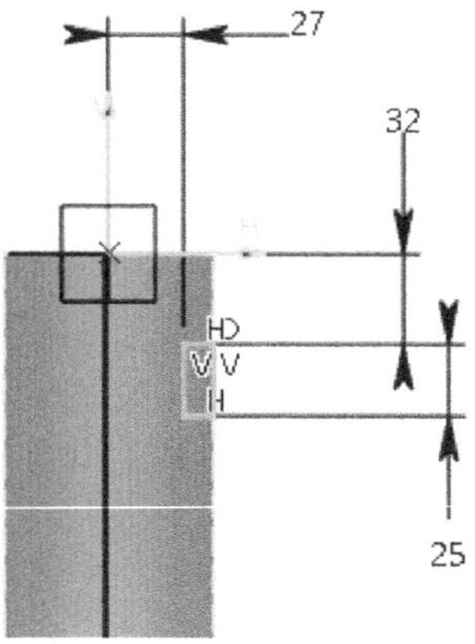

Figure 13–38

9. Sketch a vertical (Axis) coincident with the vertical axis.
10. Exit the Sketch app.
11. With the sketch highlighted, click (Groove). Note that the sketch axis is automatically selected as the rotational axis for the Groove feature.

12. Ensure the First Angle is set to **360deg** and the Second Angle is **0deg**.

13. Click **OK** to complete the feature. The part displays as shown in Figure 13–39.

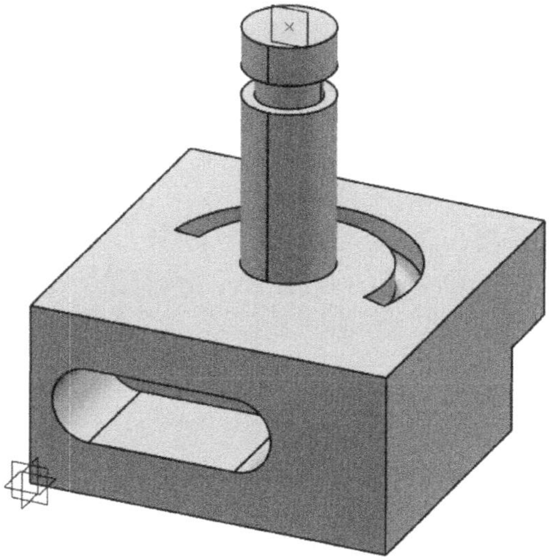

Figure 13–39

14. Save the file and close the tab.

Practice 13c (Optional) King Chess Piece

Practice Objective

- Create Pad and Shaft features without instructions.

Create a new part titled **King_Piece**, as shown in Figure 13–40. Exact dimensions are not required.

Figure 13–40

Practice 13d (Optional) Creating Shafts and Grooves

Practice Objective

- Create Shaft and Groove features with minimal instruction.

In this practice, you will create a model of a spinning top using Shaft and Groove features. The completed model is shown in Figure 13–41. As a good practice, create an axis system in the drawing as a foundation for building features.

Figure 13–41

Chapter Review Questions

1. You mistakenly use a sketch to create a Pad feature, when you really intended to create a Shaft. What do you need to do to fix this?
   a. Right-click the pad and select **Convert to Shaft**.
   b. Right-click the Pad and select **Pad.object>Definition**. In the Pad Definition dialog box, select **Shaft**.
   c. Delete the Pad and use the sketch to create a Shaft feature.
   d. None of the above.
2. Which of the following profiles is not valid for use in creating a Shaft feature?

   a. 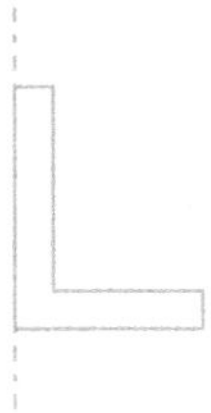

   b. 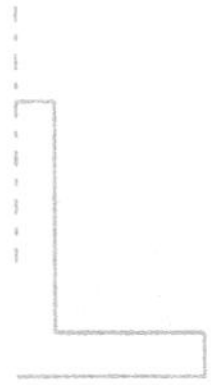

   c. 

   d. 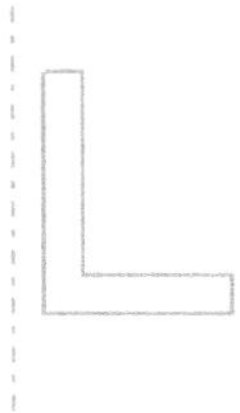

3. Which of the following are valid selections as an axis for a Shaft or Groove feature? (Select all that apply.)
    a. An axis created inside the sketch.
    b. An existing edge.
    c. The vertical absolute axis of a sketch.
    d. The implicit axis of an existing feature.
4. The profile for a Groove feature must lie completely to one side of the axis of revolution.
    a. True
    b. False
5. A Groove is required on the side of the cylindrical feature shown in Figure 13–42. What feature is required to aid in the creation of the Groove feature?

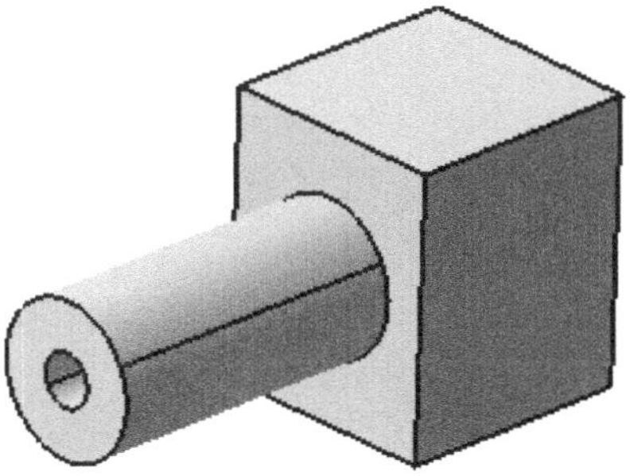

Figure 13–42

    a. A construction line.
    b. A sketch support.
    c. A point.
    d. None of the above.

6. What is going to be projected onto the sketch if the Cylindrical feature, shown in Figure 13–43, is projected using the **Project 3D Canonical Silhouette Edges** icon?

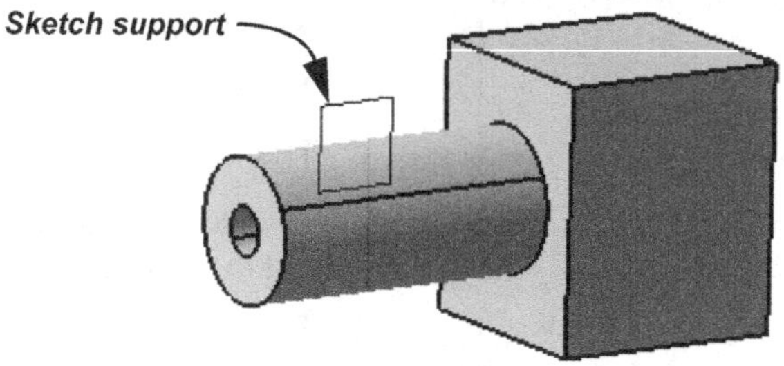

Figure 13–43

a. The silhouette edges of the cylinder.

b. The implicit axis of the cylinder.

c. The edges of the hole in the cylinder.

d. None of the above.

Answers: 1c, 2c, 3abcd, 4a, 5b, 6a

Made in United States
North Haven, CT
04 November 2026

21730355R00291